Michigan Biographies

INCLUDING MEMBERS OF CONGRESS, ELECTIVE STATE OFFICERS,
JUSTICES OF THE SUPREME COURT, MEMBERS OF THE
MICHIGAN LEGISLATURE, BOARD OF REGENTS OF
THE UNIVERSITY OF MICHIGAN, STATE
BOARD OF AGRICULTURE AND
STATE BOARD OF
EDUCATION .

VOL. I. A - K

CLEARFIELD

Originally published
Lansing, Michigan 1924

Reprinted for
Clearfield Company, Inc. by
Genealogical Publishing Co., Inc.
Baltimore, Maryland
1999

International Standard Book Number: 0-8063-4931-X
Set Number 0-8063-4930-1

Made in the United States of America

PREFACE.

IN 1888 a volume entitled *Early History of Michigan, with Biographies of State Officers, Members of Congress, Judges and Legislators* was published by the State under the impulse of the semi-centennial anniversary of Michigan's admission to the Union. Since that time the book has become somewhat rare. Much new material has come to light which was not then accessible, and many new names have been added to the list of Michigan's distinguished sons. It has seemed well to revise this earlier volume and bring it up to date. For this purpose much use has been made of the several editions of the Michigan *Manual*. It is believed that the bringing together of these scattered sources of information into a compact record will be increasingly valued as the years go by.

MICHIGAN BIOGRAPHIES

ADRIAN O. ABBOTT

Representative from the Third District of Lenawee County, 1887-8 and 1889-90. Was born at Munnsville, Madison County, N. Y., Aug. 26, 1842. Three years later his parents moved to Oriskany Falls, Oneida County, where his boyhood was spent. In 1856, at the age of fourteen, he left school and sold goods in a general store in the village where his parents resided. He remained in the store for about two years, after which he served time as a schoolmaster. In 1860 he secured a position in a dry goods store at Clinton, N. Y., where he remained until the summer of 1861, when he enlisted in Co. A, 1st N. Y. Artillery. In the spring of 1862 he was discharged for physical disability, and for the remainder of that year his health was so poor that he was unable to do any business. In 1863 he secured a position as clerk in a dry goods house in Utica, N. Y., where he remained until he came to Michigan. In 1866 Mr. Abbott located at Adrian and opened a ladies' furnishing goods store, and the business increasing he finally went into the general dry goods business, which he conducted until 1873. After 1873 Mr. Abbott was engaged in the manufacturing and selling of his own inventions, some of which proved very useful and secured a reputation over the whole country. For over three years he held the position of President of the village of Hudson. He was elected Representative as a Republican to the House of 1887-8, and re-elected for 1889-90.

ISAAC C. ABBOTT

Representative from Calhoun County, 1863-4. Was born in the State of New Hampshire, Apr. 5, 1819. He came to Romeo, Mich., in 1843. He was a Methodist Episcopal minister for seventeen years, when he became a farmer in Leroy, Calhoun County. Later he lived in Galesburg. In politics he was a Republican. He died Apr. 11, 1890.

JOSHUA K. ABBOTT

Representative from Genesee County, 1850. Was born in Concord, N. H., in 1810. He came to Michigan in 1838. By trade he was a bookbinder. On coming to Michigan he became a merchant and farmer at Grand Blanc. He was Postmaster for twenty years. He went to the war as sutler of the 30th Iowa, of which his brother was Colonel. He was taken sick in front of Vicksburg and died on his way home at Cairo, Feb. 4, 1863.

ROBERT ABBOTT

Treasurer of Michigan Territory, 1813-30; and Auditor General, 1836-9. Was born in Detroit in 1770. After reaching maturity he became a partner with his father, James Abbott, who was prominently connected with the fur trade of the Northwest. Mr. Abbott held the position of Treasurer of the territorial funds 1813 to 1836;

auditor of public accounts, 1809 to 1836, and was a U. S. Master in Chancery. His name also appears in local offices of all grades, and in benevolent and church enterprises, especially in advancing the interests of the Methodist Church, to which he was devoted. He was a Democrat in politics. He died in 1852.

WILLIAM L. ABBOTT

Representative from Lapeer County, 1877-8 and 1879-80. Was born in the county of Beauharnois, Parish of Ste. Martine, Canada East, Mar. 29, 1835. He received a common school education, and resided in Canada until the year 1856, when the family emigrated to the United States, with the intention of settling in Kansas; but owing to the political disturbances in that State at the time, they retraced their steps and settled in Goodland, Lapeer County, Mich., where he engaged in lumbering and farming. Later occupation was that of farming. He held the office of Township Clerk, Supervisor and other minor offices. In politics he was a Republican.

SYLVESTER ABEL

Senator from Washtenaw County, 1857-8. He was an early member of the Ann Arbor bar, was an excellent man, of fair abilities as a lawyer, and was honored with many public offices. In politics he was a Republican. Deceased.

OLIVER C. ABELL

Senator from Wayne County, 1867-8. Was born at Augusta, Ga., July 3, 1827, and was the son of a wealthy cotton dealer and slaveholder. In 1830 he removed to Detroit, Mich., and the next year to Dearborn, Wayne County, where he spent a portion of his time teaching until 1851, when he went to California, and remained there until 1856. On his return he was elected Treasurer of Dearborn. He followed farming until 1862. He held the office of Enrolling Officer of the Draft Department and Deputy Provost Marshal during the war. He was also Deputy Assessor and Collector of Revenue, which office he held until removed by Andrew Johnson. Exempted from the draft by disability, he furnished a substitute at a cost of eight hundred dollars. In 1867 he was State Senator and chairman of the committee on railroads. He was a director of the Detroit, Lansing & Northern Railroad. He removed to Nankin, laid out a village, and was the first hardware merchant there. He was Postmaster five years, President of the village, and Trustee. From 1875 to 1878 he had charge of the Wayne County Poorhouse. He removed to Detroit in 1884. In politics he was a Republican.

EDWARD T. ABRAMS

Representative from the Second District of Houghton County, 1907-8. Was born at Eagle River, Keweenaw County, Mich., Nov. 20, 1860, and was the son of Michael and Lydia Abrams, who were pioneers in the Copper Country. He received his primary education in the public schools of Houghton County. At the age of thirteen years, he was apprenticed to a blacksmith, continued this occupation for nearly six years and then taught school, acquiring sufficient money in this way to permit him to procure an education. Mr. Abrams was graduated from Dartmouth College and also attended the Detroit Medical College and the Long Island

Hospital, New York City. After graduation from college he spent two years in the study of law. He resided at Dollar Bay after 1890 and was employed as surgeon by a number of industries at that place. His main office, however, was located at Hancock. In 1902 Olivet College conferred on him the degree of Master of Arts. He was vice president of the Michigan State Medical Society, a member of the American Medical Association and of the American Association of Obstetricians and Gynecologists. In politics a Republican. He died at Dollar Bay, May 20, 1918.

HENRY ACKER

Representative from Jackson County, 1839-40. He was an early settler in the town of Concord, and was Supervisor in 1838. Politics and occupation are unknown.

WILLIAM H. ACKER

Delegate from the Twelfth District, Oakland and Macomb counties, in the Constitutional Convention of 1907-8. Was born in Portage, N. Y., in 1851 and was of English descent. He graduated from the Rushford Academy in 1870, afterwards taking a business course in a commercial college at Buffalo. He was married to Mary C. Gordon in 1873 and came to Michigan the same year, locating at Carson City, Montcalm County, where he engaged in the lumber and banking business. In 1878 he sold out his business and went to Richmond, where he established the Richmond bank, at that time the third bank in Macomb County. He was one of the organizers of the Higgins Land Co. and the Olean Land Co. of Minnesota, and a director in both companies. In 1896, he, with others, organized the Richmond Elevator Co., of which he was president. He was a director in the Parker Plow Co. of Richmond, a member of the Michigan Bankers' Association, and chairman of the private Bankers' Executive Committee. In politics a Republican.

FRANCIS ACKLEY

Representative from Saginaw County, 1873-4. Was born Dec. 16, 1826, in the town of Stowe, Portage County, O. Mr. Ackley received a common school education. In 1840 he emigrated to Michigan and settled in Shiawassee Township, Shiawassee County. In 1863 he removed to the village of St. Charles, Saginaw County. Mr. Ackley was President of the village of St. Charles, and held other important offices in the town. His business was that of a merchant.

WILLIAM ADAIR

Senator from Wayne County, 1861-2 to 1869-70, 1875-6 and 1877-8. Was born near Glasgow, Scotland, in 1815. In 1834 he settled at Detroit, Mich. He worked as a carpenter until 1840, when he began business as a gardener and horticulturist, in which he was very successful. He held several local positions of honor in Detroit, among them president of the Detroit Mechanics' Society and president of St. Andrew's Society. In politics he was a Democrat. A quiet, unassuming gentleman, he became one of the most influential members of the Senate, and probably exercised greater influence than any other Democrat. He died at Detroit May 19, 1895.

JOHN J. ADAM

Delegate from the Third District to the Constitutional Convention of 1835; Delegate from Lenawee County to the Second Convention of Assent; Representative from Lenawee County, 1839, 1847 and 1871-2; member of the Board of Regents of the University, 1837-40; Senator from the Second District, 1840-1; State Treasurer, 1842-5; and Auditor General, 1845-6 and 1848-51. Was born at Paisley, Scotland, Oct. 30, 1807. He received a good education, graduating at Glasgow College in 1826 with honor. The same year he emigrated to this country and arrived at Baltimore July 4, 1826. He taught Latin, Greek and mathematics at an academy in Meadville, Pa., for a year, and returned to Scotland. In 1831 he settled in Lenawee County, Mich. He taught school at Clinton, and in 1832 enlisted as a private in Captain Hickson's company to serve in the Black Hawk War, but the company only went to Niles. He took part in the "Toledo War" as a Lieutenant. Afterwards he was appointed paymaster of the 5th Division Mich. Militia, and in 1841 Aid-de-Camp of Gen. Davis Smith, same command. In 1835 he was a Delegate to the Constitutional Convention, and took an active part in framing the first State Constitution. He was Secretary of the State Senate for the first three legislative sessions. In 1839 he was a Representative from Lenawee County, and State Senator in 1840 and 1841 from the Second District, comprising Monroe, Lenawee and Hillsdale counties. In January, 1842, he was elected State Treasurer to fill an unexpired term, and was twice re-elected, serving from Jan. 13, 1842, to May 24, 1845, when he resigned at the request of Gov. Barry to take the position of Auditor General, which he held until Jan. 28, 1846. In 1847 he again served as Representative, was chairman of the committee on ways and means, and took an active part in locating the capital at Lansing. He was again elected by the Legislature Auditor General, May 9, 1848, and served until 1851. From that time until 1868 he was in the service of the Michigan Southern road, and was their construction agent in building the Airline, the Jackson branch, the Three Rivers road and the Detroit & Toledo road. From 1858 to 1868 he was auditor of the company, when he resigned. He was again Representative in the Legislature of 1871-2. For several years he was president of the Council of the village of Tecumseh, and was president of the State Pioneer Society in 1878-9. He died at Tecumseh, Mich., July 4, 1888.

C. SPENCER ADAMS

Representative from Van Buren County, 1901-2 and 1903-4. Was born in Joliet, Ill., Feb. 25, 1851. He moved to Lawton, Mich., at the age of five and received his education in the common schools at that place. Mr. Adams was married, and was a successful hardware merchant for twenty years. He was an enthusiastic devotee of fraternalism, being a member of the Maccabees, Modern Woodmen of America, Knights of Pythias and for years was an active worker in the Masonic fraternity from the blue lodge to the mystic shriners. In politics a Republican. He held the various village offices of President, Trustee, Recorder, Assessor and Treasurer.

EDGAR J. ADAMS

Representative from the First District of Kent County, Grand Rapids, 1897-8 and 1899-1900; and a member of the Constitutional Convention of 1907-8. Was born in Branch County, Mich., Aug. 6, 1866. When six years of age his parents moved to Monroe County, locating on a farm. Six years later his father sold out and

. moved to Elwell, Gratiot County, where he started a small country store; later moving to Dushville, Isabella County. His early education was acquired in the district schools of Monroe County. At the age of seventeen he taught school one term at the close of which he entered the employ of Hopkins & Lyon at Mt. Pleasant, as fire insurance and abstract clerk, where he continued for four years, and then engaged in the same business for himself. In 1888 he chose law for his profession, but being prevented by circumstances from entering an office or college, he pursued the course alone, and passed his examination before Judge Grove of the Kent County Bar. After that he devoted his entire time to his profession. In politics a Republican. He held the office of Justice of the Peace; was elected to the House of 1897-8 on the general legislative ticket of the city of Grand Rapids, and re-elected to the House of 1899-1900. Mr. Adams was chosen Speaker of the House of 1899-1900 on their organization.

EZRA C. ADAMS

Representative from the First District of Kalamazoo, 1861-2 and 1885. Was born at Collins Centre, Erie County, N. Y., July 14, 1823. At the age of fourteen he moved with his parents to Wayne County, N. Y., and subsequently to Franklin, Portage (now Kent County), O., where he commenced the study of medicine. At the age of twenty-one he graduated from the medical department of the Willoughby University. After practicing as a physician three years in Cuyahoga County, O., he returned to New York, where he engaged in his profession seven years at Collins, the town of his birth. In 1854 he removed to Kalamazoo County, Mich., and after that time resided in that and Allegan County as a medical practitioner. He was President of the village of Plainwell, and was a Republican member in the House from the First District of Kalamazoo County in 1861. In 1872 he was nominated as a member of the Legislature by the Democrats and Liberal Republicans of the Second District of Allegan, which nomination was declined. In 1874 he was nominated by the Democrats of his district and defeated by a small majority. In 1882 he was the Fusion candidate from the First Representative District of Kalamazoo County, and was defeated. In 1884 he was again nominated and elected.

ISAAC ADAMS

Representative from Oakland County, 1838. Was born at Andover, Mass., Apr. 23, 1767, and was by profession a physician, in politics a Free Soil Democrat. As a resident of Michigan he first settled in St. Joseph County in 1829, but removed from there to Oakland County in 1835. When he first went to White Pigeon the nearest postoffice was at Tecumseh, and there was no flour mill in St. Joseph County. Dr. Adams was a graduate of Harvard College. He was one of the committee on education in the House, of which Alpheus Felch was chairman, and assisted in preparing the bill to establish the University of Michigan, and took an active interest in that institution during his life. He died at Troy, Oakland County, in 1852.

JOHN Q. ADAMS

Representative from Marquette County, 1883-4. Was born in Cornwall, Litchfield County, Conn., Nov. 2, 1837. He remained with his parents until eighteen years of age, working upon the farm except during the winter months, a portion of which were spent in school. From 1856 to 1859 he was clerk in the drug store of J. M. Gardner, in the village of West Cornwall, Conn. In 1863 he commenced the study of law in the office of George Wheaton, of West Cornwall. His studies were pursued during evening hours, while the days were devoted to labor at such employments as he could engage in. He was admitted to the bar at Litchfield in April, 1865, and immediately entered upon the practice of law as the partner of his tutor, Mr. Wheaton, who died six months later, when Mr. Adams succeeded to his practice, and continued the same until March, 1872, when he removed to Negaunee, Marquette County, Mich., where he resided, and continued in the practice of his profession. In 1874 he was elected Circuit Court Commissioner of Marquette County, serving in that office until 1876, when he was elected Prosecuting Attorney of that county, and re-elected in 1878, and again in 1880, thus serving six consecutive years. In September, 1879, he formed a partnership with James F. Foley, of Negaunee, for mining purposes, and in the following month the firm discovered what is now known as the Milwaukee mine, in Negaunee, and which they sold in February, 1881. He was also interested largely in the New York Hematite Mine, and in other valuable mining properties in the mining districts of Lake Superior. Politically he was a Republican.

OLIVER ADAMS

Representative, Macomb County, 1853-4. His postoffice address was Utica. (Further information not obtainable).

OLIVER HOLT ADAMS

Representative from Isabella County, 1905-6 and 1907-8. Was born in the township of Coe, Isabella County, Mich., Apr. 28, 1860, and received his education in the district schools and Detroit Business University, from which he graduated in 1884. He was a successful farmer, lumberman and banker, and was vice president of the Commercial State Bank of Shepherd. He superintended his large farm in Coe, part of which his father located in 1854. He was married in June, 1901, to Mabel E. Curtiss of Reading, Mich. Mr. Adams always took an active part in politics and was chairman of the Republican County Committee. He held the office of Township Clerk; Supervisor six years and for four years chairman of the Board of Supervisors; was elected County Treasurer in 1898 and re-elected in 1900 by an increased majority.

OSCAR ADAMS

Representative from Genesee County, 1871-2. Was born in Harpersfield, Delaware County, N. Y., Apr. 16, 1827. At the age of twenty, he commenced the study of law at Buffalo, graduated from the Ballston Spa law school, and was admitted to the bar in 1850. He began practice in Erie County, N. Y., then removed to Wisconsin for two years. In 1855 he came to Flint, Mich. In 1860 he was elected Circuit Court Commissioner of Genesee County. During the war he was an army paymaster. He was several years president of the School Board at Flint and also its Treasurer. It was while he was a member that the fine high school building was erected in Flint. He was a lawyer by profession. In politics he was a Republican.

PETER R. ADAMS

Delegate from Lenawee County to the Constitutional Convention of 1850. Was born in Tioga County, Pa., studied law, and was admitted to the bar in 1825. He moved to Tecumseh, Mich., in 1830, where he practiced his profession until 1842, when he retired with a competence, and became a successful farmer. He died at Tecumseh in 1883.

ROBERT NEWTON ADAMS

Representative from Chippewa County, 1903-4 and 1905-6. Was born of English parents in Hastings County, Ont., May 13, 1844, and educated in the public schools of Ontario. He was married in 1867. Two sons were in the late Spanish War in Cuba. In 1878 he commenced farming in Chippewa County and after engaging in that ccupation for a time went into the real estate business and later became interested in the mercantile, mining and banking business. A Mason and a member of the commandery of Sault Ste. Marie. In politics a Republican after coming to Michigan. He was a member of the Board of Education of Sault Ste. Marie for ten years.

WALES ADAMS

Representative from Branch County, 1844 and 1845; and Delegate from Branch County to the Constitutional Convention of 1850. Was born at Medway, Norfolk County, Mass., Mar. 2, 1804, and was the son of a Revolutionary soldier. He received a common school education. From 1820 to 1828 he was engaged in mechanical work, most of the time in machine shops. In 1828 he went to New York City, and from there came to Bronson, Mich., in 1830, settling on a farm. With Willard Pierce he built the second sawmill in Branch County in 1831. He was for twenty years Supervisor of the township, and was for one term County Treasurer. Deceased.

ALLEN C. ADSIT

Representative from Ottawa County, 1871-2. Was born in Rutland, Jefferson County, N. Y., Feb. 20, 1837. His early life was spent upon his father's farm, receiving such education as the district school and county institute afforded. He studied law at Watertown, N. Y., and was admitted to the bar in 1859. He enlisted in the 44th N. Y. Vol. in 1861, and participated in the principal battles in which the Army of the Potomac was engaged. At the close of the war he settled at Spring Lake, Ottawa County, Mich., and engaged in the mercantile business in company with Hon. J. B. Perham. He was Supervisor of said town for six successive years, and President of the village in 1871. In 1874, having resumed the practice of law, he was elected Prosecuting Attorney for said county, and served during the years 1875 and 1876. In 1886 he was U. S. District Attorney in Judge Kent's Circuit. He removed to Grand Rapids in 1877, where he resided and engaged in the practice of the law. In politics he was a Democrat. He died Jan. 2, 1912, at Grand Rapids, Mich.

M. LIVY AGENS

Representative from Mason County, 1905-6, 1907-8 and 1909. Was born in Orange, N. J., June 17, 1855, of Scotch and Irish descent. He received his education in the public schools, coming to Kalamazoo, Mich., in 1864. He was married to Eva Holmes, Dec. 25, 1876. Mr. Agens engaged in farming and fruit growing after 1874 on his farm in Mason County. In politics a Republican. He held various offices of trust in his township; was President of the State Grange Fire Insurance Co., and President of the Grange Cyclone Insurance Co. Mr. Agens, after several weeks sickness, died at his temporary home in Lansing, March 30, 1909.

DAVID D. AITKEN

Member of Congress, 1893-5 and 1895-7. Was born in Genesee County, Mich., Sept. 5, 1854. He was educated in the public schools of Flint and admitted to the bar in 1879. He was elected to the Fifty-third Congress as a Republican and re-elected to the Fifty-fourth Congress. Mr. Aitken resumed the practice of law and became supreme counselor and attorney for the Maccabees of the World.

ROBERT P. AITKIN

Representative from Genesee County, 1865-6 and 1867-8. Was born Feb. 15, 1819, in Perth, Fulton County, N. Y., and was of Scotch parentage. He attended district schools winters until the age of seventeen, when he became a clerk in a military store in the city of New York. After six years' service in that place he emigrated in 1842 to Genesee County, Mich., and bought part of the farm later owned by him in the township of Flint, paid for it out of his small earnings and commenced the task of clearing up a farm. He married Miss Johnston in 1843. He lived on the same farm, and in 1886 was serving his 25th year as Supervisor of the town of Flint. He cast his first vote for Harrison, and remained a Whig until 1854, then a Republican. He was a member of the Episcopal Church. He was the organizer and director and secretary of the Genesee County Mutual Fire Insurance Co. He died in 1905 on the farm where he had lived 63 years.

WILLIAM H. AITKIN

Senator, 1909-10, from the Twentieth District, comprising the counties of Huron and Sanilac. Was born at Port Sanilac, Sanilac County, Mich., Nov. 16, 1860, of Scotch descent. He was educated in the public schools at Port Sanilac, supplemented by private instruction. He was clerk and bookkeeper until 1882, when he became cashier of the Sanilac County State Bank of Croswell, Mich. In 1888 he was admitted to the bar, and then engaged in banking and the practice of his profession. He was president of the Croswell Milling Company, president of the State Bank of Croswell, and connected with other banking institutions. In politics a Republican. He was a delegate to the National Republican Convention at St. Louis in 1896, and was Chairman of the Republican county and district committees but never a candidate for public office until nominated at the primaries, without opposition, for State Senator and was elected Nov. 3, 1908.

HIRAM ALDEN

Representative from Branch County, 1835-6 and 1837. Was born in Ashfield, Mass., in October, 1792. He moved with his father's family to Rome, N. J., in 1800, where he passed his boyhood days and acquired an education with the privations incident to these early days. He studied medicine with Dr. Rathburn, of Camden, N. J., completing his course in Cincinnati, in 1824, and acquired an enviable reputation in the profession. He came from Ripley, N. J., to Coldwater in 1834. In 1838 he was appointed by Governor Mason Commissioner of Internal Improvements, and was acting Railroad Commissioner at the time of the construction of the railroad from Detroit to Pontiac. He died at Detroit, Nov. 26, 1838, and was followed to his grave by six hundred officials and laborers, who insisted on paying the expenses as their tribute to a friend and an honest man.

FRANK ALDRICH

Representative from the First District of Detroit, 1899-1900. Was born in Pierpont, O., March 17, 1850; moved to Oberlin, O., in 1856, and attended the public schools there and in Pittsfield, near Oberlin, until 1865. He enlisted in the 3d U. S. artillery in 1867, and was sergeant when discharged in 1870, when he went to Iowa and taught country school for two years. In 1875 he went into the Black Hills, and was among the pioneers of the gold fields. In 1878 he went to Washington, D. C., read law for two years, and in 1880 engaged in business there with Gately & Haskell, book publishers; bought the interest of Mr. Haskell in 1885, and conducted the Washington branch of the Gately & Aldrich company until Mr. Gately's death, in 1889, when he accepted the management of the Hanson Battery Light and Power Company, and was also electrician for the company. He held several civil appointive offices during his fourteen years' residence in the District of Columbia, and in 1899 President Harrison appointed him Quartermaster-General of the D. of C. N. G., which position he held until his removal to Detroit. In politics a Republican. He was editor of the *Times-Standard*, a Washington weekly, during the Blaine and Logan campaign; was a delegate to the Chickering Hall convention, in New York, when the National Republican League was organized, and was chairman of the Republican Central Committee of the District of Columbia during the second Harrison campaign. He removed to Detroit, Mich., in 1892, and in 1893 invented and patented a car seal which was almost immediately adopted by several large railway systems. In 1894 he chartered and organized the "Aldrich Car Seal Manufacturing Company." In 1896 he sold his interest in this company, and engaged in designing and manufacturing special machinery.

FRANK B. ALDRICH

Representative from Cheboygan County, 1919-20 and 1921-2. Was born at Kingston, Ont., Aug. 8, 1864, of Irish parentage. In 1866 he removed with his parents to Defiance, O., where he received his education in the public schools. He lived on a farm with his parents until he was twenty-five years of age, when, in 1889, he moved to Cheboygan, Cheboygan County, Mich. He is chiefly interested in farming. He served three years as Supervisor and was chairman of the township war board. Mr. Aldrich is married and has one son. In politics he is a Republican.

LEVI ALDRICH

Representative from Cass County, 1863-4; Senator from the Seventeenth District, 1865; and a Delegate from Cass County to the Constitutional Convention in 1867. Was born in Erie County, N. Y., Jan. 27, 1820. His father, Levi Aldrich, was a pioneer farmer of Erie County. He received an academical education, studied Medicine, at the Albany Medical College and Buffalo Medical University, and practiced medicine successfully in Erie County until 1860, when his health failing him, he removed to Cass County and settled on a farm, but soon resumed his practice at Edwardsburg, which was extensive and lucrative. In politics he was an active Republican, and a Quaker in religion, but contributed to the support of various denominations. He died at Edwardsburg, Dec. 16, 1892.

OSCAR EMMET ALESHIRE

Representative from the Second District of Berrien County, 1889-90. Was born in Hancock County, Ill., Nov. 29, 1861. By profession editor and proprietor of the *Enterprise*, a weekly newspaper. Mr. Aleshire was brought up on a farm, graduated from Carthage College in Illinois in 1882, with first honors and valedictory of his class. He taught school until the spring of 1888, when he engaged in the newspaper business. He was superintendent of the Buchanan schools four years, the entire time of his residence in this State. He was married in Aug., 1887, to Mary M. Stepp, of Carthage, Ill. He was a candidate for the office of school inspector and member of the Common Council of Buchanan.

LORENZO P. ALEXANDER

Representative from Berrien County, 1861-2; Delegate from Berrien County to the Constitutional Convention in 1867; and Senator from the Sixteenth District, 1871-2. Was born in Angelica, Alleghany County, N. Y., Aug. 10, 1820. When twenty-one he came to Michigan, and settled at Buchanan, where he resided. In 1844 he was a Militia Captain, and in 1845 became Colonel of the 28th Regiment. During his first six years he was a carpenter; then for three years in the boot and shoe trade; and then for more than twenty years in the general mercantile trade. He was Constable and Town Treasurer five years; School Director twenty-five years; Town Clerk; Justice of the Peace; and many years Supervisor. He was a Delegate to the Republican National Convention at Baltimore in 1864, and was a member of the committee that notified President Lincoln of his renomination. He was Postmaster of Buchanan from 1862 to 1866 and again from 1877 to 1886. He was a Republican after 1854.

SYDNEY U. ALEXANDER

Representative from the First District of Clinton County, 1867-8. Was born in Westfield, Medina County, O., May 22, 1835. His father removed to DeWitt in 1837. In 1850 he entered the printing office of the Clinton *Express*, at DeWitt, and learned the trade of a printer, under the direction of Mark A. Childs. After five years' service as printer he became a farmer. In 1860 he was elected Supervisor of Olive, and held the position five years; was Supervisor of Watertown two years. In politics he was a Democrat. He died in Eagle Township Aug. 26, 1897.

SYLVANUS ALEXANDER

Representative from the Wexford District, comprising the counties of Wexford and Lake, 1889-90 and 1891-2. Was born in Cass County, Mich., Sept. 16, 1852. By occupation a farmer. In politics a Republican. He held the office of Supervisor two terms.

RUSSELL A. ALGER

Governor of Michigan, 1885-7; Secretary of War, 1897-9; and United States Senator, 1902-7. Was born in Lafayette Township, Medina County, O., Feb. 27, 1836. At the age of eleven years his parents died and for seven years he labored on a farm, attending the Richfield Academy, in Summit County, O., in winters, and subsequently taught country school. Later he studied law at Akron, O., and was admitted to the bar by the Supreme Court of that State March, 1859; the degree LL.D. was conferred upon him by Hillsdale College in May, 1855. In December, 1859, he moved to Grand Rapids, Mich., and extensively engaged in the lumber business and other industries. In Aug., 1861, he enlisted in the Army and mustered into service as captain of Company C, Second Michigan Cavalry, Sept. 2, 1861, and was promoted until he became brevet major-general U. S. Volunteers, June 11, 1865, for gallant and meritorious services during the war, having participated in 66 battles and skirmishes. He was elected commander in chief of the Grand Army of the Republic in 1889. In politics he was a Republican. He was a Delegate to the Republican National Convention of 1884, and elected Governor of Michigan in the same year, declining a renomination in 1886. He was first elector at large of his State in 1888 and in March, 1897, was appointed Secretary of War by President McKinley, resigning Aug. 1, 1899. On Sept. 27, 1902, he was appointed United States Senator by Governor Bliss, of Michigan, to fill the vacancy caused by the death of James McMillan; took his seat Dec. 1, 1902; was elected by the Legislature in Jan., 1903; and served until his death at Detroit, Jan. 24, 1907.

HOMER L. ALLARD

Representative from St. Joseph County, 1919-20 and 1921-2. Was born June 10, 1867, at Sturgis, Mich., of New England parentage. He received a common school education and began work at fifteen years of age. He became a cigar maker at nineteen and worked in various parts of the State until 1898, when he purchased an interest in a cigar store and factory in Sturgis. He is still engaged in the cigar business. Mr. Allard is married. He served as alderman three terms, and as mayor two terms. In politics he is a Republican.

ABRAM ALLEN

Representative from Oakland County, 1865-6. Was born in Monroe County, N. Y., June 18, 1817. He came to Michigan in 1835, and settled in Commerce, Oakland County. He was Supervisor of that town in 1860, 1861 and 1863. He was Republican in politics. He removed to Lansing in 1867 and engaged in manufacturing sash, doors and blinds; also in the lumbering business. He died at Lansing Oct. 2, 1899.

ARTEMAS ALLEN

Representative from Lenawee County, 1839. Was born in the State of New York, and before coming to Michigan was a contractor for building an aqueduct for the Erie Canal over Tonawanda Creek, and came to Michigan from Medina, N. Y., as early as 1836, settling at Medina, Lenawee County, where he was engaged in milling and mercantile business. Later he was a resident of Coldwater, where he died, Nov. 1, 1873. In politics he was a Democrat.

EDWARD PAYSON ALLEN

Representative in 1877-8 and 1879-80; member of Congress, 1887-9 and 1889-91; and member of the State Board of Agriculture, 1899-1905. Was born in Sharon, Washtenaw County, Mich., Oct. 28, 1839; worked on a farm until twenty years old, attending school and teaching during winters; graduated from the State Normal School in March, 1864; taught the Union School in Vassar, Mich., for the three months following, when he enlisted and helped to raise a company for the Twenty-ninth Michigan Infantry; was commissioned First Lieutenant in that regiment in the following September, and went with it southwest, where the regiment was engaged in active campaigning until the 1st of April. In Sept., 1865, he was mustered out of the service with his regiment as Captain; entered the law school at Ann Arbor, graduating in March, 1867; and formed a partnership with Hon. S. M. Cutcheon. Upon the removal of Mr. Cutcheon to Detroit, in 1875, he continued the practice alone at Ypsilanti; was elected Alderman of Ypsilanti in 1872 and 1874 and Mayor in 1880; and was Prosecuting Attorney of Washtenaw County in 1872. He was elected to the Lower House of the Legislature in 1876, serving as chairman of the Committee on Education; was again elected in 1878, at which time he was elected Speaker *pro tem;* was appointed Assistant Assessor of Internal Revenue in 1869; was United States Indian Agent for Michigan in Aug., 1882, which office he held until Dec., 1885; ran for Congress in 1884, and was defeated by Col. Eldridge, Democrat, and was elected to the 50th Congress as a Republican, and re-elected to the 51st Congress. He was appointed a member of the State Board of Agriculture Jan. 25, 1899, to succeed Arthur C. Bird, who had resigned.

GEORGE W. ALLEN

Representative from Kent County, 1859-60 and 1865-6. Was born in Enfield, Hartford County, Conn., Sept. 17, 1818. When three years of age he was taken by his mother (his father being dead) to the Connecticut Western Reserve, O., where she settled in the town of Painesville. Mr. Allen remained in Painesville until 1853, when he, with his family, removed to Grand Rapids, Mich. The session of 1859 was noted for the passage of three important acts, viz.: The act abolishing the grand jury system, the swamp land road act, and the act to encourage and develop the salt interest, by offering a bounty of ten cents per bushel on all salt manufactured in the State. Mr. Allen was chairman of the house select committee on salt. In 1886 he was appointed U. S. Pension Agent for Western Michigan. He held several important positions connected with city affairs. Politically he was a Whig as long as the Whig party existed, after which he was a Republican of a pronounced type. His death was reported as Jan. 12, 1898.

GILES B. ALLEN

Representative from the Second District of Eaton County, 1895-6. Was born in Freedom, Washtenaw County, Mich., March 2, 1843. At the age of four years he removed with his parents to Lodi, where two years later his father died; he attended district school, the Ann Arbor High School, and Lodi Academy. On June 1, 1861, he enlisted in Company F, 6th Mich. Infantry, remaining in the service until Aug., 1864, when he was honorably discharged as Sergeant Major. On his return he entered the medical Department of the University of Michigan, receiving the degree of M.D., March, 1867; began the practice of medicine in Norvell and Grass Lake, Jackson County, and two years later moved to Charlotte, where he continued in the practice of his profession. In politics a Republican. He served as Alderman four years, member of the Board of Education six years; and was President of the Pension examining surgeons at Charlotte during President Harrison's administration.

HARMON ALLEN

Representative from Monroe County, 1857-8. Was born in the State of Vermont in 1810. By occupation he was a farmer and civil engineer. In politics he was a Democrat until the Dred Scott decision, then a Republican. Several times he was Supervisor of Milan, Town Clerk, and filled the position of County Surveyor several times. He settled in Monroe County in 1832 and later lived in Milan.

HIRAM MURRAY ALLEN

Representative from the Second District of Eaton County, 1887-8. Was born in the township of Tecumseh, Lenawee County, Nov. 16, 1834. His parents were pioneers, having moved from Vermont to this State in 1829. In 1835 they moved to Marshall, Calhoun County. His boyhood was spent on the farm, and he attended the district school winters. At the age of seventeen he began teaching winters, and working on his father's farm summers. At the age of twenty-five he married Mary L. Hewitt, and in the spring of 1860 he moved on a new farm in Bellevue, Eaton County. In 1876 he sold his farm and bought one of the finest in Central Michigan, known as the "Captain Fitzgerald farm." He held the offices of Township Treasurer, School Inspector, and Village Trustee, and for a number of years was a member of the county committee. In politics he was a Republican. He died at Bellevue June 21, 1918.

JOHN ALLEN

Senator from the Second District, 1845-6 and 1847-8. Was born in Augusta County, Va., May 17, 1796. His parents were James and Elizabeth (Tate) Allen, both native Virginians. Mr. Allen spent his early life in Virginia, where he received his education. In January, 1824, he came to Michigan, and, in company with E. W. Rumsey, located the site of Ann Arbor. He engaged in land speculation and at one time owned thousands of acres of land in the western part of the State, much of which was lost in the panic of 1837. In company with Samuel W. Dexter, he published for a time the *Western Emigrant*, the first paper in Washtenaw County. He studied law with James Kingsley, and was admitted to the bar in 1832, but gave little time to the profession. He went to California in 1850 and died there Mar. 11, 1851.

LEWIS ALLEN

Representative from Washtenaw County, 1839. Was born Aug. 19, 1797, at Morristown, N. J. His father moved to Seneca County, N. Y., in 1803. The county was then a wilderness. He lived in Seneca County until 1832, when he moved to Sharon, Washtenaw County. On the organization of the township in 1834, he was elected its first Supervisor, which office he held repeatedly, as also that of Justice of the Peace. He was one of the founders of the Presbyterian Church in the adjoining village of Manchester, for many years was a ruling elder therein, and always gave much time and attention to educational and religious matters in his neighborhood. In politics he was a Democrat. He died in Sharon on the farm where he first settled, on the 14th day of October, 1854, aged 57 years.

LOVATUS C. ALLEN

Representative from Washtenaw County, 1863-4. Was born Sept. 21, 1816, at Huntington, Vt. He received a common school education and taught at eighteen. He worked summers and taught winters in his native town until 1841. He then taught in the vicinity of Deckertown, N. Y., continuously for five years. He then took an interest in a woolen factory for three years at Branchville, N. J. He came to Michigan about 1850 and settled on a farm in York, Washtenaw County. He held various town offices. He was a Democrat in politics.

MARVIN ALLEN

Member of the Board of Regents of the University, 1843-52. Was born at Fabius, N. Y., Nov. 4, 1800, son of Peter and Rowena (Pearce) Allen. His early life was spent on a farm. He studied at Hamilton College, N. Y., and was graduated from the Theological Department in 1826. Sept. 12, 1826, he was married to Julia Ann Green, of Auburn, N. Y. After holding pastorates in the Baptist churches at Williamson, Manchester, and Canandaigua, New York, he came to Michigan in 1837 and was settled as pastor over the Baptist Church at Adrian. In 1843 he accepted a call to the Baptist Church in Ann Arbor, where he remained three years. In 1846 the State Baptist Convention appointed him general missionary to the churches of the State, and he spent the next four years travelling over the State, forming new churches and encouraging the feeble ones. In 1850 he took up his residence in Detroit, where he conducted a bookstore and published "The Michigan Christian Herald." He was appointed Regent of the University, Mar. 9, 1843, and was continued in office by successive reappointments till Jan. 1, 1852. He was an unusually punctual and active member of the Board. He died at Detroit, June 13, 1861.

MORRIS S. ALLEN

Representative from Clinton County, 1849. Was born Apr. 10, 1809, in Richfield, Otsego County, N. Y. In 1836 he came to Clinton County, Mich., and remained until 1838, when he removed to Iowa; remained two years, then returned to New York, and back to DeWitt, Mich., in 1840. In 1844 he was elected Sheriff of Clinton County. In 1856 he removed to Sabula, Ia., and was clerk for P. S. Stiles in a grain and pork packing establishment. In 1867 he was elected Sheriff of Jackson County, Ia., and held the office six years. From 1875 to 1884 he was in business at Miles, Ia. In politics he was a Democrat. He died Jan. 13, 1886, at Sabula, Ia.

THOMAS J. ALLEN

Senator, 1907-8, from the Thirteenth District, comprising the counties of Genesee and Livingston. Was born on his father's farm in the township of Arbela, Tuscola County, Mich., Nov. 13, 1863, where he lived until he was eighteen years of age. His education was obtained in the public schools of Tuscola County and in the high school at Flint. After teaching in the district and village schools of Tuscola

County, he entered the Michigan School for the Deaf at Flint, remaining there as an instructor until Jan. 1, 1901, a period of sixteen years. In politics a Republican. He was elected county clerk of Genesee County in Nov., 1900, serving two terms. In the meantime he studied law, was admitted to practice, Oct. 16, 1903, and immediately after the expiration of his second term as County Clerk formed a law partnership under the firm name of Martin and Allen.

FREEMAN W. ALLISON

Representative from Livingston County, 1897-8. Was born in Pinckney, said county, Apr. 24, 1845, and acquired his early education in the district schools supplemented by four years of select school and two terms at Ypsilanti; taught school seven winters, devoting his summers to work on the farm. In 1869 he moved on the farm and engaged in farming. In politics a Populist. He was candidate for Supervisor and Register of Deeds; was a member of the Board of Review and elected Representative to the House of 1897-8 on the Democratic People's Union Silver Ticket.

WILLIAM ALLMAN

Representative from St. Joseph County, 1857-8 and 1877-8. Was born in England, May 12, 1818. He completed his education at Asbury University, Ind., and in 1839 removed to Sturgis, Mich., where he was a merchant tailor. He was secretary of the Grand Rapids & Indiana Railroad Company at its organization and for years thereafter; filled many local offices; was trustee of Albion College for several terms; president of the First National Bank of Sturgis. In politics he was a Republican. He died Dec. 31, 1894, at Sturgis.

WILLIAM H. ALLSWEDE

Senator, 1913-14, from the Twenty-fourth Senatorial District, comprising the counties of Bay and Midland. Was born at Red Keg, Midland County, Mich., Jan. 22, 1874, of German parentage. He was educated in the common schools. He was married June 30, 1897, to Lola M., daughter of Mr. and Mrs. Charles Sanford, and they have one son. Mr. Allswede worked the old homestead three years, later associating with his brother under the firm name of Allswede Brothers. Afterwards this firm was consolidated with E. A. Lane under the name of Sanford Mercantile Company. On the retirement of E. A. Lane he took over the grain department of the firm and engaged in the grain and produce business at Sanford. In politics a National Progressive.

JOHN ALMY

Representative from Kent County, 1837. Was a native of Rhode Island, and was educated as a civil engineer. He was for years a resident of Geneseo, N. Y., where he married Eliza Pierce. He came to Detroit in 1834, where he had been appointed City Engineer, remained there several years and laid out the system of sewers and street grades for that city. In 1855 he laid out the village of Kent, now Grand Rapids, for Lucius Lyon and N. O. Sargeant. Mr. Lyon sold out his interest to Charles H. Carroll of Groveland, N. Y., and Mr. Almy was placed in charge. He built the first stone dwelling in Grand Rapids. He was Judge of the county court,

City Engineer, engineer of the Kalamazoo and other river improvements, and chief clerk in the office of the Surveyor General. He was a man of much learning, of fine physical form and a courteous, genial gentleman. He was an Episcopalian. He died in 1863.

CHARLES H. ALVORD

Representative from Hillsdale County, 1907-8. Was born at Camden, Oct. 16, 1872, on a farm. He is a son of Nathan A. Alvord, who represented the First District of Hilldale County in the Legislature of 1881-3. During the session of 1883 he served as messenger in the House. He graduated from Hillsdale High School in 1890, attended Hillsdale College the two succeeding years and entered the Michigan Agricultural College in 1893, graduating with the class of 1895. Following his graduation he located on a farm in Camden but in the fall of 1897 he returned to the Agricultural College to accept an appointment as assistant agriculturist and foreman of the college farm. In 1899 he removed to College Station, Texas, where he was made Assistant Professor of Agriculture in the Texas Agricultural College, which position he resigned in 1902, and returned to the farm in Camden which in the meantime he had purchased. In 1896 he was married to Lottie L. Hicks of Hudson, Mich. He was connected with the farmer's institute work as State lecturer and a director of the Hillsdale County Agricultural Society. In politics a Republican.

HENRY J. ALVORD

Senator from the Twenty-ninth District, 1855-6. His postoffice address was Lapeer, Lapeer County. (Further data not obtainable).

NATHAN ALVORD

Representative from the First District of Hillsdale County, 1881-2 and 1883-4. Was born Aug. 17, 1834, in the town of Cancadea, Alleghany County, N. Y., and removed with his father to Williams County, in northwestern Ohio, in the fall of 1842. His early life was spent on his parents' farm, attending district school whenever possible. When seventeen years of age, he attended a summer term of the union school at West Unity, O., and taught a district school the next winter near that place. In the following spring, in company with an elder brother, he went to Princeton, Ill. There he worked on a farm during the summer months, and the following winter attended Princeton Academy. After spending about five years in Illinois, Minnesota, and Iowa, he returned to Ohio. He was married to Miss Melinda Landon in the fall of 1856. In the following spring he moved to Camden, Hillsdale County, this State, and engaged in the mercantile business, following that pursuit until the spring of 1869, when he bought a farm in Camden. He then engaged in farming and dealing in live stock. In politics he was a Republican. He died at Hillsdale Jan. 22, 1892.

ROBERT ALWARD

Representative from the Second District of Ottawa County, 1897-8, 1899-1900 and 1901-2. Was born in Norfolk County, Province of Ontario, Nov. 12, 1844. His parents were of Pennsylvania Dutch descent. After the death of his mother the family became separated and young Robert found a home with a farmer in Canada, where he lived until nineteen years of age; during which time he acquired a common school education. He came to Michigan in the fall of 1863, and worked in the mills and lumber woods for four years. On Apr. 14, 1867, he was married to Miss Alvevra Barton of New York State, and settled on a farm in the township of Georgetown. In politics a Republican. He was Township Treasurer four years; Supervisor seven years; Vice President and Chairman of the Board of Directors of the Kent, Allegan and Ottawa Counties Farmers' Mutual Fire Insurance Company; represented his county before the Board of Equalization; was a candidate to the House of 1892-3, but was defeated by the Democratic landslide; was elected to the House for the terms of 1897-8 and 1899-1900, and re-elected to the House of 1901-2.

VERNE C. AMBERSON

Senator, 1913-14, from the Nineteenth District, comprising the counties of Lenawee and Monroe. Was born in Ogden Township, Lenawee County, in 1883, of Scotch and English parents. He graduated from the Blissfield High School in 1899, from the Adrian High School in 1900, and taught school two years, after which he entered the literary department of the University of Michigan. He remained there two years and in 1907 graduated from the law department. After 1908 Mr. Amberson engaged in the practice of law. In politics a Democrat.

WILLIAM E. AMBLER

Senator from the Twenty-seventh District, 1879-80. Was born at Medina, O., Dec. 18, 1845, and resided there until his parents removed to Hillsdale, Mich., in 1859. He entered Hillsdale College, but in 1865 left that institution, going to Albion College, where he graduated in the scientific course. In 1866 he entered the Law School at Albany, graduated, and was admitted to practice. In 1867 he finished the classical course at Adrian College, graduating with the degree of A. B. The same fall he established himself as a lawyer at Minneapolis, Minn., but in 1868 he returned to Michigan and began the practice of law at Pentwater, where he continued to reside. He was President of the village, and was a member of the firm of Neilsen & Co., bankers. In 1870 Adrian College conferred on him the degree of A.M., and in 1875 Hillsdale College did likewise. Mr. Ambler was chosen a trustee of the latter institution. He was Judge of Probate for Oceana County. In 1893 he moved to Cleveland, O., and engaged in the real estate business.

HARVEY S. AMERSON

Representative from Antrim County, 1911-12. Was born in Illinois, Nov. 29, 1875, of German and English descent, and received his education in the Chicago Public Schools. For ten years he was traveling salesman for the John V. Farwell Company and later embarked in the mercantile business at Elk Rapids. He married Louise E. Dougherty, youngest daughter of Hon. A. K. Dougherty. He was treasurer of the Antrim County Republican Club, a member of the Antrim County Executive Committee and active in promoting his section. He is a Shriner, Knight Templar, Odd Fellow and a member of the Elks. In politics he is Republican.

JAMES W. AMES

Representative from the First District of Wayne County, 1901-2. Was born in New Orleans, La., Oct. 12, 1864. At the age of eleven he was apprenticed to learn the cooper's trade, which he completed when seventeen years old. He entered the literary department of Straight University in his native city, after which he entered the medical department of Howard University, Washington, D. C., from both of which colleges he graduated, coming to Michigan in June, 1894, after which time he was in the active practice of medicine. Married. In politics a Republican. He was elected to the Legislature of 1901-2, on the general legislative ticket.

JOSEPH G. AMES

Representative from Berrien County, 1844. Was born in New Hampshire in 1808. He settled in the town of Weesaw, Berrien County, in 1837, and was the first Supervisor of that town in 1839. He, with three others, were owners of the village of New Troy, platted in 1837. In 1839 he removed to a farm in Bertrand, where he was Supervisor in 1842. Afterwards he became a resident of Three Oaks and was the first Postmaster there in 1854. He died Aug. 12, 1855.

MICHAEL E. AMES

Representative from Wayne County, 1846, was a practicing attorney, and settled in Plymouth about three years prior to his election. He was an Eastern man, but the time and place of his nativity are unknown. He removed to Detroit after his legislative term, and soon thereafter went to Stillwater, Minn., and in 1850 was elected a member of the second territorial Legislature and was speaker of the Assembly Jan. 1 to March 31, 1851. Politics he was presumably Democratic. He is supposed to have died some years prior to 1888.

EDMUND S. AMIDON

Representative from the county of St. Joseph, 1895-6. Was born in Sturgis, Mich., Jan. 5, 1840. His school education was acquired in the union schools of Sturgis; taught school for several terms, and in 1856 began the mason trade, in which occupation he continued until Aug., 1862, when he enlisted in Company E, 19th Mich. Infantry. He was chosen First Sergeant of his company, and was serving in that capacity when in the battle of Thompson Station, Tenn., he received a minnie ball through his right arm and a contused shell wound of his right hip; discharged for wounds July, 1863. The following year he engaged in the business of contractor and builder, in which occupation he continued until 1888; then engaged in the lumber business at Sturgis and Athens. In politics a Republican. He held the office of Village Clerk, President of the Village of Sturgis; Director in the Citizen's State Bank, member of library board, and President of the Michigan Retail Lumber Dealers' Association.

AARON AMON

Representative 1915-16 and 1917-18 from Mecosta County; and Senator, 1919-20 and 1921-2, from the Twenty-fifth District comprising the counties of Gratiot, Isabella and Mecosta. Was born on a farm in Waterloo County, Ont., Nov. 5, 1859. At the age of five years he removed with his parents to Caledonia, Kent County, Mich., where he received his education. In 1882 he located in the village of Remus, Mecosta County, and platted a part of the village. His principal occupation is farming. Mr. Amon is married and has three children. He held the office of Supervisor of Wheatland Township for twenty years and was chairman of the board for four years. In politics a Republican.

ANDREW F. ANDERSON

Representative, 1915-16 and 1917-18, from the Leelanau District, comprising the counties of Benzie and Leelanau. Was born at Blekinge, Sweden, Oct. 3, 1857. He came to America in 1869, and after a short stay at Chicago and Evanston, Ill., he removed to Galesburg, Ill. Clerked in a store and worked on farm and was railway newsboy out of Galesburg. In the fall of 1880 he came to Michigan. Clerked in a store at Suttons Bay until 1883, when he embarked in the mercantile and lumbering business at Omena. Mr. Anderson was married in 1883 to Marit Bahle, of Suttons Bay; fraternally a member of the F. & A. M., R. A. M., and I. O. O. F. In politics a Republican.

DAVID ANDERSON

Senator from the Thirteenth District, 1873-4. Was born Nov. 26, 1825, in the town of Clarendon, Orleans County, N. Y., and received a common school education. He emigrated to Michigan in 1854, and settled in the town of Madison, Branch County. In 1865 he removed to the town of Columbia, where he resided. He held various offices of trust in his township. In 1862 he joined the 19th Mich. Infantry, received the commission of First Lieutenant, and in the same year was promoted to the rank of Captain. In 1864 he was commissioned as Major, and at the close of the war received a Colonel's commission. His occupation was that of a lumber manufacturer.

JEREMIAH H. ANDERSON

Representative from the First District of Kent County, 1893-4, 1897-8, 1899-1900, 1903-4 and 1907-8. Was born in Walker Township, Kent County, May 22, 1843, of Scotch descent. He acquired his education in the district schools. In 1865 he moved to Grand Rapids, secured work in a factory and in 1892 began the manufacture of furniture, but two years later burned out. He lost nearly everything invested in the plant and resumed work in a furniture factory. Married. In politics a Republican. He held the office of Alderman of Grand Rapids, three terms, and was Deputy County Clerk.

ROBERT H. ANDERSON

Delegate from Jackson County to the Constitutional Convention of 1850. Was born in Ireland in 1810, and came to this country in 1817. He settled in Tompkins, Mich., in 1835, helped organize the town and named it from Tompkinsville, N. J., where he had lived. He was a Judge in Jackson County in 1838. He was a farmer and a Democrat.

SAMUEL F. ANDERSON

Representative from Cass and Van Buren counties, 1842 and 1843. Was born in Ira, Rutland County, Vt., Feb. 19, 1803. His father, John Anderson, served in the Revolution, and was for eleven years a member of the Vermont Legislature. The son, when a young man, emigrated to Western New York and cleared up a farm. In 1835 he removed to La Grange, Cass County, Mich., and bought a farm of 200 acres. He was Associate County Judge in 1845-6. In politics he was first a Democrat, he became a Freesoiler in 1852, and a Republican in 1854. He sent two sons to the army in 1861, of whom one was killed. He died Apr. 14, 1877.

WILLIAM A. ANDERSON

Representative from Newaygo County, 1887-8. Was born in Elgin County, Ont., in 1843, the son of a farmer. At a very early age he acquired a thirst for knowledge which was gratified as well as the public schools and academies of the province would permit. At twenty years of age he was employed in one of the largest nurseries in the province, and he remained until 1863, when he came to Newaygo County, where he resided. He built the Aetna flouring mills, on White River, and operated them for many years; he cleared up a large farm; he engaged in logging at various times, and at one time in the manufacture of lumber and shingles, and for six years represented the township of Denver on the Board of Supervisors, holding that office at the time he removed from the town. Mr. Anderson conceived the idea of building a flouring-mill at Fremont, and in February, 1886, the "Crescent Mill" was in operation at Fremont. In politics he was a consistent Republican. He served one term as chairman of the Republican County Committee, and was unanimously re-elected to a second term. He held the offices of Supervisor and School Director.

CHARLES ANDREWS

Senator from the Fourth District, 1867-8 and 1869-70. Was born at Putney, Vt., Aug. 28, 1820. In 1828 he removed with his father, Rev. Elisha D. Andrews, to West Bloomfield, Ontario County, N. Y., and from there to Mendon, Monroe County, in 1829, and in 1831 to Pittsford, same county. In 1841 the family removed to Armada, Mich., and settled upon land previously purchased of the government. His education was received principally at a private school and at the Rochester, N. Y., Collegiate Institute. In politics he was a Whig until the organization of the Republican party, and remained a Republican ever since. He was a farmer. He owned his farm, but retired from its active management, and lived in Armada village. He was sixteen times elected and appointed Supervisor of his township. He was Senator from Macomb County in 1867-8 and 1869-70, where he gained the reputation of a valuable committee worker. He was Deputy U. S. Collector for Macomb County four years, and was honorably discharged. He was nominated for Judge of Probate in 1880, but failed of an election. He was a member of the Congregational Church since 1841. He was two years president of the Macomb County Agricultural Society, and six years president of the Armada Agricultural Society. For many years he was a director and the vice president of the Macomb County Mutual Insurance Co., and held various other positions of responsibility and trust. He died at Armada Nov. 14, 1902.

JOHN ANDREWS

Representative from Cass and Van Buren Counties, 1843, 1845 and 1849. Was born in Schuyler, Oneida County, N. Y., June 1, 1808, and removed from there to Cayuga County, N. Y., when young, where he lived until 1840, when he removed to Van Buren County, Mich., first living at Paw Paw and later at Lawrence. He was a farmer and was also engaged in lumbering. In politics a Democrat.

JOHN L. ANDREWS

Representative from the Third District of Oakland County, 1871-2. Was born in Chili, Monroe County, N. Y., Apr. 8, 1822. He resided in that and the adjoining town of Wheatland until 1836, when his father settled in Brighton, Mich. In 1841 he went to Milford and learned the miller's trade, at which he worked until 1859. He then bought the Pettibone mills and ran them until 1872, when he sold out, and established the Milford Exchange Bank, which he sold in 1876 to the Wilhelm Brothers, and bought a farm of 410 acres adjoining the village of Milford. He married Delphia Bartlett in 1846. She died in 1854, and he married Laura E. Fuller in 1859. He was a director of the Wayne & Monroe R. R. Company from its organization until its sale to the F. & P. M. Company. He was a member of the School Board for over thirty years. He was a Whig but was a Republican after the organization of that party. He died at Milford Feb. 17, 1897.

JOSIAH ANDREWS

Representative from Cass and Van Buren counties, 1846. Was born at Metz, Cayuga County, N. Y., June 28, 1812, and received his early education in the common schools, and at Cazenovia. He studied medicine and graduated with the highest honors from Fairfield Medical College in 1838, and settled at Paw Paw, Mich. He was surgeon of the 3rd Mich. Cavalry until 1864, when he was made Staff Surgeon, and transferred to the Army of the Potomac. In 1865 he returned home to a successful practice. He was a Collector of Internal Revenue from 1869 to 1873. In politics he was a Republican. He died at Paw Paw, Aug. 26, 1886.

WESLEY P. ANDRUS

Senator from the 25th District, 1877-8. Was born Feb. 19, 1834, in the town of Potter, Yates County, N. Y. He followed farming until attaining his majority; was educated at Franklin Academy and Genesee College, N. Y.; removed to Michigan in 1856, where, up to the time of the breaking out of the war, he was principally engaged in teaching school. In 1861 he entered the 42nd Ill. Vol. Infantry, and was commissioned First Lieutenant about two months after; was promoted to Captaincy for meritorious service at Stone River. At the Battle of Missionary Ridge he was severely wounded, and was discharged on account of disability in May, 1864. At the close of the war he engaged in mercantile business in Michigan, and was a hardware merchant at Cedar Springs, Kent County. He was a member of its Common Council and a President of that village. In politics he was a Republican. He died at Cedar Springs in 1898.

WILLIAM W. ANDRUS

Delegate from Macomb County to the Constitutional Convention of 1867; Senator from the Twentieth District, 1881-2. Was born in Middlebury, Wyoming County,

N. Y., July 25, 1821. He came with his father to Michigan in 1822, and resided in Macomb County. He was a physician and surgeon and druggist. In politics a Republican. He was Assessor of Internal Revenue under Grant in the old Fifth Congressional District. He died at his home at Utica, Macomb County, Aug. 28, 1910.

CHARLES ANGERER

Representative from the Second District of Monroe County, 1889-90. Was born in the township of LaSalle, Monroe County, Mich., Sept. 26, 1843. He attended the German school of Raisinville and spent his early life on a farm with his parents. From 1865 to 1869 he traveled through eleven States of the Union learning the trades of carpenter, bridge builder and architect. On Apr. 1, 1869, he married Miss Mary Reinhard. Mr. Angerer resided in Monroe City from 1869 to 1875, engaged in building railroad and highway bridges. In 1875 he removed to the township of Exeter and engaged in the manufacture of lumber and charcoal. Mr. Angerer was elected Justice of the Peace in 1884 and re-elected in 1888. He voted his first Republican ticket in 1868 and continued to be a Republican. He was elected to the House in a strong Democratic district.

JOHN N. ANHUT

Senator from the Fourth District of Wayne County, 1909-10. Was born at Detroit, Jan. 8, 1884, of German descent. He received his education in the parochial high school and Detroit College of Law. He began his career as a lawyer under the tutelage of John D. Conley and met with marked success at the bar. He was a member of the firm of Miner & Anhut with offices in the Moffat building. He was single and the youngest member of the forty-fifth Legislature. In politics a Republican.

FERNANDO C. ANNABLE

Representative from Van Buren County, 1842. Was born at Metz, Cayuga County, N. Y., Dec. 28, 1805. By occupation he was a farmer, in politics a Democrat. He came to Michigan in 1836, and settled on a farm in Almena, Van Buren County, where he resided until his death, Oct. 2, 1886. He was Supervisor and Treasurer of the town a number of terms.

EMIL ANNEKE

Auditor General, 1863-7. Was born in Dartmund, Prussia, Dec. 13, 1823. His father was a royal counselor. The son was educated at the University of Berlin, and, taking part in the unsuccessful revolution of 1848, with others came to this country in 1849. He taught school in Pennsylvania; was one of the editorial staff of the *Staats Zeitung* in New York; then corresponding clerk in a New York house; in 1855 came to Detroit and was editorial manager of a German paper; then a clerk in the office of the Auditor General; was nominated and elected Auditor General of Michigan in 1862, and served two terms, from 1863 to 1867; was admitted to the bar and practiced at Grand Rapids; for several years was United States Receiver at the land office at Traverse City; then he resided at East Saginaw; but after 1874 he lived at Bay City, where he engaged in law, real estate and abstract business. He died Oct. 27, 1888, at Bay City.

HENRY HARRISON APLIN

Representative from the Second District of Bay County, 1895-6; Auditor General, 1887-91; and member of Congress, 1901-3. Was born on a farm in the township of Thetford, Genesee County, Mich., Apr. 15, 1841. In 1848 his father moved to the city of Flint, where they remained until 1856, when the family again returned to the farm, where he remained until the breaking out of the Civil War in 1861, when he enlisted as a private in Company C, 16th Mich. Infantry, serving until the close of the war. He was made a Second Lieutenant in 1865. Returning to Michigan at the close of the war he entered into the mercantile business at Wenona, now West Bay City, and was identified with its growth and progress. He immediately took an active and prominent part in local politics, and was appointed Postmaster by President Grant in Nov., 1869, succeeding Newcomb Clark, which office he held until June, 1886. Always a staunch Republican, as well as a strong advocate of the rights of labor, he represented his town and county in local and State conventions for many years and his State in the National Convention which nominated Blaine and Logan at Chicago, in June, 1884. He was elected Auditor General by the Republicans in 1886 and was re-elected in 1888. He was elected a member of Congress from the Tenth District Oct. 15, 1901 to fill the vacancy caused by the death of R. O. Crump. He died at Bay City July 23, 1910.

WILLARD B. ARMS

Senator from the Fifth District, 1855-6, from the Sixth District, 1857-8, and from the Twenty-third District, 1867-8. Was born in Penfield, N. Y., Feb. 12, 1827, the youngest of six children. He came to Michigan with his parents in 1834, who settled in Milford, Oakland County. He had limited school advantages only attending to the age of twelve, but became a self-educated man by diligent study after working hours. He became apt in discussions and debate at an early age and often took part in them. In 1846 he engaged in business for himself at White Lake, Oakland County, where he remained until 1860, when he removed to Fenton, Genesee County. He devoted his energies entirely to his large mercantile business at Fenton for several years, and in 1872 removed to Marquette, Mich. After residing there four years he removed to Chicago, where he lived until his death, which occurred Nov. 8, 1878. He was a Republican in politics, and a consistent church member.

JOHN H. ARMSTRONG

Representative from the Second District of Hillsdale County, 1870. Was born in Poughkeepsie, N. Y., Aug. 30, 1815. Three years later, his parents removed to Bethel, and in 1821 to Plattsburg, N. Y., where he lived until the death of his parents, receiving only a common cchool education. In 1831 he returned to Poughkeepsie, and learned the machinist and other trades. In 1837 he came to Michigan and located at Grass Lake. His principal business from that time until 1857 was putting in running works for flouring mills in southeastern Michigan. In 1857 he removed to Hillsdale, where he resided, and engaged in the hide and leather trade until 1883. He was Trustee of the village of Hillsdale in 1862, and its President in 1863-4 and a part of 1865; chairman of the Republican County Committee for two years, and for some years Justice of the Peace. He was elected Representative in place of Harvey Rowlson resigned. He was director of the Second

National Bank of Hillsdale after 1865, and a director of the Hillsdale Savings Bank. At first he was a Whig, but a Republican after 1854; was often Delegate to State and other conventions. He died at Hillsdale June 7, 1897.

SULLIVAN ARMSTRONG

Representative from Newaygo County, 1873-4 and 1875-6. Was born Mar. 3, 1821, in the town of Riga, Monroe County, N. Y. In 1826 he emigrated to Michigan and settled in Oakland County. In 1852 he removed to Ashland, Newaygo County. He was Supervisor of his town, and County Treasurer several times. Mr. Armstrong's occupation was that of a farmer, lumberman and storekeeper. He died at Fremont, Mich., Jan. 31, 1890.

JOSEPH ARNOLD

Representative from Oakland County, 1842. He was a farmer in the town of Addison, Oakland County; was Supervisor in 1846, and later a Justice of the Peace. His estate was probated in 1859 or 1860.

SEYMOUR ARNOLD

Representative from Oakland County, 1845. Was born in New York State and educated there. He was an early settler in the town of Addison, Oakland County. He was Supervisor from 1840 to 1844, and a School Commissioner in 1837, at the first organization of the town. By occupation he was a farmer, miller and merchant. He was accidently killed about the year 1859, and buried at Mt. Vernon, Macomb County, Mich.

WILLIAM P. ARNOLD

Representative from Branch County, 1853-4. Was born at Clarendon, Vt., Aug. 23, 1806. He removed with his parents to western New York in 1818, where he lived until 1833, when he removed to Coldwater, Mich., and bought a large farm. He sold out in 1839 and purchased a farm in the township of Quincy, now the site of the village of Quincy. He was Supervisor of the town for twenty years, and held other official positions. He with his wife, Theresa Hewitt of Niagara County, N. Y., celebrated their golden wedding in 1877. He died at Quincy in 1884.

ALEXANDER M. ARZENO

Representative from Monroe County, 1847; Delegate from Monroe County to the Constitutional Convention of 1850; and Senator from the Eighth District, 1853. Was an early settler in Monroe County. By occupation he was a stave and lumber dealer, politically a Democrat. He was Supervisor, Justice of the Peace, and a leading citizen for many years. He was called "Black Hawk" from his complexion and characteristics as a leader.

ALFRED ASHLEY

Member of the Legislative Council from the Second District (Macomb County), 1832-3. He came to Mt. Clemens in 1821. He was Postmaster of Mt. Clemens in

1828. He erected the Phelps House at Mt. Clemens. He died at New Baltimore, Sept. 7, 1857.

JAMES ASHLEY

Representative from Cass County, 1869-70. Was born in Toronto, Canada, Nov. 18, 1815. In 1826 the family removed to Huron County, O., where his father followed farming. The son learned the trade of a blacksmith, which avocation he followed at intervals. In 1841 he commenced preaching as a Free Will Baptist minister. He removed to Mason Township, Cass County, Mich., in 1855, where he held a pastoral relation for more than twenty-five years. He preached at Summerville for twelve years and organized the church at Berrien Center and preached there nine years. He also did much missionary work and was never idle, working as a carpenter to supply his needs. Through his instrumentality the churches at Adamsville and Mason were built. He was a man of positive character and decided opinions, which he had the boldness to express on all suitable occasions. In politics he was a Republican. He died Mar. 23, 1882.

NOBLE ASHLEY

Representative from the First District of Wayne County, 1903-4, 1911-12, 1913-14 and 1915-16; and Senator from the Third District, 1905-6. Was born at Lincolnshire, England, Sept. 30, 1863, and located in the city of Detroit in 1880; married in 1888. Mr. Ashley was a printed by trade and was clerk of municipal concessions of the city of Detroit. He was Alderman from the tenth ward of Detroit in 1896-7; Supervisor Wayne County, 1896-7, and State Senator from the Third District in 1905-6. In politics a Republican. He was a member of the House of Representatives in 1903-4, 1911-12 and 1913-14 and re-elected Nov. 3, 1914. He died at Boston, Mass., Apr. 7, 1917.

SAMUEL ASHMAN

Representative from Chippewa County, 1840. His postoffice address was Sault Ste. Marie. (Further data not obtainable).

HENRY C. ASHMUN

Representative from Midland County in 1855-6 and 1857-8. Was born at Mackinaw and was by profession a lawyer and politically a Republican. He was a half blood Indian, and with the Indian type of eyes, hair and complexion. He served as the First Sheriff of Midland County and was a grandson of the great Chief Pontiac. He was an excellent Legislator, and in every sense of the word a gentleman. He died in 1858.

BENJAMIN D. ASHTON

Representative from the Grand Traverse District, comprising the counties of Grand Traverse and Kalkaska, 1887-8. Was born in Claremont County, O., Sept. 15, 1828. Mr. Ashton's early life was spent on a farm. He was a physician, and a resident of Michigan many years; held the offices of Supervisor and President of the village of Traverse City. He was elected Representative on the Republican ticket.

JOHN ATKINSON

Representative from the First District of Wayne County, Detroit, 1897-8. Was born at Warwick, Lambton County, Ont., May 24, 1841. He came to Michigan in 1854, locating at Port Huron, where he acquired his early education; he studied law in the office of William T. Mitchell and Harvey McAlpine of Port Huron and attended the law department of the University of Michigan, where he graduated in March, 1862. He returned to Port Huron and immediately commenced following the practice of his profession. On July 25, 1862, he enlisted and was commissioned Second Lieutenant, and in the following ten days he organized Company C of the 22d Mich. Infantry, of which he served as Captain from Aug. 14, 1762, until July 29, 1864. Captain Atkinson was promoted to be Major of the 22d regiment and on Oct. 13, 1864, he was made Lieutenant Colonel of the 3d Mich. Infantry. He was mustered out of service Feb. 24, 1866. He was married to Miss Lida Lyons while at San Antonio, Texas, in 1866. Soon after the war he returned to Port Huron and was appointed Collector of Customs at that place, by Andrew Johnson in 1866, and served until March 4, 1867, at the same time following the practice of his profession. In 1870 he moved to Detroit, where he engaged in the practice of law. In politics he was raised a Democrat and remained one until the tariff issue became prominent in 1882, after which time he became an ardent Republican. He was a Democratic candidate for Attorney General in 1870, and a Republican candidate for Congress in 1884; was elected to the House of 1897-8 on the general legislative ticket of Detroit. He died in Detroit.

JOHN GUEST ATTERBURY

Member of the Board of Regents of the University of Michigan, 1848-52. Was born in Baltimore, Md., Feb. 7, 1811, son of Louis and Katherine (Boudinot) Atterbury. His paternal ancestors were English; on the mother's side he was descended from a French Huguenot family. After a preparatory training in the public schools of Newark, N. J., he entered Yale College, and was graduated Bachelor of Arts in 1831. He was married Sept. 1, 1840, to Catherine Jones Larned. In 1843 he also received the degree of Master of Arts from Yale. He studied law and was admitted to the Bar in New York City, and began the practice of his profession there; but he soon removed to Detroit, Mich., where he relinquished the practice of law to enter the Christian ministry. He was called to the pastorate of the Presbyterian Church of Flint, Mich., and held the position for six years, when, owing to failing health, he sought a change of climate and removed to New Albany, Ind. Here he remained a pastor of the Second Presbyterian Church until a further failure of health made it necessary for him to give up this charge. After a season of rest he was appointed Secretary of the Presbyterian Board of Education with residence in New York. He held this position until the reunion of the old and new schools in 1870. Returning to Detroit he organized the Calvary Church and acted as its pastor for three years. Feb. 14, 1848, he was appointed Regent of the University and served until Jan. 1, 1852. In 1863 Marietta College conferred upon him the degree of Doctor of Divinity. He died in Detroit, Aug. 24, 1887.

ROBERT ATTRIDGE

Representative from Sanilac County, 1905-6 and 1907-8. Was born in Ontario, Canada, Nov. 6, 1854, of Irish parentage. He was raised on a farm and received his education in the common schools of Ont., Canada. He went to work on a farm at an early age, was employed for a time in the great Comstock mines in Nevada, and later taught school. Mr. Attridge later engaged in farming. In politics a Republican. He held the offices of Clerk, Justice of the Peace, Supervisor of his township, and was a member of the school board.

REUBEN ATWATER

Secretary of the Territory of Michigan, 1808-14. Was born in Wallingford, Conn., May 11, 1768. He was Collector of the port of Detroit. Atwater street in Detroit was named in his honor. The census of the Territory in 1810 was taken under his direction. He acted as Governor in 1811-12, for which Congress awarded him $500 extra compensation. He also acted as Land Commissioner, deciding 613 claims in February, 1811. The British destroyed the records when they captured Detroit and thus much information was lost. He died Feb. 8, 1831.

HENRY P. ATWOOD

Representative from Tuscola County, 1855-6. Was born in the State of New York in 1825. By profession he was a lawyer, and was Prosecuting Attorney of Tuscola County, and a Supervisor. Later he became a resident of Grand Traverse County, and engaged in farming. In politics a Republican.

MARCUS M. ATWOOD

Representative from Ingham County, 1861-2 and 1871-2. He came with his father's family from Cayuga County, N. Y., and settled in the town of Ingham, Ingham County, in 1836. He practiced law in the township and resided in the village of Dansville. He held the offices of Supervisor, Town Clerk, Justice of the Peace, and from 1868 to 1879 was President of the village of Dansville. In politics he was a Democrat. He died at Lansing Sept. 24, 1898.

ORVILLE E. ATWOOD

Representative from Newaygo County, 1919-20 and 1921-2; and Senator from the Twenty-sixth District, 1923—. Was born on a farm near Morgan Park, Ill., Feb. 23, 1880, of English parentage. At the age of twelve years he removed with his parents to Kansas. His education was received in the public schools, Ottawa Academy, of Ottawa, Kan., and the University of Chicago, from which institution he graduated in 1903. After working two years as a traveling salesman, he moved to a farm near Newaygo, where he now lives. Mr. Atwood is married and has one daughter. In politics he is a Republican.

THERON W. ATWOOD

Senator from the Twenty-first District, 1899-1900 and 1901-2; and Delegate from the Twenty-first District, Tuscola County in the Constitutional Convention of 1907-8. Was born in White Oak, Ingham County, in 1854, but was a resident of Tuscola County since infancy. His early education was obtained in the schools of that county, graduating from the law department of the University of Michigan in 1875.

He engaged in the practice of law after that time. He was Prosecuting Attorney for four terms, State Senator for two terms and served as Commissioner of Railroads from 1903 to 1907. Married. He died Sept. 27, 1917.

WILLIAM A. ATWOOD

Senator from the Thirteenth District, comprising the counties of Genesee and Livingston, 1887-8. Was born in the town of Newfane, Niagara County, N. Y., Apr. 11, 1835. He spent his early boyhood upon a farm and had the educational advantages of a common school, and one term at the Wilson Academy. At the age of seventeen he learned the jeweler's trade and three years after went to Galt, Canada, where he engaged in the stave, cooper and shingle business with his brother, Jesse B. Atwood. In 1859 he sold out his interest and returned to Niagara County and engaged in farming, and built a shingle mill which was burned in 1863. He again went to Canada and was in the lumber business. In 1866 he removed to Flint, with his brother, J. B. Atwood, and B. W. Simington, and with them built a large saw mill and began the lumber business on Flint River, and continued the same up to 1879. He continued with his brother in the lumber business in Clare County until 1883. In 1876 he associated himself with Orren Stone, in the woolen manufacturing business in the Flint Woolen Mills. In 1883 he purchased an interest in the hardware business. He was a director and vice president of the Genesee County Savings Bank. In 1881 he was elected Mayor of Flint. In politics a Republican.

ANDREW V. AUSTIN

Representative from the Second District of Oakland County, 1903-4 and 1905-6. Was born in Milford, Dec. 4, 1844. His parents were pioneers of Oakland County, settling in Milford in 1836. He enlisted in Company E, 185 New York Volunteers, and was wounded in the head at the battle of Five Forks, Apr. 1, 1865, and reported dead. In 1868 he returned to Milford and engaged in the grocery business, continuing the same for nearly thirty-five years, when he retired on account of ill health. He was at one time a member of the common council of Milford. He was a member of Heber Le Favour Post, G. A. R., No. 181, was three times elected its commander and was its quartermaster. He was married Dec. 19, 1888, to Hattie M. Foote. He was formerly married to Lizzie Bartlett, by whom he had three children.

CHARLES AUSTIN

Representative from Calhoun County, 1881-2; and Senator from the Eighth District, 1883-4 and 1885-6. Was born in London, England, Apr. 19, 1834. He received his education in one of the schools of the British and Foreign School Society. He emigrated to America in February, 1852, and resided in the State of New York until the spring of 1854, when he removed to Concord, Jackson County, Mich. There he made the acquaintance of Miss Lucy D. Taylor, whom he married Jan. 1, 1855. In the fall of the same year he removed to Homer, and two years later to Bedford, Calhoun County. In 1872, he, as senior member, formed a copartnership with Mr. Hoffmaster, and engaged in the dry goods business in Battle Creek. In 1875 he was elected an Alderman of his ward; was elected Mayor in

1876 and re-elected in 1877. In politics he was a Republican. He was for several years president of the Union Mutual Insurance Company. He died at Battle Creek Dec. 3, 1921.

DANIEL AUSTIN

Representative from Mason County, 1889-90. Was born in the town of Cannon, Kent County, Mich., Nov. 16, 1857. His father died in 1864, leaving the mother with eight children without any means for their support. He was compelled to make his own way in the world, and in the spring of 1868 he began working by the month on a farm, attending district school in the winter. In the Spring of 1872 he went to Mason County, where for eight years he spent the greater portion of his time working in the lumber woods. In 1880 he was employed by Chauncey Gibbs, of Ludington, to take charge of a fruit farm, in whose employ he remained until 1882, when he was engaged by the George W. Roby Lumber Co., as foreman and salesman of their lumber yard until 1886. Mr. Austin married Miss Josephine Malliott, of Ludington. In the Spring of 1887 he was candidate for Supervisor of the Fourth ward of Ludington, but was defeated by fourteen votes. The Common Council appointed him Deputy Marshal, which office he held until elected to the House of Representatives.

HARRISON H. AVERILL

Representative from the Second District of Ottawa County, 1919-20 and 1921-2. Was born July 25, 1859, in Polkton Township, Ottawa County, Mich., on the farm on which he now resides. He received his education in the district school of that township. Mr. Averill is a widower and has four sons. He is a member of the I. O. O. F. and Grange. He has held the office of Township Treasurer two years and Supervisor thirteen years, and was Chairman of the County Board of Supervisors four years. In politics he is a Republican.

PAUL J. AVERILL

Representative from the First District of Kent County, 1911-12 and 1915-16. Was born at Berlin, Ottawa County, Mich., Mar. 20, 1857, of English parentage. He was educated in the Coopersville High School. His early life was spent on a farm; later he became a traveling salesman, and then engaged in the real estate business. In politics a Republican.

JOHN AVERY

Representative from Montcalm County, 1869-70; and a member of Congress 1893-5 and 1895-7. Was born in Watertown, N. Y., Feb. 20, 1824. Came to Michigan with his parents in 1836; was educated in the common schools and Grass Lake Academy; studied medicine with Wm. B. Watson, of Duplain, Clinton County, Mich.; graduated from the Cleveland Medical College in 1850; and then engaged in the practice of his profession. In 1862 he was appointed surgeon for the 21st Mich. Infantry; served with the Army of the Cumberland in Kentucky and Tennessee, and was with Sherman on his march to the sea. In politics a Republican. He was a member of the State Legislature from Montcalm County in 1869-70; was a member and President of the State Board of Health; United States Pension Examiner; a member and President of the Stanton Board of Examiners; member of the school board and common council of Greenville and Supervisor of the first ward for twelve years; was a member of the 53d Congress of the United States, and re-elected to the 54th Congress.

LINCOLN AVERY

Member of the State Board of Education, 1901-4. Was born in the township of Pickering, province of Ontario, Canada, Oct. 24, 1860, removing with his parents to Michigan when less than one year of age. His education was obtained in the district schools of St. Clair County, the State Normal School, Michigan Agricultural College, where he took the degree of B.S. in 1882, and the University of Michigan, where the degree of LL.D. was conferred upon him in 1886. In July of 1886 he began the practice of law in Port Huron, in partnership with A. R. Avery, under the firm name of Avery Brothers. In politics a Republican. He was elected County Superintendent of Schools in 1892, holding the office for three years, and elected as Prosecuting Attorney for the terms of 1892-4. Interested in the St. Clair County Savings Bank of Port Huron and the Yale National at Yale and a member of the Port Huron Club. He was appointed a member of the State Board of Education Apr. 10, 1901, by Governor Bliss to fill a vacancy caused by the resignation of Frederick A. Platt. He was married Aug. 23, 1892, to Miss Elizabeth Northrup of Port Huron.

SAMUEL AXFORD

Delegate from the Sixth District to the Constitutional Convention of 1835; Representative from Macomb County, 1839, 1840 and 1843; and Senator from the Sixth District, 1851. Was born Aug. 6, 1809, in what was then known as the "Long Point" country in Ontario, Canada. His parents were originally from New Jersey. His mother, Rachael Morgan, was a niece of General Morgan of the Revolution. His parents settled in Shelby, Macomb County, where he lived until 1833, when he settled on a farm in Oxford, Oakland County, and was the third settler in that township. He held nearly all town offices. In politics he was a Democrat.

WILLIAM AXFORD

Representative from Oakland County, 1850; and Delegate from Oakland County to the Constitutional Convention of 1850. Was born in Windom, Ont., Canada, Mar. 28, 1813. He came with his parents to Michigan in 1822, who settled in Macomb County, about three miles east of the village of Rochester. As a young man, he was a teacher, and afterwards became a merchant at Avon. In 1842 he removed to Clarkston, where he was a successful merchant for twenty-five years. He was a Democrat in politics, and eminently a leader. As a business man he contributed largely to the prosperity of Clarkston. He died Sept. 16, 1886.

CHARLES V. BABCOCK

Senator from the Fifth District, 1863-4 and from the Twentieth District, 1875-6. Was born in Orwell, Addison County, Vt., June 4, 1823. He removed with his parents to Southfield, Oakland County, Mich., in 1830, and was brought up on a farm. He received a common school education, with three terms at the Ypsilanti Seminary. He taught school several winters. He was for twenty times Supervisor of Southfield, the last in 1885; held other township offices; Clerk of Oakland County from 1859 to 1861; also Justice of the Peace. His occupation was farming; in politics a Democrat.

CHRISTOPHER G. BABCOCK

Representative from Branch County, 1897-8 and 1899-1900. Was born in Portage County, O., Jan. 9, 1837. He was raised on a farm and acquired his education in the district schools and supplemented by a two years' course at Hiram College. He came to Michigan in 1858, where he engaged in farming and shipping stock. In politics a Populist. He was Supervisor of his township and elected to the House of 1897-8 on the silver ticket and re-elected to the House of 1899-1900. He died at Bronson, June 9, 1916.

HENRY S. BABCOCK

Delegate from Oakland County to the Second Convention of Assent, 1836; and Representative from Oakland County, 1842. Was born in Orwell, Vt., Aug. 23, 1798. He settled in Southfield, Mich., in 1829, and purchased of the government four hundred acres of land. He was appointed a Justice of the Peace in 1830. At the first township meeting in Southfield, held Apr. 4, 1831, he was elected Supervisor. He held the office of Justice of the Peace several terms. In politics he was a Democrat. He died Oct. 26, 1842.

HERBERT BABCOCK

Representative from the First District of Eaton County, 1897-8. Was born on a farm in Berlin Township, Ionia County, Mich. His early education was acquired in the district school supplemented by a course in the Ionia High School. In 1890 he located on a tract of two hundred and sixty acres of hardwood timber in Eaton County, where he engaged in farming and lumbering. In politics a Democrat. He was not a candidate for any office before he was elected to the House on the Democratice People's Union ticket.

JONATHAN W. BABCOCK

Senator from the Sixteenth District, comprising the counties of Lapeer and Sanilac, 1887-8. Was born in Williams Township, Ontario, Canada, Apr. 19, 1849. At the age of three years he removed with his parents to Romeo, Macomb County, Mich. He resided with his parents in Macomb County until he was fourteen years of age, when he removed with them to the township of Elk, Sanilac County. As soon as he was large enough to do any work, he began making hoops and staves. He attended school three months the winter that he was fifteen years old. This, with a few months' schooling when a small boy, is all the schooling he ever had. He continued at his former business until he was nineteen years old, when he was appointed as sub-agent for the purchase of hoops for the Salt Company at Onondaga, N. Y., which business he carried on in the Saginaw Valley for three years, when he returned to Sanilac County. During these years he had bought and read a great many books and was considered a well-informed man on general topics. He held the offices of Town Clerk, Supervisor, School Inspector, and many minor offices, and in 1872 was elected Sheriff of Sanilac County on the Republican ticket; declined a second nomination and decided to be a lawyer, and at the expiration of his term as Sheriff purchased law books, removed to the township of Elmer, and being without means he worked to support his family, studying nights and odd moments, until 1877, when he was admitted to the bar as an attorney. In 1880 he was elected Prosecuting Attorney; was re-elected in 1882 and again in 1884, and discharged his duties very satisfactorily. He died before June, 1890.

ROBERT SIMEON BABCOCK

Delegate from the Twenty-sixth District, Manistee County, in the Constitutional Convention of 1907-8. Was born in Milwaukee, Wis., in 1868, of English and American descent. He was educated in the public schools of Milwaukee and Chicago and graduated from the high school at Manistee. He attended the University of Michigan, being a member of the class of '89. Engaged in the lumbering business after he left college. He was a member of the Michigan National Guard for seven years, leaving the service with rank of Lieutenant Colonel. Also a member of the Masonic order, Elks and Foresters.

SAMUEL S. BABCOCK

Member of the State Board of Education, 1886-92. (Further data not obtainable).

W. IRVING BABCOCK

Senator from the Ninth District, Berrien and Cass counties, 1887-8 and 1889-90. Was born at Troy, N. Y., July 7, 1833. When he was but nine years old his father died. He attended school at Troy until sixteen years of age, when he entered the Collegiate Institute at Charlotteville, N. Y., and finished his studies at Genesee College, Lima, N. Y. He was engaged as teacher and contractor until 1858, and removed to Van Buren County, Mich., and engaged in farming until 1866, when he removed to Niles, where he engaged in the lumber trade. In politics a Republican. In 1885 he was elected Mayor of the city of Niles. In 1886 he was again elected. In 1884 he was alternate delegate to the Republican National Convention from the Fourth Congressional District, and he was an earnest supporter of James G. Blaine for the nomination. Also Grand Master of the Masonic Grand Lodge of Michigan. He was on the Republican ticket for State Senator, 1887-8, and re-elected to the Senate for 1889-90.

HENRY T. BACKUS

Representative from Wayne County, 1840; Delegate from Wayne County to the Constitutional Convention of 1850; and Senator from the Third District, comprising a part of Wayne County, 1861-2. Was a native of Connecticut, born in 1821, was a lawyer by profession, and was for some years a leading practitioner in Detroit. He was Alderman from the ninth ward, 1860-1. He was appointed by President Grant a Judge of the Territorial Court of Arizona, and served as such for seven years. He was a Whig and Republican in politics, and died in 1877.

WILLIAM BACKUS

Representative from Montcalm County, 1875-6. Was born Sept. 14, 1825, in the State of New York. He received a common school education, removed to Michigan in 1836 and settled in Oakland County. In 1848 he removed to Montcalm County. Mr. Backus was Supervisor in Greenville four years, and served as County Clerk of Montcalm County in 1861-2. His occupation was dealing in real estate and lumbering. In politics he was a Democrat.

CYRUS BACON

Representative from Cass County, 1849. Was born in Ballston, Saratoga County, N. Y. (Further data not obtainable).

DANIEL S. BACON

Member of the Legislative Council from Monroe County, 1832-3 and 1834-5; and Representative from Monroe County, 1839. Was born in Onondaga County, N. Y., in 1798. He came to Michigan at an early day, and taught school on the River Raisin in 1822, settled at Monroe, paid considerable attention to farming, and became a partner of Levi S. Humphrey in various kinds of business. He became a lawyer and practiced his profession with great success. He was for many years Judge of Probate for Monroe County, was president of the bank of Monroe and a director of the Michigan Southern Railroad Company. He held other positions, in all of which he acquitted himself with ability. He was one of the most popular men in the early history of Monroe County. In politics he was a Democrat. He died at Monroe, May 18, 1866.

JOHN BACON

Representative from Keweenaw County, 1851. Was a mining agent in Keweenaw County as early as 1846, and is said to have gone from Pontiac to the Upper Peninsula. He went to Detroit, where he resided several years, and from there to one of the western territories, where he died.

LEVI BACON, JR.

Representative from Oakland County, 1857-8. Was born in Ellington, Conn., in 1819. He emigrated to Michigan in 1838, and was a resident of Pontiac, from 1842 to 1875, engaged in mercantile business. In 1875 he was appointed by Secretary Chandler cashier of the Patent Office, which position he held until his death, June 22, 1887. He was Mayor of Pontiac in 1866-7, and a Republican in politics.

MARK R. BACON

Member of Congress, 1917. A native of the State of Illinois; of English-German descent, his grandfather being an officer in the American Revolution. His education was obtained in the public schools of Illinois, and his boyhood days were spent on a farm. He engaged in the practice of law and real estate, and in the manufacturing business. Married. At the primary election Aug. 29, 1916, he was nominated for the office of Congressman, and was elected Nov. 7, 1916. Lost his seat in the election contest with Samuel W. Beakes, who was seated by the House of Representatives Dec. 13, 1917.

NATHANIEL BACON

Justice of the Supreme Court, 1855-8. Was born at Ballston, N. Y., July 14, 1802, and graduated at Union College in 1824. He studied law at Rochester, N. Y., and practiced there several years. He came to Niles, Mich., in 1833, and held several offices, including that of Prosecuting Attorney. In October, 1855, he was appointed Circuit Judge and one of the Judges of the Supreme Court, in place of Judge Whipple, deceased. He acted in the Supreme Court until Jan. 1, 1858, when the present Supreme Court was organized. In 1857 he was elected Circuit Judge for six years; was elected again in 1866 to fill vacancy caused by the death of Perrin M. Smith, and was re-elected in 1869 for six years. In politics he was a Republican. He died at Niles, Sept. 9, 1869.

JOHN JUDSON BAGLEY

Governor of Michigan, 1873-7. Was born in Medina, Orleans County, N. Y., July 24, 1832. His father, John Bagley, was a native of New Hampshire, and his mother, Mary M. Bagley, a native of Connecticut. He attended district school at Lockport, N. Y., and at Constantine, Mich., where his parents removed when he was eight years of age. At thirteen years of age he became a clerk in a country store at Constantine, where he remained one year. His father removed to Owosso, where he again became a clerk. In 1847 he went to Detroit, and secured employment in a tobacco factory, where he remained five years. In 1854 he began business as a manufacturer of tobacco, and the business became very large and profitable. He also engaged in other enterprises, such as banking, mining and manufacturing. He was one of the organizers of the Michigan Mutual Life Insurance Co., and several years its president; president for years of the Detroit Safe Co.; a director for many years of the American National Bank, and stockholder and director in other corporations. He was for six years one of the Police Commissioners of Detroit; was an Alderman two years; and two years a member of the Board of Education. He was an active Republican from the organization of that party, and was chairman of the State Republican Committee from 1868 to 1870. In 1872 he was nominated and elected Governor of Michigan, and was re-elected in 1874, serving four years, from 1873 to 1877. Under his administration, the State Fish Commission was established, and a law was passed creating the State Board of Health. The successful exhibition made by Michigan at the Centennial Exhibition at Philadelphia in 1876 was largely due to him. He largely changed the character of government of the Reform School, throwing away bolts and bars, and trusting to the honor of the boys for government. He was an Unitarian in belief, but liberal in his views as to other creeds. His wife, Francis E. Newberry, was the daughter of Rev. Samuel Newberry, a pioneer missionary in Michigan. In 1881, Governor Bagley was a candidate for United States Senator, and came within one vote of receiving the caucus Republican nomination. He had accumulated a large fortune, and among other bequests gave several thousand dollars for a public fountain in Detroit. He died in San Francisco, Calif., Dec. 27, 1881, leaving a wife and seven children.

RICHARD W. BAGOT

Representative, 1893-4, from the district composed of the counties of Antrim, Charlevoix and Kalkaska. Was born in England, 1832. He came to America in 1854, landing in New York. Three years later he came to Michigan and located at Elk Rapids. Shortly after locating he was married to Miss Mary E. Radley, of New York, and engaged in business as manager for a mercantile firm, and later engaged in banking. In politics a Republican and held the office of County Treasurer, Clerk and Register of Deeds.

JOSEPH BAHORSKI

Senator from the Second District of Wayne County, comprising the fifth, seventh and ninth wards of Detroit, 1923—. Was born in St. Cloud, Minnesota, March 10, 1882. At the age of eight years he removed with his parents to Detroit, and Michigan has since been his home. His early education was obtained in district, parochial, and central high schools and he is also a graduate of the Detroit College of Law. For six years Mr. Bahorski was engaged in the baking business with the Morton Baking Co., after which he was in business for himself for a period of fifteen years. In 1915 he was appointed by Mayor Oscar B. Marx a member of the Board of Education, to fill vacancy, being elected to the same position in 1914. In 1916 he was elected member of the Detroit Common Council and in 1918 he entered the Wayne County prosecuting attorney's office as assistant, which position he holds at the present time. He is a member of Union Lodge of Strict Observance No. 3, F. & A. M., Michigan Sovereign Consistory and Shriner Moslem Temple. Mr. Bahorski is married and has five children, four boys and one girl. He was elected State Senator on the Republican ticket November 7, 1922.

ALVIN W. BAILEY

Representative from Barry County, 1853-4. Was born in Cayuga County, N. Y., Sept. 29, 1814. He came to Michigan soon after its organization as a State, and settled at Marshall. He soon after removed to Barry County, and settled at Hastings. He was the first President of the village of Hastings. He was a merchant and farmer. Politically he was a Democrat. He died Mar. 6, 1887.

CHARLES A. BAILEY

Representative from the Second District of St. Clair County, 1893-4. Was born in Port Huron, July 21, 1850. He acquired his early education in the public schools of Port Huron. He lived on the farm bordering the city limits, and was manager of the Port Huron Gas Company. In politics a Democrat. He held the office of Supervisor and Township Clerk.

FREDERICK G. BAILEY

Representative from Shiawassee County, 1873-4 and 1875-6. Was born in Bath, England, May 29, 1828. In 1832 he emigrated to the United States and settled in the city of New York. In 1845 he came to Michigan and settled in the town of Hadley, Lapeer County. Mr. Bailey received an academic education. In 1861 he removed to the town of Venice, Shiawassee County, and in 1863 removed to Keweenaw County, where he resided four years. In 1868 he returned to the town of Venice, Shiawassee County, where he resided. Mr. Bailey was chairman of the Republican County Committee of Shiawassee County, and held other offices of trust in his township. His occupation that of a farmer. Politics Republican.

ISAAC G. BAILEY

Representative from St. Joseph County, 1840. His postoffice address was Ft. Pleasant. (Further data not obtainable).

NORMAN BAILEY

Senator from the Twenty-first District, 1861-2. Was born in Cayuga County, N. Y., Jan. 1, 1822. He came to Michigan, in 1853, and resided at Hastings, except when absent at headquarters in Grand Rapids during the war and two years at Ionia. He was a Captain in the service during the war, and was Provost Marshal of the 4th Congressional District, and held several minor offices. He made a splendid record as Provost Marshal, his district taking in the Upper Peninsula and the Lower, north of Barry County. For correct reports, strict discipline, and just decisions he especially distinguished himself. As a legislator he was a Republican, later a Democrat. His business was that of a merchant. His death occurred at Hastings, Feb. 15, 1896.

THOMAS GILBERT BAILLIE

Representative from the First Representative District of Saginaw County, 1905-6. Was born at Saginaw, Mich., Mar. 8, 1881, of Scotch parentage. He attended the public and high schools of Saginaw. He entered the employ of Symons Bros. & Co., wholesale grocers, remaining with them six months, then entered the office of general traffic manager of the P. M. Railroad Co., remaining there until he entered the University of Michigan in 1900. During the summer months of 1901 to 1903 he was employed in the Savings Bank of East Saginaw, graduated from the law department of the University of Michigan in June, 1903, after which time he practiced law in the city of Saginaw. In politics a Republican.

JOHN BAIRD

Representative from the Second District of Saginaw County, 1895-6; Senator from the Twenty-second District, comprising Saginaw County, 1901-2, 1903-4 and 1905-6; and member of the Constitutional Convention of 1907-8. Was born in Quebec, Canada, Feb. 11, 1860, and received his education in the common schools of Seaforth, Canada. He came to Michigan when fourteen years of age and was employed in the manufacture of salt for many years. In politics a Republican. Mr. Baird represented his township on the Board of Supervisors, and has served as chairman of the Republican County committee.

FRANCIS BAKER

Representative from Oakland County, 1848. Was born at Sheffield, Mass., Oct. 9, 1804. He came to Michigan from Caro, near Catskill, N. Y., in 1838, and settled in Holly, Genesee County, where he always resided with the exception of four or five years in business at Flint. He was Supervisor, Town Clerk, and held other offices, and was Justice of the Peace. In politics he was a Democrat. He died Dec. 6, 1887.

FREDERICK A. BAKER

Representative from Wayne County, 1877-8. Was born at Holly, Oakland County, Mich., June 14, 1846. He received a good common school education at the public schools in Holly, Clarkston and Flint, and was a member of the freshman class in the State Agricultural College in 1863. He commenced the study of the law in 1865, was admitted to the bar in 1867, and engaged in active practice. Democrat in politics.

FREDERICK KESSLER BAKER

Senator, 1899-1900, from the Thirtieth District, comprising the counties of Chippewa, Delta, Luce, Mackinac, Menominee and Schoolcraft. Was born at Fleming, Cayuga County, N. Y., Jan. 5, 1861. His early education was derived from the common schools, and the Cayuga Lake Academy at Aurora, N. Y. He taught school during 1879-80. In 1881 he entered the Mercantile National Bank of New York, where he was employed until May, 1882, when he came to Michigan and accepted the position of bookkeeper in the Fourth National Bank of Grand Rapids. He was subsequently elected assistant cashier. In 1887 while yet a resident of Grand Rapids, Mr. Baker was a candidate for City Treasurer on the Republican ticket, but went down to defeat with his ticket in the "landslide" of that year. A year later he removed to Menominee and engaged in lumbering. In politics a Republican. He was favored by his fellow townsmen of Menominee with the positions of Alderman and President of the Council, and was chairman of the Republican County Committee.

HERBERT F. BAKER

Representative from Cheboygan County, 1907-8, 1909-10 and 1911-12; and Senator, 1919-20 and 1921-2, from the Twenty-ninth District, comprising the counties of Alpena, Charlevoix, Cheboygan, Emmet, Montmorency, Otsego and Presque Isle. Was born Jan. 13, 1862, on a farm in Dover Township, Lenawee County, Mich. He removed to Cheboygan County in 1889 and engaged in farming. Mr. Baker is married and has two sons. In politics a Republican. Was elected to the Legislature in 1906 and was re-elected to the sessions of 1909-10, and 1911-12, serving as speaker in the latter session. Was elected to the Senate Nov. 5, 1918, and re-elected Nov. 2, 1920.

LEWIS C. BAKER

Representative from the Second District of Lenawee County, 1891-2. Was born Feb. 18, 1844, on the farm, which his parents took up from the government in 1832, they having moved here from Ontario County, N. Y. He was married in 1868 to Miss Mary J. Thomas of Adrian. A member of the Masonic Fraternity and a Knight Templar. Always active in politics and a supporter of the Democratic party. He held the offices of Highway Commissioner, Justice of the Peace, and served as Supervisor for seven years, 1880-7, and was chairman of the board in 1885-6. He was elected to the House of 1891-2 on the Democratic ticket. He died at his home Dec. 8, 1917, as the result of an accident occurring five weeks before his death.

MILO S. BAKER

Representative from Ionia County, 1861-2. Was born in Morganville, Genesee County, N. Y., Mar. 20, 1828. He removed with his parents to Oneida, Eaton County, Mich., in 1836. Their teams made the first wagon track from a point nine miles west of Howell, through Williamston and Lansing, to Grand Ledge. The Indians had a corn-field at the mouth of Cedar River, now in the city of Lansing, but there were no white inhabitants along the river for many miles. In 1848-9 he helped organize the first Masonic lodge in Lansing. The same year he crossed the plains to California, returning to Michigan in 1853. He was in the foundry business in Lansing from 1864 to 1875, when he removed to Los Angeles, Calif., where he owned and ran an extensive foundry and machine shop.

NEWTON BAKER

Representative from Clinton County, 1877-8. Was born in Walworth, Wayne County, N. Y., July 13, 1833. He received a common school education. In 1865 he removed to Michigan, and settled in the township of Bengal, Clinton County. He held the offices of Justice of the Peace and Supervisor. By occupation he was a farmer and fruit grower. In politics a Democrat.

SEWARD BAKER

Representative from the Second District of Monroe County, 1885-6 and 1887-8. Was born in the township of Ash, in that County, Oct. 11, 1858. He lived on a farm until twenty-one years of age, attending school during the winter terms. Mr. Baker then entered the Northern Indiana Normal School and graduated in the teachers' department in 1882. He taught select school in Canandaigua, Lenawee County, the winter of 1882. He entered the law department of the University in October, 1885, and was admitted to the bar in June, 1886. After that time he practiced law in Carlton, Monroe County. In politics a Democrat.

WILLIAM A. BAKER

Representative from the First District of Berrien County, 1887-8 and 1889-90. Was born at New Pittsburg, Wayne County, O., Mar. 17, 1845. He was brought up on a farm, and when seventeen years of age he enlisted in the 102d Ohio Infantry, and later in the war served in Company K, 178th Ohio Infantry. After his return from the army he attended school at an academy at Canaan, O., and acquired a medical education at the University of Michigan. Also a graduate of Rush Medical College, Chicago. In 1868 he was married to Miss Alice M. Clark at Coloma, Mich., where he later held the offices of Township Clerk, Justice of the Peace and Supervisor. Dr. Baker was elected as a Republican to the House of 1887-8, and re-elected to the House of 1889-90.

WILLIAM BAKER, JR.

Senator from the Tenth District, 1861-2. Was born in Fort Ann, Washington County, N. Y., Oct. 21, 1818. He came to Michigan in 1838, stopped one year at Adrian, settling in 1839, at Hudson. He was a merchant and general produce dealer, politically first Whig, then Republican. He was a man of energy and enterprise in business, generous in the social relations of life, an active political worker, and a firm adherent to party principles. He was Postmaster of Hudson in 1841. and a member of the Board of Control of railroads. He died several years before 1888.

NATHANIEL A. BALCH

Senator from the Fifth District, 1847-8. Was born at Athens, Vt., Jan. 22, 1808, and was one of the twelve children of Nathaniel and Sarah Balch. He was possessed of a remarkable memory, and after receiving an academical education, he graduated from Middlebury College with high honor. He took the position of principal of an academy in Bennington, Vt., and was very successful as a teacher. In 1837 he came to Kalamazoo and opened and organized the school now known as Kalamazoo College. In 1838 he accepted a professorship of mathematics in Michigan College established in Marshall. The endowment of the institution being only wild lands, for which there was no sale, it closed, and Mr. Balch returned to Kalamazoo, and resumed the study of law which he had commenced before coming to Michigan. He was admitted in 1840, and continued in practice. He was Prosecuting Attorney for Barry County in 1840 by appointment, and the next year of Kalamazoo County. He was Senator at the time of the removal of the capital from Detroit to Lansing, and Mr. Balch gave efficient aid in the passage of general railroad, plank road, homestead and telegraph laws. Under Buchanan he was Postmaster of Kalamazoo for four years. In 1860 he was the Democratic nominee for Congress but was defeated. After that he was a candidate for no office. He was a professing Christian, a devoted Bible student, a strong temperance advocate, and a highly liberal and benevolent man. He was a Democrat in politics. He died at Kalamazoo Feb. 1, 1894.

JOHN L. BALCOMBE

Representative from Calhoun County, 1851. His postoffice address was Battle Creek. (Further data not obtainable).

AUGUSTUS C. BALDWIN

Representative from Oakland County, 1844 and 1846; and member of Congress, 1863-5. Was born at Salina, Onondaga County, N. Y., Dec. 24, 1817. His father was a merchant, but died when his son was five, leaving little for the support of the family. The son went to live with an uncle at Canterbury, Conn., where he went to school and at the age of nineteen engaged in teaching. The next year he attended the Academy at Plainfield, Conn. In 1827 he came to Oakland County, Mich., and taught school in Southfield. For the next five years he taught and studied by turns. He began reading law wth John P. Richardson, of Pontiac, in 1839. He was admitted in 1842, and opened an office at Milford. For nearly seven years he practiced at that place, but in 1849 removed to Pontiac. He was School Inspector in Bloomfield in 1840; Representative in the Legislative sessions of 1844 and 1846; Speaker pro tem in 1846; Brigadier General of the state militia from 1846 to 1862; Prosecuting Attorney in 1853-4; member of Congress from 1863 to 1865; Mayor of Pontiac in 1874; for eighteen years member of the Board of Education of Pontiac; Trustee of the Eastern Insane Asylum and Trustee of the Michigan Military Academy; president of the Oakland County Agricultural Society;

president of the County Pioneer Association; Judge of the Sixth Judicial Circuit from 1875 to 1879; when he resigned from insufficient salary; delegate to the Democratic National Conventions of 1860 and 1864; member of the Peace Convention at Philadelphia in 1866; member of the Democratic National and State Committee, and a prominent Mason and Knight Templar. He married Isabella Churchhill in 1842. In politics he was a Democrat; in religion a Presbyterian. He died at Pontiac.

CHARLES BALDWIN

Representative from the Third District of Oakland County, 1846, 1879-80 and 1881-2. Was born Oct. 9, 1803, in New Haven County, Conn., and removed to western New York, then almost a wilderness, in 1814. He received his education in the common schools, and taught school six terms. He spent the summer of 1825 in Michigan, but did not remove to this State permanently until 1830. He was a farmer, and held the office of School Inspector, Highway Commissioner, Justice of the Peace for several terms; Supervisor some fifteen years, and many years one of the Board of Trustees of the Pontiac union school. Mr. Baldwin was a Republican and senior member of the Legislature. He was a Democratic member of the House of 1846. He died at Pontiac May 25, 1889.

CLARKE E. BALDWIN

Delegate from the Fifth District, Lenawee and Monroe counties, in the Constitutional Convention of 1907-8. Was born in 1871 at Canandaigua, Mich., of English descent. He attended the country schools until he was sixteen years of age and graduated from the Adrian High School in 1892 and from the University of Michigan in 1896. He was married to Adelia A. Wing in 1900. He worked on a farm during his boyhood and moved to Adrian in 1888, where he practiced law.

ELIAS J. BALDWIN

Representative from Lenawee County, 1851. Came from Berkshire County, Mass., to Morenci, Mich., about 1834. He lived at Morenci until he died, being over eighty years of age. In politics he was first a Whig, then a Republican.

EZRA P. BALDWIN

Representative from Oakland County, 1848. Was born at Claremont, N. H., Dec. 22, 1800. He received only a district school education, but by extensive reading later in life became an authority upon history, law, and the current news of passing events. He came to Detroit in 1817, and in 1819 settled upon a farm in Bloomfield, Oakland County, near Birmingham. A few years later he went to Buffalo, N. Y., and remained several years and was Deputy Sheriff of Erie County. He returned to Birmingham and was Justice of the Peace in 1845-6 and 1849. He was admitted to the bar Dec. 11, 1843. In politics he was a Democrat. He removed to Iowa in 1853, and subsequently to Martinsville, Mo., where he died in October, 1883.

FRANK A. BALDWIN

Representative, from the district comprising Alpena, Montmorency, and Otsego counties, 1887-8. Was born at Fremont, O., Aug. 14, 1853. By his own personal efforts he maintained himself and paid his expenses through a scientific course in the Northwestern Normal School, at Republic, O., graduating in 1873. He was admitted to the bar in Fremont, O., in 1876. He also earned, by school teaching, sufficient funds to defray all of his expenses while taking a course at the law department of the Michigan University, from which he graduated in the class of 1877. He located at Gaylord, Mich., in 1879, and engaged in law and real estate business. He was married to Miss Nellie E. Osband, daughter of M. D. Osband, formerly of Lansing, Mich., March. 12, 1885. Mr. Baldwin held several offices of trust, among them, Assessor of Gaylor schools, Township Clerk, and Treasurer, and was Deputy County Treasurer; also County School Examiner. In politics a Democrat.

FREDERICK J. BALDWIN

Delegate from the Eighteenth District, Ionia and Montcalm counties, in the Constitutional Convention of 1907-8. Was born in Dexter, Mich., in 1867, of New England ancestry, being ninth in line from Richard Baldwin of Buckinghamshire, England, one of the founders of Milford, Conn., which was settled in 1639. He received his education in the public schools and Albion College. He was married in 1890 to Mary Haviland, a granddaughter of "Aunt" Laura S. Haviland. Mr. Baldwin was a messenger in the Legislature from 1883 to 1887 and was a member of the State Board of Library Commissioners. He engaged in the hardware business at Coral, Mich.

GAYLORD M. BALDWIN

Representative from the Second District of Allegan County, 1889-90. Was born in Bainbridge, Geauga County, O., Dec. 15, 1836. An active Republican. He held office of Supervisor and was elected director of the Kent, Allegan and Ottawa Fire Insurance Company. His father, James M. Baldwin, was the Republican Representative from Allegan County in 1858.

HENRY B. BALDWIN

Senator from the Second District, 1861-2; Governor of Michigan, 1869-73; and United States Senator, 1879-81. Was born at Coventry, R. I., Feb. 22, 1814. Governor Baldwin received a common school education, and became a clerk in a store at the age of twelve, and remained there until twenty years of age, devoting his leisure hours to study. He visited the West in 1837 and removed to Detroit in 1838, where he established a mercantile house. He was for several years a director and president of the Young Men's Society. In religious belief he was an Episcopalian. St. John's Church in Detroit was built through his liberality, and he generously aided churches throughout the State. He was a director of the Michigan State Bank during its existence, and president of the Second National Bank since its organization in 1863, resigning in 1887. He was State Senator in 1861 and 1862, and was chairman of the finance committee, of the select joint committee for the investigation of the State Treasury and the official acts of that officer, and was a member of other important committees. He was elected Governor of Michigan in 1868, and was re-elected in 1870, serving four years from 1869 to 1873, and was an able executive. During his administration the State School for Dependent Children was founded at Coldwater; the first steps taken towards building the Eastern Insane Asylum at Pontiac, and many improvements were made in the management of charitable and reformatory institutions. The appropriations for the present state capitol were recommended by him, and the contract was let under his administration. On the death of Senator Chandler in 1879, he was appointed by Governor Croswell to fill that position for the unexpired term, and was elected by the Legislature in 1881. He was a strong candidate for re-election in 1883. He was one of the delegates at large to the Republican National Convention in 1876; was two years chairman of the State Republican Committee, and was for many years a trustee of the Eastern Asylum at Pontiac. He died Dec. 31, 1892.

JAMES M. BALDWIN

Representative from the First District of Allegan County, 1859-60. His postoffice address was Hopkins. (Further data not obtainable).

LEVI W. BALDWIN

Representative from Clinton County, 1891-2. Was born in Jamestown, Chautauqua County, N. Y., Mar. 29, 1836, and in the fall of 1842, with his parents moved to Niagara County, finally located in the village of Olcott, where he resided until he came to Michigan in the spring of 1865, located in Clinton County, where he followed the occupation of carpenter and farmer until 1876, then engaged in mercantile business in the village of Fowler. He held the office of Commissioner of Highways, and in the spring of 1870 was elected Supervisor of Dallas Township, being re-elected many years thereafter; several years he was chairman of the Clinton County Board of Supervisors. He was elected to the House of 1891-2 on the Democratic ticket.

SIMEON L. BALDWIN

Representative from Kent County, 1877-8. Was born in Canterbury, Conn., Apr. 4, 1821. He was educated at the common schools and in 1840 he removed to Norwich, and for several terms attended the academy at that place, removing to Grand Rapids, Mich., in August, 1844. He was Alderman of Grand Rapids. His occupation was brick making. In politics he was a Republican. He died at Grand Rapids Aug. 10, 1901.

WILLIAM L. BALDWIN

Representative from the First District of Lenawee County, 1909-10, and 1911-12. Was born in Cambridge Township, Lenawee County, Feb. 28, 1855. While he was yet an infant in arms his mother died, and shortly after her death his father and grandparents, with whom he lived, removed to a farm in Palmyra Township. His early education was acquired in the district schools of his township. Occupation, a farmer. For years he was connected with the Lenawee County Agricultural Society. Married. In politics a Republican. He served as Supervisor.

BYRON D. BALL

Senator from the Twenty-ninth District, 1871-2; and Attorney General, 1873-5. Was born in Rochester, N. Y., July 19, 1844. His father, David Ball, came to Michigan in 1835 and founded the city of Owosso. In 1840 he removed with his family to Grand Rapids. In 1851 the son was apprenticed to learn the machinist trade with Ball & McRay of Grand Rapids. He served two years at the trade. He married in 1854, and in 1855 bought a half interest in the shop in which he had been employed, and carried on the business two years. In 1857 he commenced the study of law and in 1859 entered the law department of the State University, and graduated in the class of 1861. He commenced practice in Grand Rapids, and was Prosecuting Attorney of Kent County nearly four years. He was elected Attorney General of Michigan in 1872 and served in 1873 and up to Apr. 1, 1874, when he resigned on account of ill health. He built a block of stores at Grand Rapids and was interested with his father in other enterprises. He was a man of large stature, compactly built, of immense strength, and one of the best amateur boxers ever seen on the University grounds. He was genial, jovial, kind hearted and popular, and had many warm friends. In politics he was a Republican. He died Feb. 4, 1876.

JOHN BALL

Representative from Kent and other counties, 1838. Was born at Tenny Hill, Grafton County, N. H., Nov. 12, 1794. He had a common school and academical education, obtained by his own exertions. He graduated from Dartmouth College in 1820. He studied law two years at Lansingburg, N. Y., and then went to Darien, Ga., where he taught school five years. He then returned to Lansingburg. N. Y., completed his law studies and was admitted to the bar in 1824. He continued in practice several years and then abandoned it to take charge of an oilcloth factory for his sister, and placed it in a flourishing condition. In 1832 he traveled across the continent, went to Fort Vancouver, and taught the first school ever opened in Oregon. He returned via the Sandwich Islands and Cape Horn in 1833-4. In 1837 he settled at Grand Rapids, Mich., and represented eastern capitalists in locating lands. He also opened a law office and had as partners at various times, Hon. George Martin, formerly Chief Justice of Michigan, and Solomon L. Withey, late United States District Judge. From 1852 until the death of Mr. Ball, Feb. 5, 1884, he was the senior member of the firm of Ball & McKee. In 1842 he was appointed by Governor Barry, to select 300,000 of the 500,000 acres of land granted to Michigan by Congress for internal improvements. These were mainly selected about Grand Rapids, and were mostly taken up with internal improvement warrants, and as these warrants could be bought for about forty cents on the dollar, it resulted in a speedy settlement of the Grand River Valley. Mr. Ball was largely identified with Grand Rapids interests. He was interested in schools, geology, lyceums and all local enterprises. In politics he was a conservative Democrat. He died Feb. 5, 1884.

JOHN C. BALL

Representative from Lenawee County, 1842. His postoffice address was Tecumseh. (Further data not obtainable).

WILLIAM BALL

Representative from Livingston County, 1865-6, 1867-8 and 1881-2; and Senator, 1889-90, from the Thirteenth District, comprising Genesee and Livingston counties. Was born in Cayuga County, N. Y., Apr. 7, 1830. He received a collegiate education and was a teacher several years. He was engaged in farming and stock-growing. He held the offices of Supervisor, and Superintendent of Schools of Livingston County. He was a member of the Legislature in 1865-6, 1867-8 and 1881-2. The latter term he was speaker *pro tem*. In politics a Republican since the formation of the party.

WILLIAM HAZEN BALL

Representative from the Second District of Berrien County, 1909-10 and 1911-12. Was born at Boylston, Worcester County, Mass., Aug. 24, 1858, of American parentage. When two years of age he removed with his parents to Michigan, locating first at Dowagiac, at which place they resided two years. They then removed to Niles, where they resided two years thence moving to Coloma. Mr. Ball received his education in the public schools of Berrien County, supplemented by a business course at the Northern Indiana Normal College. He was identified for many years with the business interests of Coloma. In politics a Republican. He served his township as Clerk and Supervisor. He died Oct., 1922.

JESSIE BALLARD

Representative from Lenawee County, 1837. His postoffice address was Tecumseh. (Further data not obtainable).

SILAS L. BALLENTINE

Representative from the First District of St. Clair County, 1901-2. Was born in St. Andrews, New Brunswick, Nov. 3, 1845. His education was acquired in the common schools. He came to Michigan in 1850, and after spending three years on a farm he entered the dry goods business as clerk in a store in Port Huron. He continued in the business until 1867, when, in company with his brother, he formed the dry goods firm of S. L. & D. Ballentine. Married. He was a member of the Board of Education; was also one of the founders of the Commercial Bank and a promoter of the narrow gauge railroad into the Thumb of Michigan. He was interested in the Port Huron City Electric Railway and other commercial interests in city and county. In politics a Republican.

WILLIAM H. BALLENTINE

Representative from the Third District, of St. Clair County, 1881-2. Was born in St. Andrews, New Brunswick, July 11, 1832. He received a common school education, and at sixteen years of age removed to Calais, Me., where he became an apprentice to the hatter's trade. He lived in Calais until October, 1856, when he removed to Brockway, St. Clair County, Mich. Having purchased a farm, he followed farming until the fall of 1864. He then engaged in mercantile business in the village of Brockway. In politics a Republican.

JAMES M. BALLOU

Member of the State Board of Education, 1884-90. Was born in Mayfield, O., Jan. 24, 1886, moved to Parkville, St. Joseph County. He graduated from the State

Normal College at Ypsilanti in 1862, and was Superintendent of Schools. Engaged in manufacturing and milling business in Otsego. He held many local offices. He was elected a member of the State Board of Education Nov. 4, 1884, for a term of six years. He died at Otsego, Jan. 26, 1892.

EDWARD C. BANCROFT

Representative from St. Clair County, 1845. Was born in Westfield, Mass., in 1808. He came to Detroit in 1835, and moved to St. Clair County in 1842. In later years he was extensively identified with lake marine interests and lived in Detroit. Politically he was a Democrat. He was a merchant and vessel owner. He died at Syracuse, N. Y., in 1873.

WM. L. BANCROFT

Representative from St. Clair County, 1859-60; and Senator from the Twenty-fifth District, 1865-6. Was born at Martinsburg, Lewis County, N. Y., Aug. 12, 1825. His father removed to Michigan when he was seven years of age, and he received his education at Detroit in the high school kept by D. B. Crane. His father removed to Milwaukee, and in 1842 Mr. Bancroft was in the office of the *Courier*, a newspaper of that thriving village. In 1844 he returned to Michigan and became editor and proprietor of the *Observer* at Port Huron, where he remained until 1848. He then studied law with Hon. W. F. Allen, of Oswego, N. Y., later Judge of the Court of Appeals. He returned to Port Huron, in 1851, and entered into a lucrative practice. This he was obliged to abandon in 1857 from an affection of the eyes, which threatened total blindness. He then established in Port Huron its first banking office, although his name did not appear in the firm of John Miller & Son, now merged in the First National Bank of that city. He also engaged in lumbering. He was secretary of the State Senate in 1849. He was Democratic nominee for Congress and for Secretary of State. He was the first Mayor of Port Huron, and was Postmaster of that city. For eight years he was collector of the port, and after many years was again appointed collector of the Port Huron District in 1885 but failed to be confirmed by the Senate. He labored for many years to secure railroad connection between Port Huron and Chicago, and after every kind of opposition, in 1876 saw the final completion of the Chicago & Grand Trunk Railroad. In politics he was a Democrat.

ARTHUR D. BANGHAM

Senator, 1901-2 and 1903-4, from the Ninth District, comprising the counties of Calhoun and Kalamazoo. Was born in the township of Marengo, Calhoun County, Mich., Nov. 8, 1859. When twelve years of age he began work on the farm summers, and attended schools winters until 1876, when he entered Albion College, after leaving which he taught school in Springport, Jackson County. He graduated from the regular medical department of the University of Michigan in 1882. In 1883 he settled in Homer, where he practiced his profession, and was proprietor of the Central Drug Store. Married. In politics a Republican. He held numerous village offices; also a member of a number of fraternal organizations: The Masonic Order, K. of P., K. O. T. M., Modern Woodmen, O. E. S., and I. O. O. F.

PETER C. BARBEAU

Representative from Chippewa County, 1845. His postoffice address was Fort Brady. (Further data not obtainable).

DANIEL BARBER

Representative from Eaton County, 1840. Was born in Benson, Vt., in 1799. He was one of the original colony from that State that came to Michigan in 1836, and founded Vermontville. He was a farmer by occupation; a Republican in politics.

HOMER G. BARBER

Senator from the Twentieth District, 1871-2. Was born in Benson, Rutland County, Vt., in 1830, and came with his parents to Vermontville, Mich., in 1839. He was educated at the Vermontville Academy, and after serving one year as clerk in the postoffice at Kalamazoo, sailed around Cape Horn in 1850, engaged in mining in California for two years and was successful. He returned to Vermontville, and became a merchant and in 1871 engaged in banking. In 1861 he was appointed Postmaster of Vermontville, and held that position eleven years. In politics a Republican. He was a man of liberal views in religion, and had a choice library.

JOHN BARBER

Senator from the Third District, 1851. Was born in Perham, Mass., in 1792. He emigrated first to Vermont, and then to Walworth, Wayne County, N. Y. Afterwards he lived at Marion, same county, where he was a Justice of the Peace; also Clerk of Wayne County for six years, and was an Associate Judge of the County Court. He then became a resident of Clyde, N. Y., and was there a merchant. He settled in Adrian, Mich., in 1836, and held among other offices, those of County Clerk, Register of Deeds and Justice of the Peace. In politics he was first a Democrat, and later a Republican. He died Apr. 15, 1867.

JULIUS S. BARBER

Representative from Branch County, 1867-8; and Delegate from Branch County to the Constitutional Convention of 1867. Was born in Rutland County, Vt., Apr. 6, 1824. He removed with his father's family to Vermontville, Mich., in 1836. He received a fair education and became a teacher at the age of twenty-three. From 1847 to 1849 he clerked in a store at Whitehall, N. Y. In 1849 he went to California and was engaged as a farmer, miner and trader for five years. He then located at Coldwater, where he engaged in mercantile business. He was a Republican in politics. He was Alderman of Coldwater four years; was appointed by President Grant Assessor of Internal Revenue for the Second District, and held it until the office was abolished; two years Commissioner of the State Public School; and Postmaster of Coldwater.

JOHN BARBOUR

Representative from Calhoun County, 1846. Was born in Eaton, Madison County, N. Y., Sept. 15, 1807. He settled at Monroe in 1837, removed to Battle Creek in

1841, and to Detroit in 1867, where he died Oct. 17, 1867. By occupation he was a farmer; in politics, first a Democrat, then a Republican.

LEVI LEWIS BARBOUR

Regent of the University of Michigan, 1892-8 and 1902-8; and Delegate from the Second District, Wayne County, in the Constitutional Convention of 1907-8. Was born in Monroe, Mich., Aug. 14, 1840, of American parents. He received his education at the State University, graduating with the class of '63, literary department, and the class of '65, law. Practiced law after his graduation and was twice appointed to fill a vacancy in the regency of the University. Married. He was elected to the Constitutional Convention during his absence from the country and gave no pledges in order to receive the election.

JONATHAN S. BARCLAY

Representative from Saginaw County, 1855-6. Was born in Northumberland County, Pa., Aug. 18, 1807. He came to Michigan and settled at Albion in 1835. He lived in Detroit from 1846 to 1849, when he removed to Lower Saginaw, now Bay City, where he was prominent in the business circles of that thriving city until age and infirmities unfitted him for the active duties of life. In business he was a millwright, politically a Democrat. He was Sheriff of Bay County in 1861-2. He died Aug. 4, 1887, leaving a widow, two sons and a daughter.

HIRAM H. BARDWELL

Representative from the Second District of Genesee County, 1885-6. and 1887-8. Was born in the township of Burton, of that county, Apr. 2, 1839. He spent his early years on a farm, received a good education, enlisted in Co. K, 23d Regiment Mich. Vol. Infantry. At the expiration of his term of service he returned home and began the study of medicine, entering the medical department of the State University in 1865, remaining there until 1866, when he went to the Rush Medical College at Chicago, from whence he graduated in 1869, after which year he engaged in the practice of his profession, having built up a large practice and gained a fine reputation as a physician and surgeon. Mr. Bardwell was a practical farmer, and the owner of a valuable farm of one hundred and twenty acres about one and a half miles east of the village of Mt. Morris. He filled the office of Township Superintendent of Schools, Justice of the Peace, President of the village two terms, Councilman for five terms, and township and village Health Officer. In politics a Republican.

RICHARD P. BARKER

Representative from Berrien County, 1847. Was born in New York City in September, 1805. He settled at Niles in 1838 and was a merchant. Politically he was a Democrat. He died in 1871.

THOMAS E. BARKWORTH

Representative from the First District of Jackson County, 1891-2 and 1893-4. Was born in Lincolnshire, England, July 21, 1851. He acquired a common school education. At the age of twenty he came to Michigan, locating in a rural district in Liberty Township, Jackson County. He worked on a farm during the summer months and taught school winters, at the same time being privately engaged in the study of law. In 1878 he moved to Jackson city, was admitted to the bar and began the practice of law. In politics a Democrat.

NATHAN BARLOW

Representative from Barry County, 1841 and 1848. Was born in the State of Vermont, in 1785, came to Michigan in 1837, and settled in the township of Yankee Springs, Barry County. By occupation he was a merchant and farmer, in politics a Whig. He served as Associate Judge, and in company with his son, Nathan jr., erected a saw mill at the outlet of Barlow Lake in 1840. He died Jan. 25, 1899.

NATHAN BARLOW, JR.

Representative from Barry County, 1850. Was born in Canandaigua, N. Y., Jan. 1, 1818. He left his home in New York and first went to St. Louis, Mo., but came to Barry County in 1840, and was one of the early pioneers—engaged in active business, built the first frame hotel in Hastings, was early in mercantile and milling business, which he followed until declining health compelled him to retire. Various county offices were filled by him, and he always filled the place to the satisfaction of the people. Politically he was a Democrat.

HORACE T. BARNABY

Representative from Gratiot County, 1869-70 and 1871-2. Was born at Angelica, N. Y., Apr. 26, 1823. By profession he was a clergyman, politically a Republican. He was County Clerk of Gratiot County in 1861-2, and filled all town offices from Constable to Supervisor. He came to Hillsdale County in 1842, removed to Gratiot County in 1854, and to Gaines, Kent County, in 1875.

HORACE THOMAS BARNABY, JR.

Representative from the Second District of Kent County, 1901-2 and 1903-4; member of the Constitutional Convention of 1907-8 from Kent County; and Senator 1909-10 and 1911-12 from the Seventeenth District, comprising every township of Kent County and the sixth, seventh, eighth and ninth wards of the city of Grand Rapids. Was born in North Star Township, Gratiot County, Mich., Oct. 24, 1870, descending from the old English family of Barnabys who settled about Cape Cod early in Colonial times. His education was obtained at Hartsville College, Hartsville, Ind., Kalamazoo College, and the Ferris school at Big Rapids, Mich. He was a successful school teacher, and was graduated from the law department of the University of Michigan, in June, 1902. Married. Held the offices of School Inspector, Township Clerk and Supervisor. A staunch Republican.

EDMUND M. BARNARD

Representative from the Second District of Kent County, 1891-2; and Senator, 1893-4, 1895-6 and 1897-8. from the Seventeenth District, composed of the tenth and eleventh wards of the city of Grand Rapids, and the townships of Kent County. Was born in Hudson, N. Y., May 28, 1860, and came to Michigan with his parents at the close of the war, locating on a farm in Grand Rapids Township. His education was obtained in the public schools and at Olivet College. In connection with farming he engaged in real estate and insurance business, being a member of the insurance firm of L. K. Bishop & Co. In politics a Republican. He was elected to the House of Representatives from the Second District of his county in 1891; was a member of the Senate of 1893-4, and elected to that of 1895-6 and 1897-8. He has taken important part in maters of legislation; was the author of the joint resolution committing this state to the election of U. S. senators by popular vote; was instrumental in restoring to the soldiers of the Michigan Soldiers' Home the right of franchise through a constitutional amendment. after it had been denied them by the courts; was instrumental in the measure requiring the vestibuling of street cars, and several other measures affecting the purification of conventions and elections; was chairman of the Committee on Banks and Corporations during the session of 1895.

ELY BARNARD

Representative from Livingston County, 1843 and 1844; and a Delegate from Livingston County to the Constitutional Convention of 1850. Was born in Madison County, N. Y., Sept. 9, 1887. He came to Michigan in 1834 and settled on a farm in Genoa, Livingston County, where he died Sept. 9, 1871. He was a Democrat. He was a good farmer, and held in high esteem.

GEORGE S. BARNARD

Representative from the Second District of Berrien County, 1919-20, 1921-2, and 1923—. Was born in Berrien County, Jan. 19, 1876, of French and English parentage. He was educated in the public schools, Ferris Institute of Big Rapids, and Benton Harbor College. After teaching school five years, he engaged in the drug business, in which he is still interested. He served as Supervisor six years and Alderman two years. Mr. Barnard is married. In politics he is a Republican.

NEWELL BARNARD

Representative from the First District of Saginaw County, 1883-4. Was born in Thornton, Grafton County, N. H., Mar. 19, 1825. The family removed to Oldtown, Me., in September, 1830, remaining there until 1853. Mr. Barnard was married at Boston, Mass., Sept. 12, 1854, and soon after moved to Michigan, settling in Saginaw the following spring. On his arrival in Saginaw he commenced the business of lumbering, handling about 15,000,000 feet of lumber annually. Being a man of superior organizing ability and executive force, he largely aided in the advancement which the lumber and salt interests of the State have reached. He was active in organizing, and he was president of the second salt manufacturing company on Saginaw River, which commenced operations in 1861. In 1872 the firm of Barnard & Binder built the iron front block, corner of Franklin and Hamilton Streets, Saginaw, one of the finest business blocks in the Saginaw valley. Mr. Barnard was one of the most active and influential in securing the building of the J. L. & S. R. R. to and through Saginaw; was one of the directors and one of the executive committee of the Saginaw Valley & St. Louis R. R. Company, and foremost in aiding every church and public improvement. He was one of the first to recognize the practicability of utilizing the farm districts in the vicinity of lumber operations, by starting many years since a six hundred acre farm, and which has proved entirely successful. In politics he was a Republican. He died July 9, 1883.

ELEAZAR BARNES

Representative from Monroe County, 1851. Was born in Pittsford, Vt., June 10, 1807. By occupation he was a farmer, politically a Republican. He came to Michigan in 1833, and resided in London, Monroe County. He held the office of Supervisor several times from 1838 to 1865.

GEORGE BARNES

Senator, 1903-4, from the Thirteenth District, comprising the counties of Livingston and Genesee. Was born in England in 1846, of English parents, who came to the United States and settled in Jackson County, Mich., in 1851, and three years later moved to Gratiot County. He attended the district schools until he was seventeen years of age, at which time his father was drafted and Mr. Barnes volunteered to take his place, was accepted, and served his country in the 23d regiment, Mich. Volunteers, Company H. After returning from the war Mr. Barnes worked on a farm summers and taught school winters until the fall of 1870 when he entered the State Normal College and graduated from the classical course in 1873. He graduated from the classical course of the University of Michigan in 1877, receiving the degree of M. A. He was Superintendent of Schools at Alma, Stanton, Howell and the School for the Blind at Lansing. He was married in 1877 to Miss Augustie D. Johnson, a teacher in the public schools of Jackson, Mich. In 1889 Mr. Barnes purchased the Livingston *Republican*, at Howell. Interested also in agriculture, having purchased a farm of 240 acres. In politics a Republican.

GEORGE ALBERT BARNES

Senator, 1915-16, from the Thirteenth District, comprising the counties of Genesee and Livingston. Was born at Howell, Mich., Feb. 1, 1885, of English parentage. He was educated in the Howell High School and the University of Michigan, graduating from the literary department of the latter in 1906. During the following two years he assisted his father, George Barnes, in editing the Livingston *Republican* at Howell. In 1909 he purchased the Bellevue *Gazette* at Bellevue, Eaton County, Mich., and Jan. 1, 1910, was appointed Postmaster by President Taft, which position he resigned after selling the newspaper and going to Flint to engage in the publishing and printing business. In politics a Republican.

HENRY BARNES

Senator from the Second District, comprising a portion of the city of Detroit and Wayne County, 1859-60. Was a native of England, born in 1816. He was a printer by trade, and came to this country at quite an early age. In the early days of the State he published a paper for a time at Niles. He was associated with the publication of the Detroit *Free Press* in 1837, and subsequently with some minor publications in Detroit. His principal newspaper venture, however, was as one of the originators of the Detroit *Tribune* in 1849, with which he remained connected under various auspices until about 1863. He was clerk of the House of Representatives under the first Republican ascendancy in 1855. Under authority of the Secretary of War in 1862, he recruited the first regiment of colored troops mustered into the service of the United States. In 1866 he was appointed by President Johnson Postmaster at Detroit, and served for some time, but the refusal of the Senate to confirm his appointment (by reason of its disagreement with the President) threw him out of this position. He was subsequently appointed and served as Pension Agent at Detroit, 1867-9. He was a Whig and Republican in politics, although sympathizing with the Johnson defection, as implied by official positions mentioned foregoing. He died in 1871.

NORMAN BARNES

Representative from Monroe County, 1850. His postoffice address was LaSalle. (Further data not obtainable).

ORLANDO M. BARNES

Representative from Ingham County, 1863-4. Son of John and Anna Barnes, was born at Cato, N. Y., Nov. 21, 1824, and was a descendant of John Barnes, one of the early pilgrims. His parents removed to Aurelius, Ingham County, Mich., in 1837, where he was brought up upon a farm. He received a fine education, and was a graduate of the University of Michigan in 1850. He studied law and settled down to the practice at Mason. He soon stood among the leaders of the bar in central Michigan. In 1853 he was appointed Prosecuting Attorney to fill a vacancy, and in 1854 was elected to that office. He continued in practice with great success until 1867, when he became secretary of the Jackson, Lansing & Saginaw Railroad Company and its general counsel and attorney. He was general manager of the road from 1869 to 1871, when it was leased to the Michigan Central. He was the Land Commissioner of the J. L. & S. and had charge of the large land grant received from Congress to aid in building the road. In 1877 he was elected Mayor · of Lansing, and in 1878 was the Democratic candidate for Governor. He served as chairman of the Democratic State Central Committee from 1880 to 1884. He was a Democrat. In religion he was a Presbyterian. In 1852 he married Amanda W. Fleming. He accumulated a fine fortune, and was president of the Lansing National Bank and the Lansing Gas Company. He died at Lansing Nov. 11, 1899.

ORSAMUS S. BARNES

Representative from Eaton County, 1879-80. Was born in Broome County, N. Y., Aug. 7, 1830. In 1839 he removed to Oberlin, O. In 1846 he removed to Wisconsin. He enlisted in the Mexican War Aug. 16, 1847. Returning at the close of the war, he spent the next seven years in Wisconsin, attending school, teaching and working in wagon shops. He received a common school education, and in 1855 returned to Oberlin, O., where he married and removed to Lenawee County, Mich., and from thence to Eaton County, in 1863. He was a farmer and minister by occupation. He held nearly every town office from Constable to Supervisor. In politics a Republican.

JAMES FOOTE BARNETT

Delegate in the Constitutional Convention of 1907-8 from the Sixteenth District, Kent County. Was born in Grand Rapids in 1869, of American descent. He attended the public schools of Grand Rapids and graduated from Yale and Columbia universities. Mr. Barnett was admitted to the bar in 1896 and engaged in the practice of law.. He contributed articles to magazines, chiefly to the legal journals.

EZRA C. BARNUM

Senator 1895-6 and 1897-8, from the Twenty-ninth District, composed of the counties of Alpena, Cheboygan, Emmet, Otsego, Presque Isle and Montmorency. Was born in Castleton Township, Barry County, Mich., Mar. 8, 1850. His primary education was obtained in the district school, supplemented by a three years' course at Olivet College. He then entered the law department of the University of Michigan, and on his graduating therefrom in 1876 engaged in the practice of his profession at Hastings, Mich. In 1879 he moved to Petoskey, where he engaged in the practice of his profession and the real estate and insurance business. In politics a Republican; held the office of Township Clerk, Justice of the Peace, Village Attorney of Petoskey and Circuit Court Commissioner for Emmet County.

JOHN E. BARRINGER

Senator, 1887-8 and 1889-90, from the Fifteenth District, comprising the counties of Macomb and St. Clair. Was born in the township of Bristol, Ontario County, N. Y., July 16, 1841. He received a common school education in the district schools of his native township, and at the academy at Canandaigua, N. Y. His early life (when not in school) was passed upon the farm until he was eighteen years of age, when he commenced teaching in the public schools. In the meantime he studied medicine and attended the Medical Department of the University of Michigan. In the fall of 1863 he located at Armada, Macomb County, and commenced the practice of medicine, which he followed with success until the spring of 1878 when, on account of ill-health, he was obliged to give up practice. More or less identified with public affairs of his township and county he held several official positions. He was President of Armada village two terms, Secretary and Master of Armada Grange, Master of Masonic Lodge for many years, twelve years Secretary and two years President of Armada Agricultural Society, director of Union school for several years, Township Treasurer two terms, and Treasurer of Macomb County two terms. Owner of a fine farm. In politics a Democrat.

HIRAM BARRITT

Delegate from Oakland County to the Second Convention of Assent, 1836; and Representative from Oakland County, 1846. Was born in Alford, Berkshire County, Mass., Feb. 10, 1799. By occupation he was a farmer and surveyor, in politics a Democrat. He settled in Commerce, Oakland County, in 1833, and built the first frame house, and the first frame schoolhouse, in that township. He was Supervisor several terms, Justice many years, Town Clerk and served as County Surveyor. He removed to Ovid in 1864, and later resided at Muskegon, where he died Apr. 5, 1878.

JOHN A. BARRY

Representative, 1907-8, from the Wexford district, comprising the counties of Lake and Wexford. Was born in the township of Handy, Livingston County, July 29, 1848, of Irish descent. He lived on a farm until fourteen years of age when he removed with his parents to Muskegon County; worked in saw mills and in the lumber woods summers and attended school winters until eighteen years of age when he engaged in the drug business with Dr. H. D. Root at Newaygo, Mich. Graduated from the medical department of the University of Michigan in 1873, locating at Coral, Montcalm County, and there practiced medicine until 1889. He then engaged in the general merchandise business at Harrietta, Wexford County, under the firm name of Barry Bros. & Curtis. Married. He held the offices of Village President, Justice of the Peace and Supervisor. In politics a Republican.

JOHN STEWART BARRY

Delegate from the Thirteenth District to the Constitutional Convention of 1835; Senator from the Third District, 1835-6 and 1837-8, and from the Seventh District, 1841; Governor of Michigan, 1841-5 and 1850-1. Was born at Amherst, N. H., Jan. 29, 1802. His parents, John and Ellen (Stewart) Barry, early removed to Rockingham, Vt., where he remained until of age, working on his father's farm, and pursuing his studies at the same time. He married Mary Kidder, of Grafton, Vt., and in 1824 went to Georgia, Vt., where he had charge of an academy for two years, meanwhile studying law. He afterwards practiced in that State. He was also a member of the Governor's staff with the title of Governor's aid, and was also Captain in the State militia. He removed to Michigan in 1831 and settled at White Pigeon, where he engaged in mercantile business with I. W. Willard. In 1834 he removed to Constantine and engaged in mercantile business. He was Justice of the Peace from 1831 to 1835. In 1841 he was elected Governor by the Democrats, receiving a large majority over Philo C. Fuller, the Whig candidate. In 1843 he was again elected Governor, and before the close of his term recommended the sale of the Michigan Central & Southern Railroads, which sale was made in 1846. The constitution did not permit a Governor to hold but two successive terms, and it was not until 1849 that he was again elected Governor over Flavius J. Littlejohn. He was not a brilliant speaker, but was versed in ancient and modern languages, and thoroughly posted in historical matters. After his retirement to private life in 1852, he held no public office, but continued his mercantile business at Constantine until his death, which occurred Jan. 14, 1870. His wife had died in 1869, and as they had no children, the large property went to relatives. He was always a Democrat of the old Jeffersonian school.

THOMAS B. BARRY

Representative from the Second District of Saginaw County, 1855-6. Was born at Cohoes, Albany County, N. Y., July 17, 1852, of Irish parentage. At an early age he entered the employ of J. H. Parsons & Co., manufacturers of knitting goods, in his native city, in whose employ he remained until he went to learn the trade of ax-making. He afterwards worked at his trade in Pennsylvania and Ontario, where he married Miss Maggie Delaney, daughter of a respected farmer, of Copetown, Ont. He moved from the latter place to Cleveland, O., where he lived a number of years. Moving with his family to East Saginaw in October, 1882, he entered the employ of the "Michigan Ax and Tool Co." He entered the political arena as the candidate for the labor party, afterwards receiving the nomination of the Greenback and Democratic Conventions.

CHARLES EDWARD BARTLETT

Representative from the First District of Wayne County, 1923—. Was born in San Francisco, California, June 16, 1887. He was educated in Chicago in the public and parochial schools and the De La Salle Institute. He is married and has one son and three daughters. He is an electrician and held a position with the Chicago Telephone Company for twelve years and since coming to Michigan eight years ago has been connected with the Michiggan State Telephone Company and the Detroit Edison Company. He is a member of the International Brotherhood of Electrical Workers, holding the office of treasurer. He is also a member of the legislative committees of the Detroit Federation of Labor and of the Michigan State Federation of Labor.

SAMUEL BARSTOW

Member of the State Board of Education, 1849-51. He was appointed Mar. 30, 1849, for a two years term. (Further data not obtainable).

IRA H. BARTHOLOMEW

Representative from Ingham County, 1873-4. Was born in the town of Waddington, St. Lawrence County, N. Y., Jan. 4, 1828. He received his education in the common schools of his town and the academies at Canton and Ogdensburg. He commenced the study of medicine in the latter village, and graduated in the college of medicine and surgery of the University of Michigan, in the spring of 1853. He commenced the practice of his profession in his native town, but in the fall of 1854 removed to Lansing, Mich. In 1863 he was elected Mayor of the city of Lansing, and was twice re-elected. He was president of the State Medical Society in 1870-1, and was physician to the Reform School. Deceased.

WALLACE R. BARTLETT

Representative from Tuscola County, 1857-8. Was born in Greensburgh, Trumbull County, O., July 10, 1828. He came to Tuscola County, Mich., in 1855; established the *Tuscola County Pioneer* in 1857; was in the mercantile business at Vassar; also Postmaster there under Lincoln; held various town and county offices; removed to Omaha in 1866; was member of the Nebraska Legislature in 1872 and 1874; Deputy Collector of Internal Revenue at Omaha for five years; removed to St. Paul, Minn., in 1882; later the head of the firm of Bartlett, Ridgway & Co., real estate brokers at Minneapolis. Politically a Republican.

WALTER W. BARTON

Representative, 1881-2; and Senator, 1887-8, from the Twenty-ninth District, comprising the counties of Antrim, Charlevoix, Grand Traverse, Leelanaw, and Manitou. Was born in Wyoming County, N. Y., June 22, 1834. When two years old he removed with his parents to the village of Tonawanda, Erie County; where he remained until 1852. Here he received a common school education. In the fall of 1852 he removed to St. Louis, Mo., and engaged in the construction of railroads and continued in that business in and about that city until the spring of 1858, when he went to Northport, Leelanaw County, Mich. There he engaged in the wooding of lake steamers and selling goods until the spring of 1863, when he removed to the village of Leland, Leelanaw County. He engaged in the drug business and the cultivation of cranberries. He was Supervisor of Leland, Justice of the Peace, and Postmaster.

HENRY BARTOW

Delegate from Ionia County to the Constitutional Convention of 1850. Was born at Freetown, Cortland County, N. Y., Mar. 31, 1813. In 1824 he was elected to the New York Assembly. He came to Michigan in 1825 and settled in the town afterward called Plymouth. He worked hard to overcome poor health and lack of education. In 1836 he settled near Portland and in 1840 began the study of law. He was Prosecuting Attorney and Circuit Commissioner for his county. He aided very largely in getting the railroads. Occupation was that of a farmer.

JOHN BARTOW

Senator from the Fifth District, 1838; and Delegate from Genesee County to the Constitutional Convention of 1850. Was born in New York in 1813. He was by profession a lawyer; in politics a Democrat. He removed to Washington, D. C., and died while in the public service. He was a man of fine talent, and would have become a leading man except for his love of drink. In spite of that he was held in high regard by those who knew him.

MOSES BARTOW

Representative from Clinton County, 1865-6 and 1875-6. Was born in Niagara County, N. Y., June 10, 1822, and received his education at Youngstown Academy. He removed to Michigan in 1831 and first lived at Lyon, Oakland County, but settled at Westphalia, Clinton County, in 1841. He was Supervisor of that town eighteen years, Justice of the Peace thirty years, and two years Circuit Court Comsissioner. By profession he was a lawyer, in politics a Democrat. He died at Portland, Ionia County, July 7, 1884.

WILLIAM BARTOW

Member of the Legislative Council from Wayne County, 1830-1. He was also Associate Judge from Detroit Jan. 24, 1830. (Further data not obtainable).

JOHN BASTONE

Senator from the Seventeenth District, Huron and Tuscola counties, 1891. Was born at Sidmouth, Devonshire, England, Feb. 28, 1831. Received a common school education, worked at the gardening business until 1857, when he came to this country and located at Redford, Wayne County, working on a farm. In 1873 he moved to his present home, a farm in Almer Township, Tuscola County. Cast his first vote for Stephen A. Douglas; was elected Supervisor of Almer, was chairman of that body, although it was strongly Republican. He served as master of a Masonic Lodge, and High Priest of Caro Chapter, R. A. M. He was nominated to the office of Senator in 1890 by the Industrial Party and endorsed by the Democrats. He resigned July 3, 1891.

JOHN LAWRENCE BATCHELDER

Representative from the First District of Wayne County, 1903-4. Was born in Bennington County, Vt., in 1834, of English parents. He was educated in the common schools and Chester Academy, Vt. His ancestors came from England in 1637 and settled in Salem, Mass. The land John Batchelder settled on in 1637 is still in the hands of the family. Mr. Batchelder was for some time in the marble and cut stone business, but later retired from active business. He held the office of Justice of the Peace and was a member of the Detroit City Council. He was elected on the general legislative ticket of Detroit, Nov. 4, 1902.

ALFRED G. BATES

Representative from Monroe County, 1853-4. Was born in Canandaigua, N. Y., Jan. 25, 1810. He came to Monroe, 1834, resided there until his removal to Chicago, Ill., Feb., 1881. He was a member of the State Board of Agriculture, Sheriff, and Deputy United States Marshal and for twenty years connected with the office of Superintendent of the Poor. By occupation he was a farmer.

ERASTUS N. BATES

Representative from the Second District of Allegan County, 1885-6 and 1887-8; and Senator from the Eighth District, comprising the counties of Allegan and Van Buren, 1907-8 and 1909-10. Was born in Geauga County, O., Mar. 1, 1845. When twelve years of age he removed with his parents to Dorr Township, Allegan County. He received his education in the district schools. He was married to Flora I. Gilbert in 1870. His attention was given to farming and mercantile business. Mr. Bates enlisted in the 21st Mich. Infantry in 1864, marched with Sherman from Chattanooga to the Sea, and served until the close of the war. He held the office of Supervisor; represented the Second District of Allegan County in the House, 1885-6 and 1887-8; served as financial clerk of the House in 1889 under Daniel Crossman; appointed a trustee of the Michigan Asylum in 1889 by Governor Luce and reappointed by Governors Rich and Bliss. In politics a Republican.

FREDERICK BATES

Judge of the Supreme Court of the Territory of Michigan, 1805-8; Treasurer of Michigan Territory, 1805-6. Was born in Belmont, Va., June 23, 1777, and died Aug. 21, 1825. He was the son of a Quaker, Thomas Fleming Bates, and one of seven sons and five daughters. He was well taught in the rudiments and disciplined to study and work by his father, and at the age of sixteen was apprenticed to a court clerk to study law and do sufficient work for self-support. In 1795 he obtained employment in the quartermaster's department of the Army of the North-east and left home for the frontier, Detroit being his home, often visiting Mackinaw and other outposts. In a few years he made a little capital, and went into trade as a storekeeper in Detroit, studying law in spare hours. At that time Jefferson was President and Madison was Secretary of State, both friends of his father's family, and he was appointed Territorial Judge and a Land Commissioner. He resigned in 1808. On a visit to Washington to make a report as Land Commissioner, he was appointed, against his wish, Secretary of the Territory of Louisiana and U. S. Reporter of land titles, and located at St. Louis. He held the office of secretary until Missouri became a State in 1820. The other office was held by him until 1824, when he was elected the second Governor of Missouri. He died while in office, leaving a widow and several children, and a reputation without a stain. Edward Bates, Secretary of the Interior, under Lincoln, was a younger brother.

MORGAN BATES

Lieutenant Governor, 1869-73. Was born near Glens Falls, N. Y., July 12, 1806. When young he was apprenticed as a printer at Sandy Hill, N. Y. He worked as a journeyman printer at Albany, and other places. In 1826 he published the Warren *Gazette*, at Warren, Pa., and Horace Greeley worked for him as a journeyman printer, and the friendship thus formed was lasting. In 1828 he took charge of the Chautaqua *Republican*, at Jamestown, N. Y. In 1830 he went to New York City and planned the *New Yorker*, published by Greeley and McElrath. In 1833 he was foreman in the office of the Detroit *Advertiser*, with George Dawson. He bought that paper in 1839, and published it until 1844 as a Whig paper. Between 1849 and 1856 he made two trips to California via Cape Horn, and started the *Alta California* at San Francisco, the first daily west of the Rocky Mountains. In 1856 he became a clerk in the office of the Auditor General at Lansing, where he remained until 1858. He then removed to Traverse City and started the Grand Traverse *Herald*, which he published for sixteen years. He was Treasurer of Grand Traverse County for eight years, Register of the United States Land Office at Traverse City from the inauguration of Lincoln, except a short interval under Johnson, until his death in 1874. He was first a Whig, then a Republican. He died Mar. 2, 1874.

WILLIAM R. BATES

Representative from Bay County, 1871, and the Second District of Genesee County, 1897-8. Was born at Cazenovia, N. Y., June 28, 1845. He acquired an academic and partial collegiate education; came to Michigan in 1866 and located at Flint, where he resided with the exception of four years' residence in Bay County. He represented said county in the House of 1871-2, but resigned prior to the special session and was succeeded by the late Judge Isaac Marston. The same year he was appointed Register of the United States Land Office at East Saginaw, but resigned in 1876. He then served as special agent of the United States Pension Bureau until 1879, when he resigned; was secretary of the State Central Committee in 1880-1, under late Governor Baldwin, who was chairman. In 1881 he was appointed agent of the Treasury Department, serving four years, but was removed by Grover Cleveland; was again secretary of the State Central Committee under chairman Senator James McMillan, in 1886-8, 1890-4. He died at San Diego, Calif., Jan. 6, 1921.

FRED H. BATHEY

Representative from the Third District of St. Clair County, 1891-2 and 1893-4. Was born Aug. 21, 1865, on the farm which he later owned and occupied. He acquired his early education at the common schools and for a time attended the Parson Business College at Saginaw. Occupation a farmer, on the farm where he was born in Columbus Township. In politics a Democrat. He held the office of Township Clerk four terms.

WILLIAM B. BAUM

Representative from the First District of Saginaw County, 1893-4. Was born in East Saginaw, Jan. 23, 1856. He attended public schools until the age of seventeen years, when he entered his father's employ in the Sherman House. At the age of twenty-one he was admitted as a partner. Principally engaged in dealing in real estate. In politics a Democrat. He held the office of Alderman and of Mayor of East Saginaw, being the first native born Mayor of East Saginaw and the last one before the consolidation.

JACOB BAUMANN

Representative from the First District of Wayne County, 1901-2. Was born in Detroit May 8, 1860; spent his entire life in his native city. His education was obtained in the common schools, supplemented by a course in a business college. Officially connected with the Ph. Kling Brewing Company for many years. He served his constituents as Alderman from the 13th ward of the city of Detroit in 1885-7, and was elected to the Legislature of 1901-2 on the general legislative ticket.

LEONARD BAUMGAERTNER

Representative from the Second District of Saginaw County, 1899-1900, 1901-2 and 1903-4. Was born of German parents on a farm in the township of Buena Vista, Saginaw County, Mich., Dec. 30, 1859. He acquired an education in the common schools of his neighborhood, and reached the age of twenty-one years when his father died, leaving a family of six children, of which he was the eldest. He at once took control of the homestead, and engaged in farming. In politics a Republican. He was a member of the school board, School Inspector, and Township Clerk. He was elected to the Legislatures of 1899-1900, 1901-2, and re-elected Nov. 4, 1902, on the general legislative ticket.

WILLIAM G. BAUMGARDNER

Representative from Manistee County, 1887-8. Was born in Centre County, Pa., Apr. 3, 1850. He became a resident of Michigan about 1880. By occupation he was a saw-filer and millwright. Mr. Baumgardner held the office of Township Clerk and School Director. He was elected Representative on the Greenback-Labor ticket.

BENJAMIN L. BAXTER

Member of the Board of Regents of the University of Michigan, 1858-64; and Representative from Lenawee County, 1869-70. Was born at Sidney Plains, Delaware

County, N. Y., Apr. 7, 1815. He came to Tecumseh in 1831 with his father, Hon. Levi Baxter. He received a good education and was three years in college at Dartmouth, N. H. In 1843 he took charge of the Tecumseh branch of the University of Michigan for three years, and at the same time studied law with Hon. Perley Bills, and became his law partner for twenty-five years. In politics he was a Republican. He died at his home in Tecumseh June 10, 1902.

HOWARD F. BAXTER

Representative from the First District of Kent County, 1923—. Was born in Grand Rapids, June 8, 1886. He graduated from the Grand Rapids High School and from electrical engineering department of the University of Michigan. During the years 1910 and 1911 he was district engineer for the New York Telephone Co., and in 1912 became associated with the Baxter Laundry Co., of Grand Rapids, being made its president and manager six years later, which position he holds at the present time. During the world war he was a pilot in the air service. Mr. Baxter is married and has two children, a boy and a girl. He has always been active in civic and social welfare, being a director and officer of the Y. M. C. A., and associated with other civic and welfare organizations and clubs. He is also post commander of the American Legion. Mr. Baxter is a Republican.

LEVI BAXTER

Senator from the Third District, 1849-50. Was born at East Windsor, Conn., Oct. 5, 1788, and was the son of Levi Baxter, a Captain in the Revolution. When a boy he removed with his father to western New York, where he was engaged in farming, lumbering and merchandise at Sidney Plains. He settled at Tecumseh, Mich., in 1831, and built the "Red Mills," the first of any size west of Monroe, settlers coming fifty miles to this mill. Governor Cass made him Chief Justice of the Lenawee County court, hence the title of Judge. He built a mill at Jonesville in 1834, the first west of Tecumseh. He removed to White Pigeon in 1836 and built large mills. In 1840 he made large additions to his mills at Jonesville. In 1848 he made Jonesville his home. He was a Whig, then a Free Soiler, in 1848, and was elected Senator to the Legislature of 1849 and 1850 by a coalition of Whigs and Free Soilers. Through his influence Jonesville was made a point on the Michigan Southern Railroad. He was a member of the Presbyterian Church and an elder. He died at Jonesville in 1862.

WITTER J. BAXTER

Member of the State Board of Education, 1857-1881; and Senator from the Ninth District, 1877-8. Was born at Sidney Plains, Delaware County, N. Y., June 18, 1816, and was the son of Levi and Lois (Johnston) Baxter. His grandfather, Levi Baxter, was a Captain in the Revolution, and his maternal grandfather was Colonel Witter Johnston, a Colonel in the Revolution. Mr. Baxter came with his father to Tecumseh in 1831, remaining there until 1836, then removing to White Pigeon until 1848, when he came to Jonesville. He received a common school and academical education at the State University branches at Tecumseh, White Pigeon and Detroit, and received the honorary degree of A. M. from the University. In 1836 he commenced teaching and continued in that profession until 1841, when he studied law in Detroit, was admitted in 1844 and practiced until 1848, in partnership with Andrew Hervie, of Detroit, when he removed to Jonesville and became a partner of W. W. Murphy, of the firm of Murphy & Baxter, which continued until 1874. After that time he practiced alone. While in Detroit he was director and president of the Young Men's Society. He was also a member of the firm of Grosvenor & Co., bankers, and a member of the Jonesville School Board for twenty-six years; Supervisor and President of the Board; was appointed a member of the State Board of Education July 21, 1857, and served almost continuously until his resignation Apr. 6, 1881; president of the State Agricultural Society and a member of the executive board; an active Odd Fellow and Mason, in the first holding high offices. He always took an active interest in the State Pioneer Society, was its president and a member of the historical committee for many years. He was also president of the county pioneer society. For several years prior to 1886 he was secretary of the State Board of Charities, and an efficient officer. From the age of fifteen he was a member of the Presbyterian Church and the greater part of the time Sunday school Superintendent. He was first a Whig, but a Republican after 1854. He died suddenly Feb. 6, 1888.

JAMES BAYLEY

Representative from Oakland County, 1865-6. Was born in Scipio, N. Y., July 1, 1802. As a boy, he was engaged in harness making, and when older in the tanner and currier's trade. In 1825 he settled on a farm in Troy, Oakland County. In 1830 he went to Detroit and had charge of a tannery for some years. He was Supervisor in 1849 and farm superintendent at the Agricultural College from 1860 to 1863. He was president of the Oakland County and State agricultural societies, and stood high in the estimation of the farmers of Michigan. He died at Birmingham, Mich., May 1, 1867.

JOSEPH EDWARD BAYLISS

Representative from Chippewa County, 1913-14. Was born at Pakenham, Ont., Canada, Jan. 8, 1875, and received his education in the district and grammar schools. He came with his parents to Sault Ste. Marie in 1878. He was married in 1900 to Estelle McLeod, of Sault Ste. Marie. Mr. Bayliss entered county politics in 1908, when, with five candidates for Sheriff, he received sixty-five per cent of the total vote of his home city in the primary and won over his Democratic opponent at the general election. He was president of the local branch of the National Letter Carriers' Association, Master of Bethel Lodge No. 358, F. and A. M., also member of Chapter, Council and Commandery and Chancellor Commander of Red Cross Lodge No. 351, K. of P.; also president of the Michigan Association of Sheriffs, Chiefs of Police and Prosecuting Attorneys. In politics a Republican.

JOSEPH P. BEACH

Representative from Calhoun County, 1865-6. Was born in Jay, Essex County, N. Y., May 21, 1822. He settled in Penfield in 1836, as a farmer, and was Supervisor and held other township offices. He later resided at Battle Creek. Politically he was a Republican.

NOAH BEACH

Representative from the Saginaw District, 1843 and 1844; and Senator from the Sixth District comprising the counties of Oakland and Lapeer, Genesee, Shiawassee and Saginaw, 1850-1. Was born at Whiting, Vt., Oct. 17, 1788. When young he moved with his parents to central New York, where he spent his early boyhood until 1798, when the family moved to Lewiston, Niagara County, N. Y., where young Beach witnessed the border trouble growing out of the War of 1812. On reaching manhood he became an active participant in the struggle, and as a reward of merit for services rendered, was appointed Captain. Being a prominent Mason in the Morgan excitement, he became involved in the anti-Masonic complication to the extent, in the prosecution, of the loss of a good deal of property. While living at Lewiston he returned to Vermont, and married Eunice Cooley, of Rutland County. His father and mother died at Lewiston. In 1838 with his family, a wife and six children, he moved to Michigan, settling on a farm in Springfield, Oakland County, where he resided two years, filling the office of Justice of the Peace. In February, 1841, he moved to Bridgeport, Saginaw County, and from a heavy forest, improved the farm upon which he died. By force of character he held some offices, but his main occupation was that of a farmer. He was Supervisor and Justice of the Peace in Bridgeport several years and Postmaster for fifteen years. He died at Bridgeport, May 23, 1866.

HIRAM J. BEAKES

Representative from Washtenaw County, 1863-4. Was born at Middletown, N. Y., in 1827. He received his education there, studied law and was admitted to the bar in 1851. The same year he settled in Ann Arbor, and commenced the practice of law. He was Circuit Court Commissioner from 1855 to 1857, and Judge of Probate from 1875 to 1883. Later he was a member of the law firm of Beakes & Cutcheon of Detroit.

SAMUEL WILLARD BEAKES

Member of Congress, 1913-15, 1915-17 and 1917-19. Was born at Burlingham, Sullivan County, N. Y., Jan. 11, 1861. He was educated in Wallkill Academy, Middletown, N. Y., and in the literary and law departments of the University of Michigan, graduating in 1883; was private secretary to Judge Thomas M. Cooley; practiced law for a short time in Westerville, O., where he was editor and publisher of the Westerville *Review*. For two years he was editor and publisher of the Adrian, (Mich.) *Daily Record*, and for more than twenty years of the Ann Arbor *Argus*. In politics a Democrat. He was Postmaster of Ann Arbor under Cleveland, and served two terms as Mayor of Ann Arbor, four terms as City Treasurer, and four terms as City Assessor. Mr. Beakes was married July 7, 1886, to Annie S. Beakes of Ann Arbor. He was elected to the 63rd Congress and re-elected to the 64th Congress. In 1916 he was again a candidate for re-election to the 65th Congress. Mark R. Bacon received a small majority of the votes, but Mr. Beakes contested the election and was seated by the House of Representatives Dec. 13, 1917.

JUNIUS EMERY BEAL

Representative from the First District of Washtenaw County, 1905-6; and member of the Board of Regents of the University of Michigan, 1908—. Was born at Port

Huron, St. Clair County, Mich., Feb. 23, 1860, of American parentage, his ancestors having come to America with the Puritans in 1638. His education was obtained in the public schools of Ann Arbor and the University of Michigan, being given a degree from the latter institution in 1882. During his college days he was managing editor of *The Chronicle.* He was engaged in the printing and publishing business in Ann Arbor for twenty years, was manager of the Port Huron Gas Company ten years, and has been of later years connected with the Ann Arbor Electric Light Company and the Ann Arbor & Ypsilanti Railroad. He was a member of the Ann Arbor school board for twenty years. In politics he is a Republican. He was one of the presidential electors in 1888. Mr. Beal is married and has two children, a son and a daughter. He was elected to the Legislature in 1904, serving in the 1905-6 session. He was a member of the Public Domain Commission from 1908 to 1921. He was elected a member of the Board of Regents of the University in Apr. 1907, re-elected in 1915, and again in 1923.

ISAAC D. BEALL

Representative from the Third District of Branch County, 1867-8 and 1869-70. Was born at Clarendon, Rutland County, Vt., May 21, 1812. He married in 1837 and moved to Sherwood the same year, locating on a farm where he lived until his death. He was for twelve years Supervisor of the township and was Justice of the Peace five terms. He had some knowledge of medicine and was often called upon to prescribe in cases of sickness. His benevolence, kindness, good will and ripe judgment endeared him to all with whom he came in contact. In politics he was a Republican. He died at Sherwood, Mich., Sept. 3, 1880.

FERNANDO C. BEAMAN

Member of Congress, 1861-3 to 1869-71. Was born at Chester, Vt., June 28, 1814. His ancestors were early settlers in Massachusetts, Gamaliel Beaman having been an original founded of Lancaster. He was the twelfth of a family of fourteen children, thirteen of who lived to maturity. His father was a farmer. In 1819 the family removed to Franklin, N. Y., where the parents died in 1834. At sixteen, Mr. Beaman began life as a teacher and taught seven winters and three summers, and in that time fitted himself for college at the Malone Academy. In 1837 he studied law for one year in Rochester, and in 1838 emigrated to Michigan, and was admitted to the Lenawee County bar in 1839. He practiced in Manchester, Tecumseh and Clinton and in 1843, having been appointed Prosecuting Attorney, he removed to Adrian, and held that office for six years. He was for a time associated with Judge Tiffany, and afterwards with Judge T. M. Cooley and R. R. Beecher in the firm of Beaman, Beecher & Cooley, which had a large practice. At that time Mr. Beaman was attorney of the city of Adrian. He was a Democrat until 1848, when he joined the Free-soil party, and stumped Lenawee County for Van Buren and Adams. In 1854 he was one of the leaders in the organization of the Republican party and was vice president of the great convention at Jackson. He was a delegate to the first National Republican Convention at Pittsburg, in 1856. He took an active part in that campaign. In 1856 he was elected Mayor of Adrian, and was one of the presidential electors of that year, and was also elected Judge of Probate. In 1871 he was again appointed Judge of Probate to fill a vacancy, and was elected to that office in 1872 and 1876. In May, 1841, he married Mary

Goodrich. On the death of Senator Chandler he was appointed by Governor Croswell to fill the vacancy, but he declined on account of ill health, and Governor Baldwin received the appointment. He died at Adrian, September, 1882.

GEORGE K. BEAMER

Representative from Barry County, 1861-2. Was born Oct. 26, 1816, in Pekin, Niagara County, N. Y. He first came to Michigan in 1835 and returned. He settled in Barry County in 1846. He was a farmer by occupation, politically a Republican. As a member of the Legislature he presented the bill providing for a record of the soldiers of Michigan, subsequently compiled by Adjutant General Robertson. As Captain in N. Y. Light Artillery he was engaged in the Patriot War and in the Battle of Navy Island. He organized the Barry and Eaton County Insurance Company. He served in Common Council of Hastings.

ADAM BEATTIE

Senator from the Seventeenth District, 1873-4. Was born Nov. 26, 1834, in Seneca, Ontario County, N. Y. He received an academic education at the Canandaigua Academy, N. Y. In 1866 he emigrated to Michigan and settled in the village of Ovid, Clinton County. In 1862 he enlisted in the Twenty-sixth N. Y. Independent Battery, and served in the department of the Gulf and Southwest under Butler, Banks, Canby and Sheridan. Mr. Beattie's occupation that of general merchant. In politics a Republican.

LOUIS BEAUFAIT

Delegate from the First District to the Constitutional Convention of 1835; and Delegate from Wayne County to the First Convention of Assent, 1836; and Representative from Wayne County, 1838 and 1839. He was of French extraction his father, it is believed, having emigrated here contemporaneously with Cadillac. The best data fix the time of his birth about 1760. He was born in the township of Hamtramck, on the Beaufait farm. His early education was such as the frontier settlement afforded, and he spent some time as an Indian trader, was proficient in the Indian tongue, and was employed on many occasions as an official interpreter and Indian agent in Detroit. The name of Louis Beaufait occurs as early as 1788, and from that time to the close of the century, as presiding justice of the Common Pleas Court, but whether this was the father or the son spoken of, is uncertain. The son, however, was Captain of a company of militia in the War of 1812, and subsequently was appointed a Colonel of militia by General Cass. His civil service comprised many local positions of trust, and he was a presidential elector in 1844. In politics he was a Democrat. He died in 1854.

JOHN W. BEAUMONT

Member of the State Board of Agriculture, 1911-21. Was born at Elizabeth, N. J., July 20, 1858, of English parentage. He attended the Michigan Agricultural College, from which institution he graduated in 1882. Since Aug., 1886, he has been engaged in the practice of law at Detroit. Mr. Beaumont is married, and has resided in Michigan since 1875. He served in the Spanish-American War on board the U. S. S. Yosemite. He was elected a member of the State Board of Agriculture, Apr. 3, 1911, and re-elected Apr. 2, 1917.

JEFFERSON H. BECKWITH

Senator from the Twenty-fifth District, 1855-6. Was born in Ontario County, N. Y., in 1813. He studied law at Ellicottville, N. Y., and was admitted to the New York bar. He came to Michigan in 1830 and settled near Ann Arbor, and removed from there to East Plains, Ionia County, now part of the town of Lyons, where he resided until his death in 1865. He was Postmaster at Pitt, Mich., and for several terms Supervisor of the town of Lyons. He became a farmer, and was a Republican in politics. He was a positive man, tenacious of his opinions and always ready to defend them. He was respected for his honesty, and his word was as good as his note. He left a fine property, but was never married.

JACOB BEDTELYON

Representative from Genesee County, 1879-80. Was born in Erie County, N. Y., July 11, 1836. He there received a liberal education, and in the spring of 1854, then seventeen years of age, removed with his parents to Atlas, Genesee County, Mich. At the commencement of the rebellion he enlisted as a private in the Fourth Mich. Cavalry, Co. K. Soon after the battle of Stone River, he was commissioned as Captain, and placed in command of the company; but was compelled to resign on account of ill health in January, 1865, just before the close of the war. He held various township offices, and was Supervisor. Republican in politics.

JOSEPH E. BEEBE

Representative from Jackson County, 1855-6; and Senator from the Twelfth District, 1857-8. Was born at Sand Lake, N. Y., Feb. 18, 1810. He removed from Whitestown, N. Y., to Jackson, Mich., in 1842. He was by trade a wagon maker, and commenced their manufacture on a State prison contract, and continued in that business for nine years, the "Beebe Wagon" becoming well known throughout the West. In 1860 he was elected Judge of Probate of Jackson County and served from 1861 to 1865. He held all these positions as Republican. He was an active member of the Congregational Church, and was of great value to moral and religious enterprises in the early days of Jackson. He died Mar. 15, 1872.

URIAH BEEBE

Representative from Oakland County, 1859-60. Was born in Poultney, Vt., Apr. 3, 1812. He was a farmer by occupation, Republican in politics. He came to Michigan in 1845, and settled on wild land in the township of Oakland, Oakland County. He was a man of sterling integrity, temperate, charitable, and in religion a free thinker. He died May 7, 1865.

CHARLES N. BEECHER

Representative from Genesee County, 1851 and 1857-8. Was born in Livonia, Livingston County, N. Y., May 7, 1806. By occupation he was a farmer; in politics first a Whig, then a Republican. He came to Michigan in May, 1836, and settled on a farm in the town of Genesee, Genesee County, where he lived until 1854, when he removed to Flint, and there died Nov. 2, 1864. He was Postmaster seventeen years; nine successive years Supervisor; two years County Commissioner; and Associate County Judge.

NORMAN A. BEECHER

Representative from the First District of Genesee County, 1885-6 and 1887-8. Was born Apr. 22, 1830, in Rensselaerville, Albany County, N. Y.; moved with his parents to Oswego, Tioga County, when he was four years old. He was brought up on a farm and received a common school and academic education. At the age of twenty-one he removed to Orleans County, N. Y. He was married Sept. 19, 1855, and moved to Michigan in the fall of 1857, and settled on his farm in the township of Clayton, spring of 1858. Occupation was that of a farmer and fruit grower. The better instincts of his nature tended strongly to the interests of education. He was very successful as a teacher, having taught some twelve years. He held the office of Superintendent of Schools for years, and was elected to other township offices. Mr. Beecher was reared a Democrat and voted for James Buchanan. In 1860 he voted for Abraham Lincoln and became a staunch Republican. He died Mar. 23, 1892.

ROBERT R. BEECHER

Representative from Lenawee County, 1855-6. Was a leading lawyer of Adrian, and was a law partner of Judge Cooley and of Hon. F. C. Beeman. He was a leading Republican in the early history of the party. He was a good lawyer, and was honored with various county offices. He held the office of Judge of Probate from 1861 until his death in 1871. He died in the prime of manhood.

BENJAMIN F. BEEKMAN

Representative from the Second District of Eaton County, 1885-6. Was born at Chester, Eaton County, in 1848, where he resided and engaged in the pursuit of his chosen vocation as a farmer. He held the offices of Township Superintendent of Schools and Supervisor. He was elected a Representative as a Republican.

ALONZO P. BEEMAN

Representative from Cass County, 1907-8 and 1909-10. Was born in Erie County, Pa., in 1841, of American parents. He received his education in the district schools of Pennsylvania. He came to Michigan in March, 1856, worked at the carpenter's trade, and in 1862 enlisted in the 19th Mich. Infantry, remaining until the close of the war. He returned to Cass County and purchased the farm on which he resided. He married in 1862. A member of W. J. May Post, G. A. R. and was commander and quartermaster. He held the offices of Supervisor, chairman of the Board of Supervisors and County Treasurer. In politics always a Republican.

JOHN S. BEERS

Senator from the Ninth District, Berrien and Cass counties, 1891-2. Was born in the town of Marlboro, N. J., July 1, 1846. His early life was passed upon the farm except when attending school, principally at the Holmden Academy. At the age of eighteen he removed to the northern part of the State to engage in the fruit and tree culture, and in 1869 came to Michigan to continue in the same business until 1874, when he began the study of medicine and graduated at the medical department of the Northwestern University at Chicago in 1878, after which time he largely devoted himself to the practice of medicine, together with a general interest in farming and fruit culture. He was elected Supervisor of Royalton, Berrien County, in 1873; was prominent in grange work in Berrien County for several years, holding the position as master for several terms, and was secretary of the first country grange in the state, and which he took a prominent part in organizing. Several times he represented the township of Lincoln, Berrien County, in the Board of Supervisors. In politics a staunch Democrat.

PHILO BEERS

Representative from Kent and Ottawa counties, 1850; and from Grand Traverse County, 1859-60. Was born in Ithaca, N. Y., Feb. 8, 1801. Se settled as a farmer in the township of Courtland, Kent County, Mich., in 1840. Politically he was a Democrat. He was Supervisor of Courtland for twelve years, and was Postmaster eight years. He was Deputy United States Marshal under Buchanan for four years and keeper of the Traverse light-house four years. He was a Mason for fifty years. He died at Charlevoix, Apr. 3, 1872.

JACOB BEESON

Delegate from Berrien County to the Constitutional Convention of 1850. Was born in Uniontown, Pa., Sept. 7, 1807. His early youth was spent with an uncle in Hardy County, Va., and in early manhood he was engaged in mercantile business with the same uncle in Georgia and New Orleans. In 1829 he journeyed on horseback from his native town to Michigan, purchased a business site at Niles, and returned to Pennsylvania. In 1830, with his mother and three brothers, he came back to Niles and settled permanently, establishing himself in the mercantile business in which he was successful, and also engaging in the forwarding and commission business, and established a line of boats on the St. Joseph River. He was a Paymaster in the Black Hawk War, from which he derived the title of Colonel. He aided in organizing the State government and was a warm supporter of Gov. Mason. He was a member of the Democratic National Committee in 1856, and was appointed receiver of the land office at Detroit in 1857, when he removed to that city. In 1876 and 1877 he was president of the Detroit Board of Trade. He was president and principal stockholder of the Merchants' Bank of Detroit, and director of other banks. He was a man of great energy and rare business tact. In politics he was a Democrat. He died at Detroit, Apr. 19, 1885.

JESSE G. BEESON

Senator from Cass County, 1853-4. Was born Dec. 10, 1807, in Wayne County, Ind., where his parents, natives of North Carolina, settled at an early day. In

1830 he made a trip to southwestern Michigan, and in 1833 settled in LaGrange, Cass County. He was a successful farmer, widely known and universally respected. In politics he was a Republican. He died Feb. 19, 1888.

WILLIAM B. BEESON

Representative from Berrien County, 1859-60. Was born in Uniontown, Fayette County, Pa., in 1809. He moved to Niles, Mich., in 1831, and became one of the leading men of Michigan. He was elected to various minor offices, and in 1841 became President of the village of Niles. In politics he was a Democrat. He died at Niles in December, 1872.

JOSIAH W. BEGOLE

Senator from the Twenty-third District, 1871-2; member of Congress, 1873-5; and Governor of Michigan, 1883-5. Was born in Livingston County, N. Y., Jan. 20, 1815. His ancestors were of French descent, and settled at an early period in the State of Maryland. He received his early education in a log school house, and subsequently attended the Temple Hill Academy at Geneseo, N. Y. Being the eldest of a family of ten children, he was early taught habits of industry, and when twenty-one years of age he left the parental roof to seek a home in the Territory of Michigan, then an almost unbroken wilderness. He settled in Genesee County, and aided in building some of the early residences in what is now known as the city of Flint. Where this flourishing city now stands, there were but four or five houses when he selected it as his home. In the spring of 1839 he married Miss Harriet A. Miles. Immediately after his marriage he commenced work on an unimproved farm, where, by his perseverance and energy, he soon established a good home, and at the end of eighteen years was the owner of a farm of five hundred acres well improved. Mr. Begole being an anti-slavery man, became a member of the Republican party at its organization. He served his townsmen in various offices, and was in 1856 elected County Treasurer, which office he held for eight years. In 1870 he was nominated by acclamation for State Senator, and elected by a large majority. In the Senate he was known as an industrious and painstaking legislator. He was a member of the National Republican Convention held at Philadelphia in 1872. He was elected a member of Congress in 1872 and served on several important committees. In the gubernatorial election of 1883, Mr. Begole was the candidate of both the Greenback and Democratic parties, and was elected. He made a good record as Governor, and refused to be a candidate in 1885. He died at Flint, June 6, 1896.

EUGENE H. BELDEN

Representative from the Third District of Jackson County, 1881-2. Was born in the township of Spring Arbor, Jackson County, Mich., Dec. 14, 1840. He attended the district school of the neighborhood and the graded school in Jackson until he was fifteen years of age. Then he attended Michigan Central College, located in Spring Arbor, until, at the age of twenty, he attended the law department of the University at Ann Arbor, also studying in the office of Governor Blair. He never practiced law, but was connected with farming and real estate transactions. He held the office of Justice of the Peace and notary public for three terms. Politics a Republican.

FRIEND BELDING

Representative from Oakland County, 1849. Was born in Fabius, Onondaga County, N. Y., Nov. 3, 1799. He removed to Birmingham, Oakland County, Mich., in 1830. By occupation he was a farmer.

CHARLES EUGENE BELKNAP

Member of Congress, 1889-90 and 1891-2. Was born at Massena, St. Lawrence County, N. Y., Oct. 17, 1846. He resided in Michigan after June, 1855. During the Civil War he enlisted as private, Aug. 14, 1862, in the 21st Infantry, was promoted, and on Jan. 8, 1864, he was made Captain. He was mustered out June 22, 1865, when he returned to Grand Rapids and engaged in the manufacture of wagons and carriages. He served several years in the fire department, was a member of the school board, Alderman and Mayor. He was appointed by Governor Alger member of the Board of Trustees, Institute for the Deaf, for a term of six years. In politics a Republican. He was elected a member of Congress in 1888 and re-elected Nov. 3. 1891 to fill the vacancy caused by the death of Melbourne H. Ford.

JAMES W. BELKNAP

Senator from the Twenty-first District, comprising the counties of Ionia and Montcalm, in 1883-4 and 1885-6. Was born in Masena, St. Lawrence County, N. Y., Jan. 6, 1842. In 1855 he came to Michigan with his parents, and settled in Grand Rapids. While living in Grand Rapids he learned the printers' trade, in the office of the Grand Rapids *Herald*, and in October, 1860, removed to Greenville, Montcalm County, and engaged at his trade in the office of the Greenville *Independent* (Republican). May, 1862, he became editor and proprietor of the *Independent*, which he conducted successfully until 1865, when he sold out and engaged in mercantile pursuits. In 1872 he also became interested in the lumber business, running a saw mill in the township of Sidney, in Montcalm County, and a planing mill, door, sash, and blind factory in Greenville. In 1874 he went out of trade and gave his attention to the lumber branch of his business. He was twice elected Mayor of the city of Greenville. and for thirteen years was a member of the Board of Education. Deceased.

LYMAN E. BELKNAP

Representative from the Second District of Tuscola County, 1895-6 and 1897-8. Was born in Cayuga County, N. Y., Nov. 17, 1851. He came to Michigan when nine years of age and received a common school education. In 1875 he was married to Miss Julia Allen, who died in May, 1893, leaving a daughter fifteen years old, who died in 1895. By occupation a life long farmer, dealing some in lumber. In politics a Republican. He was Supervisor and chairman of the board.

ALEXANDER F. BELL

Representative from Ionia County, 1847. Was born in Charlton, Saratoga County, N. Y., Aug. 5, 1812, and was of Scotch descent. He graduated from Union College in 1836 and the same year came to Lyons, Mich., with Adam L. Roof, with whom he studied law. He was admitted in 1840, and removed to Ionia, where he was engaged in practice. He was first President of Ionia village. From 1853 to 1857 he was register of the United States Land Office at Ionia. He was a prominent lawyer, and for many years was a recognized leader in the Democratic party. He was interested in railroads and other improvements. He died at Ionia, Mar. 12, 1896.

DIGBY V. BELL

Representative from Kent County, 1840; Senator from the Fifth District, 1842-3; Commissioner of the State Land Office, 1844-6; and Auditor General, 1846-8. Was born Nov. 10, 1784, on the Island of St. Christopher, British West Indies. His father, a retired British naval officer and merchant, died when he was five years old. Under the care of an accomplished mother, he received every educational advantage the Island afforded. At the age of thirteen, from choice, he became a sailor, and followed that life for six years. Abandoning that occupation, he acted as agent of a mining company in New York city; afterwards of the New York Gas Light Company. Following the tide of emigration he came to Michigan in 1834, settling in St. Joseph County as a farmer. In a few months he was discharging the functions of seven officers, took an active part in the organization of a State government, and issued the first address to the citizens of St. Joseph County. He was elected Judge of Probate, and held other important offices. During the "wild cat" period he was State Bank Commissioner, and in that capacity helped to protect the people from frauds. Afterwards for several years, he was cashier of the Michigan Central Railroad Company. In 1850 he established in Chicago the first commercial college in Illinois, which he continued for several years. Then going to New York city, he became interested in a banking house which suspended in the crash of 1857, but resumed and paid off all liabilities. He returned to Chicago in 1858, and was there interested with Bryant and Stratton in the Chicago Commercial College, which became one of the first in the country. He was soon appointed by the Legislature of Illinois Commissioner of Claims, and charged with the duty of investigating the finances of the city of Chicago. He was also special agent of the Postoffice Department, and discharged its duties with great fidelity. He sent four sons to the war during the rebellion, three of whom served until peace was declared. He removed to Battle Creek, Mich., and died while serving at Postmaster, Oct. 28, 1871.

GEORGE W. BELL

Senator from the Thirtieth District, 1879-80. Was born Dec. 25, 1844, in Penobscot County, Me., but soon after removed to Dover, Piscataquis County. He received an academic education, taught school, and was admitted to the bar in 1868. In 1869 he removed to Cheboygan, Mich., and began the practice of his profession. He held the office of Judge of Probate of Cheboygan County; held the office of Circuit Court Commissioner; also several minor township and village offices. In politics a Republican.

JAMES C. BELL

Candidate for the Legislature from Jackson in 1852; was tied with Amos Root who was seated. (Further data not obtainable).

RUFUS B. BEMENT

Representative from Washtenaw County, 1840. His postoffice address was Dexter. (Further data not obtainable).

ARTHUR L. BEMIS

Representative from the First District of Montcalm County, 1897-8. Was born at Elyra, Loraine County, O., Mar. 20, 1858. He came to Ionia County, Mich., at the age of five years, and lived there for fifteen years, working on a farm by the month. He spent two years at the Michigan Agricultural College; he also took a commercial course and several years of private instruction in classic and modern languages. He taught school for nine years, at one time professor of chemistry, general history and penmanship in the Ionia schools; he was superintendent of Nashville and Carson City schools, and three years a member of the Montcalm County Board of School Examiners, and acting chairman of the Montcalm County Republican Committee. For several years he was owner and editor of the Carson City *Gazette* (Republican). In politics a Republican. He was never a candidate for any office before he was elected to the House of 1897-8.

ALEXANDER H. BENEDICT

Representative from Livingston County, 1867-8. He was a Democrat in politics, and a merchant in business at Fowlerville from 1863 to 1873, when he removed. He was a Justice of the Peace in 1866.

JACOB M. BENEDICT

Representative from Ionia County, 1875-6. Was born in Warwick, Orange County, N. Y., July 26, 1832, and removed to Michigan in 1853, taking up his residence in Ionia County in 1857. He received a common school education, was a Supervisor, and held other township offices, and engaged in farming and manufacturing. A Democrat in politics.

PETER H. BENEDICT

Representative from Sanilac County, 1853-4. Was born at Rensselaerville, N. Y., Nov. 25, 1811. He came to Michigan in 1837, and in 1842 bought a farm in Worth, Sanilac County. He was Supervisor and held other town offices. Politically he was a Democrat.

WILLIAM H. P. BENJAMIN

Representative from Saginaw County, 1875-6; and Senator from the Twenty-third District, 1879-80. Was born in the village of Saline, Onondaga County, N. Y., Sept. 2, 1839. He received his education at the Syracuse Institute, and graduated in medicine in 1861. He removed to Saginaw County. Mich.. in 1866. In politics a Democrat.

ADAM BENNETT

Representative from the First District of Macomb County, 1893-4. Was born in Chateaugay, Franklin County, N. Y., Mar. 18, 1832. He received no college education and his district school days were also very limited. He was early engaged as foreman on the Great Western & Canada Railroad and the Grand Trunk Railroad. In 1859 he came to Michigan and located at New Haven, Macomb County, and engaged in the mercantile business, which occupation he followed until 1870, when he engaged in real estate and insurance business. In politics a Democrat. He held most of the several township offices and was president of the village of New Haven.

ALONZO BENNETT

Representative from Berrien County, 1842. Was born in Addison County, Vt., Sept. 22, 1807. When young his father removed to Erie County, where the son remained until 1833, when he removed with his family to Berrien County, Mich. In 1838 he was elected County Clerk, and was re-elected in 1840 and 1842. He returned to New Buffalo in 1845. His occupation was merchandising until 1870 then a druggist. In politics he was a Democrat. He was the first President of New Buffalo. He was Postmaster and Supervisor. He died before 1890.

CHARLES H. BENNETT

Representative from the Fourth District of Wayne County, 1870. He was in the House in place of George W. Swift who resigned, in 1869 to become consul at Windsor, Canada. He served in the session of 1870.

DAVIS D. BENNETT

Representative from Lenawee County, 1848. Was born in Catherine, Chemung County, N. Y., Mar. 25, 1808. He left home when sixteen and worked on a farm and at lumbering until 1828, when he came to Michigan and remained one year. In 1830 he located on a farm in Adrian Township, Lenawee County. In 1837 he removed to a farm in Fairfield, same county. He was four times Supervisor of Fairfield, four terms Justice, and fifteen years Town Clerk.

FRANK TRIPP BENNETT

Representative from the First District of Jackson County, 1907-8. Was born in Jackson, Jackson County, Michigan, May 18, 1882, of Irish and American parentage. He received his education in the Jackson public schools and the University of Michigan. Unmarried. Practiced law in Jackson. In politics a Republican.

JAMES T. BENNETT

Representative from Chippewa County, 1907-8. Was born in Geneva, N. Y., Feb. 21, 1857, of Scotch and American descent. He attended the public schools of Geneva until he was sixteen years of age. In August, 1885, Mr. Bennett came to Michigan and became a resident of Chippewa County. He engaged in the mercantile and lumber business, being a member of the firm of Watson & Bennett Co., of Detour. Married. In politics a Republican. He was elected County Treasurer in 1902 and two years later was re-elected.

JOHN H. BENNETT

Representative from the First District of Branch County, 1881-2 and 1883-4. Was born in the township of Chenango, Broome County, N. Y., Dec. 6, 1826, where his paternal and maternal grandparents settled soon after the Revolution, both of his grandfathers having served under Washington. In 1833 his father and family moved to Licking County, O., and from there to Michigan, reaching Adrian in March, 1834, and settled on a farm in Dover. In 1839, the family removed to Branch County, settled in the township of Quincy, six miles from Coldwater, where he labored on a new farm until 1845, when he entered the employment of Dr. Wm. H. Hanchett, of Coldwater. Here he entered the village and also a select school, studying geometry and trigonometry in the latter. In 1847 he commenced the study of medicine. He graduated in Berkshire Medical College in 1854. In October he returned to Branch County and settled in the township of Algansee, where he practiced medicine ten years. In 1856 he married Miss Hannah M. Thompson. In 1862 he served as examining surgeon in his county, and in 1864 removed to the city of Coldwater, where he was active in practice as a physician and surgeon. He was a member of several medical associations. In politics he was a Whig until 1854; then a Republican. He was elected Coroner in 1858, and held that office twelve years. He held the office of County Surveyor twelve years, and County Drain Commissioner four years; was Alderman of the fourth ward of the city of Coldwater four years. He died July 31, 1891.

STILLMAN W. BENNETT

Representative from Lenawee County, 1879-80. Was born in Fairfield, Lenawee County, Mich. He held several minor offices in his township; was Supervisor in 1876 and 1877. He was a farmer by occupation. In politics a Republican.

THEODORE G. BENNETT

Senator from the Tenth District, 1871-2. Was born at Jackson, Mich., Feb. 27, 1845. In politics a Republican. He was engaged in the manufacture of sewer pipe and drain tile.

CHARLES P. BENOIT, JR.

Representative from the First District of Wayne County (Detroit city), 1893-4 and 1895-6. Was born in Detroit, Mar. 27, 1870; was educated at the German American Seminary and Detroit Business College. He was engaged in the real estate and insurance business for five years, and two years following as bookkeeper for the Detroit Sheet Metal and Brass Works, and then as weighmaster. In politics a Republican. He was a member of the House of 1893-4 and the youngest member elected to that of 1895-6.

JOHN R. BENSON

Senator, 1891-2, from the Thirteenth District, comprising Genesee and Livingston counties. Was born in Manchester, England, June 5, 1837. His parents moved to New York, Nov. 8, 1840, and the family came to what is now the township of Mt. Morris, Genesee County, on May 18 of the following year. There as a child he began his pioneer life, and was brought up on a farm, educated in the common schools, Flint Union School and the State Normal at Ypsilanti. He went to Philadelphia to attend Bryant & Stratton's Business College in the spring of 1862, after having spent a part of several years in teaching. He enlisted there Mar. 7, 1862, and served until the end of the war, sharing in all the vicissitudes of the Army of the Potomac. He returned to Michigan and was married to Miss Mary S. Bricet, of Bay City, Jan. 7, 1866. He resumed farming and teaching, and in the spring of 1874 sold his farm and removed to the village of Mt. Morris, adjoining which he purchased a tract of land and hewed another farm out of the wilderness; had about 214 acres in and adjoining the village. In politics a Republican, but joined the Patrons in the fall of 1889. He was delegate to all their county conventions and helped to nominate county and representative tickets. He was nominated for the senate of 1891-2 by the Patrons in Genesee County and the Industrials in Livingston County, and endorsed by the Democrats in both counties, and was elected.

ELIJAH BENTLEY

Representative from the First District of Jackson County, 1863-4. His postoffice address was Napoleon. (Further data not obtainable).

JOHN W. BENTLEY

Representative from St. Joseph County, 1883-4 to 1887-8. Was born in Rhode Island, Jan. 30, 1883. At the age of ten years he removed with his parents to the township of Byron, Genesee County, N. Y. He received a scientific and literary education at Cary Collegiate Seminary. At the age of twenty he commenced active business, tilling the soil in summer and teaching school in winter. In 1863 he removed to Leonidas, St. Joseph County, Mich., where he bought a farm and commenced farming. In 1869 he was engaged as principal of the Mendon Union School, which position he retained eleven years. Returning to his farm he was elected Supervisor of his township, serving two years on the County Board of Examiners. In 1885 he removed to the township of Mendon and was elected Supervisor there in 1886 and was re-elected in 1887 on the Fusion ticket.

CASSIUS R. BENTON

Representative from the Third District of Wayne County, 1905-6 and 1907-8. Was born in Plymouth Township, Wayne County, Mich., Nov. 12, 1862. He received his education in the district schools of the township and the Northville Union School, supplemented by a course in the Spencerian Business College of Detroit. He was united in marriage to Sophia L. Lauffer. Feb. 24, 1892. In politics a lifelong Republican. He held the offices of Highway Commissioner, Supervisor, and was unanimously elected chairman of the Board of Supervisors of Wayne County in October, 1904. He died Oct. 2, 1922.

JOHN BERK

Representative from St. Clair County, 1875-6. Was born in Germany, Jan 28. 1822. In 1836 he emigrated and settled in Lorain County, O. He removed to Michigan in 1866, and settled in Washtenaw County, and thence to St. Clair County in 1870. He held several township offices. By occupation he was a farmer, but for several years was engaged in the ministry. In politics he was a Republican.

FRANCIS H. BERRICK

Senator from the Twelfth District, 1875-6. Was born Sept. 18, 1823, in Clemsford, Middlesex County, Mass. His father was a soldier under Napoleon. Mr. Berrick received a common school education, and acquired the trade of a machinist. During the nine years he worked at his trade, down to 1852, he employed all his leisure time in the study of theology. In 1859 he entered Harvard Law School and graduated therefrom in 1861, and further continued his legal studies under Judge Perkins, of Salem, Mass., and was admitted to the bar in 1864. In 1865 he began the study of medicine. He graduated at the Hahnemann Medical College of Chicago. In 1868 he removed to Buchanan, Mich., where he continued to reside and follow the practice of medicine. He was a Democrat in politics.

ENOS G. BERRY

Representative from Branch County, 1842; and Senator from the Third District, 1848-9. Was born in the State of New York, Sept. 5, 1814. He studied medicine in Chautauqua County, N. Y., and settled in Quincy, Mich., in 1836, where he practiced medicine successfully for over thirty years. He secured the passage of the bill for the building of the Michigan Southern and Northern Indiana Railroad, over the veto of the Governor, and his speech on that occasion is said to have been "one of the most intensely interesting and soul-stirring speeches" ever delivered in the Senate. He was an intimate friend of the leading men in Michigan, and died in the prime of life in January, 1877.

JOHN G. BERRY

Senator from the Twenty-seventh District, comprising the counties of Cheboygan, Crawford, Kalkaska, Missaukee, Montmorency, Otsego, Presque Isle, and Roscommon, 1889-90; and Commissioner of the State Land Office, 1893-5. Was born in New York City, Dec. 13, 1838, and at the time of the Civil War was engaged in farming and mining in the Upper Peninsula. He enlisted in Co. A, 16th Mich. Infantry, Aug. 3, 1861, for three years, and at the expiration of his terms of service, re-enlisted for the war in the same company and regiment. He served as a private, Corporal, Sergeant, 1st Lieutenant and Captain. He received an honorable discharge at the close of the war, and for a number of years was employed as clerk in a large wholesale hardware store in Detroit, and subsequently engaged in real estate business in that city. In 1878 he removed to Otsego County and engaged in the saw-mill, grist-mill and general store business at the village of Berryville, later he ran a general store at Vanderbilt. Identified with the G. A. R., he was the first commander of Gen. Harker Post, No. 264, at Vanderbilt. and a delegate to State and National Encampments several times; also president of the Soldiers and Sailors' Association of Northern Michigan. In politics an abolitionist in early youth; then a Republican.

JONATHAN BERRY

Representative from Lenawee County, 1844. Was born in 1790. His parents came from Rhode Island to Rensselaer County, N. Y., where it is thought he was born. He removed with them first to Orleans County, N. Y., then to Mt. Vernon, O., in 1835, and to Adrian, Mich., in 1836. He was a soldier of the War of 1812. He finally settled on a farm in Rome, Lenawee County, where he died Oct. 20, 1851. He was for one term an Associate Judge of the Circuit Court. In politics he was a Democrat.

LANGFORD G. BERRY

Representative from Lenawee County, 1857-8; and Auditor General, 1861-3. Was born in Berlin, N. Y., June 19, 1812. He settled in Adrian, Mich., in October, 1835. He was a real estate dealer, then went into the banking business, and became one of the most prominent private bankers in the State. In politics he was a Republican. He was appointed Collector of the First District of Michigan, with headquarters at Detroit, prior to the expiration of his term as Auditor General. He held the position some time and resigned. The later years of his life were spent in Arkansas, where he died June 3, 1878.

CONRAD BETTINGER

Representative from the First District of Wayne County, 1883-4 and 1887-8. Was born in Doerrnbach, on the Rhine, Germany, Sept. 5, 1845. When about three years of age he came, with his parents, to the United States, landing in New York. He received a common school education by the Redemptorist Fathers of New York City. When about fourteen years of age he learned the trade of cigar-making. In 1863, when General Lee, with his army, entered Pennsylvania, he enlisted as a private in the 5th N. Y. National Guards. When they reached Harrisburg, they were recalled on account of the riot which prevailed in New York City, doing duty there until the 22d of July, 1863. He re-enlisted in 1864 as private in the 3rd N. Y. Cavalry, and served with it until the close of the war; was mustered out at Richmond, Va., Jan. 13, 1867. He was married to Miss Louise Platz, of New York City, and remained there until 1873, when he started for the West and finally settled in Detroit, with his family. He was nominated for the Legislature in 1879 by the Republicans, but declined in order to afford a fair test of the workingmen's party strength.

CHARLES BETTS

Representative from St. Joseph County, 1863-4. Was born in Port Hope, Ont., Aug. 1, 1822. He came to Detroit in 1833. He settled in Redford, Wayne County. He moved to St. Joseph County in 1848, and to Detroit in 1851, where for five years he was connected with the agricultural press, when he returned to Burr Oak. By occupation he was a farmer. Politically he was a Republican.

MENDEL J. BIALY

Senator, 1895-6, from the Twenty-fourth District, counties of Arenac, Bay and Midland. Was born in London, England, Feb. 18, 1852. He attended the common schools of London until 1863 when he came with his parents to the United States, locating at Detroit, Mich. Three'years later he removed to Bay City where he made his home, with the exception of three years' absence, from 1870-3, when he was at Au Sable and Tawas. Formerly he was engaged as accountant and clerk in mercantile trade, and then engaged in the lumber manufacturing business, being a member of the firm of Hitchcock & Bialy. He was a member of the First Presbyterian church of Bay City, of the Masonic fraternity and other secret orders. In politics, a Republican. He served his ward as Alderman, and as President of the City Council.

JOHN BIDDLE

Delegate in Congress from Michigan Territory, 1829-31; Delegate from the First District to the Constitutional Convention of 1835; and Representative from Wayne County, 1841. Was born in Philadelphia in 1792, of Revolutionary stock. He graduated at Princeton College, entered the United States Army, served with distinction during most of the War of 1812 as a Captain of Artillery, and was promoted to be Major. He was stationed at Detroit (which thereafter became his home) at the close of the war, resigning, however, after a few years to engage in civil pursuits. His principal official positions during his life were: Register of the land office at Detroit—the district including the whole territory—from the time the public lands were placed in market until 1832; Delegate in Congress from the Territory, 1829 to 1831; member and president of the first Constitutional Convention (1835); and member and speaker of the House of Representatives in 1841. A Whig in politics, he was made president of the Constitutional Convention (a Democratic body), and later on a Democratic Senate gave him its majority vote for United States Senator, although he failed of election through the adverse vote of the House. Among other responsible trusts, while Register of the Land Office, he acted as one of the Commissioners for adjusting land claims growing out of French and Indian titles at the various settlements on the lakes, and was connected in various ways with the conduct of Indian affairs; was named one of the Regents of the University as it was projected by the territorial government, and was commissioned to attend to the sale of certain University lands then subject to sale. He was the Whig candidate for Governor at the first state election. He was a vestryman and liberal patron of St. Paul's (Episcopal) Church, of Detroit, the pioneer church of that denomination in the Northwest, outside of Ohio. He died at White Sulphur Springs, Va., Aug. 25, 1859.

SAMUEL J. BIDELMAN

Representative from the First District of Barry County, 1881-2. Was born June 6, 1825, in the township of Shelby, Orleans County, N. Y. He received a common school education, was reared on a farm, and, when twenty years of age, went to work at the carpenter and joiner's trade. In 1855 he moved to Branch County, Mich., and in 1860 he moved to the township of Hastings, Barry County. His occupation was farming. He held the offices of Supervisor and County Superintendent of the Poor; was chairman of the Republican County Committee, president of the agricultural society, and vice president of the Barry County and Eaton County Insurance Company and a part of the time acting president. He died at Quimby, Barry County, April, 1915.

WILLIAM J. BIERD

Representative from the Second District of Bay County, 1907-8, 1909-10, 1911-12 and 1913-14; Senator from the Twenty-fourth District, comprising the counties of Bay and Midland, 1919-20. Was born at Carrollton, Saginaw County, Mich.,

Sept. 25, 1872, of Irish and American parentage. He received his early education in the public schools of Saginaw County, and graduated from the law department of the University of Michigan in 1893. He engaged in farming until 1910, when he entered the real estate business, which is his principal occupation at the present time. He is also a director of the Peoples State Savings Bank, of Auburn. Mr. Bierd is not married. He is a Republican and has held the office of Clerk, Treasurer and Supervisor of Williams Township.

JOHN M. BIGGERSTAFF

Representative from the First District of Kalamazoo County, 1915-16. Was born at St. Cloud, Minn., Nov. 18, 1858, of Scotch parentage. He received his education in the public schools of St. Cloud, at which place he served an apprenticeship as a builder. In 1892 he removed to Kalamazoo and was engaged in the building contracting business until 1913; then the general insurance business. He was married in 1884 to Lolita Lamb, of Kalamazoo, who died in 1897. In 1899 he was married to Effie J. Grant, of Marcellus. He was elected a member of the city council of Kalamazoo in 1904 and served one term. The following year he was elected President of the council and appointed chairman of finance. In politics a Republican.

SOLOMON L. BIGNALL

Representative from Livingston County, 1889-90. Was born at Tyre, Seneca County, N. Y., May 1, 1834. His occupation was that of a farmer and manufacturer, and during the war was a recruiting officer. He held the office of Supervisor.

SAMUEL MEAD BILLINGS

Representative from the First District of Marquette County, 1897-8. Was born in Canton, O., Mar. 3, 1838; when very young he moved with his parents to Michigan, locating at Marshall. His early education was acquired at Albion Seminary (now College), supplemented by a course at the University, from which he graduated in 1861. On Oct. 22, 1861, he enlisted in Co. G, 1st Regiment Lancers, for three years, but was mustered out of service with his company on Mar. 20, 1862. After completing his studies he went to Sault Ste. Marie, thence to Marquette in 1864, where he was engaged in the railroad business for seven years; he then went to Utah and engaged in mining for one and one-half years; returning to Marquette in 1873 to superintend iron explorations. In politics a Republican. · He was Postmaster fifteen years, County Clerk and Register of Deeds and Supervisor.

SIMEON R. BILLINGS

Representative from Genesee County, 1875-6 and 1877-8; and Senator from the Nineteenth District, Genesee County, 1879-80 and 1881-2. Was born Mar. 17, 1835, in Orleans County, N. Y. He received an academic education and removed to Michigan in May, 1867. He held various offices in New York and Michigan; was Supervisor of the township of Richfield; and County Surveyor. By occupation he was a farmer. In 1871 his farm was awarded the first premium by the agricultural society. He was appointed Railroad Commissioner by Governor Rich. Deceased.

PERLEY BILLS

Senator from the Tenth District, 1855-6 and from the Eleventh District, 1857-8; and Delegate to the Constitutional Convention of 1867. Was born in Wilmington, Vt., June 5, 1810. He was brought up on a farm, and at the age of nineteen embarked in trade at Honesdale, Pa., but soon abandoned it, and returned home. The next year he went to Ohio and engaged in teaching, then spent two years in a preparatory class at the Western Reserve College, and for two years was pupil and tutor at a seminary in Bennington, Vt. In 1835 he entered the second year at Oberlin College, O., and in 1837 settled at Tecumseh, Mich. He married Miss Caroline Brown, of Mass., in 1838, and they had three sons and three daughters. He taught school three years, was admitted to the bar in 1842, and engaged in practice. He organized the first school district in Tecumseh in 1838, and was continuously a member of the School Board for forty years. In 1861 he engaged in the banking business, and in 1865 became a director and vice president of the National Bank of Tecumseh. In 1874 he became the head of the banking firm of Bills, Lilly & Co., and was its president until his death, Nov. 7, 1880. In religion he was a Presbyterian. In politics he was first Whig, then Republican.

HENRY H. BINGHAM

Representative from Jackson County, 1848. Was born at Camillus, Onondaga County, N. Y., Jan. 7, 1814. His parents, Calvin and Betsey (Scott) Bingham, were pioneers from Bennington, Vt. Mr. Bingham came to Michigan in 1838, and settled in Leoni, Jackson County, as a merchant. He soon removed to Grass Lake and built the first store in that village and did a large business. In politics he was a Democrat; a Republican at the organization of that party in 1854. He was connected with the management of the State Prison at Jackson for many years, first as keeper, was its clerk for eleven years, and Warden from 1866 to 1871. Under his administration the prison became a source of income to the State. After his retirement as Warden he engaged in farming, dealer in produce and real estate. He was secretary and president of the County Pioneer Society and one of its most efficient members. He died at Jackson, Jan. 10, 1896.

KINGSLEY S. BINGHAM

Representative from Livingston County, 1837-42; member of Congress, 1847-9 and 1849-51; Governor of Michigan, 1855-9; and United States Senator, 1859-61. Was born in Camillus, Onondaga County, N. Y., Dec. 16, 1808. He was the son of Calvin and Betsey (Scott) Bingham. His father was a farmer and emigrated from Bennington, Vt. After receiving an academical education, he studied law with Gen. James R. Lawrence, of Syracuse, N. Y. He married a Miss Warden and in 1833 emigrated in company with his brother-in-law, Robert Warden, and settled at Green Oak, Livingston County, Mich. He at once as a Democrat took part in politics, and was first Justice of the Peace, then Postmaster, Judge of Probate, and was elected to the Legislature of 1837. He was re-elected and was speaker of the House for three terms, in 1838, 1839 and 1842, no other person ever having held it more than two terms. In 1846 he was elected as a Democrat to Congress and was re-elected in 1848, and was the only farmer in that body. To his efforts were the farmers indebted for the failure of the inventor of the Wood plow to get his patent renewed, worth millions to the farmers of the country. During his service as Representative in Congress he spoke and voted for the Wilmot Proviso in accordance with the first instructions of the Michigan Legislature, which instructions were afterwards reversed. From 1850 to 1854 he was a Free Soil Democrat and held no office. In 1854 he was nominated as the candidate of the Free Soilers for Governor. At the great union mass convention at Jackson, June 6, 1854, the Whigs and Free Soilers united on a State ticket and he was placed at the head of it for Governor, as the nominee of the new Republican party, which then and there sprang into existence, and received its name. Sanguine of success, he stumped the State and the entire ticket was elected. He was sworn into office, Jan. 3, 1855, and was again elected Governor in 1856 by a largely increased majority. During his term of office the State Agricultural College and the State Reform School were both placed in successful operation. At the close of his second term of office, in 1859, he was elected United States Senator, serving until 1861. He was stricken down with apoplexy and died at his home in Green Oak, Oct. 5, 1861.

ARTHUR CRANSON BIRD

Member of the State Board of Agriculture, 1897-9. Was born May 22, 1864 at Highland, Mich. He married Josephine S. (St. John) of Ann Arbor, Mich. in August, 1889. He attended common school until the age of fifteen when he entered the Agricultural College and graduated in 1883 with the degree of B. S., paying most of his expenses in college by his own exertions. He soon bought a farm and lived on it, succeeding so well that the State Board of Agriculture conferred on him the degree of Master of Agriculture. In 1897 Governor Pingree appointed him a member of the State Board of Agriculture which position he resigned Jan. 25, 1899. He was a prominent worker in farmers' clubs, both local and state, having served as secretary and president in the State Association; editor of the department of Farmers' clubs of the *Michigan Farmer*. On Jan. 25, 1899 he became secretary of the State Board of Agriculture which he resigned in 1901 and engaged in several kinds of business in Lansing and vicinity. For about six years he was president of the Dairy and Food Commission. In 1905 he was selected by Governor Warner to take the state census. He was a prominent figure in state politics and a close friend of Governors Pingree and Warner. He died rather suddenly, May 25, 1910.

JOHN E. BIRD

Attorney General, 1905-6, 1907-8 and 1909-10; Justice of the Supreme Court, 1910. Was born at Clayton, Lenawee County, Mich., Dec. 19, 1862. He was educated in the high school and at Adrian College. He was admitted to the bar, November, 1888. He was Prosecuting Attorney of Lenawee County from 1895 to 1899; was elected to the office of Attorney General for the terms of 1905-6 and 1907-8 and re-elected Nov. 3, 1908. He was appointed by Governor Warner June 6, 1910, Justice of the Supreme Court to fill vacancy caused by the resignation of Justice Montgomery, and was elected Nov. 8, 1910 to fill out the unexpired term. At the election held Apr. 3, 1911, he was elected for the full term and was re-elected Apr. 7, 1919. Justice Bird was Chief Justice during the year 1919.

JOHN M. BIRD

Representative from Lenawee County, 1840. Was born in Litchfield, Conn., Jan. 3, 1810. By occupation he was a farmer. He was a Whig. He was twelve years Justice of the Peace, and held other township offices. He resided in Dover, Lenawee County.

JAMES BIRNEY

Senator from the Twenty-eighth District, 1859-60; Lieutenant Governor, 1861; and Delegate from Bay County to the Constitutional Convention of 1867. Was born in Dansville, Ky., and was the son of Hon. James G. Birney, the Abolition candidate for President in 1844. He obtained his education at Centre College, Ky., and at Miami University, O., graduating at the latter in 1836. In 1837-8 he was professor of Greek and Latin in Miami University. He attended the law school of Yale College for two years, and commenced practice at Cincinnati, O., which he continued eleven years. He was an early settler at Bay City. He was elected Lieutenant Governor in 1860, and served from Jan. 1, 1861 to Apr. 3, 1861, when he resigned to accept a position as Circuit Judge to fill a vacancy, where he acted for four years. He was renominated for Judge but was defeated. In 1871 he established the Bay City *Chronicle*, and the daily in 1873. In 1876 he was a Centennial Commissioner for Michigan at the Centennial Exposition at Philadelphia. Later he was appointed United States Minister at the Hague where he remained several years. He died May 8, 1888.

JAMES C. BISHOP

Representative from the First District of St. Joseph County, 1881-2. Was born in Franklinville, Cattaraugus County, N. Y., Apr. 1, 1828. He removed with his parents to what is now the township of Burr Oak, St. Joseph County, Mich., in the year 1836. His occupation was that of farming. He held the offices of Highway Commissioner, Justice of the Peace, and Supervisor,—the latter office thirteen years,—being chairman of the Board three years. He took the State census in 1874. also the United States census of 1880. Politics a Republican.

LEVI BISHOP

Member of the Board of Regents of the University of Michigan, 1858-64. Was born in Russell, Hampden County, Mass., Oct. 15, 1815; received a good common school education; at fifteen became an apprentice in a leather manufactory, where he remained until 1836, when he emigrated to Detroit, and followed his trade for four years. In 1839 he lost an arm while engaged in firing a salute. He then studied law for three years; was admitted to the bar; in 1842 was elected a Justice; in 1846 became a member of the Board of Education, serving twelve years, much of the time as president. In 1857 he was elected a Regent of the State University, holding the position for six years. In 1860 he visited Europe; published several poems, among them one entitled "The Dignity of Labor," and "Teuchsa Grondie," a book of Indian legends, etc., in twenty-eight cantos. Mr. Bishop was a strong advocate of capital punishment, and gave much time and effort in attempting to secure the repeal of the present law in Michigan. He died at Detroit, Dec. 23, 1881.

ROSWELL P. BISHOP

Representative from Mason County, 1883-4 and 1893-4; and member of Congress. 1895-7 to 1905-7. Was born at Sidney, Delaware County, N. Y., Jan. 6, 1843; worked on a farm until Aug. 3, 1861, when he enlisted as a private in Co. C. Forty-third N. Y. Volunteer Infantry; Apr. 28, 1862, wounded at Lees Mill, Va., necessitating the amputation of his right arm; discharged in the field near Fredericksburg, Va., Dec. 1862. He subsequently attended school at Unadilla Academy, Cooperstown Seminary and Walton Academy, New York; taught school several years, and entered the University of Michigan in September, 1868, where he remained until December, 1872. He was admitted to the bar in May, 1875, at Ann Arbor, and commenced practicing law at Ludington, Mich., soon after. In politics a Republican. He was elected Prosecuting Attorney of Mason County, 1876, 1878, and 1884; elected to the Michigan Legislature, 1882 and 1892; elected to the Fifty-fourth, Fifty-fifth, Fifty-sixth, Fifty-seventh and Fifty-eighth Congresses, and re-elected to the Fifty-ninth Congress. Deceased.

NATHAN H. BITELY

Senator from the Eighteenth District, 1867-8. Was born in Moran, Saratoga County, N. Y., Jan. 22, 1822. He removed to Paw Paw in 1851, and the next year went to Lawton, where he was engaged many years in the manufacture of lumber. He was educated at the law at Ballston Springs law school. In politics he was a Republican, and for many years was a member of the state committee, and was a very forcible and able speaker in the early days of the Republican party. He never sought office and when elected Prosecuting Attorney of Van Buren County refused to serve. Later he consented to serve as State Senator in 1867 and was again elected in 1868. He did not take his seat in 1869. In later years he had a fruit farm and was president of the Lawton Pomological Society. He died in March, 1884.

DAVID A. BIXBY

Representative from the Second District of Lenawee County, 1883-4. Was born in the city of Adrian, in that county, Sept. 24, 1854. He graduated from the Adrian High School in 1870, and in the autumn of 1871 entered the literary department of the University of Michigan, from which he received his diploma in 1875. He held the office of City Recorder of Adrian four terms and County Clerk, and that of Supervisor, two terms. He also filled other minor positions. In politics a Democrat.

CHARLES MARION BLACK

Delegate to the Constitutional Convention of 1907-8 from the Twenty-third District, Muskegon and Ottawa counties. Was born on a farm near Three Rivers, St. Joseph County, Feb. 1, 1874. His ancestors came to America somewhere near the year 1740. Mr. Black is of Scotch, English, French and German descent. He received a common school education, his parents being poor, and early in life was apprenticed to the trade of cigar making. What he accomplished in life was through his own efforts. Mr. Black first came to Muskegon in 1882. Married.

CYRENIUS P. BLACK

Representative from the Second District of Tuscola County, 1883-4 and 1885-6. Was born at Alfred, Alleghany County, N. Y., Apr. 16, 1843. His early education was obtained from an old school district library, and in common schools, supplemented by a two years' course at Alfred University. After devoting some time to teaching school and clerking in a store, he began the study of law in the office of the Hon. Martin Grover, and then with Hon. Marshall B. Champlain, where he remained until 1866, when he came to Tuscola County, was soon after appointed United States Internal Revenue Assessor for Tuscola County, which office he resigned at the end of one year. He was admitted to the bar in February, 1867, and at once commenced practice. In 1873 he entered into partnership with D. H. Ball, of Marquette, continuing until 1877; was elected Prosecuting Attorney of Marquette County. The firm of Ball & Black was interested and successful in many important mining suits. When the twenty-fourth judicial circuit was organized Mr. Black was nominated by the bar of the circuit for Judge. He was defeated by the Hon. Levi L. Wixson. In 1880 he was the Democratic candidate for Congress. In politics he was a Democrat. In 1885 he was appointed United States Attorney for the eastern district of Michigan. He dropped dead in Lansing, Oct. 13. 1916 while arguing a case in the Supreme Court.

ROBERT R. BLACKER

Representative from Manistee County, 1883-4 and 1885-6; and Secretary of State, 1891-3. Was born in Brantford, Ont., Oct. 31, 1845. He came to Michigan at the age of nineteen; resided for two years at Buchanan and located at Manistee. At first he worked about the mills as a common laborer, until he became an expert in the sorting of lumber when he engaged as inspector of lumber. In 1879 he became a member of the firm of Davies, Blacker & Co., which firm was merged into the State Lumber Company, of which he was secretary and treasurer. He was one of the organizers of the First National Bank of Manistee; also a director in the following enterprises: Manistee Water Company, Eureka Lumber Company and Manistee Filer City and Eastlake Electric Railway Company. In politics a Democrat. He was appointed Secretary of State, Dec. 24, 1891, by Governor Winans, to fill vacancy caused by the resignation of Daniel E. Soper, and served the remainder of the unexpired term.

HENRY E. BLACKMAN

Representative from Allegan County, 1879-80. Was born in Aurora, Portage County, O., Jan. 6, 1820. He came to Michigan in 1839, and settled in the township of Trowbridge, Allegan County, in 1841. He received a common school education, and followed the occupation of a farmer. He held the offices of County Superintendent of the Poor, County Drain Commissioner, Supervisor, and Justice of the Peace. In politics he was a National.

SAMUEL H. BLACKMAN

Senator from the Nineteenth District, 1863-4; and Delegate from Van Buren County to the Constitutional Convention of 1867; and Representative from Van Buren County, 1873-4. Was born in Aurora, O., Apr. 6. 1814. He received a common school education, came to Michigan in 1842, first settling in Allegan

County, but in 1844 removed to Paw Paw. He studied law and was admitted to the bar in 1841. He was Treasurer, Register of Deeds, and Prosecuting Attorney of Van Buren County. In politics he was a Republican. Deceased.

ALBERT O. BLACKWELL

Senator, 1889-90, from the Thirtieth District, comprising the counties of Alger, Chippewa, Delta, Emmet, Luce, Mackinac and Schoolcraft. Was born on the Western Reserve, at Avon, Lorain County, O., Oct. 21, 1858. His early life was passed on a farm except when attending school. At the age of eighteen he removed to the Upper Peninsula of Michigan, where he taught school and read law for two years. In 1880 he entered the law department of the University and graduated in 1882, meanwhile having been admitted to the bar in 1881. In 1883 he entered the law office of Collins & Pierce at Appleton, Wis., and soon after formed a partnership. Mr. Blackwell was one of the first residents of Gladstone, and was prominently identified with the growth of that new city. Closely connected with politics, and, among others, he held the office of Superintendent of Schools and School Examiner. For three years he was a member of the Board of Supervisors of Schoolcraft County, and was the first Prosecuting Attorney of Alger County. In politics a Republican.

WILLIAM BLADES

Representative from Genesee County, 1848. Was born in Worcester County, Md., Sept. 27, 1798. He learned the trade of a hatter. He left Maryland in 1828, on account of his aversion to slavery, and lived first at Newark, N. J., then at East Avon, N. Y. He came to Michigan in 1834, settled and lived in Genesee County until his death, Mar. 14, 1877. He lived in Grand Blanc first ten years, afterwards at Flint. He was Justice of the Peace from 1835 to 1844; and Sheriff from 1844 to 1846. He was an old time Whig, later a Republican. He was a farmer at first in Genesee County, but a local preacher of the Methodist Episcopal Church for the last twenty-five years of his life, and is said to have buried and married more people than any other man in Genesee County. He was also a Superintendent of the Poor in later years.

AUSTIN BLAIR

Representative from Jackson County, 1846; Senator from Jackson County, 1855-6; Governor of Michigan, 1861-5; member of Congress, 1867-9, 1869-71 and 1871-3; and Regent of the University of Michigan, 1882-90. Was born at Caroline, Tompkins County, N. Y., Feb. 8, 1818; graduated from Union College, Schenectady, N. Y., in 1839; studied law in Oswego for two years, and moved to Michigan, where he began practicing in 1842. He was County Clerk of Eaton County, and Prosecuting Attorney for Jackson County; member of the State Legislature serving in both branches; elected Governor of Michigan in 1860; elected as a Representative from the Third District of Michigan to the Fortieth, Forty-first, and Forty-second Congresses; Regent of the University of Michigan for the term, Jan. 1, 1882—Dec. 31, 1889. In politics a Republican. He died at Jackson, Mich., Aug. 6, 1894.

CHARLES BLAIR

Representative from Lenawee County, 1842 and 1845. His postoffice address was Tipton. (Further data not obtainable).

CHARLES A. BLAIR

Attorney General, 1903-5; and Justice of the Supreme Court, 1905-12. Was born at Jackson, Jackson County, Mich, Apr. 10, 1854, of Scotch descent. His father was Austin Blair, the famous "War Governor" of Michigan. Mr. Blair was graduated from the Jackson High School in June, 1872, and from the literary department of the University of Michigan in June, 1876. He studied law in his father's office and was admitted to practice Sept. 5, 1878. He was Prosecuting Attorney of Jackson County, besides holding several minor offices. He was married Oct. 8, 1879, to Miss Effie C. North. Mr. Blair was elected to the office of Attorney General, Nov. 4, 1902, and was the unanimous choice of the Republican State Convention, held at Detroit, June 30, 1904, for the second term nomination to that office. Mr. Blair's name was placed before the judicial convention at Saginaw, Sept. 8, 1904, as a candidate for Justice of the Supreme Court, and was nominated for the five year term. He withdrew his name as a candidate for Attorney General, and was elected to the Supreme Bench. At the Republican State Convention held at Grand Rapids, Feb. 12, 1909, Justice Blair was the unanimous choice of the convention for the nomination to succeed himself and was elected Apr. 5, 1909. Justice Blair was chief justice during the year 1909. He died Aug. 30, 1912.

JOHN E. BLAKE

Representative from the First District of Ottawa County, 1869-70. His postoffice address was Lamont. (Further data not obtainable).

WILLIAM A. BLAKE

Representative from the Second District of Kalamazoo County, 1891-2. Was born in Livingston County, N. Y., in 1832. Married and by profession a farmer. He held the offices of Township Treasurer, Justice and Supervisor; was elected to the House of 1891-2 on the Democratic ticket.

EDWIN A. BLAKESLEE

Senator, 1897-8 and 1899-1900, from the Seventh District, composed of the counties of Berrien and Cass. Was born in Galien, Berrien County, Mich., July 18, 1865. His early education was acquired in the Galien High School; entered the State Normal at Ypsilanti in the fall of 1882, where he remained three and one-half years. In the fall of 1887 he entered the University of Michigan, spending two years on special work in the literary department and one year in the law department. Owing to the death of his father in the fall of 1890 he was compelled to leave college and return home, where he actively engaged in farming, banking, and mercantile business, and became a director of the Citizens' National Bank, of Niles, Mich. In politics a very active Republican. He held the offices of Township Clerk and Councilman of the village of Galien; and Supervisor of his township.

GEORGE BLAKESLEE

Representative from Oakland County, 1861-2. Was born in Oakland County, Mich., in 1826. He lived on a farm until about the age of fifteen when he went to Detroit and shipped for the ocean under the noted Captain Blake, on the steamer Illinois. The next year he apprenticed himself to learn the carpenter and joiners' trade, at which he worked for four years under the master builders, mostly at Detroit, attending select school four months in the year. He then taught school one winter. In 1848 he married, and lived in Detroit several years, working as a builder and contractor. In 1850 he was elected Assessor of the first district, comprising the first, second and eighth wards, and was appointed Fire Warden in 1851. The same year he purchased a farm and saw mill at Birmingham, and moved his family there in 1854. He was two years Supervisor of Bloomfield Township. He was a Democrat in early life but became a Republican in 1856. He was in 1863 special agent of the Provost Marshal of the Fifth District, and afterwards became Deputy. He carried on a mercantile business in Birmingham and also dealt in real estate.

ABRAM R. BLAKLEY

Representative, 1893-4, from the district comprising the counties of Alpena, Montmorency, Otsego, Oscoda and Crawford. Was born in Delaware County, N. Y., Oct. 19, 1841. He came with his parents to Michigan in 1853, locating in Meridian Township, Ingham County, where he supplemented his common school education with a short course at the agricultural college. He was the first railroad agent and grain buyer at the village of Okemos, and was Supervisor of his township for several terms. In 1865 he moved to Alpena and engaged in the mercantile business and later in farming and real estate dealing. In politics a Republican. He held the office of Supervisor, Comptroller and Alderman, and was elected to the House of 1893-4. He resigned Oct. 15, 1894.

JOSEPH EDWARD BLAND

Representative from the First District of Wayne County, 1901-2 and 1905-6; and Senator from the Third District of Wayne County, 1907-8. Was born in London, Ont., May 5, 1866. His parents were of the Irish branch of the English family of Blands. He attended the public schools and business college, and afterward the University of Michigan where he received the degrees of Bachelor of Laws and Master of Laws. Mr. Bland engaged in the practice of law in the city of Detroit where he resided with the exception of a few years' residence in California. During the Spanish-American war, Mr. Bland enlisted in the U. S. Navy, and was one of the crew of the U. S. S. Yosemite. He remained active with the naval militia. In politics an ardent supporter of the Republican party.

JOHN BLINDBURY

Representative from Wayne County, 1844. Was born Feb. 22, 1806, in Lyons, N. Y., emigrated to Michigan in 1825 and purchased a farm in Southfield, Oakland County, erected a log house, and sent for his father's family. He hired out to chop at four and a half dollars per acre, paying his father for his time until he was twenty-one. In 1837 he removed to Greenfield, eight miles from Detroit, and began keeping hotel. He was Supervisor of Greenfield thirteen successive years, and held other local offices. In 1852 he removed to Detroit and built the Blindbury Hotel, later known as the Antisdel House. In politics he was a Democrat, in religion a Methodist. He died Mar. 1, 1867.

CHARLES OSCAR BLINN

Representative from Tuscola County, 1917-18 and 1919-20. Was born at Perrysburg, O., July 20, 1857, and was educated in the public schools of that place. His first political job was an appointment by the Board of Public Works of the State of Ohio to take charge of the Western Reserve Pike. In 1886 Mr. Blinn removed with his family to Michigan to take charge of the William Peters' stock farms, located at Columbiaville, Lapeer County, and East Dayton, Tuscola County. He was appointed Deputy Oil Inspector in 1905 and served in that capacity for five years, but resigned before the expiration of his term in order to take charge of the oil business. Married. In politics a Republican. He served as Sheriff of Tuscola County.

AARON PITT BLISS

Member of the State Board of Agriculture, 1903-9. Was born July 27, 1860, at Peterboro, Madison County, N. Y. He was the son of Eli S. Bliss and Mariette Hoffman, both of the town last mentioned. He married Mary Brockway in Saginaw, Mich., Dec. 12, 1882. He was educated at Evans Academy, then in Saginaw and Detroit. A member of the Methodist Church and a Republican in politics. His occupation that of lumbering and farming.

AARON T. BLISS

Senator from Saginaw County, 1883-4; member of Congress from the Eighth District, 1889-91; Governor of Michigan, 1901-5. Was born May 22, 1837, in Smithfield, Madison County, N. Y. He was the seventh child of Lyman and Anna (Chaffee) Bliss. He spent his early life on the farm, obtaining his education in the little schoolhouse near by. At seventeen he left home and secured employment in a store, where he remained until the Civil War broke out and President Lincoln made his second call for troops. He then enlisted as a private in Co. D, 10th N. Y. Cavalry, taking the oath the first day of October, 1861. Later he was commissioned Captain. He spent three years and five months in the service. He was captured at Reem's Station, Va., and was held for six months as a prisoner of war in the prisons at Salisbury, North Carolina, Andersonville and Macon, Georgia, Charleston and Columbia, South Carolina. After several fruitless attempts, he escaped from Columbia prison, Nov. 29, 1864, and finally reaching the Union lines near Savannah, Dec. 16, nearly starved. In the fall of 1865, he settled in Saginaw and began his successful career as a lumberman. Mar. 31, 1868, he married Allaseba M. Phelps, of Solsville, Madison County, N. Y. The scope of his business enterprises gradually enlarged until it embraced besides the manufacture of lumber and salt, banking, mercantile and farm enterprises, giving employment to large numbers of men. In politics a Republican. He served his city as Alderman, Supervisor and member of the Board of Education. In 1882, he represented the 25th Senatorial District (Saginaw County) in the State Senate. When the board to organize and locate the Michigan Soldiers' Home was constituted, he was made a member and served thereon until he entered the 51st Congress, representing the Eighth District. While in Congress he secured the appropriation which resulted in the splendid federal building which adorns Saginaw, and the Government Indian school at Mt. Pleasant. In 1855 he was appointed aide on the staff of Governor Alger. His long service in the Grand Army of the Republic was signalized in 1897 by his election as department commander. He was nominated for Governor at the Republican Convention held at Grand Rapids in June, 1900, and was elected; was re-nominated on the first ballot at the convention held in Detroit, June, 1902, and re-elected. He died at Milwaukee, Sept. 16, 1906.

SOLOMON BOND BLISS

Representative from Saginaw County, 1863-4. Was born at Bennfield, Mass., Apr. 17, 1828, and died at East Saginaw, Nov. 12, 1884. The oldest of a family of five children, he had a limited education, and at the age of twelve years went to work, being employed in Springfield and Boston for four years, then went to Ohio, returning to Massachusetts on horseback when seventeen. He returned to Ohio in 1845, settling first at Wellington, and then at Elyria, where he married a daughter of Dr. O. L. Mason in 1850. He resided in Cleveland until 1854 when he removed to East Saginaw and engaged in the grocery trade with Curtis Bros. for some years, finally buying out the business. He also engaged in the banking and the lumber business, and built the Bliss block in East Saginaw. He was also Postmaster under President Johnson. He was a Republican, a Knight Templar, an Odd Fellow, and a charter member of the Unitarian Church. He was a genial, pleasant gentleman, and highly esteemed. He died Nov. 12, 1884.

AMOS C. BLODGET

Representative from Washtenaw County, 1857-8. Was born in Vermont, Jan. 30, 1822, coming with his parents to Michigan in 1836, and settling in Ypsilanti in 1840. His education was academic, and his first occupation that of teaching. He was admitted to practice as an attorney at Ann Arbor in 1847. He held the office of Justice of the Peace and other local offices at Ypsilanti, and in 1864 was elected Prosecuting Attorney of the County. Mr. Blodget was a Democrat, but was nominated for the Legislature on the Republican ticket by reason of local considerations, and elected. He removed to Philadelphia in 1872, taking a position with an insurance company, and came to Detroit in 1883. He made a special study of insurance law.

CALVIN A. BLOOD

Representative from the First District of St. Clair County, 1881-2. Was born in Vermont in 1823. He received a common school education, and in 1845 came to the State of Michigan and settled in St. Clair County, where he followed the occupation of carpenter and joiner eight years. In 1853 he engaged successfully in mercantile business. He held the office of Collector of Customs fifteen years, Postmaster eight years, express agent and telegraph operator five years, and steamboat agent twenty-five years. In politics he was a Democrat previous to 1856. In 1860 he commenced active labors with the Republican party.

ADAM E. BLOOM

Representative from the First District of Wayne County, 1881-2. Was born in Cincinnati, O., Sept. 5, 1849. He was a graduate of the public schools of that city.

At an early age he engaged in the mercantile business with his brothers at Fayetteville, Tenn. In the spring of 1868 he returned to Cincinnati, where he remained until the fall of 1870, when he located at ElDorado, Kan. While there he began to read law with Judge William P. Campbell, and in the spring of 1872, was admitted to practice in the Supreme Court of Kansas. Having returned to Cincinnati in the summer of 1872, he entered the law office of Lincoln, Smith & Stephens. While there he attended law lectures in the law department of the Cincinnati University, graduating in May, 1873. In June he came to Detroit, where he resided, and succeeded in building up quite a lucrative and extensive law practice. In politics he was a Republican. He was a member of the Detroit Board of Education. He died previous to Mar. 10, 1916.

FRANK P. BOHN

Senator from the Thirtieth District, comprising the counties of Chippewa, Delta, Luce, Mackinac, Menominee and Schoolcraft, 1923—. Was born at Charlottsville, Hancock County, Indiana, July 14, 1866, of German-English parents. His early education was obtained in the common schools of Indiana. In 1890 he graduated from The Medical College of Indiana, and has since been engaged in active practice. He has been a resident of the Thirtieth Senatorial District since 1890; has been village president five terms; a member of the board of supervisors and of the school board; was a trustee of Newberry State Hospital for twenty years, acting as president for twelve years, and has been president of the Newberry State Bank since 1909. He is a member of the B. P. O. E. and of the following Masonic orders: Blue Lodge, Chapter, Commandery, Shrine and Eastern Star. Mr. Bohn is married and has one daughter. He was elected senator on the Republican ticket November 7, 1922.

HENRY M. BOIES

Senator from the Ninth District, 1855-6 and from the Tenth District, 1857-8. Was born in Blandford, Mass., Jan. 12, 1818. He came to Michigan in 1840, settling at Hudson, Lenawee County. He was a pioneer merchant of that town. He was President of the village of Hudson in 1854 and 1855. He was appointed one of the Inspectors of the State Prison by Governor Blair in 1860. He removed to New York City in 1862, and was in mercantile business there several years, and in 1873 he changed his residence to Chicago, where he established the wholesale grocery house of Boies, Fay & Conkey, continuing at the head of that concern until his death from pulmonary disease, which occurred at Chicago on Nov. 5, 1880.

JOHN K. BOIES

Representative from Lenawee County, 1865-6 and 1867-8; and Senator from the Eighth District, 1869-70 and from the Sixth District, 1875-6. Was born in Blandford, Mass., Dec. 6, 1828. He came to Michigan in 1845, settling at Hudson, Lenawee County. He engaged in mercantile business, and also in banking. He was President of the village of Hudson in 1863 and 1867. He was a member of the State Board of Control of Railroads from 1871-4, and again from 1878-86. He was president pro tem of the State Senate, 1875-6. Was several times chosen president of State Republican Conventions. He was appointed by President Garfield in 1881, a member of the United States Board of Indian Commissioners, holding that position until he resigned it, Jan. 15, 1886. He died at Washington, D. C., Aug. 21, 1891.

GEORGE LEWIS BOLEN

Senator, 1917-18, from the Ninth District, comprising the counties of Branch and Calhoun. Was born near Staunton, Va., Oct. 31, 1861. His father's people came to Virginia in colonial times from England. His mother's people were colonial Pennsylvania Germans. His first twelve years were spent in the country. From twelve to fifteen he learned to be a printer. From fifteen to eighteen he was on a farm in summer, and at school in winter. From eighteen to twenty his school work in winter was changed to teaching. He then spent a year and a half as a printer in Providence and Boston, a year at Valparaiso (Indiana) Business College, a year and a half (1884-6) at the University of Michigan, and nearly five years as a newspaper writer and manager at Houghton, Michigan. In 1890 he returned to Virginia and organized a company and established the Staunton *News*, the town's first daily paper. In 1893 he returned to Michigan and started a small job printing shop in Jackson. He remained there twelve years and on January 1, 1906, he went to Battle Creek and bought the Phoenix Printing Company business. He devoted his spare time to the study of economics, being the author of two books on this subject. In politics a Democrat.

ROBERT E. BOLGER

Representative from the Fifth District of Wayne County, 1881-2 and 1883-4. Was born in Wexford, Ireland. When a child he came with his parents to Detroit, where he received a common school education. When the war broke out he enlisted in the 24th Mich. Infantry; served during the war. He was twice wounded in action, once at Gettysburg, and once at the Wilderness, Va. He was taken prisoner at the Battle of Weldon Road. He remained a prisoner six months and a half, when he was paroled and returned to his regiment, and was mustered out with the same at Detroit, July 1, 1865. He served on the lakes and rivers surrounding Michigan for years as pilot, clerk, etc. He did not sit in the extra session of 1882.

ARTHUR J. BOLT

Senator, 1921-2, from the Twenty-third District, comprising the counties of Muskegon and Ottawa. Was born Mar. 2, 1892, at Grand Haven, Mich., of Holland American parentage. He received his education in the public school of Grand Haven, University of Chicago and the University of Michigan, and is now engaged in the practice of dental surgery. Mr. Bolt is married and has one daughter. During the World War he was stationed at Camp Custer in the Medical Corps. In politics he is a Republican.

TOM J. G. BOLT

Senator, 1909-10, from the Twenty-third District, comprising the counties of Muskegon and Ottawa. Was born in Devonshire, England, Apr. 16, 1848. He came to America and landed at New York, March, 1857. He went to London, Canada, and in the winter of 1858 located in Ottawa County, Michigan, and lived on his

father's farm which he helped to clear. He attended school at Lisbon, Ottawa
County, and graduated from Grand Rapids High School in 1867. He taught district
and village schools in Kent, Ottawa and Muskegon counties for twenty-one successive years. He was married to Ola A. Minnich, Dec. 25, 1874. Owner of a large
farm. He held the offices of School Inspector, Township Superintendent of
Schools, Township Treasurer, Supervisor and County School Commissioner. He
was in the employ of the State Tax Commission for five years doing expert field
work and was elected Supervisor first in 1882. In politics a Republican.

ABRAHAM F. BOLTON

Representative from Jackson County, 1836. He settled in Napoleon, Jackson
County, Mich., in 1832. The town was so named at his request. He was the
first settler in the town. He was Supervisor in 1835. He was in the extra session
of the Legislature only in the place of Townsend E. Gidley resigned. He became
a General of State militia. Deceased.

EARL B. BOLTON

Representative, 1901-2 and 1903-4, from the Presque Isle District, comprising the
counties of Crawford, Montmorency, Oscoda, Otsego and Presque Isle. Was born
in Leslie, Mich., Feb. 13, 1862, and received his education in the high schools
of Leslie and Mason. Married and a resident of Gaylord, being one of its heaviest
property holders—a member of the E. B. Bolton hardware company and a member
of the firm of Buck & Bolton, commission merchants, vice-president of the Gaylord
State Savings Bank and half owner of the bank at Wolverine. Always a staunch
Republican.

WILLIAM S. BOND

Representative from Detroit, 1865-6. Was born in Massachusetts in 1831, and came
to Michigan when a boy. He was a printer by trade, with a fondness for politics,
being of the Democratic school. In 1856 he was interested for a short time in the
publication of a daily paper called the *Evening News*, and in 1862 in an agricultural
paper. He was Alderman from his ward, 1862-5, and 1808-9, the latter year
being president of the Council. He left Detroit, several years prior to 1888 and
is understood to have died soon after leaving the city.

ASHER BONHAM

Representative from St. Joseph County, 1850. Was born in Flemington, N. J., Oct.
27, 1808. By occupation he was a carriage maker, in politics a Democrat. He
settled in Nottawa, Mich., in 1835. He was four years County Clerk, Justice
of the Peace sixteen years, Master in Chancery four years, and Town Clerk.
After becoming a resident of Michigan he was a farmer, but from 1851 to 1877
was in railroad business in Indiana. He died at Nottawa, Mar. 9, 1891.

EVAN J. BONINE

Representative from Cass County, 1853-4 and from Berrien County, 1865-6, 1867-8
and 1873-4; and Senator from the Sixteenth District, 1869-70. Was born at

Richmond, Ind., Sept. 10, 1821, of Quaker descent. Until seventeen years of age he worked on his father's farm, attending school winters. After one year as clerk in a store he studied medicine and graduated at the Ohio Medical College in Cincinnati in 1843. In 1844 he settled at Niles, where he had a large medical practice, and was prominent in politics. He resigned as Representative before the extra session of 1874, and was succeeded by Ethan A. Brown. He went into the army as Surgeon of the 2nd Mich. Infantry, and became Surgeon-in-chief of the Third Division of the Army Corps. In this capacity he acquired a great reputation as a surgeon. He was twice Mayor of Niles. and was Postmaster from 1870 to 1885. He was Division Surgeon of the Michigan Central Railroad. In politics he was a Republican.

BENJAMIN C. BONNELL

Representative from the district consisting of Lake, Wexford, Kalkaska, and Missaukee counties, 1883-4. Was born in Elizabeth City, N. J., in 1841. His opportunities for education were those of free schools. He removed with the family to Westchester County, N. Y., and five years later to Pike County, Pa., where he was married in 1861. He enlisted in the 151st Pa. Vol., in 1862; was engaged in the Battle of Chancellorsville, May 2, and 3, 1863, and at the Battle of Gettysburg, July 1, where he was taken prisoner, but paroled on the 3d of that month, after which he was discharged. He then joined a construction corps, serving until Gen. Sherman started for the sea, when he returned to Pennsylvania. After the war he lived two years in Jersey City, N. J., and two years in Minnesota, engaging there in farming. In 1870 he came to Michigan, settling upon a homestead claim in Missaukee County, and was elected Supervisor, twice elected County Treasurer. He was elected County Surveyor in 1872, continuing in that office ten years. In politics a Republican.

JOHN E. BONSER

Representative from the Third District of Bay County, 1901-2. Was born in London, Ontario, in 1859. His education was obtained in the high school of that place. He removed to Detroit, when 18 years of age, after which time he had varied experiences in newspaper work, acting as compositor on the Bay City *Tribune*, and that of publisher on the Pinconning *Press*. Married. In politics a staunch Republican.

MARTIN V. BORGMAN

Representative from the First District of Wayne County, 1881-2. Was born in Auglaize County, O., Dec. 1, 1839. Having been educated in the common schools of Cincinnati, O., he commenced to learn the printer's trade, but failing health caused him to abandon that and seek employment not so confining. He, therefore, in 1859, removed to Detroit, Mich., where he found employment more suited to his taste and health. At the breaking out of the war he entered the army in the 16th Mich. Infantry and served nearly three years. At the close of the war, in 1865, he was appointed on the Detroit police force, then just organizing, and obtained the Superintendency of the force in 1867. He remained with the police force until 1873, when he resigned to accept the position of Superintendent of the Detroit House of Correction. He was an Alderman, and Assistant Superintendent of the Detroit police.

ALBERT H. BOSCH

Representative from the Second District of Ottawa County, 1915-16 and 1917-18. Was born at Holland, Mich., Apr. 5, 1869, of Holland parentage. He received his early education in the public schools and afterwards took a business course. He taught school for fifteen years, afterwards engaging in farming. After 1911, he devoted his time to notary work and auctioneering being secretary of the Jamestown Cooperative Creamery Company; secretary-treasurer of the Farmers' Mutual Fire Insurance Company of Ottawa and Allegan Counties and Township Clerk of Jamestown. In politics a Republican.

WILLIAM EDWIN BOSLEY

Representative from the First District of Calhoun County, 1905-6. Was born at Geneseo, Livingston County, N. Y., Mar. 30, 1837. The Bosley family emigrated from England and were among the early settlers of Maryland. He acquired his education in the high schools of Geneseo, N. Y. He enjoyed a successful business career. From 1859 to 1871 he was interested in a general store at Lakeville, N. Y., and came to Michigan in 1871. He resided in Marshall after 1876, and for six years carried on a carriage and implement business. In 1882 he established a general hardware business which he carried on until 1893 when he took his son, D. W. Bosley into partnership with him under the firm name of W. E. Bosley & Son. Aside from his varied mercantile interests Mr. Bosley owned two farms. Married. In politics a Republican. He held the offices of Alderman and Mayor of Marshall. He died at Marshall in May, 1916.

ALFRED J. BOSS

Senator from the Fourth District, 1855-6. Was a resident of Pontiac, Oakland County. He kept a livery stable there. He was a man of fine personal appearance, a warm partisan, and took an active part in the Legislature.

EDWARD E. BOSTWICK

Senator, 1897-8, from the Sixth District, comprising the counties of Branch, Hillsdale and St. Joseph. Was born on a farm in Otisco, Onondaga County, N. Y., May 27, 1840. His early education was acquired in the common schools of his native town, supplemented by a course in the Onondaga Academy, N. Y., Homer Academy, N. Y., and the Cazenovia (New York) Seminary. Soon after leaving school he was married, and for a short time was engaged in business at Syracuse, N. Y. In the fall of 1864 he moved to Union City, Branch County, Mich., where he engaged in farming. In politics he was an ardent Republican during the war, being a member of the Loyal League, and voted the Republican ticket until 1884, when he joined the Prohibition Party; upon the division of the party at Pittsburg he united with the Nationalists or broad guage wing. In 1884 he was a candidate for Representative on the Prohibition ticket; was a candidate for Senator in 1886 and 1890; was Supervisor one term; being a warm advocate of the union on reform forces, he received the nomination for State Senator on the Democratic People's Union Silver Ticket and was elected to the Senate of 1897-8.

EZRA BOSTWICK

Representative from Branch County, 1869-70. Was born in Otisco, Onondaga County, N. Y., Feb. 27, 1826. He was brought up a farmer, and received a common school education. He came to the town of Union, Branch County, in 1846, and settled on a farm of two thousand acres, purchased by his father in 1835, of which he improved over one thousand acres. He became prominent at Union City. He was several years President of the village. and director of the Union City National Bank.

PHILIP V. M. BOTSFORD

Representative from the Second District of Shiawassee County, 1891-2. Was born in Scottsville, N. Y., in 1839, and removed to Michigan shortly after. In politics a Democrat. He held the offices of Town Clerk, Supervisor and Circuit Court Commissioner. He was nominated and elected to the State Legislature by a combination of the farming and labor interests.

THOMAS BOTTOMLEY

Representative from St. Clair County, 1873-4. Was born in the town of Southouram, Yorkshire, England, Oct. 5, 1837. Mr. Bottomley was educated at the Saltrauble Academy, Yorkshire, England. In 1854 he emigrated to the United States, and settled in the city of Buffalo. In 1856 he emigrated to Michigan, and settled in New Baltimore, Macomb County. He removed to Romeo in 1865, and in 1872 removed to the town of Capac, St. Clair County. Mr. Bottomley held various offices of trust in the different places where he resided. His occupation was that of a merchant.

CHARLES B. BOUGHNER

Senator from the Fourteenth District, comprising the county of Oakland, 1891-2. Was born in Flemington, N. J., 1825. In the year following his parents removed to the village, now city of Waterloo, Seneca County, N. Y. In 1835 he came to Monroe County, Mich. In November, 1837, he settled in Oakland County, Mich., and remained there. He followed the profession of teacher until 1852, when he engaged in farming. He was twice nominated to the office of Representative, but declined the nomination. In politics a Democrat. He died Sept. 15, 1920 at West Bloomfield. Oakland County.

CHARLES O. BOUSSUM

Representative from St. Joseph County, 1909-10. Was born at Union City, Mich., Apr. 26, 1870, of American descent. He received his education in the common schools, supplemented by a course in several high schools. Married. After finishing his school work, he engaged in farming for a few years, later accepting a position as foreman with the Lamb Knit Goods Co., Colon, which place he creditably filled for a continuous period of thirteen years, during which time he served Colon Township as Treasurer two terms; afterwards chosen Justice of the Peace and in the fall of 1904 was elected Treasurer of St. Joseph County and re-elected in 1906; also held the office of President of Centerville village and did efficient work during the campaign of 1908 as chairman of the Republican County Committee.

CASPER L. BOWEN

Representative from Barry County, 1891-2. Was born in Maple Grove, Barry County, Mich., June 17, 1850. Occupation that of farming. He held the offices of School Inspector, Highway Commissioner, and was Supervisor. He was elected to the House of 1891-2 on the Patron ticket.

JESSE BOWEN

Representative from Branch County, 1863-4. Was born in Greenfield, Saratoga County, N. Y., Feb. 27, 1805, and spent his boyhood days upon a farm. In 1837 he married Lucy Morehouse, and the same year settled on a farm in Butler, Branch County, Mich. He was Supervisor of the township for many years. In 1863-4 he was Representative from the Third District of Branch County as a Republican, and died during the extra session, Feb. 7, 1864. Three of his sons served in the war of 1861-5.

OZRO A. BOWEN

Representative from Ingham County, 1879-80. Was born in Butler Township, Branch County, where he lived on a farm until 1861. He enlisted as a private in the 11th Mich. Infantry, and served three years. After being mustered out of the service he entered Hillsdale College, where he remained three years. He then purchased an interest in the Coldwater *Republican*, and there remained for some time. He was Deputy Commissioner of the State Land Office for five years, and a member of the firm of Dart, Bowen & Co., of Lansing. In politics a Republican. Later he was a resident of the Upper Peninsula and of Chicago.

JOHN H. BOWMAN

Representative from St. Joseph County, 1838 and 1845. Was born in Columbia County, Pa., in 1797. He settled at Three Rivers, Mich., in 1832, named the village, and owned a part of the land on which it stands. In 1836 in connection with the Smiths, he built what is known as the Three Rivers mill. He built a flouring mill at Colon in 1838, and in 1848 purchased an interest in what was later known as the Hoffman mill, and ran the business with Phillip Hoffman up to the time of his death, May 2, 1855. He died of cholera at Lexington, Mo., while traveling in the West. He brought about $10,000 to Michigan and left an estate of $50,000. He started the village of Three Rivers by giving every man a lot who would build a house upon it; and was noted for public spirit and great benevolence. By occupation he was a miller and farmer. In politics he was a Whig.

JOHN BOWNE

Representative from Barry County, 1849; and Senator from the Seventh District, 1850 and 1851. Was born in Cold Springs, N. Y., Jan. 14, 1796, and died May 17, 1861. He lived in and around New York city for some years, and at the age of twenty-one moved to Courtland County, N. Y., where he married Sarah P. Owen, and resided until he moved to Barry County, Mich., in 1837. By occupation he was a farmer; in politics a Democrat.

WILLIAM BOYD

Representative from the First District of Calhoun County, 1901-2. Was born in Antrim County, Ireland, May 30, 1839, and received his earlier education in the national schools of that country. He came to America with his parents in 1851 and remained in New York State two years, attending district school during that time. In 1853 his parents removed to Lenawee County, Mich., and in 1867 he bought a farm in the township of Sheridan, Calhoun County. His first vote was cast for Abraham Lincoln, and he voted the Republican ticket until 1896 when he joined the D. P. U. S. party. Married. He held the offices of Township Clerk, Justice of the Peace and Supervisor.

WILLIAM EDWARD BOYDEN

Member of the State Board of Agriculture, 1895-7. Was the son of Edward Luther Boyden, of Washtenaw County, Mich. and Frances A. (Burnett) Boyden of Phelps, N. Y. William Edward was born in Webster township, Washtenaw County, Mich., July 15, 1860. He married Nettie Adella Robison, of Sharon, Washtenaw County. She was reared, educated and married in Ann Arbor. He was educated in a public school of Detroit, having frail health. In politics a Republican. By occupation a farmer, preferring live stock, living on the old home farm until Nov. 13, 1901, when as manager of a farm, he cast his lot with Eugene Fifield of Bay City. He was director and moderator of the old home district school and for some years a director of the American Shorthorn Association.

DANIEL BOYNTON

Representative from Jackson County, 1885-6. Was born in Grass Lake, Mich., Sept. 9, 1842. He lived at home, working on the farm summers, and attending district schools winters until he was seventeen years of age; he then went to school at the Michigan Collegiate Institute, located at Leoni village, for a couple of years. He canvassed one summer as agent for the Michigan State Fire Insurance Company, of Adrian, and taught school the next winter. He then worked his father's farm two summers, and taught school winters. He was married July 3, 1864, to Mary A. Burkhart, of Leoni. He bought a farm in the township of Leoni, in the spring of 1865, and removed there May 11. In the year 1874 he, with his partner, Wm. A. Watts, built the grist mill later known as the Boynton mills. He bought out his partner in the spring of 1877. He was elected Township Treasurer, served three years; was elected Supervisor in 1881. He was elected Representative as the candidate of the Fusion party.

NATHAN S. BOYNTON

Representative from the First District of St. Clair County, 1869; and Delegate in the Constitutional Convention of 1907-8 from the Eleventh District, St. Clair County. Was born in Port Huron, June 23, 1837, of English and German descent, his father's ancestry descending from Sir Mathew Boynton, of England, and his mother's from Capt. Louis Rendt of the German army. Mr. Boynton attended the country district schools and graduated from the Waukegan, Ills., High School when sixteen years of age. He lived on a farm until he was twenty years old. In 1859 he married Miss Annie Fields German, at Cincinnati, O. He spent five years of his life in mercantile business and another five in the real estate and insurance business. Mr. Boynton became Great Commander of the Knights of the Maccabees in 1881 and held the position twenty-seven years. He held the position of City Clerk at Marine City, and was also President of that village. He was Supervisor from 1866 to 1870 and was also Mayor of Port Huron.

FREDERICK BRAASTAD

State Treasurer, 1891-3. Was born in Ringebo, Guldbrandsdalen, Norway, in the year 1847, and received a common school education. His early life, when not in school, was passed upon the farm of his parents until sixteen years of age, when he entered a store as clerk in the city of Lillehammer, which position he held for five years. In the year 1868 he came to the United States, and arrived at Marquette, Mich., in the month of October. He commenced working as a common day laborer, and in the year 1869 engaged as clerk with J. P. Pendell, of Negaunee, Mich., at which place he remained until 1873, when he engaged in mercantile business at Ishpeming, Mich., for himself, which became one of the finest and largest businesses in the Upper Peninsula; also vice president and general manager, and one of the principal owners of the Winthrop and Mitchell Iron Mines.

SAMUEL K. BRADBURY

Representative from the Third District of Bay County, 1895-6. Was born in Buxton Centre, York County, Me., Mar. 27, 1859, and received his early education in the common schools of that State. In 1874 he came to Michigan and cleared up a farm. For five years he was also engaged in lumbering. In politics a Republican, and for a number of years a member of the Republican Executive Committee. He held the office of School Inspector and was a member of the Board of Review.

THOMAS D. BRADFIELD

Representative from Keweenaw and Ontonagon counties, 1875-6 and 1879-80. Was born Jan. 12, 1843. He received an academic education, and prosecuted his medical studies at the University of Michigan during the years 1867-8, and graduated at the Detroit Medical College in 1869. He practiced his profession in Keweenaw County.

VINCENT L. BRADFORD

Senator from the Third District, 1838, and from the Seventh District, 1839. Came from Philadelphia to Niles in 1835, and engaged in the practice of the law. He was a ripe scholar, and a man of eminent ability, and immediately took rank among the first lawyers of the State, and acquired a State reputation. He returned to Philadelphia in 1843, became one of the first lawyers of that city, and afterwards a judge. He died at Philadelphia, Pa., Aug. 7, 1884.

EDWARD BRADLEY

Senator from the Fourth District, 1843. Was born at East Bloomfield, N. Y., in 1808, brought up on a farm, and received a fair common school and academical education. In 1836 he was a Judge of the Common pleas court in Ontario County, N. Y. He came to Michigan in 1839 and studied law, first at Detroit and then at Marshall, and engaged there in practice with Gibbs & Sanford. In 1847 he was elected to Congress, but never qualified, dying at New York while on his way to Washington, and Charles E. Stuart was elected to fill the vacancy. He was a fine lawyer and a great orator. In height, five feet ten; fine eyes, light complexion, curly, bushy head of brown hair; easy in manner, fluent in speech, a master of wit and ridicule, logical, argumentative, enthusiastic and inspiring, he was by many considered the ablest Democratic speaker in those early days of Michigan. He gloried in the life of a pioneer.

GEORGE BRADLEY

Member of the Board of Regents of the University of Michigan, 1858-64. Was born at Hopewell, Ontario County, N. Y., May 31, 1810. In 1837 he was licensed to preach by the Northern Ohio Conference of the Methodist Episcopal Church, and the following year, at Tiffin, O., he was appointed "junior preacher" to the Copley circuit, then included in the Michigan Conference. In 1839 he was appointed to the Saline circuit, which brought him to Michigan. From 1841 to 1847 he was Missionary to the Indians, with headquarters at Flint, Mich. During the two following years he was presiding elder of the Grand River District, which extended across the State from Saginaw to Lake Michigan. In 1850 this district was divided, and he was made presiding elder of the eastern half, still residing at Flint. In 1852 he was placed in charge of the Methodist work in Lower Saginaw, now Bay City, where he built the first Methodist Church. From 1853 to 1857 he labored at Albion, Marshall, and Jackson; and from 1857 to 1859 he was presiding elder of the Indian Mission District and Missionary to the Indians in Isabella County. For the following two years he was presiding elder of the Lansing District, and in 1862 he was super-annuated. He died Apr. 15, 1871, being at the time in New York City, whither he had gone on business for the Indian Agency. He was buried at Mt. Pleasant, Mich., his home for some years prior to his death. He was married in 1832 to Miss Sophia Blakesly. He was elected Regent of the University in 1857 and took his seat the following January, serving the full term of six years.

HARMON BRADLEY

Representative from Calhoun County, 1879-80. Was born in Vermont in 1817. He received a common school education, and in 1835 came to Michigan and settled in Calhoun County, where he followed the occupation of a farmer. He held the office of Supervisor and other minor offices. In politics he was a Republican.

JAMES B. BRADLEY

Auditor General, 1905-9. Was born on a farm in Middlebury Township, Shiawassee County, Mich., Nov. 19, 1858. He obtained his early education in the public schools of Shiawassee County. Dr. Bradley lived in Laingsburg and vicinity until he came to Eaton Rapids in 1880, entering the employ of Hamilton Bros., druggists, and remained with them until he entered Rush Medical College of Chicago. He was graduated from that institution in the spring of 1886, and returned to Eaton

Rapids, where he practiced his profession; conducted a large farm, and other extensive business interests. Dr. Bradley was married to Miss Jennie A. Frost of Genesee County, September, 1885. A Mason, member of Charlotte Commandery, and Saladin Temple of Mystic Shriners of Grand Rapids; also belonged to the orders Knights of Pythias and Maccabees. He was twice elected Mayor of the city of Eaton Rapids, and was a member of the Board of Pension Examiners of Eaton County twelve years. In politics always a Republican. At the Republican State Convention held at Detroit, June 30, 1904, he was placed in nomination for Auditor General.

MARTIN R. BRADLEY

Representative from Menominee County, 1923—. Was born in Newberry, Michigan, April 1, 1888, of Irish parentage. While still a child his parents removed to a farm in Huron County and his early education was acquired in the district school there. He later attended the Ferris Institute and the Central State Normal and then taught in rural schools for several years. In 1909 he was married to Jennie Wallen of Midland and went to Hermansville as Superintendent of Schools. He held the Postmastership eight years, under the Wilson administration, and is Supervisor of Meyer Township. He was elected to the Legislature on the Democratic ticket, November 7, 1922.

MILTON BRADLEY

Delegate from Kalamazoo County to the Constitutional Convention of 1867. Was born in Stockholm, St. Lawrence County, N. Y., Mar. 13, 1812. He graduated from Middlebury College in 1835. He was married in 1838 and on account of his wife's health came to Michigan where he settled in Richland in 1843, going from there to Kalamazoo in 1844. His pastorate at Richland was the longest then known. In 1850 he was defeated for the convention by Samuel Clark but succeeded in the Constitutional Convention of 1867. He was deeply interested in all educational matters. He died at Richland, Feb. 3, 1896.

NATHAN B. BRADLEY

Senator from the Twenty-seventh District, 1867-8; member of Congress, 1873-5 and 1875-7. Was born in Lee, Mass., May 28, 1831. He moved with his father's family to Ohio in 1835. He received a common school education and came to Michigan in 1852. He settled at Bay City in 1858. He served in the village and city Council and was elected Mayor in 1865. He was elected State Senator and served in the session of 1867. In 1872 and 1874 he was elected to Congress and served in the 43d and 44th sessions. In that position he made a good record. He engaged in the manufacture of lumber and salt.

WILLIAM HERBERT BRADLEY

Senator, 1909-10 and 1911-12, from the Eighteenth District, comprising the counties of Ionia and Montcalm. Was born in Spencer Township, Kent County, Mich., Feb. 26, 1859, and received his education in the public schools, and at Eastman's Business College, Poughkeepsie, N. Y. He worked for three years in his father's store, and five and one-half years in a printing office. From 1880 to 1884 he was engaged in the retail general merchandise business, and from 1884 to 1903 was in the wholesale and retail grocery business. After 1903 he conducted an exclusive wholesale grocery business. Married. He served as Alderman of Greenville, was Mayor in 1908 and again in 1909. In politics a Republican.

ELIAS BRADSHAW

Representative from Wayne County (residence Van Buren Township), 1835 and 1836; Delegate from Wayne County to the First and Second Conventions of Assent, 1836. Was a native of Canada, and of Quaker extraction. The dates of his birth and death are unknown. By reason of his religious tendencies, or from some other cause, he refused to bear arms in the British service in the War of 1812, and was imprisoned for a time as an American sympathizer. After regaining his liberty he came to Michigan, though at what time is unknown. He is first mentioned as a Justice of the Peace in 1831, and was subsequently Supervisor of the then township of Huron, and of Van Buren after it was set off from Huron. He was a man of intelligence and education, numbered surveying among his pursuits, and was County Surveyor in 1837-41, and Associate Judge in the last named year. The period of his public service would define his politics as presumably Democratic.

DAVID H. BRAKE

Representative from Newaygo County, 1923—. Was born in Waterloo, Ontario, Canada, in 1864. In 1865 his parents came to Michigan and located on a farm in Kent County, where he lived until 1897 when he removed to Newaygo County. With the exception of a little more than three years spent in the mercantile business, Mr. Blake has lived all his life on a farm. He was educated in the district school, Caledonia High School and Sweensburg Business College in Grand Rapids. Fraternally he is a member of the Masonic lodge, the Grange and Maccabees. He is a Republican and has held various township offices, being Supervisor of Dayton Township for the past six years.

OSCAR W. BRAMAN

Representative from the Third District of Kent County, 1919-20, 1921-2 and 1923—. Has lived in Kent County all his life, having been born in Plainfield Township, Nov. 2, 1875, of American parents. He was educated in the district school, and the Grand Rapids Business College. Later he took a special course at the Michigan Agricultural College. Both his father and grandfather were fruit growers and Mr. Braman has devoted his life to general farming and fruit growing, specializing on apple culture. He has served as Treasurer of Grand Rapids Township and also Plainfield Township. Mr. Braman is married and has two sons and one daughter. He is a Republican.

NORRIS H. BRANCH

Representative from the First District of Jackson County, 1901-2. Was born in Jackson, Mich., Jan. 25, 1871. He was educated in the high school of that city, and was married Feb. 11, 1891. He successfully engaged in the bakery business, and was elected Alderman of the 4th ward. In politics a Democrat.

CALVIN K. BRANDON

Representative from Wayne County, 1885-6. Was born in New Carlisle, O., Sept. 6, 1841. When one year old his parents removed to Indianapolis, Ind., where they both died within five years. He was then taken to Pennsylvania, the home of his parents. In the common schools he received a limited education. At the age of nineteen he removed to Illinois. Seven days after the siege of Fort Sumpter he enlisted in the Sixteenth Ill. Infantry for three months, but on the 26th of April, 1861, he was mustered into the three years' service. At the expiration of that time he spent a short time in Quincy, Ill., but soon re-enlisted in the 14th Ill. Infantry, and was chosen Captain of Co. E of said regiment; was detailed as commissary of subsistence and general ordnance officer of General Stolbrand's brigade, 17th army corps, and served in this capacity until he was mustered out of the service September, 1865. He settled in Saline County, Mo., in 1866, as a stock farmer. He removed in July, 1872, to Hamtramck, Mich. He engaged in manufacturing cooperage materials and dealing in real estate. In politics a Republican.

LYMAN A. BRANT

Representative from Wayne County, 1883-4 and 1885-6. Was born at Great Bend. Pa., Jan. 20, 1848, and is descended from the early Dutch settlers of New Jersey. He received his primary instruction in the village school, and pursued advanced studies in the graded schools of Binghampton, N. Y., and the Susquehanna Seminary. In 1861 he began an apprenticeship in the printers' trade in the office of the Binghampton *Republican*. Having learned his trade, he made an extended tour through the southwestern and western states, which terminated in October, 1868, when he took up his permanent abode in Detroit. Since that date a large portion of his time was employed in the job rooms of the *Free Press* of that city. Mr. Brant took an active interest in political affairs for a number of years, and his first aspirations in that direction were rewarded by his election as Representative by the Democrats and workingmen of Detroit, to the Legislature of 1883-4. In 1884 he was nominated by the Labor party and endorsed by the Democrats. He was also a State Fish Commissioner.

GUS A. BRAUN

Representative from Huron County, 1923- . Was born in Ann Arbor, March 15, 1865, of German parentage. He was educated in the public schools of Detroit and for ten years followed the occupation of painting and decorating; since then he has engaged in farming. He is married and has a family. Mr. Braun has held the offices of Treasurer and Supervisor of Chandler Township, and Treasurer of Huron County. He is a Republican.

BARTLEY BREEN

Representative from Menominee County. 1887-8. Was born in the province of New Brunswick, Jan. 22, 1834. His business was that of buying and selling pine and mineral lands. During the Civil War he was a member of Battery L, 1st Ill. light artillery, three years and seven months. He was Supervisor of the 4th ward of Menominee city, and was elected Representative on the Fusion ticket. He was defeated for Congress in February, 1888.

EDWARD BREITUNG

Representative from Marquette County, 1873-4; Senator from the Thirty-first District, 1877-8; and member of Congress, 1883-5. Was born Nov. 10, 1831, in the city of Schalkan, Duchy of Saxe-Meiningen, and was the son of a Lutheran clergyman. He graduated from the college of mining at Meiningen in 1849, and came to Michigan the same year, making his home in Kalamazoo County. He attended school at Richland several months to acquire a knowledge of the English language. Then he became a clerk in a store at Kalamazoo. In 1851 he went to Detroit, where he remained four years, and removed to Marquette in 1855. There he engaged in mercantile business, also in exploring and buying and selling mineral lands. He removed to Negaunee in 1859 and continued his mercantile business until 1864, when he gave his entire attention to mining and mining interests. He was engaged in running the Pioneer Furnace at Negaunee; was superintendent of the Washington and Republic Iron Companies; located iron mines in the Menominee and Vermillion ranges; and was interested in gold and silver mining in Colorado. He was Mayor of Negaunee in 1880, 1882 and 1883, and held other positions. In politics he was an ardent and leading Republican. He was a delegate to the National Republican Convention of 1876. After serving one term in Congress he declined a second term. He acquired a large fortune and was a leading operator in mining property. In religion he was a Lutheran. He died Mar. 3, 1847.

VINCENT M. BRENNAN

Senator from the Second District of Wayne County, 1919-20; and member of Congress, 1921-2. Was born at Mt. Clemens, Mich., Apr. 22, 1890, of American descent. He was educated at Sts. Peter and Paul's Parochial School of Detroit, the Detroit College and Harvard University, graduating from the law department of the latter institution in 1912. In October of that year he was admitted to practice in the Supreme Court of Michigan. Two years later he received the degree of A. M. from the University of Detroit. During 1914 he was associated in the law business with former Attorney General Otto Kirchner, and during the following year with Hon. Alexander J. Groesbeck, present Governor of Michigan. In June, 1915, he won a civil service appointment of assistant corporation counsel of the City of Detroit. The following March he was admitted to practice before the Supreme Court of the United States. Mr. Brennan is married and has one daughter. In politics a Republican.

CHARLES E. BRENNER

Representative from the First District of Saginaw, 1893-4. Was born in Overath, Rhine Province, Prussia, Jan. 1, 1838. At the age of eleven years he came to America, landing at New York, where he remained one year and came to Saginaw with his parents in 1850. He acquired his early education at the public schools in Germany and New York, and attended school two years after coming to Saginaw. From 1857-65 he was in the mines of Colorado, Montana, British Columbia, Idaho and Washington. He returned to Saginaw for a short visit but was detained in an official capacity. He was appointed City Marshal in 1866, and in 1868 was made Deputy Sheriff. In 1880 he was elected Recorder of the city. From 1868 to 1875 he served as Constable and from 1875-85 as Justice of the Peace. In the fall of 1885 he was admitted to the bar and engaged as practicing attorney and

real estate dealer. In 1890 he was elected the first Recorder of the consolidated
city of Saginaw. In politics a Democrat.

JOHN BREWER

Representative from Washtenaw County, 1835 and 1836. His postoffice address
was Ypsilanti. (Further data not obtainable).

MARK S. BREWER

Senator from Oakland County, 1873-4; and member of Congress, 1877-9, 1879-81,
1887-9 and 1889-91. Was born Oct. 22, 1837, in Addison, Oakland County, Mich.
He worked upon his father's farm until he was nineteen years of age; was educated
at Romeo and Oxford academies; commenced reading law in 1861 with ex-Governor
Wisner and Hon. M. E. Crofoot, and in 1864 was admitted to the bar at Pontiac,
in his native county. He was Circuit Court Commissioner for Oakland County in
1866-7-8-9; was City Attorney of Pontiac in 1866-7; was elected to the State Senate
of Michigan in 1872 and served two years; was elected to the 45th Congress, and
re-elected to the 46th Congress; was appointed Consul General at Berlin, Germany,
June 30, 1881, by the late President Garfield, and served in that position until
June 8, 1885, when he returned to Pontiac, his home, and entered once more
upon the practice of his profession. On Sept. 10, 1886 he was unanimously renominated by the Republican party as its candidate for the 50th Congress, and
on Nov. 2 was duly elected, and was re-elected to the 51st Congress. Deceased.

WILLIAM W. BREWSTER

Representative from Hillsdale County, 1859-60. Was born in Waterloo, N. Y.,
Apr. 11, 1820, and was a lineal descendant of Elder William Brewster, of the
Mayflower. His childhood and youth were spent in different localities in New
York State until 1837, when he moved to Medina, Mich. Later he resided in
Hillsdale County, and in Detroit, removing to Hudson in 1870, where he resided
until his death, Nov. 28, 1886. He was a scholarly man, a close student and
constant reader. Leaving school from ill health at the age of fourteen he ultimately gained a fund of information seldom equalled by those who complete a
college course. He was Clerk of Hillsdale County, Deputy Internal Revenue Collector at Detroit for three years, and for a considerable period Recorder of Hudson.
In politics he was a Republican. In religion he was a Presbyterian. Tolerant
of opinions differing from his own, he was a self-reliant man and a consistent
christian. He died at Hudson, Nov. 28, 1886.

WILLIS FILLMORE BRICKER

Representative from Ionia County, 1897-8, 1911-12 and 1913-14. Was born at Ada,
Hardin County, O., May 20, 1854, of Dutch and English descent. His education
was acquired in the district schools. He came to Ionia County, Mich., in 1867,
locating in Boston Township. He engaged in the dry goods, bazaar and clothing
business and was owner of two large farms near Belding; also dealt extensively
in Belding real estate. In politics a Democrat. He was elected Alderman of
Belding and Mayor several terms.

HENRY P. BRIDGE

Senator from the Sixth District, 1840-1. Was born at Littleton, Mass., in 1808. He came to Michigan in 1836, and settled at Grand Rapids, then called Kent. Meeting with pecuniary reverses, he went to Detroit in 1845, and formed the commission house of Bridge & Lewis, with Alexander Lewis for partner. This house became the leading one in that line of business in the State. He was the first president of the Detroit Board of Trade in 1856, and held that position three years, and on his retirement was elected a life member of the Board. He was for several years Collector of Detroit, and was so universally esteemed by all that he received the nomination of Mayor, both from Democratic and Republican parties. He was in politics a Democrat. He died Jan. 20, 1884.

CHARLES BRIGGS

Representative from Houghton County, 1879-80. Was born at Cincinnatus, Cortland County, N. Y., November, 1837. He received an academic education, and came to Michigan from Wisconsin, August, 1864. By occupation he was merchant. Politics was Republican.

DANIEL B. BRIGGS

State Superintendent of Public Instruction, 1873-7. Was born at Adams, Mass., Feb. 13, 1829. His parents were natives of that State. He received an academical education, and entered Williams College in 1844, graduating in 1848. He studied law and was admitted to practice in 1850. For three years he was principal of the high school in his native town, and also a member of the school committee. He removed to Romeo, Mich., in March, 1854, and entered upon the practice of law. In 1855 he became principal of the Dickinson Institute, formerly a branch of the State University, where he remained three years. In 1858-9 and 1860 he was principal of the High School at Ann Arbor; then for five years held the same position at Jackson. In 1867 he returned to Macomb County and engaged in farming. In April, 1867 he was elected Superintendent of Schools for Macomb County, which position he held for four years. During his last official term he was president of the State Association of County Superintendents. He was director of the Romeo union school district for eight years; and was for many years secretary of the County Agricultural Society. In 1879 he became Deputy Secretary of State and held that position until 1883. He was a Republican in politics. He died at Lansing, Jan. 7, 1902.

EDWARD L. BRIGGS

Representative from Kent County, 1873-4 and 1875-6. Was born in the town of Skaneateles, Onondaga County, N. Y., July 30, 1830. Mr. Briggs was educated in a common school. In 1834 his parents removed to Michigan and settled in Washtenaw County. In 1850 he removed to Grand Rapids. He was timber agent for the State land office from 1859 to 1865. Mr. Briggs' occupation was that of a farmer.

F. MARKHAM BRIGGS

Senator, 1895-6, from the First District, composed of the ninth, eleventh, thirteenth and fifteenth wards of the city of Detroit, and the townships of Greenfield, Grosse

Pointe, Hamtramck, Livonia, Plymouth and Redford, Wayne County. Was born in Livonia Township, Aug. 19, 1840. He attended the Plymouth High School and the State Normal; settled on a farm in Livonia Township where he lived for many years. In politics a Republican. He held the office of Justice of the Peace of his township.

GEORGE G. BRIGGS

Representative from Kent County, 1869-70. Was born in Wayne County, Mich., Jan. 25, 1838. When young he became a clerk in a store at Battle Creek where he remained three years, afterwards for a time attending Olivet College. In 1862 he enlisted in the 7th Mich. Cavalry and served with his regiment in the army of the Potomac during the war, the regiment forming part of the Michigan Cavalry Brigade under General Custer and taking part in sixty-three battles. He was promoted from grade to grade, and became Colonel of the regiment in 1864. At the close of the war his regiment was sent West and remained in Utah until late in 1865. He was a merchant and manufacturer. In 1868 he was a delegate to the Republican National Convention.

HENRY C. BRIGGS

Senator from the Nineteenth District, 1861-2. Was born June 29, 1831, at West Haven, Rutland County, Vt. His parents, Noah and Sarah (Kenyon) Briggs, removed to Michigan in 1836, and settled on a farm in Allegan County. He attended district school, and as a student first entered Kalamazoo College, and afterwards the State University. In 1856 he was elected Clerk of Allegan County, and held the office four years. He was State Senator in 1861-2 and served one regular and one special session, when he resigned, was admitted to the bar, and removed to Kalamazoo, where he served as Prosecuting Attorney for four years. In 1868 he was elected Judge of Probate of Kalamazoo County, and held the position for eight years. He took a strong interest in religious and temperance questions, and aided in educational matters, especially those relating to Kalamazoo College. In politics a Republican. He was a member of the Baptist Church, and for many years was a Sabbath School superintendent.

ROBERT V. BRIGGS

Representative from Wayne County, 1869-70; and Senator from the Third District, 1871-2. Was born at Potter, Yates County, N. Y., Aug. 12, 1837. He received an academic education, and at the age of nineteen commenced the study of law, and was admitted to the bar in 1858. In 1859 he came to Michigan and commenced the practice of the law at St. Johns, and the next spring was elected village Clerk. In the fall he went to Mississippi and remained until the fall of 1861, when he returned and settled at Wayne. In 1864 he removed to Wyandotte, where he engaged in practice. He was Justice of the Peace, and many years City Attorney. In 1872 he was a delegate to the convention at Louisville, which nominated Charles O'Connor for President. He was always a Democrat.

JOHN BRISKE

Representative from the First District of Bay County, 1889-90. Was born in Prussia, of Polish parents, June 14, 1845. By occupation he was a general merchant.

He held the office of Supervisor. Mr. Briske was elected to the House of 1889-90 on the Democratic ticket.

ELI H. BRISTOL

Representative from Oakland County, 1853-4. Was born in Livingston County, N. Y., Apr. 27, 1803. By occupation he was a farmer, in politics a Whig. He came to St. Joseph County, Mich., in 1835, removed to Commerce, Oakland County, in 1846, and died at Pontiac, July 29, 1871. For several terms he was a Supervisor.

FRED W. BRISTOW

Representative from the Second District of Wayne County, 1923—. Was born in Greenfield Township, Wayne County, June 7, 1875. Mr. Bristow is married and has four children; he has always resided on a farm. He has held the offices of Township Clerk, Township Treasurer and Supervisor, which last named office he has held for the past seven years. He is also director and vice-president of the Strathmoor State Bank. Mr. Bristow is a Republican.

CALVIN BRITAIN

Member of the Legislative Council, 1832-3 and 1834-5; Senator from the Third District, 1835-7; Representative from Berrien County, 1847-8 and 1850-1; Delegate from Berrien County to the Constitutional Convention of 1850; and Lieutenant Governor, 1852-3. Was born in Jefferson County, N. Y., in 1800, came to Michigan in 1827, and was the first settler in the town of St. Joseph, Berrien County. He was for a short time connected with the Carey mission. He preempted land in 1827 and 1829, but the survey was not made by government until 1830. He remained a citizen of the town from 1829 until his death, Jan. 18, 1862. He was one of the prominent men of Michigan in pioneer days. In politics he was a Democrat. He never married. He laid out the village of St. Joseph, first known as Newberry.

ROSWELL BRITTON

Representative from Kent County, 1835 and 1836. Was born in the State or Vermont, June 16, 1789, and died June 2, 1850. He came to Michigan in 1824, and settled in Kent County in 1834, where he built a sawmill and operated it for a number of years, when he engaged in farming. Politically he was a Democrat. He died June, 1850.

MARTIN W. BROCK

Representative from the Second District of Bay County, 1887-8. Was born in Danby, Tompkins County, N. Y., July 21, 1838. His early life was passed partly in New York and partly in Pennsylvania. He came to Michigan in 1856, remaining in Oakland County until October, 1865, when he removed to Bay County. He was elected Alderman of what was Lake City, afterwards Wenona, now West Bay City, and continued to hold that office for four years; he was Supervisor from 1871 to 1874. He was elected Sheriff of Bay County and held that office four years, was manager of the West Bay City Manufacturing Company. He was a farmer. In politics a Republican. In 1885 he was elected Treasurer of the township of Monitor. He was married Apr. 5, 1860, to Miss Sarah J. Armstrong, of New York.

JAMES E. BROCKWAY

Representative from the First District of Bay County, 1905-6. Was born at Brockway, St. Clair County, Mich., Nov. 30, 1872. He lived at Brockway and Port Huron until thirteen years of age, and then went to Au Sable and Oscoda, and tallied and inspected lumber during the summer months, attending school winters. He graduated from the Au Sable High School, paid his way through college, and finished his education at the Northern Indiana Normal University. He was admitted to the bar in 1895, practiced his profession separately until 1899, when he formed a partnership with Hon. Devere Hall, of Bay City, under the firm name of Hall & Brockway. Mr. Brockway was in active service in the Santiago campaign in Cuba with the 33d Mich. Vol. Inf. In 1901 and 1902 he was Assistant Adjutant General of Spanish War Veterans in the United States; also Senior Vice Commander of the Michigan Corps Spanish War Veterans and Judge Advocate General for the United States in the National League of Veterans and Sons. In politics a Republican. He held the office of Circuit Court Commissioner from 1898 to 1902.

WILLIAM H. BROCKWAY

Senator from the Fourteenth District, 1855-6; and Representative from Calhoun County, 1865-6 and 1871-2. Was born in Morristown, Orleans County, Vt., Feb. 24, 1813. In 1820 he removed with his parents to Malone, N. Y., where he worked with his father, who was a blacksmith, and had little opportunity for an education. He came to Detroit in 1831, and worked as a blacksmith in Dexter and Ypsilanti. He taught the first school in Dexter, then taught the Wyandot Indians at Flat Rock. He was licensed as a Methodist preacher in 1833, and had many locations, including the Indian mission at Lake Superior. He was Chaplain at Fort Brady for eight years. From 1848 to 1855 he was financial agent of what is now Albion College, and its first success is largely due to his exertions. After 1858 he was largely engaged in real estate and general business. He was the contractor in building the division of the Lake Shore railroad from Jonesville to Lansing. He was sergeant-at-arms of the Senate in 1863; Trustee of the village of Albion for many years and several years its President; trustee of Albion College for a long period and many years its treasurer; for sixteen months Chaplain of the 16th Mich. Infantry; and was a member of many societies. At first a Democrat, he was a Republican after 1854. He died at his home in Albion, Oct. 21, 1891.

THORNTON F. BRODHEAD

Senator from the Sixth District, 1850, and from the Third District, 1859-60. Was a native of New Hampshire, born, 1822, and came to Pontiac when a stripling, residing with his brother there. In 1845 he was secretary of the State Senate, having previously served a year or two as Assistant Secretary of State. In the summer of 1846 he took a commission as Lieutenant in a company formed at Pontiac for service in the Mexican War, and soon after reaching the field he was assigned to duty on the staff of Gen. Pierce, where he served until the close of the war. He subsequently removed to Detroit and was connected with the management of daily paper there, 1849-52. In 1853 he was commissioned by President Pierce as Postmaster at Detroit. He held the office during the Pierce administration, and at the close of his term took up his residence on Grosse Ile. Upon the breaking out of the Civil War he sought service and was commissioned to raise the first regiment of Mich. Cavalry, of which he became Colonel. Col. Brodhead was mortally wounded at the second battle of Manassas (or Bull Run), Aug. 30, 1862, and died Sept. 5. His remains were brought to Detroit for burial, and the funeral services, with military honors, were held at St. Paul's Episcopal Church. Sept. 10. In politics he was a Democrat.

CLARK L. BRODY

Member of the State Board of Agriculture, 1921—. Was born at Three Rivers, February 1, 1879. He acquired his education in the Constantine High School, Three Rivers Business College and Michigan Agricultural College, graduating from the last named institution with the class of '04. Always interested in agriculture in all its branches, he developed a splendid herd of registered Holstein cattle during the ten years following his graduation. In 1915 he became county agricultural agent in St. Clair County and held that position until called by the State Farm Bureau, in 1921, to become its secretary and manager. On October 7, 1921, he was appointed by Governor Alex J. Groesbeck, to fill the vacancy on the State Board of Agriculture caused by the resignation of John W. Beaumont. He was elected April 2, 1923.

FLAVIUS LIONEL BROOKE

Justice of the Supreme Court, 1908-21. Was born in Norfolk County, Ont., Canada, Oct. 7, 1858. He was educated in the Canadian common schools; Albert University, Belleville, Ont.; and Osgoode Hall, Toronto, Ont. At the age of nineteen he entered the University, taking a two years's course in art; at the age of twenty began the reading of law and spent one year in Belleville and four years in Toronto, the four years in Toronto being in the law offices of Mowat, MacLennan & Downey. Mr. Mowat was then Attorney General for Ontario and leader of the Liberal party. Mr. Brooke was admitted to practice at Toronto in 1884, removed to Detroit in 1885, and entered the office of Col. John Atkinson and Judge Isaac Marston. In 1887 the firm of Atkinson, Carpenter and Brooke was formed and conducted for several years until Judge Carpenter went on the bench. The law firm of Brooke & Spaulding was then formed and continued from 1892 to 1896, after which Mr. Brooke continued the practice of law alone until 1900. He was married Nov. 24, 1884. He was appointed by President McKinley supervisor of the census for the first district of Michigan. Mr. Brooke was elected Judge of the Third Judicial Circuit, to fill vacancy, in November, 1900, and re-elected Apr. 3, 1905. He was appointed a Justice of the Supreme Court, Nov. 7, 1908, and was elected to fill the vacancy, caused by the resignation of Justice Carpenter, Nov. 3, 1908. Was re-elected Apr. 5, 1915, for the term ending Dec. 31, 1923. He died Jan. 21, 1921.

JOHN A. BROOKS

Representative from Newaygo and other counties, 1857-8 and 1859-60. Was born in Haverill. N. H.. May 14. 1803. He settled at Newaygo in 1841, and founded the village of Newaygo in 1852. He constructed a canal across the Muskegon flats.

planning the work, and made it a success. Previously, he had obtained an appropriation of internal improvement lands for the purpose. He engaged in lumbering, and by his energy built up the village, established the county seat, erected a first-class hotel, built a church, procured capital to dam the river, followed by the building of mills, and the manufacture of lumber on a large scale. He was originally a Whig, but became a Republican in 1854. During the war he was in the pay-master department in Missouri. He was a born leader, and had by his suavity of manner and fine address, great control over men. He was a man of great intelligence and energy, and did more for the place of his adoption than any other man. He died May 20, 1866.

NATHANIEL W. BROOKS

Representative from St. Clair County, 1847. Was born in Castine, Me., Aug. 27, 1808. He moved with his father's family from Maine to Columbus, O., in 1828, came to Detroit in 1836, and was in the grocery business there until 1843; then engaged in lumbering at Algonac, St. Clair County, where he resided thirteen years, when he returned to Detroit. He was an active Republican, and served as Alderman of the First Ward, and received the nomination for Mayor, but declined to run. He died at Detroit, Sept. 30, 1872.

ARCHIBALD BROOMFIELD

Delegate in the Constitutional Convention of 1907-8 from the Twenty-fifth District, Newaygo, Mecosta, Isabella and Osceola counties. Was born on a farm in Isabella County in 1875, of Scotch descent. He was educated in the district schools and worked on the farm until 1896, when he attended the Ferris Institute at Big Rapids. He graduated from the University of Michigan in 1902, taking the degree of LL. B. He immediately began the practice of law in Big Rapids, forming a partnership with A. B. Cogger. In 1909 he was appointed City Attorney of Big Rapids.

P. C. H. BROTHERSON

Representative from Washtenaw County, 1846. Was born in the State of New York in 1811. He was a miller by occupation, and in politics a Whig. He died in Manchester, Sept. 16, 1852.

CHARLES A. BROTT

Representative, 1907-8, from the Missaukee District, comprising the counties of Kalkaska and Missaukee. Was born in Casnovia Township, Muskegon County, Mich., Oct. 24, 1858, of Dutch and English parents. He lived on a farm and attended a district school until he was twenty-three years old, when he learned the carpenter's trade, following that occupation for five years. Mr. Brott then went to Moorland where for eight years he was quite extensively interested in the manufacture of lumber and shingles, also in the mercantile business. Then engaged in the mercantile business in the village of Boardman. In politics a Republican. He held the offices of Postmaster of Moorland, Clerk of Moorland Township, Muskegon County, and Supervisor of Boardman Township, Kalkaska County.

BURNEY E. BROWER

Representative from the First District of Jackson County, 1917-18 and 1919-20; and Senator from the Tenth District, 1921-2 and 1923—. Was born on a farm in Ingham County, June 18, 1880, and is of Dutch-Irish descent. He was educated in the district schools and Stockbridge High School from which he graduated in 1900. After teaching three years he entered Valparaiso University, graduating from the law department in 1906 and from Northwestern University Law School, Chicago, in 1907, since which time he has engaged in the practice of law. He is married and has one daughter. In politics he is a Republican. He was assistant Prosecuting Attorney of Jackson County in 1913-14.

AARON B. BROWN

Senator, 1891-2 from the Twenty-third District, comprising the counties of Mecosta and Montcalm. Was born at Chagrin Falls, O., Mar. 20, 1845; came to Michigan with his parents in 1861, and settled in Montcalm County, near the banks of Crystal Lake, when that country was a wilderness. When he became of age he came into possession of the homestead, which he sold in 1877, and moved to a farm in the town of Bushnell, Montcalm County. His early education was obtained in the country schools of his native place; at twelve he entered the Chagrin Falls Academy, where he remained until coming to Michigan; one year at the Lansing High School, in 1863 and 1864, completed his education. He taught fifteen winters in the country schools of Montcalm County, and was principal of the Sheridan School in 1883 and 1884. He held several township offices and was a member of the county board of school examiners, and was a candidate for Representative on the Fusion ticket in 1884. In politics a Republican until 1874; in 1876 joined the Greenback movement and voted for Peter Cooper, and subsequently acted quite independent politically, voting for Garfield in 1880, although no longer acting with the Republican party. He was nominated for the Senate of 1891-2 by the Patrons of Industry.

ADDISON MAKEPEACE BROWN

Senator, 1899-1900, from the Ninth District, comprising the counties of Kalamazoo and Calhoun. Was born at Schoolcraft, Kalamazoo County, Mich., Feb. 15, 1859. His early education was acquired in the public schools of his native village, and in 1883 he was graduated from the University of Michigan with the degree of A. B. At the close of his university studies he assumed control of his father's farms. He served as Director of the Board of Education at Schoolcraft. He was twice elected Justice of Peace; was President of the village of Schoolcraft two terms; was for several years secretary of the Kalamazoo County Pioneer Association; also President of the Kalamazoo County Husbandman's Club. In politics a Republican.

ALVARADO BROWN

Representative from Branch County, 1847 and 1848; and Delegate from Branch County to the Constitutional Convention of 1850. Was born in Newport, Herkimer County, N. Y., Jan. 15, 1809. He received a common school and academical education. He went at an early day to York, Ind., and took up several lots, which he afterwards exchanged for a farm in Quincy, Mich. He was a Town Clerk from 1841 to 1847. Deceased.

AMMON BROWN

Delegate from the First District to the Constitutional Convention of 1835; from Wayne County to the First Convention of Assent, 1836; and from Wayne County to the Constitutional Convention of 1850; and Representative from Wayne County 1835-7. Was born in Dutchess County, N. Y., Jan. 15, 1798, subsequently removed to Wayne County, that State, and to Wayne County, Mich., in 1824 settling in the township of Nankin as a farmer, his early occupation having been that of a teacher. His services were always in demand in his township in local offices of all grades. He held an influential position in the politics of Wayne County for more than forty years. He also held the position of County Auditor of Wayne County, for a number of years, and of County Superintendent of the Poor. He enjoyed in a marked degree, throughout his life, the confidence of his fellow citizens. He was a Democrat in politics. He became a resident of the village of Wayne, in 1854, and died there May 19, 1882.

AMOS S. BROWN

Representative from Van Buren County, 1867-8. Was born in Essex, Chittenden County, Vt., in 1819. He settled in Michigan in 1835, and the present village of Breedsville, Van Buren County. Commencing life with little, by industry and superior financial ability, he accumulated a large property, being alike successful in farming, lumbering and milling. He aided liberally in all public improvements, and never forgot the needy. He was for twenty-five years Supervisor of the town of Columbia. In politics he was a Republican. He died at St. Paul, Minn., where he had gone for health, Sept. 4, 1872.

ASAHEL BROWN

Delegate from Branch County to the Constitutional Convention of 1850, also that of 1867; and Senator from the Fifteenth District, 1857-8 and 1859-60. Was born in Stafford, N. J., Apr. 9, 1803. He removed with his parents to western New York when young, where he was brought up to farming and received a common school education. In 1833 he came to Michigan, first settling on a farm in Palmyra, but in 1836 removing to a farm in Algansee, Branch County. The first town meeting was held in his log cabin in 1838, and he was elected the first Supervisor, which he held consecutively until 1851, also in 1853, 1856, 1857 and from 1861 to 1865. He was also for several years Justice of the Peace. He was a strong Whig until 1854, then a Republican. He owned a large farm, and for several years was president of the Branch County Farmer's Mutual Fire Insurance Company. He died June 8, 1874.

BENJAMIN BROWN

Representative from Oakland County, 1859-60. Was born in Yarmouth, England, Nov. 1, 1818, and came to America with his father in 1827. His father purchased a farm near Rochester, N. Y., where they lived five years. His father removed to Novi, Mich., in 1832, and located a farm, where the family encountered all the hardships of the first pioneers. The son worked on the farm until 1844, receiving a common school education, and then went into mercantile business at Walled Lake, which he continued until 1871, when he removed to Ann Arbor. He was Postmaster at Walled Lake ten years. Justice fourteen years, was Supervisor at Ann Arbor, and a candidate for Mayor. He was a Republican after 1854.

CHARLES BROWN

Representative from Lenawee County, 1875-6. Was born in the town of Scipio, County of Cayuga, N. Y., Jan. 8, 1808. He received a common school education and engaged in teaching for several years. He removed to Medina, Lenawee County, in 1852. He held the offices of Township Clerk, Postmaster, and County Superintendent of the Poor. His business was that of a merchant. In politics he was a Republican.

CHARLES BROWN

Representative from the Second District of Kalamazoo County, 1883-4 and 1885-6. Was born in the township of Brady, Kalamazoo County, Mich., in 1847. He was reared upon a farm. After attaining manhood he engaged in teaching school for several years. Occupation was that of farming, residing on the farm his father located in 1835. Mr. Brown held at different times several official positions in his township. In politics he was a Republican. He was Postmaster at Vicksburg for seven years, president of the Farmers' State Bank and member of the Board of Education. He died Oct. 30, 1916.

CHARLES A. BROWN

Representative from the Second District of Genesee County, 1921-2. Was born June 5, 1868, at Athens, O., of Scotch-Irish parents. He was educated in the public schools of Athens, O., and Ohio State University, Columbus, O. He has engaged in the wholesale dry goods business, was for ten years a public accountant. coming to Michigan seven years ago, since which time he has engaged in real estate, loans and insurance business. Mr. Brown is married and has one daughter. He was a member of Genesee County Draft Board and inspector of draft boards of the Lower Peninsula of Michigan, and also served with the American Red Cross overseas during the World War. In politics he is a Republican.

CHARLES H. BROWN

Representative, 1903-4, from the Iron District, comprising the counties of Baraga, Iron, Keweenaw and Ontonagon. Was born in Defiance County. O., on the 13th day of March, 1870. His parents emigrated from Germany to Ohio in 1854, and settled on a farm where he spent his boyhood days. Mr. Brown was educated in the Columbus school. At the age of twenty he moved to Saginaw, Mich., and secured employment as scaler of logs. The following year he moved to Ontonagon, Mich., where he was employed in saw milling. In 1898, he enlisted in the 35th Michigan, which was under Colonel Irish, and was promoted to Corporal. He was mustered out of service in 1899, and moved to Greenland, Ontonagon County. In politics a Republican. He served as member of the Board of Review of Greenland, and chief of the Fire Department.

CHARLES R. BROWN

Representative from Berrien County, 1867-8. Was born in Columbia, Lorain County, O., in 1836; was educated at the Baldwin University; was for a time principal of the Fredonia Academy in Portage County; and in 1855 published a paper in Cuyahoga County. He studied law and in 1860 removed to St. Joseph, Mich. He was Circuit Court Commissioner of Berrien County. He removed to Kalamazoo in 1867, and in 1869 was elected Judge of the 9th Circuit. He edited and published two volumes of "Michigan Nisi Prius Cases."

DANIEL E. BROWN

Member of the State Board of Education, 1863-73. Was born at New Lebanon, Conn., Sept. 7, 1794, educated in the public schools. He served in the War of 1812. He engaged in farming in New York State and afterwards entered the ministry. He was Superintendent of the Indian Mission School at Green Bay, Wis. for four years. He was sent as a home missionary to Flint in 1839 where he built a very fine church. He resigned Aug. 11, 1846 and occupied several pulpits throughout the State. He was elected a member of the State Board of Education, Nov. 4, 1862, and re-elected Nov. 3, 1868. He died at Flint, Aug. 6, 1873. .

DAVID E. BROWN

Representative from Kalamazoo County, 1839 and 1840. Was born in Loudon County, Va., June 20, 1795. He was a graduate of the medical department of the University of Pennsylvania, and was a remarkably well educated physician for that time. He settled at Schoolcraft, Mich., in 1830. He was Whig until that party ceased to exist, then a Democrat. For sometime he was a professor of a medical school established at La Porte, Ind. In 1852 he moved upon a farm in Pavillion, which he made his home until about the time of his death, which occurred May 13, 1871, at Boone, Ia. He was buried at Schoolcraft.

EBENEZER LAKIN BROWN

Representative from Kalamazoo County, 1841; Senator from the Twenty-first District, 1855-6 and from the Eleventh District, 1879-80; and member of the Board of Regents of the University of Michigan, 1858-64. Was born at Plymouth, Vt., Apr. 16, 1809, and was the son of Thomas and Sally Brown. His ancestors came over about 1640. He received a fair academical education, and at the age of twenty-one came to Ann Arbor, thence to Kalamazoo County. At Prairie Ronde he found employment in a store, and afterwards became a partner, and continued in the mercantile business until 1848, when he retired to a farm near Schoolcraft. In politics he was a Whig, then Republican. He was active in 1855 in securing a prohibitory law, and was a strong anti-slavery man. For six years he was president of the Schoolcraft and Three Rivers Railroad, and pushed it through to success. In religious persuasion he was a Baptist. He perfected an incomplete education by hard study, and as a classical scholar translated the Greek odes of Horace, and wrote fine, original, descriptive poems. He died at Schoolcraft, Apr. 12, 1899.

ETHAN A. BROWN

Representative from Berrien County, 1874-5. Was born Aug. 22, 1820, at Willoughby, O. He received a common school education. He removed to Michigan in the spring, 1830. Mr. Brown held the office of Supervisor, Treasurer, and other minor offices. In politics he was a Democrat. He succeeded Evan J. Bonine as Representative in 1874, and died Apr. 28, 1875.

GEORGE BROWN

Representative from Barry County, 1855-6. Was an early settler in that county and was a farmer. He was a member of the forces that turned out in the Toledo War. He died many years ago.

GEORGE BROWN

Representative from the First District of Wayne County, 1919-20 and 1923—. Was born in Dublin, Ireland, in 1863. He was educated at Fearnside Academy, a private school in Dublin. After coming to the United States he worked as reporter on New York and Detroit papers and was war correspondent for the Detroit *News* during the Spanish War. Following the war he entered the commercial field and for several years represented concerns in Brooklyn and Chicago which manufactured farm implements. He moved to Detroit in 1906, and engaged in the general insurance business. He served as secretary of the Board of Education and also a member of the City Board of Estimates. In politics he is a Republican, married and has three sons and one daughter.

GEORGE I. BROWN

Representative from Calhoun County, 1871-2. Was born in Dutchess County, N. Y., in 1816. He was a Republican in politics, and a farmer by occupation. He came to Michigan in 1866, was a wealthy farmer, and a prominent officer and member of the Methodist Church. He died in 1883.

GEORGE W. BROWN

Representative from Jackson County, 1859-60. Was born in Litchfield County, Conn., May 5, 1825. He learned the trade of a miller. He came to Michigan in 1833, resided in Concord and Jackson up to 1850, went to Branch County, studied law and was admitted at Coldwater in 1852. He returned to Jackson in 1853, and resided there until 1861, when he removed to Sault Ste. Marie, which was his home, except two years at Albion. In 1861 he was appointed superintendent of the St. Mary's Falls Ship Canal, and held that position until 1865. He was Prosecuting Attorney and Circuit Court Commissioner of Chippewa County from 1868 to 1876; Register of Deeds and County Clerk from 1876 to 1887. In politics he was first a Republican, then a Democrat.

GILES T. BROWN

Senator from the Twenty-eighth District, comprised of Midland, Gratiot, Clare, Gladwin and Roscommon counties, 1881-2. Was born at Green Oak, Livingston County, Mich., Jan. 28, 1837. Having received an academic education at the Seminary and the Normal School at Ypsilanti, he engaged in teaching for several years. He graduated from the law department of the Michigan University in the spring of 1865, and was admitted to the bar in the same year, by the Supreme Court, in session at Detroit. He removed to Ithaca, Gratiot County, in 1866, practicing law a portion of the time. He held the office of County Superintendent of Schools from 1867 to 1871, and again from 1873 to 1875. He was renominated for the same office, when it was abolished. He held several minor local offices, such as President of the village of Ithaca, and Justice of the Peace. From 1876 to 1881 he was Judge of Probate of Gratiot County. In politics a Republican.

JEFFERSON G. BROWN

Delegate in the Constitutional Convention of 1907-8, from the Eleventh District, St. Clair County. Was born in Kenockee Township, St. Clair County, in 1872, of English and Irish descent. His father was Delmere Brown of the same township, prominent lumberman and farmer. He graduated from the Flint High School. In 1893 he married Edna Green. Mr. Brown was engaged in lumbering and the mill business for seven years; and then a farmer. He held the office of Supervisor for six years.

JOHN S. BROWN

Representative from Hillsdale County, 1843. Was born in Livingston County, N. Y., about 1810, and came to Michigan in 1838. He was a farmer and a Democrat. He removed from Michigan to the West in 1845. Nothing further is known of him.

JOSEPH W. BROWN

Member of the Board of Regents of the University of Michigan, 1839-40. Was born in Falls Township, Bucks County, Pa., Nov. 26, 1793, was of Quaker descent and the youngest of eleven children. In 1824 he removed to Tecumseh, Mich., the village site having been bought by Brown, Evans & Wing. They erected the first saw mill in the county in 1825 and the first grist mill in 1826. In 1832 he was General in the Black Hawk War. From 1833 to 1837 he was largely engaged in the staging route between Detroit and Chicago. Among positions held by him were the following: Adjutant in regular cavalry of New York veterans in 1847; Captain in 1818 and Lieutenant Colonel in 1819 of the 108th New York; first Judge of Lenawee County, 1826; Colonel 8th Mich. Militia, 1829; Commander of Michigan troops in the Toledo War; Register of the land office at Ionia, 1836; Brigadier General, 1839. He was a member of the Michigan Pioneer and Historical Society. He died at Tecumseh, Mich., Dec. 9, 1880.

NORRIS J. BROWN

Representative from the First District of Montcalm County, 1889-90. Was born in Granby Township, Oswego County, N. Y., Apr. 21, 1852. His parents removed to Branch County, Mich., when he was three years old, and shortly afterwards to the township of Danby, in Ionia County, where he continued to reside on a farm until he was fourteen years of age. He then removed with his parents to Portland, Mich., where he attended the Union School for two years, and then began teaching district schools. In 1872 he commenced the study of law with Hon. A. Williams of Ionia, and was admitted to the bar in 1874. He afterwards taught the Union School of Sheridan, Mich., and commenced the practice of law in that village in April, 1875. He removed to Stanton in December, 1876. He served as Township and City Clerk, City Attorney, Circuit Court Commissioner, and from 1881 to 1885 was Prosecuting Attorney of Montcalm County. At the judicial convention in 1887 he received the unanimous support of the delegates of his own county for Circuit Judge—O. L. Spaulding of St. Johns being finally nominated. He was elected to the house of 1889-90 on the Republican ticket.

ROBERT BROWN

Representative from the county of Isabella, 1895-6. Was born in Hamden, Delaware County, N. Y., Apr. 20, 1847, of Scotch parents. His early education was acquired in the common schools, supplemented by one term at the Andes Collegiate Institute, N. Y. With the exception of teaching school one term and clerking one year in a country store, he was continually engaged at farm labor until 1876, when he came to Michigan and engaged as traveling salesman for a nursery firm, which occupation he followed for about twelve years, and engaged in the hotel business at Dushville, Isabella County. During President Harrison's administration he was Postmaster at Dushville, and in 1892 removed to a farm. In politics a Republican. He was never a candidate for any office before he was elected to the House of 1895-6.

SAMUEL B. BROWN

Representative from Hillsdale County, 1877-8 and 1879-80. Was born in Pittstown, Rensselaer County, N. Y., Oct. 23, 1820. He was educated in the common schools, and removed to Michigan in 1862. In April, 1864, he settled in Ransom, Hillsdale County; in 1865 was elected Justice of the Peace and held the office ten years. In 1873 and 1874 he was chosen Supervisor of the town. By occupation he was a farmer, in politics a Republican.

STEPHEN F. BROWN

Representative from Kalamazoo County, 1857-8 and 1859-60; and Senator from the Twentieth District, 1861-2 and 1865-6, and from the Tenth District, 1885-6. Was born in Loudon County, Va., Dec. 31, 1819. When a lad of eleven years of age, he came with his parents to the township of Schoolcraft, Kalamazoo County. Mr. Brown was a farmer all his life-time and was elected the first master of the State Grange, upon its organization, and then held the office of treasurer of that body continuously from the expiration of his term as master, until the annual meeting in December, 1884, when he declined another re-election. In politics he was a Republican. He died June 2, 1893.

THOMAS H. BROWN

Delegate to the Constitutional Convention of 1907-8; and Representative from the Second District of Wayne County, 1909-10, and 1911-12. Was born in Greenfield

Township, Wayne County, Mich., Jan. 30, 1860, of English descent. He acquired his education in the district schools of Wayne County. He was married to Louise Granzow in 1887. By occupation a farmer. In politics a Republican. He served as Supervisor of Greenfield Township for many years.

WILLIAM BROWN

Member of the Legislative Council from Wayne County, 1828-9 and 1830-1. Was a physician by profession, but no information is obtainable as to his nativity or the time of his death. The records, however, show him to have been a man of marked prominence in the local councils. He was a trustee of the corporation of Detroit in 1805, was one of the signers of the protest against the British General Proctor's order of expulsion in 1813, a director of the newly organized bank of Michigan in 1818, County Commissioner in 1820 and Trustee of the University in 1821. Politically he was doubtless in sympathy with the prevailing sentiment of the time.

WILLIAM E. BROWN

Senator, 1903-4 and 1905-6, from the Twenty-first District, comprising the counties of Lapeer and Tuscola; and Delegate to the Constitution Convention of 1907-8 from the Twenty-first District. Was born on his father's farm in the township of Hadley, Lapeer County, Mich., Dec. 25, 1863. He was educated in the public schools and afterward taught in district and village schools for five years. He graduated from the law department of the University of Michigan in 1887, and was admitted to practice the same year by the Supreme Court. He commenced the practice of law at Imlay City and continued to live there until elected Prosecuting Attorney in 1892, when he moved to Lapeer. He was married in 1890 to Grace E. Palmer of Imlay City. Mr. Brown served two terms as Prosecuting Attorney, and subsequently engaged in the practice of law. An active member of several secret societies.

WILLIAM G. BROWN

Representative from Jackson County, 1867-8. Was born in Tompkins County, N. Y., Mar. 9, 1821. In 1836 he came with his father and settled at Parma. He received most of his education in the State of New York. He was Supervisor of his town many years. He was successful in business and owned one of the largest farms in Jackson County. In religion he was a Methodist, in politics a Republican.

HENRY WHEELOCK BROWNE

Representative from the First District of Ionia County, 1889-90. Was born in Medway, Mass., Nov. 24, 1831. He received his education in the Medway common and high school, and entered Harvard University Medical Department in 1853, graduating in March, 1856. He practiced his profession in his native town until the beginning of the War of the Rebellion. May, 1861, he raised a company, which was mustered into the 2d Mass. Vols. In the fall of 1861 he enlisted as private in Company I, 16th Mass. Vols.; was later commissioned Surgeon 76th U. S. C. T.; mustered out and honorably discharged, Dec. 31, 1865. In the summer of 1869 he removed to Michigan, and with the exception of a short time spent in the township of Lebanon, in Clinton County, resided at Hubbardston, engaged in the practice of his profession. He was admitted to the bar in the Circuit Court of Clinton County in January, 1883. He served as Justice of the Peace of the township of Lebanon, Trustee and President of the Village of Hubbardston, and commander of G. A. R. Post No. 234; represented his township on county committees, etc., and was elected to the Legislature in 1888 on the Republican ticket.

EDMUND BROWNELL

Representative from Lapeer County, 1889-90. Was born at Metamora, Lapeer County in May, 1853, received his education in the common schools of that township, and resided there until 1891, when he removed from the old homestead to his own farm in the township of Hadley. His father, Hon. Ellery A. Brownell, served in the State Legislature in 1867 and again in 1869. Edmund Brownell served as Supervisor of Hadley Township, Vice-President of the First National Bank of Lapeer and one of its directors for a number of years. He was elected to the House of 1899-1900 to fill a vacancy caused by the death of Henry Lee.

ELLERY A. BROWNELL

Representative from Lapeer County in 1867-8 and 1869-70. Was born in Genesee County, N. Y., Mar. 7, 1816. By occupation he was a farmer, in politics a Republican. He settled in Metamora, Lapeer County, in 1838, and moved to Hadley, same county, in 1872. He died in June, 1888.

FRANKLIN BROWNELL

Representative from the First District of Cass County, 1855-6. His postoffice address was Dowagiac. (Further data not obtainable).

GEORGE BROWNELL

Representative from Oakland County, 1835 and 1836. Was born at New Lisbon, N. Y., in May, 1802. He married Clarissa Grant and emigrated to Michigan in 1825, settling at Farmington, where he resided 31 years. He held the office of Postmaster many years, was Captain in the "Toledo War," and filled many minor positions. In 1856 he removed to Utica, Macomb County. He was appointed Justice of the Peace in 1833, and he held that position over forty years. Politically he was a Democrat. He died Aug. 15, 1879.

SEYMOUR BROWNELL

Senator from the Fourth District, 1872. Was born at Farmington, Mich., Feb. 27, 1837. He received a common school education and in 1856 became a merchant at Utica, Mich. He married Helen A. Lawrence in 1857. He was Deputy Postmaster four years, and Postmaster from 1858 to 1861, at Utica, when he resigned, raised Co. "H" of the 2d Mich. Cavalry, went into the field, was commissary of subsistence, with the rank of Captain, served on the staffs of several generals, and in 1864 became chief of subsistence on the staff of General Hunter. He resigned in 1864 and was brevetted Colonel for meritorious services. He was a Supervisor, was one of the directors of the Detroit & Bay City Railroad, and in 1872 built the first thirty miles of that road. In 1873 he removed to Lake Superior, and was manager of the Munising furnace and the Marquette brown stone quarry. In 1879 he was one of the purchasers of the Duluth blast furnace, the company purchasing another furnace and an iron mine in 1882. He sold out in 1884, removed to Detroit and engaged in the mercantile business. He was delegate to the Democratic National Convention in 1868, and was a member of the Democratic State Committee. He was elected Senator to succeed Gilbert Hathaway, deceased.

WILLIAM BROWNELL

Representative from Macomb County, 1857-8 and 1861-2. Was born at Farmington, Mich., Nov. 16, 1830. He was educated in district and select schools. He studied medicine and graduated in the class of 1852 at the Michigan University. He settled at Utica, Macomb County, and except three years in the army, was in practice there until his death, May 22, 1844. He married Jane E. Scudder in 1856, and they had three children. He was a prominent physician and surgeon, and had a large practice. He was for sixteen years a director of the Utica schools. He went out in 1861 as surgeon of the 2nd Mich. Cavalry, and served until the regiment was mustered out in the fall of 1864. In politics a Democrat.

FERDINAND BRUCKER

Member of Congress, 1897-9. Was born Jan. 8, 1858, at Bridgeport, Saginaw County, Mich.; received a common school education and graduated from the law department of the University of Michigan in the class of 1881. He was a lawyer by profession. He served as Alderman of the city of East Saginaw two years, 1882-4; held the office of Judge of Probate for Saginaw County two terms, 1888-96; and was elected to the Fifty-fifth Congress as a Silver Democrat. After leaving Congress he resumed the practice of law.

CHARLES L. BRUNDAGE

Senator, 1893-4 and 1895-6, from the Twenty-third District, composed of the counties of Muskegon and Ottawa. Was born in Steuben County, N. Y., Aug. 17, 1830; was a graduate of the Alfred University and State Normal School, N. Y., and was Superintendent of Schools of Allegany County, N. Y., for six years. In 1874 he came to Michigan, locating at Muskegon. During the war he served in 130th New York and 1st New York Dragoons, was commissioned First Lieutenant, and Nov. 9, 1862, promoted to Captain. At his home in Muskegon he engaged in the drug business. In politics a Republican.

JOHN C. BRUNSON

Representative from Clinton County, 1873-4. Was born in the town of East Bloomfield, Ontario County, N. Y., July 20, 1822. He received an academic education. In 1845 he removed to Michigan and settled in the town of Victor, Clinton County.

He held several offices of public trust in his township. Mr. Brunson was a farmer by occupation. He was long Postmaster at Victor. He died at St. Johns, Feb. 3, 1893.

ELIJAH BRUSH

Treasurer of the Territory of Michigan, 1806-13; and Attorney General, [1807?]-1809. Was born in Bennington, Vt., in 1772. He graduated at Dartmouth College, studied law and settled in Detroit at any early day. He was Attorney General of Michigan Territory until 1809. He served in the War of 1812 as Colonel, and was counsel in the first case to test the right to hold slaves in Michigan. He died, Dec. 14, 1814.

EDWARD C. BRYAN

Representative from the Second District of Wayne County, 1897-8 and 1899-1900. Was born at Portsmouth, O., Aug. 2, 1867; came to Michigan, locating at Wyandotte in 1868, where he acquired his education, graduating from the public schools of said city in 1885. He went to Detroit and engaged in wholesale houses for five years, after which he returned to Wyandotte and engaged in business. In politics a Republican. He was City Clerk for two years.

SIMON D. BRYAN

Representative from Eaton County, 1919-20, 1921-2 and 1923—. Was born on a farm in Brookfield Township, Eaton County, Mich., Aug. 31, 1859, of American parents. He received his education in the district schools of that township, the Charlotte High School and the Northern Indiana Business College at Valparaiso, Ind. He taught school winters for six years, working on his farm in Walton Township, Eaton County, when not teaching. At the same time he acted as school inspector. He served as Supervisor for thirteen years and while holding this office was elected Register of Deeds. Following his election to the latter office, he moved to Charlotte but still retained his interest in his farm. He is a member of Olivet F. & A. M., and of the Charlotte Commandery. Mr. Bryan is married. In politics he is a Republican.

ERNEST J. BRYANT

Representative from the Second District of Lenawee County, 1907-8 and 1909-10; and Senator, 1917-18, 1919-20 and 1921-2, from the Nineteenth District, comprising the counties of Lenawee and Monroe. Was born in Michigan, May 2, 1873, of English parents. He was educated in the Fayette Normal College and the Fayette Business University, of Fayette, O. Mr. Bryant has always been a farmer. He is married and resides on his farm in Lenawee County. In politics a Republican.

PHILIP H. BUCK

Representative from St. Joseph County, 1849. Was born at Amherst, Erie County, N. Y., Jan. 7, 1811. He removed to Sturgis Prairie, Mich., in December, 1828.

He was bred a farmer, but became a merchant. He was several times a Whig candidate for the Legislature. He died at Chicago, Aug. 9, 1886.

WALTER A. BUCKBEE

Representative from Washtenaw County, 1838. Was born in the State of Vermont, in 1807. He was educated in his native State, at an early age commenced to study law, and was admitted to the bar prior to his coming to Ypsilanti in 1837, where he had purchased a fine residence property. He devoted himself to his profession. He died in 1850, leaving a wife and four children.

CHESTER BUCKLEY

Representative from the Third District of Calhoun County, 1857-8 and 1863-4. His postoffice address was Battle Creek. (Further data not obtainable).

PHILO H. BUDLONG

Representative from Calhoun County, 1875-6. Was born in Frankford, Herkimer County, N. Y., May 28, 1821. He removed to Michigan in 1835, and settled in the town of Eckford, Calhoun County. He received a common school education. Mr. Budlong filled two or three township offices, and that of Supervisor for several years. By occupation he was a farmer and lumberman; in politics a Democrat. He died at Harbor Springs, May 26, 1886.

ALEXANDER W. BUEL

Representative from Wayne County, 1838, 1848 and 1859-60; and member of Congress, 1849-51. Was born in Poultney, Vt., in 1813, early manifested an aptness for study, and took the bachelor's degree in college at the age of sixteen, spending, thereafter, some three years in teaching, in literary pursuits, and in legal studies. Coming to Detroit in 1834, he completed his law course in the office of the late Judge Witherell, and was admitted to practice in the spring of 1835. His official career, except as above sketched, was confined to a term or two as Prosecuting Attorney of Wayne County (then by appointment), 1843-6, a further appointment having been declined. He also served as president of the Detroit Young Men's Society (1836) and as a member of the School Board of the city. That he was so early and repeatedly honored with public trusts is evidence of his attainments and of the estimation in which he was held. He was defeated for a re-election to Congress in 1850 by reason of the then rising anti-slavery feeling, he being a Democrat and having supported in Congress the so-called compromise measures of that year. He died at Detroit, Apr. 17, 1868.

AHASUERUS W. BUELL

Representative from Oakland County, 1863. Was born at Northampton, Fulton County, N. Y., Nov. 25, 1819. He settled in Rose, Oakland County, in 1846, built the Buckhorn hotel and kept it for nearly two years, when he sold out. He built a store, was successful as a dealer in general merchandise, and also ran a small tannery, where buckskins were tanned and mittens made. He removed to Holly in 1854, opened the first store there, shipped the first car load of wheat over the Detroit & Milwaukee road to Detroit, and became a leader in business. He held various offices, including those of School Director and Supervisor. Politically he was a Republican. An ardent supporter of the Union during the war, he allowed a son under fourteen to enlist, and being chided for it, said, "If I had a hundred sons old enough to carry a sword they should all fight for the American flag." While serving as a member of the House he died at Lansing, Mar. 20, 1863.

DARIUS D. BUELL

Representative from Branch County, 1891-2 and 1893-4. Was born, Dec. 13, 1853, on a farm near Union City. He acquired his early education at Olivet College, graduating in 1877. His life occupation was that of a farmer, with some special attention to stock raising. He was a delegate to the Farmers' National Congress at Montgomery, Ala., also to Council Bluffs, Iowa; at which last named place he was elected vice-president of said Congress; also vice-president of the Farmers' National Bank of his native village. In politics a Republican. He held the offices of School Inspector and Justice of Peace of his township.

EMMONS BUELL

Senator from the Seventeenth District, 1863-4. Was born in Newport, Sullivan County, N. H., Feb. 15, 1821. He moved to Genesee County, N. Y., in 1850. He was educated at the common schools and at Lima Seminary. By occupation he was a farmer. He read law for a time with Judge Hastings, of Rochester, N. Y., but ill health compelled him to return to the farm. He was Colonel of the 62d N. Y. Regiment in 1852. He moved to Cass County, Mich., in 1854. In politics he was a Republican. He resided at Kalamazoo in 1888.

HENRY S. BUELL

Representative from Oakland County, 1859-60. Was born in Castleton, Vt., in 1821. He was a physician and surgeon by profession, in politics a Democrat, He first came to Michigan in 1836, went back to Vermont, in 1840 and graduated at the Medical College of Vermont in 1843, returning to Michigan the same year. He resided at Franklin, Oakland County, in 1888 and was engaged in the practice of his profession.

JOHN L. BUELL

Representative from Delta and other counties, 1873-4. Was born in Laurenceburg, Ind., Oct. 12, 1835. He was educated in the public schools and took a two years' course in the Norwich Military Academy, Vt. In 1857 he went to Kansas and Colorado where he spent a few years. At the outbreak of the Civil War he entered military service for two years. In 1863 he entered Harvard University, studied law for six months and returned to his home in Laurenceburg where he engaged in farming until August, 1866. On account of ill health he came to Menominee, Mich. In 1871 he visited the Menominee range and laid bare the first merchantible iron ore on the range in a mine which he named the Quinnesec. He died Jan. 30, 1917.

HARRY C. BULKLEY

Member of the Board of Regents of the University of Michigan, 1911-17. Was born at Monroe, Mich., Mar. 7, 1870. He was educated in the University of Michigan where he received the degree of Bachelor of Arts in 1892 and of the Bachelor of Laws in 1895. He married Cora Buhl Strong of Rockwood, Mich., Aug. 13, 1899. A lawyer by profession he began to practice in Detroit in 1895; a member of several clubs and societies. He was appointed a member of the Board of Regents of the University Apr. 7, 1911, to succeed George P. Codd resigned.

FREDERICK G. BULLOCK

Representative from the First District of Lapeer County, 1891-2. Was born Dec. 16, 1841, on a farm in Elba Township, Lapeer County. He was an active and practical farmer, devoting his entire attention to farming and taking an active interest in agricultural fairs; connected with the Lapeer County Agricultural Society. He held the offices of Highway Commissioner, Township Treasurer, County Superintendent of the Poor and Supervisor of his Township, which latter position he occupied for eight years in succession. In politics a Democrat.

HORACE E. BUNCE

Representative from St. Clair County, 1861-2. Was born in Windsor, Vt., June 18, 1820. He removed with his father's family to Desmond, now Port Huron, in 1825. In 1830 his father removed to Brownsville, N. Y., where the son worked on a farm until 1839. He attended the Black River Institute and was a teacher. In 1844 came back to Michigan and was in the employ of Z. W. Bunce and James Abbott at Clyde, St. Clair County, until 1849, when he with a brother bought out the firm, including a saw mill, grist mill and pine lands, and engaged in lumbering and farming. After 1863 he resided on a farm in Port Huron Township. He held many town offices. In politics he was first a Whig, then a Republican. He died at Marysville, Feb. 22, 1899.

ZEPHANIAH W. BUNCE

Member of the Legislative Council, from St. Clair County, 1824-5 and 1826-7. Was born at Hartford, Conn., in 1787. Both of his grandfathers, Bunce and Drake, were sea captains, owning their own vessels, and among the earliest settlers of Hartford. The famous Charter Oak was on the Bunce farm. His father while a student in Yale College enlisted on a privateer, aided in taking several prizes from the British, was taken prisoner and confined at Halifax, from which he escaped, and was disinherited. His father died when he was young, and he went to live with his Grandmother Drake on the farm where the Connecticut State House now stands. At the age of seventeen he went to work as a hatter, and earned money to send him to school. He went into the hatting business at Claremont, N. H., for three years, then went to Chester, Vt., for four years, then was in the dry goods trade at Albany, N. Y., in 1817 he came to Michigan, settled in St. Clair County. For many years he was a Judge of the county court of St. Clair County. When he first settled there were but nineteen families in St. Clair County. He lived on the same place at St. Clair for more than sixty years. He was still alive in 1887.

ARCHIBALD F. BUNTING

Representative, 1905-6 and 1907-8, from the Leelanau District, comprising the counties of Benzie and Leelanau. Was born at Albion, Ill., May 17, 1871, of English descent. He obtained his education at Benzonia College and was graduated from the law department of the University of Michigan in August, 1894. He was principal of the Thompsonville schools in 1890 and 1891 and of the Empire schools in 1892, was admitted to the bar in 1893, locating at Empire where he practiced his profession. He was married July 21, 1895. In politics a Republican. He held the offices of Deputy County Clerk, Register of Deeds, Prosecuting Attorney for two terms, and was alternate delegate to the national convention at Philadelphia in 1900; was elected Lieutenant Colonel of Michigan Sons of Veterans in 1893.

WILLIAM BURBANK

Representative from Oakland County, 1837. Was born in the State of Maine in 1792. He was by occupation a furniture dealer; in politics, first Whig then Republican. He removed from Maine to New York in 1806, from that State to Missouri in 1820 and from Missouri to Michigan in 1822. He was for several years Justice of the Peace in the village of Rochester, where he died Jan. 29, 1878.

JOHN BURCH

Senator from the Third District, 1842-3. Was a native of Jefferson County, N. Y. He came to Monroe in 1834, where he followed the business of a warehouse man, and was in politics a Democrat. He was a Supervisor, and Treasurer of the city of Monroe. He died at Monroe.

LOU J. BURCH

Representative from the First District of Wayne County, 1899-1900. Was born at Eaton Rapids, Eaton County, Mich., Feb. 28, 1863, and was educated at the public schools of his native village. At the age of eighteen years he entered a job printing office to learn the trade, and one year later, when but nineteen years of age, he, in company with C. M. Seger, began the publication of the Eaton Rapids *Times*, thus becoming the youngest publisher in the State at that time. He was married to Miss Ida M. Bryant of Albion, May 29, 1884. He went to Detroit in 1887 to engage in newspaper work, and became the senior member of the firm of Burch & LaRiviere, publishers and commercial printers, and editor of *Truth*, the official organ of the organized liquor interests of Michigan. In politics a Republican. He was President of his ward club, and an active worker in the interests of his party.

MARSDEN C. BURCH

Senator from the Twenty-seventh District, 1877-8. Was born at Canoga, Seneca County, N. Y., June 25, 1847. While he was quite young his parents removed to Waterloo in the same county. His education was obtained at Waterloo Academy, Falley Seminary, Fulton, N. Y., and Hobart College, Geneva, N. Y. He studied law in New York, attended one session of the law department of the Michigan University, and commenced the practice of his profession at Rochester, Oakland

County, at the age of twenty-one. Two years afterward he removed to Hersey, Osceola County, was soon after appointed Judge of Probate by Gov. Baldwin to fill a vacancy, and was subsequently elected to the same office for the full term. He was a Republican in politics and was the youngest member of the Senate of the Legislature of 1877. After leaving the Legislature he was U. S. District Attorney of Western Michigan for several years, and then in the practice of his profession at Grand Rapids. He died at Rochester, Mich., June 14, 1921.

CYREN BURDICK

Representative from Kalamazoo County, 1835 and 1836. His postoffice address was Bronson. (Further data not obtainable).

NOAH WHITTIER BURDICK

Representative from Antrim County, 1907-8. Was born at Dexter, Penobscot, Me., Sept. 6, 1855, of English and Welsh descent. Remaining at home and attending school until the fall of 1870 he entered a harness shop an an apprentice. In 1875 he opened a harness shop at Monson, Me., remaining there about three years when he came to Millbrook, Mecosta County, and established a harness shop. In 1881 he removed to Traverse City and in 1883 to Mancelona, continuing in the harness business for about three years at the latter place when he disposed of this business to give his sole attention to official and private interests. He was married in 1881 to Lillie M. Bartlett. Active in public affairs he held the office of village Clerk and Assessor, School Inspector, Township Treasurer, Justice of the Peace, member of Board of Education and Supervisor; held the office of Grand Chief Templar of the Grand Lodge of Good Templars of Michigan and was granted a life certificate of membership by the Grand Lodge. In politics a Republican.

EDMUND BURFOOT

Representative from the First District of Kent County, Grand Rapids, 1899-1900. Was born in England in 1858, and removed with his parents to Canada in 1867. He acquired his education in the public schools of Toronto, Canada, supplemented by private study, having learned the art of wood carving, came to the United States in 1880, working at his trade in different parts of the country, and in 1887 settled in Grand Rapids, still plying his trade by day and studying nights, and in 1895 was admitted to practice law, which profession he followed. He was elected to the Legislature of 1899-1900 on the general legislative ticket of the city of Grand Rapids.

ANDREW L. BURK

Representative from Berrien County, 1849. Was born in Giles County, Va., Sept. 6, 1810. He removed to Preble County, O., in 1824, and in 1828 emigrated to Cass County, Mich. In 1836 he removed to a farm in Berrien, Berrien County. By occupation a farmer; in politics a Democrat.

FRANCIS X. BURKE

Representative from the Fourth District of Wayne County, 1913-14. Was born in the township of Ecorse, Wayne County, in 1866, and was educated in the public schools of Detroit and Ecorse. His mother came from an old French family whose ancestors came to Detroit with Cadillac in 1701. Mr. Burke was Postmaster at River Rouge during Grover Cleveland's second administration, and served as Justice of the Peace of Ecorse Township. In politics a Democrat.

WILLIAM BURKE

Representative from Cass County, 1837 and 1838. Was an Associate County Judge of Cass County from 1831 to 1836 and was a prominent citizen.

JOHN L. BURLEIGH

Senator from the Fourth District, 1877-8. Was born in Middlesex County, Mass., Oct. 15, 1842. He received a common school education, supplemented by instructions from a private tutor, and was a graduate of the law department of the Michigan University. He removed to Michigan in 1874. By profession he was a lawyer. Immediately after the attack on Sumter he entered the service as Second Lieutenant in a New York Regiment. Within a year he was promoted to First Lieutenant for general good conduct, and Captain for bravery on the field at Hanover Court House, May 27, 1862. He received several wounds; was brevetted Major, Lieutenant Colonel and Colonel. was appointed Lieutenant Colonel of a new regiment, but on account of his wounds left the service, and commenced business in the West Indies. In consequence of impaired health he returned to New York, where he was engaged for several years in the commission business. He studied law. In politics he was a Democrat. In later years he was an actor.

WILLIAM BURNETT

Representative from Washtenaw County, 1848. Was born in Phelps, Ontario County, N. Y., Dec. 21, 1809. His father was Gen. William Burnett, and his mother was a daughter of Gen. Granger, of Revolutionary fame. He was a farmer and settled with his family in Washtenaw County in 1833. He held all town offices, and was a Justice of the Peace. He was treasurer of the Washtenaw County Agricultural Society at the time of his death. By occupation he was a farmer, in politics a Whig. He was one of the best and most influential members ever sent from Washtenaw County. He died in Scio, Oct. 8, 1856.

CHARLES F. BURNHAM

Representative from Sanilac County, 1921-2. Was born in North Township, Sanilac County, Jan. 29, 1875, and is of French, Scotch and Irish descent. He received his education in the district schools, Lexington High School, Lake View Academy and Valparaiso University, receiving the degrees of LL.B. and B. A. He is married and has a family of five children. He is engaged in farming. In politics a Republican. He has been Supervisor, Township Clerk and Director of the First standard school of Sanilac County, and is secretary-treasurer of the South Worth Threshing Association, and a member of the Grange and Gleaners.

FRED J. BURNHAM

Representative from the Third District of Wayne County, 1909-10 and 1911-12. Was born in Wayne County, Jan. 28, 1867, of English and German descent. He acquired his education in the common schools of Huron Township. Married and by occupation a farmer. In the year 1882, he was elected Supervisor and served four successive terms. In politics an active Republican.

DAVID E. BURNS

Representative from the First District of Kent County, 1901-2; and Senator 1903-4, from the Sixteenth District, comprising the city of Grand Rapids, except the sixth, seventh and eighth wards. Was born in Coldwater, Mich. He was educated at Albion College, and later graduated from the law department of the University of Michigan in 1892, and in the fall of that year located in Grand Rapids, where he practiced law. He was appointed Assistant Prosecuting Attorney of Kent County in January, 1893, for two years, was subsequently a member of the Advisory Board in the Matter of Pardons from June, 1899, to August, 1900, when he resigned. In politics a staunch Republican. Mr. Burns was married Oct. 22, 1902, to Miss Elsie McKinley of Ashland, Newaygo County, Mich. He was father of the first primary law ever enacted in Michigan for the nomination of candidates by a direct vote of the people.

JAMES BURNS

Representative from Wayne County, 1873-4. Was born in northern New York, Nov. 10, 1810. Mr. Burns received a common school education. In 1834 he emigrated to Michigan, settling in Detroit. Mr. Burns was engaged from 1836 in the mercantile business and accumulated a fortune. His death occurred at Detroit, Dec. 7, 1883.

JAMES A. BURNS

Representative from the First District of Wayne County, 1923—. Was born in Detroit, Jan. 8, 1899, of American parentage. He was educated in the parochial schools, graduating from Assumption high school and the literary department of Assumption College. He has also attended the University of Detroit Law School and will graduate the coming year. During the world war he served in the naval aviation department and upon his return took the management of the St. Claire hotel. Mr. Burns is a Republican.

WILLIAM R. BURNS

Representative, 1909-10, from the Schoolcraft District, comprising the counties of Alger, Luce, Mackinac and Schoolcraft. Was born in Athens, Bradford County, Pa., Nov. 15, 1872. He received his education in the Athens High School. He was united in marriage in 1902 to Elizabeth J. Lobb, of Negaunee, Mich. He served two terms as President of the village of Munising. In politics a Republican.

HENRY BURR

Representative from Isabella County, 1887-8. Was born in Plymouth, Wayne County, Mich., Aug. 31, 1837. He assisted his father on the farm and received the advantages afforded by the common schools, until the breaking out of the late war, when he enlisted in Co. H, 1st Mich. Cavalry. He participated in three general engagements, the second battle of Bull Run, Gettysburg, and Winchester; was wounded at Gettysburg. Early in 1863 he was promoted to Commissary Sergeant and on Dec. 31, 1863, re-enlisted, and at Winchester was again wounded. In June, 1865, he was discharged for disability, at St. Louis, Mo., when he returned to this State. In 1866 he was married to Alice D. Jones, of Dexter, Washtenaw County. One year after this he removed to Jackson County, remained two years, then moved to Pontiac. In 1869 he purchased 80 acres of heavily timbered land in Lincoln Township, Isabella County. Here he experienced the trials and difficulties incident of pioneer life. Mr. Burr held the offices of Justice of the Peace and Supervisor and other minor offices. In politics he was a Republican.

DELABAR BURROWS

Representative from Oakland County, 1850. Was born in Montgomery, Orange County, N. Y., Jan. 24, 1813. By occupation he was a farmer, in politics a Democrat. He settled in 1836 in Independence, but bought land in Rose, Oakland County, Mich., where he farmed it for thirty-three years. Later he resided at Fenton.

JULIUS C. BURROWS

Member of Congress, 1873-5, 1879-81, 1881-3, 1885-7 to 1893-5; and United States Senator, 1895-1911. Was born at North East, Erie County, Pa., Jan. 9, 1837; acquired a common school and academic education. In 1859 he came to Michigan and in 1860 was admitted to the bar and engaged in the practice of law in Kalamazoo. During the war he served as Captain in the 17th Michigan Infantry. Returning to Kalamazoo he continued the practice of law; was Prosecuting Attorney for Kalamazoo County for two terms, 1867-70 inclusive. He received the degree of LL.D. from Kalamazoo College. In politics he was a strong advocate of the principles of the Republican party and very active in campaigns; was a member of the 43d, 46th, 47th, 49th, 50th, 51st, 52nd, 53d and 54th Congresses; twice elected speaker pro tempore of the House. On the convening of the Legislature, in January, 1895, he was chosen United States Senator for the unexpired term of the late Senator Stockbridge. In 1899 he was chosen by the unanimous vote of the Republican members of the Legislature to succeed himself in the United States Senate for the term of six years from 1899 to 1905; and in 1905 was chosen for another term of six years by the unanimous vote of the Legislature. He was temporary chairman of the Republican National Convention held at Chicago in 1908. He died Nov. 16, 1915.

EDWIN BURT

Representative from Isabella, Montcalm and Clare counties, 1863-4. His postoffice address was Isabella City. (Further data not obtainable).

HIRAM AUSTIN BURT

Member of the Board of Regents of the University of Michigan, 1868-75. Was born in the township of Avon, Oakland County, Mich., Dec. 31, 1839, son of John and Julia Ann (Calkins) Burt. He is of mixed ancestry, English, Scotch, Dutch, and Irish. His paternal ancestor, Richard Burt, came from England and settled at Taunton, Mass., about the middle of the seventeenth century. The seventh in line from this Richard, William Austin Burt, grandfather of Hiran Austin, came to Michigan as early as 1817 and was a pioneer land surveyor under government employ for many years. In 1840 he was commissioned to survey the northern peninsula of Michigan and was assisted in this work by his oldest son, John. It is said that they made the first discovery of the rich iron deposits of Marquette County. Later these men became very active in promoting the building of a ship canal at Sault Ste. Marie. John Burt took up his residence in Detroit, where the son was prepared for college. He entered the Kalamazoo College in 1858, and after two years changed to the University of Michigan, where he graduated Bachelor of Arts in 1862. The degree of Master of Arts followed in 1865. He settled at Marquette, Mich., where he became prominent in mining and other iron interests. In 1867 he was elected Regent of the University and served the full term of eight years from Jan. 1 following. He was chairman of the committee on the museum and on the literary department. From 1869 to 1874 he was Collector of Customs for the Lake Superior District. Laterly he lived in retirement at Gardiner, Me.

WELLINGTON R. BURT

Senator from the Twenty-second District, 1893-4; and Delegate from Saginaw County in the Constitutional Convention of 1907-8. Was born in New York in 1831. Eight years later he came with his parents to Michigan locating in Jackson County. He attended school at Albion and the Michigan Central (now Adrian) College. He spent three years in a trip through Central and South America and Australia and after returning located at Saginaw. He was originally extensively engaged in the manufacture of lumber and salt, but later engaged in manufacturing and banking. In politics a Democrat. He held the office of Mayor of East Saginaw and was the Democratic candidate for Governor of the State of Michigan in 1888. He was elected to the Senate of 1893-4; elected a Delegate to the Constitutional Convention of 1907-8 from Saginaw County on a non-partisan ticket. He died at East Saginaw Mar. 2, 1919.

WILLIAM A. BURT

Member of the Legislative Council, from Macomb County, 1826-7; and Representative from Macomb County, 1853-4. Was born at Worcester, Mass., June 13, 1792. His parents in 1798 removed to Montgomery County, N. Y., where in the absence of schools, he had great difficulty in obtaining an education. Through the aid of a neighbor who had been a teacher, he learned surveying and astronomy at an early age. He served for a time in the War of 1812, and at the age of twenty-one married Phoebe Cole. After a few years of mercantile business, not a success, he came to Michigan in 1822, settled in Washington, Macomb County, in 1824, and from time of his arrival until 1833 was engaged in mill-building and local surveying. He was appointed district surveyor by Gov. Porter in 1832, and was County Surveyor of Macomb County from 1831 to 1834. He was also Postmaster of Mt. Vernon, a position he held twenty-four years. In 1833 he was also Associate Judge of the Macomb circuit. In the autumn of 1833 he was appointed United States Surveyor and left for the field north of Fort Gratiot, on the shore of Lake Huron. At this time he had conceived the idea of the solar compass— the crowning achievement of his life. He exhibited the model before the Franklin

Institute at Philadelphia in 1835, and was unanimously awarded a Scott's legacy medal. He became engaged in the land surveys in Wisconsin and Iowa for some time. In 1838 he was elected one of the Commissioners of Public Improvements for the State of Michigan. In 1840 he exhibited a perfect solar compass, for which he received the highest commendation as to the value of his invention. From 1840 to 1847 he was occupied in land surveys in the Upper Peninsula, but published a manual for the use of his compass. He discovered more than twenty beds of iron ore from 1844 to 1846, thus turning the public attention to the vast mineral wealth of northern Michigan. He visited Europe in 1851. In 1852 he returned. In 1856 he secured letters patent on an equatorial sextant, both in this country and Europe, but died before it was perfected. He was a member of the Baptist Church and a Democrat in politics.

CLARENCE MONROE BURTON

Delegate to the Constitutional Convention of 1907-8 from the Second District, Wayne County. Was born in California, Nov. 18, 1853, of English parents. He received his education in the common schools of Hastings, Mich., and the University of Michigan. He graduated from the law department of the University in 1874, and has since been engaged as a lawyer and abstractor of titles in Detroit. Mr. Burton has been a resident of Michigan since 1855. He held the offices of member of Board of Estimates and Board of Education in Detroit, and for several years was president of the Pioneer and Historical Society of Michigan; and now a member of the Michigan Historical Commission.

PORTER BURTON

Representative from Barry County, 1879-80. Was born in Perryville, Madison County, N. Y., July 22, 1821. He received a common school education. In 1844 he moved to Napoleon, Jackson County, and engaged in farming. In 1856 he removed to Barry County. He held the office of Justice of the Peace. In politics he was a National. He died at Hastings Apr. 17, 1895.

CHARLES P. BUSH

Representative from Livingston and Ingham counties, 1840 and 1841, and from Livingston County, 1842 and 1843; and Senator from the Second District, 1846-7 and from the Twenty-sixth District, 1853-6; and a Delegate from Ingham County to the Constitutional Convention of 1850. Was born Mar. 18, 1809, at Ithaca, Tompkins County, N. Y. He came to Michigan in 1836, and was one of the first settlers in Handy, Livingston County. He was an earnest advocate of the doctrines and policy of the Democratic party. As State Senator he cast in 1847, the deciding vote that removed the state capital from Detroit to Lansing. Soon after, he became a resident of Lansing. In 1852 he was a delegate to the Democratic National Convention at Baltimore. He drafted and supported the bill by which capital punishment was abolished in Michigan. He was a successful business man, and his farm of 1,700 acres in Livingston County, was one of the best in the State. On the stump he was an effective and forcible speaker, and was possessed of a memory that was never at fault. In the prime of life he suffered years of illness, and died at Lansing about 1856.

DAVID BUSH

Representative from Livingston County, 1859-60. Was born in Danby, Tompkins County, N. Y., June 12, 1822, and came to Michigan in 1837. He lived in Handy until 1845, but became a farmer in Conway, Livingston County. He held a number of local offices. In politics he was a Democrat.

DANIEL P. BUSHNELL

Representative from Wayne County, 1859-60. Was a native of Albany, N. Y., born in 1810. At the age of sixteen he entered the employ of the American Fur Company, working in the northwest. In 1834 he was appointed by President Jackson, Deputy Indian Agent for the Northwest Territory, serving in that capacity seven years. He settled in Detroit in 1843. He interested himself in politics, and was clerk of the House of Representatives, sessions 1851-2, and a member of the House as above stated. He was Sergeant of Arms in the Constitutional Convention of 1850. He was City Treasurer of Detroit at the time of his death, May 4, 1862. He was a democrat in politics.

WILLIAM B. BUSHNELL

Representative from Branch County, 1901-2. Was born in Noble Township, Branch County, Mich., Feb. 21, 1849. He was raised on a farm and acquired his education in the district school, supplemented by a short course at the Orland Academy. He went west at the age of twenty years, and followed the painter's trade seven years. He returned to Michigan in 1876 and followed the occupation of farming. Mr. Bushnell was married Sept. 17, 1879. In politics a staunch Republican. He was Supervisor many years.

HENRY FRANKLIN BUSKIRK

Representative from the Second District of Allegan County, 1897-8 and 1899-1900; and a member of the State Board of Agriculture, 1905-7. Was born at Hopkins, Allegan County, Mich., Nov. 26, 1856, and lived on a farm until he was sixteen years of age. His education was acquired in the Otsego High School, and in 1876 he attended the Agricultural College; taught school during winters; paid his own tuition, and graduated in November, 1878, with the title of B. S. After completing his course of education he located in Wayland Township, where he engaged in farming, also dealing in lumber and hay. He was married in 1881. In politics a Republican. He held township and village offices, and was appointed a member of the State Board of Agriculture Jan. 3, 1905, to fill the vacancy caused by the resignation of Charles F. Moore.

ABRAM G. BUTLER

Representative from the Second District of Eaton County, 1893-4. Was born in Marshall, Calhoun County, Aug. 15, 1841. He attended common school, also private seminary, and at the age of seventeen entered Albion College. Dec. 6, 1865, he was married to Lovinia M. Balch, of Marshall, who died July 12, 1887, leaving him eight children. While in Marshall, he was engaged in handling wool; he went to Detroit and later to New York City, where he more extensively continued in the wool business. After the great fire of Chicago he went to that city and was for ten years an active and successful member of the board of trade, exporting largely American breadstuffs and provisions. In the meantime, he made several trips to the British Isles and the continent of Europe. In 1884 he moved to Bellevue, Mich., where he became proprietor of the National Lime Works, also an extensive dealer in wool and grain. In politics a Republican. He served as President of the Village of Bellevue and Supervisor of his township.

DAVID H. BUTLER

Representative from Lapeer County, 1921-2 and 1923—. Was born in Tuscola County, Apr. 15, 1887, of English and Dutch parentage. His education was acquired in the public schools of Tuscola County and after graduating from high school he worked for two years in the mercantile business. He then completed a course in salesmanship and was a commercial salesman for six years, when failing health forced him to discontinue that work and he took up farming in which occupation he is now engaged. Mr. Butler was married Apr. 6, 1910, to Edna A. Folsom. He is a Republican; has held several township offices, and was elected to the Legislature in 1920 and re-elected November 7, 1922.

EDWARD H. BUTLER

State Treasurer, 1883-7. Was born in Detroit in 1841. He was prepared in the public schools of his native city for the University at Ann Arbor, entering there in 1857; abandoned his college course in 1859 by reason of ill-health, returned to Detroit, became clerk in the banking office of Wm. A. Butler & Co., and was admitted to the firm in 1863. In 1870 the Mechanics' Bank of Detroit was organized, and he was made cashier, a position he held many years. He carried a torch in the first Republican procession ever had in Detroit (in 1856), was a member and treasurer of the Republican city committee, of Detroit, for the years 1877-8 and 1879, and chairman during the campaign of 1880; also a member of the Wayne County Republican Committee for the years 1880-1; and one of the presidential electors in 1880. In 1882 he received the solid vote of the Wayne delegation in the Republican Convention at Kalamazoo, where he was nominated for the office of State Treasurer and elected. In 1884 he was renominated and re-elected on the Republican ticket.

ORANGE BUTLER

Representatives from Lenawee County, 1837. Was born in Pompey, Onondaga County, N. Y., Mar. 5, 1794. He graduated at Union College, studied law with Victor Birdseye, at the same time teaching classics. He commenced practice at Vienna, N. Y., then at Gaines, N. Y., where he had a large practice and was prominent in the famous Morgan trials, during the Anti-Masonic excitement, and was Prosecuting Attorney. He came to Adrian, Mich., in 1835. He removed to Delta, Eaton County, in 1847, and purchased the Ingersoll mills. He sold the property in 1849 and removed to Lansing, where he died July 11, 1870. He practiced law and was Justice of the Peace for many years. In politics he was a Democrat.

RICHARD BUTLER

Representative from Macomb County, 1838. Was born at Grosse Isle, Wayne County, Mich., Apr. 1, 1797, but removed with his parents to Gosfield, Canada. His father died when he was young and he was apprenticed to a Pennsylvania farmer, until he attained his majority. He had no chance for education, and commenced a course of self education in 1821, removing the same year to Detroit, He there continued his studies, and subsequently taught school for a term of years, numbering the children of Gen. Cass and other prominent Detroit citizens among his pupils. He also taught at Mt. Clemens and other places in Macomb County. He engaged in mercantile business for a short time at Detroit, and removed to Mt. Clemens in 1828. In 1829 he was commissioned as County Clerk of Macomb County by Gen. Cass, also Justice of the Peace. He was appointed Register of the land office at Sault Ste. Marie and held that office during one term. He studied law and was admitted to the Macomb County bar in 1834, and practiced successfully until 1865; was Prosecuting Attorney 1857-8; and started the Macomb *Statesman* in 1837. He married Abagail Hayes in 1827, and they had four children.

ARCHIBALD BUTTARS

Senator from the Thirtieth District, 1881-2 and from the Twenty-eighth, 1883-4; and Lieutenant Governor, 1885-7. Was born in Manchester, England, Nov. 21, 1838, and has been a resident of Michigan since 1852. He received but a limited education, then followed the occupation of wood-cutter, lumberman, and land looker, and as such endured all the privations of frontier life. He was elected Senator in the State Legislature in 1880, and re-elected in 1882. He was chosen president pro tem. of the Senate of 1883. Having received the nomination for Lieutenant Governor, from the Republican State Convention in 1884, he was elected. He was not a candidate for re-election in 1886. His residence is Charlevoix.

IRA H. BUTTERFIELD

Senator from the Twenty-fifth District, 1861-2, and from the Twenty-third District, 1873-4. Was born Dec. 6, 1812, in Gainesville, Wyoming County, N. Y. He received a common school education. He came to Michigan in 1838 and settled at Shelby, Macomb County. He was a leading farmer and largely interested in agricultural matters in the county of Macomb and the State. He helped to organize the Macomb County Agricultural Society, and was for many years one of its officers. He was one of the executive committee of the State Agricultural Society in 1853, 1854 and 1861. He was one of the first to introduce merino sheep in eastern Michigan, and brought to Macomb County the first herd of Devon cattle. He was engaged in milling as well as farming, both in Lapeer and Macomb counties. He was an active Whig but was a Republican after 1854. He died at Lapeer May 10, 1884.

IRA HOWARD BUTTERFIELD

Member of the State Board of Agriculture, 1889-93. Was born Dec. 22, 1840, at Utica, Macomb County, Mich., and took the same name as that of his father, hence for the early part of his life, wrote after it "junior". The name of his mother was Rachel (McNeil) B. He married, Aug. 29, 1866, Olive F. Davison, Lapeer, Mich. He was brought up on a farm, educated in the common schools, Westfield Academy, N. Y., and the State Normal School, Mich., a total schooling of approximately that of a high school. When twenty, he started overland for California having in charge a drove of cattle and sheep for his father and John D. Patterson.

He returned in about two years. In 1865 he began on his own farm breeding Holstein cattle and Merino sheep, continuing until 1893. In 1879 he was appointed Deputy Collector and Inspector of Customs at Port Huron, serving until 1885 and again in 1889, resigning in 1893; was appointed a member of the State Board of Agriculture 1889, serving until 1893 when he was elected their secretary serving until February, 1899, also serving as Postmaster until 1902; in 1881 was a member of the Executive Committee of the State Agricultural Society; 1891 elected Secretary of that Society, serving for four years; vice-president three years, 1898 President; 1899-1900 Secretary; 1910-11 General Manager of the Connecticut Fair at Hartford.

JOHN W. BUTTERFIELD

Representative from Berrien County, 1851. Came to Michigan in 1840, and was a manufacturer at Niles. He was a Democrat in politics. Deceased.

ROGER WILLIAMS BUTTERFIELD

Member of the Board of Regents of the University of Michigan, 1888-1904. Was born at Elbridge, N. Y., Apr. 23, 1844,· son of the Rev. Isaac and Sarah A. (Templeton) Butterfield. His father, a prominent minister of the Baptist denomination, removed to Iowa at an early date. After a preparatory training in the public schools the son entered Princeton College, from which he was graduated Bachelor of Arts in 1866. He now entered the law department of the University of Michigan and was graduated Bachelor of Laws in 1868. In that year he opened a law office in Grand Rapids, Mich.; also interested in various commercial enterprises, notably the Grand Rapids Chair Company and the Widdicomb Furniture Company. In 1887 he was elected a Regent of the University for the full term and re-elected in 1895. During the sixteen years that he sat in the Board he did important service as a member of the Library Committee of the Board and as Chairman of the Committee on the Literary Department, of the Medical Department, and on the Department of Law. In 1870 was married to Leonora Ida Drake, of Fort Wayne, Ind.

JOHN H. BUTTON

Representative from Oakland County, 1840. Was born near Springfield, Mass., Oct. 14, 1805. He came to Michigan in 1831, and settled with his family on a farm in Farmington, Oakland County, having located the land in 1828. He was Supervisor of the town from 1845 to 1854, for eight years was one of the County Superintendents of the Poor, and for four years was a justice of the Peace. He affiliated with the Republican party. He was for several years Postmaster at North Farmington. He died at Fentonville, Dec. 1, 1876.

FRED C. BUZZELL

Representative from the Second District of Macomb County, 1893-4. Was born at Romeo, Mich., in 1856. His early education was acquired in the public schools of Romeo. He afterwards studied law and after a short practice drifted into the more active pursuits of journalism and politics. He was at times connected with the Chicago *Daily News*, the *Rocky Mountain News*, and the Detroit *Free Press*. He, with a younger brother, founded the Romeo *Hydrant.* He also owned the Mt. Clemens *Press,* selling out 1890. In politics a Democrat. He was store-keeper of the port at Port Huron under Cleveland's first administration.

CHARLES J. BYRNS

Representative from the Second District of Marquette County, 1901-2, 1903-4, 1905-6 and 1907-8. Was born Jan. 6, 1861, in Altona, N. Y. When eight years of age he moved with his parents to Port Henry, N. Y., where he received his education in the high school. He moved to Michigan when eighteen years of age and located at Ishpeming where after an experience of several years as bookkeeper and manager of different lumber concerns, he purchased and successfully conducted a retail lumber business for two years. He engaged with the Wisconsin Land & Lumber Co. of Hermansville, Mich., as traveling salesman and remained with them for nearly four years. An ardent advocate of fraternal societies, he served as state deputy head consul of the Modern Woodmen of America for nine years, and was elected by acclamation, June, 1903, national director of the Modern Woodmen of America; also a past grand master workman of the Michigan Grand Lodge of the A. O. U. W., and past grand commander of the military branch of the same order, and a member of the K. O. T. M., Royal Arcanum, B. P. O. E., Knights of Columbus, and C. O. F. Married, and in politics a Republican.

WARREN D. BYRUM

Representative from the Second District of Ingham County, 1919-20, 1921-2 and 1923—. Was born Oct. 19, 1887, on a farm in Onondaga Township, Ingham County, of American parents. He attended the district school and graduated from the Leslie High School. After teaching in the rural schools he attended the State Normal College at Ypsilanti, and the University of Michigan, graduating from the literary department of the latter institution in 1912. He has since resided on the old homestead which was taken up by his grandfather from the government. Mr. Byron is married and has three daughters. He served as Supervisor of Onondaga Township and as Chairman of the County Board of Supervisors. In politics he is a Republican.

BURT DUWARD CADY

Senator, 1907-8, from the Eleventh District, comprising the county of St. Clair. Was born at Port Huron, St. Clair County, July 25, 1874. He attended the public schools of Port Huron and at the age of eighteen entered the law offices of Avery Brothers and Walsh as a student. He was admitted to the bar July 25, 1895, and began the practice of law in October, 1897. May 10, 1900, he formed a partnership with Clifford W. Crandall under the firm name of Cady and Crandall, which partnership is still in existence. Mr. Cady has held the offices of Police Justice, Circuit Court Commissioner, Prosecuting Attorney, was elected secretary of the State League of Republican Clubs in 1897 and later president; also secretary of the Republican County Committee.

CHARLES H. CADY

Representative from the Third District of Wayne County, 1887-8. Was born in Nankin, of that county, July 20. 1842, and has been a resident of Michigan since that time. Mr. Cady was a farmer and a Democrat, held the offices of School Inspector, Township Treasurer, Justice of the Peace, and Supervisor for seven years.

CHARLES T. CADY

Representative from Monroe County, 1855-6. Was born at Putney, Vt., May 11, 1811. By occupation he was a hotel keeper and farmer, in politics a Republican. He came to Dundee, Monroe County, in 1843. He was Sheriff of Monroe County. In religion he was a Congregationalist. He expended money liberally for the building of churches, establishing schools, and in the cause of temperance. He was a prime mover in building a plank road from Tecumseh to Monroe. He died Mar. 11, 1886.

CHAUNCEY G. CADY

Representative from Macomb County, 1849. Was born in Otsego County, N. Y., Aug. 20, 1803. He received a common school education, and came to Mt. Clemens, Mich., in 1820. In 1833 he settled on a farm in the towns of Clinton and Sterling, same County. He held the offices of Supervisor, Town Clerk, Justice, and Drain Commissioner. He was Pay master, with the rank of Major, in the territorial militia from 1826 to 1829. He was a Democrat until 1854, then a Republican. He was the first president of the Macomb County Pioneer Society. He died at the home of his daughter in Detroit December, 1893.

HORACE H. CADY

Representative from Macomb County, 1843, 1865-6 and 1873-4. Was born in Hadley, Windham County, Conn., Feb. 20, 1801, and received a common school education. He emigrated to Michigan in 1821, and settled in Mt. Clemens, where he remained until 1837, when he removed to Macomb, Macomb County. He was Supervisor of that town fifteen years, Justice of the Peace, Treasurer of Macomb County, and president of the Pioneer Society, 1882. By occupation he was a farmer.

EDWARD CAHILL

Justice of the Supreme Court, 1890. Was born in Kalamazoo, Mich., Aug. 3, 1843. His father, Abraham Cahill, was a tanner and had settled at Kalamazoo in 1831, and in 1841 married Frances M. Marsh, the daughter of John P. Marsh, also an early settler. Miss Marsh was a niece of Epaphroditus Ransom, a former judge of the Supreme Court and Governor of the State from 1848 to 1850. When the subject of this sketch was two years old his father sold his tanning business and bought a farm on Grand Prairie, three miles west of Kalamazoo, to which he removed in 1845, and where he continued to live until the winter of 1854. During these years after he was old enough his son attended district school. In 1854 Abraham Cahill sold his farm and removed to Holland, in this State, where he bought considerable tracts of land, intending to erect a mill and engage in the lumber business. In August 1854 however he died leaving a wife and six children, of whom Edward was next to the oldest and very little besides wild land for their support. In the spring of 1855 the family moved back to Kalamazoo. Here Edward attended the public schools for a while, and in the fall of 1856 entered the preparatory department of Kalamazoo College. In 1860 he entered the office of the Kalamazoo *Gazette* as an apprentice to the printer's trade, and remained there and in the office of the Kalamazoo *Telegraph* until he entered the army as a private in Co. A, 89th Ill. Inf., in August, 1862; was taken sick and discharged. Upon recovering his health in the spring of 1863, he commenced the study of law in the office of Miller & Barns in Kalamazoo. In the fall of that year he raised a company of colored men for the 1st Mich. Col. Inf., afterwards 102 U. S. C. T., with which he went to the field first as a First Lieutenant and afterwards as Captain and served for the remainder of the war, and until October, 1865. Upon his return from the army he resumed the study of the law at St. Johns, Mich., and was admitted to the bar there in June, 1866. In September following he removed to Hubbardston in Ionia County, where he was engaged in the practice of his profession until elected Circuit Court Commissioner in 1870, when he removed to Ionia. In June, 1871, he resigned his office and removed to Chicago, he was engaged in practice until in August, 1873, he removed to Lansing. In politics a Republican. He was twice elected Prosecuting Attorney of Ingham County. In 1889 he was appointed by Gov. Luce a member of the Advisory Board in the Matter of Pardons. On the death of Judge Campbell in March, 1890, he was appointed by the Governor Justice of the Supreme Court to fill the vacancy until the next general election. At that election he was the Republican candidate but was defeated. Judge Cahill was married in 1867, to Lucy C. Crawford of Milford.

DAVID J. CAHOON

Representative from Isabella County, 1897-8. Was born in Waterloo Township, Jackson County, Mich., Jan. 11, 1842, where he acquired a common school education, attending school winters and working on his father's farm summers. He was married Nov. 27, 1864, and two years later with his wife and one child moved to Union Township, Isabella County, and located on a farm. Principal occupation that of farming and lumbering. In politics a Populist. He was elected to the House of 1897-8, on the Democratic People's Union Silver ticket.

JOHN CALDWELL

Representative 1897-8 and 1899-1900, from the Wexford District, comprising the counties of Wexford, Missaukee and Clare. Was born in Medina, Orleans County, N. Y., July 4, 1850, and came with his parents to Litchfield, Hillsdale County, Mich., in 1856. He worked on his father's farm summers and attended school during winters. At the age of seventeen he went north and worked in the lumber woods for four years, and then took up a homestead which became one of the best farms in Missaukee County. In politics a Republican. He held the office of Highway Commissioner, Town Clerk, Township Treasurer, Justice of the Peace, County Treasurer and Supervisor.

NORMAN CALHOUN

Representative from Lenawee County, 1851. Was born in Coventry, Conn., Feb. 13, 1807, and died Aug. 15, 1876. By occupation he was a farmer, and politically a Republican. He settled in the town of Bridgewater in 1837, and lived there until 1865, then was a resident of the village of Clinton until his death.

ALANSON CALKINS

Representative from Tuscola County, 1851. Was born in Scipio, N. Y., Sept. 19, 1815. By occupation he was a farmer, politically a Whig. He settled in Oakland County, Mich., in 1836, but removed to Tuscola County in 1847. He died May, 13, 1854.

EPHRAIM CALKINS

Delegate from the Sixth District to the Constitutional Convention of 1835; and Representative from Macomb County, 1837. Was born in Greenbush, N. Y., Oct. 7, 1792. By occupation he was a millwright, surveyor and farmer; in politics first a Democrat, then a Free Soiler. He came to Michigan in 1831. He was County Surveyor of Macomb County, three years County Commissioner; and vice president Clinton and Kalamazoo Canal Celebration, Mt. Clemens, July 20, 1838. He helped to organize the Free Soil party in Michigan in 1848, and was their candidate for Congress in that year. He was a man of sound judgment, and noted as an arbitrator and peace-maker. He died at Gratton, Kent County, Mar. 8, 1853.

WILLIAM DUDLEY CALVERLEY

Delegate in the Constitutional Convention of 1907 8 from the Thirty-second District, Houghton County. Was born in Canada in 1853, of English and Irish descent —the nephew of Charles Stuart Calverley, author and Dean of Oxford. Mr. Calverley attended the public schools at Houghton, but left school when he was fourteen years old. He sailed the lakes as a sailor for six years and then entered train service as a brakeman and afterwards conductor. He then went into the employ of the Sheldon estate as bookkeeper and served in that capacity for twenty-three years. Later he was an officer of the Sheldon Estate Company and was interested in mines, real estate and banking. In 1904 he married Miss Mary Temby Roberts. Mr. Calverley served as Supervisor of Portage Township.

LEVI CAMBURN

Representative from Montcalm County, 1865-6, and 1867-8. Was born in Lockport, N. Y., Feb. 7, 1828. His occupation was farming, politics Republican. He came to Michigan in 1832, first living at Tecumseh, removed to Montcalm County in 1856, and was County Treasurer from 1861 to 1865.

THOMAS M. CAMBURN

Representative from the First District of Lenawee County, 1895-6 and 1897-8. Was born Sept. 6, 1835, on a farm in Franklin Township. He received a common school education, and attended a seminary at Tipton, conducted by Joseph Estabrook, Superintendent of Public Instruction. In occupation he was a life-long farmer. In politics a Republican. He held the office of Township Clerk, and Supervisor.

ALEXANDER CAMERON

Representative from Kalamazoo County, 1869-70 and 1871-2. Was born in Deerfield, Oneida County, N. Y., Sept. 29, 1813, of Scotch descent. He came to Michigan in 1834. He was brought up to farm work and had a limited education. He acquired a skillful use of tools and in 1834 settled at Kalamazoo, Mich., working as a carpenter, also dealing in real estate and buying and selling live stock. In 1849 he went to California and engaged in gold mining. He has held many local offices. He was first a Whig, a Republican from 1854. He died at Kalamazoo Mar. 18, 1894.

THEODORE J. CAMPAU

Representative from Wayne County, 1859-60. Was the son of Joseph Campau. He was born Apr. 26, 1825, and was educated at Notre Dame College, Ind. Although an active Democrat, he was not an aspirant for political honors, his official life being comprehended by his term in the Legislature and by one or two nominal appointments under the city government. He died Mar. 10, 1875.

ABNER E. CAMPBELL

Representative from Calhoun County, 1848. Was born at Camillus, N. Y., in 1811. By profession he was a lawyer, in politics a Democrat. He located at Battle Creek in 1842, and established a large and lucrative law business. He was an able lawyer, and a genial, cultivated gentleman. He died Aug. 2, 1856 .

ALLEN CAMPBELL

Representative from Oakland County, 1875-6. Was born in Perthshire, Scotland, in 1817, removed to this country in 1827. He took up his residence first at Paterson, N. J., and afterwards at Stockport, N. Y. He received a common school education. In 1834 he went to sea from New Bedford, Mass., and filled all positions on shipboard from boy to master. He was master of a United States transport during the Mexican War. He came to Michigan in 1847, and purchased and improved the farm in Groveland, Oakland County. He held various township offices. In politics a Democrat. He was twice married and was the father of thirteen children. He died June 22, 1883.

ANDREW CAMPBELL

Senator, 1897-8, from the Tenth District, comprising the counties of Jackson and Washtenaw. Was born in Laurenston, parish of Dalrymple Ayrshire, Scotland, May 29, 1832, where he acquired his early education; came to Michigan in 1842 and taught school a number of terms; was graduated from the State Normal School in April, 1859, and was married to Miss Catharine Fisher, Oct. 26 of the same year. A farmer by occupation; a member of the Congregational Church and of the Grange. In politics an unwavering Republican from the organization of the party.

BRADFORD CAMPBELL

Representative from Livingston County, 1849. Was born in Campbell, N. Y., in 1802. He emigrated to Canton, Mich., in 1827, lived there two years, removed to Nankin, Wayne County, where he kept hotel on the old Chicago road for six years. He then removed to Hamburg, Livingston County, where he engaged in milling, wool carding, cloth dressing, and farming.

COLIN PERCY CAMPBELL

Representative from the Third District of Kent County, 1907-8 and 1909-10. Was born in Walker Township, Kent County, Mich., June 3, 1877, of Scotch and American parentage. He received his early education in the district schools, attended Albion College and graduated from the law department of the University of Michigan. He was employed on the editorial staff of the Lawyers' Cooperative Pub. Co., of Rochester, N. Y., having been directly engaged in the preparation of the second edition of Abbott's *Trial Brief Civil-Jury Issues.* In April, 1900, he severed his connection with the Rochester firm to prepare a digest of the New York Court of Appeals *Reports* which he completed in July, 1901, and in the following September opened a law office in Grand Rapids. He was one of the original publishers of the *Michigan Serial Digest*, later sole owner, finally sold his interest in the publication but was retained as editor. He was also law editor for several technical trade magazines. A Republican in politics.

DANIEL CAMPBELL

Senator from the Twenty-fifth District (Arenac and Bay Counties), 1887-8. Was born in Caithness-shire, Scotland, in 1836, and came to Michigan in 1861. By occupation he was a builder. He was a member of the City Council. He was elected to the Senate of 1887-8 on the Greenback and Republican ticket.

GORDON R. CAMPBELL

Delegate in the Constitutional Convention of 1907-8 from the Thirty-second District, Houghton County. Was born in Middlesex County, Ont., in 1870, of Scottish descent. He was educated in the public schools and graduated from the Collegiate institute at Strathroy, Ont., and also from the law department of the University of Michigan in 1893. He was married in 1902 to Miss Lou C. Holly, of Milwaukee, Wis. Mr. Campbell practiced law from 1893 to 1901 and then engaged in the mining business; was secretary of the Calumet & Arizona Mining Company and the Superior & Pittsburg Copper Company, both operating in Arizona. He came to Michigan to attend the law school in 1891, and located in Marine City in 1893, where he stayed until 1898 when he moved to Calumet.

H. FRANK CAMPBELL

Representative, 1893-4 and 1895-6, from the Wexford District, composed of the counties of Wexford, Missaukee and Clare. Was born in Branch County, Mich., in 1851. He acquired his education at the public schools at Grand Ledge, and at the age of fifteen began the trade of printing. In 1877 he moved to Wexford County and entered the office of the *Clam Lake News* (now the Cadillac *News and Express*); he remained here but a short time when he went to Sherman and bought one-half interest *Wexford County Pioneer.* In 1878 he sold his interest in the paper to accept the position of Postmaster, which he held until 1881, when he removed to Manton and engaged as a clerk in a general store. Two years later he purchased the Manton *Tribune,* and once more engaged in his favorite occupation. Soon afterwards he was again appointed Postmaster, which position he held until removed by the Democratic administration. He then sold his paper and returned to Sherman where he engaged in the drug business. In politics a Republican. He held several local offices.

HENRY MUNROE CAMPBELL

Delegate to the Constitutional Convention of 1907-8 from the First District, Wayne County. Was born in Detroit, Apr. 18, 1854, the eldest son of the Hon. James Valentine Campbell, Associate Justice and Chief Justice of the Supreme Court of Michigan for over thirty-two years, who married Cornelia Hotchkiss, a daughter of Chauncey Hotchkiss, one of the builders of the Erie Canal. He is of wholly American descent. Mr. Campbell received his education in the public schools of Detroit and at the University of Michigan, where he was graduated from the literary department in 1876 with the degree of Ph. B. and from the law department in 1878 with the degree of LL.B. In 1878 he formed a partnership with Henry Russel, later general consul of the Michigan Central Railroad. In 1880 he was appointed a Master in Chancery of the United States Circuit Court. Nov. 22, 1881, he married Caroline Boardman Burtenshaw, a daughter of James Burtenshaw, a well known Detroit merchant. In addition to membership in the American Bar Association, the Michigan Bar Association and the Detroit Bar Association, he was also identified with many non-professional and social organizations. He was an original member of the Michigan Naval Brigade and president of the Detroit Naval Reserves during the Spanish War.

JAMES H. CAMPBELL

Representative from the Second District of Calhoun County, 1879-80 and 1881-2. Was born Nov. 12, 1850, in the township of Lee, Mich. His education was received in the common schools. Mr. Campbell was by profession a lawyer, and was admitted to the bar in 1872. He was City Recorder of Marshall five years, from 1866 to 1870, inclusive; City Attorney in 1873, 1876 and 1879. As Republican candidate in 1878 he was elected Representative.

JAMES VALENTINE CAMPBELL

Justice of the Supreme Court, 1858-90. Was born in Buffalo, N. Y., Feb. 25, 1823. His father, Henry Campbell, was a merchant who brought his family to Detroit in 1826, and who held in New York, and afterward in Michigan, the position of County Judge. The son was educated at Flushing, L. I., and graduated at St. Paul's College in July, 1841. He was admitted to the bar at Detroit in October, 1844. In 1857, upon the establishment of the present Supreme Court, he was elected one of the Judges, held the office the remainder of his life. He was closely identified with the advancement of educational and refining influences, especially in Detroit, where he was president of the young men's society in 1848, and a member of the Board of Education for several years. In 1859 he was chosen Marshall professor of law in the law department established that year in the University of Michigan, and he held the chair for many years. He received the degree of Doctor of Laws from that University in 1866, being the first of a few very eminent men upon whom the University has conferred the degree. In 1876 he published his "Outlines of the Political History of Michigan." In politics he was a Whig so long as the Whig party maintained a political existence, then a Republican. He died at Detroit Mar. 26, 1890.

JOB T. CAMPBELL

Representative from the Second District of Ingham County, 1893-4 and 1895-6. Was born in Onondaga Township, said county, July 9, 1855. His early education was acquired at the district school and Leslie High School, working on a farm summers and attending school winters; taught school two winters, was Deputy Clerk of Ingham County from 1880-3; then engaged in newspaper work, publishing the Leslie *Local* from 1883-6 and the Pinckney *Dispatch* in 1887. In 1888 he spent five months in the law department of the University of Michigan, and was admitted to the bar June 19th of that year. In November, 1889, he purchased the *Ingham County News*. In politics a Republican. He held the office of Township Clerk, Circuit Court Commissioner, member Board of Education, and Supervisor of his ward.

JOHN K. CAMPBELL

Representative from the Second District of Washtenaw County, 1897-8. Was born in Augusta Township, Washtenaw County, June 7, 1849. His parents came from Ayrshire, Scotland, in the fall of 1842, and in the spring of 1843 settled on the farm where he later resided. His early education was acquired in the district school, supplemented by a classical course in the State normal; was graduated in 1875; entered the literary department of the University in the fall of 1875; remained but a short time owing to his eyes troubling him; went home and worked on his father's farm. He was married in 1877 to Miss Emma A. Jennings, of Ionia County; after renting his father's farm a number of years he purchased it. In politics he was a Republican. He was Township Superintendent of Schools and School Inspector for several terms; an active member of the grange and lecturer for Fraternity grange; and was chairman of the committee of legislative action at the State Grange sessions of 1894-5. He died at his home in Augusta Township, Washtenaw County, in April, 1913.

MILO D. CAMPBELL

Representative from the First District of Branch County, 1885-6. Was born at Quincy, Branch County, Mich., on the twenty-fifth day of October, 1851. He was a graduate of the high school at Coldwater, Mich., and of the State Normal School at Ypsilanti. At the age of twenty-one years he was elected to the office of Superintendent of Schools of Branch County. He was twice elected a member of the Board of School Examiners of said county, and three times elected secretary of such board, and Mayor of Coldwater three terms. He held the office of Circuit Court Commissioner two terms. He studied law with Loveridge & Barlow, of Coldwater, Mich., and was admitted to practice in 1877. After his admission to the bar he was in the active practice of his profession. He was a Republican in politics. Mr. Campbell was appointed private secretary to Governor Luce Jan. 1, 1887. Gov. Winans appointed him member Board of Corrections and Charities; Gov. Rich appointed him to the Board of Crossings; Gov. Pingree appointed him Insurance Commissioner, also a member of State Tax Commission. He belonged to many fraternal orders. His residence was in Branch County until his death.

THOMAS G. CAMPBELL

Representative, 1901-2, from Midland District, comprising the counties of Midland, Gladwin, and Arenac. Was born in Carlisle, Middlesex County, Ont., June 28, 1858. His early education was obtained in the common school and Toronto University, where he graduated with the degree of A. B. He came to Michigan in

1871, and entered the University of Michigan, graduated in 1888 with the degree of LL.B. He taught school for a time, and in 1888 settled in Gladwin where he practiced law. Married. In politics a strong Republican. He was Commissioner of Schools and Prosecuting Attorney for Gladwin County, and Mayor of the city of Gladwin.

ISRAEL CANBY

Representative from Cheboygan, Emmet, and Charlevoix counties, 1883-4. Was born in Logan County, O. He was raised on a farm and received a common school education. Soon after he became of age he took charge of a railroad freight and ticket office, continuing in that occupation three years. He then engaged in the milling business until the war of the rebellion. In April, 1861, he enlisted, and was elected Captain of his company, the company was assigned to the 23d O. Vol. Infantry. After serving three years and four months he was mustered out by reason of expiration of term of service. He then engaged in various occupations with varied success, until the year of 1872. In the spring of 1875 he moved to Emmet County and took a homestead; was elected three time Supervisor, also two terms County Treasurer; was elected on the Republican ticket a member of the Legislature from his district. Deceased.

IRVIN S. CANFIELD

Representative from Alpena County, 1905-6. Was born at Tyrone, Schuyler County, N. Y., May 12, 1863. In 1871 he came with his parents to Michigan locating at Lyons, removing two years later to a farm in Hamlin Township, Eaton County. His education was obtained in the district school from which he graduated in 1885, afterwards taking a course in the Detroit University. He taught school winters and read law at intervals in the office of John M. Corbin of Eaton Rapids. In 1886 he removed to Alpena where he was engaged as assistant teacher in the Alpena High School four years, was admitted to the bar in 1888, then practiced law at that place. Married. In politics a Republican. He held the office of County School Examiner, City Attorney of Alpena, and was chairman of the Republican County Committee, 1900-2.

LUCIUS H. CANFIELD

Representative from the First District of Macomb County, 1877-8, 1899-90 and 1891 2. Was born in Chester County, Conn. In 1838 he came with his parents to Chesterfield, Macomb County, Mich., being then eight years of age, where he remained working on a farm and getting a common school education. He afterwards learned the mason's trade, which trade he worked at for 10 years. After his father's death he resumed the occupation of farming. He was Township Treasurer of Chesterfield and held the office of Supervisor.

SAMUEL P. CANFIELD

Representative from the First District of Macomb County, 1853-4. His postoffice address was New Haven. (Further data not obtainable).

WILLIAM CANFIELD

Senator from the Twenty-fifth District, 1857-8 and 1859-60. Was born in Saybrook, Conn., May 26, 1809. Educated in the schools of Hartford, he became a clerk at the age of sixteen. He settled as a merchant at Mt. Clemens, Mich., in 1829, and married Ann, daughter of Judge Clemens, 1830. He was appointed Sheriff of Macomb County in 1832, and was a Brigadier General of State militia. In 1835 he settled on a farm near Mt. Clemens, where he died, Sept. 6, 1877. He was an officer in both county and State agricultural societies, and from 1862 to 1865 Assistant Assessor of Internal Revenue. He was a candidate for Congress in 1844. In politics he was a Republican.

STEPHEN CANIFF

Representative from Hillsdale County, 1867-8. Was born in Knollsville, N. Y., May 30, 1816. When a young man he taught winters and worked at farming summers. He settled on a farm at Pittsford, Hillsdale County, in 1836. In 1843 he sold out and bought a farm in Litchfield, where he resided until his death, Nov. 23, 1876. He was a Republican.

ELLERY CHANNING CANNON

Representative from the Osceola District, 1885-6 and 1887-8; and Senator, 1901-2 and 1903-4, from the Twenty-fifth District, comprising the counties of Isabella, Mecosta, Newaygo and Osceola. Was born in Macomb County, Mich., Dec. 28, 1842, a son of Rev. John Cannon, a pioneer minister of the Christian Church in this State. He obtained his education in the district schools, being pre-eminently a self-made man. He served his country three years during the Civil War, being a member of Co. B, 22d Mich. Inf. Married. In politics a Republican. He held various township offices.

JAMES CAPLIS

Representative from Wayne County, 1873-4; and Senator from the First District, 1881-2. Was born in Barncourt, Ireland, Mar. 28, 1841. He received a common school education. He emigrated to the United States in 1854, and subsequently settled in Detroit. In 1857 he was station master for the Great Western Railroad. He was also employed in the same capacity in 1858-9, for the Detroit & Milwaukee Railroad. He studied law and was admitted to the bar in 1862. He continued in the practice of his profession and dealt in real estate. He was Prosecuting Attorney of Wayne County. He died July 23, 1888.

HENRY WESTONRAE CAREY

Member of the Board of Regents of the University of Michigan, 1902-10. Was born in the city of New York, Sept. 21, 1850, son of William and Mary (Ramsay) Carey. His ancestors were English and Scotch. He received an elementary education in the public schools, and entered the college of the city of New York, where he was graduated Bachelor of Arts in 1870. After graduation he spent several years in the publishing business and in other activities. In 1881 he came West and entered the employ of Mr. R. G. Peters, of Manistee, Mich. When the R. G.

Peters Salt and Lumber Company was organized, he became its secretary and treasurer. Later he was instrumental in organizing the Michigan Maple Company and the Hemlock Bark Company; also president of the Lakewood Lumber Company of Grand Rapids and treasurer of the Gillette Roller Bearing Company, also of that city. He was for some time a member of the twenty-second regiment, National Guard, State of New York, from which he retired with the rank of Captain of the veteran corps. For years he was chairman of the Manistee County Republican Committee, and for a term served as secretary of the Congressional Committee, of the Ninth District of Michigan; a member of the Republican Central Committee from 1888 to 1902 and a member of its Executive Committee. For four years he served as Paymaster General of the Michigan troops. For twenty years he was on the school board of Eastlake. He was elected a Regent of the University in April, 1901, for the full term of eight years, and took his seat Jan. 1, following. In 1879 he was married to May M Ransom, daughter of Jonathan Ransom, of New York.

EZRA C. CARLETON

Member of Congress, 1883-5 and 1885-7. Was born at St. Clair, Mich., Sept. 6, 1838. He remained upon his father's farm and attended the district school until 1856, when he entered a more advanced school at Port Huron. In 1859 he began as clerk in mercantile business. He engaged with Wm. Stewart, hardware merchant, 1863, and four years later became partner with Mr. Stewart and Peter B. Sanborn. After ten years of successful business the firm was changed to Sanborn, Carleton & Co. In 1881, Mr. Carleton became the head of the firm. He was elected Mayor of Port Huron in 1881, and was chairman of the Port Huron fire relief committee in the same year. He was elected to the United States Congress on the Fusion Ticket.

PALMER S. CARLETON

Representative from St. Clair County, 1879-80. Was born in Hoosick, N. Y., Nov. 29, 1831. He removed to St. Clair, Mich., in 1866. He received an academic education, and spent ten winters in teaching school. He held the office of Suprvisor in his township for nine years, and was chairman of the board for three years. He was appointed delegate to represent his county on the Board of State Equalization in 1866. His occupation was a farmer; politics Democrat. He left the farm about 1862 and resided at St. Clair where he died July 2, 1917.

AUBERN D. CARLTON

Representative from Eaton County, 1885-6. Was born in Pittsfield, Mich., Feb. 18, 1846. He remained with his parents on a farm until he was fourteen years of age. In 1864 he enlisted in the 10th Mich. Cavalry, Co. D, and remained in the regiment until the close of the war. Upon being discharged he came to Windsor, Eaton County, where he worked on a farm summers and attended school winters until 1869. He engaged in farming for himself, in Windsor. He held the office of Supervisor for six successive years.

ISRAEL E. CARLTON

Representative from Oceana County, 1865-6; and Senator from the Thirtieth District, 1867-8 and 1869-70. Was born in New Hampshire, Mar. 26, 1819. By occupation he was a lumberman, politically a Republican. The exact date of his first residence in Michigan is unknown. He was a practical business man, and as a Legislator was a man of tact and influence. He died Mar. 28, 1871.

SHERLOCK H. CARMER

Representative from the First District of Ingham County, 1881-2. Was born Jan. 29, 1842, in Portage County, O. His parents were formerly from New Jersey. He was in active business from his youth up, and held many positions of trust, both public and private. He came to Lansing, Mich., 1869, engaged in mercantile business, and went from that into milling. He was senior member of the firm of Carmer, Parmelee & Co., "Capital Mills," Lansing. He was a Democrat. Deceased.

CHARLES K. CARPENTER

Representative from Oakland County, 1859-60. Was born in Hornellsville, N. Y., Jan. 23, 1826. In 1837 he came with his parents to Orion, Oakland County, and worked clearing land and in a saw mill, receiving only six months' schooling after he was ten years of age. By occupation he was a farmer. He helped organize the Oakland Agricultural Society, was president for two years, and a director twenty years. He was also director of the Detroit & Bay City railroad. In politics he was a Democrat. After 1861 he did not act with the Democrats, but was a leader in the Prohibition party, and was a candidate at various times for Governor, Auditor General and Presidential Elector on that ticket.

DAVID CARPENTER

Member of the State Board of Agriculture, 1861-3 and 1865-71. Was born at Potsdam, N. Y., Apr. 19, 1815. He received an academical education, taught school two winters, and in 1836 came to Toledo, O., and was first a clerk, then engaged in the grocery and baking business. In 1838 he removed to Blissfield, Mich., and became the junior member of the firm of G. & D. Carpenter, merchants. He also owned a large farm. He was engaged in mercantile business until 1852. In 1867 he again went into mercantile business as the head of the firm of Carpenter & Brown, and with Mr. Furnam built the first brick block at Blissfield. He was also interested in "Bay View," the summer resort near Petoskey; built a residence there, purchased a large farm, and invested largely in real estate. He died at Mt. Dora, Fla., Dec. 22, 1891.

GUY CARPENTER

Representative from Lenawee County, 1843. Was born at Potsdam, N. Y., Dec. 13, 1809. He received an academical education, studied higher mathematics and civil engineering, and came to Michigan in 1830, taught school, and from 1832 to 1835 was a farmer, then became a merchant at Blissfield, continuing in that business until his death in 1849. He held the office of Supervisor, Justice and County Commissioner. He was an anti-slavery Democrat. As a Legislator he drafted the first law for the drainage of swamps, marshes, and other low lands. He died at Blissfield, 1849.

HENRY D. CARPENTER

Representative from Wayne County, 1850. His postoffice address was Detroit. (Further data unobtainable).

JOEL CARPENTER

Senator from the Eleventh District, 1859-60 and 1861-2. Was born in Potsdam, N. Y., Sept. 3, 1818. He graduated from St. Lawrence Academy in 1837, came to Adrian, Mich., 1838, read law and was admitted to the bar in 1842. He was a Whig, but in 1841 with others, organized the anti-slavery party in Lenawee County. He was a delegate to the Free Soil Convention at Buffalo in 1848. He became a Republican in 1854, was Supervisor and Postmaster of Blissfield, Deputy U. S. Assessor, Enrolling Officer during the war, Census Enumerator, and was an alternate delegate to the Chicago Republican Convention in 1880. He died at Blissfield, Mich., Jan. 1891.

MANSON CARPENTER

Representative from Lenawee County, 1879-80 and 1881-2; and Senator from the Sixth District, 1885-6. Was born in the township of Greenfield, Saratoga County, N. Y., Oct. 2, 1830. With his parents he came to Woodstock, Lenawee County, in 1836, and resided there. His education was principally obtained in the common schools. He held various township offices, including that of Supervisor for two years. His occupation that of a farmer. He was elected to the Senate on the Republican ticket.

WILLIAM ELMORE CARPENTER

Representative from the Second District of Oakland County, 1883-4 and 1891-2. He owned the farm and lived in the house in which he was born, the farm consisting of 280 acres. His business was that of farming, though he taught school several terms at the same time. He held the offices of School Inspector, Superintendent of Schools, Justice, Town Clerk and Supervisor.

WILLIAM LELAND CARPENTER

Justice of the Supreme Court, 1902-8; and member of the State Board of Agriculture, 1910-12. Was born near Orion, Oakland County, Mich., Nov. 9, 1854; there he lived with his parents on their farm until 1872, when he entered the Michigan Agricultural College. He was graduated from that institution in 1875 and from the law department of the University of Michigan in 1878. He practiced law in the city of Detroit from 1878 until Jan. 1, 1894, when he became one of the judges of the Third Judicial Circuit of this State. He became president of the Detroit College of Law in January, 1903. He was elected Justice of the Supreme Court of Michigan, Nov. 4, 1902, to fill a vacancy caused by the death of Hon. Charles D. Long; re-elected, but resigned Sept. 15, 1908. He was elected a member of the State Board of Agriculture on Apr. 5, 1909, for a two year term.

NATHAN T. CARR

Representative from Midland County, 1859-60. Was by trade a printer, and a Republican in politics. He published a Republican paper at Midland City for some years. He removed from Midland City in 1862 or 1863, went into the army, and afterwards resided in Indiana. Reported deceased.

WILLIAM S. CARR

Representative from Washtenaw County, 1840; and Delegate from Washtenaw County to the Constitutional Convention of 1850. Was born in Columbia County, N. Y., in 1808, came to Michigan in 1833, and settled in Manchester, Washtenaw County. In politics he was a Whig in 1840; after that a Democrat. He served as Justice of the Peace, Supervisor and Councilman. He still resided at Manchester in 1888.

EDWARD ROSS CARTER

Representative from Delta County, 1923—. Was born in Ontario, Canada, Apr. 18, 1883, of Irish parentage. Leaving school when only twelve years of age, he began earning his own living working on a farm. At the age of seventeen he went on the railroad as a locomotive fireman, coming three years later to the Michigan Soo where he was employed as engineer on the Sabin Lock, hauling out the first ten cars of rock. Later he returned to railroad work and is at present a freight brakeman. He is a member of the Brotherhood of Railway Trainmen and for seven years has held the office representing the trainmen on legislative matters. He is also local chairman, representing the trainmen on the Soo railroad east of Minneapolis. Mr. Carter is married and has two daughters. He was elected to the Legislature on the Republican ticket Nov. 7, 1922, without opposition.

HARLEIGH CARTER

Representative from Macomb County, 1845 and 1850. Was an attorney and was admitted to the Macomb County bar in 1837. His residence was at Utica, Macomb County. He was appointed United States Judge in one of the western territories, and died there. He was long a Justice of the Peace at Utica, and was Prosecuting Attorney of Macomb County from 1842 to 1844.

JOHN CARTER

Representative from Livingston County, 1873-4. Was born in Queen's County, Ireland, Oct. 10, 1820, and received a common school education. In 1845 he emigrated to the United States and settled at Amboy, N. Y. In 1848 he emigrated to Michigan and settled in Milford, Oakland County. In 1856 he removed to Brighton. He held the position of Justice of the Peace many years, and was Supervisor several years. By occupation he was a farmer. He died at Oakwood, Nov. 9, 1890.

AUGUSTUS C. CARTON

Senator from the Twenty-eighth District, 1907-8; and Commissioner of the State Land Office, 1913-15. Was born on a farm in Clayton Township, Genesee County, in 1869, of Irish parentage. He received his education in the district school of Clayton Township, high school at Flint and the Michigan Agricultural College. He was married in 1904 to Miss Josephine Grace Hazelton, of Lansing, and they have two children. After leaving the Agricultural College he taught school, manufactured lumber and shingles in Ogemaw County, was employed in the State Land Office for five years and represented that department in the survey of the St. Clair Flats; was agriculturist for the Tawas Sugar Company and in 1907 represented the Twenty-eighth Senatorial District in the State Senate. At the expiration of his term as Senator he was appointed Deputy Commissioner of the State Land Office and later was made Secretary of the Public Domain Commission and Commissioner of Immigration. In politics he is a Republican. He was elected Commissioner of the State Land Office, Nov. 5, 1912.

JOHN J. CARTON

Representative from the Second District of Genesee County, 1899-1900, 1901-2 and 1903-4; and Delegate in the Constitutional Convention of 1907-8, from the Thirteenth District, Genesee County. Was born in Clayton, Genesee County, in 1856, and is of Irish descent. He was educated in the district schools in the township of Clayton, afterwards attended the Flushing High School and for a time attended the school in Flint. He was by turns a farmer, clerk and school teacher until 1877, when he worked in a drug store at Flushing until August of that year, then accepting a position with Niles & Cotcher, merchants at Flushing, as bookkeeper. He remained there until December, 1880, in which year he was elected Clerk of Genesee County, serving four years in that capacity. In the meantime he studied law and was admitted to the bar in 1884. He at once formed a partnership with George H. Durand, under the firm name of Durand and Carton. Mr. Carton was City Attorney for two years. He was a member of the House of Representatives from 1899 to 1905 and served as Speaker of the House in 1901 and 1903. At the opening of the Constitutional Convention of 1907, he was unanimously chosen its president and served in that capacity until the convention adjourned.

CHARLES ERNEST CARTIER

Senator, 1911-12, from the Twenty-sixth District, comprising the counties of Lake, Manistee, Mason, Newaygo and Oceana. Was born at Manistee, Mich., Mar. 24, 1875. He was educated in the Ludington public schools and the University of Michigan. He was manager of a factory for seven years, manager of a general store and in the lumber and coal business six years. He served as Mayor of Ludington, a director of the First National Bank of Ludington, vice-president of the Cartier Lumber Company and the Cartier Manufacturing Company. In politics a Republican.

JOHN F. CARTWRIGHT

Representative from the First District of Genesee County, 1893-4. Was born Dec. 19, 1846, in the township in which he lived. He attended the public schools until the war, when he enlisted in the Thirtieth Michigan Infantry. On returning he attended school at Flint and Pontiac until the fall of 1868, when he began teaching, in which he continued for three successive winter terms. In 1872 he was married to Miss Mercy A. Cole, of Davison, and engaged in the mercantile business at Davison, which he followed for three years. From 1875-7 he managed a flour and lumber mill; the two summers following he spent in the West. On returning he engaged in the mercantile business, which, in connection with banking, was his occupation for many years. In politics a Republican. He held most of the various township and village offices.

RICHARD B. CARUSS

Representative from Clinton County, 1881-2. Was born in Stafford, N. Y., Feb. 3, 1828. In May, 1833, he moved with his parents to Commerce, Oakland County, and worked on his father's farm until March, 1858. Having married in 1857, he removed to Farmington. In 1861 he enlisted in Co. "D," 2d Mich. Infantry, and participated in many battles. He was prostrated by sun-stroke, and was discharged on account of disability. He returned in 1864, and removed to Clinton County. His business was farming and stock-raising.

LYMAN CARVER

Representative from Washtenaw County, 1848. His postoffice address was Saline. (Further data not obtainable).

JOHN CARVETH

Senator from the Thirteenth District, 1885-6, consisting of Barry and Eaton counties. Was born at Saranac, Ionia County, Mich., Mar. 12, 1841. He was formerly a teacher, but later a lawyer, the senor member of Carveth & Hendrick, of Middleville, Barry County. He moved to Grand Rapids where he died May 14, 1910.

ARTHUR T. CASE

Representative from the Leelanaw District, 1885-6 and 1887-8, comprising the counties of Benzie and Leelanaw. Was born at Andover, O., Oct. 6, 1835. He had been a resident of Michigan twenty-five years. He held the offices of County Superintendent of Schools four years, County Clerk and Register six years, Supervisor fifteen years, and Justice of the Peace seventeen years. He was elected Representative as a Republican. He died Apr. 15, 1888, at his residence, Wildon Township, Benzie County.

BARNABAS CASE

Senator from the Second District, 1851. Was born Nov. 19, 1799, in Livingston County, N. Y. He came to Michigan in 1832, and settled in Manchester, Washtenaw County, in 1836. He was a farmer and distiller, and in politics a Democrat. He was Supervisor of Manchester in 1842 and 1849, was Postmaster and was elector on Breckenridge ticket, 1860. He died at Manchester July 2, 1880.

BERNIE L. CASE

Senator from the Twenty-fifth District, comprising the counties of Gratiot, Isabella and Mecosta, 1923—. Was born in Lorain County, O., Feb. 23, 1872. He came to Gratiot County, Mich., with his parents in 1887 and helped to clear the farm on which they settled. With the exception of the summers of 1891 to 1898, when he sailed the Great Lakes, Mr. Case has always lived on a farm. His education was obtained in the common schools of Ohio and Michigan. He is a member of the Presbyterian Church and the I. O. O. F. Always an active Republican, he has served several terms on the Board of Supervisors, held the offices of Township Clerk and Treasurer and in 1914 was elected County Clerk of Gratiot County, which office he held when elected to the Legislature Nov. 7, 1922 without opposition.

DANIEL L. CASE

Representative from Ionia County, 1851; and Auditor General, 1859-61. Was born in 1811, near Three Rivers, Canada, where his father was stopping for a time. He studied law with Wm. J. Moody at Penfield, N. Y., and came with Mr. Moody to Jackson, Mich., in 1834. In 1836 he went to Louisiana and Texas practicing law in both states. In 1843 he settled in practice at Mason, Mich., and was Prosecuting Attorney of Ingham County for three terms. In 1845 he engaged in mercantile business which he removed to Lansing in 1847. He was a Democrat until 1856, then wrote a powerful address, giving his adhesion to the Republican party, and became a party leader, and a most effective stump speaker. In 1864 he was appointed Paymaster in the army with the rank of Major, which he held until after the close of the war. Then he became a merchant, and later resided on a farm. Held many honorary positions, and was a trustee of the Institute for the Blind, at Lansing, and resident manager. Deceased.

EMANUEL CASE

Delegate from the Fourth District to the Constitutional Convention of 1835; and Representative from Livingston and Washtenaw counties, 1837. He only sat in the adjourned session of 1837 in place of Thomas Lee resigned. He built the first mill at Manchester for Major John Gilbert in 1832.

GEORGE F. CASE

Delegate from Montcalm County to the Constitutional Convention of 1867. Was born in Franklin County, Vt., Jan. 20, 1830. He removed with his father's family to Jackson, Mich., in 1846; and in 1850 engaged in the lumber business at Greenville. He went to Stanton in 1863 and continued the same business. He was twelve years a Supervisor, was two years Clerk of Montcalm County, and filled other local offices. In politics he was a Republican.

JAMES A. CASE

Representative from the district composing the counties of Alpena, Montmorency and Presque Isle, 1885-6. Was born at Farmersville, Ont., July 29, 1832. He came to Michigan in 1852, and resided for a number of years in Shiawassee County; removed to Alpena in 1864. He resided in the township of Alpena, where he followed the occupation of a farmer. At one time he edited the *Alpena County Pioneer*, of which paper he was the first editor. He held the offices of Justice of the Peace, Township Treasurer, member of the Board of Education, and Superintendent of the County Poor. He was elected Supervisor of the Township of Alpena five years in succession, during which time he was twice chosen chairman of the Board of Supervisors. He was appointed by the board a delegate to represent his county at the meeting of the State Board of Equalization in 1881. In politics he was a Republican. Deceased.

LEON D. CASE

Senator, 1913-14, from the Seventh Senatorial District, comprising the counties of Berrien and Cass. Was born at Ellsworth, Pierce County, Wis., Jan. 15, 1877, of English and French parentage. He was educated in the Ellsworth, Wis., and Watervliet, Mich., public schools. In 1891, he removed, with his parents, to Michigan, where he worked on several country newspapers and five years in the Watervliet paper mills. In 1900 he went into business with his father, as publisher of the Watervliet *Record*, under the firm name of E. F. Case and Son; also interested in farming at Watervliet. Married. In politics a Democrat.

OVID N. CASE

Representative from Wayne County, 1883-4 and 1885-6. Was born at Windsor, Ashtabula County, O., Nov. 13, 1853. After receiving a common school education he removed to Lenawee County, Mich., where for some years he worked on his father's farm. He was married in 1872. In 1875 he graduated from Adrian College. The same year he became Superintendent of Schools for Cambridge and later he entered upon the study of law in the office of Stacy & Underwood at Adrian. He began the practice of his profession at Vermontville, Eaton County, in 1877. The following year he came to Detroit, where he rose to a high place at the bar, and to a commanding political position. He was elected to the Legislature of 1887 but died Dec. 26, 1886.

SPAULDING M. CASE

Representative from Livingston County, 1851. Was born in Oswego County, N. Y., Nov. 7, 1813. By occupation he was a merchant, in politics first a Democrat then a Republican. He came to Michigan in 1837. He was four terms Supervisor of the town of Brighton. He died June 18, 1867.

WILLIAM L. CASE

Representative from the Leelanau-Benzie District, 1919-20 and 1921-2; and Senator from the Twenty-fifth District, 1923—. Was born in Gustavus, O., Aug. 21, 1856, of American parents. With his father's family, he came to Benzonia in 1860 and received his education in the local schools. After taking a business course in the Bryant and Stratton Business College of Chicago, he engaged in the lumber business in Benzonia. In 1889, he, with two of his brothers, incorporated under the name of Case Brothers Lumber Company and engaged in the manufacture of hardwood lumber and the business was continued until the charter expired in 1819. He is married and has eight children. Mr. Case held the office of Justice of the Peace almost consecutively for twenty-eight years and for many years was a member of the school board. In politics he is a Republican.

LEWIS CASS

Governor of the Territory of Michigan, 1813-31; member of the Board of Regents of the University of Michigan, 1843-4; United States Senator, 1845-8, 1849-57. Was born in Exeter, N. H., Oct. 9, 1782. His ancestors were early settlers in New England. His father was a commissioned officer in the revolutionary army, participated in the battles of Bunker Hill, Saratoga, Trenton, Princeton, Monmouth and Germantown, and was afterwards a Major in Wayne's army. In 1799 he removed to Marietta, O., finally settling in the vicinity of Zanesville, where he died in 1830. General Cass was educated at an academy in Exeter, N. H., and studied law at Marietta, under Governor Meigs. In 1806 he was elected to the Ohio Legislature, was one of a committee to investigate the enterprise of Colonel Burr. In 1807 he was appointed U. S. Marshal of Ohio, which office he resigned in 1813. In 1812 he volunteered his services to the force called out to join the army under General William Hull, and was elected Colonel of the 3d regiment of Ohio Volunteers. He marched with his regiment through the trackless wilderness to Detroit. After the surrender of General Hull he went to Washington and made a report to the government. The next spring he was appointed Colonel of the 27th Infantry, and was soon after promoted to Brigadier General. He joined the army of Gen. Harrison, was present in the pursuit of Proctor, and participated in the triumph at the Moravian towns. At the end of the campaign he was left in command of Michigan, with headquarters at Detroit. On the ninth of October, 1813, he was appointed Governor of the Territory of Michigan, which he held until July, 1831, when he became Secretary of War under President Jackson. During these eighteen years he stamped the impress of his mind on the institutions of Michigan. He negotiated Indian treaties by which settlers were enabled to become possessors of the soil. In October, 1836, he was appointed Minister to France, which he held until December, 1842. By the force of argument and weight of character he was able to break the treaty, already partly signed, between England, France, Russia, Austria and Prussia, which would have made England mistress of the seas by giving her the right of search. He was appointed Regent of the University Apr. 1, 1843, in the place of Oliver C. Comstock who had resigned, and completed the term the following year. In 1844 he was the leading Democratic candidate for President, at the Baltimore Convention, and received 125 votes, but was defeated by Polk. The same year he was elected United States Senator from Michigan, took his seat in 1845, and was chairman of the military committeee. In 1848 he was nominated as the Democratic candidate for President, but was defeated by General Taylor. In the Democratic National Convention of 1852 he at first received the most votes, but the choice ultimately fell on General Pierce. He was re-elected Senator in 1849 to fill the balance of term, also in 1851 and served until 1857. By the natural rise of real estate owned by him in Detroit, he became possessed of a large fortune in those days, and was hospitable and highly esteemed in social as well as political life. He was Secretary of State under President Buchanan from Mar. 4, 1857, to December, 1860, when he resigned, not agreeing with Buchanan and a portion of the cabinet, in their failure to make efforts to avert civil war and the division of the federal republic. He resided thereafter at Detroit until his death in July, 1866.

LEMUEL CASTLE

Representative from Shiawassee County, 1840 and 1841. Was born in Genesee County, N. Y., May 2, 1793. He received a common school education, enlisted as a

Sergeant in the War of 1812, took part in several battles and became a Captain. In 1820 he settled on a farm in Bloomfield, Mich., was seven terms Supervisor, also many terms a Justice. He was a Lieutenant in the militia in 1827. In 1837 he settled on a large farm in Shiawassee, Mich., and was again Supervisor and Justice. He died Oct. 28, 1882.

JOHN G. CATHCART

Representative from St. Joseph County, 1840. Was born in Watsontown, Pa., Jan. 1, 1799. His father and grandfather were both soldiers in the Revolution. He settled on a farm in Constantine, Mich., in 1831, and was the first Supervisor of the township, serving in 1837-8 and 1839. He was County Commissioner in 1839. In politics he was a Democrat.

JOHN J. CATHRO

Representative, 1895-6, from the Alpena District, composed of the counties of Alpena, Montmorency, Otsego, Oscoda and Crawford. Was born on a farm in Forfarshire, Scotland, Apr. 3, 1842; four years later his father died, and his mother moved the family to the burgh of Forfar, where he learned the business of decorator, which was subsequently his occupation. In 1862 he moved to Glasgow, and after several trips across the Atlantic, in October, 1874, removed his family from the old country, locating at Alpena, Mich., where he took up a homestead, also continuing in his chosen occupation until about 1893 after which he engaged in farming, and to a limited extent in lumbering. In politics a Republican. He held the office of Township Treasurer, Supervisor, and Justice of the Peace.

ASHMON H. CATLIN

Representative from the Second District of Ingham County, 1911-12 and 1913-14. Was born at Hudson, Lenawee County, Mich., Apr. 19, 1869, of Irish and French ancestry. He received his education in the district and public schools of Wayland. In 1881 he removed with his parents to LeRoy Township, Ingham County. Married. He was elected President of the Webberville State Bank at their annual meeting in 1909; a member of the I. O. O. F. and the Gleaners. He held the office of Township Treasurer and Supervisor. In 1909 he was chairman of the Board of Supervisors of Ingham County. In politics a Democrat.

VOLNEY W. CAUKIN

Representative from Kent County, 1857-8. Was born in the State of New York, June 25, 1819. By occupation he was a farmer and land surveyor; in politics a Democrat up to 1848, a Free Soiler until 1854, then a Republican. He held nearly all township offices and those of County Surveyor and Deputy U. S. Surveyor. He came to Macomb County, Mich., in 1831, and from 1844 to 1884 was a resident of Kent County. In 1884 he became a resident of Jordan, Antrim County. He died May 16, 1888, at Almira, Antrim County.

MARTIN J. CAVANAUGH

Delegate in the Constitutional Convention of 1907-8 from the Tenth District, Jackson and Washtenaw counties. Was born in the township of Manchester, Washtenaw County, on July 23, 1866, and attended the district school in the township of Sharon until about fourteen years of age, when he went to the village of Manchester and graduated from the Manchester High School in 1883 and from the literary department of the University of Michigan with the degree of Bachelor of Arts in 1887. The same year he was admitted to the bar and commenced the practice of law in the village of Chelsea, and shortly thereafter removed to the city of Ann Arbor, where he subsequently resided. Mr. Cavanaugh was married Nov. 6, 1889, to Miss Mary C. Seery. He was a Commissioner of Schools of Washtenaw County and President of the Board of Education for the city of Ann Arbor for a number of years, and was elected Delegate to the Constitutional Convention by the Tenth Senatorial District as a Democrat, although the district was overwhelmingly Republican.

JAMES P. CAWLEY

Senator from the Eighth District, 1871-2. His postoffice address was Morenci, Lenawee County. (Further data not obtainable).

MERRIT N. CHAFEY

Representative from the counties of Manistee and Mason, 1873. Was born in Attica, N. Y. He received an academic education. In 1861 he enlisted as a private in the 5th N. Y. Cavalry, and participated in many battles. In 1864 he received a First Lieutenant's commission. He was mustered out of service June, 1865. In 1866 he emigrated to Michigan, and settled in Free Soil, Mason County. He was a farmer, and held various offices of trust in both town and county. He resigned as Representative before the extra session of 1874, and was succeeeded by Andrew J. Dovell.

ELI B. CHAMBERLAIN

Representative from the Chippewa District, comprising the counties of Alger, Chippewa, Mackinac and Schoolcraft, 1887-8. Was born in Oxford County, Ont., in 1834. He became a resident of Michigan about 1856. He engaged in real estate business, and was County Surveyor. In politics a Republican.

FRANK CHAMBERLAIN

Representative from the Second District of Allegan County, 1911-12 and 1913-14. Was born in Branch County, Mich., Aug. 31, 1858, of English parentage. He was educated in the public schools and at the Valparaiso, Ind., Normal. His parents died when he was five years of age and he afterwards resided with Dr. Daniel Wilson, a physician and farmer of Branch County, until the death of the latter in 1879. He attended school at Valparaiso in the fall of 1880 and the summer of 1881, being employed as a teacher in Allegan County in the winters of 1880-1. He went to Wayland in the fall of 1881 and resided there, with the exception of one year spent in Lake and Osceola counties. He was married in 1884 to Miss Ella J. Furber, of Leighton Township, Allegan County. Mr. Chamberlain settled on a farm in Wayland Township in 1890 and resided there until 1906 when he located at Wayland. He was Treasurer four years, Supervisor six years and President of Wayland two years. In politics a Republican.

FREMONT C. CHAMBERLAIN

Representative, 1893-4 to 1899-1900, from Gogebic District, composed of the counties of Gogebic, Ontonagon, Keeweenaw and Isle Royal. Was born in Ripon, Wis., Oct. 6, 1856. He acquired his education at the Ripon College; came to Marquette County, Mich., in 1875; taught school twelve years, moved to Gogebic County in 1887, where he engaged in the practice of law. He was married to Miss Etta Bartle, of Negaunee, Feb. 8, 1897. In politics a Republican. He held the offices of Supervisor, School Inspector, and Circuit Court Commissioner, and was connected with the popular fraternal orders of the State.

HARMON CHAMBERLAIN

Representative from St. Clair County, 1850. His postoffice address was St. Clair. (Further data not obtainable).

HENRY CHAMBERLAIN

Representative from Berrien County, 1849; and member of the State Board of Agriculture, 1883-9 and 1891-7. Was born at Pembroke, N. H., Mar. 17, 1824. He received an academical education. In 1836 he became a clerk at Concord, N. H. He removed with his father to Three Oaks, Mich., in 1843, and in 1854 became a merchant, but was also engaged in farming. He was Supervisor from 1845 to 1851, and often held that office after that time. In politics a Democrat. A member of the Congregational Church. Several times he was a Democratic candidate for Congress and for other offices, and in 1872 was a candidate for elector, and 1874 was the Democratic nominee for Governor, and the result was very close. As a Mason, he was grand master of the Grand Lodge in 1872; was a member of the Semi-centennial Commission in 1886, and presided at the meetings held in the Hall of Representatives, June 15, 1886. In 1883 he was appointed a member of the State Board of Agriculture for six years, and was again appointed in 1891. He died at Three Oaks, Feb. 9, 1907.

WILLIAM CHAMBERLAIN

Representative from Berrien County, 1871-2 to 1875-6; and Senator from the Thirteenth District, 1877-8 and 1879-80. Was born in Pembroke, N. H., Feb. 7, 1834. He was educated at Concord, and came to Michigan with his father in 1843. In business he was for many years a merchant, in politics a Republican. He was Postmaster, and was Superintendent of the Poor for twenty years, and held other local offices. He was president pro tem. of the Senate in 1879, and was president of the State Agricultural Society; was an authority in agricultural matters. He died in Chicago, Nov. 7, 1901.

SAMUEL CHAMBERLAIN

Representative from Oakland County, 1855-6. Was born in Amherstburg, Canada West, Sept. 15, 1820. He came to Michigan in 1821, where he made his home until

1863. He was long a resident of Pontiac, Mich. By occupation he was a merchant, in politics a Democrat. He was in the service of the government for eight years; was a hardware merchant after 1863; later Postmaster of Waupun, Wis. He died Oct. 23, 1893.

CLIFTON J. CHAMBERS

Representative from Gratiot County, 1907-8, 1909-10, 1911-12. Was born in Crawford County, O., Sept. 23, 1864, of American parentage. He came to Michigan with his parents in 1878 and settled in New Haven Township, Gratiot County. He obtained his education in the district schools of Ohio and at the Valparaiso, Ind., Normal School and Business College. For a number of years he taught school during the winter season and was engaged in building and contracting during the summer months. Later he purchased a farm on which he lived until 1907, when he moved to Ithaca. Mr. Chambers was married to Emma A. McWilliams in 1890. He held the offices of Township Treasurer, Supervisor for seven consecutive years and was elected County Clerk in 1902 and re-elected in 1904. In politics a Republican.

MICHAEL CHAMBERS

Representative, 1889-90, from the Chippewa District, comprising the counties of Alger, Chippewa, Luce, Mackinac and Schoolcraft. Was born at St. Ignace, Mich., in 1851. By profession a merchant. In politics a Democrat.

SCHUYLER CHAMPION

Senator, 1893-4, from the Fourteenth District, composed of the counties of Ingham and Shiawassee. Was born in Homer, Calhoun County, Mich., Feb. 14, 1847. When one year of age he moved with his parents to Sturgis, Mich. He attended public school, and at twelve years of age began the trade of carriage painter. In 1878 he began the practice of dentistry. He was married to Miss Agnes Clark, of Lansing, in 1871. In 1886 he moved to Lansing, where he continued in the practice of dentistry. He was elected to the Senate of 1893-4 on the Democrat and People's party tickets.

ELISHA POWELL CHAMPLIN

Representative from Hillsdale County, 1838 and 1840; and Senator from the Second District, 1841 and from the Third District, 1842. He came to Michigan in 1824, and located at Tecumseh, where he stayed two years and returned to New York. He again came to Tecumseh in 1830, and remained there until 1834, when he sold out and removed to Jonesville, engaging in the mercantile business with George C. Munro, and built a block of stores. He retired from business in 1851. He owned a farm east of the village. He was Postmaster from 1840 to 1844. In politics he was a Whig. He died in 1855.

JOHN WAYNE CHAMPLIN

Justice of the Supreme Court, 1884-91. Was born at Kingston, Ulster County, N. Y., Feb. 7, 1831. His prominence as an attorney made him a frequent candidate with his party for judicial honors; was Judge of the Recorder's Court in Grand Rapids in 1861, candidate for Circuit Judge in 1863, Prosecuting Attorney of Kent County in 1864, was Mayor of Grand Rapids in 1867, and candidate for the same office again in 1868. He was nominated for Justice of the Supreme Court by the Fusion party in 1883, and elected. He died at Grand Rapids July 24, 1901.

DAVID G. CHANDLER

Representative from Grand Traverse County, 1909-10 and 1911-12. Was born at Flushing, Genesee County, Mar. 3, 1847. He received his education in the district schools of Lenawee and Monroe counties. He removed to Grand Traverse County in 1864, his attention having been given to lumbering and farming. In politics a Republican. He held the offices of Sheriff, Supervisor and member of the Board of Education.

GEORGE CHANDLER

Representative from Monroe County, 1851. Was born in Granville, N. Y., May 16, 1800. By occupation he was a wagon maker, in politics a Democrat. He came to Romeo in 1845, and held the positions of Postmaster and Justice of the Peace. He died Feb. 18, 1867. His three sons graduated at the State University.

JOSEPH H. CHANDLER

Senator from the Thirty-second District, consisting of Houghton, Ontonagon, Keweenaw, and Isle Royal counties, 1881-2. Was born at Niles, Cayuga County, N. Y., July 30, 1842. He came to Michigan in 1857, and resided in Washtenaw County until 1868; then he went to Houghton County. In 1862 he went to the army and served until 1866. He was admitted to the bar in 1869, at Houghton. He held the office of Prosecuting Attorney for Houghton County, and was Collector of Customs for the District of Superior.

MERRITT CHANDLER

Delegate in the Constitutional Convention of 1907-8 from the Twenty-ninth District, Presque Isle County. Was born in Lenawee County, Nov. 29, 1843, of English and Welsh ancestry, who located at Philadelphia about 1680. His father's sister was an anti-slavery poetess. He finished his education in a seminary. Mr. Chandler was born on a farm and lived there twenty-seven years. After that he became a lumberman, living in Cass County for five years, and moved to Cheboygan where he built the state road from Petoskey to Presque Isle Harbor, also seventeen miles of state road crossing at Onaway. In 1887 he moved to Onaway and platted the village of Onaway in 1892. In 1898 he secured the location of a railroad and later the establishment of saw mills and hardwood manufacturing plant employing several hundred men. This raised the population from seventy-five to 3,000 people in five years. He was married in 1886.

WILLIAM CHANDLER

Representative, 1899-1900 and 1901-2, from the Chippewa District, comprising the counties of Luce, Mackinac and Chippewa. Was born of Quaker parentage, in

Raisin Township, Lenawee County, Apr. 27, 1846, and spent his early life on a farm, receiving his education at a Quaker seminary near his home. In 1862 he went to Indianapolis, Ind., to serve an apprenticeship at a trade, but before completing it he changed his mind and went into a wholesale paper business on his own account. This naturally brought him into constant intercourse with newspaper men, and in 1870 he became the editor and publisher of a Republican paper in Muncie, Ind. The venture failed because of the libel suits and consequent expensive litigation, and in 1872 he returned to Michigan and took the editorship of the newly established Adrian *Press*. By a change of ownership and politics he left the *Press* and joined the staff of the Adrian *Times*, remaining there until 1875, when he established the Cheboygan *Tribune*. In 1876 he was elected a member of the Republican State Central Committee; in 1877 was appointed collector of tolls of St. Mary's Falls Ship Canal, and in 1878 established the Sault Ste. Marie *News*. In 1881 the canal passed under the control of the United States and Mr. Chandler became Superintendent, holding that position until 1885. In 1886 he organized the Sault Savings Bank, and became its first cashier and manager. In the same year he was instrumental in organizing a central station electric light plant at the "Soo." In 1892 he organized the Chandler-Dunbar Water Power Company at the "Soo," laying the foundation for one of the largest water-power developments in the country. In 1875-6 he secured a swamp land appropriation, and established the famous "Inland Route" between Cheboygan and Petoskey.

ZACHARIAH CHANDLER

United States Senator, 1857-75 and 1879. Was born in Bedford, N. H., Dec. 10, 1813, and with the advantages of a common school education, became a resident of Detroit in 1833. He engaged in trade and in a few years the firm of which he was the head became the leading wholesale dry goods house in Michigan. In politics a Whig, and strongly anti-slavery in his sentiments, he soon became a leading politician, more through the action of his friends than from personal ambition. He was elected Mayor of Detroit in 1851, and was the Whig candidate for Governor in 1852, when he stumped the State vigorously, and made as strong a fight as possible with a minority party, personally running ahead of the ticket. In 1857 he was elected the first Republican United States Senator from Michigan. He was re-elected in 1863, and in 1869, serving continuously eighteen years, from Mar. 4, 1857, to Mar. 4, 1875. In 1862 he secured the passage of a resolution on the conduct of the war, and declining to be chairman, was an active member of that committee during the war. He had the full confidence of President Lincoln, and made his influence felt, especially at the time when disaster and defeat followed our armies in the field. In 1875 he was defeated as a candiate for Senator by several members who refused to go into Republican caucus, their votes combining with the Democrats to defeat him, and to elect Judge Christiancy, also a leading Republican. He was soon appointed Secretary of the Interior by President Grant, and became a most efficient and able cabinet officer, serving until the close of the second term of Grant. From 1876 to 1880 he was chairman of the National Republican Committee, and in 1878 was chairman of the Republican State Committee. Senator Christiancy having resigned in 1879, to accept the position of Minister to Peru, Mr. Chandler was elected Mar. 18, 1879, to fill the vacancy. Soon after he made the short and thrilling speech in the Senate that defeated the attempt to place Jefferson Davis on the Mexican pension roll, which gave him a host of friends in the Northern States. The same year, on invitation, he made many speeches to large meetings, but died suddenly at Chicago, Nov. 1, 1879, after addressing the young Republicans of that city.

CALEB M. CHAPEL

Representative from the Third District of Jackson County, 1853-4. His postoffice address was Gidley's Station. (Further data not obtainable).

CHARLES W. CHAPEL

Representative from Chippewa and the counties thereto attached, 1855-6. His postoffice address was Sault Ste. Marie. (Further data not obtainable).

WORDEN R. CHAPELL

Representative from the First District of Shiawassee County, 1887-8. Was born in the township of Dexter, Washtenaw County, in 1848. Mar. 9, 1883, he received the appointment by President Arthur of Postmaster at Corunna, which office he held until Aug. 1, 1886. Mr. Chapell was Treasurer of his city and Supervisor of the 3d ward of Corunna, and was elected Representative on the Republican ticket.

SAMUEL A. CHAPIN

Representative from St. Joseph County, 1839. His postoffice address was White Pigeon. (Further data not obtainable).

THEODORE N. CHAPIN

Representative from Antrim County, 1915-16, 1917-18 and 1919-20. Was born at Grattan, Kent County, Mich., Dec. 10, 1862, of Welsh parentage. He was educated in the public schools of Green Bay, Wis. At the age of fourteen he began working in the lumber woods, and in 1881 he removed to Bellaire, where he subsequently resided. His chief occupation was farming. He served as School Director, School Treasurer, Justice of the Peace and Sheriff. Married. In politics a Republican.

ADELBERT R. CHAPMAN

Representative from Hillsdale County, 1885-6 and 1887-8; and Senator, 1889-90, from the Sixth District, comprising the counties of Hillsdale and Jackson. Was born in the township of Ash, Monroe County, Mich., Feb. 24, 1846. A dealer in real estate and hard-wood lumber. In former years he was a farmer, merchant and banker. During the war he served in the 11th Mich. Cavalry.

IRA GARDNER CHAPMAN

Representative from Macomb County, 1901-2 and 1903-4. Was born at Sterling, Macomb County, Nov. 20, 1841. His education was obtained at the district school supplemented by one year at the Utica High School. In February, 1878, he was married to Miss Mary Wilcox of Oakland County. He was appointed Census Enumerator in 1890 and again in 1900. In 1891 he was elected Supervisor of his township which for thirty years, had elected a Democratic Supervisor.

LEANDER CHAPMAN

Representative from Jackson County, 1849. Was born in Oswego County, N. Y. He came to Jackson, Mich., in 1835, and commenced the practice of law. He was Judge of Probate from 1836 to 1840, also Prosecuting Attorney during a portion of that time. He was County Treasurer from 1842 to 1846. He was a man of high standing both as a lawyer and a citizen. In politics he was a Democrat. He finally removed to Cedar Falls, Ia., where he died in 1863 or 1864.

WARREN CHAPMAN

Senator from the Eighteenth District, 1865-6 and from the Sixteenth District, 1867-8. Was born at New Market, N. H., July 24, 1812. He was educated at Bracket Academy, Greenland, and at the age of twenty-one engaged in the mercantile business at New Market. In 1836 he lost his means in land speculations, and learned the trade of a machinist, at which he worked five years. He emigrated to St. Joseph, Mich., in 1843, where he was a lumber merchant for eight years. From 1855 to 1859 he was County Register of Deeds; from 1859 to 1867 was in the real estate business; and after 1864 was the owner of a large farm. He was first a Whig, a Republican after 1854.

ALEXANDER CHAPOTON

Representative from Wayne County, 1863-4. Was born in Detroit, Feb. 3, 1818. He was descended from the early French stock as was his brother William, elsewhere mentioned. He was by profession an architect, contractor and builder, and filled many places of trust, both under the city and State governments. His politics were Whig and Republican. He did not sit in extra session of 1864. He died May 2, 1893.

WILLIAM CHAPOTON

Representative from Wayne County, 1861-2. Was a descendant of one of the earliest French families by whom Detroit was settled, and was born in 1825. He was a contractor and builder. His political faith was first to the Whig party, and afterwards to its successor, the Republican party.

FRANCIS CHARTER

Representative from Monroe County, 1835-6 and 1838. His postoffice address was LaSalle. He was Supervisor of his township from 1831-5. (Further data not obtainable).

EUGENE V. CHASE

Representative from Clinton County, 1877-8 and 1879-80. Was born in Trumbull County, O., Sept. 6, 1833. He graduated as a physician from the State University, first practicing at Ovid, Mich., then at Elsie. In 1861 he enlisted in the 1st Mich. Cavalry and served through the war, rising to the rank of First Lieutenant. He was several times Supervisor of Duplain, and chairman of the County Board. In politics a Republican.

IRVING CHASE

Representative from Osceola County, 1919-20 and 1921-2. Was born in Walden, Orange County, N. Y., June 27, 1851, of American parents. He removed with his parents to East Saginaw, Mich., in 1868, and was educated in the public schools of that city. He served as clerk in the City Clerk's office for two years, and at the same time acted as reporter for the Saginaw *Enterprise and Courier*. In 1873 he moved to Evart, where he published the Evart *Review* from 1873 to 1881. Since that time he has been engaged chiefly in the real estate and insurance business. He has served the township as Clerk, Justice of the Peace, and Supervisor, and the village as Assessor, Clerk, Trustee and President. He was Assistant Postmaster for four years and Judge of Probate eight years. Mr. Chase is a widower and has one son. In politics he is a Republican.

JONATHAN CHASE

Delegate to the Constitutional Convention of 1835 from the Fifth District; and Representative from Oakland County, 1839. Was born in Richfield, N. Y., in June, 1795, and died Mar. 8, 1882, in Royal Oak, Mich. He came to Michigan in 1825 and settled at Royal Oak. He was a mason by trade, in politics a Democrat. He was Town Clerk, Supervisor and Justice of the Peace.

MARCUS A. CHASE

Representative from Wayne County (Detroit), 1857-8. Was born in Ontario County, N. Y., May 24, 1832, and came with his parents to Detroit in 1841. His education was academic, including three years at the University of Michigan. His legal education was acquired by private study and by attendance at the State and National law school at Poughkeepsie, N. Y. He was admitted to the bar in Detroit in 1854, and was continuously in practice in Detroit. A Democrat in politics.

WILLIAM CHASE

Representative from Branch County, 1861-2. Was born in Westford, N. Y., Nov. 12, 1815. At eight years of age he came with his father to Michigan. He received a common school education and learned the trade of a carpenter. He settled on a farm in Kinderhook, Branch County, in 1841. He was the first Justice of the town, was Supervisor eight years, and chairman of the County Board and filled other local positions. Deceased.

CHESTER C. CHATFIELD

Representative from Eaton County, 1855-6. Was the first attorney in Eaton County, and was admitted to the bar in 1845, and practiced law at Eaton Rapids. He was Prosecuting Attorney from 1850 to 1852. He attained good standing as an attorney, held an influential position in the Democratic party, and was an able political writer and speaker. He published a Know Nothing paper in 1854. He died about 1856.

CHARLES B. CHAUVIN

Representative from Wayne County, 1867-8. Was born in Grosse Pointe, Nov. 11, 1832. His official career was confined to several years' service as Township Clerk and School Inspector. He was a lineal descendant of M. Chauvin, Governor of New France, of which Michigan and the Northwest formed a part, 1603 to 1612. Occupation was a farmer. He was a Democrat in politics, but took a prominent part in the Greenback or National party.

HENRY MARTYN CHEEVER

Representative from the First District of Wayne County, 1899-1900. Was born at Stillwater, Saratoga County, N. Y., June 20, 1832. His father, Rev. Ebenezer Cheever, D. D. (1791-1866), was a leading Presbyterian divine in the eastern states for many years. He received his education in classical and private schools in New Jersey, and at the University of Michigan, where he was graduated in 1853 with the highest honors, taking the full college course, and receiving the degree of A. B., and three years later that of A. M. He then studied law and was admitted to the bar in his twenty-first year, and from that time forward devoted himself almost exclusively to his profession. He was a member of the Board of Education of Detroit from 1857 to 1861, and of the State Board of Visitors to the University of Michigan in 1857 and 1858. A staunch Presbyterian, he was one of the organizers of the Westminster Church of Detroit, a member of the Board of Trustees for many years, and was four years its president. In politics a Republican. At the outset of his professional life Mr. Cheever married Sarah Buckbee, eldest daughter of Hon. Walter Buckbee, a prominent lawyer in the State. Mrs. Cheever died in 1890.

AMHERST B. CHENEY

Representative from Kent County, 1877-8 and 1879-80. Was born in Ripley, O., Oct. 27, 1841. He removed with his father to Homer, Mich., in 1845. In 1862 he enlisted as a private in the 21st Mich. Infantry, took part in many battles, was promoted to First Lieutenant and was mustered out in 1865. He taught school two years, and engaged in a general collection, insurance and real estate business, and was Justice and Town Treasurer at Sparta. In politics a Republican.

HENRY P. CHERRY

Representative from Barry County, 1871-2. Was born in Bethany, N. Y., May 21, 1823, and removed with his father to Ohio in 1831, and to Johnstown, Mich., in 1838, where he was Postmaster. In politics he was a Whig; after 1854 a Republican. He was one of the members of "Under the Oaks" convention at Jackson. He was County Clerk in 1863-4, and bookkeeper in the State Land Office for eight years. Later he resided at Bedford, Mich., where he was for several years Town Clerk, also a Justice of the Peace. He died at Johnstown July 17, 1895.

EASTON T. CHESTER

Representative from Hillsdale County, 1844. Was born at Mexico, N. Y., Mar. 3, 1807. In 1837 he removed to Camden, Mich., and took up a farm. He built the first barn and the second saw mill in the town. He also built a carding mill. He increased his farm until he owned 1,400 acres. The carding mill was converted into a grist-mill, and was one of the best mills in southern Michigan. He dealt extensively in black walnut lumber, and shipped over $200,000 worth from Camden. He was Supervisor ten years, Justice of the Peace nine years, and always a prominent man.

JACOB E. CHEW

Representative from Charlevoix County, 1917-18 and 1919-20. Was born in Drake County, O., Sept. 25, 1863, of English parents. He was educated in the public schools. He removed to Charlevoix County in 1879, and resided there. He taught in the district schools for three years, and for ten years was engaged in the flour and grain business, then in farming. Married. He served five years on the Board of Supervisors, two years on the Village Board, eight years as School Director, and eight years as Justice of the Peace; a member of the F. & A. M., I. O. O. F., and Charlevoix Grange. In politics a Republican.

AARON CHILDS

Representative from Washtenaw County, 1871-2. Was born in Henniker, N. H., Dec. 1, 1806. In early life he worked in a woolen factory, and became foreman. He settled on a farm in Augusta, Mich., in 1833. The first election was held at his house and he was the first Town Clerk, which office he held six years, and was Supervisor for eighteen years. In politics he was a Democrat. He died Mar. 4, 1881.

AUGUSTUS W. CHILDS

Representative from Lenawee County, 1851. Was born in the State of New York in 1814. He came to Michigan in 1836, and resided at Hudson, Lenawee County. He was Supervisor, Town Clerk, and held other office. By occupation he was a farmer, politically a Republican.

J. WEBSTER CHILDS

Representative from Washtenaw County, 1859 and 1861-2; Senator from the Eighth District, 1865-6, from the Sixth District, 1867-8, and from the Fourth District, 1873-4 and 1879-80; and member of the State Board of Agriculture, 1869-82. Was born in Henniker, N. H., June 16, 1826. He received an academic education and settled as a farmer in Augusta, Mich., in 1848. He held the office of Supervisor seven years, School Inspector twenty years, and Drain Commissioner. He was a man of force and character, and made his mark as a Legislator. He died at Ann Arbor, Nov. 11, 1882.

ARTHUR H. CHILVER

Representative from the First District of Kent County, city of Grand Rapids, 1895-6. Was born in Aurora, Ill., 1860, and came with his parents to Grand

Rapids, Mich., in 1866; attended the city schools; learned the trade of bookbinding and blank book manufacturing in his father's establishment. Later he purchased the business. In politics a Republican. He was secretary of the Republican City Committee in 1892; member of the Board of Education, and was elected to the House of 1895-6, on the general legislative ticket of the city of Grand Rapids.

HENRY C. CHIPMAN

Judge of the Supreme Court of the Territory of Michigan, 1827-32. Was born in the State of Vermont, July 25, 1784, and was the son of Nathaniel Chipman, Judge, U. S. Senator and legal writer. The son was a graduate of Middlebury College in 1803, was admitted to the bar, practiced law in South Carolina, and removed to Detroit in 1823 and engaged in practice. He was a Chief Justice of the court of Wayne County. From 1841 to 1843 he was Judge of the criminal Court of Wayne County. He continued in practice until his death, Mar. 31, 1867. He was a Whig in politics, a Conservative after 1854; in religion an Episcopalian.

J. LOGAN CHIPMAN

Representative from the First District of Wayne County, 1865-6; and a member of Congress, 1887-9 to 1893. Was born at Detroit, Mich., June 5, 1830. He was educated in the schools of that city and at the University of Michigan. He engaged in the Lake Superior region as an explorer for the Montreal Mining Company in 1846, was admitted to the bar in 1854, and participated in making the treaty of Detroit with the Ottawas and Chippewas of Michigan. In politics a Democrat. He was Assistant Clerk of the State House of Representatives of Michigan in 1853; was elected City Attorney of Detroit in 1856, and held that position until 1861; was elected to the Michigan Legislature in 1864; was appointed attorney of the Police Board of Detroit in 1865; ran for Congress in 1866, but was defeated; retained the office of attorney of Police until May 1, 1879, when he was elected Judge of the Superior Court of Detroit to which position he was re-elected at the end of six years; was elected to the Fiftieth Congress, and re-elected to the Fifty-first, Fifty-second and Fifty-third Congresses. He died Aug. 17, 1893.

JOHN S. CHIPMAN

Representative from St. Joseph County, 1842; and member of Congress, 1845-7. Was born about 1801 in Vermont, where he received his education, graduating at Middlebury College in 1823. He came to Michigan in 1838, and settled at Centerville, St. Joseph County. At the expiration of his term he settled at Niles. In 1849-50 he removed to San Francisco, Calif., where he died some twelve years later. He was a lawyer, a natural orator, and listening to one of his speeches was like reading one of Cooper's novels. He was over six feet in height, slender, large head, dark complexion, hair black, straight and thick, forehead low and broad; his eye dark and piercing; his appearance that of an Indian Sachem. He was universally called "Black Chip." He was a Democrat. His expression in Congress that "Education was at war with democracy," gave him notoriety in the old world.

JOSEPH S. CHIPMAN

Senator from the First District, 1845-6. Was born in Shoreham, Vt., in September, 1803, and was a descendant of a family which contained some of the most distinguished lawyers of that State. He graduated from Middlebury College in 1828, was admitted to the Vermont bar in 1833, and practiced law at Middlebury for several years. He settled in Niles, Mich., in 1836, and practiced his profession there. He died at Niles in November, 1870.

CLYDE C. CHITTENDEN

Senator, 1895-6, from the Twenty-seventh District, counties of Antrim, Benzie, Charlevoix, Grand Traverse, Kalkaska, Leelanau and Wexford. Was born in Cattaraugus County, N. Y., Aug. 19, 1860. He acquired an academic education, taught school a few terms and attended Hamilton College, N. Y. He studied law with a law firm at Little Valley, N. Y.; came to Michigan in the fall of 1883 and engaged in the insurance and law business, being admitted to the bar in March of 1884; also engaged in real estate business and lumber, being a stockholder in the Wexford Lumber Company, and vice president of said company. In politics a Republican. He was elected Circuit Court Commissioner in the fall of 1884, and Prosecuting Attorney for the terms of 1887-8, 1889-90 and 1891-2.

WILLIAM F. CHITTENDEN

Representative from Wayne County, 1849 and 1853-4. Was born Mar. 28, 1812, in Kent County, England. He emigrated to this country in 1825, and worked in Utica, N. Y., learning the trade of a blacksmith, from 1826 to 1832. He came to Detroit, Mich., in 1835, and was Alderman of that city in 1839, 1841, and 1846. He served in the war with Mexico as Quartermaster and Commissary. In politics he was a Democrat.

EMERSON CHOATE

Delegate to the Constitutional Convention of 1850 from Monroe County; and Representative from Monroe County, 1861-2. Was born in North Carolina in 1808. He was Postmaster in Monroe, was Supervisor, and was Justice of the Peace, in his town for some twenty consecutive years. He was a farmer by occupation; in politics a Democrat.

HUGH CHRISHOLM

Representative from Gratiot County, 1891-2. Was born in Ross shire, Scotland, Apr. 29, 1855, came with his parents to Ingham County, Mich., when three years of age, and went to Gratiot County four years later. At that early day Gratiot County was an almost unbroken wilderness, and the subject of this sketch endured with his parents, the privations and hardships incident to pioneer life. He resided in Emerson Township on a farm cleared by his own hands. In politics a staunch Prohibitionist. He was nominated in 1890 for Representative by the Patrons of Industry and endorsed by the Democrats and Prohibitionists.

ISAAC P. CHRISTIANCY

Senator from the Third District, 1850-1; Justice of the Supreme Court, 1858-75; United States Senator, 1875-9. Was born at Johnstown, N. Y., Mar. 12, 1812. His education was that of common schools, and he was early a teacher. He studied law, came to Monroe, Mich., in 1836, and completed his studies. He took high rank as a lawyer and from 1838 to 1857 was in practice at Monroe. From 1841 to 1846 was Prosecuting Attorney; in 1848 was a delegate and leader at the National Free Soil Convention at Buffalo; and Free Soil candidate for Governor in 1852. He was the leader and prime mover in the political combination of the Whig and Free Soil parties in 1854, from which sprang the Republican party. He was a delegate to the First National Republican Convention at Philadelphia in 1856. He purchased and edited the Monroe *Commercial.* In 1857 he was elected Associate Justice of the Supreme Court of Michigan, and was re-elected in 1865 and 1873, serving part of the time as Chief Justice. In 1875 he was elected United States Senator, and after a service of two years was appointed Minister to Peru, and resigned. He remained at Lima, Peru, several years. After his return he was for a part of the time engaged in practice before the courts. He was an able Judge and a courteous and honorable man in every position. He died at Lansing, Sept. 8, 1890.

HARVEY CHUBB

Representative from Washtenaw County, 1846 and 1847. His postoffice address was Ann Arbor. (Further data not obtainable).

LUCIUS L. CHURCH

Representative from the Second District of Montcalm County, 1891-2 and 1893-4. Was born in the township of Ada, Kent County, Apr. 1844. He moved with his parents to Illinois when five years of age, where two years later his father died; he then moved to Wisconsin where he stayed until twelve years of age, when he returned to his home in Michigan. His education was received in the district schools, which he left during the second year of the war and enlisted in the 21st Mich. Infantry, where he served until the close of the war, when he returned to Michigan, locating in Montcalm County. By occupation a farmer; in politics a Republican. He held the offices of Justice of the Peace and Highway Commissioner, Treasurer and Supervisor.

THOMAS B. CHURCH

Delegate to the Constitutional Convention of 1850 from Kent and Ottawa counties; and Representative from Kent County, 1851 and 1855-6. Was born in Dighton, Bristol County, Mass., in September, 1821. His grandfather, Thomas Church, was a Colonel in the War of the Revolution, and he was a direct descendant of Benjamin Church who commanded in the Indian War which resulted in the death of King Philip. As a boy he was a sailor for several years, then entered Washington, now Trinity College, and graduated. He went south and engaged some years in teaching; spent one year in Cambridge law school, then finished his studies at Marshall and commenced practice in Grand Rapids in 1843. He was Prosecuting Attorney of Kent County two years; and in 1852 Mayor of Grand Rapids. He was three times the Democratic candidate for Congress in the Grand Rapids District. He married Mary E. Stuart.

WORTHY L. CHURCHILL

Representative from Alpena County, 1875-6. Was born in Batavia, Ill., Dec. 14, 1840. He was educated in the schools at Geneva, N. Y. He came to Michigan in 1872, resided at Alpena, and was largely engaged in manufacturing lumber. He was proprietor of the Churchill House at Alpena. In politics a Democrat.

ROBERT H. CLANCY

Member of Congress, 1923—. Was born in Detroit, Mar. 14, 1882, of colonial ancestry. He is a graduate of the Detroit Eastern High School and of the University of Michigan, with the degree of A. B. After his graduation he was political and court reporter on the Detroit *News* and traveled in Europe six months. He held the position of private secretary to Congressman F. E. Doremus two years, and to Secretary of Commerce E. F. Sweet four years. He was appointed U. S. customs appraiser of Michigan, serving five and one-half years. During the war he was in charge of the Detroit district of the U. S. war trade board and was appointed chief inspector of purchases of the medical corps of the War Department. He was also one of the organizers, and a member of the executive committee, of the Detroit patriotic relief fund and of the home service section of American Red Cross. He is a Democrat. He was elected to the Sixty-eighth Congress Nov. 7, 1922.

FRANK W. CLAPP

Representative from the Second District of Calhoun County, 1891-2; and Senator, 1893-4 and 1895-6, from the Ninth District, composed of the counties of Calhoun and Kalamazoo. Was born in Bedford, O., Nov. 25, 1844, and came to Battle Creek, Mich., the following year. He was a graduate of Olivet College and law department of Michigan University. By occupation he was a lawyer; in politics a Republican. He was City Attorney of Battle Creek and Prosecuting Attorney Commissioner of the State Land Office, 1873-7. Was born in Mottville, Mich., of Calhoun County. He died at Battle Creek May 9, 1916.

LEVERETT A. CLAPP

Commissioner of the State Land Office, 1873-7. Was born in Mottville, Mich., June 24, 1837. He received an academic education. In 1856 he was appointed Deputy Register of Deeds of St. Joseph County, a position he held until 1872, except two years when he was Register. In politics he was a Republican; in business at White Pigeon in 1887.

ALBERT K. CLARK

Representative from Washtenaw County, 1875-6. Was born in Jersey City, N. J., Nov. 1, 1810. He removed with his father's family to Seneca County, N. Y., and in 1836 came to Michigan, settling in Saline. He received a common school education, and was a farmer. In politics he was a Democrat. He died at Saline, Mich., Dec. 21, 1879.

ARTHUR MERRILL CLARK

Member of the Board of Regents of the University of Michigan, 1884-92. Was born at Landaff, N. H., Aug. 4, 1833, son of Daniel and Mary (Merrill) Clark. His parents both sprang from New England families. He attended the common schools of his native State till he was sixteen years of age. He then entered the Seminary and Collegiate Institute at Newbury, Vt., where he was graduated in 1853. He taught for a year and then came to Michigan as Principal of Schools at Lexington. He held this position for five years and then turned to commercial pursuits. In 1875 he disposed of his business and became Grand Lecturer of the Grand Lodge, of F. and A. M. of Michigan. He held this office till 1901 and then resigned it on account of failing health. He was married Aug. 16, 1855, at Stowe, Vt., to Mary E. Robison. She died July 27, 1862. He married a second time, at Littleton, N. H., Sept. 7, 1863, to Martha Hale. She died Aug. 22, 1896. Jan. 11, 1898, he was married to Emma Church Alford, who survived him. He was elected a Regent of the University on the Democratic ticket in April, 1883, and took office Jan. 1, 1903. He died at Lexington, Oct. 27, 1903.

BENJAMIN CLARK

Representative from Calhoun County, 1869-70. Was born in Eaton, N. Y., May 3, 1811. He resided in western New York until 1836, when he went to Indiana. He removed to Albion, Mich., in 1852. By occupation he was a farmer, in politics a Whig until 1854, then a Republican. He was present at the birth of the Republican party "Under the Oaks." He was an earnest supporter of Albion College. He died Aug. 16, 1889, at Albion.

CHARLES W. CLARK

Representative form the Second District of Ingham County, 1915-16 and 1917-18. Was born in Ingham County, Mich., in 1862, of American parents. He was educated in the rural schools and the Dansville High School. He lived on a farm until about 1910 when he removed to Dansville. In 1904 he was appointed County Drain Commissioner by the Board of Supervisors and held the office for three years. He was elected Supervisor in 1908 and was re-elected each succeeding year; a director of the Farmers Bank of Mason for several years and also did quite an extensive business as an auctioneer. Mr. Clark was married. A Republican in politics. He died Dec. 16, 1921.

DARIUS CLARK

Representative from Calhoun County, 1851. Was born in Ovid, Seneca County, N. Y., in 1814. He came to Michigan and settled in Marshall in 1836, where he continued to live until 1852. He was a contractor on the M. C. R. R. and other railroads. He went to New York City in same year as general ticket agent of the M. C. R. R. in New York City, and remained there until he died in 1872 or 1873. He was a Whig in politics, and subsequently a Republican.

DAVID CLARK

Representative from Clinton County, 1851. Was born in Castleton, Vt., June 13, 1817. His parents removed to New York in 1822, where they resided until 1833, when they came to Pontiac, Mich. In 1835 they settled in Eagle, Clinton County, where the son lived, following the occupation of a farmer. He was a Democrat until 1856, then a Republican. He served as Supervisor and held other town offices.

EDWIN G. CLARK

Representative from Oakland County, 1877-8. Was born Apr. 8, 1815, in the town of Manlius (now called DeWitt), Onondaga County, N. Y. He received a common school education. He came to Michigan in 1831, first settling in Detroit. He removed to Independence, Oakland County, in 1836. He was the first School Inspector elected in his township, was Constable nine years, Justice of the Peace twelve years, and Supervisor four years. His occupation was farming; politics Democratic. He died at Clarkston, Mich., Dec. 14, 1908.

ELIJAH B. CLARK

Representative from Oakland County, 1847. Was born in Groton, Conn., Nov. 23, 1792, and died July 10, 1884. He came from Pennsylvania in 1830 and purchased a farm in Orion, Oakland County, settling upon it in 1831. He was Supervisor in 1837 and 1838, and was several times Assessor and Treasurer. In politics he was first Whig, then Republican. He was orginally a millwright, but followed farming in Michigan.

ELIHU L. CLARK

Representative from Lenawee County, 1848. Was born in Walworth, N. Y., July 18, 1811. He commenced business as a clerk in a dry goods store in Palmyra, N. Y., in 1830. In 1832 he began business for himself. In 1835 he removed to Adrian, Mich., and opened a store, selling only for cash. From 1838 to 1842 he invested in state warrants and state script, which he bought at a discount and held until he received par value. He continued in the dry goods trade until 1847. After that time engaged in loaning money. He was several years president of the Lenawee County Savings Bank. He died before 1888, leaving the largest fortune in Lenawee County.

FREDERICK O. CLARK

Representative from Delta and other counties, 1875-6. Was born at Girard, Pa., in 1842, and received an academic education. He removed to Michigan in 1862, and took up his residence in the Upper Peninsula. For four years engaged as a civil engineer on the Northwestern Railroad, and also in the iron mines. He was admitted to the bar in 1870. In 1871 he was elected president of the village of Escanaba, and served one term. In 1872 he was elected Prosecuting Attorney of Delta County. In politics a Republican. He was practicing law at Marquette in 1888.

GEORGE M. CLARK

Justice of the Supreme Court, 1919—. Was born at West Williams, Ont., Nov. 21, 1875, of Scotch parentage. He received his education in the high school and studied law in offices at Bad Axe. Mr. Clark engaged in the practice of law Jan. 1, 1905. He is a widower. For six years he was County Clerk of Huron County; was appointed by Governor Albert E. Seepler, a Justice of the Supreme Court, Dec. 30, 1919, to fill vacancy caused by the resignation of Franz C. Kuhn, and at the general election Nov. 2, 1920, he was elected for the full term which will expire Dec. 31, 1925.

JASPER N. CLARK

Representative from Mason County, 1895-6 and 1897-8. Was born in Cavendish, Vt., May 1, 1844. He acquired his early education at the country schools, attending winters and working at the tanner's trade with his father during summers. At the age of sixteen years he moved with his father's family to a farm, where shortly afterwards his father died. One year later he enlisted in Co. I, 2d Vt. Inf. Returning from the army, he learned the blacksmith trade, which occupation he soon discontinued, and then engaged in farming. In 1885 he came to Michigan, bought wild lands in Victory Township, Mason County. In politics a Republican. He held the office of Supervisor of his township.

JEREMIAH CLARK

Representative from Oakland County, 1839 and 1841. Was born in the State of Vermont, Sept. 19, 1790. When young he removed with his father to Madison County, N. Y. As a young man he was interested in the manufacture of salt for several years in Onondaga County, then at Albany, filled contracts on public works for the State. He came to Detroit in 1831, where he controlled a bakery and grocery for several years. He removed to a farm in Independence, Oakland County. In 1838 he built a grist mill at Clarkston. He served as Supervisor, Justice, and County Judge. He died at Syracuse, N. Y., Aug. 29, 1847.

JOHN CLARK

Senator from the Fifth District, 1835-6 and 1837-8; Delegate to the Constitutional Convention of 1850 from St. Clair County; and Representative from St. Clair County, 1857-8. Was born at Bath, Me., July 29, 1797. He was a clerk from 1812 to 1818, then became a merchant. He opened a store in Detroit in 1830, and in 1832 purchased large tracts of land on the St. Clair River and removed to Port Huron. In 1835 he removed to a farm in China, which remained his home through life. He was a Commissioner to settle Indian claims in Michigan. He was a Democrat until 1856, then a Republican; a prominent Mason and leading pioneer.

JOHN R. CLARK

Representative from Lenawee County, 1859-60. Was born in Ontario (Now Walworth), N. Y., Sept. 4, 1822. He received a common and select school education. He came to Adrian with his father in 1836, and resided there. He was a clerk from 1840 to 1845, then a merchant. He was a farmer and stock dealer. He was for five years Supervisor of Madison, and several times an Alderman and always prominent business man.

JUDSON BEECHER CLARK

Representative, 1905-6, from the Schoolcraft District, comprising the counties of Alger, Luce, Mackinac and Schoolcraft. Was born at Ashtabula, O., Mar. 24, 1859, of American parentage. His father served in Battery G, 1st Mich. Inf., and at the close of the war Mr. Clark, Sr., came to Michigan and settled on a farm in Grand Traverse County. Young Clark attended district school, Traverse City High School, and later attended school at Downer's Grove, Ill., while living at the home of his uncle. His first work for himself was in a saw mill. Next he engaged in the meat and grocery business at Fife Lake, Mich., coming to St. Ignace in 1886, and continuing this business until 1903 when he took up the real estate business. A married man. In politics a Republican. He held the offices of Supervisor, Mayor, and Treasurer of St. Ignace City; prominent in Masonic, Maccabee and Odd Fellow circles, and was master of St. Ignace Lodge, No. 369, F. & A. M. for seven years, and high priest of Mackinac Chapter R. A. M., one year.

MYRON W. CLARK

Senator, 1893-4, from the Tenth District, comprising the counties of Jackson and Washtenaw. Was born in Jackson County, on a farm in Henrietta Township, Sept. 15, 1840. He attended district school and the Albion College. In 1860 he quit school, went to Van Buren County and began farming; three years later he moved to Jackson City and engaged as mechanic. He continued in this occupation for three years and then engaged in the mercantile and milling business in Jackson city. In 1892 he moved on a farm near his old home in Jackson County. He was Republican in politics until 1872, when he joined issues with the Democratic party. He was elected to the Senate of 1893-4 on the Democratic ticket.

NEWCOMB CLARK

Representative from the Second District of Bay County, 1883-4 and 1885-6. Was born in the State of New York. He resided in West Bay City, and was a Republican. Upon the organization of the House of Representatives he was chosen to fill the office of speaker. He was the first president of the village of Wenona, now West Bay City, served as Major and Lieutenant Colonel of the 102d U. S. C. T. and was for a time in command of the regiment.

ORMAN CLARK

Representative from Washtenaw County, 1869-70. Was born at Batavia, N. Y., Mar. 9, 1809. In 1831 he married Sarah A. Pierson, and removed in 1836 to Lyndon, Washtenaw County, Mich., near Chelsea, and purchased a farm where he resided. The farm was one of the best in that part of the county, and he made the raising of fine horses and Durham cattle a specialty. He was Supervisor, and held other local offices. In politics he was a Democrat.

ROBERT E. CLARK

Representative from Wayne County, 1863-4. Was born in New Hampshire, Jan. 10, 1810, and came to Michigan in 1835. By occupation he was a farmer, a Democrat in politics, and resided at Belleville in 1887.

ROY CLARK

Senator, 1919-20 and 1921-2, from the Seventh District, comprising the counties of Berrien and Cass. Was born Aug. 7, 1860, in Pipestone Township, Berrien County, Mich., of American parents. He was educated in the district schools and at the Cheboygan, Wis., High School. He lived on a farm all his life except while attending school. Mr. Clark is married. He is a member and Past Exalted Ruler of Benton Harbor Lodge No. 544, and a 33rd degree Mason. He was Supervisor four years, County Clerk four years, and at present Chairman of the Republican County Committee.

SAMUEL CLARK

Delegate to the Constitutional Convention of 1850 from Kalamazoo County; and a member of Congress, 1853-5. Was born in Cayuga County, N. Y., in January, 1800. He was brought up on a farm, graduated at Hamilton College, read law with Judge Hulburt, of Auburn, and commenced practice at Waterloo, N. Y., in 1828. In 1833 he was elected to Congress and served one term, resuming practice at Waterloo until 1842, when he removed to Kalamazoo. He immediately took high rank in his profession, and was recognized as one of the leading lawyers of the State. He died at Kalamazoo, Oct. 2, 1870.

WALTER H. CLARK

Representative from the Second District of Ottawa County, 1911-12 and 1913-14. Was born in Robinson Township, Ottawa County, Dec. 31, 1866, of English parents. He was educated in the public schools and West Michigan Business College. He was married June 28, 1895. Mr. Clark was Supervisor, and County Treasurer of Ottawa County; taught school two years and was engaged in the lumber business and in farming for several years. In politics a Republican.

WILLIAM A. CLARK

Senator from the Twenty-third District, 1863-4. Was born at Ballston Spa, N. Y., Sept. 9, 1823. He moved with his father to Brighton, Mich., in 1837. He worked on his father's farm until 1841, ran the Brighton Mills two years, studied law in 1836, and began practice in 1844. He was Supervisor of Brighton in 1849-50; and Prosecuting Attorney 1851-5. He removed to Saginaw in 1864, was City Attorney in 1879-80, and was a Democratic candidate for Regent and Lieutenant Governor. From 1856 to 1862 he was a Republican, then a Democrat. He died Jan. 21, 1892.

HOVEY K. CLARKE

Representative from Calhoun County, 1850. Was born July 11, 1812, in Sterling, Mass., where he lived until 1816; then in Utica, N. Y., until 1831; then in Canandaigua, N. Y., till 1836; then in Allegan, Mich., until 1843; then in Marshall, Mich., until 1852; and from that time in Detroit. In politics he voted with the Democratic party until 1848; then with the Free Soil party until 1854; and then with the Republican party. He was admitted to the bar in 1839. He held the offices of Prosecuting Attorney of Allegan and Calhoun counties, Commissioner to examine the compilation of laws, (1857) appointed by Gov. Bingham, member of the Board of Control of Railroad land grants, appointed by Gov. Blair, State reporter, and register of bankruptcy for the eastern district of Michigan. He died at Grace Hospital, Detroit, July 21, 1889.

LUTHER W. CLARKE

Senator from the Twenty-second District, 1853-4. Was born in Marietta, O., in 1825. By profession he was a physician, politically a Democrat. He settled in Michigan in 1847, and was a resident of Eagle River, Keweenaw County. He died in 1869.

JOHN CLARKEN

Representative from the First District of Wayne County, 1909-10. Was born at Ann Arbor, Washtenaw County, Mich., in 1871, of Irish descent. He received his education in the public and parochial schools of Ann Arbor. Not married. At the beginning of the Spanish American wwar, he enlisted in the United States Navy with the Michigan State Naval Brigade and was assigned to the U. S. Steamer Yosemite, and served until the close of the war. A molder by trade and prominent in labor movements, he was identified as business agent of the Molder's Union, general organizer and vice president of the Brass Molder's International Union, also of the Metal Polisher's District Council. In politics a Republican.

JOSHUA CLEMENT

Representative from Jackson County. 1871-2. Was born in Orange County, N. Y., Sept. 3, 1818. He was brought up on a farm, taught school several years, came to Michigan in 1843, and was a farmer in Leoni, Jackson County. He was Supervisor ten years, and filled minor town offices.

JAMES CLEMENTS

Representative from the Second District of Washtenaw County 1865-6. His post-office address was Ann Arbor. (Further data not obtainable).

WILLIAM LAWRENCE CLEMENTS

Member of the Board of Regents of the University of Michigan, 1910—. Was born Apr. 1, 1861, at Ann Arbor, Washtenaw County, Mich., of Scotch-English parents. He was educated in the public schools of Ann Arbor and at the University of Michigan, graduating from the latter institution with the degree of B. S. in 1882. He entered the employ of the Industrial Works, at Bay City, Mich., as engineer but was soon promoted to the position of superintendent and manager. In 1896 he became president of that organization, which office he still holds. He has been president of the First National Bank of Bay City, and of the Bay County Savings Bank since 1914. A member of the American Antiquarian Society and of the American Historical Association and in 1916 was appointed a member of the Michigan Historical Commission. He was first elected member of the Board of Regents of the University in 1909 and was re-elected Apr 2, 1917.

ANDREW CLIMIE

Representative from St. Joseph County, 1871-2 and 1873-4; and member of the Board of Regents of the University of Michigan, 1874-82. Was born in Whitestown, N. Y., Feb. 4, 1834. He was educated at Vernon Academy, N. Y., and in

1860 removed to Leonidas, St. Joseph County, where he engaged in milling and lumbering. He held several local offices. He was elected Regent of the University of Michigan in 1873 and filled that position six years. In politics he was a Republican. He died at Pontiac May 14, 1897.

WILLIAM M. CLINE

Senator from the Seventeenth District (St. Clair County), 1885-6. Was born in Ontario, July 31, 1851. He lived with his parents on a farm and began life as a teacher in the public schools of Sanilac and St. Clair counties. He then became a lawyer. He was elected on the Fusion ticket.

CHARLES W. CLISBEE

Senator from the Fifteenth District, 1867-8. Was born at Cleveland, O., July 24, 1833. He came to Cassopolis, Mich., in 1838. He was at Oberlin College from 1846 to 1851, and a graduate of Williams College in 1856. He studied law and was admitted in 1858; was Circuit Court Commissioner four years; two terms Prosecuting Attorney; delegate at large to the Republican National Convention of 1864; and secretary of the national conventions of 1880 and 1884; Circuit Judge in 1878; presidential elector in 1868; and for many years secretary of the Cass County Pioneer Society. From 1869 to 1873 he was reading clerk in the House of Representatives at Washington, D. C., and again in 1881. He died Aug. 18, 1889.

HENRY S. CLUBB

Senator from the Twenty-ninth District, 1873-4. Was born in Colchester, England, June 21, 1827. He came to this country in 1853 and became a shorthand reporter on the New York *Tribune;* was then a congressional reporter, and also reported for the South Carolina Legislature. He settled at Grand Haven in 1856 and published the *Clarion* from 1857 to 1862; was Assistant Quartermaster with the rank of Captain in the army, and became Chief Quartermaster of the 17th army corps; was wounded, and served until 1866. He founded the Grand Haven *Herald* in 1869, which he published several years. He was a Republican. He died at Philadelphia, Pa., Oct. 29, 1921.

HENRY ALSON CLUTE

Representative from the First District of Calhoun County, 1897-8. Was born in Wayne County, N. Y., Mar. 24, 1840. When four years of age he came with his parents to Michigan and located on a farm five and one-half miles north of the village of Marshall, Calhoun County. He attended the district school until his father died in 1855, when he was compelled to look after the management of the farm; two years later his mother rented the farm and moved to Corunna, Shiawassee County, where he attended the Corunna public schools for two years. He returned to the farm in the spring of 1860. Two years later he enlisted in the 2d Missouri Cavalry or "Merrill Horse," remaining in the service until June 15, 1865, when he was mustered out under general order 83. In 1874 he was elected Supervisor on the Republican ticket and re-elected to the same position in 1876; was elected Supervisor in 1880 on the Greenback ticket and elected to the House of 1897-8 on the Democratic People's Union Silver ticket.

WILLIAM L. CLYBURN

Representative from Summerville, Cass County, 1851. Was born in Virginia. He was Supervisor of Pokagon Township for the years 1847, 1849, 1855 and 1857; Treasurer, 1838-42; Clerk, 1843-6. Occupation was a farmer.

MATHIAS COAD

Representative from the Second District of Ingham County, 1897-8. Was born in Eastport, Me., May 27, 1836. His early education was acquired in the Eastport High School, supplemented by a course in the Berkshire Medical College, from which he graduated with the class of 1865. He then moved to Massachusetts and in 1862 enlisted in the 52d Massachusetts Infantry; commissioned as surgeon in the 76th U. S. C. T., where he served until he was honorably discharged, and mustered out of service Dec. 31, 1866. He came to Michigan, locating at Williamston in 1868, where he engaged in the practice of medicine. In politics a member of the People's Party. He was a Republican candidate for Representative in 1870; was President of the Village, and member of the Board of Education; was elected to the House of 1897-8 on the Democratic People's Union Silver ticket.

JOSEPH COATES

Representative from Oakland County, 1841. Was born in England, Dec. 6, 1791. He came to Michigan in 1832, and settled in Pine Lake, Oakland County, where he died Mar. 12, 1876. By occupation he was a farmer, in politics at first a Democrat, then a Republican. He was reporter for the first Michigan Legislature that met at Detroit, and for many subsequent years reported the legislative debates for State and Detroit papers. He also reported the proceedings of the Constitutional Convention of 1850. He was a man of liberal education; was master of several languages. For years he was the only man in Michigan who could write shorthand, and was frequently called upon to report arguments in the courts at Detroit.

LINTSFORD B. COATES

Representative from Allegan, 1847. Was born in Elkland, Pa., July 22, 1806. He came to Allegan County in 1835, and practiced as a physician at Otsego. In politics he was a Democrat. He died Aug. 15, 1879.

GEORGE P. COBB

Representative from the First District of Bay County, 1881-2. Was born Apr. 13, 1841, in York, Livingston County, N. Y., and shortly afterwards his parents removed to Rochester. In 1855 he removed to Macon, Mich., and lived a farmer's life for several years, some times attending district school in the winter. In the winter of 1859-60 he attended the union school at Ypsilanti. He served one year in the 5th Mich. Vol. Cavalry. Having entered the law department of the University of Michigan in October, 1866, he graduated in 1868. He settled in Bay City. He was Supervisor of the third ward in 1873. In politics a Republican.

JAMES P. COBB

Representative from Kalamazoo County, 1863-4 and 1865-6. Was born at Orwell, Vt., May 18, 1823. He moved with his father in 1834 to Brighton, N. Y., where he was educated, and taught several terms. He lived in Vermont several years. He settled on a farm near Kalamazoo in 1854, and also engaged in commercial business. He was County Treasurer, and held other positions, including Supervisor. In politics he was a Republican. He was a large wool buyer for many years, and took great interest in State and county fairs. He died May 8, 1899.

THOMAS S. COBB

Representative from Kalamazoo County, 1873-4; and Senator from the Fifteenth District, 1875-6. Was born in Springfield, Vt., Oct. 4, 1819. He removed to Boston in 1835, where he remained until 1855, when he came to Michigan and settled at Kalamazoo. He finished his education at the Kimball Union Academy, Meriden, N. H. He was a member of the School Board of Kalamazoo, was cashier of the National Bank of Kalamazoo, and held other positions of trust. By occupation he was a merchant; in politics a Democrat. He died Mar. 21, 1891, while on his return from Florida.

VARNUM B. COCHRAN

State Superintendent of Public Instruction, 1881-3. Was born in Argentine, Genesee County, 1845. He received his early instruction in the schools of Linden and Fenton, completing his studies preparatory to the University, at the high school at Ann Arbor. Meantime he taught three terms in the schools of his native town, and for somewhat more than a year was in charge of the schools of Marquette. In the fall of 1866 he entered the literary department of the University, where, however, he was unable, on account of ill health, to complete the full college course. Returning to the Upper Peninsula he again became Superintendent of the City Schools of Marquette. Thereafter he was for some years engaged in the drug business, during part of the time holding the office of County Superintendent of Schools for Marquette County. Subsequently he was at the head of the public schools of Negaunee, whence, in the spring of 1881, he was called to the office of Superintendent of Public Instruction, upon appointment by Governor Jerome to the vacancy caused by the resignation of Hon. C. A. Gower. At the commencement in 1882 the University conferred on him the honorary degree of master of arts. Nominated by the Republican State Convention in 1882, he was elected in November. He resigned during his term of office, to become Register of the U. S. Land Office at Marquette, which he held several years.

JAMES W. COCHRANE

Senator from the Twenty-eighth District, 1879-80. Was born at Attica, N. Y., June 1, 1840. He received an academic education and was admitted to the bar in 1862, and commenced practice at Warsaw. He came to Midland, Mich., in 1864 and continued in his profession until 1871, when he began the lumbering and land business. He held important local offices, such as Supervisor and Justice of the Peace. In politics a Republican.

LYMAN COCHRANE

Representative from Wayne County, 1871-2. Was born in New Hampshire, Aug. 6, 1825. He was educated at the University of Michigan and graduated in 1849. He studied law and graduated at the Ballston, N. Y., law school in 1852. He engaged in practice in Detroit, became well skilled as a special pleader, and his opinion on intricate matters of law was held in high regard by the Detroit bar. In 1873 he was elected Judge of the Superior Court, of Detroit. He was a Democrat in politics. He died at Detroit, Feb. 5, 1879.

WILLIAM JOHNSON COCKER

Member of the Board of Regents of the University of Michigan, 1890-1906. Was born at Almondbury, Yorkshire, England, Mar. 17, 1846, son of Benjamin F. and Mary (Johnson) Cocker. His parents emigrated to Australia in 1850, and thence to the United States. The son was prepared for college at the Ann Arbor High School, where he was graduated in 1864, and entered the University of Michigan the same year. At the end of his Junior year he accepted a position as assistant in the General Library of the University for one year. He then resumed his studies and was graduated Bachelor of Arts with the class of 1869. Settling in Adrian, Mich., soon after graduation, he was appointed Principal of the city High School, which position he held for ten years. Mr. Cocker was married Mar. 25, 1870, to Isabella M. Clark of Adrian. From 1879 to 1885 he was Superintendent of the Adrian schools, and 1885 to 1888 a member of the School Board. In 1888 he became president of the Commercial Savings Bank of Adrian and continued in the banking business there up to the time of his death. In 1889 he was elected Regent of the University, and at the end of eight years was re-elected for a second term. He was chairman of the Finance Committee for some years and instituted the present system of managing the budget. He died suddenly at Ann Arbor, May 19, 1901.

GEORGE P. CODD

Member of the Board of Regents of the University of Michigan, 1910-11; and member of Congress from the First District, 1921-2. Was born in Detroit, Dec. 7, 1869, of Scotch-Irish parentage, and was educated in the public schools of that city. Later he entered the University of Michigan from which he was graduated in 1891, with the degree of B. A. He studied law in the offices of Alfred Russell and Griffin & Warner and was admitted to the bar in 1892. Mr. Codd is married and has three children. In politics a Republican. He was Assistant City Attorney of Detroit, 1893-6; member Common Council, 1901-5; Mayor 1905-6; Regent of State University, 1910-11, Circuit Judge, Third judicial district, 1911-12; and was elected to Congress Nov. 2, 1920.

FRANK CODY

Member of the State Board of Education, 1913—. Was born at Belleville, Wayne County, Mich., Dec. 31, 1870, and received his elementary education in the public schools of that county. After graduating from high school he taught in the schools of his native village for three years. He then entered the State Normal College at Ypsilanti, and in 1891 was appointed Superintendent of the Delray schools, holding that position until Delray was annexed to Detroit in 1907, when he was appointed to the Principalship of the Detroit McMillan High School. In 1914 was made Assistant Superintendent of the Detroit public schools, and in April, 1919, was appointed Acting Superintendent. On June 26, 1919, the appointment was made permament. He served for a number of years as treasurer of the Detroit Teachers' Association and president of the Detroit Schoolmen's Club. In 1893, he organized the night school for Detroit newsboys and was its principal for five years. Later he was elected president of the Detroit Newsboys' Association. In 1895, he was elected a member of the Wayne County Board of School Examiners, holding the office until 1907. He is a Knight Templar and 32nd degree Mason and also a member of the I. O. O. F. and K. of P. Mr. Cody is married and has three children.

GEORGE ALONZO COE

Senator from the Fourth District, 1846, and from the Third District, 1847; Representative from Branch County, 1849; and Lieutenant Governor, 1855-8. Was born in Rush, N. Y., Aug. 16, 1811. When young he became a resident of Illinois, and was brought up on his father's farm until fourteen, then attended or taught school until of age. Then he studied law with Judge Pratt, at Rochester, N. Y., and began practice at Coldwater, Mich., 1839. He was a good lawyer, a Whig in politics. He filled many local positions of trust and honor, among them Prosecuting Attorney and Justice. He died Oct. 21, 1869.

BELA COGSHALL

Representative from Oakland County, 1869-70. Was born at Glennville, N. Y., Feb. 16, 1816. He received a common school education; became clerk in a store; in 1836 removed to a farm in Groveland, Oakland County, where he remained until 1867, when he sold his farm, removed to Holly and commenced legal practice and insurance business.   In 1853 he was Sergeant-at-arms of the House. In 1867 and 1871 he was President of the village of Holly, and was president of the Board of Education from 1867 to 1873. He was a distinguished Mason and held high offices in that order. In politics he was a Democrat. He died October, 1881.

ALEX. COHEN

Representative from the First District of Ingham County in the Extra Session of 1907. He succeeded Stanley D. Montgomery who had resigned.

LEMUEL COLBATH

Delegate from the Second District to the Constitutional Convention of 1835; and Representative from Monroe County, 1837. Was born in Maine, Dec. 27, 1788, where he lived until twenty-one years of age, when he removed to Sodus, Wayne County, N. Y., and settled on a farm. In 1832 he removed to Erie, Monroe County, Mich., where he purchased a farm and resided until his death, July 22, 1837. He was succeeded in the Legislature by Peter Picott.

SHERIDAN J. COLBY

Representative from the First District of Wayne County, 1899-1900, 1901-2, 1903-4, 1907-8 and 1909. Was born in Woodhull Township, Shiawassee County, Mich., Dec. 2, 1864. He worked on a farm until of age, attending school winters. In the year 1888 he removed to Detroit, canvassed about one year, worked as a street car conductor about six years, attending the evening sessions of the Detroit College of Law. He was admitted to the bar in June, 1894, and practiced law. He was an advocate of the nomination of candidates for public office by a direct vote of the people and introduced the first bill in the Michigan Legislature providing for the direct nomination of State, County and District officers. In politics a Republican. He died May 19, 1909.

EZRA COLE

Representative from St. Joseph County, 1846. Was born in Yates County, N. Y., Nov. 17, 1799, and died at Three Rivers, Mich., July 30, 1884. He came to Michigan in 1839, bought land near Three Rivers, and farmed it for several years. He sold his farm about 1850, and with his son opened a produce store in Three Rivers, which he continued until about 1860, when he retired from business. He was for several years Justice. Politically he was a Democrat.

HENRY S. COLE

Attorney General of the Territory of Michigan, 1833-6. Was a native of Canandaigua, N. Y., and became a resident of Detroit about 1828, and was an able lawyer. He died in 1836.

MINER T. COLE

Representative from the First District of Lenawee County, 1887-8 and 1889-90. Was born at Spencer, Lucas County, O., July 3, 1839. His parents were pioneers from Seneca County, N. Y. His education was acquired at Maumee City, O., and Kalamazoo, Mich. He enlisted in the 14th Ohio Inf. under Col. Steedman, at Toledo, Aug. 26, 1861, serving in nearly every rank from eighth corporal to First Lieutenant. He re-enlisted Dec. 14, 1863, and had charge of a forage party from "Atlanta to the sea," and was mustered out Oct. 16, 1865. On May 30, 1867, he married Mary J. Taylor, daughter of an enterprising farmer of Spencer, O., and then settled in Palmyra, Lenawee County, May 11, 1868. He was an officer in the Lenawee County Agricultural Society more than fifteen years; a regular correspondent for several agricultural as well as other journals. In politics a Republican.

WILLIAM B. COLE

Representative from Mason and Manistee counties, 1875-6. Was born in Ellisburgh, N. Y., Dec. 22, 1822. He became a physician in 1846, and began practice at Pottsville, Pa. In 1848 he removed to Fenton, Mich., engaged in practice, and was elected Censor of the Genesee County Medical Society. He remained in practice until 1871, then purchased the Pontiac *Jacksonian*, and removed to Pontiac. In 1873 he removed to Ludington, and started the Ludington weekly *Appeal*. He held the office of Justice several years. He was a Democrat in politics. He died in 1878.

GEORGE COLEMAN

Representative from Livingston County, 1883-4 and 1885-6. Was born in Minisink, N. Y., Sept. 7, 1833. He removed to Livingston County, Mich., with his parents in the fall of 1843, and they settled on a farm in Marion Township. His early life was divided between the active duties of the farm and a regular attendance of the common school. His business was farming and stock raising; in politics a Democrat. He held the office of Justice of the Peace for four terms, Supervisor of his township four years, and president of the Livingston County Mutual Fire Insurance Company.

HAMMOND J. COLEMAN

Representative from the First District of Calhoun County, 1919-20 and 1921. Was born at Galt, Ont., Nov. 5, 1855, of English and Irish parents. The next year he removed with his parents to a farm near Homer, Calhoun County, Mich. He was educated in the district schools and the Marshall High School. He lived with his parents on the farm until he was twenty-eight years of age, when he moved to Marshall, where he engaged in the general merchandise business. Four years later he became interested in three farms, which he operated, one of which he operated for twenty-eight years; was also interested in wool, grain and coal. He served as Alderman and Mayor of Marshall. Mr. Coleman was married. In politics a Republican. He died May 30, 1921.

HENRY COLEMAN

Representative from Van Buren and Cass counties, 1840. His postoffice address was Kendall. (Further data not obtainable).

PHILIP T. COLGROVE

Senator, 1889-90, from the Eleventh District, comprising the counties of Barry and Eaton. Was born in Winchester, Ind., Apr. 17, 1858. On his twenty-first birthday he was admitted to practice law by the Supreme Court of this State. In 1879 he married Rose Altoft of Hastings, and moved to Reed City, where he remained until 1880, engaged in the practice of the law, and was a member of the firm of Colgrove & Cooper; he then removed to Hastings and entered into co-partnership with Judge Clement Smith. He was elected Prosecuting Attorney in the fall of 1882, and in the fall of 1884 re-elected; was again re-elected in the fall of 1886. At the session of the Grand Lodge of the Knights of Pythias, held in Detroit in 1887, he was elected Grand Chancellor of the grand jurisdiction of Michigan.

VICTORY PHELPS COLLIER

Senator from the Thirteenth District, 1865-6, and from the Eleventh District, 1867-8; State Treasurer, 1871-7; and member of the Board of Regents of the University of Michigan, 1877-8. Was born at Victor, N. Y., Apr. 25, 1820. He was educated in the common schools and at a seminary at Lima, N. Y. In 1835 he removed with his parents to Battle Creek, Mich., and in 1837 to Johnstown, Mich. At twenty years of age he began to teach school, and taught for three successive winters. In 1847 he returned to Battle Creek and entered mercantile business.

His success was immediate and for many years he was a leading merchant of the place. He also engaged in banking and was president of the First National Bank of Battle Creek for a number of years. He was actively interested in politics and held several offices. He was for some time a member of the State Republican Committee. He was Mayor of Battle Creek in 1875. In 1876 he was United States Centennial Commissioner at Philadelphia. Mar. 8, 1877, he was appointed Regent of the University in place of Jonas H. McGowan resigned; but he in turn resigned the office on Sept. 24 of the same year. At the spring election of 1877 he had been chosen Regent for the full term from Jan. 1, following, but declined to qualify. He died at Battle Creek, June 28, 1898.

CHARLES BARNARD COLLINGWOOD

Senator, 1899-1900, from the Fourteenth District, composed of the counties of Ingham and Shiawassee. Was born at Plymouth, Mass., May 1, 1860. During his early years he attended the public schools of Plymouth and Boston, and at the age of fourteen entered the publishing house of James R. Osgood & Co. Mr. Collingwood remained in Boston until 1878, when he turned his face toward the "Great West" and went to Colorado, but retraced his steps eastward, and one year later his name was enrolled as a freshman on the roster of the Michigan Agricultural College. Leaving college soon after the close of his first year, Mr. Collingwood spent two years in Utah and California, engaging in civil engineering and other occupations until he had earned sufficient to complete his college course, when he returned and graduated from that institution in the class of 1885. After graduation he taught school at Pewamo and Howard City, where he also studied law. In 1888 he was appointed adjunct professor of chemistry in the University of Arkansas, and went from there to Tucson, Arizona, as chemist in the new university of that State. He returned to Lansing in 1894, was admitted to the bar, and engaged in the practice of law. In politics a Republican.

ALPHEUS COLLINS

Delegate from the Fourth District to the Constitutional Convention of 1835. Was born near Rutland, Vt., Sept. 24, 1790. His parents in 1799 moved to Phelps, N. Y., where he remained until 1811, when he married Betsy Hall, and purchased a farm in Rose, Wayne County, N. Y. He resided there until 1829, when he came to Michigan and settled on a farm in Pittsfield, Washtenaw County. He afterwards settled on a large farm in Lyndon, same County, and was several years Supervisor and Justice of the Peace. He was generally a Democrat, but sometimes a Republican at general elections. He died May 16, 1862.

DAVID COLLINS

Representative from Newaygo County, 1889-90 and 1891-2. Was born at Susquehanna, Pa., July 26, 1832. At the age of 18 he went to New York City and engaged in a saw mill, where he learned the trade of sawing ship timber. He remained here three years, then went to New Haven, Conn., where he worked a year in a saw mill. He then spent one year at home in Pennsylvania and in 1856 came to Croton Township, in Newaygo County, and worked by the month in the lumber woods, after which he began jobbing for himself. When the war broke out he enlisted in Co. A, 6th Mich. Cavalry, for three years; was transferred, made Orderly Sergeant, same regiment, and promoted to First Lieutenant, and served until the close of the war; was wounded at the Battle of Gettysburg. He held the office of Sheriff, Supervisor and School Director.

FREDERICK W. COLLINS

Representative from Barry County, 1873-4. Was born in Rose, N. Y., Feb. 16, 1828. He received a common school education. In 1837 he came to Pittsfield, Mich. He removed to Barry County in 1869, and settled in Thornapple. He served in several local positions of trust. By occupation he was a farmer.

LUCIUS H. COLLINS

Representative from the First District of Wayne County, 1885-6. Was born at Romeo, Mich., July 17, 1855, where his early education was obtained, graduating from the high school of that village in 1873. He entered the class of 1877 in the literary department of the State University, remaining through the freshman year. In the fall of 1874 he began the study of law and was admitted in 1876. He was elected to the Legislature as the candidate of the Democratic party. He died at Detroit May 16, 1916.

SAMUEL B. COLLINS

Representative from the First District of Jackson County, 1899-1900. Was born at Parma, Monroe County, N. Y., Oct. 18, 1846. He received his early education in the schools of that county, and in 1864, at the age of eighteen years, he entered the University of Rochester, graduating four years later, in the class of 1868. He obtained a position as traveling salesman, and after an experience of eight years as a "knight of the grip" he removed to Galion, O., and entered the wholesale grocery business. After nine years experience in that line Mr. Collins removed to Jackson, Mich., in 1884, and founded the transfer house of Smith Bros. & Collins. In 1887 he founded the Collins Manufacturing Company, and three years later the National Wheel Company; sold his interest in the last named company in 1894, and became president and general manager of the Harmon-Whitmore Co.; also senior partner in the firm of S. B. & H. C. Collins, wholesale coal dealers in the city of Jackson. In politics a Republican. He held but one public office (that of Alderman) previous to his nomination to the House of 1899-1900.

WILLIAM A. COLLINS

Senator, 1909-10 and 1911-12, from the Twenty-fourth District, comprising the counties of Bay and Midland. Was born at Saginaw, Mich., Feb. 19, 1879, and received his education in the public and high schools of Bay City. Leaving school in 1896, he began teaching in the country schools of Bay County, continuing teaching for six years, in the meantime studying law. He was admitted to the bar on passing examination before the State Board of Law Examiners in 1901, and began the practice of law in 1902. Married. He was a member of the Bay County Board of School Examiners from 1899 to 1902, and Circuit Court Commissioner from 1902 to 1906. In politics a Republican.

HUTSON BENEDICT COLMAN

Senator, 1897-8, from the Ninth District, composed of Calhoun and Kalamazoo counties. Was born in Oakland County, Mich., June 8, 1855. His early education was acquired in the public schools supplemented by a course at the Kalamazoo College, from which he was graduated in 1877 with the degree of A. B.; taught school for three years in Hastings and Kalamazoo, then engaged in business. In politics a Republican. He was elected Alderman of the city of Kalamazoo, in which capacity he served two years. He died at Kalamazoo.

BENJAMIN COLVIN

Representative from the Third District of Saginaw County, 1897-8 and 1899-1900. Was born in Cato, Cayuga County, N. Y., Aug. 3, 1827. His grandsire came from Scotland, and located on Long Island; later removed to Rutland, Vt., where Benjamin's father was born, and later served in the War of 1812. When Mr. Colvin was seven years of age his father died and he was bound out to a farmer, where he remained for seven years, then started life for himself, and in 1849 he went to Salt Lake City; returned in 1853, and located on a farm in Brant Township, Saginaw County. Mr. Colvin was one of the pioneers and organizers of Brant Township. In politics he was a member of the People's Party. He was a candidate for Congress, and held several township offices.

OLIVER D. COLVIN

Representative from Branch County, 1850. Was a farmer. He was Supervisor of Kinderhook from 1842 to 1847, and six years Justice of the Peace. He died about 1858.

DAVID G. COLWELL

Representative from Livingston County, 1865. Was born in Seneca, N. Y., Mar. 14, 1825. He came to Michigan in 1838, and settled at Tyrone, Livingston County, where he lived for twenty-nine years. He resided in Fenton in 1887.

HENRY J. COLWELL

Representative from Marquette County, 1874. He was in the extra session, taking the place of Edward Breitung who resigned. (Further data not obtainable).

WILLIAM M. COLWELL

Representative from the district consisting of Chippewa, Delta, Mackinac, and Schoolcraft counties, 1883-4. Was born in Chenango County, N. Y., May 17, 1839. In 1841 he moved with his parents to Addison, Steuben County, N. Y., where he remained until he reached his majority, receiving a common school and academic education. He worked about three years in the printing business, then engaged in sash and door making. In 1860 he removed to northern Pennsylvania, where he embarked in the lumbering trade. In 1863 he volunteered, joining the 21st Pa. Cavalry, and was mustered out at the close of the war as a member of the 210th (re-enlisted) regiment Pa. Infantry; was twice wounded in action. He returned to lumbering in the employ of Messrs. Weston Brothers, of Olean, N. Y. In 1872 he came to Manistique, this State, having taken an interest in and management of the Chicago Lumbering Company. The business of his company was very prosperous, manufacturing annually from thirty to fifty million feet of lumber. In politics a Republican.

RUSSELL COMAN

Representative from Hillsdale County, 1849. Was born in 1802, in Eaton, Madison County, N. Y., and was brought up on a farm, living with his parents until 1825, when he removed to Dearborn County, Ind., where he lived ten years principally engaged in trading down the Ohio and Mississippi Rivers. He married in 1829, and removed to Wright, Hillsdale County, Mich., in 1835, and settled on a farm.

HENRY P. COMBES

Representative from Lenawee County, 1857-8 and 1863-4. Was born in the State of New York in 1820. By profession he was a physician, in politics a Republican. He came to Michigan in 1838, and resided at Rome, Lenawee County. He died. Jan. 1, 1895.

JOHN H. COMBS

Representative from the First District of Lenawee County, 1901-2 and 1903-4. Was born in Rome Township, Lenawee County, Mich., Dec. 22, 1861, on the farm. His father, Dr. Henry P. Combs, was a member of the Michigan Legislature from Lenawee County from 1857 to 1864, and gave his son a common school education until 1879, when he attended Adrian College two years and entered Goldsmith's Business College at Detroit in 1882, from which he graduated. Mr. Combs was married in 1884 to Miss Nellie E. Williams of Detroit. In politics a strong Republican. He held different offices in his township, being also identified with the grange and the farmers' interests in his locality.

HENRY COMPTON

Senator from the Second District, 1843-4; and Representative from Washtenaw County, 1845. Was born in Deposit, N. Y., Oct. 22, 1803. He had an excellent education, and when young engaged in teaching. Later, he was a merchant in western New York. In 1833 he came to Ypsilanti, where he engaged in the dry goods trade. He held various offices; Associated Judge of the County Court and Supervisor. In politics he was a Democrat. He died in Ypsilanti, May 2, 1863.

ADDISON J. COMSTOCK

Delegate from Lenawee County to the Second Convention of Assent, 1836; and Delegate from Lenawee County to the Constitutional Convention of 1850. Was born in Palmyra, N. Y., Oct. 17, 1802. He received a good business education and moved with his parents to Lockport, N. Y., in 1820, where he worked for his father, who had the contract for building the locks at that place on the Erie Canal. In 1825 he came with his father to Michigan and purchased a section of land where now stands the city of Adrian. In 1826 he built a log house, the first in the city, and a saw-mill. In 1828 he laid out and platted the village of Adrian. In 1829 he was appointed Postmaster, was Town Clerk, and built a grist-mill. In 1832, with his father, Darius Comstock, he projected the Erie and Kalamazoo Railroad, which was completed from Toledo to Adrian in 1836, he being secretary and treasurer of the road. In 1853 he was Mayor of Adrian. He was the prime mover in the early prosperity of Adrian. He was a leading member of the Methodist Church, and largely interested in the early banking houses of Adrian. He died Jan. 20, 1867.

CHARLES C. COMSTOCK

Member of Congress, 1885-7. Was born at Sullivan, N. H., Mar. 5, 1818, and was brought up on a farm, receiving a common school education. In 1842 he engaged in the lumber business and soon owned several saw mills; in 1853 he removed to Grand Rapids, Mich., and engaged in the same business. In 1857 he bought a furniture factory, failed, but in the next four years paid his debts, and in 1862 inaugurated the first successful wholesale furniture business in Grand Rapids. He sold out to his sons in 1865, but continued the lumber business and the manufacture of pails, sashes, blinds, and doors. He also had several farms, and was a leading business man of Grand Rapids. In 1863-4 he was Mayor of Grand Rapids; in 1870 Democratic candidate for Governor; in 1872 and 1878 Democratic candidate for Congress. He served as member of Congress from the Fifth District in 1885-6, but declined a renomination in 1886. He died Feb. 20, 1900.

DARIUS COMSTOCK

Delegate to the Constitutional Convention of 1835; and Delegate from Lenawee County to the First Convention of Assent, 1836. Was born in Cumberland, R. I., July 12, 1768. He removed to western New York with his father in 1790. In 1820 he took and completed a large contract on the Erie Canal, which included the locks at Lockport. In 1826 he removed to Logan (now Raisin), Lenawee County, and settled on lands purchased the previous year. In 1827 he was the first Supervisor, and in 1835 was a member of the Constitutional Convention. He was a Quaker and remained a member of that sect. He was prominently identified with the early history of Michigan and Lenawee County, and did much to secure the building of the railroads through southern Michigan. He died June 2, 1845.

HORACE H. COMSTOCK

Senator from the Third District, 1835-6 and 1837-8; and Representative from Allegan County, 1849. Came from Cooperstown, N. Y., in 1831, and founded the village of Comstock, Kalamazoo County, which for a time was a rival of Kalamazoo. Possessed of ample means, he built mills, and gave a schoolhouse to the people. His wife was a niece of James Fenimore Cooper, the novelist. He was a Democrat in politics. He was supervisor of Comstock from 1840 to 1845. In 1844 he removed to Kalamazoo, having bought a one-fourth interest in the village plat for $17,000. His wife died in 1846. He removed to Otsego, Mich., and afterwards to New York City, where he died.

OLIVER C. COMSTOCK

Member of the Board of Regents of the University of Michigan, 1841-3; State Superintendent of Public Instruction, 1843-5; and Representative from Branch County, 1849. Son of Adam Comstock, was born in Warwick, R. I., Mar. 1, 1781. His father was a Lieutenant Colonel in the Revolution. After the war he removed to Schenectady, N. Y. Mr. Comstock studied medicine and practiced near Cayuga Bridge. He there married Lydia Smith, daughter of Judge Grover Smith, and removed to Trumansburg, N. Y. He was the first Judge of Seneca County, and first Postmaster of Trumansburg. He was three times elected to Congress from that district, where he was an able member. He was one of the Commissioners to settle the claims of war sufferers on the Niagara frontier. He was ordained to the Baptist ministry, declined a re-nomination to Congress, and continued the practice of medicine until 1825. For several years he was pastor of the First Baptist Church in Rochester, N. Y., then became Chaplain to Congress. He afterwards preached in Norfolk, Va., but ultimately emigrated to Michigan, and settled in Detroit. As a young man he was a member of the New York Assembly. He was appointed Regent of the University March, 1841, in the place of Samuel W. Dexter. He resigned in 1843. He was a Democrat in politics. He died Jan. 11, 1860.

HARRY A. CONANT

Senator from the Fifth District, 1879-80; and Secretary of State, 1883-7. Was born at Monroe, Mich., May 5, 1844. He prepared for college at Monroe and entered the Michigan University class of 1865. Mr. Conant was admitted to the bar in February, 1878. After leaving college he engaged in mercantile and manufacturing pursuits for some years. In politics a Republican. He served as Mayor, Alderman and Supervisor. In 1880 he received the appointment of Consul at Naples, which he resigned after a residence abroad of seven months.

GEORGE M. CONDON

Senator from the Fourth District of Wayne County, 1917-18 to 1923—. Was born at Fort Covington, Franklin County, N. Y., Dec. 27, 1860, of American parentage. He was raised on a farm and received his education in the public schools of Fort Covington. After teaching school for five years, he entered the dry goods business at Bombay, N. Y. Two years later he went into business at Atlanta, Ga., but soon moved to Detroit, Mich., where he was employed by the Standard Oil Company. Being interested in law he entered the Detroit College of Law, from which institution he received his degree of LL.B. He has practiced law in Detroit ever since and is now senior member of the firm of Condon, Nellis & Condon. He organized and is director of the Condon Literary Club, Incorporated, through which organization more than five hundred young men have received training as debaters and public speakers. He served eight years as member of the Detroit Board of Education. He is a widower and has one son who is associated with his father in business as junior member of the firm. In politics he is a Republican.

EDWIN F. CONLEY

Representative from Wayne County, 1877-8. Was born in the city of New York, Sept. 7, 1847. In 1853 he came with his parents to Brighton, Mich. He received a common school education, and graduated from the law department of the University of Michigan. By profession he was a lawyer, in politics Democratic. He was Superintendent of Police in Detroit.

ELISHA CONGDON

Delegate from Washtenaw County to the Second Convention of Assent, 1836; and Representative from Washtenaw County, 1863-4. Was born at Norwich, Conn., in 1799. In 1832 he came to Michigan and settled in Sylvan, Washtenaw County. He was a man of great energy and untiring activity, and was known as an upright, earnest, capable man. The village of Chelsea owed its origin, name and largely its prosperity to his energy and enterprise. A large part of his life was spent in mercantile business. He held many minor offices, was President of the village of Chelsea, first Postmaster and held the office eight years; as a Democrat, supported the Union and sent three sons to serve through the rebellion. He died May 20, 1867.

JAMES M. CONGDON

Representative from Washtenaw County, 1871-2. Was born Mar. 23, 1805, at the city of Norwich, Conn., and removed to Michigan in 1834. He settled in Sylvan, Washtenaw County, upon land whereon part of the village of Chelsea is now located. Occupation was machinist and farmer; politics Democratic. He died June 16, 1888, at Chelsea.

JAMES L. CONGER

Member of Congress, 1851-5. Settled at Belvidere, Macomb County, Mich., as early as 1836, where he built a large house and purchased several hundred acres of land. His home was a favorite place of resort for the young people of Mt. Clemens. He was a man of fine personal appearance, a good lawyer, a brilliant debater and orator, and few equaled him as a stump speaker. In later years he was a resident of St. Clair, where he died. He was a brilliant writer, and wrote works on religion, and extracts from these written works caused great excitement from the liberal views of the writer. He was averse to their publication while living.

OMER D. CONGER

Senator from the Thirty-first District, 1855-6 and from the Twenty-sixth District, 1857-8 and 1859-60; Delegate to the Constitutional Convention of 1867 from St. Clair County; member of Congress, 1869-71 to 1881; and United States Senator, 1881-7. Was born in 1818, at Cooperstown, N. Y. He removed with his father to Huron County, O., in 1824. He pursued his academic studies at Huron Institute, Milan, O., and graduated in 1842 at Western Reserve College; was employed in the geological survey and mineral explorations of the Lake Superior copper and iron regions in 1845-6 and 1847; and, in 1848, engaged in the practice of law at Port Huron, long his home. He was elected Judge of St. Clair County in 1850, and was elected Presidential Elector on the Republican ticket in 1864.

EBENEZER H. CONKLIN

Delegate from Washtenaw County to the First Convention of Assent, 1836. Was born in Rutland, Vt., May 4, 1790. He was by occupation a physician, and in politics a Whig. He came to Michigan at an early day, settled in practice at Sharon, Washtenaw County, and was the second Supervisor of that town. He died June 11, 1851.

HENRY C. CONKLING

Senator from the Ninth District, 1869-70. Was born at Middletown, N. Y., Jan. 26, 1824. He came to Michigan with his parents in 1833, and was brought up on a farm until nineteen years of age. He was clerk in a store in Tecumseh for three years. He went to New York City in 1846 and was employed seven years in a wholesale grocery house; returned to Tecumseh, Mich., in 1854. From 1862 to 1869 he was engaged in general grocery and produce business; later railroad transportation agent. His politics were Republican. He was County Clerk of Lenawee County from 1872 to 1876; was County Superintendent of Poor, 1879 to 1888. He died at Rochester, N. Y., Nov. 25, 1916, on his way to spend the winter at Washington, D. C.

JOHN CONLEY

Senator, 1911-12, from the Twenty-first Senatorial District, comprising the counties of Lapeer and Tuscola. Was born in Lapeer Township, Lapeer County, Mich., in 1863, of Irish parentage. He lived on a farm until the age of twenty years and was educated in the district schools. He worked in the lumber woods for six years. He was Township Clerk, Supervisor, and held other offices. Married. In politics a Democrat. He was elected to the Senate at the special election held on Monday, Jan. 30, 1911, to fill the vacancy caused by the death of Edwin G. Fox.

WILLIAM M. CONNELLY

Senator, 1919-20 and 1923, from the Twenty-third District, comprising the counties of Muskegon and Ottawa. Was born Jan. 15, 1881, at Moundsville, W. Va., of American parentage. He was educated in the public schools of Moundsville and at the Carnegie Night Technical School of Homestead, Pennsylvania. Upon completing his schooling he entered the electrical department of the Carnegie Steel Works at Homestead. Later in connection with this work, he had headquarters at Chicago, Ill., and while living there bought a farm near Spring Lake, Mich., as a summer home. Later he made the farm his permanent home. After coming to Michigan he has been active in the good roads movement and served as director of the West Michigan Pike Association and the Michigan Good Roads Association, and as secretary of the Michigan Road Commissioners' Association and the Grand Highway Association. He is married. In politics he is a Republican.

HENRY CONNOR

Member of the Legislative Council, 1826-7 and 1828-9. Was born in Ohio, 1780. When an infant, he was brought to Michigan with his father's family, who came with a party of Moravian missionaries and Indian converts, taken captives near Sandusky, O., in 1782, by the British. These captives formed a settlement near

the present site of Mt. Clemens, their only subsistence the first winter being veni-
son, of which they obtained an abundance, by reason of a deep crusted snow. His
acquaintance with the Indian language gave him a position as an interpreter, and
secured him the appointment of sub-Indian agent for the State, which he held
many years, visiting different points, and supervising the payment of annuities.
He was with Gen. Cass at the making of the first treaty with the Indians at Fond-
du-Lac. Mr. Connor became possessed of hundreds of acres of land on the river
above Detroit, which has become valuable. Through it passes Connor's Creek,
named after him. He was Supervisor in 1818. In politics he was a Democrat. He
died in 1840.

RICHARD H. CONNOR

Representative from Wayne County, 1859-60. Was born July 26, 1814, in Grosse
Point. He lived on the farm where he was born. He purchased a white girl
named Miss Myers for goods amounting to $200 who was taken prisoner at four
years of age in Ohio during the Revolutionary War by the Chippewas and who
afterwards became Mrs. Connor. He served his township as Supervisor and Justice of the Peace at various times, and in 1849 was sergeant-at-arms of the House
of Representatives at Lansing. In politics he was a Democrat.

ROWLAND CONNOR

Representative from the Second District of Saginaw County (east side of city of
Saginaw), 1889-90 and 1891-2. Was born in New York City, June 16, 1842; was
graduated from the College of New York in 1860, and after teaching a year entered the theological department of St. Lawrence University, from which he was
graduated in 1863. He preached 12 years in New Hampshire and Massachusetts,
and then engaged in literary pursuits, contributing to newspapers and magazines,
and for a time was one of the editors and owners of the New York *Nation*. He
was married in 1869 to Miss Emma Hilton of Boston. In 1880 he came to East
Saginaw, Mich., and founded the First Unitarian Society of that city, though he
did not relinquish his literary work, and gave numerous lectures on social and
scientific as well as political subjects. A Mason, a K. P., a past exalted ruler of
the Order of Elks, and past grand commander of the Knights of the Maccabees.
A member of the Board of Education of East Saginaw. He was elected on the
Democratic ticket to the House of 1889 90, and re-elected to the House of 1891-2.

WILLIAM CONNOR

Delegate from St. Joseph County to the Constitutional Convention of 1850. Was
born in New Hampshire in 1803. He settled in Michigan in 1825 and took part in
the Black Hawk War. He was an interpreter for C. C. Trowbridge, and a messenger for Gen. Harrison to Commodore Perry. He held several local offices. He was
married. Occupation was a farmer. He died before 1877.

JAMES CONNORS

Representative, 1897-8, from the Chippewa District, composed of the counties of
Chippewa, Luce and Mackinac. Was born in Prescott County, Ont., May 7, 1856.
His early education was acquired in the common schools of Ontario. He engaged

in farming at an early age and continued it until 1879, when removed to Carson City, Nev. In August, 1880, he moved to St. Ignace, Mich., and entered the employ of the Martel Furnace Company; became manager of their plant at Allanville, where he remained until 1884. In 1885 he engaged in the business of lumbering, in connection with the Mackinaw Lumber Co. of St. Ignace. In politics a Republican. He was Supervisor of Brevort Township in 1883; Alderman at St. Ignace in 1888-9, and Mayor of St. Ignace in 1895.

LUTHER FITCH CONRAD

Representative from the Second District of Clinton County, 1885-6. Was born at Sharon, Medina County, O., May 23, 1839. He was engaged in the Civil War, his regiment being the 180th O. He moved to Michigan in 1868. Mr. Conrad was formerly a teacher, later engaged in farming. He held various township and county offices, having served one term as member of the County Board of School Examiners.

EZRA CONVIS

Delegate to the Constitutional Convention of 1835 from the Tenth District; Representative from Calhoun County, 1835-7. Speaker of the first Legislature of Michigan, was born in Vermont. When young his parents removed to Chautauqua County, N. Y., where he received a common school education, and taught several terms. He came to Michigan in 1832 and was so well pleased that in 1834 he settled in Calhoun County, where he aided in building up Verona, for several years a rival of Battle Creek. While a resident of New York he served as Justice, was Brigadier General of State troops, and was considered an able officer. In 1835 Gen. Convis was elected a member of the first Legislature of Michigan and became speaker of the House. He was a Democrat, and a supporter of the administration of Jackson. He was also a Mason, and a member of the Baptist Church. In the winter of 1837-8, while on his way home from a wedding he received injuries which resulted in his death at Detroit, Feb. 27, 1837. He was succeeded in the Legislature by Sands McCamly.

ALBERT BALDWIN COOK

Senator, 1903-4, from the Fourteenth District, comprising the counties of Ingham and Shiawassee; and Delegate from Shiawassee County in the Constitutional Convention of 1907-8. Was born at the Michigan Agricultural College, Aug. 11, 1873, of New England descent. He was educated at the Agricultural College, was graduated in 1893, and a farmer by occupation. Married and lived on his farm near Owosso. In politics a Republican.

ASA B. COOK

Representative from Calhoun County, 1857. Was born in Joy, N. Y., May 30, 1809. In 1826 he went to Keesville, N. Y., and learned the wagon maker's trade. In 1832 he emigrated to Marshall, Mich., and began the making of wagons in 1833, making the first in Calhoun County. In 1837 in company with others he built the first stone flouring mill, and the first merchant mill at Perrinville. The company operated the mill until 1842, then sold it. He then became a merchant and remained in that business until 1875. He was originally a Whig and later a Republican.

AUGUST C. COOK

Representative, 1895-6, from the Dickinson District, composed of the counties of Baraga, Dickinson and Iron. Was born in Germany, May 14, 1857; came to America, locating at Marquette, Mich., in May, 1867; attended high school; studied law; was admitted to the bar, and after 1880 engaged in the practice of the profession. He was appointed Prosecuting Attorney of Dickinson County on its organization in 1891. In politics a Republican. He was Prosecuting Attorney of Menominee County in 1888 and Supervisor of fifth ward, Iron Mountain, in 1893-4.

DAVID R. COOK

Senator from the Fifteenth District, 1877-8 and 1881-2. Was born in the town of Canajoharie, N. Y., Sept. 1, 1830. He was reared a farmer; received a common school education and came to Michigan in 1854, where he settled on a farm in Prairieville, Barry County. In 1863 he removed to Hastings, and served as Deputy Register of Deeds six years, then engaged in the abstract and real estate business. He served several terms as Supervisor, also as Mayor and Alderman of Hastings. In politics he was a Republican. He died at Hastings, Feb. 7, 1907.

ELIJAH F. COOK

Delegate to the Constitutional Convention of 1835 from Oakland County; and Senator from the Fifth District, 1838, and from the Third District, 1839. Was born in Montgomery County, N. Y., in 1805. By occupation he was a lawyer, in politics a Democrat. He settled in Rochester, Mich., in 1831. He was trustee of Hillsdale College. He died in 1886.

FRANCIS W. COOK

Representative from the First District of Muskegon County, 1883-4 and 1891-2. Was born in the village of Chemung, Chemung County, N. Y., Oct. 30, 1848. At the age of eight years he came to Michigan, remaining for about one year in the town of Commerce, Oakland County. From there he removed to the township of Victor, Clinton County, residing there until 1867, working at farm labor summers and attending district school winters. Having acquired a common school education he entered the law office of John Q. Patterson, at Ovid, in 1867, and was admitted to the bar at St. Johns, Clinton County, at the April term, 1870. In the winter of 1870 he located at Muskegon and commenced the practice of his profession. In politics he was a Greenback Democrat, but in the fall of 1881 and spring of 1882 he espoused the cause of the laboring men at Muskegon, then engaged in a struggle against the aggressions of capital. The working classes of Muskegon City and County elected him Representative in 1882. He had the honor of being the first Representative ever elected in Michigan by a purely workingman's party.

HERVEY COOK

Representative from Calhoun County, 1840. Was born at Palestine, N. Y., Feb. 16, 1788. He came to Saline, Mich., in 1831, moved to Homer in 1832, and settled on a farm near the village of Homer, in the present town of Eckford where he lived until his death, Sept. 4, 1874. He was Moderator of the first town meeting in Homer, and afterwards held several offices. He was an elder of the Presbyterian Church. Politically he was a Republican.

JACOB COOK

Representative from Washtenaw County, 1841. Was born in Morris County, N. J., Dec. 24, 1800. He removed to Wayne County, N. Y., while young, and emigrated to York, Mich., in 1831. He held the office of Justice of the Peace while Michigan was a Territory. In politics he was a Whig; by occupation a farmer. He died Jan. 18, 1884.

JOHN P. COOK

Representative from Hillsdale County, 1846; Senator from the Third District, 1847-8, and from the Ninth District, 1874; and a Delegate from Hillsdale County in the Constitutional Convention of 1850. Was born in Plymouth, N. Y., Jan. 27, 1812. When young he was engaged in farming, teaching and carpentry. He was educated in common schools, built a foundry at Detroit in 1832, removed to Jonesville in 1834, and was the first merchant in Hillsdale County. He settled at Hillsdale in 1837 which then contained only two houses, built a flour mill and was a merchant until 1862. He was a large contractor in the building of the Lake Shore Railroad; engaged in banking from 1855 to 1863; then in the hardware and lumber trade, and a large land owner; was the first Treasurer of Hillsdale County; the first Postmaster of Hillsdale, long a member of the Board of Education, and trustee of Hillsdale College. In politics he was a Democrat. In 1874 he was Senator in place of William Stoddard deceased.

LEVI COOK

Treasurer of the Territory of Michigan, 1830-6; and Representative from Wayne County, 1838. Was born in Norfolk County, Mass., in 1792. He was for many years a leading merchant of Detroit, and closely identified with its interests. He was County Commissioner, 1824 to 1837; Trustee of Detroit, 1821-2; Mayor in 1832, 1835 and 1836; Alderman at large in 1828, and Alderman of the second ward in 1840-1; City Treasurer in 1822; chief engineer of the Fire Department, 1833 to 1835, and held other offices of trust. He was a director and president of the Farmers and Mechanics' Bank for many years. He was prominent in educational interests and railroad enterprises, was liberal in church and society affairs, and was grand master of the Masonic fraternity for several years. He was originally a Whig and afterwards a Republican. He retired from active business some twenty years before his death, Dec. 2, 1866.

PETER COOK

Representative from Washtenaw County, 1873-4. Was born in Phelps, N. Y., June 5, 1827. In 1831 he settled in York, Mich. He received a common school education, was Supervisor, and held other places of trust. By occupation he was a farmer.

PETER J. COOK

Representative from Allegan County, 1845. He came to Saugatuck in 1843 as an agent of a lumbering company, which was not very prosperous, made no permanent home there and stayed but a few years.

PETER NAPOLEON COOK

Member of the Board of Regents of the University of Michigan, 1892-1900. Was born in the township of Antrim, Shiawassee County, Mich., Aug. 1, 1840, son of Peter Gordon and Elizabeth (DuBoice) Cook. On the paternal side he is descended from the Scotch Gordons; his mother was of French Hugenot origin. His parents came to Michigan from New York State in 1834, and were among the first settlers in Shiawassee County. He received his early education in the district school and completed his preparation for college at Lodi Academy, Washtenaw County, in 1860. He then engaged in teaching, for a time, and in the summer of 1863 assisted in raising a company for the 10th Michigan Cavalry. On July 25 he was mustered in as Captain of Company H, and was promoted to be Major on Feb. 18, 1865. In April of the same year he was sent to take command of the dismounted cavalry of the Department of Tennessee, where he continued until they were mustered out of service in June. In October, 1865, he was detailed on a military commission by the War Department and went to Memphis, Tenn., remaining on duty there until ordered to join his regiment to be mustered out. He was married on Dec. 6, 1868, to Mary A. Rutan. In 1872 he entered the law department of the University of Michigan and was graduated with the class of 1874. He took up the practice of his profession at Corunna, Mich.

WILLIAM COOK

Representative from Calhoun County, 1861-2 and 1863-4; and Senator from the Eighth District, 1875-6 and 1877-8. Was born in Rome, N. Y., in 1819. He received a common school education; removed to Michigan in 1831. He was a Supervisor for many years. Occupation was a farmer and grain dealer; a Republican in politics. He died at Homer, Oct. 30, 1901.

ANTHONY COOLEY

Representative from Kalamazoo County, 1838. Was born in Hampshire County, Mass., in 1794. He came to Prarie Ronde, Kalamazoo County, in 1829, and was a farmer and amateur painter. Politically he was first a Whig, then a Democrat. He died at Paw Paw in 1860.

SLOAN COOLEY

Representative from Oakland County, 1861-2. Was born Nov. 24, 1816, in Cheshire, Mass. His parents removed to Galen, N. Y., in 1818, and in 1836 he came to White Lake, Mich. By profession he was a farmer and surveyor. He was County Surveyor in 1849, and holding a fifth term of that office in 1887. In politics he was a Prohibitionist.

THOMAS McINTYRE COOLEY

Justice of the Supreme Court, 1864-85. Was born at Attica, N. Y., Jan. 6, 1824. His father was a farmer, descended from an early family of New England farmers. After a good academic education he taught school three terms and in 1842 began the study of law with Hon. Theron R. Strong, of Palmyra, N. Y., afterwards one of the Supreme Judges of that State. He came to Adrian, Mich., in September, 1843, and completed his law studies with Tiffany & Beaman. He was admitted to the bar in January, 1846, and for a while was a partner of Judge C. A. Stacy, of Tecumseh, but returned to Adrian in 1848. There he became one of the firm of Beaman, Beecher & Cooley, and afterward of Cooley & Croswell. In 1857 he was elected by the Legislature to compile the laws of the State, and completed the work within a year. In January, 1858, he was appointed reporter of the Supreme Court, and while in that position published eight volumes of reports. In 1859, with Judge J. V. Campbell and C. I. Walker, he was appointed a professor of the law department of the State University, and removing to Ann Arbor became the dean of the faculty. In 1864 he was elected a Justice of the Supreme Court, and was re-elected in 1869 and in 1877, continuing in that position until Oct. 1, 1885; when he resigned. During two years of each term he was Chief Justice. In 1868 he published a treatise on constitutional limitations which has passed through many editions, and is recognized authority wherever the English language is spoken. He also wrote works on the law of taxation, also on the law of torts, which take high rank. He also edited editions of Blackstone's commentaries, and Story on the Constitution, to which works he added many valuable notes and citations. He was the author of the legal articles in the American Encyclopedia. He wrote largely for reviews, and in 1885 wrote a valuable contribution to history, entitled "Michigan, a History of Governments," especially commenting upon constitutional questions that have arisen in the progress of Territory and State. He resigned his position of professor of law, but accepted and ably filled the position of professor of history in the literary department of the University at Ann Arbor. For two seasons, in 1877 and 1878, he delivered courses of lectures at the John Hopkins University at Baltimore. As a law writer he takes high rank. In 1846 he married Mary E. Horton, of Tecumseh. He served a few months as receiver of the Wabash and was chairman of the Interstate Commission at Washington. He died at Ann Arbor, Sept. 12, 1898.

HENRY H. COOLIDGE

Delegate to the Constitutional Convention of 1867 from Berrien County. Was born at Leomister, Mass., Aug. 9, 1811. He was educated at Amherst College in 1836, emigrated to Cass County, Mich., and was admitted to the bar in 1844. He was successful in law practice, and in 1872 was appointed Judge of the Circuit Court, and in 1876 was elected to that position. He held other local offices. In religion he was a Presbyterian, in politics a Republican after 1854. He died prior to 1887.

GEORGE W. COOMER

Representative from the Second District of Wayne County, 1885-6; and Delegate in the Constitutional Convention of 1907-8. Was born on a farm in the township of Troy, Oakland County, Nov. 4, 1843, of English and Holland descent. Both of his great grandfathers were soldiers of the Revolution. He received an academic education and was also a graduate of the law department of the University of Michigan, class of 1871. He was admitted to the bar in April of that year and continued in the practice of the law. Married.

MYRON COON

Representative from Wayne County, 1877-8. Was born in Ontario County, N. Y., May 26, 1822. He removed to Redford, Mich., in 1831, and to Greenfield, same county, in 1857. He was educated in the district schools. He served as Deputy Sheriff, and held the office of Commissioner of Highways. Occupation was farming.

GEORGE B. COOPER

Senator from the Fourth District, 1837-8; Representative from Jackson County, 1842; State Treasurer, 1846-50; and member of Congress, 1859-61. Was born at Longhill, N. J., in 1807. He came to Michigan in 1829, settled at Jackson and was a merchant. He was Postmaster of Jackson in the early history of that city. He was appointed State Treasurer Mar. 17, 1846, and served in that position until Mar. 13, 1850. In politics he was a Democrat. He went into the banking business at Jackson in 1851. In 1859 he ran for Congress against William A. Howard, of Detroit, and took his seat as a member, but was finally ousted and Mr. Howard was declared by the House entitled to the seat. Later he removed to New Jersey and died at Shark River, in that State, in 1866.

GEORGE H. COOPER

Representative from the First District of Shiawassee County, 1881-2. Was born in Sterling, N. Y., July 12, 1840. He came to Michigan in 1856, and began the study of dentistry in the city of Detroit, Jan. 1, 1861. Having completed the studies in 1864, he began the practice of his profession, which he continued to follow until the autumn of 1872, when he abandoned it and engaged in the drug business in Vernon, Shiawassee County.

WALTER H. COOTS

Representative from the First District, Wayne County, 1883-4. Was born in Braintree, Essex County, England, in 1833. He came with his parents to this country in 1844, and resided in Brooklyn, N. Y., where he received a common school education. He spent six years in a provision house, and in 1854 settled in Detroit. Then he established himself in the city hall market, and carried on a successful business until Jan. 10, 1877, when he assumed the duties of Sheriff of Wayne County. In politics a Republican. As the Republican nominee for Sheriff, in the election of 1876, he was elected, and was re-elected in 1878. Mr. Coots three times became a member of the Common Council of Detroit (representing the old fifth ward), and served in that capacity five years. He also served a term of three years as member of the Board of Sewer Commissioners of the city of Detroit, and remained on duty until the board was replaced by the Board of Public Works.

BENJAMIN COPELAND

Representative from Jackson County, 1839 and 1841. Was born in Norton, Mass., May 14, 1791, and graduated at Brown University, R. I., in 1815. He engaged in teaching and had a son of Audubon for a pupil while teaching near Natchez, Miss. He settled in Brooklyn, Mich., in 1835, built a large flouring mill, and for years was a prominent and enterprising citizen. In 1843 he removed to Clarendon, N. Y., and engaged in trade. He died Jan. 15, 1879.

JOSEPH T. COPELAND

Senator from St. Clair County, 1850-1; and Justice of the Supreme Court, 1851-7. Was born in New Castle, Me., May 6, 1813. By profession he was a lawyer, in politics a Democrat. He settled at St. Clair, Mich., in 1844, and was Judge of the County Court from 1846 to 1849. In 1859 he was elected Circuit Judge, which made him also a Judge of the Supreme Court, and served from 1851 to 1857. He removed to Pontiac in 1851 and resided there until 1878, when he removed to Florida. He enlisted in 1862, was made Lieutenant Colonel of 1st Cavalry, Aug. 22, 1861; Col. 5th Cavalry, Aug. 14, 1862; Brigadier General Volunteers, Nov. 29, 1862. He resigned Nov. 8, 1865, and was honorably discharged.

ALEXANDER B. COPLEY

Representative from the First District of Cass County, 1865-6 and 1871-2, and the First District of Van Buren County, 1875-6 and 1881-2. Was born in Champion, N. Y., Mar. 11, 1822. He subsequently resided with his parents at several manufacturing villages of that State, removing to Dayton, O., in 1829, and from there to Little Prairie Ronde, Mich. His education was limited to the common schools of Michigan. His occupation was farming until 1874, when he removed to Decatur. His time was partly occupied in the First National Bank of that place, of which bank he was president. He was Supervisor of Volinia Township, Cass County, for six terms. In politics he was a Republican. He died Mar. 27, 1899.

ALMON WARD COPLEY

Representative from the First District of Wayne County, 1909-10, 1911-12, 1913-14, 1917-18, 1919-20 and 1921-2. Was born in 1867 in Cass County, Mich., of American parentage. His grandfather, Alexander Copley, was one of the pioneers of Cass County, and his father, Hon. Alexander B. Copley, was Representative in the State Legislature for five terms. Mr. Copley was educated in the public schools. He graduated from the law department of the University of Michigan in 1892 and is now engaged in the practice of law at Detroit. Mr. Copley is married. In politics a Republican.

SANFORD H. CORBIN

Representative from Macomb County, 1851. Settled in Armada, Mich., in 1831. He was a house builder, and built the grist-mill in that town in 1834.

WILLIAM CORBIN

Senator from the Ninth District, 1863-4; Delegate from Monroe County in the Constitutional Convention of 1867; and Representative from Lenawee County, 1881-2. Was born in Nichols, N. Y., July 30, 1825. He received a common school education, and came to Michigan in 1843. In 1847 he became a merchant at Petersburg and remained in that business fifteen years. He held the offices of Town Clerk, Supervisor and Justice. He was engaged in farming, real estate, insurance, hardware and other business, and held other local positions.

JEREMIAH D. COREY

Representative from Washtenaw County, 1867-8; and Senator from the Fourth District, 1875-6. Was born in Otisco, Onondaga County, N. Y., Apr. 17, 1816. He was educated at the Onondaga Academy, came to Michigan in 1833, settled in Washtenaw County, and then resided at Manchester. He was a farmer, and a Democrat. He was Supervisor, Justice of the Peace, Town Clerk, School Inspector, and a member of the School Board and Village Council for many years. He was a railroad and bank director, and was vice president of the People's Bank at Manchester. Deceased.

JOHN BLAISDELL CORLISS

Member of Congress, 1895-7 to 1901-3. Was born in Richford, Vt., June 7, 1851, and was educated at the Methodist University of that State. Graduating in 1871, he chose the profession of law and entered the office of Noble & Smith, counsel for the Vermont Central Railroad. After two years' preparation he matriculated in the Columbian Law College at Washington, D. C., and was graduated from that institution in 1875; came to Detroit, where he engaged in the practice of his profession. In politics a Republican. He was City Attorney for the terms 1882-5, and revised the charter of the city as it was passed by the Legislature of 1883. He was elected to the 54th, 55th and 56th Congresses and re-elected to the 57th Congress of the United States.

JOHN BLAISDELL CORLISS, JR.

Representative from the First District of Wayne County, 1923—. Was born in Detroit, Nov. 3, 1877, of New England ancestry. He was educated in the public schools of Detroit. For twelve years he held the position of treasurer of the Michigan Lubricator Co., but at present is engaged in study and research. He was elected to the Legislature on the Republican ticket.

TERRY T. CORLISS

Senator, 1913-14 and 1915-16, from the Twenty-first District, comprising the counties of Lapeer and Tuscola. Was born at Almont, Lapeer County, Mich., Feb. 10, 1867, and is of Yankee descent. He was educated in the public schools of Almont. He is married and has always resided in Michigan and for over twenty-seven years conducted the Mayville Monitor. He held the offices of Village Clerk and Township Clerk, Director and Treasurer of school district and was Postmaster at Mayville; served as proofreader and assistant secretary of the Senate. In politics he is a Republican.

JERRY G. CORNELL

Representative from Jackson County, 1837. His postoffice address was Spring Arbor. (Further data not obtainable).

PATRICK CORRIGAN

Representative from Monroe County, 1851. Was born in Ireland, Jan. 7, 1815. He was a brother of the famous Sir Dominic Corrigan, doctor in Dublin. By occupation he was a farmer, in politics a Democrat. He settled in Exeter, Monroe County, in 1835, held the offices of Supervisor, Town Clerk, Justice of the Peace, and filled other town offices. He resided at Monroe in 1887.

ALVA H. CORWIN

Representative, 1901-2, from the Osceola District, comprising the counties of Lake and Osceola. Was born Aug. 7, 1855, in Cattaraugus County, N. Y., and in 1865 removed to Clinton County, Mich., where his parents settled on a farm near St. Johns. His education was received in the common schools, after which he taught school for ten years. Mr. Corwin was married in 1882 and six years later removed to Marion, Osceola County, where he engaged in the mercantile business. In politics a Republican. He held various township and village offices.

CHARLES H. COSSITT

Representative from Shiawassee County, 1885-6. Was born in Oconomowoc, Wis., July 10, 1848. At an early age he removed with his parents to Michigan, settling at Detroit, afterwards removing to Wayne, and from there to Lansing. He enlisted in the 6th Mich. Cavalry, and served in the Army of the Potomac, and in Utah territory, where he was mustered out of the service. Returning to Michigan, he located at Owosso, where he engaged in the foundry and machine business for many years. In the year 1881 he was elected Mayor and re-elected the following year. In politics a Democrat.

WILLIAM A. COTTON

Member of the State Board of Education, 1907-10. Was born at Saranac, Ionia County, Mich., Nov. 30, 1863. He received his education in the public schools of Saranac and Grand Rapids, and the University of Michigan, graduating from the Homeopathic department of the University in 1889. He located in Escanaba the same year and retired from the practice of medicine in 1903, and engaged in manufacturing and lumbering. Married. He served as state surgeon of the Sons of Veterans, member of school board and board of public works and chairman of the Board of Supervisors. He was appointed by Governor Warner, January, 1907, a member of the State Board of Education to fill the vacancy caused by the resignation of Luther L. Wright. He was nominated to succeed himself at the Republican State Convention, held in Grand Rapids, Feb. 14, 1907, and elected Apr. 1, 1907.

EBER W. COTTRELL

Representative from the Third District of Wayne County, 1879-80 and 1881-2. Was born Feb. 17, 1842, in Cottrellville, St. Clair County, Mich., where his father and grandfather were also born and reared. He was educated at the Newport (now Marine City) Academy, and, at an early age, commenced a maritime life upon the Great Lakes, where he became proficient in all branches of that profession. He made several sea voyages, and spent some time upon the Mississippi and other southern rivers. In 1868 he married and removed to Greenfield, Wayne County. He there entered upon agricultural pursuits, successfully managing one of the finest stock farms in the State. He devoted considerable time to the interests of stock-breeding, and wrote extensively upon agricultural topics for the press. He wrote a series of letters from the West Indies for the Detroit *Tribune*, while making a tour among those Islands in 1866-7. He filled the offices of Justice of the Peace, Supervisor, and Superintendent of Schools for the township of Greenfield, and member of the Republican State Central Committee.

JOHN F. COULTER

Representative from Berrien County, 1871-2. By occupation he was a farmer and stock raiser, in politics a Republican. In 1874 he removed to Fillmore County, Nebr., and 1878 represented the Twenty-third Senatorial District, comprising the counties of Fillmore and Clay, in the Senate of Nebraska, and was also a member of the Capitol Building Board, which commenced the building of the new .capitol at Lincoln. In 1882 he removed to Kansas, and in 1884 was elected Representative from the Fortieth District to the Kansas Legislature. He resided at Kinsley, Kan., in 1887.

JOSEPH COULTER

Senator from the Thirty-second District, 1861-2. His postoffice address was Ontonagon, Ontonagon County. He did not sit in the extra sessions of 1861 and 1862. (Further data not obtainable).

JAMES COUSINS

Representative from the county of Hillsdale, 1895-6 and 1897-8. Was born in Hertfordshire, England, Mar. 3, 1849. His early education was acquired in the common schools of England. In 1868 he came to America, locating in Hillsdale County, Mich., where he was engaged in the manufacture of brick and tile until 1884; subsequently his occupation was that of a farmer. In politics a Republican. He held the offices of Highway Commissioner and Supervisor.

JAMES COUZENS

United States Senator, 1922—. Was born in Chatham, Ontario, Canada, Aug. 26, 1872. He was educated in the Chatham High School, and came to Detroit in 1890. He was married to Margaret A. Manning in 1898 and they have four children, one boy and three girls. As a boy and young man Mr. Couzens was clerk, news butcher and railway operator, being connected with the Michigan Central Railway from eighteen years of age until twenty-five. Following this he was interested in the coal business for several years. In 1903 he, with others, organized the Ford Motor Company. He was made secretary and business manager and under his administration the company not only prospered, but grew with startling rapidity.

In 1916 Mr. Couzens resigned as vice-president and treasurer, which positions he had held for several years, and in 1919 all connection with the Ford company was entirely severed. In the spring of 1916 he accepted an appointment as Police Commissioner of Detroit, and in 1919 was elected Mayor, being re-elected in 1921. In November, 1922, he resigned to accept the appointment of Governor Alex J. Groesbeck to United States Senator, to fill the vacancy caused by the resignation of Truman H. Newberry.

GEORGE C. COVELL

Representative from Grand Traverse, Benzie and Leelanau counties, 1893-4 and 1895-6; Senator, 1897-8, from the Twenty-seventh District, composed of the counties of Antrim, Benzie, Charlevoix, Grand Traverse, Kalkaska, Leelanau and Wexford. Was born in Dundee, Mich., Oct. 16, 1860. His early life was spent upon the farm attending union school at the village of Dundee. He was a member of the Junior law class of 1885 in the Michigan University, and continued his reading until 1887, when he was admitted to the bar. In August of the same year he located at Benzonia, where he practiced his profession until 1892, when he removed to Traverse City. In politics a Republican. While in Benzie County he was Prosecuting Attorney for two terms. In Traverse City he engaged in the practice of his profession, being the junior member of the firm of Dodge & Covell. He died at Ashville, N. C., Apr. 11, 1918.

FRANK L. COVERT

Senator, 1915-16 and 1917-18, from the Twelfth District, comprising the counties of Oakland and Washtenaw. Was born in Waterford Township, Oakland County, Mich., Nov. 23, 1867, of American parents, being a son of Hudson P and Nancy J. Covert, who were early pioneers of Oakland County. He was educated in the district schools and the Pontiac High School. In 1890 he was admitted to the bar and engaged in the practice of law. He was married Oct. 2, 1895, to Catherine Cruice and had one son, Hudson C Covert. He served three terms as Circuit Court Commissioner of Oakland County, three terms as Prosecuting Attorney and Superintendent of the Poor for about three years. In politics a Republican.

LEWIS M. COVERT

Representative from Oakland County, 1851. Was born at Romulus, N. Y., Apr. 5, 1818. He was by occupation a teacher and farmer. He came to Michigan in 1832, and settled in Oakland County. In politics he was a Democrat. He was Treasurer of Troy; and Supervisor of Waterford Township in 1854 and 1856. He died Jan. 11, 1857.

ALEXANDER COWAN

Representative from the First District of St. Clair County, 1915-16 and 1917-18. Was born at North Street, St. Clair County, Mich., May 29, 1874, of Scotch parents. He was educated in the North Street schools and the State Normal College at Ypsilanti, after which he returned to Clyde Township and engaged in general farming and stock feeding. He was married Dec. 12, 1900, to Flora Beard. He served as chairman of the School Board and Treasurer of Clyde Township, In politics a Republican.

GEORGE Y. COWAN

Representative from Eaton County, 1863-4. Was born in Cayuga County, N. Y., Dec. 25, 1812. He came to Michigan in 1836. He was a farmer by occupation, and politically a Republican. He resided at Eaton Rapids in 1887.

GEORGE D. COWDIN

Representative from the Second District of Oakland County, 1907-8. Was born in Livingston County, N. Y., Oct. 21, 1835, of Scotch and Irish descent. He received his education in the district schools of Oakland County. He always gave his attention to farming, spent two years in the Rocky Mountains, 1859-61. He married in 1863. He held the offices of Justice of the Peace and Supervisor; was president of the Oakland County Farmers' Mutual Insurance Co., master of the Masonic Lodge. In politics a Republican.

ROBERT COX

Representative from Hillsdale County, 1861-2. Was born in North Branch, N. J., Apr. 30, 1813. When young was a resident of the State of New York, and came to Lenawee County, Mich., in 1829. In 1834 he located on a farm in Wheatland, Hillsdale County. In politics he was a Whig until 1854, then a Republican. He held several local offices. He died at Wheatland June, 1890.

JAMES CRAIG

Representative from Wayne County, 1875-6. Was born in Ticonderoga, N. Y., Dec. 2, 1823. He received an academic education. He removed to Detroit in 1847, where he continued to reside, pursuing the business of a merchant. In politics he was a Democrat. He died at Detroit, Nov. 11, 1894.

LOUIS C. CRAMTON

Representative from Lapeer County, 1909-10; member of Congress, 1913-15—. Was born in Hadley Township, Lapeer County, Dec. 2, 1875, of American parents. He was educated in the Lapeer High School and the University of Michigan, graduating from the latter in 1899. He was law clerk of the State Senate three times; was a member of the Michigan House of Representatives in 1909-10; Deputy Commissioner of Railroads from Feb. 1, 1907, to the establishment of the commission, and secretary of the Michigan Railroad Commission from Sept. 30, 1907, to Dec. 31, 1908. He has been Grand Master of the Grand Lodge of Michigan I. O. O. F. He was elected to Congress in November, 1912, and has served continuously since that time. He is a Republican.

GEORGE W. CRANDELL

Representative from Wayne County, 1877-8. Was born in Dearborn, Mich., in 1834. He was a student at Adrian College, but enlisted, serving through the rebellion. He was a farmer in Dearborn in 1887. In politics a Republican.

ARCHER H. CRANE

Representative from Lenawee County, 1869-70 and 1871-2. Was born in Onondaga County, N. Y., Mar. 30, 1821. By occupation he was a farmer, in politics a Republican. He held the office of Supervisor ten years. He settled in Freedom, Washtenaw County, in 1834, but later lived in Lenawee County. He resided at Hudson in 1887.

ELISHA CRANE

Member of the Board of Regents of the University of Michigan, 1842-6. Was born at Bethel, Vt., Nov. 2, 1800. He entered the ministry of the Methodist Episcopal Church and removed to Detroit in 1835, where he preached two years. He was afterwards pastor in succession of the churches in Marshall, Ann Arbor, Monroe and Ypsilanti. He was presiding elder of the Detroit district for a time, and later was pastor in succession of the churches at Coldwater, Constantine and Litchfield. He was active in establishing Albion College, and was for many years president of the Board of Trustees. He was a member of the Board of Regents of the University of Michigan from 1842 to 1846. He died at Litchfield, Mich., Apr. 22, 1868.

FLAVIUS J. B. CRANE

Representative from Livingston County, 1838. Was born in Canandaigua, N. Y., in 1812; with a common school education, he was for years a clerk, and came to Detroit in 1835. He, with Edward Brooks, owned and platted the village of Howell, and was the first Postmaster in 1836, also the same year was County Clerk. Later he resided at Ann Arbor, where he was Postmaster and a real estate dealer. From 1851 to 1872 he was a resident of Detroit, and acquired a fortune in real estate. From 1872 until his death, in 1886, he was a resident of Denver, Col., where he was largely interested in Sunday School work.

GEORGE CRANE

Representative from Lenawee County, 1851. Was born in Norton, Mass., Mar. 30, 1783. He removed to Wayne County, N. Y., in 1804, and lived in Macedon until 1833, when he settled in Palmyra, Mich., where he took up 2,500 acres of land. He built the first frame house in the town in 1833. He was a stockholder and director of the Erie & Kalamazoo Railroad Company, organized in 1834 to construct a railroad from Toledo to Adrian. He was one of three commissioners to locate the road. At a later date he was president of the road, holding that position several years, during which time he executed a lease of the road for ninety-nine years to the Michigan Southern Railroad Company. He was the first Supervisor of Palmyra, and was several times re-elected; and was for several years a County Commissioner. He was one of the most prominent men of Lenawee County in its early history. In religion he was a Quaker. He was generous, honest, pure and unselfish, and had the respect and confidence of all classes of people. He died at Palmyra, Apr. 17, 1856.

GEORGE L. CRANE

Representative from Lenawee County, 1863-4. Was born in Palmyra (now Macedon), N. Y., Nov. 20, 1810. He came to Palmyra, Mich., in 1833, where his father located 2,500 acres of land, and took an active part in building the railroad from Toledo to Adrian, of which he was a leading stockholder and director. The son settled on a farm in Madison, Lenawee County, in 1835, and for many years followed surveying. He was Supervisor, and held many other town offices, and was a Representative in 1863-4, as a Republican.

JESSE D. CRANE

Senator, 1893-4, from the Thirteenth District, composed of the counties of Genesee and Livingston. Was born in New York, in 1841. When five years of age he came with his parents to Michigan, locating on a farm in Fenton Township, Genesee County, being now located in Fenton village. His life occupation was that of a farmer. His early education was acquired in the public schools. In politics a Republican.

OZRO N. CRANOR

Delegate in the Constitutional Convention of 1907-8 from the Twenty-sixth District, Mason County. Was born in Wayne County, Ind., 1855, of English, German and Scotch-Irish descent. Mr. Cranor, after receiving a common school education, spent one year at the Hartsville University, Ind, and one year in Otterbein University, Westerville, O. He farmed, taught school and lumbered until 1888. After that time he practiced law; a resident of Michigan since 1901. He was appointed to fill the vacancy occasioned by the resignation of Hon. Roswell P. Bishop. He served as Representative and State Senator in the Indiana Legislature, and held the office of Justice of the Peace.

HENRY HOWLAND CRAPO

Senator from the Twenty-fourth District, 1863-4; and Governor of Michigan, 1865-9. Was born at Dartmouth, Bristol County, Mass., May 22, 1804. His father was of French descent, and was very poor, cultivating a farm which yielded little. The son fitted himself for teaching and took charge of the village school at Dartmouth. When this was changed to a high school he became its principal. In 1832 he removed to New Bedford, where he followed the occupation of a land surveyor. He was soon elected Town Clerk, Collector of taxes, and Treasurer, which office he held for many years. He was also Alderman; Police Justice for many years; chairman of the council committee on education, and in that capacity made a report that led to the establishment of a free public library in New Bedford, the first in Massachusetts. In interested himself to a large extent in horticulture, and started a nursery which he filled with fruit and ornamental trees, shrubs, flowers, etc. He was also a regular contributor to the New England *Horticultural Journal*, while he lived in Massachusetts. He was also engaged in the whaling business, and took an active interest in the State Militia, of which he was a Colonel. He was president of the Bedford County Mutual Fire Insurance, and secretary of the Bedford commercial insurance companies. He removed to Flint, Mich., in 1856, to care for large pine interests, in which he had invested in 1837 and 1856. He engaged largely in the manufacture and sale of lumber in Flint, Fentonville, Holly and Detroit, and was one of the largest and most successful dealers in the State. He was instrumental in securing the building of the Flint & Holly railroad, and was its president until it was merged in the Flint & Pere Marquette

Railroad Co. He was early elected Mayor of Flint, and took an active part in its educational and municipal affairs. In 1864 he was elected Governor of Michigan and was re-elected in 1866. The striking features of his administration were his veto of bills granting railway aid legislation, and his refusal to pardon convicts, except upon the clearest proofs of their innocence, or of extreme sentence. During the last years of his life he was a regular contributor to the Albany *Country Gentleman*. He was a member of the Christian, sometimes called the Disciples Church. In 1825 he married Mary Ann Slocum, of Dartmouth, Mass. They had ten children—one son and nine daughters. His son, William W. Crapo, for many years was member of Congress from New Bedford, Mass. Mr. Crapo in early life was a Whig, but was an active member of the Republican party from its organization. He died at Flint, July 22, 1869.

BERT F. CRAPSER

Representative from the First District of Genesee County, 1913-14. Was born at Swartz Creek, Mich., on Feb. 11, 1874, of German parentage. Married. His occupation that of a farmer. Politically, affiliated with the National Progressive Party.

ISAAC E. CRARY

Delegate to the Constitutional Convention of 1835 from the Tenth District; member of Congress, 1835-7 to 1839-41; Representative from Calhoun County, 1842 and 1846; member of the Board of Regents of the University of Michigan, 1837-43; Delegate to the Constitutional Convention of 1850 from Calhoun County; and member of the State Board of Education, 1850-4. Was born Oct. 2, 1804, at Preston, Conn. He received a good education, and graduated at Trinity College. In 1833 he came to Marshall, and engaged in a successful law practice. He was elected the first and then the only member of Congress from Michigan in 1835, and was re-elected in 1837 and in 1839, serving six years as the sole Representative. In this position he secured the passage of the first law of its kind, giving section sixteen in every township of the State for the benefit of common schools. All previous grants has been given to townships and effected little good. It was by his advice that John D. Pierce was appointed the first Superintendent of Public Instruction in this State. He was early and closely connected with the educational interests of the State. He always acted with the Democratic party. He was appointed member of the State Board of Education, Mar. 29, 1850, in the place of Samuel Newberry resigned; elected Nov. 2, 1852, for term of six years. He died May 8, 1854.

ISAAC M. CRAVATH

Senator from the Twenty-first District, 1871-2. Was born Feb. 14, 1826. He was brought up on a farm, and was in politics first Free Soil, and then a Republican. In 1855 he became a clerk in the Auditor General's office, where he held a place many years. He also was for a time editor of the Lansing *Republican*. He went to war as Captain in the 12th Mich. Infantry, was engaged in the Battle of Shiloh, but resigned from ill health. His wife, Mira E. Fiske, was a sister of President Fiske, of Albion College. He died May 4, 1872.

ROBERT E. CRAVEN

Representative from Clinton and Gratiot counties, 1853-4. Was born in King-wood, N. J., Apr. 13, 1811. He removed to the State of New York in 1830, and in 1835 came to Michigan. In 1841 he settled in Duplain, Clinton County, where he resided until his death, Nov. 16, 1855. He was three terms County Commissioner and for many years a Supervisor. By occupation he was a farmer, and for twelve years a lumberman; in politics a Republican.

JAMES CRAWFORD

Representative from Keweenaw County, 1869-70. Was born in Washington, D. C., Nov. 20, 1820. He spent most of his early life in New York City, from whence he came to the Upper Peninsula in 1846. He was an explorer and surveyor, and a Democrat in politics. He was an energetic political worker. He died at Eagle River, Aug. 18, 1882.

JOHN G. CRAWFORD

Senator from the Sixth District, 1865-6. Was born in Massachusetts, Apr. 21, 1834. By profession he was a lawyer, in politics a Republican. He came to Michigan in 1861, resided in Holly until 1867, in Fenton from 1867 to 1870, in the State of New Hampshire from 1870 to 1881, and later engaged in the practice of law at Clinton, Mass. He enlisted Aug. 2, 1861, as Sergeant Major in the 2nd Mich. Cavalry, was promoted to Lieutenant in September, 1862, and became acting Adjutant. He resigned in April, 1863. He was Recorder of Holly, in 1865-6, Town Clerk of Lancaster, N. H., in 1877, was appointed Consul to Canada in 1881 and served until July, 1884. He died at Meredith, N. H., Feb. 26, 1917 or 1918.

SAMUEL E. CRAWFORD

Representative from the Second District of Washtenaw County, 1919-20. Was born on a farm near North Branch, Mich., June 15, 1876. He attended the district school, the North Branch High School, and graduated from the Michigan State Normal College at Ypsilanti. He was founder of the weekly college paper now issued by the State Normal College. After graduation he entered the life insurance business. A member of the Masonic Lodge and the K. of P. Married. In politics a Republican.

RICHARD J. CREGO

Representative from Jackson County, 1861-2 and 1863-4; and Senator from the Twelfth District, 1865-6. Was born in Newsteed, N. Y., Mar. 19, 1819. By occupation he was a farmer, in politics first a Whig then Republican. He came to Michigan with his father in 1834, who settled on a farm in Columbia, Jackson County. He was Supervisor of Liberty for eight terms. The son took up a farm in Liberty, where he lived until 1864, when he removed to Columbia and lived on the farm taken up by his father, until his death, Oct. 8, 1872.

ALONZO CRESSY

Representative from Lenawee County, 1837; and Senator from the Fifteenth District, 1855-6. Was born in Scipio, N. Y., in 1808. He received a fair education, studied medicine, and began practice at Lima, N. Y. There he married a daughter of Dr. Justin Smith, and emigrated to Clinton, Mich., in 1831. In 1832 he accompanied a detachment of troops sent to the Black Hawk War as far as Chicago, treating many attacks of cholera and studying the malady in hospital. In 1836 he was elected as Representative as an Independent. He removed to Hillsdale, in 1855 was Senator from Hillsdale County, and toward the close of the session was president pro tem. He was first an anti-slavery Whig, later a Republican, and the latter portion of his life a Democrat. He took high rank as a physician. He was presiding officer of the Sons of Temperance for two years. He died many years before 1887.

GEORGE D. CRIPPEN

Representative, 1897-8, from Dickinson District, comprising the counties of Baraga, Dickinson and Iron. Was born on a farm in Superior Township, Washtenaw County, Mich., May 13, 1861. His early education was acquired in the district schools; at the age of fifteen he entered the State Normal School at Ypsilanti, where he remained two and one-half years of the next five, the balance of the time was spent on his father's farm. Beginning in 1881, he taught school four winters in Pulaski, Jackson County, one year at Onondaga, Ingham County, and two winters in his own township, working on the farm when not teaching. In politics a Republican. He was Supervisor of Superior Township in 1888 and re-elected in 1889, but resigned to accept the principalship of the Stambaugh schools; at the close of his term he accepted a position as mining engineer; was Justice of the Peace, Village Clerk, and member of the Board of School Examiners.

WILLIAM W. CRIPPEN

Representative from the Second District of Oakland County, 1893-4. Was born in Highland, said county, Sept. 3, 1842. He began life as a day laborer, and later engaged in farming. He located at Milford and dealt in agricultural implements. During the Civil War he was engaged as private in Co. I, of the 22d Michigan Infantry. In politics a Democrat. He held the offices of Supervisor, Justice and President of the village of Milford.

MARTIN CROCKER

Representative from the First District of Macomb County, 1887-8; and Senator, 1891-2, from the Fifteenth District, comprising the counties of Macomb and St. Clair. Was born at New Baltimore, Mich., Feb. 7, 1858, and had the usual school experience of most young men. In 1879 he went to the Ann Arbor Law School; was admitted to the bar in 1880, and at once opened a law office and began the practice of law in the city of Mt. Clemens. He served as Alderman in 1881 and 1883, and was elected to the House of 1887-8; after serving his party in the session of 1887 he resumed the practice of his profession, and in August of that year was married to Miss Emily Sabin, of Memphis, Mich. In February, 1888, he was appointed special deputy collector of customs of Huron distrct, and removed to the city of Port Huron where he entered at once upon the discharge of the duties of his office, remaining there until the election of President Harrison. Then he practiced law at Mt. Clemens in partnership with his father. He was elected to the Senate of 1891-2 on the Democratic ticket.

THOMAS M. CROCKER

Delegate to the Constitutional Convention of 1867 from Macomb County. Was born at Pawlet, Vt., Nov. 23, 1825. His education was received at public and private schools in Granville, N. Y. At the age of eighteen he came to Macomb County, Mich., and for several years worked upon a farm summers and taught school winters. In 1852 he removed to New Baltimore, where he was Postmaster for seven years. While in that position he studied law. In 1862 he was elected Prosecuting Attorney of Macomb County, removed to Mt. Clemens, and became a law partner of Hon. Giles Hubbard, which continued until the death of Mr. Hubbard in 1876. He then formed a partnership with H. B. Hutchins until 1884. He was appointed Collector of Customs at Port Huron by Grover Cleveland. From 1864 to 1868 he was Probate Judge of Macomb County. He died Dec. 8, 1902.

GEORGE W. CROFOOT

Representative from Livingston County, 1871-2. Was born at Pavillion, N. Y., Mar. 21, 1834. His early life was passed on a farm and attending common schools. At the age of eighteen he came to Pinckney, Mich., and engaged in teaching for two years. He also engaged in farming and mercantile business, the larger portion of his life in farming. In politics a Republican. He was Supervisor of Putnam fourteen years. He was Judge of Probate of Livingston County from 1881 to 1885.

HENRY CROLL, JR.

Representative, 1913-14 to 1919-20, from the Clare District, comprising the counties of Clare, Gladwin and Roscommon. Was born at Saginaw, Mich., Apr. 22, 1875, of German parentage. His education was acquired in the public schools of Saginaw. He left school at the age of thirteen years, and obtained a position in the American Commercial and Savings Bank of Saginaw, where he remained eight years. He then located at Beaverton where he held the offices of Alderman, Supervisor and School Director. In politics he is a Republican.

JESSE R. CROPSEY

Senator, 1905-6 and 1907-8, from the Ninth District, comprising the counties of Calhoun and Kalamazoo. Was born on a farm in the township of Brady, Kalamazoo County, Mich., Apr. 27, 1866. He remained on the farm and attended the district school until twenty-two years of age, then took a course at the Vicksburg High School, and after reading law for one year was admitted to the bar at Kalamazoo, Mar. 18, 1890. He actively engaged in his chosen profession, enjoying a large practice in his and adjoining counties, as well as in the higher State and Federal courts. He was married to Carrie B. Yates of Vicksburg, Oct. 28, 1891. He held the office of Township Clerk for several terms, President of the Board of Education of the Vicksburg district and served two terms as Circuit Court Commissioner. For several years he was Village Attorney and a member of the Republican County Committee; was placed in nomination at the Republican convention for presidential elector from the Third Congressional District, but withdrew when nominated for State Senator. Deceased.

CALVIN B. CROSBY

Senator from the Second District (Wayne County), 1887-8. Was born in Pompey, Onondaga County, N. Y., Aug. 29, 1829. He had been a resident of Michigan forty-five years in 1887. During the late Civil War he served in the 24th Mich., Infantry. He was made President of Plymouth village twice, and Treasurer of Wayne County twice. He was elected on the Republican ticket to the State Senate.

D'ANIEL W. CROSBY

Representative from Oceana County, 1889-90. Was born at Barrington, Yates County, N. Y., in 1833. In earlier years he was a teacher, but later a farmer. He served as Superintendent of Schools, Township Clerk, Supervisor, County Cler!:, and Register of Deeds. In politics a Republican.

HALE E. CROSBY

Representative from Berrien County, 1857-8. Was born in Ashburnham, Mass., Oct. 15, 1810. Occupation was a farmer; politics first anti-slavery and Republican, then Independent. He came to Michigan in 1844, and resided at New Buffalo about forty years. He published an anti-slavery paper in New Hampshire, when anti-slavery mobs were of frequent occurrence. He was Supervisor five terms and chairman of board. He resided at Three Oaks, Mich., in 1887.

MOREAU S. CROSBY

Senator from the Twenty-eighth District, 1873-4; and Lieutenant Governor, 1881-4. Was born in the town of Manchester, Ontario County, N. Y., Dec. 2, 1839. He graduated from the University of Rochester in 1863. He first came to Michigan in 1857, and settled in Grand Rapids. He was a member of the Board of Education of that city for four years; was for several years trustee of the Kalamazoo College; was president of the Young Men's Christian Association of Grand Rapids for five years, and of the Young Men's State Christian Association for two years, and was for some years a member of the State Board of Charities. He engaged in the real estate and insurance business, as a member of the long established firm of J. S. Crosby & Co. He died Sept. 12, 1893, at Boston, Mass.

WILL A. CROSBY

Representative from the Second District of Calhoun County, 1899-1900. Was born in Battle Creek Township, Calhoun County, June 11, 1863, was educated in the home schools, and graduated from the high school at Battle Creek. He engaged in book-keeping in Battle Creek in the fall of 1880, remaining until the spring of 1881, and in the same year was employed in a broker's office in Detroit. During the latter part of 1881 he engaged in soliciting for a life insurance company in Detroit and vicinity. He was admitted to the bar in 1885, and commenced practice at once, locating at Reed City. After several years of practice he was compelled, in March, 1890, to cease on account of ill health (of some two years duration at that time) and returned to Battle Creek. In October of the same year, having fully recovered, he resumed practice in that city, and was active in his profession until his election on the Republican ticket to the Legislature of 1899-1900.

JOHN S. CROSS

Representative from the Second District of Van Buren County, 1885-6 and 1887-8. Was born at Bangor, Mich., May 4, 1849. He received his education in the district and village schools, with the exception of one term at Hillsdale College. In 1870 he entered the service of the C. & M. L. S. R. R. as assistant in the surveys and construction of that road, and for years was engaged in similar work, filling various positions. In April, 1884, he resigned his position as civil and mining engineer for the Lehigh Coal and Navigation Company of Pennsylvania, and engaged in the real estate and insurance business at Bangor, where he resided. In politics a Republican.

ALANSON CROSSMAN

Representative from Washtenaw County. 1835 and 1836. Was born at St. Johnsbury, Vt. He was educated at Montpelier, Vt. He came to Michigan in 1831, settling at Dexter, and was at first engaged in the "wagon and blacksmith" business. He built the first storehouse for the Michigan Central Railroad at Dexter. He held office of some kind until his death, in 1853. He was a Democrat in politics.

DANIEL L. CROSSMAN

Representative from the Second District of Ingham County, 1867-8 and 1869-70. Was born in Brutus, Cayuga County. N. Y., Nov. 4. 1836. the youngest of five children. His father, a native of Connecticut. was a farmer until 1844, when, his older children being married. his wife. dead, he married a second wife, and with this son removed to Michigan, and settled on land he had taken up from the government in 1836, in the town of Ingham, Ingham County, where he commenced the business of selling goods; thus the son when not in school had the education of a country and village store, supplemented by two years at Michigan Central College, then located at Spring Arbor, Jackson County, Mich. In 1855 the father moved to Ann Arbor, and the son succeeded to the business, which he continued until 1871. He was always familiarly known as "Dan," so when in 1856 the village was platted by him, it was named "Dans"ville. He was married in 1859; was one of Lincoln's Postmasters from 1861 to 1865; corresponding clerk of the House of Representatives in 1865; several times Supervisor, both of Ingham and Williamston Townships; chairman of the Board of Supervisors; member of the Board of Control of the State Reform School from 1869 to 1875; Treasurer of that board, 1873 to 1875; chief clerk of the House of Representatives continuously since 1873 —seven terms—several times elected to that position by the unanimous vote of 100 members (all parties); served 1876 as one of the Hayes electors, and was secretary of the Special Tax Commission of 1882. In politics he was a Republican. In 1871 he removed to Williamston, Mich., and engaged in the business of grain buying and milling, opening in connection therewith a private exchange bank. He died at Williamston, Mar. 7, 1901.

JOHN S. CROSSMAN

Representative from Ingham County, 1851. Was born at Elbridge, N. Y., Aug. 19, 1820. He came to Michigan in 1839 and settled in Ingham, Ingham County, and for two years was Supervisor of that town. He went to the Pacific coast, and in November, 1852, was elected a Delegate to the Constitutional Convention at

Carson, Nev. In 1864 he was elected Lieutenant Governor of Nevada, which office he held for two years and one month, and was ex-officio Warden of the Nevada State Prison. He returned to Michigan in 1875. He was Postmaster of Williamston, Mich., from 1878 until his death, Sept. 17, 1884. He was also one of the County Superintendents of the Poor for several years. He was a Republican in politics.

CHARLES M. CROSWELL

Senator from the Tenth District, 1863-4 and 1865-6, and from the Eighth District, 1867-8; Delegate from Lenawee County to the Constitutional Convention of 1867; Representative from Lenawee County, 1873-4; and Governor of Michigan, 1877-81. Was born at Newbury, N. Y., Oct. 31, 1825, and was the son of John and Lottie (Hicks) Croswell. His father, of Scotch-Irish extraction, was a paper maker, and carried on business in New York City. When seven years of age his mother and sister died, and three months later, he lost his father. An orphan, his uncle, James Berry, a house builder and contractor, took charge of him. He came with him to Adrian in 1837, and until the age of twenty was a portion of the time working at the trade with his uncle, and the balance in school. In 1846 he was appointed Deputy Clerk of Lenawee County, and during the four years he held that office he pursued the study of the law. In 1850 he was elected Register of Deeds on the Whig ticket, and was re-elected in 1852. He was a Delegate in 1854 to the Convention at Jackson which organized the Republican party, and was its secretary. In 1855 he became a partner of Judge T. M. Cooley in the law business, which continued until Judge Cooley became law professor at Ann Arbor. and removed there. In 1862 he was appointed City Attorney of Adrian, and the same year was elected Mayor. He was active in legislative matters and strongly supported President Lincoln in his emancipation proclamation, and vigorously opposed legislation in favor of municipal aid to railways. He was president of the Constitutional Convention of 1867. He was a Presidential Elector in 1868. In 1873 he became secretary of the State Board of Charities, serving until 1877. He was an attendant of the Presbyterian Church at Adrian, and enjoyed in private life the respect and esteem of the people of Michigan. He died suddenly at Adrian, Dec. 13, 1886.

ROBERT CROUSE

Representative from Livingston County, 1848; Delegate from Livingston County to the Constitutional Convention of 1850; and Senator from the Twenty-third District, 1859 60. Was born in Avon, N. Y., Oct. 2, 1813. He came to Michigan in 1832, and from 1834 to 1841 was a merchant at Kensington, then became a mill owner and farmer in Hartland. In 1860 he became interested in real estate and the manufacture of salt at East Saginaw, and in 1862 built the Crouse block and the Everett House. He died in February, 1869.

JAMES A. CROZER

Representative from Menominee County, 1885-6. Was born in Hillsboro, O., in 1844, and went to Ontonagon, in 1857. He belonged to Co. A, 27th Mich. Infantry, and was Color Sergeant of that regiment. He was wounded three times. He was raised a printer, and occupied editorial positions on several papers in this State, but for several years was in the lumber business, and president of the Menominee Bay Shore Lumber Company, the Wancedah Lumber and Cedar Company, a director in the First National Bank and Electric Light Company of Menominee, and member of the Common Council of that city. He was Commandant of the Soldiers' Home at Grand Rapids, 1897-8. He was elected to the Legislature on the Republican ticket. He died July 3, 1901.

ROSSEAU O. CRUMP

Member of Congress, 1895-7 to 1901. Was born at Pittsford, Monroe County, N. Y., May 20, 1843, and received his education in the Pittsford and Rochester schools; followed the lumber business and established his first home in Plainwell, Mich. He was a Republican in politics. He served West Bay City as Alderman for four years, and in the spring of 1892 was nominated and elected Mayor of West Bay City, and was re-elected in 1894; elected a Representative to the Fifty-fourth Congress; re-elected to the Fifty-fifth, Fifty-sixth and Fifty-seventh Congress. He died at West Bay City, Mich., May 1, 1901.

CHARLES HERBERT CULVER

Representative from the First District of Wayne County, 1915-16, 1917-18, 1921-2 and 1923—. Was born Feb. 5, 1870, at Detroit, of American parentage. He was educated in the public schools and Detroit College of Law, being admitted to the bar in 1893. He was connected with the Detroit Police Department during the years 1884-1893. He has for the past fifteen years been engaged in the publishing business, at present being publisher and editor of the *Little Stick*, a weekly newspaper devoted to political reform through education, and also publisher and editor of the Springwells *Tribune*. Mr. Culver is married and has one son. In politics he is a Republican.

JONATHAN H. CULVER

Representative from Branch County, 1847. Was born in Canandaigua, N. Y., Feb. 1, 1819, and died Jan. 20, 1873. He came to Michigan in 1836, settled as a farmer in Matteson, Branch County, where he always lived. He was for many years Supervisor of the town.

GEORGE JOHNSON CUMMINS

Representative from the Clare District, 1909-10 and 1911-12. Was born Nov. 4, 1853, at Vienna, Warren County, N. J., and came with his parents in 1863 to Clarkston, Oakland County, Mich., where .the family resided, returning to Ann Arbor in 1871. He attended the Clarkston and Ann Arbor public schools and was graduated in 1875 from the law department of the University of Michigan. In 1876 he went to Farwell, Mich., and in 1885 he removed to Harrison. He practiced his profession in Clare County. In politics a Republican. He was twice elected Mayor of the city of Harrison, and held the office of Prosecuting Attorney of Clare City for four terms. He died at Harrison, Mich., Jan. 26, 1921.

GILBERT A. CURRIE

Representative from Midland County, 1909-10, 1911-12 and 1913-14; and member of Congress, 1917-18 and 1919-20. Was born in Midland Township, Midland

County, Mich., Sept. 19, 1882, of Scotch parents. His father came to Midland County in 1859 and was one of its earliest settlers. Mr. Currie received his education in the common schools and the Midland High School, and graduated from the law department of the University of Michigan in 1905, since which time he has been engaged in the practice of law in Midland. When twenty-three years of age, was elected Supervisor of his township and served three successive terms, and in 1908 was elected chairman of the Board.

JAMES L. CURRY

Representative from Genesee County, 1869-70; Senator from the Nineteenth District, 1873-4. Was born Dec. 30, 1825, in Enfield, N. Y., and received a common school education. He went to New Haven, O., in 1847, and in 1856 to Bath, Ill., for four years. He returned to Tontogany, O., in 1860, where he remained until 1865, when he settled in Clio, Mich. He served from 1861 to 1864 in an Ohio regiment, rising to the rank of Colonel. By occupation he was a lumber merchant, in politics a Republican.

SOLOMON S. CURRY

Representative from Marquette County, 1875-6. Was born in Lancaster, Canada, June 12, 1840; received a common school education; removed to Michigan in 1861, and settled in Houghton County. In 1862 he went to Marquette, where he resided. He was a mining superintendent for several years; followed the business of contractor. In politics a Democrat.

FREDERICK W. CURTENIUS

Senator from the Twenty-first District, 1853-4; and from the Nineteenth District, 1867-8. Was born in the city of New York, Sept. 30, 1806. His father, Peter Curtenius, was a General in the War of 1812, Marshal of the State of New York, and for many years member of the New York Legislature. Mr. Curtenius graduated at Hamilton College in 1823, studied law, then went to South America, enlisted as a Lieutenant, and helped free them from the yoke of Spain. In 1831 he was Colonel of New York militia. In 1835 he removed to Michigan, and commenced farming at Grand Prairie. In 1847 he raised a company for the 1st Mich. Infantry, was Captain, and under Colonel Stockton served through the war with Mexico. In 1855 he was appointed Adjutant General of Michigan, and held that position until 1861. He then became Colonel of the 6th Mich. Infantry, served in Louisiana, but being under arrest for refusing to surrender slaves to their masters, he indignantly resigned. He was Collector of Internal Revenue two years; President of Kalamazoo; for many years treasurer of the Michigan Asylum; president of the Kalamazoo City Bank; and an ardent friend and strong financial supporter of the female seminary. He was first a Whig, then a Republican; was a Presbyterian, and leading Odd Fellow. He died at Kalamazoo, July 13, 1883.

GEORGE M. CURTIS

Representative from the Second District of Genesee County, 1893-4 and 1895-6. Was born in Burton Township, Genesee County, Jan. 4, 1843. His early education was acquired at the district school and the Flint High School, supplemented by a short course at the State Normal. After completing his course he taught school for several winters, devoting his summers to work on the farm. In 1876 he was married, and two years later he gave up teaching and then devoted his whole attention to farming. In politics a Republican. He held the office of Township Clerk, Treasurer, School Inspector and Supervisor.

ISRAEL CURTIS

Representative from Macomb County, 1849. Was an early settler in the town of Erin, where he was Justice of the Peace as early as 1838. He was Supervisor of that town in 1844 and 1845.

JAMES B. F. CURTIS

Representative from the First District of Shiawassee County, 1889-90. Was born at Warsaw, N. Y., Nov. 17, 1839. By profession he was a physician, and during the war was hospital steward of the 102d U. S. C. T. He was Alderman of the city of Flint and also City Clerk; was elected on the Republican ticket to the House of 1889-90.

LESTER CURTIS

Representative from Marquette County, 1877-8. Was born in Yates County, N. Y., Jan. 29, 1829. He removed to Michigan in 1842, and settled in Northfield, Washtenaw County. In 1867 he removed to Rio, Wis., and engaged in mercantile pursuits, and from thence to Ishpeming, Mich., in 1874, where he engaged in mercantile business. He received a common school education. In politics a Republican.

MILES S. CURTIS

Representative from the Second District of Calhoun County, 1895-6 and 1917-18 to 1923—. Was born in Kingsville, Ashtabula County, O., Apr. 1, 1852. His early education was acquired in the district schools and the Grand River Institute at Austinberg, O. At the age of twenty-one years he came to Michigan and commenced the study of law at Jonesville, but soon gave up his studies to help his father on a farm near Battle Creek. Later he purchased a farm adjoining the city, a part of which he still owns. Mr. Curtis is married. He was Grand K. of R. & S., Knights of Pythias, nearly twelve years. Politically he is a Republican. He was Supervisor of his township for two years, and was elected to the Legislature of 1895-6. Later he served one term as Mayor and was then appointed Postmaster, which position he held eight years.

NORMAN D. CURTIS

Senator from the Second District, 1838-9. Was born in Madison County, N. Y., in 1803. He came to Michigan in 1827, and practiced as a physician until his death in December, 1860. He was several times Supervisor of the town of Monroe. In politics he was a Democrat.

THOMAS CURTIS

Delegate from the Fifth District to the Constitutional Convention of 1835; and Representative from Oakland County, 1841. Settled as a regular physician on a farm, the present site of New Hudson, Oakland County, in 1832. He built the first hotel in Kensington, and was the first Postmaster of New Hudson in 1834. He was admitted to the bar and removed to Albion, Mich., and afterwards to Holly where he died.

WILLIAM H. CURTIS

Representative from Ottawa County, 1873-4 and 1878-9. Was born in Lysander, N. Y., July 15, 1828. He received a common school education. In 1853 he settled in Waterloo, Mich. In 1856 he removed to Georgetown, Ottawa County, and in 1886 to Jamestown. He held several responsible offices of trust. By occupation he was a farmer, in politics a Republican.

WILLIAM L. CURTIS

Representative from the Cheboygan District, 1901-2; and Senator, 1903-4 and 1905-6, from the Twenty-ninth District, comprising the counties of Alpena, Cheboygan, Emmet, Mackinac, Montmorency, Otsego and Presque Isle. He was born in the township of Richland, Kalamazoo County, Mich., Jan. 29, 1842, and obtained his education in the district schools and Prairie Seminary at that place. He taught school for three years, and at the age of twenty, in partnership with his brother, assumed the entire control of his father's large farm, and for nineteen years was known as one of the most successful farmers in that section of the country. In 1882 he removed to Petoskey and purchased the interest of Thomas Quinlan in the banking firm of Wachtel & Quinlan, later purchasing the balance of interest and in partnership with his son formed the First National Bank of Petoskey. In politics a staunch Republican. He held the office of Mayor of the city of Petoskey, being endorsed by both parties and having but one vote against him.

DARWIN Z. CURTISS

Representative from the First District of Wayne County, 1909-10. Was born in Huron County, O., Oct. 5, 1861, of French-Spanish descent. He lived on a farm until fifteen years of age, and acquired his education in the high school at Plymouth, O., supplemented by a one year's course at Oberlin College. He taught school at the age of sixteen and two years later entered the railway and telegraph service continuing that work for ten years. In 1882 Mr. Curtiss began newspaper work on the Minneapolis *Tribune* and in 1885 founded the *Daily Journal* at Saginaw, and also published daily papers in Battle Creek and Marquette. In 1901 he became resident manager of the American Press Association in Detroit, resigning his position in 1906 and later being employed by the Hearst Syndicate until 1908. He was married in 1886. In politics a Republican.

JOHN L. CURTISS

Senator from the Twenty-second District, Kent County, 1885-6. Was born at Brooklyn, Wyndham County, Conn., in 1835. When he was eleven years of age his parents moved to Ontario County, N. Y. He received a liberal education at Lima Seminary, and at the age of nineteen taught school in the village of Naples, in the same State. The money he thus realized he expended in a thorough course of instruction at Bryant & Stratton's Commercial College, Buffalo. At the breaking out of the Civil War Mr. Curtiss enlisted at Geneva, N. Y., but was rejected upon a physical examination by the surgeons, in consequence of an injury to his left hand received previously to enlistment, and incapacitating him for military service. He then came West to Milwaukee, Wis., where he was married in 1865. Leaving there soon after he took a position as traveling salesman for a Chicago wholesale house, where he remained five years. In 1871 he started a paper and oil house in Grand Rapids on a moderate scale. By strict integrity, close application to business, and managing all the details thereof himself, he was in 1887 at the head of the extensive wholesale house of Curtiss, Dunton & Co., of that city. Mr. Curtiss was elected to the office of Alderman for the first ward in 1878, and served two years with satisfaction to his constituents. He was elected a member of the Greenback State Central Committee in 1882 and re-elected in August last at their State Convention at Detroit. He was elected Senator on the Fusion ticket.

JOHN W. CURTISS

Representative from Isabella County, 1891-2 and 1893-4. Was born in Oakland, Genesee County, N. Y., Feb. 13, 1846. He received his early education at the common schools supplemented by one term at the Cary Collegiate Seminary of Oakfield, N. Y. In 1868 he came to Michigan and began work on a farm, in which occupation he continued for six years, and entered the employ of a lumbering company, serving in the different capacities from common laborer to scaler, foreman, bookkeeper and cashier. After nine years of lumbering experience he again went to the farm, where he remained. During the war he enlisted in the Ninth New York Heavy Artilley, but was rejected on account of his age. He held the offices of Township Clerk, Supervisor, County Surveyor; was elected to the House of 1891-2 by the Democrats and Patrons of Industry, and re-elected to that of 1893-4 by the Democrats and Populists. He died May 22, 1920.

EDWIN J. CURTS

Senator, 1913-14, from the Thirteenth District, comprising the counties of Genesee and Livingston. Was born at Saginaw, Mich., Oct. 23, 1870, of German parents. His education was received in the Flushing· public schools. He was for some time engaged in the clothing business, and held the office of County Treasurer from 1902 to 1906. In politics a National Progressive.

EDWIN M. CUST

Senator from the Second District, 1842-3 and 1844-5; and member of the Board of Regents of the University of Michigan, 1849. Was born in Devonshire, England, Sept. 25, 1800. He was the son of wealthy parents, attended college at Eton, and Cambridge, studied law, was admitted to the bar, but never practiced on account of ill health. He traveled extensively in Europe and India. He married Marianna Ward in 1828 and came to Hamburg, Mich., in 1837, and settled on a farm, later occupied by his only daughter, Mary, the wife of Adolph Buck. Mr. Cust was a Democrat. He was appointed Regent of the University Feb. 2, 1849, but resigned the same year. He was president pro tem of the Senate in 1844. He was a thoroughly educated English gentleman, and received an annuity from England which made him independent as to means. He greatly enjoyed society, spending much of his time in Detroit, where he numbered many friends. He died at Detroit, Jan. 9, 1852, and was buried at Elmwood.

BYRON M. CUTCHEON

Regent of the University of Michigan, 1876-84; and member of Congress, 1883-5 to 1889-91. Was born at Pembroke, Merrimack County, N. H., May 11, 1836; pursued his preparatory studies at Pembroke and completed them at Ypsilanti, Mich., where he moved in 1835; graduated from the University of Michigan, classical course, in 1861; became principal of the high school at Ypsilanti, 1861. He served as Captain, Major, Lieutenant-Colonel, and Colonel of the 20th Mich. Inf., 1862-64; Brevet Colonel and Colonel of the 27th Mich. Inf., and Brevet Brigadier-General, "for conspicuous gallantry," 1864-65; and assigned to the command of the Second Brigade, First Division, Army of the Potomac, in 1864; mustered out in 1865. He studied law with Hon. S. M. Cutcheon, Ypsilanti, Mich., 1865-66; graduated from Michigan University Law School, 1866, and admitted to practice at Ann Arbor, Mich.; and commenced the practice of law at Manistee, Mich., in 1867. In politics a Republican. He was a member of the Board of Control of Railroads of Michigan, 1866-83; Presidential Elector in 1868; City Attorney, 1870-1; County Attorney, 1873-4; Regent of the Michigan University, 1876-84; Postmaster at Manistee City, 1877-83; elected to the Forty-eighth Congress; re-elected to the Forty-ninth, Fiftieth and Fifty-first Congresses; and appointed the civilian member of the Board of Ordinance and Fortifications by President Harrison in July, 1891, serving until Mar. 25, 1895. He then became editorial writer on the Detroit *Daily Tribune* and Detroit *Journal*, 1895-7; and resumed the practice of law at Grand Rapids, Mich. He died at Ypsilanti, Apr. 12, 1908.

OTIS E. M. CUTCHEON

Representative from the Midland County District, 1879-80 and 1881-2. Was born in Dryden, N. Y., Aug. 8, 1845. His parents moved to Albion, Mich., in 1846, and settled upon a farm. He received his education at Albion College, and for a time followed teaching. Having pursued the study of law at Charlotte, Mich., he was admitted to the bar in 1872. He was elected Prosecuting Attorney of Iosco County, 1872; was re-elected in 1874; was appointed County Superintendent of Schools in February, 1873; was elected to the same office in April following, and was elected Circuit Court Commissioner in 1874. He moved to Idaho Falls, Idaho.

SULLIVAN M. CUTCHEON

Representative from Washtenaw County, 1861-2 and 1863-4; and member of the Constitutional Commission of 1873. Was born in Pembroke, N. H., Oct. 4, 1843. He graduated at Dartmouth College in 1856, and the same year became a resident of Ypsilanti, there taught until 1858, when he became Superintendent of Schools at Springfield, Ill., for two years, and was admitted to the Illinois bar. He practiced law at Ypsilanti until 1875, then at Detroit. He was chairman of the Constitutional Commission of 1873, and from 1877 to 1885 was U. S. District Attorney of eastern Michigan. He was president of the Dime Savings Bank, trustee of Harper Hospital and Olivet College, and director in several corporations. In politics he was a Republican. He was chairman of the Michigan delegation at the Republican National Convention in 1868. He was the head of the law firm of Cutcheon, Crane & Stellwagen. During many campaigns he was a leading Republican speaker. In religion he was a Presbyterian. He married Josephine Moore in 1859. He died May 18, 1900, at Detroit.

VINCENT P. DACEY

Representative from the First District of Wayne County, 1921-2 and 1923—. Was born in Detroit July 3, 1895, of Irish-American parentage. He received his early education in Detroit parochial grammar schools, subsequently graduating from the Detroit High School and the literary department of the University of Detroit, where he received the degree of A. B., in 1916. While at college he was prominent as an athlete and upon completion of his course was appointed City Athletic Director, serving in that capacity for the past four years exclusive, however, of time spent in military service. He entered the army in July, 1918, and was later assigned to 14th ammunition train detachment of the 14th Division at Camp Custer. From there he was sent to the Field Artillery Central Officers Training School at Camp Taylor, Ky., where he was discharged in December following the signing of the Armistice. In politics he is a Republican.

LEMUEL G. DAFOE

Representative from Alpena County, 1891-2, 1919-20 and 1921-2. Was born at Dunville, Ont., Oct. 2, 1857. At the age of five years he removed with his parents to Alpena, where he received his early education in the public schools of that city. After attending the State Normal College at Ypsilanti he taught school four years, and then began the study of law in the office of Hon. J. D. Turnbull, of Alpena. In 1882 he entered the law department of the University of Michigan, and the next year was admitted to the bar. He immediately took up the practice of law at Alpena, in which he is still engaged. Mr. Dafoe is married and has one daughter. He was first elected to the Legislature in 1890 and represented the counties of Alpena, Montmorency and Otsego in the session of 1891-2. In 1898 he was appointed by President McKinley Postmaster at Alpena and was re-appointed in 1902 by President Roosevelt. He was twice elected delegate-at-large from Michigan to the national convention of Republican Clubs League and in 1904 was elected vice-president from Michigan of that organization. The same year he was selected as a delegate to the Republican National Convention at Chicago that nominated Theodore Roosevelt for President. He served as Mayor of Alpena from 1910 to 1914.

SAMUEL E. DAIGNEAU

Representative from the Second District of Berrien County, 1915-16 and 1917-18. Was born at Brandon, Vt., May 17, 1852, of French parentage. His parents removed to Battle Creek in the fall of 1854 where he received his education in the public schools. He was married Dec. 31, 1874, to Carrie Stone, at Hillsdale, and resided in that city for about six years when he removed to Battle Creek, residing at the latter place until 1891. After 1891 he resided at Benton Harbor where he engaged in the laundry business. He served as Alderman of Benton Harbor,

member of the Board of Public Works and represented the second ward on the
Board of Supervisors for seven years. In politics a Republican.

MILO H. DAKIN

Representative from Saginaw County, 1885-6 and 1887-8. Was born in the town
of Ingham, Mich., Oct. 1, 1848. His parents both dying when he was but thirteen
years of age, he was thrown upon his own resources. At fifteen he enlisted in Co.
C, 9th Regiment, Mich. Cavalry, and served until the close of the war, eighteen
months in all, when he went to Ionia County, where he was engaged in work upon
a farm for nearly four years; he then went to Montcalm County, obtained a place
in a saw mill, remaining there four years and then removed to Saginaw County,
where he resided, being employed in the mills during the summer and in the woods
in winter as a shingle inspector and packer. Politics, Labor.

JAMES DALTON

Representative from Ottawa County, 1859 60. His postoffice address was Dalton's
Mills. (Further data not obtainable).

JOHN W. DALTON

Representative from the Second District of Lenawee County, 1889-90. Was born
in Adrian. His father and mother were pioneers in what is now the city of Adrian.
When a boy he removed with his parents to a farm in Madison, a short distance
south of Adrian, and continued a resident of that township. In politics an active
Republican. He was elected on the Republican ticket to the offices of Township
Treasurer, Clerk and Supervisor.

LAWRENCE DALTON

Representative from the Second District of Wayne County, 1871-2. His postoffice
address was Dalton's Corners. (Further data not obtainable).

JAMES DALY

Representative from Wayne County, 1875-6. Was born in Roscommon County,
Ireland, Jan. 25, 1830. In 1836 he emigrated to America with his father's family,
settling in Alleghany County, N. Y., where he received a common school education. In 1847 the family removed to Michigan, near Detroit, in which city he resided. He held several ward offices, including that of school inspector, and served
two terms as Alderman. By occupation he was a merchant, in politics a Democrat.

JOHN ADAMS DAMON

Representative from the First District of Tuscola County, 1887-8 and 1889-90; and
Senator, 1915-16 and 1917-18, from the Twenty-fifth District, comprising the coun-
ties of Gratiot, Isabella and Mecosta. Was born at Madison, O., June 4, 1850, of
Scotch and English parentage. His education was acquired principally at the
Wisconsin University. When he was five years of age his parents moved to Deane

County, Wis. In 1872, he went to Beloit, Wis., where he was married to Ella G. Jewett, who died in August, 1913. He was married in September, 1915, to Mrs. E. M. Cooper, of Mt. Pleasant. He came to Michigan in 1876 and located at Millington, Tuscola County; moved to Mt. Pleasant in December, 1906. In politics a Republican. He served on school boards for years, was Township Clerk, County Treasurer of Isabella County in 1906 and 1908, and Alderman of Mt. Pleasant in 1913 and 1914.

EPHRAIM B. DANFORTH

Senator from the Seventh District, 1847-8; and Delegate from Ingham County to the Constitutional Convention of 1850. Was born in Massachusetts in 1807. He settled at Mason, Mich., in 1837, as agent of Noble & Co., who owned the site of that city. He was one of the firm. He named the place after Gov. Mason. He was the first Postmaster, and Associate County Judge in 1838 and 1842. With Hon. Alvin Hart and H. H. Smith he built the first grist mill in Lansing in 1848. He was a leader in locating the capital at Lansing. He was married; occupation a farmer. He removed to Lansing in 1850 and died in 1853.

GEORGE DANFORTH

Senator from the Second District, 1851. Was a lawyer, and settled in practice at Ann Arbor about 1835. He was a man of wit and genial qualities, and kept everybody around him in good humor. In politics he was a Democrat. He died about 1856.

DAVID I. DANIELS

Representative from Clinton County, 1859-60. Was born in Scipio, N. Y., Apr. 16, 1817. He came to Watertown, Mich., at an early day. He studied law late in life, was admitted to the bar in 1852, and practice until his death, Apr. 11, 1874. He was Supervisor, and for four years Circuit Court Commissioner. In politics he was a Republican.

EBENEZER DANIELS

Representative from Lenawee County, 1841; and Delegate from Lenawee County to the Constitutional Convention of 1850. Was born in New York in 1803. By occupation he was a merchant, in politics a Whig. He settled at Medina, Mich., in 1803; was Postmaster at Medina in 1851. He died June 1, 1862.

GEORGE DANZ

Representative from Monroe County, 1921-2. Was born at Monroe, Mich., Mar. 15, 1877, of American parents. He was educated in the parochial and union schools of Monroe. He was for seventeen years agent and salesman for I. E. Ilgenfritz & Sons and in 1908 he accepted a position with the Weiss Manufacturing Company, which position he now holds. Mr. Danz is married and has one daughter and two sons. In politics he is a Republican.

JOHN DAPRATO

Representative from Dickinson County, 1913-14 to 1919-20. Was born at Barga, Italy, in May, 1852, and was educated in a private school. He came to America in 1868, going directly to Chicago, where he worked for and eventually became manager of J. Daprato Statuary Company, now the Daprato Statuary Company. In 1876 he entered the employ of J. B. Fish & Company, of Chicago, as hat pattern maker, working for them until 1890. On account of ill health he removed to Iron Mountain, Mich., where he was a member of the firm of Daprato & Rigassi. A widower. Member of the F. & A. M., R. A. M., K. T., and the S. P. R. S. In politics a Republican.

HENRY DARLING

Representative from Lenawee County, 1851. Emigrated from the State of New York to Macon, Mich., where he died. In politics he was a Whig.

ARCHIBALD B. DARRAGH

Representative from Gratiot County, 1883-4; and member of Congress, 1901-3 to 1907-9. Was born in Monroe County, Mich., Dec. 23, 1840. He received a common school and collegiate education and was graduated from the University of Michigan in the class of 1868. He taught school for two years, and on Aug. 14, 1862, enlisted as private in the 18th Mich. Inf. After being captured by the enemy he was exchanged and transferred to the 9th Mich. Cavalry, with which regiment he served until the close of the war. Married. He held the offices of County Commissioner of Schools, County Treasurer, President of the village, Mayor of the city of St. Louis, and member of the Lower House of the State Legislature. In politics a Republican. He was elected to the 57th, 58th, and 59th Congresses of the United States and re-elected Nov. 6, 1906.

LEWIS DARRAH

Representative from Monroe County, 1847. Was born in McConnellsburg, Pa., Apr. 29, 1809. He came to LaSalle, Monroe County, in 1833. His occupation was that of Justice of the Peace, his politics Democratic. He died July 5, 1887.

SAMUEL J. DAUGHERTY

Representative from Tuscola County, 1907-8. Was born at Zanesville, O., Aug. 14, 1873, of Irish descent. He received his education in the district schools of Tuscola County. He was married to Rhoda S. Dickinson, in December, 1893. His general occupation that of a farmer. He served as keeper of the County Poor Farm, and in 1902, was elected Sheriff of Tuscola County. In politics a Republican.

GEORGE DAVENPORT

Senator from the Twenty-fifth District (Saginaw County), 1885-6. Was born in Saginaw City, Mich., Jan. 11, 1840, his parents having moved to Saginaw June 2, 1835. Senator Davenport received a common school education, and at the age of twenty years commenced teaching; taught thirteen years. He was successfully engaged for eight years in the manufacture of lumber and shingles; was engaged in farming; served six years as Alderman; was twice appointed to fill a vacancy on the Board of Supervisors. In politics he was a Democrat. He was killed by lightning at Saginaw, July 2, 1901.

GEORGE DAVENPORT

Representative from Lapeer County, Mich., in 1881-2 and 1883-4. Was born in the city of New York, Mar. 23, 1833. In 1837 he removed, with his parents, to Hadley, Mich. He resided there, except in the years 1857-8, which he spent in New York. He afterwards returned to Hadley and engaged in farming. He held various township offices, having been elected Township Treasurer in 1861 and again in 1862, which position he resigned. Aug. 9, 1862, he enlisted as a private in Co. K, 4th Mich. Cavalry. When discharged, at the close of the war, he was First Sergeant. He participated in the capture of Jefferson Davis. He filled the office of Supervisor several terms. He was a farmer by occupation; in politics a Republican.

JAMES I. DAVID

Representative from Wayne County, 1859-60; and Senator from the Third District, 1875-6. Was born at Catskill, N. Y., Aug. 20, 1811, and came to Michigan in 1842. His early business life was as a contractor in canal and bridge work. He settled on Grosse Isle in 1848, and his general business was lumbering. He was a Lieutenant in Broadhead's cavalry in 1861, and subsequently Captain and Commissary; was Colonel of the 9th Mich. Cavalry in 1862, and in 1863 commanded a division in Burnside's corps, Shackleford's division, mustered out in 1864, having resigned by reason of disability. He was appointed by President Cleveland, in 1886, Indian agent at the Osage Agency. In politics he was a Democrat. He died at Ecorse, Wayne County, Oct. 13, 1872.

ORRIN DAVID

Representative from Wayne County, 1849. Was born at Catskill, N. Y., in 1822, and moved to Grosse Isle in 1843. He was a lumberman and had flour mill interests at Trenton. He held local offices in the township of Monguagon, of which Grosse Isle forms a part. In politics he was a Democrat. He died in 1851.

ALEXANDER P. DAVIS

Senator from the Twenty-fourth District, 1859-60 and 1865-6. Was born in Cayuga County, N. Y., about 1814. He came to Michigan in 1837, and first settled in Livingston County, removing to Flint in 1842. He was by profession a lawyer, and was also engaged in milling. In both occupations his reputation was that of a thoroughly honest man. He was an able lawyer and successful advocate before a jury. He was Prosecuting Attorney from 1852 to 1858. He removed to Fentonville about 1870, and died Mar. 4, 1871.

ALEXANDER W. DAVIS

Representative from Genesee County, 1861-2. Was born at Waterloo, N. Y., Oct. 30, 1824. In 1836 he removed with his parents and settled in Tuscola, Mich. He removed to Grand Blanc, in 1844. In 1847 he enlisted and served eighteen months in the war with Mexico, and was severely wounded at Churrubusco. He returned to Grand Blanc, and was Justice for many years.

ALONZO C. DAVIS

Representative from the District comprising Ontonagon, Isle Royal, Baraga, and Keweenaw counties, 1877-8 and 1885-6. Was born Sept. 4, 1823, in Genesee County, N. Y. He removed to Michigan in 1827. Since 1846 he had been engaged much of the time as superintendent of copper mines in Ontonagon, Keweenaw, Houghton, and Isle Royal counties. In politics he was a Republican. He died Feb. 20, 1886, at Detroit.

AMMOS DAVIS

Representative from Oakland County, 1839 and 1840. Was born at Ware, Mass., Dec. 15, 1799, and died at Birmingham, Mich., Dec. 20, 1884. At the age of nine he moved with his parents to Bennington, Vt., where he was apprenticed to learn the trade of a woolen manufacturer. When a young man he removed to Truxton, N. Y. In 1825 he removed to Chillicothe and ran a woolen mill owned by Gen. Worthington. On account of malaria he was compelled to return East in 1826. The next year returned to Ohio and ran a woolen mill at Xenia. In 1829 he settled on a farm in Southfield, Oakland County, Mich., where he lived until 1851. In 1849 he established a branch store at Birmingham, having one at Southfield, and removed there in 1851, continuing in business until 1880. In politics he was first Whig then Republican.

BAYARD G. DAVIS

Senator, 1919-20 and 1921-2, from the Eighth District, comprising the counties of Allegan and Van Buren. Was born on a farm in Aurelius Township, Ingham County, Mich., in 1868, of English and Irish parents. He received his education in the Eaton Rapids High School and the State Normal College at Ypsilanti. After teaching four years in Jackson County, he went to Chicago where he entered the employ of the Anchor Line Transportation Company. He remained with this company seventeen years, the last ten years as general superintendent. In 1908 resigned this position and bought a farm near Lawton, Mich., where he now resides. At present he is vice-president of the Wolverine Fruit Association, of Paw Paw, Mich. Mr. Davis is married. In politics a Republican. He has been chairman of the County Committee, and for the past ten years one of the speakers for the State Central Committee.

CALVIN DAVIS

Representative from Macomb County, 1845. Was born at Hubbardston, Mass., Apr. 27, 1793. He settled on a farm in Shelby, Mich., in 1824. He was Associate County Judge in 1826, and filled that place until the court was abolished. He removed to the town of Macomb in 1832, and in 1838 was Sheriff of Macomb County. He was for twenty-three years Postmaster of Macomb, and twenty-four years a Justice. He was a Democrat until 1856, then a Republican. He died Feb. 10, 1870.

CHAUNCEY DAVIS

Representative from Muskegon County, 1861-2 and 1863-4. Was born in Jefferson County, N. Y., Mar. 15, 1812, and died Feb. 9, 1888. He received a common school and academic education, and taught school several terms. In 1835 he went to Kenosha, Wis., and was engaged in house building for twelve years. He removed to Muskegon, Mich., in 1848, where he became a leading business man, especially in the lumber business. He was the first Mayor of Muskegon in 1860 and again in 1871. He filled important positions in business corporations, and was liberal in aiding schools, churches, railroads, etc. In politics he was a Democrat until 1854, then a Republican.

GEORGE B. DAVIS

Representative from the Second District of Macomb County, 1895-6 and 1897-8; and Senator, 1899-1900, from the Twelfth District, comprising the counties of Macomb and Oakland. Was born in Detroit, Mich., June 23, 1858. His early education was acquired in the public schools. At the age of sixteen he clerked one year in the wholesale oil house of M. V. Bently, of Grand Rapids, after which he traveled for a wholesale house in Detroit. In 1882 he started in business for himself in Utica, Macomb County, as manufacturer and dealer in hardwood lumber. In 1890 he organized the Utica Hoop and Lumber Company, also organized the Detroit Sand and Gravel Company, and was later its sole owner. In politics a Republican.

HENRY DAVIS

Representative from Branch County, 1853-4. Was born in Pennsylvania in 1812, studied medicine and commenced the practice of his profession in his native State. He came to Michigan in 1840, settling in the town of Bronson, and was soon after married to Miss Helen Wheeler. He practiced his profession there until 1861, when he removed to California. In politics he was a Democrat. He was an industrious legislator and served well his constituents. He was in personal appearance tall and slim, grave almost to melancholy, and was a close, hard-working student. He died in California.

IRA DAVIS

Representative from Wayne County, 1861-2. Was a native of Canada, born in 1818. He was by profession a lake captain, and was interested with John Owen, of Detroit, in the Cleveland line of steamers, and had other vessel interests, and was also interested in lumbering. He was a Republican in politics. He had also considerable real estate interests in and about Detroit, where he died Dec. 4, 1873.

JAMES M. DAVIS

Representative from the Second District of Kalamazoo County, 1899-1900. Was born on his father's farm at Orchard Grove, Lake County, Ind., Sept. 11, 1844. His early life was spent on the farm, and he attended the district school until about fifteen years of age, after which he spent about one year at high school at Crown Point, Ind.; then attended college at Valparaiso, Ind., for three years, and then entered Indiana Asbury University—now DePauw University—at Greencastle, Ind., from which he graduated with the degree of A. B. in 1868, and A. M. in course in 1871. He attended the University of Michigan Law School at Ann Arbor during the year 1869-70 and came from there to Kalamazoo County in March, 1870. He taught two years in the district schools of Indiana, and while doing his collegiate work taught mathematics and Greek one year at Valparaiso College, and Latin, Greek, and mathematics for two years at Danville Academy in Hendricks County,

Ind.; also acted as a tutor at DePauw University for two years. He was admitted to the bar in November, 1870, and practiced law in Kalamazoo. He was married Mar. 22, 1867, to Miss Estella Eldred of Climax, Mich. In politics a Republican. He held the office of Justice of the Peace in Kalamazoo, was Circuit Court Commissioner and United States Circuit Court Commissioner for the Western District of Michigan. In the fall of 1888 he was elected Judge of Probate of Kalamazoo County, which office he held for eight years. For many years, he was president of the Kalamazoo County Sunday School Association, and also for nine years member of the executive committee of the Michigan State Sunday School Association, having served as its president one year.

JOHN DAVIS

Representative from Oakland County, 1844 and 1846. His postoffice address was Birmingham. (Further data not obtainable).

JOHN M. DAVIS

Representative from Wayne County, 1857-8. Was a native of New Hampshire, born in 1806. The time of his coming to Detroit is not known, although he was a road district supervisor in the city in 1838. He was Alderman in 1850, Superintendent of Sewers in 1854, City Assessor in 1856, and a member of the Board of Education, 1853-7. He was a teacher and a wood-working mechanic. Democratic in politics. He died in 1861.

JONATHAN B. DAVIS

Delegate from the First District to the Constitutional Convention of 1835; and Senator from the First District, 1835-7. Was born at Hanover, N. Y., June 29, 1795. He acquired by his own efforts an academic and medical education, paying his way as teacher, clerk in store, etc. After residing in the State of New York, he came to Michigan in 1828, located land in Plymouth, and began life as a farmer and doctor. He was a Justice under the territorial regime, was Postmaster at Plymouth for some years, and president of the Wayne County (wild cat) bank there. He removed to Jackson in 1842, where he held the position of prison physician, but subsequently removed to Albion for its educational advantages, and died there May 15, 1853. In politics he was a Democrat.

LEWIS C. DAVIS

Senator from the Thirtieth District, 1885-6. Was born at Amsterdam, N. Y., in 1832. He was formerly engaged in farm and mechanical work, but was later a physician and surgeon. He held the offices of Township Clerk, Health Officer, School Inspector and Village Trustee. Having been in the south at the outbreak of the rebellion, he was conscripted into the Confederate army, but soon made his escape and took the oath of allegiance to the United States. In politics Fusion.

ROBERT W. DAVIS

Representative from Oakland County, 1849. Was born in Boston, Mass., Feb. 20, 1816, and lived in that State until 1837, when he removed to Detroit, and from there to Oxford, Oakland County, 1842. He was by trade a carriage maker, but owned a foundry at Oxford. Under Buchanan he was United States Marshal of Michigan. He was a Democrat in politics.

WILLARD DAVIS

Representative from Eaton County, 1857-8. Was born in Worcester, Mass., Dec. 23, 1805. When four years of age, his parents removed to Chenango County, N. Y., where he resided until of age. He was a student in Hamilton College, but was forced to leave from ill health. He came to Michigan in 1844 and was engaged two years teaching. From 1838 to 1844 he was in mercantile business at Honesdale, Pa. He returned to Vermontville in 1844. In early life he was a Whig, then a Free Soiler, after 1854 a Republican. He held many local offices. He died Dec. 19, 1873.

WILLIAM DAVIS

Representative from Newaygo County, 1907-8 and 1909-10. Was born in Tuscarawas County, O., Oct. 4, 1847, of Dutch and Irish parentage. He lived the life of a farmer's boy, attended district school winters and worked on his father's farm summers. By occupation a farmer. In politics a Republican. He held the offices of School Inspector, Township Clerk, Supervisor, and served as County Treasurer.

WILLIAM R. DAVIS

Representative from the Fourth District of Kent County, 1869-70. His postoffice address was Oakfield. (Further data not obtainable).

NORMAN DAVISON

Delegate from the Fifth District to the Constitutional Convention of 1835; and Delegate from Lapeer County to the Second Convention of Assent, 1836. Was born in Susquehanna Valley, N. Y., August, 1786. He emigrated from Avon, N. Y., and settled with his family in 1831, in Atlas, Mich., where now stands the village of Davisonville. He built a saw mill in 1833 and a grist-mill in 1836. The first town meeting was held at the Davison mills in 1836, and there was established the first Postoffice. Mr. Davison was the first Postmaster. He was the first Supervisor of Grand Blanc, in 1833, and at an early day, when Atlas formed a part of Lapeer County, was a County Judge. He held other offices and was a man highly respected and esteemed. He was a Democrat. He died in Mar. 26, 1841.

OLIVER P. DAVISON

Representative from Oakland County, 1847. Was born in Parma, N. Y., Aug. 31, 1810; came with his father's family to Davisonville, Mich., in 1831, but subsequently settled in the town of Highland, where he owned a fine water power. He was in 1845 the first Postmaster at Highland Corners, and served two terms. He was also a Justice of the Peace. He died at Milford, Oakland County, Mar. 6, 1879.

HARLOW P. DAVOCK

Representative from the First District of Wayne County, 1893-4. Was born in Buffalo, N. Y., Mar. 11, 1848. He lived with his parents and attended public school until the fall of 1866, when he entered the University of Michigan. He graduated from the literary department of that institution in 1870, and from that time until 1882 he practiced as civil engineer upon the public works throughout the United States. In 1882 he located at the city of Detroit and engaged in the practice of law. In politics a Republican. He was elected to the House of 1893-4 upon the general legislative ticket of the city of Detroit.

DENIAS DAWE

Representative from Monroe County, 1923—. Was born in Newport, Wales, Oct. 31, 1860, of English-Welsh parentage. He is a graduate of the Deerfield High School and the University of Michigan and has been a practicing physician and surgeon for forty years. Mr. Dawe is a Democrat.

WILLIAM DAWSON

Delegate in the Constitutional Convention of 1907-8 from the Twentieth District, Sanilac County. Was born in 1845 at Markham, Ont., of English and Dutch descent. He attended district school until twelve years of age and studied with his father while working on the farm for three years. In 1865 he was married to Lorania Allen, daughter of Chancy Allen, and old pioneer of Sanilac County. He resided at Peck, where he was engaged in mercantile business and farming. He held the office of Postmaster from 1865 to 1871, and was elected County Clerk in 1876 and removed to Lexington, where he was instrumental in having the county seat moved to the center of the county, now city of Sandusky. In 1880 he was elected Register of Deeds and afterwards held the office of Circuit Court Commissioner and Judge of Probate. He was alternate delegate to the Republican National Convention that nominated President Roosevelt. In politics a pronounced Republican. He was identified with almost all the business interests of the city, and owner of a farm of 700 acres within and adjoining the city, which he developed and improved. He held all the various school, township and village offices and prominent in Masonic circles, being a member of Custer Lodge No. 393, Sanilac Chapter No. 145 and Lexington Commandery No. 27; also a member of Port Huron Lodge No. 343, B. P. O. Elks.

DANIEL DAYTON

Representative from Genesee County, 1849. Was born in Sandgate, Vt., in 1800. He came to Michigan in 1839, and settled in Genesee County. He held various offices, and was Judge of the Genesee County court, and during his term sent two persons, a man and a woman, to State Prison for life for murder. He removed to Harmony, Fillmore County, Minn., in 1854, where he resided in good health in 1887. By occupation he was a farmer.

JOHN G. DEAN

Representative from the First District of Bay County, 1919-20 and 1921-2. Was born May 6, 1875, at Saginaw, Mich., of American parents descended from German stock. He was educated in the public schools of that city. He has been foreman of the planing mills at Mathew Lamont Sons Company, of Bay City, for the past 22 years. Mr. Dean is married and has one child. He served four terms as Alderman of the fourth ward, and Supervisor six years. In politics he is a Republican.

HENRY STEWART DEAN

Member of the Board of Regents of the University of Michigan, 1894-1908. Was born at Lima, N. Y., June 14, 1830, son of William Whetten and Eliza (Hand) Dean. His ancestors were English and Dutch. He was educated chiefly in two schools,—the Academy of West Bloomfield, N. Y., and Mutting's Academy, Lodi Plains, Washtenaw County, Mich. At the completion of his course in the latter institution in 1852 he was fully prepared for college; but immediately upon leaving the Academy he went to California to engage in mining and general business pursuits. After one year he became president and general maanger of the Union Tunnel Company of Calaveras County, and so continued until his return to Michigan in 1857. He settled in Livingston County, where, until 1862, he was a Justice of the Peace and conducted a milling business, dealing in flour and lumber. In 1862 he volunteered his service to the United States Government as Second Lieutenant and Recruiting Officer of the Twenty-second Mich. Inf. On July 31, 1862, he was commissioned Captain, and later promoted to Lieutenant Colonel. He was married Aug. 24, 1865, to Delia Brown Cook. After the close of the war he engaged in business in Ann Arbor as a member of the firm of Dean and Company. Some of his business connections have been as follows: Secretary and treasurer of the Ann Arbor Printing and Publishing Company, 1872-8; president of the Ann Arbor Milling Company since 1892; president of the Michigan Milling Company since 1899; and director of the Owosso Gas Light Company in 1898-9. He was Postmaster of Ann Arbor from 1870 to 1874. In public life he held numerous offices of trust, notable as member of the Board of State Prison Inspectors from 1886 to 1890; president of the Washtenaw County Agricultural Society in 1898-9; director of the University School of Music after 1895; a member of the National Council of Adminstration of the Grand Army of the Republic in 1886; Commander of the Department of Michigan of the Grand Army in 1893; Commander of the Michigan Commandery of the Military Order of the Loyal Legion in 1897; and Supervisor of the first ward of Ann Arbor in 1898-9. June 1, 1894, he was appointed Regent of the University in place of Henry Howard, deceased, and in 1899 was elected to succeed himself for the full term beginning the following January.

CHAS. W. DEANE

Representative from Newaygo, Oceana and Mecosta counties, 1867-8. His post-office address was Pentwater. (Further data not obtainable).

HENRY W. DEARE

Representative from Wayne County, 1863-4. Was born in England in 1825. He was Judge of Probate of the county in 1864, serving the four years' term, and also represented Hamtramck in the Board of Supervisors. By profession he was a teacher and was still living in 1887. He was a Democrat in politics.

WILLIAM DeBOER

Representative from the First District of Kent County, 1915-16. Was born in Michigan on Oct. 5, 1871. He was educated in the public schools of Grand Rapids after which he was employed for three years in a grocery store and later served an apprenticeship as a machinist for nearly twenty years. He was superintendent of the Michigan Free Employment Bureau at Grand Rapids for a little more than two years and operated a licensed employment bureau until May, 1914, when he entered the real estate business. He was elected Alderman of the fourth ward of Grand Rapids in 1906 and re-elected each succeeding year for several years. Married. In politics a Republican.

FREEMAN L. DECKER

Representative from the Missaukee District, 1909-10 and 1911-12. Was born at Pinckney, Livingston County, Mich., June 4, 1854. His education was obtained in the Pinckney public schools. While a resident of Livingston County, he served several terms as Supervisor of his home township and also acted as Deputy Sheriff of the county. He removed to Missaukee County in 1881, resided in Lake City. Most of the time he was engaged in farming, having improved a large amount of land, and also built a number of residences in the village of Lake City. In politics a Republican. He held the offices of Village Assessor, School Assessor, Justice of the Peace and Supervisor; also president of the Missaukee County Agricultural Society. He died at Lake City, June 20, 1917.

JESSE DECKER

Representative from Oakland County, 1838 and 1839. Was born in the State of New Jersey and settled as a farmer in Orion, Oakland County, in 1825. He was accompanied by several other settlers from the same State, was the leader, and the place was known as the "Decker settlement." He purchased first land in Brandon, 1831. He became a leading man of the town, and was the first Post-master in 1832.

PATRICK DEE

Representative from the First District, Detroit, of Wayne County, 1889-90. Was born in Ireland, Oct. 14, 1837. Occupation a contractor and builder. He was a member of the Board of Estimates of the city of Detroit; was elected to the House of 1889-90, on the Democratic ticket.

MURL H. DeFOE

Senator, 1919-20, from the Fifteenth District, comprising the counties of Barry, Clinton and Eaton. He is a native son of Eaton County; editor of the Charlotte *Republican* and served his city as City Clerk and Alderman.

JOHN G. DEHN

Representative from the First District of Bay County, 1919-20. Was born May 6, 1875, at Saginaw, Mich., of American parents. He was educated in the public schools of that city. He was foreman of the planing mills of Matthew Lamont Sons Company, of Bay City, for many years. Married. He served three terms as Alderman of the fourth ward of Bay City. In politics a Republican.

ANSON H. DELAMATER

Representative from Jackson County, 1844. Was born in Pompey, N. Y., Apr. 13, 1811. He was educated at Cazenovia Seminary, and at the age of sixteen commenced teaching, and was engaged in teaching and farming until 1834, when he came to Columbia, Mich. and located a farm. In 1837 he was elected Surveyor of Jackson County, and held that position twelve years. He was the first Supervisor of Columbia Township, and filled that position several times. In 1880 and 1881 he was president of the Jackson County Pioneer Society.

CHARLES J. deLAND

Delegate from the Tenth District to the Constitutional Convention of 1907-8; Senator from the Tenth District, 1915-16 to 1919-20; and Secretary of State, 1921—. Was born Dec. 18, 1879, at Saginaw, Mich., of American parentage. He was educated in the Jackson public school and the Michigan Agricultural College. He lived on the home farm until 1900, when he removed to Jackson and in 1903 was appointed Deputy County Treasurer. Upon his arrival in Jackson, he began the study of law and in 1905 was admitted to the bar. From 1906 to 1910 he was chairman of the Republican County Committee and was a member of the Constitutional Convention of 1907. Mr. DeLand is married and has one son, a daughter having died in October, 1918.

CHARLES V. DELAND

Senator from the Twelfth District, 1861-2, and from the Twenty-fifth, 1873-4. Was born in North Brookfield, Mass., July 25, 1826, of French Huguenot descent, his ancestors coming to New England in 1636. His father was in the War of 1812, and coming from northern New York, settled with his family on land now forming part of Jackson, in 1830. His family and two other families were the first permanent settlers in Jackson County. The son in 1836 began the trade of a printer and followed it until 1861. He established the Jackson *Citizen* in 1848, owned and edited it until 1861; was Clerk of the Michigan House in 1857; Alderman and Supervisor several years; Senator from Jackson County in 1861-2; Senator from Saginaw County in 1873-4; entered the service in 1861 as Captain of Co. "C," 9th Mich. Infantry, served until the close of the war, and was promoted as Colonel of the 1st Mich. Sharpshooters, and Brevet Brigadier General "for faithful and meritorious services;" in 1865 removed to East Saginaw, and was connected with the *Enterprise*, the first daily in the valley; held there the offices of Street Commissioner, Marshal, City Controller, Chief Engineer, Supervisor and Tax Collector; was for six years Collector of Internal Revenue; started the Saginaw *Morning Herald* in 1872 and published it until 1882; then removed to his old home near Jackson, and became a farmer. He was a Whig until 1854, then a Republican. He died Sept. 21, 1903.

PETER B. DELISLE

Representative from the Fourth District of Wayne County, 1903-4. Was born in the township of Ecorse, Wayne County, Jan. 21, 1846. He was educated in the district school and Paterson's classical and mathematical school. He was a contractor and builder for some time. He was engaged in the grocery business in Detroit for three years, after which he moved to Toledo, O., and conducted a coal and wood business, after a few years he disposed of his business in Toledo and moved to Delray, Mich., and engaged in the real estate and insurance business. Prominent member of several fraternal societies. Married. In politics a Democrat.

DANIEL H. DEMING

Representative from Lenawee County, 1847-9. Was born in Sharon, Conn., Sept. 25, 1804. He was brought up as a farmer. At the age of twenty-four he removed to Poughkeepsie, N. Y. After one year there he was four years at Penn Yan, N. Y., in a drug store. He emigrated to Michigan in 1834 and became a farmer in Dover, Lenawee County. In politics he was a Democrat. He held several local offices. He died Apr. 7, 1871.

DAVID E. DEMING

Senator from the Sixth District, 1841, and from the Fifth District, 1842. Was born in Cornish, N. H., June 14, 1796. He was a physician by profession, in politics a Whig. He was the first settler in the town of Cooper, Mich., in 1833, and the first Supervisor, holding that office several terms. He had a large practice, but in later years was a farmer. He died Sept. 5, 1879.

THEODORE E. DEMING

Representative from the Third District of Wayne County, 1889-90. Was born at Ypsilanti, Mich., May 11, 1846. He held the offices of Township Clerk, Justice of the Peace, member of the Common Council, and member of the Board of Education.

JAMES WARD DEMPSEY

Representative from Manistee County, 1893-4. Was born in Manistee, Feb. 10, 1867. His early education was acquired at the Manistee High School. He was for five years in the First National Bank which position he resigned to accept the charge of the books of the Manistee and the Eureka lumber companies. In politics a Democrat.

EDWIN DENBY

Representative from the First District of Wayne County, 1903-4; and member of Congress from the First District of Michigan, 1905-7 to 1909-11. Was born of American and English parentage at Evansville, Ind., Feb. 18, 1870. He acquired his education in the Evansville High School, and the University of Michigan, from which he was graduated in 1896 with degree of LL.B. Mr. Denby accompanied his father to China in 1885, then appointed United States Minister to that country. In June, 1887, he joined the Chinese Imperial Maritime Customs' service, as foreign service under Sir Robert Hart, Bart., and served seven years in various parts of China. He returned home in 1894 on a two years' leave of absence, with half pay, and entered the law department of the University of Michigan. In June, 1896, he entered the law firm of Kenna and Lightner of Detroit, Mich., continuing with them until April, 1898, when he enlisted in the United States navy, with the Michigan State Naval Brigade and was assigned to the U. S. Steamer Yosemite with rating of gunner's mate, third class. Mr. Denby was honorably discharged in September, 1898, returning to Detroit, and resumed the practice of law. In politics he is a Republican.

JACOB DEN HERDER

Senator, 1889-90, from the Twenty-first District, comprising the counties of Muskegon and Ottawa. Was born in the Netherlands Jan. 11, 1834. He came with his parents to the United States in the spring of 1847, arriving at Black Lake, in Ottawa County, after a continuous journey of fully three months, settled in the township of Zeeland, where he continued to reside. At the age of 19 he began teaching school, and continued in that occupation for ten years. He then entered the mercantile business. In 1878 he started a private bank at Zeeland. At the age of 22, and for fifteen years thereafter, he was elected Township Clerk, was Supervisor four terms, and Justice of the Peace one term. He was Presidential elector in 1876, and cast his vote for Hayes and Wheeler. In politics a Republican ever since the party came into power. He died at Zeeland, December, 1916

HENRY B. DENMAN

Representative from the First District of Cass County, 1863-4. His postoffice was Dowagiac. (Further data not obtainable).

MOSES R. DENNING

Representative from Manistee County, 1891-2. Was born in Maine in 1848; was raised on a farm in the lumbering district of that State. Upon leaving school he went to Pennsylvania and worked at lumbering on the Susquehanna River until the war broke out. On the "three months' call" he helped to raise the famous "Bucktail Regiment" and take them to Camp Curtin. Afterwards he helped to raise and get to the front the 84th and 110th Pennsylvania regiments. In 1863 he went to the western territories and engaged in farming and mining. He came to Manistee in 1866, and engaged in lumbering, driving logs on different rivers, and dealing in pine, farming and coal lands in Michgan, Florida and Arkansas; also director of the Manistee National Bank. In politics a Democrat. He served as member of the School Board and Alderman a few times; was elected to the House of 1891-2. He did not sit in the extra session of 1892.

DAVID B. DENNIS

Representative from Lenawee County, 1848 and 1850. Was born in Farmington, N. Y., June 12, 1817. By occupation he was an attorney and banker, politically a Democrat. He came to Michigan with his father's family in 1827, and settled at Adrian. He resided at Adrian for twenty-five years, and became a resident of Coldwater. He was a leader in the Democratic party, and repeatedly its candidate for State and other offices.

ORVILLE DENNIS

Representative, 1901-2 and 1903-4, from Missaukee District, comprising the counties of Missaukee and Kalkaska. Was born in the township of Milton, Cass County, Mich., Mar. 28, 1873. He graduated from the Reed City High School in 1890 and was employed for a time in the law office of Hon. S. Wesselius of Grand Rapids, after which he spent several years teaching successfully in district and village schools of Osceola and Missaukee counties. During this time he served as principal of the schools at Tustin and McBain. In 1894 he published the *Chronicle* at McBain, which he conducted until 1897, when he sold out and bought the Missaukee *Republican* at Lake City. Married. In politics a Republican. He also held several village and township offices and for two terms was member of the Board of School Examiners of Missaukee County.

SAMUEL DENTON

Delegate from Washtenaw County to the Second Convention of Assent, 1836; member of the Board of Regents of the University of Michigan, 1837-40; and Senator from the Second District, 1845-6 and 1847-8. Was born at Wallkill, N. Y., July 2, 1803. In 1826 he came to Ann Arbor, where he practiced his profession as a physician, until his death, Aug. 17, 1860. He was the first physician in Ann Arbor and a member of the State Historical Society. He was president of the State Medical Association. He was also one term Regent of the State University, and was professor in the medical department of "theory and practice," from its organization until his death. He was a man of remarkable depth and vigor of intellect, a profound thinker, and in the lecture room was noted for his originality and felicity of expression. In politics he was a Whig. He died at Ann Arbor, Aug. 17, 1860.

SOLOMON W. DENTON

Representative from Oakland County, 1848. His postoffice address was Pontiac. (Further data not obtainable).

WILLIAM J. DESHANO

Representative from the Second District of Bay County, 1923—. Was born in Montreal, Canada, Sept. 10, 1867, of French parentage. When he was a child, his parents removed to Michigan, locating in Arenac County, and four years later moved to Bay County, where he has since lived in the Township of Beaver. In early life he worked at lumbering, river driving and mill work. He was married in July, 1894, and settled on a farm where he has since resided. Mr. Deshano is a Republican; has held the office of Township Treasurer four years and has been Supervisor for the past eight years.

PETER DESNOYERS

State Treasurer, 1839-40; and Delegate from Wayne County to the Constitutional Conventions of 1850 and 1867. Was born in Detroit, Apr. 21, 1800, and died Mar. 6, 1880. He reeived a good education, principally at Clinton, N. Y. He became a Detroit merchant in 1821, and was successful. He was Treasurer of Wayne County in 1826, serving two terms; Alderman in 1827; U. S. Marshal from 1831 to 1836; again County Treasurer in 1838, also in 1843 and 1851. For the last twenty years of his life was not in business, but resided in Hamtramck. He was a Democrat in politics, in religion a Catholic. He died at Detroit Mar. 6, 1880.

ANDREW L. DEUEL

Delegate from the Twenty-ninth District in the Constitutional Convention of 1907-8; and Representative from Emmet County, 1917-18 and 1919-20. Was born in Oakland County, Mich., Aug. 23, 1850, of American parentage. His education was secured in the public schools, the State Normal College at Ypsilanti, and the University of Michigan. He taught school five and a half years, and practiced law and engaged in the real estate and insurance business for thirty-seven years. He held the offices of County School Commissioner, Prosecuting Attorney, Judge of Probate, Village President, Justice of the Peace, President of the School Board, and was a member of the Constitutional Convention of 1907-8; was director and member of the executive board of the Western Michigan Development Bureau for a number of years. Married. In politics a Republican.

JOHN DEVLIN

Representative from Wayne County, 1883-4. Was born in Minersville, Pa., June 10, 1846. He spent his boyhood on a farm. On the 12th of August, 1861, he enlisted in "F" Co., 48th Regiment, Pa. Vol., and served with his regiment up to the close of the war, participating in nearly all the engagements and marches of the command. He was seriously wounded in the right hand and arm by a canister shot at the storming of Petersburg, Va. He received a common school education at the Dickinson Seminary, Williamsport, Pa., afterwards taking up a course in bookkeeping at the Union Business College, Philadelphia, Pa. He started in the mercantile business at Shenandoah City, Pa., and continued in it for a number of years. Afterwards he removed to Philadelphia, Pa., and again started the mercantile business, but in 1879 removed with his family to Detroit, Mich., where he was employed at the finishing trade in the Pullman Palace Car Works. He was Consul at Windsor, Canada, for five years. In politics he was a Democrat. He died at Detroit, June 20, 1918.

GEORGE E. DEWEY

Representative from Osceola County, 1905-6 and 1907-8. Was born at Pennline, Crawford County, Pa., July 31, 1854. He acquired his education in the district schools of Ashtabula County, O. He was married to Kate Rankin in 1880. He was a successful business man and for a number of years was engaged in the lumber business, and the sale of agricultural implements. In politics a Republican. He held the offices of President of Shelby village, Trustee, Township Treasurer, also Register of Deeds of the County.

GEORGE M. DEWEY

Senator from the Sixteenth District, 1873-4. Was born in Lebanon, N. H., Feb. 14, 1832. He became a resident of Lowell, Mass., and graduated from the State Normal School in 1848. In 1851 he was principal of the Mann School at Lowell,

BIOGRAPHICAL SKETCHES

removed to Wisconsin in 1852 and taught in union schools of that State until 1856, and then for a year as principal of the union school at Buchanan, Mich. In 1857-8 was Deputy Superintendent of Public Instruction. He was editor and publisher of the Niles *Enquirer* from 1858 to 1866, then owned and edited the Hastings *Banner* for several years. He was in the postal serve six years, and was several times clerk of important legislative committees. In 1887 he owned and edited the Owosso *Times*. In politics he was a Republican. He died at Owosso in 1897.

HEZEKIAH RANNEY DEWEY

Representative from the First District of Genesee County, 1889-90. Was born at Rochester, Monroe County, N. Y., Apr. 14, 1838. He engaged in farming, breeding thoroughbred American merino sheep, and general agent for D. S. Morgan and Co.'s harvesting machinery. He served as Justice of the Peace, member of the executive board of Genesee County Agricultural Society, and member of the executive board of State Agricultural Society. In politics a staunch Republican.

JOHN W. DEWEY

Representative from Shiawassee County, 1881-2. Was born June 3, 1818, at Clarence, Erie County, N. Y. He moved to Michigan with his parents in 1823, and settled on a farm in Bloomfield, Oakland County, where he received a common school education. In 1839 he removed to Shiawassee County and settled on a farm in Owosso. He held the office of Highway Commissioner for several terms, and was a member of the School Board over twenty years, besides holding other minor offices. He died at Owosso, Sept. 11, 1896.

THOMAS DUSTIN DEWEY

Member of the State Board of Agriculture, 1881-7. Was born at Broomfield Center, Oakland County, Mich., Feb. 22, 1823. His father's name was Apollos Dewey, Jr., of Vermont; his mother's name was Abigail (Wetmore) Dewey of Connecticut. Mr. Dewey married Philena Bould, of Cayuga County, N. Y., on Apr. 10, 1849; she died in 1885. He married Elizabeth Cramer, Nov. 2, 1887. She died June 29, 1904. Mr. Dewey was educated in the common schools. He was a Presbyterian and a Republican. He was a merchant's clerk, later a miller at Owosso. In company with Mr. Stewart, he was a breeder of fine horses, including Jerome Eddy, sold for $25,000. He was Mayor of Owosso; Chief of the Fire Department; interested in fairs. He died Mar. 22, 1906.

FRANCIS B. DEWITT

Representative, 1921-2, from the Iosco District, comprising the counties of Alcona, Arenac, Iosco and Ogemaw. Was born in Jackson County, Ind., Mar. 11, 1849, of American parentage. He was educated in the district schools of Ohio and the National Normal, Lebanon, O. At the age of twelve years he enlisted in 46th Ohio Infantry and served with the 46th and 121st Ohio Infantry, in the Western Department until the close of Civil War in 1865. He was in Salsbury, Danville and Libby prisons. For seventeen years he practiced law in Ohio, serving in Ohio

Legislature, and as Congressman from Ohio, moving to Michigan in 1902, since which time he has been engaged in farming. In politics he is a Republican.

ERNEST R. DEXTER

Representative from Isabella County, 1923—. Was born in Washington County, Illinois, Feb. 23, 1875, of English and Welsh parentage. In 1883 he removed with his parents to Michigan and they settled on a farm in Saginaw County where he received a public school education. He held the offices of School Director, Township Supervisor and Deputy County Road Commissioner. In March, 1911, Mr. Dexter moved his family to Mt. Pleasant, Isabella County, and engaged in the mercantile business, which occupation he still follows, together with running a farm. He has held the offices of City Treasurer and secretary of the County Poor Commissioners, which latter position he still holds. Mr. Dexter is married and has four children. He is a Republican.

GEORGE W. DEXTER

Representative from Ionia County, 1842. He was born in Herkimer County, N. Y., Aug. 4, 1795. He came to Michigan in 1844, and was sergeant-at-arms of the first Senate in 1835. He was a farmer, politically a Democrat. He died Aug. 4, 1848.

JOHN C. DEXTER

Senator from the Twenty-eighth District, 1871-2. He located 120 acres near Ionia in 1838.

SAMUEL DEXTER

Delegate from Kent County to the Second Convention of Assent, 1836. Was born in Rhode Island, Dec. 15, 1787. He removed from Herkimer County, N. Y., and settled on the present site of Ionia, Mich., in 1832. He married Anna Fargo. He had been a member of the New York Assembly. He built the first saw and grist mills at Ionia. He held the offices of Justice, County Judge, and Receiver of the U. S. Land Office. In politics he was a Whig. He was a leading pioneer of the Grand River Valley. He died Aug. 6, 1865.

SAMUEL W. DEXTER

Member of the Board of Regents of the University of Michigan, 1840-1. Was born in Boston, Mass., in 1792. His father, Samuel Dexter, was a distinguished lawyer, and a member of the cabinet of John Adams. The son settled at Dexter, Mich., in 1824, and was the founder of that village. He was Chief Justice of Washtenaw County from 1827 to 1833, and was the Anti-Masonic candidate for Congress in 1831, and later of the Free Soil party. He started the first newspaper in Washtenaw County, The Emigrant. He located Byron, Saginaw City, and Elk Rapids and Tecumseh. An orthodox Unitarian, he preached at country stations without pay, and was a man of strong convictions, a graduate of Harvard, and a powerful reasoner. With ample means he was a leading pioneer, and his charities were numberless. He died Feb. 6, 1863.

CHARLES I. DEYO

Senator from the Fourteenth District, 1887-8. Was born in Parma, N. Y., July 10, 1839. When he was fourteen years of age, his parents removed to Michigan, locating at Richland, Kalamazoo County. He spent his early life on a farm, attending the public school during the fall and winter terms. At the age of twenty he commenced his public life as a minister of the gospel, uniting with the Christian Church. For a few years he devoted nearly all his time to preaching and study, thoroughly preparing himself for his profession. With the exception of two years in Illinois, and one year in Naples, N.Y., his work was confined to Michigan, including various localities. After 1880 he lectured in several states on labor and other economic questions. He was appointed Chaplain of the State House of Correction under Governor Begole in 1883. In politics he was a National Greenbacker.

CORNELIUS DeYOUNG

Representative from Montcalm County, 1909-10. Was born at Grand Rapids, Mich., Jan. 23, 1860. His education was acquired in the Grand Rapids public schools. In 1877 he removed with his parents to Crystal Township; was lumber inspector four years and in the general merchandise business three years in Fishville; removed in 1890 to Crystal, was Town Clerk, and Township Treasurer; member of K. O. T. M., president of the Montcalm County K. O. T. M. Association and Great Second Master of the Guards of the Great Camp K. O. T M. Married. In politics a life long Republican.

ALBERT DICKERMAN

Senator from the Ninth District, 1881-2. Was born in Masonville, N. Y., Mar. 26, 1840. He received an academic education, and for a few months attended Oberlin College. He taught in Missouri and Ohio. In 1862 he enlisted in the 105th O. Vols., and rising to the rank of Adjutant served until the close of the war. He graduated from the Union Law College at Cleveland in 1865, and the next year commenced practice at Hillsdale, Mich. He was Circuit Court Commissioner four years, Judge of Probate four years, and held other offices. In politics a Republican.

CHARLES DICKEY

Representatives from Calhoun County, 1859-60; and Senator from the Fifth District, 1850-1, and from the Thirteenth District, 1853-4. Was born in Londonderry, N. H., Apr. 13, 1813. When young he became a resident of Livingston County, N. Y., and was there engaged in business. He moved to Marshall, Mich., in 1836, engaged in the manufacture of fanning mills, and in 1838 bought the first wool sold in southern Michigan. He was Sheriff of Calhoun County from 1845 to 1849. He was a Colonel on the staff of Gov. Mason; was U. S. Marshal of Michigan from 1861 to 1866, and Judge of Probate from 1873 to his death, Jan. 13, 1879. He took an active part in the organization of agricultural societies, and was president of the State society in 1858-9, and a member of the executive committee from 1845 during life. He was a charter member of the Michigan Pioneer and Historical Society. Politically he was a Whig until 1854, then a Republican.

JOSEPH H. DICKINSON

Representative from the First District of Wayne County (Detroit), 1897-8 and 1899-1900. Was born at Chatham, Ont., June 22, 1855. His parents, Samuel and Jane Dickinson, were native born citizens of the United States, and returned to Michigan and settled at Detroit in 1856, where he acquired his education. At the age of fifteen he shipped on board the United States revenue cutter Fessenden; served two years, then entered the employ of Simmons & Clough, organ manufacturers, where he remained ten years; then went to Lexington, Mich., where he established the Dickinson & Gould Organ Company. After remaining at the head of said firm four years, he sold out his interest to Messrs. Gould and returned to the employ of the Clough & Warren Organ Company of Detroit. In politics a Republican. He was elected to the House of 1897-8 on the general legislative ticket of the city of Detroit, and was re-elected to the House of 1899-1900.

LUREN D. DICKINSON

Representative from Eaton County, 1897-8, 1905-6, and 1907-8; Senator from Eaton County, 1909-10; and Lieutenant Governor 1915-7 to 1919-21. Was born in Niagara County, N. Y., Apr. 15, 1859, of English and Irish descent. His parents removed to Eaton County, Mich., in 1860, where he lived, receiving his education in the district schools and the Charlotte High School. He taught school during the winter for nineteen years and was at one time principal of the Potterville High School. He was married in 1888 to Zora D. Cooley. He was interested in farming, fruit-growing and stock-raising for many years; a stockholder in the First National Bank of Charlotte, The Duplex Truck Company, of Lansing and Charlotte, trustee of the Eaton M. E. Church and a member of the order of K. of P. In politics a Republican. He has been a member of the County Committee, chairman of the representative committee, Assessor of school district, Town Clerk, Superintendent of Schools under old system and Supervisor several terms.

WILLIAM E. DICKINSON

Senator from the Thirty-second District, 1859-60. Was born in the city of New York, May 31, 1824. He attended school at New Haven and Litchfield in 1846. For the next three years he was traveling in foreign lands. He returned in 1850 and engaged in study as a mining engineer. He went to the Upper Peninsula in 1851 and resided in Ontonagon and Houghton counties. In 1856 he moved to Eagle River, Keweenaw County. In 1870 he removed to Marquette, and in 1881 to Commonwealth, Wis. He was first a Whig, then a Republican. He held town and county offices in every county where he lived.

ROBINSON J. DICKSON

Representative from Cass County, 1883-4 to 1887-8. Was born in Wayne County, Ind., Apr. 3, 1823. His father was a native of Pennsylvania, and his mother a native of New York. Mr. Dickson was the second son of a family of nine children. His parents settled on McKinley's Prairie, in LaGrange Township, Cass County, Mich., in the year 1828, engaging in farming. By occupation he was a farmer, in 1887 owned a farm in Pokagon Township. He held various township offices. In politics he was a Republican.

BARNEY DIEHL

Representative from Macomb County, 1917-18. Was born in Buffalo, N. Y., in 1871. He came to Michigan in 1865. He received his education in the Mt. Clemens High School. He was married Nov. 26, 1895, to Mary Wolff. He was Alderman and Supervisor and Deputy Sheriff. Fraternally a member of the K. of P. and K. O. T. M. In politics a Republican.

GERRIT J. DIEKEMA

Representative from Ottawa County, 1885-6 to 1891-2; and member of Congress, 1907-9 and 1909-11. Was born at Holland, Mich., Mar. 27, 1859. He was educated at Hope College, graduating in 1881, and at the University of Michigan, graduating from the law department in 1883; began the practice of law in his native city. Entering political life early, he served as School Inspector, member of the local Harbor Board, member of the Board of Education, Mayor, City Attorney, and member of the Legislature four consecutive terms, beginning in 1885, at the session of 1889 he was chose speaker of the House of Representatives; was chairman of the Republican State Central Committee in four campaigns; was a delegate to the national convention in 1896, which nominated Major McKinley for President, and by him appointed a member of the Spanish Treaty Claims Commission, which position he resigned to make the race for Congress. In 1884 he was chosen to deliver the annual oration before the alumni association of the University of Michigan and was the orator on Netherlands Day at the Columbian Exposition and World's Fair, Chicago, 1893. He was elected to the 60th Congress, Apr. 27, 1907, to fill the vacancy caused by the resignation of William Alden Smith and re-elected Nov. 3, 1908.

HENRY B. DILLER

Representative from Genesee County, 1881-2 and 1883-4. Was born in Clarence, N. Y., Aug. 15, 1840. Having received a liberal education there, in the spring of 1874 he removed to Genesee, Mich., where he engaged in farming. In politics a Republican. He held the office of Supervisor several terms.

LOUIS DILLMAN

Representative from Wayne County, 1877-8. Was born Dec. 25, 1830, in the city of Friedrichshalen, Wurtemburg, Germany. In 1849 he emigrated to the United States, and after working some time at his trade (tanner) in Buffalo, he came to Detroit in 1853, and started a leather and finding store. At the outbreak of the rebellion he enlisted as Captain of Co. A, of the 2nd Mich. Infantry, under the command of Col. Richardson. Captain Dillman was promoted to be Major in March, 1862, and was made Lieutenant Colonel July 26, 1862. He participated in many battles, also in the Morgan raid in Kentucky. In 1863 he resigned and came to Detroit, where he became proprietor of the Hotel Mauch. He engaged in the wine trade. He was a candidate for State Land Commissioner and for Auditor General. In politics a Democrat.

JOSEPH DILLON

Representative from Kent County, 1887-8. Was born in Lowell, Mass., in 1850. When twelve years old he entered a woolen factory. At fifteen he was apprenticed at the carver's trade at Wilson, N. H., but afterwards went to Greenville, N. H., where he worked at his trade until he was twenty-three. In 1873 he moved to Washington, D. C., where he worked at carving and picture frame work for a year, and then for six years carried on the business as an employer. In 1880 he moved to Grand Rapids, where he resided and worked at the carver's trade in the various shops and factories. He was elected Representative on the Republican and Labor ticket

REUBEN B. DIMOND

Representative from St. Clair County, 1848; and Delegate from St. Clair County to the Constitutional Convention of 1850. His postoffice address was Lexington. (Further data not obtainable).

EDWARD NELSON DINGLEY

Representative from the First District of Kalamazoo County, 1899-1900 and 1901-2. Was born in Auburn, Me., Aug. 21, 1862. His parents moved to Lewiston in 1863; was educated in the public schools of Lewiston, graduating from the high school in 1879. He spent one year in Bates College, Lewiston, Me., then entered the sophomore class at Yale University, graduating in 1883 and receiving the degree of A. B.; spent two years in the law school of Columbia University, Washington, D. C., graduating in 1885 and receiving the degree of LL.B. He spent a year in Boston on the *Advertiser and Record*, as a political writer, and a like period in Leavenworth, Kan., doing newspaper work; moved to Kalamazoo, Mich., in 1888, purchasing (with others) the Kalamazoo daily and weekly *Telegraph*. In February, 1897, he was elected president of the Michigan League of Republican Clubs and was Michigan's candidate for president of the National League of Republican Clubs in July, 1898, at Omaha, Neb. He was a candidate for member of the Michigan House of Representatives in 1890 and 1892 and failed to be nominated both times, but received a unanimous nomination for that office in the Republican Legislative Convention of his district, held August, 1898. In June, 1898, he was appointed clerk to the ways and means committee of the National House of Representatives, which position he held until Jan. 1, 1900.

DANIEL W. DINTURFF

Representative from Livingston County, 1873-4. Was born July 24, 1830, in the town of Potter, N. Y. He received a common school education. In 1885 he emigrated to Michigan and settled in Pittsfield. In 1856 he removed to Handy, Livingston County. By occupation he was a farmer.

JOHN DIVINE

Representative from Sanilac and Huron Counties, 1855-6; and Delegate from Sanilac County to the Constitutional Convention of 1867. His postoffice address was Lexington. (Further data not obtainable).

JOSEPH DIVINE

Representative from Hillsdale County, 1885-6. Was born in Cayuga County, N. Y., on Apr. 1, 1820. He received a common school education and settled in Hillsdale County, Mich., in 1842. In politics he was a Whig, then a Republican. He held the office of Justice. He died Sept. 14, 1914, at Cambria, Hillsdale County.

ROSEKRANS K. DIVINE

Representative from Montcalm and counties thereto attached, 1855-6. His post-office address was Eureka. (Further data not obtainable).

WESTBROOK DIVINE

Senator from the Twenty-eighth District, 1863-4 and 1865-6. Was born at Rochester, Ulster County, N. Y., Aug. 4, 1822. By occupation he was a farmer, politically a Republican. He settled on a farm in Montcalm County, Mich., in 1843, which he occupied until 1883, when he sold out and removed to Belding, Mich. Among other offices held by him are the following: Register of Deeds for four years, Justice of the Peace, Town Clerk, Supervisor of Eureka for twenty-eight years, Assessor of Internal Revenue six years, and president of a fire insurance company for fourteen years. He was a member of the State Pioneer Society. He died at Grand Rapids Sept. 13, 1888.

ROSCOE D. DIX

Commissioner of the State Land Office, 1887-9 and 1889-91; and Auditor General, 1897-9 and 1899-1901. Was born in the county of Jefferson, State of New York, June 11, 1839, and came, with his parents, to Michigan in April, 1852. The family located on a farm in Bainbridge Township, Berrien County, where young Dix lived until the age of seventeen, working on the farm and teaching the district school in winter. At a later period he attended Albion College. On the 26th of April, 1861, he enlisted at Kalamazoo in Co. K, 2d Mich. Inf., and was with his regiment and company in every engagement in which it participated as private, corporal and sergeant, until he was severely wounded at Knoxville, Nov. 24, 1863. He was in hospital until May 25, 1864, when he was honorably discharged, permanently disabled. Returning to Berrien County, he was nominated and elected Register of Deeds, in the fall of 1864, and re-elected in 1866, 1868 and 1874. He was President of the village of Berrien Springs, and a member of the School Board, taking a deep and active interest at all times in the material and educational advancement of his own locality in the State. He was the founder and organizer of Kilpatrick Post No. 39, G. A. R. In 1869 Mr. Dix formed a partnership with Thomas L. Wilkinson, and engaged in the abstract and real estate business, with office at St. Joseph.

JOHN S. DIXON

Representative from Charlevoix and other counties, 1863-4. Was born in Mexico, N. Y., Aug. 24, 1818. By occupation he was a farmer, in politics a Republican. He graduated at Oneida Institute, N. Y., in 1837. He came to Lenawee County, Mich., in 1838, and followed teaching until 1854. He removed to Charlevoix in 1855. He was Justice, County Clerk, County Surveyor, and Superintendent of Schools. He platted Charlevoix, and suffered greatly from the depredations of Mormons from Beaver Island at an early day.

JAMES DOCKERAY

Representative from Kent County, 1863-4. Was born in Westmoreland County, England, May 1, 1815, came to this country in 1838, and settled at Albion, N. Y., where he worked at day labor and studied and practiced surveying. In 1846 he removed to Cannon, Mich., and settled on a farm. He was Supervisor sixteen years and held other offices. In 1874 he removed to Rockford, and was the proprietor of the Exchange Bank in that place. He served one term as County Surveyor. In politics he was a Democrat, up to 1856, then a Republican.

FRANCIS HENRY DODDS

Member of Congress, 1909-11 and 1911-13. Was born in St. Lawrence County, N. Y., June 9, 1858. He came to Isabella County with his parents in 1866 and there received his early education in the common schools. He was a graduate of Olivet College and of the law department of the University of Michigan; was president of the law alumni of the latter institution during the years 1880-1. From 1874 to 1878, he taught school, and after 1880 engaged in practice of law. He is married. He was elected to the 61st Congress and re-elected Nov. 8, 1910. In politics a Republican.

CHARLES D. DODGE

Representative from the Second District of Monroe County, 1891-2 and 1893-4. Was born in the village of Dundee, said county, Feb. 19, 1853. He acquired his early education at the Dundee Union School and Adrian College. At the close of his school days, 1873, he engaged in dealing in produce and real estate in his native village, which he followed until 1883, when he exchanged the village property he had acquired for the farm in London Township. In politics a Democrat.

FRANK L. DODGE

Representative from Ingham County, 1883-4 and 1885-6. Was born at Oberlin, O., Oct. 22, 1854. He attended school until fourteen, was engaged in railroading and traveling several years, for two years in the hotel business at Eaton Rapids, then studied law, and became a partner of I. M. Crane, at Eaton Rapids, until 1881. In 1887 he was a resident of Lansing, engaged in law practice. In politics a Democrat.

HENRY M. DODGE

Representative from Chippewa County, 1848. His postoffice address was Sault Ste. Marie. One Henry Dodge was a member of the Legislative Council, 1832-3, for the Seventh District (Chippewa and other counties). (Further data not obtainable).

HIRAM DODGE

Representative from Lenawee County, 1835-6. His postoffice address was Clinton. (Further data not obtainable).

JOHN A. DOELLE

Member of the State Board of Agriculture, 1921-2. Was born on a farm at Yale, St. Clair County, Mich., Feb. 10, 1878, and was the thirteenth and youngest of his father's family. He worked on the farm, doing all the various kinds of work incident to pioneer farm life. Later he graduated from the University of Michigan after which he took up teaching, his first position being principal of Benton Harbor school. Going from there to Houghton, he became Superintendent of Schools, and foreseeing the possibilities of the Upper Peninsula as an agricultural district, he conceived the idea of inaugurating agriculture into the public schools, and was instrumental in establishing the first agricultural school in the State, at Otter Lake. In 1917 he took active charge of the war industries resources committee in the Upper Peninsula, with offices at Ishpeming, after which he was made secretary of the Upper Peninsula Development Bureau. He was elected member of the State Board of Agriculture, Apr. 4, 1921; resigned in April, 1922.

JOHN SEYMOUR DOHANY

Representative from the Second District of Wayne County, 1903-4. Was born on a farm at Southfield, Oakland County, July 9, 1868. At the age of seventeen he commenced teaching district schools, continuing in this work for four years. After preparatory courses at Fenton Normal School and the State Normal College, he entered the Detroit College of Medicine in 1891, receiving his degree of M. D. with the class of 1894. He then located in Greenfield, Wayne County, where he practiced medicine. A prominent member and medical examiner of Greenfield Tent, 325 K. O. M. M. In politics a Democrat.

ALFRED J. DOHERTY

Senator, 1901-2, 1903-4 and 1905-6, from the Twenty-eighth District, comprising the counties of Alcona, Arenac, Clare, Crawford, Gladwin, Iosco, Missaukee, Ogemaw, Oscoda and Roscommon; and member of the State Board of Agriculture, 1907-19. Was born in the state of New York, May 1, 1856. His education was obtained at Genesee Seminary, Belfast, N. Y. He came to Michigan in 1878 and engaged in the mercantile business, which he conducted successfully for twenty years. Mr. Doherty is married. In politics a staunch Republican.

SIDNEY DOLE

Member of the Second Legislative Council from Oakland County, 1826-7. Was born in Troy, N. Y., in 1787. In 1816 he owned and improved land on which is now the site of Syracuse, N. Y. He came to Detroit in 1818, and the next year removed to Pontiac. He was the first Clerk and Register of Deeds of Oakland County, from 1820 to 1827, and was a Justice of the Peace. He died at Pontiac, July 20, 1828.

LEVI E. DOLSON

Representative from Wayne County, 1841. Was a native of Riley, Upper Canada, born Jan. 1, 1813. He came to Detroit while a boy, where he acquired a business and social standing and raised a family. He served for a number of years as a member of the Board of Education of the city. His occupation was that of a tanner, and he was a Republican in politics. He died, Jan. 23, 1887.

JOHN C. DONNELLY

Representative from Wayne County, 1879-80. Was born in Plympton, Ont., Nov. 27, 1851. He received a common school education, and removed to Michigan in 1870. In 1873 commenced the practice of law in Detroit. Was second lieutenant of Co. C, 1st Regiment Mich. State Troops, and was elected Captain of the Montgomery rifles in 1877. He was the youngest member of the House.

JOHN DONOVAN

Representative from the First District of Bay County (Bay City), 1895-6 and 1897-8. Was born in Hamilton, Ont., May 26, 1843. When two months old he removed with his parents to Youngstown, Niagara County, N. Y., where by private tutors and in the high school he received his early education; was principal of the high school of Youngstown one year; came to Michigan in 1865 and taught school for twelve years, then engaged in the occupation of contractor and builder. In 1873 he located at Flint, and the following year was married to Miss Sarah Isham, of Kennedy, N. Y.; remained at Flint until 1878, when he removed to Bay City. In politics a Democrat, and the only Democratic member in the House of 1895-6; elected to that of 1897-8 on the Democratic People's Union Silver Ticket.

PETER DORAN

Senator from the Sixteenth District (Kent County), 1891-2 and 1893-4. Was born in London, Canada, Apr. 16, 1848, of Irish descent, his parents coming from Belfast, Ireland. He acquired a common school education and began life as wheelsman and clerk on vessels on the Great Lakes. He afterwards taught school, managed a general store, studied medicine for a time, and finally began privately the study of law. He was admitted to the bar; began practice in Detroit in 1872. Four years later he moved to Grand Rapids, where he continued in the practice of his profession. In politics a Democrat; a member of the Democratic county, congressional and State committees, and for a number of years chairman of the city committee.

FRANK E. DOREMUS

Representative from Ionia County, 1891-2; and member of Congress, 1911-13 to 1919-21. Was born in Venago County, Pa., Aug. 31, 1865, of Holland and English parentage. He was educated in the Portland, Mich., High School, later entering the Detroit College of Law. He was editor of the Portland Review from 1885 to 1899, and then practiced law. He was Assistant Corporation Counsel for the city of Detroit four years and City Controller three years. He is married. In politics he is a Democrat.

ANDREW DORSEY

Representative from Calhoun County, 1838. Was born in Frederick, Md., Apr. 25, 1786. He located at Lyons, N. Y., in 1800. He was a Captain in the War of 1812. By occupation he was a farmer, in politics a Democrat. He settled in Homer, Mich., in 1836. He was a Justice in New York and Michigan for eighteen years. He died, Apr. 12, 1842.

EDWARD DORSCH

Member of the State Board of Education, 1873-9. Was born in Wurzenburg, Bavaria, Germany, Jan. 10, 1822. In 1840 he entered Munich University. He was exiled in 1849 and came to New York. In October he commenced the practice of his profession. He was the author of several valuable books which attracted much attention. He practiced medicine in Monroe for thirty-seven years. He gave his very valuable library to the University of Michigan and his home to the city of Monroe. He died at Monroe, Jan. 10, 1887.

TITUS DORT

Delegate from Wayne County to the First Convention of Assent, 1836; Representative from Wayne County, 1839, 1842 and 1865-6; and Senator from the First District, 1849-51. Was born at Bridgeport, Vt., June 17, 1806, and removed with his father to Ohio in 1811. He settled at Detroit in 1826, and was engaged in the manufacture of brick. He served as Justice, several times Supervisor, and Superintendent of the Poor. In politics he was a Democrat. He died, Oct. 7, 1879, at Dearborn, Mich.

JAMES DUANE DOTY

Member of the Legislative Council from the Seventh District (Brown, Chippewa and other counties), 1834-5. (Further data not obtainable).

PHILO DOTY

Representative from Clinton County, 1869-70 and 1871-2. Was born in Sweden, N. Y., in Mar. 8, 1816. He received a common school education. He removed to Eagle, Clinton County, Mich., in 1839, cleared up a large farm and lived there. He was a Democrat until Gen. Cass wrote the Nicholson letter, then a Republican. He was Supervisor and Treasurer each five years, and held other town offices. He was the Republican candidate for State Senator in 1872. He died at Eagle, Jan. 27, 1896.

SAMUEL DOTY

Representative from Washtenaw County, 1838. Was born in Rensselaer County, N. Y., May 10, 1795. He emigrated to Ann Arbor, 1832. He removed to Manchester' same county, in 1839, where he was a Justice of the Peace and a merchant. He retired from business on account of poor health about 1848, and lived at Tecumseh with his son, A. S. Doty until his death, Feb. 27, 1884.

THOMAS E. DOUBLE

Representative, 1905-6 and 1907-8 from the Presque Isle district, comprising the counties of Crawford, Montmorency, Oscoda, Otsego and Presque Isle. Was born in Wayne County, O., Feb. 28, 1866, of German descent. He moved with his parents to Williams County, Ohio, when three years of age, and lived at the place until eighteen years of age, working on the farm and attending the public schools. He finished his education in the Pioneer high schools. In 1884 he removed to Montmorency County, Mich., and taught in the public schools for six years after which time he engaged in farming. Mr. Double was married in September, 1893. In politics a Republican. He held the offices of Township Clerk, Supervisor and County School Examiner. In January, 1895, he took charge of the County Clerk's office as Deputy County Clerk, and was elected County Clerk in 1896 and re-elected to that office in 1898.

ANDREW B. DOUGHERTY

Attorney General, 1923—. Was born in St. John, New Brunswick, October 17, 1863. He came to Charlevoix, Mich., with his parents, Archibald K. and Mary M. Dougherty in November, 1868. He resided in Charlevoix for ten years. Since that time he has lived in Elk Rapids. He was educated in common schools of Charlevoix and Elk Rapids, read law in the office of Fitch R. Williams, was admitted to the bar in the Antrim County circuit court May, 1899, and was principal examiner in General Land Office of Washington, D. C., during the Harrison administration. He returned to Elk Rapids in 1894, and was elected Prosecuting Attorney of Antrim County and re-elected in 1896 and 1898. He practiced law in Elk Rapids until January 1, 1913, when he was appointed Deputy Attorney General by Hon. Grant Fellows; served with him four years. He served in same capacity for another four years with Hon. Alex. J. Groesbeck, and for two years and nine days under Hon. Merlin Wiley, when he was appointed Attorney General by Governor Groesbeck.

ARCHIBALD K. DOUGHERTY

Representative from the counties of Antrim, Charlevoix, and Manitou, 1887-8. Was born in St. John, New Brunswick, June 26, 1835. His education was limited. He became apprenticed to learn the trade of a ship-builder, and followed it as his principal occupation. In 1868 he removed to Charlevoix, Mich. In 1876 he located at Elk Rapids, where he was foreman in the shipyard of the Elk Rapids Iron Company. He held the office of Supervisor three years, and was eight times in succession elected Township Clerk of Elk Rapids. In politics a Republican.

COLUMBUS C. DOUGLAS

Representative from Houghton County, 1861-2. Was born in Springville, N. Y., Aug. 22, 1812. He came to Michigan in 1825 and assisted Dr. Houghton in the geological survey of the Upper Peninsula, and settled at Houghton, where he was largely interested in mining and real estate. He died at London, England, Dec. 17, 1874.

FRANK A. DOUGLASS

Representative from Houghton County, 1887-8. Was born in Tennessee, July 16, 1851. His business was that of general insurance agent, but for thirteen years was Postmaster at Houghton. He was elected on the Republican ticket a Representative.

SAMUEL T. DOUGLASS

Judge of the Wayne Circuit Court (the Circuit Judges then also constituting the Supreme Court of the State), 1851-7. Was born in Rutland County, Vt., Feb. 28, 1814, but was raised in Fredonia, N. Y., where his parents removed, and was educated at the Fredonia Academy. He came to Detroit in 1837, and was admitted to practice as an attorney the following year, having previously studied in New York. He was appointed reporter of the Supreme Court in 1845, serving until 1849, when he resigned, having during his service, published the two first volumes of Michigan reports. His election to the judgeship was by an independent movement outside of both parties, the Whig candidate, however, ultimately withdrawing in his favor. Judge Douglass' official life was comprised as above, and in part of a term as City Attorney and several terms on the Board of Education. He also served a year as president of the Detroit Young Men's Society. He lived the latter part of his life on a farm on Grosse Isle, giving little attention to law business. Politically he was a Democrat. He died Mar. 5, 1898.

ANDREW J. DOVEL

Representative from Manistee County, 1874. Was born in Pickerington, O., June 19, 1850. By profession he was a lawyer, politically a Democrat. He was City Attorney of Manistee four terms, Mayor, and Prosecuting Attorney of Manistee County three terms. After graduating at the Michigan University in 1871, he became a resident of this State. He was elected Representative to succeed Merritt N. Chafey, resigned.

JOHN DOW

Representative from Eaton County, 1863-4. Was born in Somerset County, N. J., Jan. 5, 1804. He settled as the first pioneer in Roxand, Eaton County, Mich., in 1837. He was Supervisor of Roxand thirteen years, removed to Sunfield, and was Supervisor there for thirty-two years—in all forty-five years. He for five times represented the county before the State Board of Equalization. He died Sept. 30, 1885.

PETER DOW

Senator from the Sixth District, 1863-4 and from the Eighteenth District, 1879-80 and 1881-2; and Representative from Oakland County, 1875-6. Was born Feb. 27, 1821, in the parish of Ballingray, Scotland. He settled at Orchard Lake, Mich., in 1830. He was educated in the common schools, and held several township offices. He was twice Town Treasurer and three times Supervisor. He was a farmer and a Republican. He died Oct. 21, 1887, at Richland, Dakota.

MICHAEL A. DOWLING

Representative from Bay County, 1877-8. Was born at Toronto, Ont., in 1834. He received a fair education in the common schools and seminary. He came to Michigan in 1867. He was Justice of the Peace and Village Attorney of Wenona. He lived eight years in Minnesota previous to coming to Michigan. He was admitted to the practice of law in that State. In politics a Democrat.

ALONZO DOWNING

Representative from the Second District of Sanilac County, 1891-2. Was born in Richmond County, N. Y., Apr. 2, 1829; worked on a farm until the age of twenty-one, when he removed to Niagara County and engaged in coopering and making hoops, moving to Michigan in 1858, where he continued the business of hoop making and also lumbering. In 1873 he purchased the farm at the village of Downington, a member of the firm of Downing and Southworth, general store. He held the office of Supervisor, and was elected on the Democratic ticket to the House of 1891-2.

CHARLES E. DOWNING

Representative, 1913-14, from the Third District of Wayne County, comprising the townships of Brownstown, Canton, Huron, Livonia, Northville, Plymouth, Romulus, Sumpter, Taylor and Van Buren. Was born at Romulus, Mich., Sept. 13, 1873, of English descent. His education was acquired in the district schools. He worked for his father until the age of twenty-one, when he began farming on his own account. He always took a lively interest in everything pertaining to country life, having served several years as president of the Wayne County Farmers' Institute, and also took an active interest in the grange, of which he was a state deputy. He was married, Oct. 20, 1910, to Marian White, of Marshall, Mich. Fraternally, a member of the A. O. O. G. and F. and A. M. In politics a Democrat.

PETER DOX

Representative from Oakland County, 1850. Was born in Albany, N. Y., in October, 1813. When young he went with his mother to Geneva, N. Y., where he lived until of age. In 1838 he removed to Birmingham, Oakland County, where he kept a hotel and was elected Supervisor in 1846. In 1847 he was elected Supervisor of Bloomfield, also in 1848-9, 1852-3. In 1853 he was appointed agent of the State Prison at Jackson, and held that position until 1855, when he removed to Chicago. In 1860 he was appointed to a position in the Custom House at Chicago, which he resigned, and became assistant keeper of the Bridewell Prison, which he filled for seventeen years, and resigned from ill health. He was always a Democrat.

MICHAEL J. DOYLE

Representative from the Chippewa District, 1891-2. Was born Oct. 1, 1854, at Memphis, Tenn. While an infant he was removed with father (his mother having died in child-birth) to Toronto, Ont., and in this city he was educated, primarily at the Christian Brothers' School, and later at De La Salle Institute. He studied law in the office of Hon. John O'Donohoe, later a member of the Canadian Senate, and attending the law course at Osgoode Hall, the only authoritative seat of legal learning in Ontario. In 1879 he was admitted to practice, and shortly thereafter moved to Detroit, where he engaged in business for several years, and in 1887 resumed the practice of law at Sault Ste. Marie. In 1889 he was appointed City Attorney by the Common Council, which position he held until after his election to the Legislature. A Democrat in politics, a Roman Catholic in religion, and of Irish parents on both sides. In 1880 he married Marie Fitzpatrick, the daughter of the late Kenny Fitzpatrick, of Hamilton, Ont. He was elected to the House of 1891-2, but vacated his seat by removal from the district before the extra session of 1892.

MICHAEL S. DOYLE

Representative from Clinton County, 1899-1900 and 1901-2. Was born in New Brunswick, Dominion of Canada, in 1842, and educated in the New Brunswick district schools. He removed to Ontario, Canada, in 1859 and was employed in farming in 1871, when he removed to Elsie, Clinton County, Mich. His occupation in the State various—six years in mercantile business and twenty-three years in cheese making and farming.

THOMAS J. DRAKE

Member of the Legislative Council from Oakland County, 1828-9, and 1830-1; Senator from the Third District, 1839-41; and Acting Lieutenant Governor, 1840-1. Was born in Scipio, N. Y., Apr. 18, 1799. He settled at Pontiac, Mich., in 1822, and was a leading lawyer for more than fifty years. He was the author of our liberal exemption laws, and the only member who at first dared to vote for them. He was president pro tem of the Senate in 1840-1, and Acting Lieutenant Governor in 1841-2, by the election of Gov. Woodbridge to United States Senate. He was Prosecuting Attorney; Register of Probate; Presidential Elector in 1840 and 1856; Chief Justice of Utah from 1862 to 1869; and publisher of a paper, first at Flint, then at Pontiac. At first he was a Whig, then a Republican. He was a good lawyer and a remarkable man, and especially strong in the use of sarcasm. He died Apr. 20, 1875.

WILLIAM DRAKE

Representative from Hillsdale County, 1873-4. Was born in the town of Lyons, N. Y., Mar. 22, 1828. He received his education in a common school. In 1838 he emigrated to Michigan, and settled in Amboy, Hillsdale County. He held various official positions. By occupation he was a farmer.

CHARLES DRAPER

Senator from the Fifth District, 1867-8. Was the first clerk of the courts under the State Constitution of 1835, and held that position until 1838. He was a law partner of his father, Hon. William Draper, for many years. He held the position of Prosecuting Attorney and ranked high in his profession. In politics a Republican.

CHARLES STUART DRAPER

Member of the Board of Regents of the University of Michigan, 1886-92. Was born at Pontiac, Mich., Aug. 26, 1841, son of Charles and Mary (Chamberlain) Draper. He was of New England ancestry. Both his father and his grandfather, William Draper, were graduates of Harvard College. He was prepared for college in the public schools of Pontiac, and entered the University of Michigan in 1858. On the breaking out of the Civil War he enlisted as Quartermaster Sergeant in the Fifth Michigan Infantry and served throughout the war. He was wounded at Antietam while serving on General Richardson's staff. While in the field the degree of Bachelor of Arts was conferred upon him by the University with the class of 1863. On returning to civil life he studied law in his father's office at Pontiac and eventually became a member of the firm. On Dec. 12, 1867 he was married to Sarah Thurber. In 1869 he removed to Saginaw, where he entered into partnership with H. H. Hoyt, Esq. Some time afterwards this partnership was dissolved and a new one was formed with Oscar F. Wisner, Esq., which was only terminated by Mr. Draper's death. At one time he was City Attorney of East Saginaw and later held the office of City Controller. On the resignation of Regent

Joy at the end of 1886, Mr. Draper was appointed to the vacancy and served out the term ending Jan. 1, 1890. In April, 1889, he was elected for the full term to succeed himself, but did not live to complete it. In the summer of 1892, his health having become seriously undermined, he went to Europe in the hope of finding relief. This hope proved vain. He started home, but died at sea, Aug. 5, 1892, and was buried in the family lot at Pontiac.

WILLIAM DRAPER

Delegate from Oakland County to the First Convention of Assent, 1836; member of the Board of Regents of the University of Michigan, 1840-4. Was an early resident of Pontiac, and was admitted to the Oakland County bar in 1833. He was president of the First Convention of Assent, which met at Ann Arbor in 1836. He was a good lawyer, well read, and had an extensive practice. He had been in law practice in Massachusetts prior to his coming to Michigan. He died in July, 1858, while on a visit to Mackinac.

WILLIAM P. DRAPER

Representative from Lapeer County, 1838. His postoffice address was Lapeer. (Further data not obtainable).

JOHN A. DREW

Representative from Mackinac County, 1841. His postoffice address was Mackinac. (Further data not obtainable).

JOHN F. DREW

Representative from Jackson County, 1873-4. Was born in the town of Shelby, N. Y., Dec. 3, 1828. He received a common school education. In 1866 he emigrated to the township of Rives, Jackson County. He had his share of town offices. While a resident of the State of New York, he served his district in the Assembly of that State. By occupation he was a drover.

ALFRED L. DRIGGS

Representative from St. Joseph County, 1847. Was born in Albany County, N. Y., Aug. 25, 1807. By occupation he was a farmer and lumberman, politically a Democrat. He came to Michigan in 1831 and bought land in Constantine, but went to Branch County and built a saw mill, where he remained until 1836, when he returned to Constantine and cleared up and cultivated his farm. He was Supervisor of Constantine for many years.

JOHN F. DRIGGS

Member of Congress, 1863-5 to 1867-9. Was born in Kinderhook, N. Y., Mar. 8, 1813, and received a good common school education. He was a master mechanic and builder, and also dealt in lands. He was superintendent of the New York Penitentiary in 1844, and came to Michigan in 1856. He was President of the village of East Saginaw in 1858. Near the close of the Civil War he raised a regiment of soldiers in sixty days. In 1872 he was an Independent candidate for Congress. He died Dec. 17, 1877.

HUGH DRUMMOND

Representative from the Second District of Genesee County, 1919-20. Was born Oct. 9, 1877, at Stirling, Scotland, where he attended the common schools. He went to work at the age of twelve years and at fifteen was indentured to the carpenter trade. Before coming to the United States in 1905 he lived three years in South Africa. Married. He was a member of the carpenters' union for many years and held the office of business agent two years, and president of the Flint Federation the same length of time; a member of the F. & A. M.; and was a member of the City Charter Commission. In politics a Republican.

ANTHONY DUDGEON

Senator from the First District, 1859-60. Was born Jan. 8, 1818, at Stewartstown Island. He came to Detroit at the age of eighteen, and for several years was attached to the American Fur Company. He was afterwards the head of the firm of Dudgeon, Lewis & Graves, in the forwarding and commission business, and was successful. He was Alderman of Detroit in 1854, president of the Board of Alderman in 1855. He retired from active life in 1855, and purchased an estate and erected a beautiful residence on Grosse Isle. In 1869 he became auditor and afterwards president of the Republic Insurance Company of Chicago, which went down with the great fire of 1871. He died at Grosse Isle, Dec. 22, 1875.

HARLAN J. DUDLEY

Representative from Newaygo County, 1897-8 and 1899-1900. Was born in Newfield, Tompkins County, N. Y., Sept. 27, 1853, and came to Michigan in 1867, attending school at Hastings, while working for his board on a farm. He obtained a state certificate from the State Normal School in 1879; conducted a teachers' normal department during the last half of the same year for the convenience of teachers at Freeport, Mich.; removed to Newaygo County to assist his father in establishing a lumbering enterprise, and closed his school work by being principal of Fremont schools, Newaygo County, in 1880-1. He commenced the manufacture of shingles in 1882, and later, in connection with the manufacturing of shingles, he became a general wholesale dealer in lumber, lath and shingles. In 1892 he handled for the trade, 1,670 car loads of forest products. In politics a Republican.

WILLIAM J. DUFF

Representative from the First District of St. Clair County, 1899-1900. Was born at Pittsburg, Pa., Aug. 17, 1856. As the son of Lieut. George Duff, of the first U. S. Infantry, he was born amidst military surroundings, and always evinced a lively interest in that profession. Coming to Michigan with his parents in 1868, when but twelve years of age, he received his education in the common schools, finally entering the University of Michigan, and graduating from the medical department in 1885, after which he practiced the profession of physician and surgeon. He joined the Michigan National Guard, and was promoted from rank to rank until in 1887 he obtained the rank of Captain, but owing to the growing demands of his profession he was forced to resign. Upon the declaration of war with Spain, Dr. Duff sent his name to the Governor for a commission, but not meeting with satisfactory recognition, he enlisted as a private in Co. F, 33d Mich. Inf., and was assigned to duty as a Corporal. In this capacity he served through the Battle of Santiago du Cuba, but after the surrender the necessities of the troops demanded his professional services. He remained with his regiment until it was mustered out, when he returned to his home in Port Huron and resumed his practice. He was nominated for the Legislature of 1899-1900 on the Republican ticket.

D. BETHUNE DUFFIELD

Member of the State Board of Education, 1856-7. Was born in Carlisle, Cumberland County, Pa., Aug. 29, 1821. In 1835 he removed with his parents to Philadelphia; in 1840 he entered Yale College and received his degree of A. B. In 1839 he came to Detroit, his father being the pastor of the First Presbyterian Church. He studied law and was admitted to the bar in 1843. He became the City Attorney in 1847 and was appointed to the State Board of Education in 1856 to succeed G. O. Whittemore resigned, and served as its president. His work for the department was highly commended. He was the author of several poems. In politics he was allied with the Republican party. He died at his residence in Detroit, Mar. 12, 1891. A fine memorial volume was gotten out in his city.

GEORGE DUFFIELD

Member of the Board of Regents of the University of Michigan, 1839-43 and 1844-8. Was born at Strasburg, Lancaster County, Pa., July 4, 1794; son of George and Faithful (Schleiermacher) Duffield. His father was a merchant, an elder in the Presbyterian Church, and his grandfather, of the same name, a graduate of Princeton College, in 1752. He entered the University of Pennsylvania and was graduated Bachelor of Arts in 1811. The degree of Master of Arts followed in 1815. He proceeded from the University to the Theological Seminary of New York City, where he studied for three years, and in 1815 was licensed to preach by the Presbytery of Philadelphia, and served the Presbyterian Church there for nineteen years. He was then pastor of the Fifth Presbyterian Church of Philadelphia for two years, resigning this charge to accept at the Broadway Tabernacle of New York City. In 1838 he removed to Detroit at the invitation of the First Presbyterian Society, and was pastor of that Church until his death in 1868. He was appointed Regent of the University of Michigan, July 1, 1839, in place of Lucius Lyon resigned, and served out the term, retiring in February, 1843. Mar. 12, 1844 he was appointed Regent for the full term of four years. He was the first clergyman to sit in the Board. He published the following: Regeneration, Claims of Episcopal Bishops Examined, Travels in the Holy Land, and numerous discourses and addresses. In 1841 he received the degree of Doctor of Divinity from the University of Pennsylvania. He died at Detroit, June 26, 1868, being struck with glottal paralysis while addressing a convention of Young Men's Christian Association in that city. His wife was Isabella Graham Bethune, of New York City, and there were thirteen children. Only six of these reached adult years.

GEORGE DUFFIELD

Member of the Board of Regents of the University of Michigan, 1877-86. Was born at Carlisle, Pa., Sept. 12, 1818, son of the Rev. George and Isabella Graham

(Bethune) Duffield. His father was one of the early Regents of the University of Michigan. He was prepared for college largely under the tutorship of his father and entered the sophomore class of Yale in 1834. Three years later he was graduated Bachelor of Arts, being the youngest member of a class that afterwards became famous. He took up the study of theology at Union Seminary, N. Y., and completed the course there in 1840. He was immediately settled as pastor of a church in Brooklyn, and remained there seven years. He then accepted a call to the Presbyterian Church in Bloomfield, N. J., and continued in that pastorate for six years. In 1853 he removed to a church in the Northern Liberties of Philadelphia where he found a wide field for pastoral work. About the time of the Civil War he came to Michigan and was settled, first at Adrian, and later over the Lansing Church. On the resignation of Regent Collier in September, 1877, he was appointed to the vacancy; and at the end of the year was reappointed for the full term, Regent Collier who had been elected to the office the preceding April having declined to qualify. On Oct. 22, 1840, he was married to Augusta Willoughby, of Brooklyn, N. Y., and they had three children. He died at Bloomfield, N. J., July 6, 1888, and was buried in the family lot in Elmwood, Detroit.

WILLIAM W. DUFFIELD

Senator from the Third District, 1879-80. Was born at Carlisle, Pa., Nov. 19, 1823. He graduated from Columbia College in 1842. He became a resident of Detroit in 1836. By profession he was a civil engineer, also a member of the Detroit bar. He was Adjutant of the 2d Tennessee in the Mexican War; was engineer and superintendent of railroads in New York; surveyed the Detroit and Milwaukee Railroad in 1852 from Pontiac to Grand Haven; also the road from Detroit to Port Huron, and from Mendota to Galesburg, Ill. He was appointed by President Cleveland to the position of Superintendent of the coast and geodetic survey. He went out in 1861 as Lieutenant Colonel of the 4th Mich. Infantry, and became Colonel of the 9th Infantry; commanded 23d brigade, was Military Governor of Kentucky, and was wounded and compelled to resign in 1863; had charge of coal mines in Pennsylvania and iron mines in Kentucky, and was chief engineer of the Kentucky Union Railroad. He was a Whig until 1854, then a Democrat.

DANIEL DUNAKIN

Representative from Calhoun County, 1855-6. Was born in Niagara County, N. Y., Apr. 19, 1810, and in 1834 settled on a farm in Eckford, Calhoun County. He was several years Supervisor. Through his influence a bill was passed giving a charter to Hillsdale College. In politics he was a Republican, in religion a Free Will Baptist. He died May 16, 1875.

ADDISON E. DUNBAR

Representative from the First District of Monroe, 1885-6 and 1887-8. Was born in Bedford, Monroe County, in 1834. He followed the business of farming and settling of estates; was a resident of Michigan all his life. He was Justice of the Peace, School Inspector, and Drain Commissioner; was County Surveyor four years, Superintendent of Poor six years, and Township Clerk twenty-two years. Mr. Dunbar was elected Representative for 1887-8 on the Democratic ticket.

WILLIAM DUNBAR

Representative from Monroe County, 1857-8, and 1859-60. Was born in West Stockbridge, Mass.. Feb. 22, 1807. He was a Democrat in politics, a farmer by occupation. He settled in Bedford, Monroe County, in 1832. He was the first Supervisor of the town; seven years Town Clerk; Superintendent of the Poor two terms; and was elected Sheriff of the county for two terms. He died Aug. 27, 1870.

DELAMORE DUNCAN

Representative from Kalamazoo County, 1850; and Delegate from Kalamazoo County to the Constitutional Convention of 1867. Was born at Lyman, N. H., Nov. 24, 1805. He received a common school education and worked in his father's mill at wool carding and cloth dressing. He was a lumberman in Vermont, and settled on a farm in Prairie Ronde, Mich.. In 1829. He was the first Sheriff of Kalamazoo County from 1830 to 1834: was nine years Supervisor; was Assessor and Justice, a merchant from 1855 to 1865; president of the Schoolcraft & Three Rivers Railroad, giving liberally of time and means to secure its completion: and a director of the National Bank at Three Rivers from 1864 until his death, May 1, 1870.

GEORGE W. DUNCAN

Representative from the First District of Wayne County. 1903-4, 1905-6 and 1906-7. Was born at Lockport, N. Y., June 28, 1857, of Scotch-Irish parents, his father serving throughout the Civil War. He received his education in the public schools of Lockport and later learned the printers' trade. Mr. Duncan came to Michigan in 1879, and for many years was connected with the Detroit *Journal*. He was actively identified with the organized labor movement for many years, having filled the offices of president and secretary of the Detroit Trades Council and Detroit Typographical Union No. 18, and was the first secretary and treasurer of the Michigan Federation of Labor. In politics a Republican.

LAWSON A. DUNCAN

Senator from the Eleventh District, 1883-4. Was born at Columbus, Ind., Jan. 21, 1832; entered the volunteer service of his country at the time of its struggle with the southern rebellion, serving three years, and to the close of the war, as Adjutant and Major of the 40th Iowa Infantry, gaining the highest rank in his regiment in which there was a vacancy; was Presidential Elector for the Fourth District Michigan in 1872. Mr. Duncan was editor of the Niles *Republican* for many years.

ROBERT W. DUNCAN

Representative from Ottawa County. 1855-6. Was born in Rutland, Vt., Feb. 24, 1824. He came to Grand Haven in 1851. By profession he was a lawyer, politically a Democrat. He was Circuit Court Commissioner six terms; Prosecuting Attorney two terms; Mayor in 1868; Supervisor several times; and repeatedly the Democratic candidate for Circuit Judge.

WILLIAM C. DUNCAN

Senator from the Second District, 1863-4. Was born in Lyons, N. Y., in 1820 and acquired a business education at Rochester, N. Y. He began business for himself in 1821. He came to Detroit in 1849, and went into business as a brewer and malster. He was Alderman from 1854 to 1858, and Mayor of Detroit in 1862-3. He was a member of the Board of Estimates in 1873, and was tendered the nomination for Mayor but declined. He retired from business about 1865, and died Dec. 19, 1877.

CLARENCE DUNCOMBE

Delegate from Van Buren County to the Constitutional Convention of 1867. Was born at Ancaster, Canada, May 30, 1822. He settled with his father's family at Keeler, Van Buren County, in 1844. In politics he was first a Whig, later a Republican. He went to California in 1849 and engaged in mercantile trade, returning in 1852. He owned several farms, was for several years cashier of the Decatur National Bank, owned the mills at Decatur, also several stores and a hotel.

ROBERT F. DUNDASS

Representative from the counties of Mason and Lake, 1881-2. Was born Dec. 12, 1847. He was a Republican, in politics, and by profession a physician.

NELSON DUNHAM

Representative from Monroe County, 1840, 1844 and 1846; and Senator from the Third District, 1848-9. Was born in Madison, N. Y., in 1803. By profession he was a physician, politically a Democrat. He settled in Dundee, Monroe County, in 1836, where he resided until 1856, when he removed to Petersburg, where he remained until his death, Apr. 30, 1866.

ABIJAH B. DUNLAP

Representative from Grand Traverse and adjoining counties, 1865-6 and 1867-8. Was born in Ovid, N. Y., Aug. 29, 1810. He graduated at Yale College in 1833. He taught, then farmed for several years. In 1853 he married May A. Wright of LeRoy Seminary, and served several years as a missionary in the Levant. He was several years professor of ancient languages and literature at the Michigan Un'versity, then principal of the high school at Jonesville, then taught the languages and literature at Elmira Female College, N. Y. He removed to a farm in Leelanau County, near Traverse City. First he was a Whig, then a Abolitionist, later a Republican; a Democrat in 1888. He was Prosecuting Attorney of Leelanau County. In religion he was a Presbyterian.

FRED E. DUNN

Representative from Sanilac County, 1911-12 and 1913-14; and from the Second D'strict, Wayne County, 1919-20 and 1921-2. Was born on a farm in Port Huron Township, Clair County, Mich., Aug. 25, 1877. He received his education in the district schools of that township, Fenton Normal, Albion College and the University of Michigan. Before entering Albion College he taught four years in the district schools. He received the degree of A. B. from Albion College in 1903. The next fall he moved to Sanilac County and for six years was engaged as

Superintendent of Schools, three years at Brown City and three at Sandusky. He received the degree A. M. from the University of Michigan in 1916 upon completion of a year's post-graduate work. Mr. Dunn is married and has lived in Highland Park for the last six years. He is engaged in the real estate and insurance business, being president and general manager of the Dunn Realty Co. In politics he is a Republican.

JAMES DUNN

Representative from St. Clair County, 1901-2 and 1903-4. Was born in the county of Perth, Canada, Feb. 18, 1861. He came to Michigan in 1878 and settled on a farm. His education was obtained in the district schools of Canada. Married, and a successful farmer. President of the St. Clair County Farmers' Institute, of which organization he was for many years secretary. In politics a strong Republican.

WILLIAM M. DUNNING

Representative from the First District of St. Clair County, 1907-8. Was born in Canada, July 24, 1845, of Scotch and Irish parentage. He received his education in the common schools and resided in Michigan after November, 1864. From 1864 to 1875 he was identified with the lumbering interests in eastern Michigan, and then for many years engaged in farming. He married Miss Ella Hollister, June 16, 1875. In politics a Republican. He held the offices of member of the Board of Review and Township Treasurer, and was elected to the Legislature, Nov. 6, 1906.

JAMES C. DUNSTAN

Representative from the Second District, Houghton County, 1903-4 and 1905-6. Was born in the county of Cornwall, England, 1847. He was educated in the common schools of England and at the State Normal College at Ypsilanti, Mich. Mr. Dunstan came to Michigan in 1869, settling in Keweenaw County where he worked two years in the copper mines, and then prepared himself for the work of teaching in which he engaged for fifteen years. In 1888 he engaged in the local management of a lumber and real estate business, and later occupied a clerical position connected with the various copper manufacturing establishments at Dollar Bay. In politics a Republican.

THOMAS B. DUNSTAN

Representative from the Keweenaw District, 1883-4; Senator from the Thirty-second District, 1889-90; and Lieutenant Governor, 1897-9. Was born at Camborne, Cornwall County, England, Jan. 4, 1850. His parents emigrated to America in the spring of 1854 and settled in Ontonagon County, Mich. He graduated at Lawrence University, Appleton, Wis., June, 1871; attended the law department of Michigan University during the winter of 1871-2 and was admitted to the bar in the Keweenaw Circuit in June, 1872. In November of the same year he was elected to the offices of Judge of Probate and Prosecuting Attorney for the county of Keweenaw. He held these offices until July, 1879, at which date he resigned the same and removed to Pontiac, Mich. He resided in Pontiac until the mid-summer of 1882, when he removed to his former home at Central Mine, Keweenaw County. In the fall of 1882 the Republicans of the Representative District comprising the counties of Keweenaw, Baraga, Ontonagon and Isle Royal placed him in nomination for the Legislature. He was elected by a large majority. In the autumn of 1883 he removed to Hancock, Houghton County. In 1884 he was nominated for the office of Prosecuting Attorney by the Republicans of Houghton County, and elected. In 1886 was again placed in nomination by the Republicans for the same position and endorsed by the Democratic Party of his county. In 1888 was one of the delegates at large from Michigan to the Republican National Convention at Chicago; a member of the Board of Control of the Michigan College of Mines.

CHARLES DUPONT

Representative from the First District of Wayne County, 1901-2. Was born in Detroit, Mich., Feb. 12, 1844, and obtained his education in the common school. He enlisted in the Civil War, May 16, 1861, in Company K. Fourth Regiment Michigan Volunteer Infantry, and was wounded while serving as Corporal in said company. At the Battle of Gaines Mill, June 27, 1862, he was taken prisoner and confined in Libby Prison. In December, 1863, he was commissioned First Lieutenant, Thirteenth Mich. Battery, Light Artillery, and was made Captain, June 11, 1864. Unmarried, and engaged in the laundry business. A Democrat in politics. He held the office of Register of Deeds of Wayne County from 1874 to 1876 and was elected to the Legislature of 1901-2 on the general legislative ticket.

JAMES DUPUY

Representative from Jackson County, 1855-6. Was born in Pompey, N. Y., Oct. 20, 1815. By occupation he was a farmer, in politics a Republican. He held the position of Town Clerk, several times Supervisor, Trustee of Michigan Central College, and other offices. Deceased.

GEORGE H. DURAND

Member of Congress, 1875-7; and Justice of the Supreme Court, 1892. Was born at Cobleskill, N. Y., Feb. 21, 1838. He removed to Flint, Mich., in 1858. By profession a lawyer. He was elected Mayor of Flint in 1873 and again in 1874. In politics a Democrat. In 1874 he was elected to Congress; was defeated as a candidate for Congress in 1876 by Mark S. Brewer. He then engaged in the practice of his profession at Flint. He was appointed in 1892 Justice of the Supreme Court to fill temporary vacancy. He died at Flint, June 8, 1903.

MILLARD DURHAM

Representative from the Second District, Ottawa County, 1903-4 and 1905-6. Was born in the township of Polkton, Ottawa County, Mich., July 26, 1856, of German parentage. He was educated in the Coopersville graded schools, and lived on a farm until 1894, when he purchased the elevator at Coopersville, after which time he engaged in the grain and coal trade. He was married to Sarah Pierce, Jan. 3, 1880. He was a member of the firm of Durham & Moore, engaged in local fire insurance business, and president of the Coopersville State Bank. He held the offices of Village Trustee, Township Treasurer and Supervisor.

LEWIS DURKEE

Senator from the Fifteenth District, 1881-2. Was born at Farmersville, N. Y., May 29, 1834. He received an academical education, studied law, and in 1864 went into business as a merchant at Hickory Corners, Barry County. He was admitted to the bar in 1877, and engaged in practice. He was four terms a Supervisor. In politics he was a Republican. He died Apr. 11, 1881.

LAURENT DUROCHER

Member of the Legislative Council from Monroe and Lenawee counties, 1826-7 to 1834-5; Senator from the Second District, 1835-6; and Representative from Monroe County, 1839. Was born at St. Genevieve Mission, Mo., in 1786. He received a collegiate education at Montreal, Canada, and settled at Frenchtown, Mich., in 1805. In the War of 1812 he served in the army of Gen. Hull, and after his surrender of Detroit, rendered important services to the government. He was made County Clerk on the organization of Monroe County in 1818, and held that office many years. He also held the offices of Justice of the Peace, Probate Judge, Circuit Clerk, and Clerk of the city of Monroe, where he died, Sept. 21, 1861. He was an accomplished gentleman and the great legal authority among the French population on the River Raisin.

JOEL J. DUSSEAU

Representative from Monroe County, 1867-8. Was born at Erie, Monroe County, Mich. By occupation he was a merchant, in politics a Democrat. He was in mercantile business at Toledo, O., in 1887.

VICTOR A. DUSSEAU

Representative from Monroe County, 1865-6 and 1869-70. Was born in Erie, Mich., Nov. 20, 1835. He was a farmer until 1862, and was a teacher, the first child of French descent to engage in teaching in that locality. He was Town Clerk from 1863 to 1873. He was in the nursery business from 1876 to 1882, teaching winters. He held many town offices.

FRANK H. DUSENBURY

Representative from Isabella County, 1909-10 and 1911-12. Was born at Mt. Pleasant, Mich., May 26, 1878, of American descent. He received his education in the Mt. Pleasant High School, the Saginaw common schools, and in June, 1902, he was graduated from the law department of the University of Michigan. In the same year he was elected Prosecuting Attorney of Isabella County and re-elected in 1904. In 1906 Mr. Dusenbury was married to Edith E. Gorham, and for several years engaged in the practice of law at Mt. Pleasant. In politics a Republican.

WILLIAM T. DUST

Representative from the First District of Wayne County, 1907-8. Was born in Germany, July 25, 1853, of German parents. He received his education in the public and German-American schools of Detroit. Married. Mr. Dust was lithographic printer for twenty-one years and for many years a prominent manufacturer and jobber of stove castings. In politics a Republican. He held the offices of Alderman, City Clerk, Member of the Board of Estimates of Detroit city and member of the Board of State Tax Commissioners.

AARON SMITH DYCKMAN

Member of the State Board of Agriculture, 1873-9. Was the son of Avery Brown Dyckman of Greenbush, N. Y., and Harriet (Hinckly) D. He was born Feb. 16, 1826, at Clay, N. Y. He married Amorita Blood of South Haven, Mich., Feb. 25, 1856. He was born in Utica, N. Y., in 1836. Mr. Dyckman was educated in the common school and at Kalamazoo College; attended the Congregational Church and voted the Republican ticket. In early life he ran a saw mill and engaged in the lumber business; was a most successful grower of peaches and some other fruits; served as County Treasurer, 1860-64; president of the State Pomological Society. He died Dec. 12, 1899, living for much of his active life at South Haven, Mich.

EVERT B. DYCKMAN

Representative from Kalamazoo County, 1847. Was born at Greenbush, N. Y., Sept. 25, 1800. He had a limited education. He became a resident of Onondaga County, N. Y., assisted in the construction of the Oswego canal, established a boat yard, and carried on an extensive coopering business. He purchased one thousand acres of land and settled at Paw Paw, Mich., in 1838, and built the Dyckman House, and a grist mill and store. He removed to Schoolcraft in 1842. In 1853 he purchased the present site of South Haven, and built a pier, saw mill, store and several houses. He was engaged in important enterprises at Schoolcraft, and was also engaged in banking.

WALTER RICHARDSON DYER

Representative, 1889-90, from the Iosco District, comprising the counties of Iosco, Alcona and Arenac. Was born at Boston, Mass., Apr. 20, 1855. By occupation a lumberman and live stock breeder; his former profession was the law. In politics a Republican. He held the offices of Supervisor and School Treasurer.

ATE DYKSTRA

Representative from the First District of Kent County, 1923—. Was born in the Netherlands, December 1, 1865, where he followed the occupation of farmer until he came to America in 1890 and located in Grand Rapids. Here he was employed in furniture factories for a time and then conducted a grocery and dry goods store for twenty-five years, now being retired from business. Mr. Dykstra is married and has two children. He is a Republican and served five years on the Kent County Board of Supervisors, three terms as Alderman of Grand Rapids and was a candidate for Mayor in 1910.

JAMES EAKINS

Representative from Huron County, 1881-2. Was born in Toronto, Ont., Nov. 13, 1846, and was educated in Toronto University College, and took the degree of

Bachelor of Medicine from that college in 1870. He engaged in practice at Port Crescent, Mich., and also engaged in salt manufacture there. He held various local and county offices. In politics a Republican.

BARNEY EARL

Representative from Kalamazoo County, 1849 and 1851. Was born in Providence, N. Y., Jan. 29, 1803. He lived there twenty years, then worked in a woolen factory four years, then moved to New Jersey. From 1826 to 1835 he was in the grocery business in the city of New York. He removed to Cooper, Mich., and became a farmer. In politics he was a Whig.

HORATIO S. EARLE

Senator, 1901-2, from the Third District, comprising the fourth, sixth, eighth and tenth wards of the city of Detroit; and State Highway Commissioner, 1905-9. Was born at Mt. Holly, Vt., Feb. 14, 1865. His education was acquired in the common school, supplemented by a course in the Black River Academy at Ludlow, Vt. He followed the occupation of farming for a number of years, and then became a traveling salesman and manufacturer. In politics a Republican. He was appointed the first State Highway Commissioner, July 1, 1905.

J. MILTON EARLE

Senator, 1893-4 and 1895-6, from the Eighteenth District, composed of the counties of Ionia and Montcalm. Was born in Oneonta, N. Y., Sept. 1, 1851; a resident of Michigan since 1867. He was educated at Fairfield Academy, N. Y., Newton High School, Mass., and Michigan State Normal; taught school in New York and Michigan about seven years. On coming to Michigan he located at Smyrna, Ionia County, where he remained until 1875, when he removed to Belding, where he engaged in the mercantile business, and in real estate and insurance; president of the Belding Building and Loan Association and director in the Belding Savings Bank; had a large interest in the Lansing Pants and Overall Company of Lansing, Mich. In politics a Republican. He held the offices of Township Clerk and Treasurer.

NATHANIEL A. EARLE

Representative from Kent County, 1881-2. Was born in Allegan County, Mich., was educated in common and high schools; from 1870 to 1874 was teacher and principal of Paw Paw schools; studied law at Grand Rapids and was admitted in 1875; went into practice, at Grand Rapids. He was an Alderman, and was long one of the law firm of Stone & Earle, and later Taggart, Stone & Earle.

AHIRA G. EASTMAN

Representative from Lenawee County, 1845. Was a practicing lawyer at Adrian and came there from the State of New York in 1835. He held the position of master in chancery. During the Mexican War he volunteered and received a Lieutenant's commission, but resigned from ill health before reaching Mexico. Later he removed to Breedsville, Mich., where he died.

DAVID J. EASTON

Representative from Branch County, 1881-2. Was born in Castile, N. Y., June 5, 1842. He came with his parents to Algansee, Mich., in 1846, removing to Coldwater in 1855. He learned the trade of a printer and became one of the publishers of the Sturgis *Journal*. He enlisted in the 19th Mich. Infantry, served from 1862 to the close of the war, was three times wounded and rose to the rank of Major. He established the Coldwater *Republican* in 1866, and in 1867 was Clerk of Coldwater. In 1869 he established the Union City *Register*.

CHARLES L. EATON

Representative from the First District of Van Buren County, 1889-90 and 1891-2; and Adjutant General, 1893-5. Was born in Orleans County, N. Y., Apr. 2, 1846. He served in the army during the War of Rebellion; came to Michigan in 1867, since which time he engaged in various business enterprises, acquiring considerable property. During the campaign of 1888 he was chairman of the Van Buren County and Fourth Congressional District Republican committees. At the State Encampment of the Grand Army of the Republic, held at Muskegon, in March, 1891, he was unanimously elected department commander for the current year. Gov. Rich appointed him Adjutant General and while holding that office dropped dead, Feb. 27, 1895, at Detroit.

CROSBY EATON

Representative from Allegan County, 1877-8, 1879-80 and 1881-2. Was born in Franklin County, Me., in 1823. He received a high school education and went to Massachusetts in 1845. He was overseer in a cotton mill for seven years, and superintendent of Dr. J. C. Ayers & Co.'s patent medicine manufactory seven years. He came to Michigan in 1858, and settled in Casco, Allegan County. He was Superintendent of Schools several years, and Supervisor of the town twelve years in succession. His occupation that of farming and fruit growing.

EBENEZER C. EATON

Representative from Wayne County, 1839 and 1847; and Delegate from Wayne County to the Constitutional Convention of 1850. His postoffice address was Rawsonville. (Further data not obtainable).

EDWIN EATON

Senator, 1895-6, from the Fifth District, composed of the counties of Lenawee and Monroe. Was born of English parents in Wilton, Franklin County, Me., Nov. 6, 1848; educated at Wilton Academy and Bowdoin College, graduating from the medical department of the latter in 1873; practiced medicine at Lewiston, Me., until 1876, when he came to Michigan, locating at Clayton, Lenawee County, where he continued in the practice of his profession; was also interested in the drug business. In 1886 he removed to Hudson, and succeeded to the practice of Dr. A. R. Smart. In politics a Republican and prominent in the affairs of his city; president of the Board of Water Commissioners of his city; great medical examiner of the K. O. T. M. of Michigan, and past commander of his tent of Maccabees;

a prominent member of the Masonic fraternity, and identified with other secret societies; also president of the Northern Tri-State Medical Association. While at Clayton he was president of the Village and member of the Council.

FRED L. EATON

Representative from the First District of Saginaw County, 1917-18. Was born in Saginaw, in 1869. He was educated in the public schools and U. S. Naval Academy. He was admitted to the bar in 1892, and was Prosecuting Attorney of Saginaw County from 1897 to 1900; resigned his office and served in the Navy during the Spanish-American War with rank of Ensign. In politics a Democrat.

JEROME B. EATON

Representative from Jackson County, 1851 and 1869-70. Was born in Columbia, Herkimer County, N. Y., Jan. 11, 1811, and was reared on a farm, working summers, attending school winters. At the age of thirteen he commenced teaching and followed it for seven successive winters. From twenty to twenty-two he was engaged in peddling. He came to Adrian, Mich., in 1833 and engaged in the dry goods trade. In 1842 he removed to Jackson and engaged in a prison contract, making barrels. In 1858 he engaged in the wholesale grocery trade. He was president of the Air Line Railroad and was a prime mover in the removal of the Michigan Central railroad shops from Marshall to Jackson. He held several local offices of trust, and was identified with the interests of Jackson for many years. In politics he was a Democrat. He was a member of the State Pioneer Society. He died at Jackson, Aug. 26, 1887.

LEVI EATON

Representative from Wayne County, 1851. His postoffice address was Romulus. (Further data not obtainable).

ROYAL C. EATON

Representative from the First District of Allegan County, 1891-2 and 1893-4. Was born in Orleans County, N. Y., May 23, 1824, and moved with his parents when a boy, to Lorain County, O., where he grew to manhood. He moved to Allegan County, Mich., in the fall of 1849, where he engaged in mercantile business for about ten years, and in 1859 moved upon the farm of 200 acres. He was an enrolling officer during the war; held the offices of Supervisor for a number of years, also Treasurer and other township offices, and director of the School Board for a number of years; also Justice for over twenty years.

WILLIAM R. ECK

Representative from St. Joseph County, 1867-8 and 1869-70. Was born at Briar Creek, Pa., Aug. 31, 1809. By occupation he was a miller, in politics a Republican. He came to Michigan in 1833, and located at what was then called Bucks, now Three Rivers, Mich., where he remained until 1845, when he removed to Colon, and later retired from business. He was Supervisor of Colon six years.

GEORGE ECKLEE

Representative from Lenawee County, 1845. His postoffice address was Rollin. (Further data not obtainable).

HIRAM S. EDDY

Representative from Lenawee County, 1855. Was born in Clarendon, Vt., June 6, 1812. He received a common school education. He was brought up a farmer and learned the trade of carpenter. He came to Michigan in 1832, settled on a farm in Palmyra and afterwards in Fairfield, Lenawee County. He was eight times Supervisor of Fairfield. He administered on many estates in Lenawee County. In 1867 he purchased large farms in Iowa, which he managed profitably.

WILLIAM R. EDGAR

Representative from the Second District of Lenawee County, 1895-6 and 1897-8. Was born in Henry County, O., June 24, 1860. When eight years of age his parents moved to Fulton County, O., where he attended district schools winters and worked on the farm summers; afterwards attended the union schools at Wauseon, O. Taking up the study of medicine he graduated from the Detroit College of Medicine, class of 1881, coming to Michigan he located at Blissfield, where he engaged in the practice of medicine. In politics a Republican.

FRANK LEWIS EDINBOROUGH

Senator, 1907-8, from the Twenty-fourth District, comprising the counties of Arenac, Bay and Midland. Was born at Bay City, Mich., July 6, 1874. He received his education in the public schools of Bay City and the University of Michigan graduating from the latter in 1895. Unmarried. He was a practicing attorney at Bay City, after graduation. In politics a Republican. He held the office of Circuit Court Commissioner of Bay County.

CHARLES A. EDMONDS

Commissioner of the State Land Office, 1871-3. Was a resident of Quincy, Branch County, when he enlisted and became First Lieutenant of battery "A," 1st light artillery. In 1862 he became Captain of the 17th Mich. Infantry. He was wounded at the Battle of South Mountain, lost an arm, and was discharged in 1863 on account of wounds. He held the office of Register in Branch County. He resided at Milwaukee in 1887. While in Michigan he was a Republican.

JAMES M. EDMUNDS

Senator from the Fifth District, 1840-1; Representative from Washtenaw County, 1846 and 1847; and Delegate from Washtenaw County to the Constitutional Convention of 1850. Was born in Niagara County, N. Y., Aug. 23, 1810. He settled in Ypsilanti, Mich., in 1831, where he was a teacher and merchant. In 1853 he moved to Detroit, engaged in the lumber business, and was several years comptroller. In 1861, under Lincoln, he was appointed Commissioner of the General Land Office, and held it until 1866, when he became Postmaster of the Senate.

In 1859 he was appointed Postmaster of Washington, and held it until his death, Dec. 14, 1879. He was chairman of the State Republican Committee from 1855 to 1861; president of the National Council of the Union League from 1862 to 1869; and for a number of years published the *Republic*, a Washington magazine. He was a man of great ability, familiar with men and events, well informed in State and National affairs, had a judicial mind, great political sagacity, and his opinion was always received with great consideration by the leading men of the nation. First he was a Whig; a Republican from 1854.

WILSON C. EDSELL

Senator from the Nineteenth District, 1865-6; and from the Fourteenth District, 1877-8 and 1881-2. Was born in Pike, Pa., July 14, 1814. Brought up on a farm, he attended common schools, and learned the carpenter's trade. In 1835 he went to Ohio and worked as a millwright; in 1835 took a four years' course at Oberlin College; and in 1843 was one of the Oberlin Colony which founded Olivet College, of which he was trustee, secretary and treasurer for six years. He removed to Otsego in 1849. He was a lawyer, Justice, trustee of the Michigan Asylum and held other positions. He was a Republican, later a Prohibitionist. He was in the banking business. Deceased.

ABRAHAM EDWARDS

Member of the Legislative Council from Wayne County, 1824-5 to 1828-9; and from Lenawee County, 1830-1. Was born at Springfield, N. Y., Nov. 17, 1781, and became a physician in 1803. He became an army surgeon in 1804; served as such in Indiana and Ohio until 1812; was member of the Ohio Legislature in 1811; was ordered to Detroit in 1812 and took charge of the medical department of the army; in 1813-14 had charge of the quartermaster stores at Pittsburgh, Pa., with the rank of Major; returned to Detroit in 1815, and was president of the Board of Trustees in 1816-17; was aid of Gov. Cass in 1823, with the rank of Colonel; in 1831 became U. S. Register of the land office of western Michigan, and held it until 1849. He was President of the Territorial Council of Michigan from 1824 to 1831. He died at Kalamazoo in 1860.

ADELBERT D. EDWARDS

Representative from the Third District of Houghton County, 1907-8 to 1917-18. Was born at Lincklaen, Chenango County, N. Y., June 15, 1856, of American parentage. He received his early education in the district schools and at the age of sixteen taught district school and worked on a farm during vacations. He also attended the Cincinnatus Academy, Cortland Normal School, N. Y., and the Michigan State Normal College and graduated from the latter in 1882. After graduation he went to the copper country to teach but soon gave up teaching for bookkeeping and was chief clerk with the Atlantic Mining Co. for twenty-two years. He was identified with the public schools for many years and held the offices of Township Clerk, Treasurer, Justice of the Peace, Supervisor, many years as chairman of the board, and County Commissioner of Schools; a Mason, having taken all of the degrees excepting the thirty-third. In politics a Republican.

ARTHUR EDWARDS

Representative from Wayne County, 1855-6. Was born in Fort Wayne, Ind., in 1805, and came to Michigan about 1815. He was a vessel builder and master

mariner, by profession, and holding the rank of Quartermaster during the rebellion
he did notable service in building steamers to facilitate the operations of Sherman
and Grant, for which he was formally thanked in the official reports and given the
honorary rank of Brevet-Colonel. Col. Edwards was devoted to the Methodist
Episcopal Church. In politics he was a Republican. He died in 1885.

EDWARD E. EDWARDS

Representative from Newaygo County, 1881-2; and Senator from the Twenty-
second District, 1885-6 and 1887-8. Was born in Broome County, N. Y., Feb. 20,
1845. He was of Welsh descent, his father a pioneer of Oceana County but moved
to Missouri where he died. Judge Edwards was admitted to the bar, March, 1870
and practiced in Pentwater until his removal to Fremont in 1875 and to White
Cloud soon after. He became a lawyer in 1870. Previously he was in various
employments, and held many local and federal offices. A Republican in politics.

GEORGE F. EDWARDS

Representative from Berrien County, 1877-8; and member of the State Board of
Education, 1879-85. Was born in 1843, at Ypsilanti, Mich. He was by profession
a lawyer, having been admitted to practice in 1873.

HENRY D. EDWARDS

Representative from Wayne County, 1873-4. Was born in Nantucket, Mass., Dec.
1, 1838. He received his education in a high school. He was sixteen years at
sea. He was in command of the gunboat Albatross and other vessels four years,
and was especially distinguished as having fired the last hostile shot in the Federal
navy during the Civil War, destroying the last blockade runner at Galveston,
Texas. In 1865 he emigrated to Michigan and engaged in dealing in mill supplies
in Detroit. Deceased.

WILLIAM J. EDWARDS

Representative from Berrien County, 1871-2. Was born at Limerick, N. Y., Mar.
17, 1830. He came to Niles, Mich., in 1855, and was Deputy Postmaster until 1858.
He enlisted as a private in Company "K," 6th Mich. Infantry, in 1864, and was
gradually promoted to Captain, going out of service in August, 1865. From 1870
to 1872 he was a Supervisor; chairman Democratic Committee, 1871-8; City
Treasurer three years; Postmaster under Johnson and in 1887 Postmaster of Niles,
and member Congressional committee, 1876-80.

FRANCIS B. EGAN

Representative from Wayne County, 1885-6. Was born at St. Johns, Newfoundland,
Oct. 13, 1846. He received a common school education at London, Ont., and learned
the printing business at Sarnia, Ont. He settled in Detroit in 1877, and was an
active worker in labor organizations, and held prominent positions in that connection. He was Deputy Commissioner of Labor in 1885-6, and in 1887 was Deputy
Secretary of State. In politics a Republican.

EBENEZER S. EGGLESTON

Representative from Kent County, 1873-4. Was born in Batavia, N. Y., May 12, 1825. He received a common school education. In 1837 he settled in Litchfield, Hillsdale County. In 1851 he removed to Grand Rapids. In 1861 he was appointed Consul to Cadiz, Spain, and remained there four years. He studied law with Lieutenant Governor Gordon, and was admitted to the bar in 1852. He died at Parma, Mich., Aug. 2, 1892.

JAMES EGGLESTON

Representative from Allegan County, 1875-6. Was born in Strongsville, O., Sept. 1, 1836. He received a common school education. He removed to Michigan in 1856 and settled in Allegan County. He was four terms Supervisor of Monterey. By occupation he was a carpenter and joiner; in politics a Republican.

PHILIP EICHHORN

Representative from the First District. St. Clair County, 1903-4 and 1905-6. Was born in Port Huron, Mich., Feb. 1, 1859, of German parents. He was educated in a private school and the Detroit Business College. Married. Mr. Eichhorn was in the postoffice at Port Huron for twelve years, Deputy Collector of Customs four years, and grocery business three years. He engaged in the hotel business for over twelve years, proprietor of the Union Hotel at Port Huron; director of the First National Exchange Bank and vice-president and director of the Port Huron Building and Loan Association.

HENRY J. EIKHOFF

Representative from the First District of Wayne County (Detroit), 1897-8 and 1899-1900. Was born of German parents, in the city of Detroit. Oct. 19, 1861, where he acquired his education. At the age of eighteen years he began the trade of metal pol'sher. He was always an ardent worker in the union labor organizations, being one of the organizers of "The Metal Polishers' International Union of America;" was a member of the national executive board four years, and became president of its national organization; one of the two members of the House who were recognized as labor union men. In politics a Republican.

GEORGE J. EISENMANN

Representative from Monroe County, 1913-14. Was born in Bedford Township, Monroe County, Mich., Oct. 25, 1860, of German parentage, receiving his education in the district schools. He was married Dec. 14, 1887, to Dora E. Willard. He always engaged in farming. He was a member of the School Board, and also held the office of Township Clerk. In politics a Democrat.

JOHN C. EISENMANN

Representative from Monroe County, 1881-2. Was born in Bedford, Mich., Mar. 30, 1847. He received a common school education. By occupation he was a farmer; in politics a Democrat.

ALVAH D. ELDRED

Representative from Calhoun County, 1885-6 and 1887-8. Was born at Canadice, N. Y., Feb. 29, 1832. He came to Michigan in 1852. He went to Macomb County to learn the carpenter and joiner's trade. In 1885 he removed to Tekonsha, where he began working at his trade as a builder, but for some time, though carrying on his trade, he was a partner in a firm dealing in agricultural implements. Mr. Eldred was Justice of the Peace two years, Highway Commissioner thirteen years, and twice President of the village of Tekonsha. He was elected to the House as a Republican.

CALEB ELDRED

Representative from Kalamazoo County, 1837. Was born in Pownal, Vt., Apr. 6, 1781, and was of English ancestry. With a common school education he became a teacher, and a resident of Otsego County, N. Y., in 1803, where he was a farmer, Justice, president of the County Agricultural Society several years, and a member of the New York Assembly. He settled at Comstock, Mich., in 1830, and later removed to a large farm on Climax prairie. He was the first Supervisor in Kalamazoo and Comstock; County Judge; and for more than thirty years president of the board of trustees of Kalamazoo College. A Democrat until 1854, he was then a Republican.

FOSS OSCAR ELDRED

Senator, 1921-2 and 1923—, from the Eighteenth District, comprising the counties of Ionia and Montcalm. Was born in Van Buren County, Mich., Mar. 15, 1884, of American parentage. He received his education at Albion College, State Normal College and University of Michigan. He was engaged in teaching for seven years, four years of such time in Michigan State Normal College as principal of training school. He is at present time practicing law, being a member of the firm of Hawley, Eldred, Gemuend. Mr. Eldred is married and has one son. In politics he is a Republican.

JAMES B. ELDREDGE

Representative from Macomb County, 1863-4. Was born at Mt. Clemens, Mich., Nov. 25, 1836. He graduated at the Michigan University in 1855. He studied law and was admitted to practice in 1858. He was Prosecuting Attorney of Macomb County four terms. He was Judge of Probate from 1877 to 1885. As a member of the firm of Eldredge & Spier he engaged in law practice at Mt. Clemens. In politics he was a Democrat. He died at Mt. Clemens, Feb. 18, 1901.

NATHANIEL B. ELDREDGE

Representative from Lapeer County, 1848; and member of Congress, 1883-5 and 1885-7. Was born at Auburn, N. Y., Mar. 28, 1813. He received an academic education; studied and practiced medicine fifteen years; then studied and practiced law thirty years; and finally settled down to farming. While a resident of Lapeer County, he was elected engrossing and enrolling clerk of the State Senate in 1845; and Judge of Probate in 1852. Having entered the Union army, June 18, 1861, he served as Captain and Major of the 7th regiment, and Lieutenant Colonel of the 11th regiment, Mich. Infantry, in the war of the rebellion. Having removed to Adrian in 1865, he was elected Sheriff of Lenawee County in 1874. In 1882 he was elected Representative to the Forty-eighth Congress on the Union ticket. He died at Adrian, Nov. 27, 1893.

ROBERT P. ELDREDGE

Secretary of State, 1842-6; and Senator from the First District, 1847-8. Was born at Greenwich, N. Y. With an ordinary education at the age of seventeen he commenced the study of law at Hamilton, N. Y. In 1826 he came to Michigan, taught school a short time in Detroit, studied law at Pontiac and taught school. Then he was a clerk at Mt. Clemens, devoting leisure time to his studies, and in 1828 was admitted, then the only lawyer in Macomb County. He soon had a lucrative practice. After that he devoted himself strictly to his profession, refusing all offers of public office. He was a prominent Mason from 1847. He died in 1884.

JOHN ELLENWOOD

Delegate from the Fifth District to the First Constitutional Convention in 1835; and Representative from Oakland County, 1835 and 1836. Was born in New Hampshire, Sept. 17, 1777. He came to West Bloomfield, Mich., in 1823. He was appointed a Justice in 1827, and held that position through life. By occupation he was a surveyor, in politics a Democrat. He surveyed nearly all the roads in his section and after his death the office was discontinued of County Surveyor. He was the first Postmaster from 1831 to 1856, and Supervisor nine years. He died May 9, 1856.

ADAM ELLIOTT

Delegate from Barry County to the Constitutional Convention of 1867; and a Representative from Barry County, 1869-70. Was born in England, Oct. 31, 1815; came to New York in 1836, and to Barry County, Mich., in 1843. By occupation he was a farmer, in politics a Republican. He was Supervisor of Barry Township nine years.

MARCUS D. ELLIOTT

Representative from Oakland County, 1877-8. Was born in Montgomery County, N. Y., Jan. 19, 1827. With a common school education he came to Holly, Mich., in 1846 and the next year settled on a farm in Rose Township. In 1861 he enlisted in the 8th Mich. Battery, 1st artillery volunteers, was promoted to the grade of Captain, and took part in many pitched battles. In politics he was a Republican.

ADOLPHUS A. ELLIS

Attorney General, 1891-3 and 1893-5. Was born in Vermontville, Eaton County, Mich., Apr. 5, 1848. In his early days he assisted his father on the farm in summer and attended the district school in winter. The fall and winter of 1864-5 he attended the Union School at Charlotte. In March, 1865, he enlisted in the Fifth Mich. Cavalry, but by reason of his age and size, he failed to pass muster. He went West in 1866, and was gone from Michigan three years, one year of which was spent in school, and the other two in managing a large farm. Returning to Michigan he spent three years at Olivet College, after which, for about five years, he was engaged in·teaching, spending his spare time and vacations in the study of law. In January, 1876, he was admitted to the bar at Ionia, and engaged in active practice of law. In politics he was a Republican prior to 1877, at which time he joined the National Labor Party and in 1880 was a delegate to the Chicago Labor Convention. In 1884 he was elected Prosecuting Attorney of Ionia County, and re-elected in 1886. In 1888 he was the candidate for Attorney General of the State on the Democrat and Greenback tickets, but was defeated. In the spring of 1890 he was elected Mayor of Ionia, and re-elected in 1891. He was renominated by the Industrial and Democratic parties for Attorney General, for the term of 1891-2, to which·he was elected; was renominated in 1892 on the People's party and Democratic tickets, and elected. He died at Grand Rapids, Apr. 25, 1921.

EDWARD D. ELLIS

Senator from the Second District, 1835-7; Delegate from the Second District to the Constitutional Convention of 1835; and Delegate from Monroe County to the First Convention of Assent, 1836. He emigrated from New England to Monroe, Mich., at an early day, where he resided many years, and published and edited a newspaper. He was a man of culture and foresight, and to him as a Legislator is given the credit of providing for the establishment of libraries, by appropriating money received from fines for non-performance of military duty. He died at Detroit in 1848.

GEORGE EDWIN ELLIS

Representative from the First District, Kent County, 1905-6. Was born at Belleville, Jefferson County, N. Y., Dec. 22, 1864, of American parentage. He received his education at the Union Academy, graduating in 1881, and at the Syracuse University from which he graduated with the class of 1885. Mr. Ellis was identified with the base ball interests for several years in Michigan, and gained an enviable reputation among the patrons of the great American game as manager and owner of the Grand Rapids Western League team. For several years he was an extensive dealer in stocks and grain; owner of two farms and considerable real estate in Grand Rapids. In politics an active Republican.

MYRON H. ELLIS

Representative from Wayne County, 1883-4. Was born at Saline, Mich., Nov. 24, 1841. In 1862 he enlisted in the 5th Mich. Cavalry and rose to the rank of Captain. After leaving the service he kept a livery stable at Ypsilanti, and was Deputy Sheriff. He engaged then in farming in Huron, Wayne County, and also in the manufacture of lumber and charcoal. A Democrat in politics.

CHARLES C. ELLSWORTH

Representative from Montcalm and other counties, 1853-4; and member of Congress, 1877-9. Was born in West Berkshire, Vt., Jan. 29, 1824. He was educated at the Bakersfield Academy, came to Michigan at an early day, and read law with his uncle, Josiah Turner, at Howell, teaching school winters. In 1849 he was appointed Prosecuting Attorney of Livingston County. In 1851 he removed to Greenville. In 1863 he was appointed Paymaster of Volunteers, and held that position until the close of the war. He was four years Prosecuting Attorney of Montcalm County. He was a Democrat until 1856, then a Republican. He was in the active practice of his profession at Greenville in 1887.

ELISHA ELY

Representative from Allegan County, 1835-7; and member of the Board of Regents of the University of Michigan, 1852-4. Was born in West Springfield, Mass., Apr. 27, 1784. He removed to Allegan, Mich., in 1833 from Rochester, N. Y., and founded the village of Allegan. He made an honorable record in the War of 1812, and as a resident of Michigan occupied many public positions of trust and honor, including those of Judge, Legislator, and Regent of the State University, holding the last position from Jan. 1, 1852 until his death at Allegan, Nov. 2, 1854.

HEMAN B. ELY

Representative from Marquette County, 1853-4. Was born in Rochester, N. Y., Mar. 15, 1815, and was the son of Judge Elisha Ely who founded Allegan, Mich., in 1833. He was a graduate of Hamilton College, N. Y. He studied law and commenced practice, but in 1849 left the profession to enter upon the construction of the telegraph line from Buffalo westward, and between Pittsburg and Philadelphia. He organized and began the construction of the Cleveland, Painesville & Ashtabula Railroad, the first section of the present L. S. & M. S. railroad. In 1852, with his brothers, S. P., G. H. and John F. Ely, he engaged in building a railroad from Marquette to the iron ore mines, then undeveloped. The country was an unbroken wildnerness, the Sault Ste Marie lock and canal not built, and great obstacles were encountered. The project was then deemed almost impracticable and somewhat visionary, but he persevered until, just on the eve of its completion, he died suddenly at Marquette, Oct. 14, 1856, and was buried at Rochester, N. Y. In politics he was a Democrat.

RALPH ELY

Senator from the Twenty-sixth District, 1873-4; and Auditor General, 1875-9. Was born in Marshall, N. Y., July 10, 1820, and died at Redmond, Mich., Apr. 12, 1883. He was brought up on a farm in Stockton, N. Y., receiving a district school education. At the age of twenty-one removed to Indiana, and remained two years, and then returned to his father's home for three years. He came to Michigan in 1846, settling at Ronald, Ionia County. In 1854 he removed to Alma, Gratiot County, and until 1860 was engaged in farming, lumbering and mercantile business. He built the first saw and grist mills in Alma, and was very liberal in aiding destitute settlers. He entered the service as Captain of Co. C, 8th Mich Infantry, and was promoted to Major, Lieutenant Colonel and Colonel of his regiment. In 1865 he was commissioned Brigadier General, and with his brigade was the first to enter Petersburgh, and received its surrender, by order of General Grant. He took part in more than thirty battles, and was not mustered out until June, 1866. He returned to Alma and engaged in lumbering and farming. In early life he was a Democrat, but became a Republican in 1854. In 1881 he engaged in lumbering and farming in Emmet County, near Cross Village, where he died.

TOWNSEND A. ELY

Senator, 1905-6, and 1907-8, from the Nineteenth District, comprising the counties of Clinton and Gratiot; and State Highway Commissioner, 1909-13. Was born in Wabash, Ind., Aug. 27, 1843, of English parentage. He came to Alma, Mich., in April, 1854, and received his education in the district schools of that place. Mr. Ely entered the army as a private of Co. C, Eighth Mich. Inf., enlisting at Arcadia, Feb. 25, 1865, and was commissioned Second Lieutenant, Apr. 25, 1865. At the close of the war he returned to Alma and engaged in farming. He served three terms as President of Alma village and was Postmaster during both the Hayes and Harrison administrations. In politics a Republican. He was appointed State Highway Commissioner, July 1, 1909.

LUTHER G. EMERSON

Representative from Ontonagon County, 1867. His postoffice address was Rockland. (Further data not obtainable).

PHILIP H. EMERSON

Senator from the Eleventh District, 1871-2; and from the Eighth District, 1873-4. Was born in Danby, Vt., Feb. 15, 1834. He was educated at the Troy Conference Academy, at Poultney, Vt. He studied law and was admitted to the bar in 1862. The same year he located at Battle Creek, Mich., and commenced practice. He resigned as Senator before extra session of 1874 and was succeeded by Wm. F. Hewitt. He was City Attorney from 1865 to 1873; trustee and president of School Board from 1868 to 1873; and U. S. Associate Justice of the Supreme Court of Utah from Mar. 16, 1873, to Mar. 17, 1885. He died at Ogden, Utah, Mar. 19, 1889.

RICHARD EMERSON ·

Representative, 1921-2 and 1923—, from the Clare District, comprising the counties of Clare, Gladwin, and Roscommon. Was born at Peterboro, Ont., Nov. 11, 1873, of Irish parents. He received his education in the public schools at Fraserville, Ont. Mr. Emerson is a farmer. He held the office of Supervisor of Grant Township from 1908 to 1918, being chairman of Board of Supervisors from 1913 to 1918. In 1918 he was appointed as member of Board of County Road Commissioners, which office he now holds. In politics he is a Republican.

JARED H. EMERY

Representative from the First District of Lapeer County, 1867-8. His postoffice address was Burnside. (Further data not obtainable).

JEP P. C. EMMONS

Representative from Wayne County, 1848. Was born in Washington County, N. Y., in 1818. His early education was partly academic. He came to Detroit as a merchant's clerk about 1836, studied law, and was admitted to practice in 1840. He was a man of marked brilliancy, and a personal favorite with the men of the time, especially with Gov. Mason. He served as Prosecuting Attorney of the

County of Wayne, 1855-7, and member of the School Board, 1853-4; was also clerk of the House of Representatives in 1838. He was in early life a Democrat, but subsequently a Republican. He became a resident of Florida after the war, and was for a time Attorney General of that State, and died there in 1877, his remains being interred at Detroit.

G. RAYMOND EMPSON

Representative from Delta County, 1915-16. Was born at Manchester, England, in 1872. He was educated in the Sault Ste. Marie High School and the Detroit College of Law. He married and was a resident of Gladstone where he engaged in the practice of law. In politics a Republican.

ALBERT J. ENGEL

Senator, 1921-2, from the Twenty-seventh District, comprising the counties of Antrim, Benzie, Grand Traverse, Kalkaska, Leelanau, Missaukee and Wexford. Was born at New Washington, O., Jan. 1, 1888, of Alsatian parentage. His parents came to America in 1871 after the Franco-Prussian War, moving to Grand Traverse County, Mich., in 1900. He was raised on a farm in Mayfield Township, where his father still resides. He worked in logging camps and saw mills, earning enough money to pay his way to Chicago and worked his way through school, graduating from Northwestern University in 1910. He engaged in the practice of law and in 1917 was elected Prosecuting Attorney of Missaukee County; served as Prosecuting Attorney until May, 1917, when he enlisted and joined the first training camp at Fort Sheridan, Ill. He was commissioned a First Lieutenant at Fort Sheridan and promoted to Captain in France. He was transferred overseas Oct. 1, 1917, and assigned to general headquarters under General John J. Pershing, and for five months served as Divisional Personnel Adjutant of the 32nd Division. While with the army of occupation in Germany he wrote the Divisional poem "Where the Thirty-Second Arrow Pierced the Line." He returned to the United States in August, 1919, and was honorably discharged, Sept. 4, 1919. He was re-elected Prosecuting Attorney while in France. Mr. Engel is married. In politics he is a Republican.

CHARLES ENGEL

Representative from Sanilac County, 1909-10. Was born at Gross Methling, Mechlenburg Schwerin. He attended school at Dargun, Germany, and night school at Detroit. At the age of twenty-one he emigrated to America, coming to Detroit, Mich., on Nov. 20, 1873. While in Detroit, he attended nights schools during the years 1876-7, and in 1878 settled in Delaware Township, Sanilac County, converting a wild piece of land into a nice farm. He held the office of Township Treasurer of Delaware Township in 1865 and 1866. In the year 1888 he was elected Supervisor of said township and held this office for eleven successive years. In 1894 he was elected chairman of the Board of Supervisors of Sanilac County; was appointed U. S. Census Enumerator in 1900, and also acted in that capacity at the last State census. In politics a Republican.

HIERONYMUS ENGLEMANN

Representative from Macomb County, 1885-6 and 1887-8. Was born at Baden, Germany, Sept. 29, 1844. He became a resident of Michigan in 1847, and served in the Civil War as member of Co. I, 3d Mich. Infantry. He was four years in college in Milwaukee, Wis. In 1875 he was appointed Postmaster at Center Line, which office he resigned to become eligible as member of the House.

JEHIEL ENOS

Representative from Berrien County, 1848 and 1857-8. Was born in Norwich, N. Y., Oct. 24, 1799. He received a common school education and at the age of eighteen became a teacher. In 1825 he came to Ann Arbor, Mich., where he remained and followed surveying as a Deputy to Lucius Lyon. He helped survey Berrien County and settled there soon after, 1830. He was the first permanent settler in St. Joseph, but later took up wild land in Royalton. He was a Representative in 1848 as a Democrat, and in 1857 as a Republican. He was also for years a Supervisor and County Surveyor. He died June 5, 1883.

MORGAN ENOS

Representative from Berrien County, 1859. Was born in Tompkins County, N. Y., Apr. 26, 1804. He came to Pipestone, Berrien County, Mich., in 1836, bought a farm, and engaged in the practice of medicine. He was successful. In politics he was a Whig until 1854, then a Republican. He died Sept. 26, 1868.

OLE ERICKSON

Representative from Delta County, 1905-6 and 1907-8. Was born in Norway, Aug. 13, 1851. He received his education in the common schools of Norway. He came to America in 1870, locating at Fairbault, Minn., where he engaged as brakeman on a construction train during the winter of 1870 and 1871. He went to Dakota in the spring of 1871, roamed from place to place, and finally located at Ford River, Delta County, Mich., in 1873. He worked for the Ford River Lumber Company in different capacities until 1884, when he started in the grocery and lumber business at Escanaba; became a successful business man, and senior member of the firm of Erickson & Bissell, which was established in 1886. Married. In politics a Republican. He was mayor of Escanaba for two terms.

JAMES ERSKINE

Representative from Sanilac County, 1857 and 1863-4. Was born in Aroostook County, Me., Jan. 21, 1824. He came to Michigan in 1854, and was a merchant and lumberman. He lived in Sanilac County many years but in 1887 was a resident of Rogers City, Presque Isle County, and Judge of Probate of that county. He was a Democrat in politics.

JOHN PAXTON ESPIE

Representative from Clinton County, 1923—. Was born in Moscow Township, Hillsdale County, February 14, 1881, on the farm on which his grandparents settled in 1836. His early education was acquired in the district school, located on his father's farm, and in the Hanover High School; later he graduated from the Armstrong Business College, of Hillsdale. He was married to Edith Sprague in 1904 and they have three sons. In 1909 he located on a farm in Eagle and has served four terms as Supervisor of his township. He has also held the offices of director of Farmers' Elevator Co., of Grand Ledge, and director of the Clinton County Agricultural Association, is a member of the Methodist Church and prominent in Masonic and I. O. O. F. fraternities. Mr. Espie is a Republican.

JOHN S. ESTABROOK

Representative from Saginaw County, 1879-80 and 1881-2. Was born at Alden, N. Y., Jan. 22, 1826. He was a descendant on his mother's side of John Alden of pilgrim fame. He received a common school education at Alden, N. Y., settled at St. Clair, Mich., in 1845, and removed to East Saginaw in 1852. At first he was a farmer, but later largely interested in lumber, salt, and lake commerce. He held many local offices, including Mayor, and was an enterprising, able man.

JOSEPH ESTABROOK

Member of the Board of Regents of the University of Michigan, 1870-8; and Superintendent of Public Instruction, 1887-9 and 1889-91. Was born in Bath, N. H., July 3, 1820. In 1843 his parents moved to Western New York, where they resided four years, moving to Michigan in the fall of 1838. He prepared for college at Tecumseh, in what was then a branch of the Michigan University, and took his college course in Oberlin, O., and taught winters and worked vacations to obtain the necessary means to pursue his studies. He spent seven winters in teaching district schools in and near Clinton, Lenawee County, taught select school two years and a half in the village of Clinton, and was three years in charge of what was then known as the Tecumseh Institute. In the spring of 1853 he took charge of the public schools of Ypsilanti, and remained there fourteen years and a half; then went to East Saginaw, organized the public schools in that city and remained in charge five years; was then appointed principal of the Normal School at Ypsilanti, of which he was the honored and successful head nine years. In 1880 he became a professor in Olivet College. The Republicans in 1870 elected him Regent of the University, which position he filled creditably for eight years. Prof. Estabrook was the first teacher in Michigan to use the word-method of teaching reading, and his love of study kept him abreast of the times in all the methods of school work; was also a minister of the Gospel. During the Civil War he was connected with the Christian Commission.

FREE ESTEE

Representative from the counties of Isabella and Clare, 1885-6. Was born on a farm in Coe, Mich., Dec. 12, 1856. His early education was obtained at a log school house. At the age of sixteen he began teaching school, which profession he followed four years, teaching winters and summers, and attending school during the spring and fall terms. He graduated from the law department of the State University in 1879. He practiced law at Greenville, O., for one and a half years. He returned to Mt. Pleasant, Mich., in 1881, held the office of Justice, School Inspector, and secretary of Board of School Examiners, and was one of the directors of the First National Bank of Mt. Pleasant.

SAMUEL ETHERIDGE

Senator from the Seventh District, 1839-40. Was born at Williamston, Mass., Apr. 15, 1788. He received a common school education and excelled in mathematics.

He taught school for a time, then learned the trade of millwright and machinist. He came to Michigan in 1835, and settled at Coldwater. In 1844 he removed to a farm in Quincy. As a millwright he employed sometimes seventy-five men, and built large mills at Ypsilanti, Saline, Leonidas, Marshall and Allegan. He was elected to various offices. He was a Democrat. He died at Quincy, Mich., Feb. 18, 1864.

CHARLES EVANS

Representative from the First District of Lenawee County, 1917-18 to 1923—. Was born at Forden, Montgomeryshire, Wales, Aug. 14, 1859, of English and Welsh descent. He married and came to the United States in July, 1880. He worked on a farm for a time and at contract work on drains. He is the owner of a good farm and is engaged in the livestock shipping business. Mr. Evans is a stockholder and director of the Lenawee County Savings Bank of Adrian, and director of the Tecumseh Co-operative Association. In politics he is a Republican. He has held various township offices.

M. L. EVENS

Representative from Branch County, 1915-16. Was born in Butler Township, Branch County, Mich., Feb. 24, 1865, of American parentage. He was educated in the district schools and Hillsdale College. By occupation he was a commercial sales-man for the Lamb Wire Fence Company and the Michigan Wire Fence Company, of Adrian. He was married, Dec. 31, 1890, to Kittie D. Willard. Fraternally a member of Tyre Lodge No. 18, F. & A. M., Temple Chapter 21, R. A. M. Mt. Moriah Council No. 6, R. & S. M., Jacobs Commandery No. 10, Coldwater Lodge 1023, B. P. O. E., and Butler Grange No. 18. In politics a Republican.

PHILANDER EWELL

Representative from Macomb County, 1855-6. Was born in Middlebury, N. Y., Mar. 3, 1809. He was brought up a farmer and received a common school and academical education. In 1820 he settled on a farm in Shelby, Mich., where he served as Supervisor in 1849-50. In politics he was a Democrat. In 1869 he sold his farm and removed to Rochester, Mich., where he resided, and owned and ran the Stony Creek Woolen Mills.

CHARLES EWERS

Representative from Wayne County, 1881-2. Was born in Detroit, Oct. 17, 1843. He enlisted in the 1st Mich. Infantry in 1861, was captured at the Battle of Bull Run and held a prisoner one year, when he was paroled. He began the study of medicine, graduating at the Detroit Medical College in 1873, and practiced in Detroit. He was City Physician two years, was Alderman of the second ward in 1876; re-elected in 1877-9, and was president of the Common Council.

ALEXANDER EWING

Representative from Washtenaw County, 1853-4. Was born in Ireland, Apr. 5, 1819. He came to America in 1833, and graduated as a physician at Geneva, N. Y., medical college. He settled at Lima, Mich., in 1840, but soon removed to Dexter.

During the war he was surgeon of the 13th Mich. Infantry, and was in charge of hospitals at Nashville and Lookout Mountain. He died Sept. 17, 1879.

ALVIN E. EWING

Representative from the county of Hillsdale, 1893-4. Was born in Jackson, O., Nov. 10, 1864. He is the son of H. McEwing, of Co. D, 2d Mich. Inf., Vol., and with his parents came to Michigan at the close of the war, locating on the farm in Woodbridge Township. His general school education was closed by a two years' course at Hillsdale College; after which he taught a few terms and then entered the Michigan University in 1890, from which he graduated in the law department with the class of 1892. Mr. Ewing was married, Apr. 5, 1893, to Miss Carlotta Bailey, of Grand Rapids. In politics a Republican.

WILLIAM S. EWING

Representative from the First District of Marquette County, 1911-12, 1915-16 to 1921-2. Was born at Marquette, Mich., July 13, 1869, of Irish and Scotch parentage. He was educated in the public schools. He served as Township Clerk, Justice of the Peace, secretary of the School Board thirty years and Supervisor twenty-two years. Mr. Ewing is married and has been engaged in farming and the implement business. He is a Mason and a member of the Patrons of Husbandry, and No. 405 B. P. O. E., of Marquette. In politics he is a Republican.

MERTON W. FAIRBANK

Representative from the Second District, Genesee County, 1905-6 and 1907-8. Was born in the town of Sweden, Monroe County, N. Y., Sept. 10, 1847, of American parents. He acquired his education in the district schools of New York State. At the age of sixteen he enlisted in the army, serving one year and three months in the Third New York Cavalry. He came to Michigan in 1867 and settled on a farm in Genesee County. Married. He held the offices of Township Treasurer, Supervisor, acting as chairman of the Board of Supervisors one year, a member of the building committee for the new court house. In politics a strong Republican.

EARL FAIRBANKS

Representative from the Wexford District, 1903-4 and 1905-6; Senator, 1907-8 and 1909-10, from the Twenty-sixth District, comprising the counties of Lake, Manistee, Mason and Oceana. Was born at Fillmore Center, Allegan County, Mich., July 19, 1860, of English parents. He attended the district schools until fourteen years of age. He taught school, worked in the lumber woods and on the railroad until he secured enough money to pay expenses in the medical department of the University of Michigan, from which he graduated in 1888. He established himself at once in the practice of medicine at Luther. He was Postmaster at Luther, President of the village, chairman of the Republican County Committee and president of the School Board; was alternate delegate to the Republican National Convention at St. Louis, 1896, and delegate to the convention of 1900 at Philadelphia from the Ninth Congressional District. Married.

EBENEZER W. FAIRFIELD

Representative from Lenawee County, 1844. Was born at Pittsfield, Mass., in 1812. By profession he was a lawyer, in politics a Democrat. He came to Ann Arbor in 1835, but shortly removed to Adrian, where he practiced his profession until his death in August, 1845.

EDMUND B. FAIRFIELD

Senator from the Fourteenth District, 1857-8; and Lieutenant Governor, 1859-61. Was born in Parkersburg, W. Va., Aug. 7, 1821. By occupation he was a teacher and minister, in politics a Republican. He was a resident of several states up to 1848, when he became president of Hillsdale College, which he filled for twenty-one years. Among other positions, he was principal of the State Normal School at Indiana, Pa., chancellor of the University of Nebraska for six years; pastor of the Congregational Church at Mansfield, O., 1870-5; and pastor of the Congregational Church at Manistee, Mich., after 1882. In all positions, he held a high place in public estimation, and in the early days of the Republican party, was an eloquent and effective speaker. He received the degrees of A. B. and A. M. from Oberlin, LL. D. from Madison University, N. Y., and D. D. from Denison University.

JOHN ARCHIBALD FAIRLIE

Delegate in the Constitutional Convention of 1907-8 from the Tenth District, Washtenaw County. Was born in Glasgow, Scotland, in 1872, and came to the United States in 1881, living for some years in the State of Florida. He attended Harvard College, and was graduated with the degree of A. B. in 1895. He then pursued post-graduate studies in history, government and economics at Harvard and Columbia Universities, receiving the degree of Ph. D. from the latter in 1898. In 1899 he was secretary to the committee on canals of New York State, appointed by Governor Roosevelt. In 1900 he was lecturer in municipal administration at Columbia University; and later in the same year was appointed to the chair of Administrative Law in the University of Michigan. Mr. Fairlie has published numerous articles and books on political and economic questions. He has served as Secretary of the Michigan Political Science Association, and the League of Michigan Municipalities, a member of the executive council of the American Political Science Association and of the council of the National Civil Service Reform League, and one of the board of editors of the *American Political Science Review*.

DELOS FALL

Superintendent of Public Instruction, 1901-3; and Delegate from the Ninth District in the Constitutional Convention of 1907-8. Was born in Ann Arbor, Mich., Jan. 29, 1848, the son of Benjamin and Ann M. (Bassett) Falls. His early life was spent on a farm near Ann Arbor, his educational training beginning in the district schools near his home, where later he was employed as teacher. His education was continued in the Ann Arbor High School and later in the University of Michigan, from which he graduated in 1875, receiving the degree of B. S. Seven years later he was granted the degree of M. S. upon examination. His professional work began in 1872, when he became teacher of science in the Ann Arbor High School. He was principal of the Flint High School from 1875 to 1878, from which position he was called to Albion College where he was head of the department of natural science until 1887 after which he held the chair of chemistry and the directorship of the McMillan chemical laboratory. In 1898, as a recognition of his twenty years of service, Albion College conferred upon him the degree of Sc. D. Mr. Fall traveled extensively, especially in South America. He was the author of numerous magazine articles on scientific subjects, and conducted much original research in his chosen lines, chemistry and sanitary science, being the author of a "Laboratory Manual in Inductive Chemistry." He was an active worker in teachers' institutes and farmers' clubs and institutes, and prominently identified with both the National and State Teachers' Association, having been president of the latter in 1897. He was a member of the American Association for the Advancement of Science, the American Public Health Association, the National Conference of Boards of Health, and vice-president of the North Central Association of Colleges and Secondary Schools. He held positions of public trust, both municipal and state. For eight years he served on the Albion city Board of Education, and from 1894 to 1896 on the City Council. For twelve years, from 1889 to 1901, he was a member of the Michigan State Board of Health, and his lectures and writings on public hygiene while a member of this board have had much to do with making the State and local health service in Michigan second to none in the world. He died February 13, 1921.

ISAAC A. FANCHER

Representative from Midland, Isabella, and Clare, 1873-4; and Senator from the Seventy-sixth District, 1875-6. Was born in Florida, N. Y., Sept. 30, 1833. He was educated at Amsterdam Academy, N. Y.; studied law at the law university at Albany, and was admitted in 1860. In 1863 he emigrated to Michigan and settled in Mt. Pleasant. He was Prosecuting Attorney of Isabella County six years; and chairman of the Republican County Committee six years. He was one of the board of control of the State School at Coldwater.

JOHN D. FARGO

Representative from Montcalm County, 1857-8. Was born in Chautauqua County, N. Y., Nov. 14, 1817. He was a farmer by occupation, a Republican in politics. He resided at Groton, Brown County, Dakota, in 1887. He was Supervisor in Montcalm County. He came to Michigan in 1838.

EDWIN FARMER

Representative from Livingston County, 1907-8 to 1913-14. Was born in Stockbridge Township, Ingham County, May 28, 1862, of American parents. He received his education in the district schools, Michigan State Normal College and Devlin's Business College of Jackson. Occupation a farmer. He lived in Ingham County until 1889 when he removed to Unadilla, Livingston County. He was married to Minnie L. Westfall in 1889. He held the office of Township Treasurer of Stockbridge Township, Ingham County, and was Supervisor of Unadilla Township, Livingston County, and chairman of the Board of Supervisors; and represented Livingston County before the State Board of Equalization in 1906. In politics a Democrat.

JOHN FARMER

Representative from Ingham County, 1833-4. Was born Feb. 14, 1827, at Redmond's Corners, N. Y. He removed to Ann Arbor in 1836, and from there to

Stockbridge, Ingham County, in 1839. He worked at manual labor from his youth. He received a common school education; principal business, farming.

WILLIAM S. FARMER

Delegate from Berrien County to the Constitutional Convention of 1867. Was born in Montgomery County, N. Y., May 24, 1815. He attended common schools and for eight years was clerk until 1839. He opened a store at Fultonville, N. Y., and carried on the business nine years. In 1838 he removed to Berrien County, purchased a farm of two thousand acres, and also acted as a land broker. In religion he was a Methodist, in politics a Republican.

ELON FARNSWORTH

Member of the Legislative Council from Wayne County, 1834-5; Attorney General, 1843-5; and member of the Board of Regents of the University of Michigan, 1846-58. Was born at Woodstock, Vt., Feb. 2, 1799. He was well educated in New England schools, came to Detroit in 1822, studied law with Judge Sibley, and went into practice. In company with Judge Goodwin he had a large professional business. From 1836 to 1842 he was Chancellor of the State, and resigned from ill health. Chancellor Kent said of him: "The administration of justice in equity in Michigan under Chancellor Farnsworth was enlightened and correct and does distinguished honor to the State." He was the Democratic candidate for Governor in 1839; was a director of the Michigan Central Railroad for twenty years, and president of the Detroit Savings Bank from 1849 to 1877; a prominent Episcopalian. Closely identified with the interests of Michigan at an early day, conscientious in the performance of every duty, he is entitled to a high place among Michigan pioneers. He died in Detroit, Mar. 24, 1877.

AUGUSTINE W. FARR

Representative from Manistee County, 1877-8; and Senator, 1901-2, 1903-4 and 1905-6, from the Twenty-sixth District, comprising the counties of Benzie, Lake, Manistee, Mason and Oceana. Was born in North Hudson, Essex County, N. Y., July 29, 1847. He came to Michigan with his parents in 1854 and spent five years in the public schools of Grand Rapids. Mr. Farr resided at Onekama after 1870, and engaged in the mercantile business and the manufacture of lumber; also interested in farming and real estate. He held various township and village offices. In politics a Republican.

GEORGE ALEXANDER FARR

Senator from Ottawa and Muskegon counties, 1879-80 and 1881-2; and member of the Board of Regents of the University of Michigan, 1896-1904. Was born in Niagara County, N. Y., July 27, 1842, son of Sylvester Archibald and Julia (Alexander) Farr. He is of English ancestry on his father's side, and of Scotch on his mother's. His early life was spent in a limited attendance at the public schools of Michigan, and in work upon the farm as means of livelihood. He was but nineteen at the outbreak of Civil War, but volunteered his services to the Government, enlisting for the ninety days' service in 1861 in the First. Mich. Inf. At the expiration of this period he went into the regular service, assigned to Battery

M, Fourth U. S. Artillery, with which command he was connected until mustered out as First Sergeant, Apr. 10, 1865. Upon return to civil life he engaged in teaching, at the same time preparing for the Michigan Agricultural College, which he entered and from which he was graduated Bachelor of Science in 1870. He took up the study of the law and was admitted to the Bar at Monroe, Mich., Mar. 30, 1873. He continued in the practice of his profession. He was married Sept. 24, 1879 to Sue C. Slayton. From 1885 and 1891 he was a member of the Board of Trustees of the Northern Michigan Asylum and was Collector of Customs for the district of Michigan from 1897 to 1901. January 11, 1896, he was appointed Regent of the University for the full term in place of Charles H. Hackley, who had been elected to the position but who had failed to qualify. He was a member of the Grand Army of the Republic and of the Michigan Bar Association.

CHARLES H. FARRELL

Representative from the First District of Kalamazoo County, 1907-8. Was born at Saginaw, Mich., May 18, 1873. He received his education in the Saginaw public schools and Ann Arbor High School, attended the University of Michigan graduating with the class of 1898 and received the degree of P. B. Later he was a student in the law department of the University of Michigan but was admitted to the bar before completing the course. He was a successful educator, having been Superintendent of Schools at Zeeland and Nashville; was a member of the law firm of Frost and Farrell at Kalamazoo. A Republican in politics.

NELSON G. FARRIER

Representative, 1917-18 to 1923—, from Presque Isle District, comprising the counties of Crawford, Montmorency, Oscoda, Otsego and Presque Isle. Was born on a farm in Rust Township, Montmorency County, Mich., in 1887. He was educated in the public schools of that county. When he was fifteen years of age he took charge of his father's farm and managed it until he was twenty-five years old. He also worked in the lumber woods during the winters. He was elected Township Treasurer when he was twenty-two years of age. Two years later he was elected County Treasurer, and held this office two terms. Mr. Farrier is married. In politics he is a Republican.

THOMAS FARRINGTON

Representative from Monroe County, 1837. His postoffice address was London. (Further data not obtainable).

ORLANDO J. FAST

Senator from the Tenth District, 1883-4. Was born Dec. 10, 1838, in Jefferson County, O. Brought up a farmer, graduating at Mt. Union College, O., in 1861. In 1862 he enlisted in 100th Ind. Vol., and became Lieutenant, Captain and Assistant Adjutant General; six times wounded, never a prisoner. He located in the hardware trade at Mendon, Mich.; sold out in 1866, studied law at Kalamazoo and was admitted in 1867. He graduated from law department of the University in 1868, and went into practice at Mendon. He was Prosecuting Attorney, Circuit Court and U. S. Commissioner. In politics a Republican.

THOMAS J. FAXON

Representative from Lenawee County, 1847. Came from the State of New York, about 1836, to Tecumseh, Mich., where he followed the trade of a carpenter, and built the Michigan Exchange Hotel at Brownsville, adjoining Tecumseh. Afterwards he became a resident of Raisin Township and was Supervisor for several terms. For the last ten years of his life he was a resident of Adrian. In politics he was a Whig and Republican. Deceased.

JONATHAN P. FAY

Representative from Wayne County, 1835 and 1836. Was a physician by profession. He died Mar. 12, 1836, during the session of the Legislature, and his funeral was attended by the two Houses in a body. He was succeeded as Representative by Charles Moran. A brief obituary in the Detroit *Free Press*, Mar. 14, says: "Dr. Fay was an old and respected inhabitant of this city, and his loss will be deeply lamented." He is supposed to have shared the prevailing political sentiment of his time, which was of course Democratic.

ALPHEUS FELCH

Representative from Monroe County, 1835-7; Auditor General, 1842; Justice of the Supreme Court, 1842-5; Governor of Michigan, 1846-7; and United States Senator, 1847-53. Was born in Limerick, Me., Sept. 28, 1806. His father was the first merchant in Limerick, a business he followed through life. By the death of both father and mother he was left an orphan at the early age of three, and found a home with his paternal grandfather, where he remained until his death. In 1821 he became a student at Phillips Exeter Academy, subsequently entered Bowdoin College, and graduated in the class of 1827. He at once began the study of law and was admitted to practice at Bangor, Me., in 1830. He began the practice at Houlton, Me., but in 1833, owing to poor health and the severity of the climate, was obliged to seek a new home. He disposed of his library and started to join his friend, Sargent S. Prentiss, at Vicksburg, Miss., but on arriving at Cincinnati was attacked with cholera, and on his recovery, finding his health too much impaired to risk a journey down the Mississippi, he determined to come to Michigan. He first began practice at Monroe, where he remained until 1843, when he removed to Ann Arbor. Early in 1838 he was appointed one of the Bank Commissioners, and in that capacity brought to light and exposed frauds, had the guilty parties prosecuted, and in many cases the banks were closed. In 1842 he was appointed Auditor General of the State, but held the position only a few weeks, when he was appointed one of the Judges of the Supreme Court, in place of Judge Fletcher resigned. In 1845 he was elected by the Democrats, Governor of Michigan, and served through the year 1846. In 1847 he was elected United States Senator, and resigned as Governor, Mar. 4, 1847, when his senatorial term commenced. He served six years as United States Senator, acting on the committee on public lands, and was four years its chairman. In 1853 he was appointed one of the Commissioners to adjust the Spanish and Mexico land claims in California, and was made president of the Commission. In March, 1856, the labors of the commission were satisfactorily finished. In June he returned to Ann Arbor and engaged once more in law practice. In the spring of 1879 he was appointed Tappan law professor in the University, a position he held several years with honor, and voluntarily resigned on account of feeble health and old age. He died June 13, 1896 at Ann Arbor.

GRANT FELLOWS

Attorney General, 1913-15 and 1915-17; and Justice of the Supreme Court, 1916—. Was born in Hudson Township, Lenawee County, Mich., Apr. 13, 1865, of English parentage. He was educated in the district schools and the Hudson High School. Mr. Fellows engaged in the practice of law Dec. 11, 1886, and in 1890 became a member of the law firm of Fellows and Chandler. From 1911 until his election to the office of Attorney General he was a member of the Board of Law Examiners. He is identified with the Republican Party. At the Republican State Convention held at Saginaw, Sept. 28, 1916, he was nominated for Justice of the Supreme Court, to fill vacancy occasioned by the death of Justice McAlvay, and was elected Nov. 7, 1916; and was re-elected Apr. 2, 1923.

ORVILLE H. FELLOWS

Representative from Kalamazoo County, 1863-4 to 1867-8. Was born in Huntington, Pa., July 24, 1820. He came to Prairie Ronde, Kalamazoo County, at an early day. By occupation he was a farmer, in politics a Republican. He was several times Supervisor.

DORMAN FELT

Representative from Ingham County, 1859-60. Was a native of New Hampshire but passed his early life in Oswego County, N. Y. He was long a resident farmer in Bunker Hill, Ingham County. He was Postmaster of what was known as Felt's postoffice in that township. He settled there in 1847. Later he removed to Jackson, where he died. Politically he was a Republican.

GEORGE H. FENNER

Representative from Sanilac County, 1869-70. Was born in Monroe County, N. Y., Mar. 21, 1821. By profession he was a Baptist minister, politically, first Whig, then Republican, later Prohibitionist. As a Whig he took the stump for Clay in 1844. He came to Michigan in 1824. He resided at Marlette, Sanilac County, in 1887.

CHARLES B. FENTON

Representative from Mackinac County, 1867-8 and 1871-2. Was born in Brooklyn, N. Y., Feb. 1, 1836. He received a good education, and it was the desire of his mother that he should become an Episcopal minister, but, declining to enter that profession, he took a position in the store of A. T. Stewart, of New York. In 1858 he came west and married Eliza J. Wendell, of Mackinaw. In 1862 he settled at that place, where he became a successful merchant. He was. in his absence, elected president of Mackinaw Island for 1888. He was a Democrat.

JOSEPH S. FENTON

Representative from Genesee County, 1851. Was born in Washington, Mass., Jan. 21, 1781. He lived in Norwich, N. Y., for twenty-one years, then in Palmyra, N. Y., until 1840, when he came to Michigan and made his home at Fenton, which was laid out and named by his son, the late Wm. M. Fenton. Mr. Fenton was a banker, and a Whig in politics. He died at Flint, Nov. 14, 1851.

WILLIAM M. FENTON

Senator from the Sixth District, 1846-7; and Lieutenant Governor, 1848-52. Was born in Norwich, N. Y., Dec. 19, 1808. He graduated at Hamilton College, N. Y., in 1826, at the head of his class. For health in 1827 he shipped as a common sailor and served four years on the ocean, becoming mate of a merchant vessel. In 1835 he married a daughter of Judge Birdsall, of Norwich, N. Y., and the same year became a merchant at Pontiac, Mich. In 1837 he purchased a large tract of land where now is the town of Fenton and village of Fentonville, both named after him, and was in mercantile, milling and real estate business. He commenced the study of law in 1839 and was admitted in 1842. He removed to Flint in 1847. He held the position of Register of the U. S. Land Office at Flint from 1852 until it was removed to East Saginaw, and was Mayor of Flint in 1858. On the breaking out of the war in 1861, he tendered $5,000 to Gov. Blair to help equip the first regiments sent out. He became Major of the 7th Mich. Infantry early in 1861, but was commissioned Colonel of the 8th Mich., and led the regiment to the front, and took part in many battles, resigning in 1863 from ill health. He was the Democratic candidate for Governor in 1864. He erected the large block and public hall in Flint that bear his name. As chief of the Fire Department of Flint, while on duty, he received an injury which resulted in his death, Nov. 12, 1871.

AUGUSTUS F. FERGUSON

Representative from the First District of Ingham County, 1889-90 and 1891-2. Was born in the township of Delhi, Ingham County, May 31, 1847. His early years were spent on a farm, where he received a common school education. In 1867 he began the study of medicine with Benjamin F. Bailey, M. D., of Lansing, attended a course of lectures at the University of Michigan, in 1868-9. Apr. 10, 1869, he was married to Miss Kate Hammond, daughter of S. W. Hammond of Mason, Mich. In 1870 he moved to Okemos and commenced the practice of medicine. In 1871-2 he attended a course of lectures at the Michigan Homeopathic College, from which he graduated, receiving his diploma Feb. 24, 1872, and continuing the practice of his profession at Okemos. He was also a leading member of the firm of John Ferguson & Sons, who carried a stock of general merchandise, and did a very successful business in the village of Okemos; owner of a farm of 120 acres in the township of Meridian where he raised fine standard bred Hambletonian horses. He held several offices of trust in the township. He was elected Representative on the Democratic ticket.

DANIEL FERGUSON, JR.

Representative from Clinton and Shiawassee counties, 1844. Was born in Cortland County, N. Y., Mar. 18, 1794. He moved to Michigan in 1838, settling in Olive, Clinton County, in 1839, where he lived until his death, Feb. 28, 1864. He served as a soldier in the War of 1812. He was Supervisor of Olive several terms, and Treasurer of Clinton County from 1847 to 1851. He for several terms held the position of Justice of the Peace. In politics he was a Democrat, by occupation a farmer.

FENNER FERGUSON

Representative from Calhoun County, 1849. Was born in Nassau, N. Y., Apr. 25, 1814. He worked on a farm until seventeen, then attended school at the Nassau

Academy. He read law, was admitted, and practiced at Albany for five years. He came to Michigan an invalid in 1844, settled at Albion, and resumed practice. In politics he was a Democrat.

JAMES E. FERGUSON

Representative from Van Buren County, 1877-8 and 1879-80. Was born in Oneida County, N. Y., in 1824, and came to Michigan in 1866. He received a common school education, supplemented by one year at the Goveneur Academy, N. Y. He studied medicine and graduated from the Jefferson Medical College, Philadelphia. He was for one year Township Superintendent of Schools, and two years Postmaster in Bangor, Mich. He was practicing medicine in 1887; in politics a Republican.

MARVIN FERGUSON

Representative from the First District of Calhoun County, 1891-2 and 1893-4. Was born in Yates County, N. Y., Mar. 7, 1843. He acquired his early education at the Penn Yan Academy of Pen Yan, Yates County, N. Y. He came to Michigan in 1883 and located on a farm in Marshall, Calhoun County; also interested in manufacturing industries in Marshall city; president of the windmill company located there and a stockholder in the Page Bros. Carriage Company. He was a member of the House of 1891-2 and re-elected to that of 1893-4 on the Democrat and Populist tickets.

THOMAS A. FERGUSON

Representative from Grand Traverse District, 1873-4 and 1875-6. Was born at Iosco, Mich., Sept. 2, 1839. He subsequently removed to Wexford County. He was a graduate of the State University in 1869. He was Prosecuting Attorney of Wexford County. He enlisted as a private in the 4th Mich. Infantry in 1864, and soon afterward received a First Lieutenant's commission. He participated in the capture of Atlanta, and also took part in the battles of Franklin and Nashville. He accompanied the fourth corps to Texas in 1865, and was mustered out of service at New Orleans the following September. By profession he was a lawyer, politically a Republican. His death occurred in 1883. .

WILLIAM W. FERGUSON

Representative from the First District of Wayne County (Detroit), 1893-4 and 1895-6. Was born in the city of Detroit, May 22, 1857. He was educated at the Detroit High School, graduating from that institution in 1876. While attending school he also learned the printer's trade, in which occupation he was engaged until 1890. His later occupation was that of real estate dealer. In politics a Republican. He was of Afro-American descent, and the first of his race elected to the State Legislature; was a member from the city of Detroit for the term of 1893-4, and elected to that of 1895-6 on the general legislative ticket of that city.

GEORGE W. FERRINGTON

Delegate from the First District to the Constitutional Convention of 1835; and Representative from Wayne County, 1835-7 and 1847. Was born in Herkimer

County, N. Y., Feb. 22, 1790. He was a carpenter and farmer by occupation, and settled in Redford in 1828. He was appointed Justice of the Peace under the territorial regime in 1830 and held the office by appointment and election until his death, Apr. 6, 1854. He also served some thirteen years as Supervisor, Town Clerk and Treasurer. He was a Democrat.

BENJAMIN F. FERRIS

Representative from Branch County, 1848. His postoffice address was Sherwood. (Further data not obtainable).

CHESTER A. FERRIS

Representative from the First District of Wayne County, 1923—. Was born in Galion, Ohio, April 5, 1885, of English and Irish parentage. His education was acquired in the schools of Dayton, Ohio, and the University of Michigan. He has been engaged in the practice of law since 1908, and was appointed Assistant Prosecuting Attorney of Wayne County, serving in 1920 and 1921. Mr. Ferris is a Republican.

JACOB FERRIS

Representative from Montcalm County, 1859-60; and Delegate 'from Kent County to the Constitutional Convention of 1867. Was born in Glenn's Falls, N. Y., Feb. 10, 1822. He came to Michigan in 1837. By profession he was a lawyer. He held the position of Prosecuting Attorney, was Captain of Co. D, 21st Mich. Infantry, during the rebellion. In politics he was for many years a Republican, and an effective stump speaker, but later an Antimonopolist. He resided at Spring Lake in 1887, but was engaged in practice at Grand Rapids.

RICHARD FERRIS

Representative from the First District of Allegan County, 1871-2. His postoffice address was Bear Lake Mills. (Further data not obtainable).

WOODBRIDGE N. FERRIS

Governor of Michigan, 1913-17; and United States Senator, 1923—. Was born in a log cabin near Spencer, Tioga County, New York, January 6, 1853. His early education was obtained in the country school, Spencer Union Academy, Candor Union Academy and Owego Academy, all of New York State. His first teaching experience was when he was only seventeen years of age. Later he entered the Oswego Normal and Training School, and it was while there he met Miss Helen Frances Gillespie, who became Mrs. Ferris in December, 1874. To them were born three sons, Carleton G., Clifford, who died at the age of three months, and Phelps Fitch. Mrs. Ferris died in March, 1917. In 1873 Mr. Ferris entered the medical department of the University of Michigan with the idea of gaining knowledge that would aid him in the teaching profession. He organized the Freeport Business College and Academy in Illinois in 1875, but gave up this work to become principal of the normal department of the Rock River University. In 1877 he organized a business college and academy at Dixon and two years later was elected superintendent of schools at Pittsfield, Illinois, remaining there five years. In the fall of 1884 Mr. and Mrs. Ferris and son, Carleton, went to Big Rapids, where he organized the Ferris Industrial School. The school grew rapidly and in 1893 the main building of the Ferris Institute was built. It was incorporated in 1894 with a capital stock of $50,000. Mrs. Ferris taught in the Ferris Institute until 1901. Her work and influence have been of great value to the institution and have made possible whatever success Mr. Ferris has attained. Mr. Ferris was a candidate for Congress in the Eleventh District in 1892. In 1904 he was a candidate for Governor on the Democratic ticket. Mr. Ferris was the Democratic choice for Governor at the primary election August 27, 1912, was elected November 5, 1912, and re-elected November 3, 1914. In 1920 he was again a candidate, but was defeated by Alex J. Groesbeck. At the election held November 7, 1922, he was elected to the United States Senate.

ASA P. FERRY

Representative from Kent County, 1871-2. Was born in Spafford, N. Y., Jan. 20, 1824. He was brought up a farmer, and educated in common and select schools; settled in Courtland, Mich., and farmed from 1849 to 1865, then moved to Cannon until 1879, and from that time was engaged in milling at Rockford; was three years Supervisor of Courtland and five years of Cannon. In politics he was a Republican.

DEXTER MASON FERRY, JR.

Representative from the First District of Wayne County, 1901-2 and 1903-4; and member of the State Board of Education, 1906-12. Was born at Detroit, Nov. 22, 1873. He was graduated from the Detroit High School in 1892, from the University of Michigan in 1896 and in 1898 Columbia University conferred on him the degree of Bachelor of Arts. He gave attention to mercantile and manufacturing business after graduation, occupying many positions of trust and responsibility such as, treasurer of D. M. Ferry & Co., treasurer of the American Harrow Co., treasurer of the National Pin Co., and director of the First National Bank and the Wayne County Savings Bank of Detroit. In January, 1906, Governor Warner appointed him to fill vacancy on the State Board of Education; was nominated by the Republican State Convention at Detroit, July 30, 1906, for the full term and was elected Nov. 6, 1906.

THOMAS W. FERRY

Representative from Kent and Ottawa counties, 1851; Senator from the Thirty-first District, 1887-8; member of Congress, 1865-7 to 1869-71; and United States Senator, 1871-83. Was born at Mackinaw, Mich., June 1, 1827, and received his education in the public schools. He was one of the vice-presidents of the Chicago National Convention of 1860; was appointed a member of the Board of managers of the Gettysburgh National Cemetery in 1864, and re-appointed in 1867. He was re-elected to the forty-second Congress but was afterwards elected United States Senator, to succeed Jacob M. Howard. While in the house, he was chairman of the sub-committee on the New York Postoffice building, and the erection of that magnificent structure was largely due to his exertions. He took his seat in the Senate Mar. 4, 1871; was elected president *pro tem* Mar. 9 and 19, and Dec. 20, 1875; became acting vice-president upon the death of Vice-President Wilson, serving as such until Mar. 4, 1877. In the absence of the president, he presided and delivered an address at the centennial exposition, July 4, 1876. He was re-elected Senator Jan. 17, 1877, he was also re-elected president *pro tem* Mar. 5, 1877, Feb. 26, 1878, Apr. 17, 1878, and Mar. 3, 1879. In the Senate he was for many years chairman of the committees on rules, and postoffices and post-roads, and a member of the committee on finance. His ability as presiding officer was tested in the impeachment trial of Secretary of War Belknap, and at the joint convention on the electoral count of 1877. He was a leading candidate for re-election in 1883, but after a long and heated contest his name was withdrawn. He died at Grand Haven, Oct., 1896.

WILLIAM MONTAGUE FERRY

Member of the Board of Regents of the University of Michigan, 1858-64. Was born at Michilimackinac, Mich., July 8, 1824, elder son of the Rev. William Montague and Amanda (White) Ferry. In 1834 he removed with his parents to Grand Haven, which continued to be his home for over forty years. He received his early training in his father's library. He also had a year's instruction at the Sanderson Academy of Ashfield, Mass., under Henry L. Dawes, afterwards United States Senator, and spent one year at the Kalamazoo branch of the University of Michigan. Active life began for him at the age of fifteen, when he was placed in charge of large gangs of men as manager of his father's lumber business on the Grand River. In April, 1857, he was elected Regent of the University for the term beginning Jan. 1, following, and serving the full term. In August, 1861 he enlisted at Grand Haven as private in the 14th Mich. Infantry, and was promoted in rank. He was honorably mustered out of the service Apr. 24, 1865. He was the originator of the systems of commutation of rations, which has now been included in the regulations of the army, having received the formal approval of Congress. In 1870 he was the Democratic nominee for Governor of Michigan, and in 1873 Governor Bagley appointed him one of the members of the commission to revise the State Constitution. He was elected Mayor of Grand Rapids in 1876. In 1878 he removed to Park City, Utah. Here he became actively interested in the mining operations of the territory and was one of the original owners of the Quincy Mine. From 1884 to 1892 he represented Utah on the National Democratic Committee. In 1893 he was Commissioner of the World's Columbian Exposition at Chicago. In 1904 he was nominated for Governor of Utah on the American ticket. He was a member of the Society of the Army of the Tennessee, and of the Military Order of the Loyal Legion. He was married Oct. 29, 1851, to Jeannette Hollister, of Grand Rapids, Mich. There were six children. He died at Park City, Utah, Jan. 2, 1905, and is buried at Grand Haven, Mich.

C. B. H. FESSENDEN

Representative from Macomb County, 1842. Was born at Sandwich, Mass., July 17, 1813. By profession he was a lawyer, in politics a Democrat until 1861, then a Republican. He settled in Utica, Mich., in 1838, where he engaged in practice. He was engrossing clerk of the Senate in 1839. After 1842 he removed to New Bedford, Mass. He was Collector of Customs at New Bedford, from 1853 to 1861, Sheriff of Bristol County, Mass., from 1862 to 1869, and held other public positions.

CONRAD FEY

Representative from Saginaw County, 1873-4. Was born in Hesse, Prussia, June 17, 1831. He received his education in a common school. In 1847 he emigrated to the United States, and settled in Detroit. In 1862 he removed to East Saginaw, where he resided in 1887. He was a member of the Board of Water Commissioners of East Saginaw. His business was insurance and dealer in foreign exchange.

JAMES FIELD

Representative from Lenawee County, 1837. Came from the State of New York, settled at Palmyra, Mich., at an early day, and afterwards removed to Adrian, where he was in business as a warehouse man. His mother was a Quaker preacher at Scipio, N. Y. While living at Palmyra he was a Justice of the Peace. He served in the extra session of the Legislature in 1837 in place of Asahel Finch, Jr.. who had resigned. He died at Adrian, Mar. 16, 1863.

MOSES W. FIELD

Member of Congress, 1873-5; and member of the Board of Regents of the University of Michigan, 1886-9. Was born at Watertown, N. Y., Feb. 10, 1828, and received an academic education at Victor Academy, N. Y. He came to Detroit in 1844, was at first a clerk, later a partner in the firm of Stephens & Field, then alone in business as a merchant; also engaged in manufacturing and real estate. He gave Linden Park to Detroit, a tract of fifty acres. He was a Whig, then a Republican. later a Greenbacker. He was Alderman, Trustee of the Asylum at Pontiac, and then a Regent of the University. In Congress he was a Republican; was a member of the State Republican Committee and chairman of the State Greenback Committee; was the Republican candidate for Congress in 1874, but was defeated. He died Mar. 14, 1889, at Detroit.

NATHANIEL L. FIELD

Representative from Chippewa County, 1909-10 and 1911-12. Was born of American parents in Shelburne Falls, Mass., in 1868, and was educated in the public schools and academy. Afterwards taught school one year; worked in country store one year; was teller in Shelburne Falls National Bank four years; bookkeeper in First National Bank of Bridgeport, Ala., three years; shipping clerk for Ara Cleshman Company, Auburn, Me., one year; and was in the general merchandise business at Rudyard for many years. Mr. Field was married at Bridgeport, Ala. He held the offices of Township Treasurer, and Supervisor; was elected chairman of the County Board of Supervisors in 1908. He was member of the following: F. & A. M., I. O. O. F., K. of P. and K. O. T. M. In politics a Republican.

FRANCIS W. FIFIELD

Representative from Oakland County, 1863-4. Was born in Ogden, N. Y., Apr. 10, 1821. By occupation he was a farmer and stock raiser, in politics a Democrat. He settled in Waterford, Mich., in 1838 and lived there until 1880, then a resident of Decatur, Mich. He was School Inspector of Waterford twenty-three years; Justice of the Peace twelve years; Supervisor nine years; Town Clerk four years, and master of the Masonic lodge for twenty-two years.

FRANCIS FILDEW

Representative from the First District of Wayne County, 1891-2. Was born in Devonshire, England, in 1851, coming to Michigan in 1867. Married. By trade a carpenter and joiner, and identified with the trades union movement, having been a member of Carpenters' Union No. 10, of Detroit; was at one time its president, and served as recording secretary for several terms, also as delegate to the biennial convention of the brotherhood of carpenters; represented the International organization of carpenters in the conventions of the American Federation of Labor at St. Louis, Boston, and Detroit. He was president of the council of trades and labor unions of Detroit in 1887, and represented that body as a delegate to the State Federation of Labor at its organization in Lansing in 1889. Politically a Democrat.

ASAHEL FINCH, JR.

Representative from Lenawee County, 1837. Came to Adrian, Mich., from the State of New York as early as 1832, and started a dry goods store in company with Nelson D. Skeels. He remained in business at Adrian for several years, and then engaged in banking at Homer, Mich. Later he removed to Milwaukee, Wis., where he engaged in law practice. He resigned before the adjourned session of the Legislature in 1837 and was succeeded by James Field. While in Adrian he served as a Justice of the Peace under the Territorial Government. Deceased.

SILAS FINCH

Senator from the Fourth District, 1835-6. His postoffice address was Saline. (Further data not obtainable).

WILLIAM FINLEY, JR.

Senator from the Second District, 1849-50. Was born in Geneseo, N. Y., Dec. 15, 1810. He was educated at Temple Hill Academy, and became a land surveyor and civil engineer. He came to Michigan in 1832 to survey lands for J. S. Wadsworth, of Geneseo, N. Y., and followed that business until 1838. He returned to New York and became Judge of the Livingston County Court in 1840. He settled at Ann Arbor in 1845. At first a Democrat, he became a Free Soiler; was a delegate to the Buffalo Convention in 1848. He was the first president of the Washtenaw County Agricultural Society. Outside of official duties he followed farming. He died June 12, 1858.

NOBLE H. FINNEY

Representative from Kent, Ottawa and Ionia Counties, 1839. His postoffice address was Grand Rapids. (Further data not obtainable).

GEORGE W. FISH

Senator from the Nineteenth District, 1875-6. Was born at Kortright, N. Y., July 16, 1816, and graduated as a physician at Castleton, Vt., in 1837. He became a resident of Michigan in 1838. He served as Consul at Ningpo, Japan; was surgeon of the 4th Mich. Cavalry, and afterwards of the first and second cavalry brigades during the war; was a trustee of the Institution for the Deaf, Dumb and Blind at Flint; Collector of Internal Revenue, and from 1868 to 1872 was editor of the Saginaw *Enterprise*. In politics he was a Republican, in later years a Democrat. He died Sept. 19, 1885.

ALONZO W. FISHER

Representative from the First District of Allegan County, 1903-4 and 1905-6. Was born in Newton Township, Calhoun County, Mich., June 21, 1845. He acquired his education in the district schools and in the high schools at Grand Rapids, O., attending school winters and working on his father's farm summers. He was married to Carrie E. Chase, Jan. 13, 1869, moved to Ganges Township, Allegan County, Mich., and settled on a piece of new land. He devoted his time to fruit growing and general farming. He served as Highway Commissioner, Township Treasurer, and as Supervisor. In politics a Republican.

DELOS FISHER

Representative from Jackson County, 1865-6. Was born in Scohairie County, N. Y., Aug. 20, 1812. By occupation he was a cooper, in politics a Republican. He became a resident of Michigan at an early day. He was Marshal of Jackson in 1855, and afterwards held the offices of Alderman and Mayor. He died at Jackson, Nov. 22, 1875.

SPENCER O. FISHER

Member of Congress from the Tenth District, 1885-7 and 1887-9. Was born in Camden, Mich., Feb. 3, 1843, a resident of West Bay City. By occupation he was a lumberman and banker, and politically a Democrat. He was an Alderman, twice Mayor, and a delegate to the Democratic National Convention of 1884. He served his second term in Congress, and secured a government building and a U. S. court at Bay City. He died at Bay City, June 2, 1919.

CHARLES H. FISK

Representative from the First District of Wayne County (Detroit), 1895-6. Was born in Manchester, Washtenaw County, Mich., June 19, 1858. His early education was acquired in the common schools of Clinton, Lenawee County, supplemented with one year at Adrian College. He was of New England descent, son of Henry C. Fisk, member of the 17th Mich. Inf., who was killed at Campbell's Station, Tenn., November, 1863. At the age of eighteen years, he taught school, and at twenty entered the law office of Alfred Russell, of Detroit; eighteen months afterwards he was admitted to the bar; practiced common law five years, and then engaged in the practice of patent law. In politics a Republican. He was elected to the House of 1895-6 on the general legislative ticket of Detroit city.

J. RUSSELL FISK

Representative from the Second District of Jackson County, 1903-4, 1905-6 and 1011-12. Was born in Tompkins Township, Jackson County, Apr. 8, 1867, of New England parentage. His education was acquired in the district schools. Married. By occupation a farmer; also extensively engaged in stock-raising. In politics a Republican.

ANDREW MASON FITCH

Member of the Board of Regents of the University of Michigan, 1842-6. Was born at Cherry Valley, Otsego County, N. Y., Mar. 15, 1815, son of Gurdon and Hannah (Leck) Fitch. His grandfather, Andrew Fitch, was Captain of the 4th Conn. Infantry in the War of the Revolution. His parents removed to Cleveland, O., in 1826. He there received a common school education, after which he entered Norwalk Seminary in 1834. He was ordained a Deacon in the Methodist Episcopal Church in 1838 and an Elder in 1840. He held pastorates at Lima and Toledo, O.; and was then called to Michigan, where he was pastor of churches at Monroe, Adrian, Detroit, Jackson, Ann Arbor, and Grand Rapids, and presiding elder of the Marshall District. Feb. 16, 1842, he was appointed Regent of the University and served the full term of four years. From 1851 to 1856 he was financial secretary of the State Indian Agent for Michigan. For many years he was a trustee of the Wesleyan Seminary and of its successor, Albion College. He served for a time on the School Board of Albion. He was married in 1841 to Cornelia Chittenden, of Adrian, who died in 1858, leaving three children. In 1862 he was married to Susan C. Searles, of Newark, N. J. He died at his home in Albion, Mich., Jan. 8, 1887.

CHARLES C. FITCH

Representative from the Second District of Ingham County, 1889-90 and 1891-2. Was born in the village of Cuylerville, Livingston County, N. Y., July 19, 1842. Mr. Fitch was a farmer until 1875, excepting the years from 1863 to 1865, when he was Deputy Register of Deeds and was employed in the abstract office of this county. He took charge of the latter office in 1878, and remained in charge of the same until the summer of 1886. He was elected Register of Deeds of Ingham County in 1884 and re-elected in 1886; also a member of the School Board of Mason. He was elected on the Democratic ticket to the House.

FERRIS S. FITCH

Superintendent of Public Instruction, 1891-3. Was born upon a farm in Ingham County, Feb. 1, 1853, where he labored till his sixteenth year, and during his school and college vacations thereafter. He received his early instruction in the common schools of his native county, was graduated from the classical course of the Michigan Normal School at Ypsilanti in 1873, and from the classical course of the University in 1877. After completing his University course he was called to the chair of Latin and Greek, and afterward to the acting presidency of Smithson College, Ind. He resigned there in 1878 to accept the principalship of the high school in Pontiac; after three and one-half years in the position he was promoted to the Superintendency of the city schools at Pontiac, which position he held nine years. At the end of the school year in 1890 he resigned to accept the position of editor and manager of the *Oakland County Post*. The same year he was unanimously nominated to the office of Superintendent of Public Instruction by the Democratic state convention, and was elected. He died Jan. 30, 1920.

FERRIS S. FITCH

Representative from Ingham County, 1853-4, and 1855-6. Was born in Shelden, N. Y., Dec. 28, 1815. He received a fair education, and was by trade a mason, working on the Croton aqueduct. He settled on a large farm in Bunker Hill,

Mich., in 1848, where he resided until his death, Mar. 27, 1883. He was several terms Supervisor of his town, and often a delegate to State and other conventions. In politics he was a Democrat.

LYMAN A. FITCH

Senator from the Twentieth District, 1855-6. Was born in Rutland, N. Y., Oct. 21, 1814. He came to Michigan in the fall of 1837, and located on a farm a short distance from Paw Paw. For the last eight years of his life he resided in Paw Paw. Politically he was first a Whig, then a Republican. He died June 19, 1887.

MORGAN L. FITCH

Representative from Van Buren County, 1851. Was born in the State of New York, Feb. 2, 1810. By occupation he was a farmer, in politics a Democrat. He removed to Van Buren County in 1837, and resided there until his death, Apr. 6, 1887.

NATHAN FITCH

Representative from Berrien County, 1863-4. Was born in Urbana, O., Oct. 12, 1810. He learned the trade of a plasterer, and came with his family to Michigan in 1835, locating a farm eight miles from Niles. He was Sheriff of Berrien County from 1857 to 1861. In politics he was first Whig then Republican. He resided at Niles in 1887.

NORTON FITCH

Representative from the Third District of Kent County, 1891-2 and 1893-4. Was born in Orleans County, N. Y., Nov. 17, 1833. In 1848 he came with his parents to Michigan and settled on a farm in Sparta, Kent County. He acquired his education at the rural district school. In 1855 he was married to Sophia Murray, of Alpine, Kent County, purchased a piece of wood land of 120 acres in Alpine Township, and began clearing it. At the outbreak of the war he enlisted as private in Co. C. First Berdan's U. S. Sharpshooters; he participated in all the battles of the army of the Potomac until he lost an arm at the second Battle of Bull Run. He declined a commission and returned to his farm. Shortly afterwards his wife died and in 1872 he was again married to Elizabeth Smith, of Norwalk, O. Later he moved to Sparta village where he made his home although continuing farming. In politics a Republican. While in Alpine he was Township Clerk and Supervisor, and President or director of the Ottawa and West Kent Agricultural Society.

VIRGIL A. FITCH

Representative from Mason County, 1919-20. Was born May 21, 1860, in Middlebury Township, Shiawassee County, Mich., of English and Irish parents. He was educated in the district school and at the Ovid High School, Spring Arbor Seminary, and the University of Michigan. He graduated from the law department of the State University, and was admitted to the practice of law at the age of twenty-one years. In 1901 he was admitted to practice in the United States Circuit

Court and in the United States District Court at Grand Rapids. In 1912 he was appointed by the National Government white slave officer for the Ludington district. He served as City Justice. In politics a Republican.

JEROME B. FITZGERALD

Senator from the Fourth District, 1847-8. Was born in southern Indiana, in September, 1822. He came with his father, Gen. Thomas Fitzgerald, to Berrien County, Mich., in 1832. He received a collegiate education, studied law and was admitted to the bar in 1844. He practiced his profession in New York City from 1850 to 1864, when he returned to Berrien County. He was father of the bill for asylum for the insane and blind. In politics he was a Democrat. He was a good counselor and a reliable friend. He died at Niles, June 5, 1878.

JOHN C. FITZGERALD

Senator from the Eleventh District, 1869-70. Was born in Berlin, O. His father was a pioneer in Springport, Mich. The son attended Albion College, studied law with Gov. Blair at Jackson; was admitted in 1858; in 1860 removed to Marshall, where he practiced until 1873; and was Prosecuting Attorney of Calhoun County from 1861 to 1865. He went to Grand Rapids in 1873, became a partner of John W. Champlin and became a leading member of the Grand Rapids bar, having a large practice in both State and federal courts. He was the Republican candidate for Congress in the Fifth District in 1884.

JOHN P. FITZGERALD

Representative from the First District of Wayne County, 1919-20. Was born June 30, 1872, at Chicago, Ill., of Irish-Scotch parentage. He was educated in private and parochial schools and at St. Ignatius College, Chicago. After some experience on the Chicago Board of Trade he entered the newspaper field and continued in that work for more than twenty-five years, except for six years when he worked in the City Clerk's office in that city. For several years he was connected with the *Michigan Manufacturer and Financial Record*, of Detroit, a periodical devoted to the interests of manufacturers and bankers of Michigan. Married. In politics a Republican.

JOHN W. FITZGERALD

Representative from the First District of Eaton County, 1895-6. Was born at Montpelier, Vt., Oct. 22, 1850. He was left an orphan when quite young, and was adopted by Daniel Barton and wife, of Lyons, N. Y. He received his education in the common schools of New York, and taught school three winters. In 1873 he came to Michigan, locating at Grand Ledge, Eaton County. For two years he worked on a farm summers and taught school winters; he then engaged in the hardware business, in which occupation he continued until 1892. During the legislative session of 1893 he was clerk of the committee on state affairs. In politics a Republican. He was a member of the School Board of Grand Ledge, and vice-president of the sewer pipe works of that city; received the nomination in the Republican convention as Representative of the First District of Eaton County for the term of 1895-6, and was elected.

THOMAS FITZGERALD

Member of the Board of Regents of the University of Michigan, 1837; Representative from Berrien County, 1839; and United States Senator, 1848-9. Was born in Germantown, N. Y., Apr. 10, 1796. His father was a soldier of the Revolution. The son enlisted in the War of 1812, had his arm shattered by a bullet, and for life was an invalid pensioner. He taught school, married Mary Baldwin in 1818, and removed to Indiana, taught school, studied law, and was admitted in 1821. He became a Democratic leader and was elected to the Indiana Legislature. In 1832 President Jackson appointed him light-house keeper at St. Joseph, Mich., and he soon became a prominent man in the Territory of Michigan, and held many offices. He was Clerk of Berrien County in 1834; Bank Commissioner in 1837; Democratic candidate for Lieutenant Governor on the ticket headed by Chancellor Farnsworth; and in 1848 was appointed United States Senator by Governor Ransom, to fill vacancy caused by the resignation of Gen. Cass. He served two sessions and won the respect of political friends and opponents. He declined the tender of Judge in a territory. While serving as Probate Judge of Berrien County he died at Niles, Mar. 25, 1855.

WILLIAM L. FITZGERALD

Representative from the First District of Kalamazoo County, 1913-14. Was born in Arlington Township, Van Buren County, Aug. 30, 1881, of Irish descent. He was educated in the Lawrence Grammar School and the Paw Paw High School, and a graduate of the law department of the University of Michigan. He taught school in 1901-2 and after Nov. 1, 1907, he practiced law at Kalamazoo; was City Attorney of Kalamazoo and also served on the Charter Commission. In politics a Democrat.

DAVID A. FITZGIBBON

Representative from the First District of St. Clair County, 1911-12; and Senator, 1913-14 and 1915-16, from the Eleventh District, comprising the counties of Macomb and St. Clair. Was born at Point Edward, Ont., Jan. 1, 1873, of Irish parentage, and was educated in the high schools of Sarnia and Toronto, Ont. He was a lawyer by profession. He served in the Spanish-American War with the Thirty-third Mich. Regiment. In politics a Republican. He was elected to the Legislature of 1911-12 at a special election held on Wednesday, Mar. 1, 1911, to fill vacancy caused by the death of Charles M. Green.

GEORGE FITZSIMMONS

Representative from Hillsdale County, 1853-4. Came from Rose, N. Y., and settled in Reading, Mich., in 1837. In 1839-40 he was Town Treasurer, and served as Justice sixteen years. He aided largely by his time, influence and means in securing a railroad through the town. He was a farmer and was prosperous. He died Oct. 9, 1870.

RICHARD C. FLANNIGAN

Delegate in the Constitutional Convention of 1907-8 from the Thirty-first District, Dickinson County. Was born at Ontonagon in 1857, of Irish descent. He attended the district school when a boy, and in 1870 moved to Marquette, where he worked for the M. H. & O. R. R. Co., with now and then a few months' schooling in the Marquette schools. From 1874 to 1877 he was employed in the law office of Parks & Hayden, lawyers, at Marquette. For six months he attended the law school at the University of Michigan. Returning to Marquette he studied law for one year in the office of Mr. Maynard, an attorney in that city, and in 1879 was admitted to the bar by the Circuit Court for the county of Marquette. He then practiced law. Married.

ALFRED M. FLEISCHHAUER

Representative from the Osceola District, 1897-8 and 1899-1900; and Delegate in the Constitutional Convention of 1907-8, from the Twenty-fifth District, Osceola County. Was born in Waterloo, Ont., in 1867, of German descent. He received a public school education. Married. In 1877 his parents removed to Reed City from Canada. He worked in his father's grocery until 1902. At that time he took up the real estate and insurance business. In politics a Republican. He held the office of Justice of the Peace for several years and was Village Treasurer in 1907; was a member of the Methodist Episcopal Church.

JOSEPH FLESHIEM

Senator, 1891-2, from the Thirty-first District, comprising the counties of Iron, Marquette and Menominee. Was born in Cleveland, O., Apr. 28, 1848, and removed to Menominee, Mich., in 1871. He served as County Clerk, County Treasurer, and as Register of Deeds. He became quite wealthy by his mining and other enterprises, and conducted at one time the largest fire insurance agency north of Milwaukee. He was elected to the Senate of 1891-2 on the Republican ticket.

FRANK WARK FLETCHER

Member of the Board of Regents of the University of Michigan, 1894-1910. Was born in Boston, Mass., May 16, 1853, son of George N. and Sarah A. G. (Miller) Fletcher. His father was born at Ludlow, Vt., and his mother at Keenebunkport, Me., the line of descent being traced in American families as far back as 1632. He had his preparatory training in the public schools of Detroit and in P. M. Patterson's school in that city. In 1875 he was graduated Bachelor of Philosophy from the University of Michigan. The following year was spent in post-graduate study at the Massachusetts Institute of Technology. After three years' service as chemist in the employ of the Detroit and Lake Superior Copper Company he entered the lumber business at Alpena, Mich., in 1879; was also president of the Fletcher Paper Company at Alpena. He was married Jan. 22, 1879 to Grace E. Parker, of Detroit. He died Dec. 17, 1922.

JOHN W. FLETCHER

Representative from Calhoun County, 1877-8. Was born in Marshall, Mar. 4, 1844. He received a common school education in his native city, and began business for himself in 1866 as a clothing merchant. Subsequently he inaugurated a branch clothing store at Charlotte, Eaton County, and one at Albion, Calhoun County. In politics he was a Democrat. He resided at Battle Creek and was Postmaster of that city in 1887.

NIRAM A. FLETCHER

Representative from Kent County, 1883-4. Was born at Oakland, Ont., Feb. 13, 1850. He was educated at a common school and became a teacher. He came to Michigan in 1870. He studied law and engaged in practice at Grand Rapids. Politically a Democrat.

WILLIAM A. FLETCHER

Member of the Legislative Council from Wayne County, 1830-1; Justice of the Supreme Court. 1836-42; and member of the Board of Regents of the University of Michigan, 1842-6. The first Chief Justice of Michigan, was born in New Hampshire, and as a young man was engaged in mercantile business at Salem, Mass. He removed to Schoharie County, N. Y., stud'ed law, and in 1821 commenced practice at Detroit. In 1823 he was appointed Chief Justice of the County Court of Wayne County. He held that position three years, and was several years Attorney General. In 1833 a judicial circuit was established including all the counties of the State except Wayne, and Judge Fletcher was appointed Judge. He removed to Ann Arbor to comply with the law as to residence. In 1836 he was appointed Chief Justice of the Supreme Court, and held that position until 1842, when he resigned. He was appointed Regent of the University of Michigan Apr. 5, 1842 in the place of Randolph Manning resigned and served until 1846. In 1837 he made a revision of the laws of the State. He died at Ann Arbor in August, 1853.

JAMES K. FLOOD

Representative from Oceana County. 1895-6; and Senator, 1897-8 and 1899-1900, from the Twenty-sixth district, comprising the counties of Lake. Manistee. Mason and Oceana. Was born of American parents in Oxford County, Ont., July 24. 1846. He was educated in the public schools; moved to Pentwater. Mich., in 1864 and worked in the mills and at lumbering until 1869. then he moved to Hart, where he was engaged in the drug business until 1878; subsequently be engaged in various mercantile pursuits. In 1874, with Judge Russel and A. S. White as co-partners, they organized the Citizens' Exchange Bank. The same company in 1892 organized the Hart Cedar and Lumber Company. In politics he was a Republican. He was Postmaster from 1881-6; and six years a member of the Board of Education of the Union Schools of Hart. He died in 1921.

JAMES FLOWER

Representative from Macomb County, 1849. His postoffice address was Armada. (Further data not obtainable).

CHARLES FLOWERS

Representative from the First District of Wayne County, 1909-10 to 1917-18. Was born in Bucks County, Pa., Dec. 14, 1845, of English and Dutch ancestors. His parents were Qua'ers. Mr. Flowers remained at home until about eighteen years of age, when he went to New York and secured a position as stenographer in the the off'ce of the Grand Trunk Railway, remaining there about one year. He then continued his education by attending the Collegiate Institute of Fort Edward, N. Y., where he remained two years. He was then employed by the government in

North Carolina, in reporting military commissions during the reconstruction period. He went from there to New York and commenced the study of law; remained there but one year; came to Detroit in 1868, and established the practice of reporting in the courts. Mr. Flowers was appointed by Governor Baldwin as the first stenographer of the Wayne Circuit Court, which position he held for thirteen years. In 1869 he was employed to report the Constitutional Convention of Illinois; in 1872 to report the Constitutional Convention of Pennsylvania; and in 1873 to report the Constitutional Convention of Ohio, continuing the study of law, while acting as stenographer. He was admitted to the bar in 1879, and in 1880 was elected Circuit Court Commissioner, and re-elected in 1882. In 1896 he was appointed Corporation Counsel of Detroit by Mayor Pingree, and held the office for four years; was also a member of the Fire Commission for four years, from 1895-9. In politics a Republican.

CHARLES FOLKS

Representative from the Second District of Jackson County, 1907-8 and 1909-10. Was born in Hanover Township, Jackson County, Sept. 30, 1858, of English descent. He received his education in the district schools and Hanover High School. He taught school several winters, married in 1880 and moved on a farm in Pulaski Township, Jackson County; owner of a fine farm of 360 acres and giving his attention to general farming and stock raising; also secretary and treasurer for several years of the Citizens' Mutual Fire Insurance Co., of Pulaski. In politics a Republican.

ELWIN B. FOLLETT

Representative, 1913-14 and 1915-16, from the Iosco district, comprising the counties of Alcona, Arenac, Iosco and Ogemaw. Was born on a farm in Fremont, Steuben County, Ind., Nov. 14, 1877, receiving his education in the Fremont High School. The early years of his life were spent on his father's farm. Nov. 5, 1908, he removed from Fremont, Ind., to Albion, Mich., and on Nov. 4, 1909, he located at Hale, Iosco County, Mich., where he purchased a large tract of land which he engaged in clearing and farming. He was married to Miss Edna Stroh, of Fremont, Ind., on Apr. 7, 1901. He served as Alderman of Fremont and Supervisor of Plainfield Township, Iosco County, Mich. Fraternally, a member of the Grange, Gleaners and F. & A. M. In politics a Republican.

MARTIN P. FOLLETT

Representative from Montcalm County, 1861-2. Was born in the State of Ohio, May 20, 1820. He came to Michigan about 1855, and settled in Fairplains, Montcalm County, as a farmer and lumberman. He was Supervisor of that town. During the war he was a sutler in the army. He resided at Chicago, Ill., in 1887.

CHARLES E. FOOTE

Representative from the First District of Kalamazoo County, 1895-6 and 1897-8. Was born in Franklin, Delaware County, N. Y., Sept. 6, 1840. His early education was acquired at the common schools, and at the age of nineteen he began the trade of carriage ironing. Eighteen months later, at the outbreak of the Civil War, he enlisted in Co. D, Third New York Cavalry; served three years, received severe sabre wounds in a duel with a confederate soldier of the Second North Carolina Cavalry. On his return from the war he finished his trade, and in 1866 was engaged by the Empire Agriculture Works of Cobleskill, N. Y., with which firm he remained until 1873, when he engaged in business for himself. He was Postmaster from 1878-82. At the close of his term he received an appointment as clerk in the pension bureau, and served successively as clerk, special examiner, assistant to the pension board of appeals, and again special examiner, until Mar. 6, 1888, when he was discharged from the department by Secretary of the Interior Lamar. He immediately returned to Kalamazoo, where he extensively and successfully engaged as pension claim agent, was Assistant Quartermaster General, Department of Michigan, G. A. R., appointed by Gen. William Shakespeare, department commander. In politics he was a Republican. He died at Kalamazoo, June 5, 1909.

CHARLES R. FOOTE

Representative from the Second District of Kent County, 1913-14, 1915-16 and 1917-18. Was born at Ionia, Mich., Dec. 13, 1871, and was educated in the Belding High School. In the spring of 1872, he removed with his parents from Ionia to a farm near Belding. He taught school two years after graduating from the Belding High School in 1887, afterwards studying law with Lyon and Dooling, of St. Johns, and was admitted to practice Dec. 22, 1892. Mr. Foote was married Nov. 23, 1897, to Josephine M. Rounds at Fremont, Mich. He practiced law in Belding until 1902, when he formed a partnership with W. A. Rounds and purchased a hotel at Hart, Mich. He sold out in 1907 and went to Alto, where he engaged in the hardware business. He is a member of the Knights of Pythias and a past chancellor of the order. In politics he is a Republican.

DAN P. FOOTE

Senator from the Twenty-third District, 1877-8. Was born in Deerfield, N. Y., Aug. 18, 1831. As a citizen of New York State he served in the Mexican War. He was a sailor several years. He settled in Saginaw County, Mich., in 1854, became a lawyer, was Prosecuting Attorney, Justice, Supervisor, City Attorney of Saginaw, and held other offices. In politics a Democrat.

HENRY K. FOOTE

Representative from Oakland County, 1837, 1840, 1861-2. Located a farm in Commerce in 1831-2, and was the first physician there. He removed to Milford in 1838, and took high rank as a physician. He went into the service and was made Lieutenant, Aug. 14, 1862, and died at Poolesville, Md., Feb. 9, 1863.

JOHN FORBES

Representative from Wayne County, 1840. Was born in Vermont in 1800, and came to Michigan in 1819, settling at Flat Rock, Wayne County, removing to Van Buren Township in 1865, where he died June 19, 1876. He held the offices of Supervisor and Justice. He was a farmer; and Whig and Republican in politics.

JOSHUA FORBES

Representative from Washtenaw County, 1865-6. Was born in Buckland, Mass., February, 1808. In 1817, with his parents, he removed to Leicester, Genesee County. In 1837 he removed to Saline, Mich., where he died Feb. 10, 1880. He was several times Supervisor and held other town offices. He was a farmer and a Democrat.

HENRY FORD

Senator from the Twelfth District, comprising Van Buren and Cass counties, 1881-2. Was born in Monroe, N. Y., Feb. 11, 1825, and received a common school education. Having become, at the age of seventeen, a clerk in the store of the Southfield Furnace Company, at the age of twenty-one he was promoted to superintendent. He held the office of Superintendent of the Poor, and Justice. He removed to Michigan in 1867 to take charge of the erection of the Lawton Iron Works. In politics he was a Republican.

MELBOURNE H. FORD

Representative from the Second District of Kent County, 1885-6; and member of Congress, 1887-9 and 1891. Was born in Saline, Washtenaw County, June 30, 1849. He was educated at the Michigan Agricultural College, and the U. S. Naval Academy at Annapolis, Md.; was a member of the Michigan Legislature of 1885; was elected to the 50th Congress; was a candidate for re-election to the 51st Congress but was defeated; was elected to the 52d Congress as a Democrat. He died, Monday, Apr. 20, 1891, at his home in Grand Rapids. He was succeeded by Charles E. Belknap.

RANSOM L. FORD

Representative from the First District of Genesee County, 1915-16 and 1917-18. Was born at Byron, Mich., Feb. 12, 1878, of English parentage. His education was acquired in the Chesaning High School. He was owner and editor of the Montrose *Record* for fourteen years, disposing of the publication Dec. 1, 1914. He was Township Clerk and Village Clerk: a member of Montrose Lodge No. 428 F. & A. M., master of same during 1911 and 1912 and patron of Montrose Chapter No. 351, O. E. S., for three years. In politics a Republican.

SHERIDAN FORD

Representative from the First District of Wayne County, 1915-16 and 1917-18. Was born in Monroe County, Mich., of Irish-American descent. His education was secured in the common schools. He began his life work as a New York newspaper man, devoting himself to criticism, both literary and art pictorial. From there he went to London as special correspondent. He was with the London edition of the New York *Herald* as art critic, later passing to the staff of the London *News.* He enjoyed the reputation of being the first critic to publicly recognize the genius of the Glasgow group of painters, then struggling for recognition at the hands of British philistinism. For several seasons he lectured upon pictures and painters in Paris, London, Scotland and Riviera resorts. Later he was publisher of the *Inside American,* a monthly magazine devoted to literature and the fine arts. Married. In politics a Republican. He died in Detroit April, 1922.

JOSEPH W. FORDNEY

Member of Congress, 1899-1901 to 1921-2. Was born in Blackford County, Ind., Nov. 5, 1853. He lived with his parents on a farm until he was sixteen years of age, received a common school education, and came to Saginaw in June, 1869. He began life in the lumber woods, logging and estimating pine timber, thus acquiring a thorough knowledge of the pine land and lumber business. Mr. Fordney is married. In politics he is a Republican. He served two years as Alderman; was elected to Congress in 1898, and has been a member of each succeeding Congress. He was re-elected for the last term, Nov. 2, 1920.

GEORGE B. FORRESTER

Senator, 1917-18, 1919-20 and 1921-2, from the Twentieth District, comprising the counties of Huron and Sanilac. Was born at Montreal, Canada, Sept. 13, 1862, of Scotch parents. He came to Michigan in 1867, locating at Richmond, Macomb County. He received his education in the public schools of that village. He has been engaged in the mercantile business more than thirty years. Mr. Forrester is married and has two children. In politics he is a Republican.

JOHN H. FORSTER

Senator from the Thirty-second District, 1865-6. Was born at Erie, Pa., May 29, 1822. When young he was a law student and schoolmaster, later, civil and mining engineer, explorer, geologist, and then a farmer. He was Assistant Engineer U. S. survey of lakes, river and harbor improvements; on the Mexican boundary survey, 1848-9; six years special engineer of Michigan for construction of Portage Lake and Lake Superior Ship Canal; several years superintendent of copper mines; Judge of Probate in California; Justice, Postmaster, member board of control of Michigan Mining School. In politics he was a Democrat. He was extensively engaged in the breeding of Jersey and other choice stock. He died at his home in Williamston, June 15, 1894.

ALEXANDER FORSYTH

Senator, 1897-8, from the Twenty-fourth District, comprising the counties of Midland, Arenac and Bay. Was born at Adelaide, Middlesex County, Canada, Aug. 16, 1860. He acquired a common school education, and spent his early days on his father's farm; at the age of sixteen he engaged in teaching and fire insurance business; became secretary and general manager of the Home Mutual Fire Insurance Company of Bay, Arenac and Ogemaw counties, and conducted a general fire insurance business. In politics, up to 1892, he was Independent; after that a Populist and a Free Silver Democrat. He was elected to the Senate of 1897-8 on the Democratic People's Union Silver ticket.

ROBERT A. FORSYTH

Member of the Legislative Council from Wayne County, 1826-7. (Further data not obtainable).

CHARLES WOODWORTH FOSTER

Senator, 1915-16 and 1917-18, from the Fourteenth District, comprising the counties of Ingham and Shiawassee. Was born in Lansing, Mar. 28, 1873. He graduated from the Lansing High School in 1891; from the literary department, University of Michigan, in 1895 and from the law department in 1896. He has since resided in Lansing, where he has been actively engaged in the practice of law, and prominently identified with the Republican party. He held the office of Circuit Court Commissioner for Ingham County from 1898 to 1902.

EUGENE FOSTER

Delegate in the Constitutional Convention of 1907-8 from Gladwin County; and Senator, 1909-10 and 1911-12, from the Twenty-eighth District, comprising the counties of Alcona, Arenac, Clare, Crawford, Gladwin, Iosco, Ogemaw, Osceola, Oscoda and Roscommon. Was born at Caroga, Fulton County, N. Y., Aug. 8, 1860. He was educated in the public schools of Fulton and Hamilton counties, N. Y.; and Cass City and Tuscola, Mich. In 1875 he began to learn the printer's trade at Midland, Mich., remaining there until 1878, when he went to Gladwin and took charge of the *Gladwin County Record* which had just been established. He held the offices of School Assessor, member of Board of Education, Clerk of Grant Township, Clerk of Gladwin village, Postmaster under President Harrison and Mayor of Gladwin city. He was a member of the Constitutional Convention of 1907-8, from the Twenty-eighth District, and a member of the Gladwin County Republican Committee and chairman thereof after 1892; a member of the F. & A. M., R. A. M., K. of P., O. E. S., Foresters, Ben Hurs, Loyal Guards and Woodmen. In politics a Republican.

GUSTAVUS LEMUEL FOSTER

Member of the Board of Regents of the University of Michigan, 1850-2. Was born in Royalton, Niagara County, N. Y., May 5, 1818. He studied theology at Auburn Seminary, and at the Yale Theological School. He was ordained a minister in the Presbyterian Church in 1842. He did pastoral work at Dexter, Jackson, Clinton, Coldwater, Howell, and Lapeer. Mar. 2, 1850, he was appointed Regent of the University in place of Austin E. Wing deceased, and served to the end of the term, Jan. 1, 1852. Died at Lapeer, Mich., Sept. 9, 1876.

SEYMOUR FOSTER

Representative from the First District of Ingham County, 1895-6. Was born in Ann Arbor, Mich., July 1, 1845. From there he removed with his father's family to Scio, Washtenaw County, and in 1856 came to Lansing, which has since been his home. He acquired his early education in the public schools and at fourteen years of age engaged as a clerk; four years later he enlisted as a private in Co. B, Second Regiment, U. S. (Berdan's) Sharpshooters, participating in all the engagements of his regiment, as a part of the Second (Hancock) Corps, from the Battle of the Wilderness to the surrender of Lee. On his return from the army, he in 1871 engaged in the real estate business, which has since been his chief occupation. In politics a Republican. He held the office of Clerk and Treasurer of the city of Lansing; was Postmaster of Lansing during President Harrison's administration, resigning that position Mar. 4, 1893.

WILDER D. FOSTER

Senator from the Twenty-fourth District, 1855-6; and member of Congress from 1871-3. Was born in Monroe, N. Y., Jan. 8, 1821. He became a blacksmith and a resident of Marshall, Mich., and then of Grand Rapids. In 1845 he entered into the hardware trade at Grand Rapids, and was ultimately the largest dealer in that line in the Grand River valley. He served as Alderman, Treasurer and Mayor of Grand Rapids. He was a Republican in politics. He was elected to the Forty-second Congress in the place of Thomas W. Ferry who had been elected United States Senator. He had the respect and esteem of everybody. He died Sept. 20, 1873.

WILLIAM HENRY FOSTER

Representative, 1897-8 and 1899-1900, from Grand Traverse District, comprising the counties of Benzie, Grand Traverse and Leelanau. Was born on South Manitou Island, Mich., May 10, 1859, where he remained on a farm until the spring of 1880; sailing that summer and fall, he then moved to Traverse City, where he commenced schooling himself; taught school three terms; graduated from Traverse City schools in 1885, and entered the State Normal School the same year; he was graduated in 1887; was principal of schools at Samonauk, Dekalb County, Ill., in 1888; entered the law department of the University in 1889, graduating in 1890, and then engaged in the practice of his profession. In politics a Republican. He was Prosecuting Attorney and Circuit Court Commissioner.

WILLIAM J. FOSTER

Representative from the Second District of Calhoun County, 1901-2 and 1903-4. Was born in Wyoming, N. Y., Feb. 11, 1839, and received his education in the public schools and Wyoming Academy. A farmer by occupation. Married. In politics a Republican. He held various offices in his township.

PERLE L. FOUGH

Representative from the First District of Allegan County, 1907-8 and 1909-10. Was born at Burnip's Corners, Allegan County, Mich., Mar. 30, 1875, of English descent. He attended the public schools, high school, the Michigan State Normal College, the Northern Indiana Law School at Valparaiso, receiving his education through his personal efforts. Mr. Fouch was reared on the farm but followed the occupation of an attorney and in active practice of the law for many years. In politics a Republican. He held the office of Circuit Court Commissioner.

JAMES FOWLE

Representative from Hillsdale County, 1850, 1861-2 and 1863-4. Was born in Monroe County, N. Y., in 1807. In 1831 he came to Michigan, settling in Blissfield, and in 1835 removed to Camden, Hillsdale County. He was Postmaster from 1837 to 1844; the first Supervisor, and held that position and Justice several terms. He was a volunteer in the Black Hawk and Toledo Wars. He died May 18, 1865.

OTTO FOWLE

Senator, 1909-10 and 1911-12, from the Thirtieth District comprising the counties of Chippewa, Delta, Luce, Mackinac, Menominee and Schoolcraft. Was born at Moscow, Hillsdale County, Mich., Jan. 9, 1852. He was educated in the district schools, Hillsdale High School, and business college, and worked on a farm until sixteen. In 1871 he entered Hillsdale College and graduated in 1875, having taught school during two winters. He later read law, and was admitted to the bar at Hillsdale, September, 1877. In 1878 he was elected Circuit Court Commissioner. Mr. Fowle was married to Jennie E. Mead, June 30, 1880. He opened the first bank in Chippewa County at the Soo in July, 1883 with E. H. Mead as partner. In August, 1886, he formed the First National Bank into which the private bank was merged, and was its president. He also held several public offices, being appointed on Board of Water Commissioners and Sewer Commissioner in village of Soo, elected first Republican Mayor in 1889, chairman Board of Supervisors, Chamber of Commerce, Commercial Club, treasurer of Public Library Board, etc. Mr. Fowle organized St. Mary's Falls Water Power Company, original of Lake Superior Power Company; was appointed by Governor Bliss on board of trustees U. P. Hospital for Insane and was chairman of board for about four years. In politics a Republican. He died at Sault Ste. Marie, Aug. 21, 1920.

FREDERICK FOWLER

Representative from Hillsdale County, 1859-60; and Senator, 1865. Was born at Perry, O., Feb. 5, 1816. He had a fair education and was brought up a farmer. He filled large contracts on the Lake Shore railroad east of Hillsdale, and in 1837 with his brother, platted seventy-six acres, known as Fowler's addition to Hillsdale, and was a merchant there. He moved upon a farm in Reading in 1840, and owned several other farms. In 1861 he went into service as Captain of a Company in the 2d Mich. Cavalry, resigning in 1863, with the rank of Lieutenant Colonel. In politics he was a Republican. He was a member of the Michigan Pioneer and Historical Society. Deceased.

RALPH FOWLER

Representative from Livingston County, 1845 and 1851. Was born in Trenton, N. Y., Oct. 20, 1808. He settled in 1836 on a farm in Handy, Mich., and was the founder of the village of Fowlerville. He was the first Supervisor in 1838 and several terms thereafter, was a Justice for twenty-five years, and was liberal in giving aid to settlers, and in charity. He was a member of the Michigan Pioneer and Historical Society. He died Sept. 26, 1887.

AARON O. FOX

Representative from Branch County, 1917-18. Was born in Summit County, O., Feb. 18, 1852, of American parentage. His education was secured in the common schools and Buchtel College at Akron, O. He taught in the district and graded schools until he was thirty-eight years of age, when he took up farming, and was one of the active farmers of Branch County for twenty years. Several years ago he gave up farming and lived a retired life. He was Supervisor of Batavia for many years. Mr. Fox was married, Apr. 3, 1876 to Ellen Kauffman. In politics a Republican.

BENJAMIN F. FOX

Representative from Jackson County, 1849. Was born at Whitesboro, N. Y., Apr. 4, 1804, and removed to Buffalo, N. Y., in 1812. He was bred to farming and was a natural mechanic. He came to Michigan in 1826. In politics he was a Democrat.

EDWIN G. FOX

Senator, 1887-8, 1889-90, 1893-4 and 1909-10, from the Twenty-first District, comprising the counties of Lapeer and Tuscola. Was born of American parents in the Province of Ontario, in 1848. He came to Michigan when a boy and lived in Lapeer County for a short time, later locating at Flint. Most of the time since, he lived in Tuscola County. He received his education in the public schools. After spending one year as clerk and bookkeeper in a general store, he went to western Iowa to take charge of a general store. Owing to failing health he returned to Mayville, Mich., where he took charge of a general store for a few years. In 1876 he engaged in the mercantile business for himself. He served six years as Town Clerk, four years as Register of Deeds, two years Village President and eighteen years on the School Board. In politics a Republican. He was a member of the Senate of 1887, 1889 and 1893; and was again elected to the Senate, Nov. 3, 1908. He died Nov. 21, 1910 and was succeeded by John Conley.

HENRY FRALICK

Representative from Wayne County, 1847; Delegate from Wayne County to the Constitutional Convention of 1850; and Senator from the Third District, 1853-4. Was born at Minden, N. Y., Feb. 9, 1812. His father was a Captain in the War of 1812, and his grandfather one of eleven brothers who served in the Revolution. He received a fair education and came with his father to Michigan in 1824. He in early life was a sailor; was a clerk at the Michigan Exchange in 1836, and then in a store at Plymouth, and was in trade there from 1838 to 1860, also owned mills. He removed to Grand Rapids in 1862 and became a banker, being a director of the City National Bank; was also a merchant, real estate dealer, and manufacturer. He was Justice, Supervisor, editor, County Auditor, president of School Board, a manager to represent Michigan at the Philadelphia exposition, member of the semi-centennial exposition in 1886, and held other positions of trust and honor. He died at Grand Rapids, Mich., Mar. 14, 1891.

THOMAS TRACY FRALICK

Representative from Manistee County, 1911-12 and 1913-14. Was born at Paris, Ont., Nov. 7, 1851, of Dutch and Scotch parentage, and came to Michigan at the age of seventeen. His early life was spent on a farm and he was educated in the public schools. In politics a Democrat.

JAMES FRANCIS

Representative from Alpena County, 1903-4. Was born in Glengary County, Ont., Nov. 23, 1857, of Irish parents. He was educated in the public schools of Van Kleek Hill, Ont., and normal school at Ottawa, Canada, receiving a life certificate as teacher in 1886. After teaching school a year in Ontario, Mr. Francis came to Alpena and entered the employment of the D. B. C. & A. Railway Company, but soon commenced teaching at Hillman, Mich., and while teaching took up the study of law. He was admitted to the bar in 1889. He was elected Prosecuting Attorney for Montmorency County on the Republican ticket in 1896 and was re-elected in 1898 but resigned before the close of his second term and moved to Alpena where he formed a law partnership with Hon. Michael O'Brien. He was elected Circuit Court Commissioner for Alpena County in 1900. Married. In politics a Republican.

THOMAS F. FRANCIS

Representative from the Second District of Marquette County, 1915-16, 1917-18 and 1921-2. Was born at Redruth, Cornwall, England, Dec. 14, 1852, of English parentage. He was educated in the Redruth schools of England. He with his widowed mother and two sisters came to America in 1871, moving to Ishpeming in 1876 where he has resided continuously since. He is a widower, and has a family of four children. Mr. Francis has been engaged in the mining business from which he is now retired. He was for three years president of the Ishpeming Co-operative Mercantile Society and for several terms served as a director. In politics he is a Republican.

WILLIAM H. FRANCIS

Representative from Leelanau and Benzie counties, 1879-80; and Senator from the Twenty-eighth District, 1885-6. Was born in Ingham County, Mich., Jan. 29, 1843. He was educated at common schools; was a clerk; served from 1861 to 1864 in the 2d Mich. Cavalry; studied law and was admitted in 1882; and went into practice at Frankfort, Mich. He held several positions, including Justice, Prosecuting Attorney, Supervisor, and Circuit Court Commissioner. In politics a Republican.

WILLIAM H. FRANKHAUSER

Republican, of Hillsdale, was elected to Congress from the Third Congressional District, Nov. 2, 1920, but, because of ill health, did not take his seat. He died on May 9, 1921, at Battle Creek.

CHARLES L. FRASER

Representative from Emmet and other counties, 1881-2. Was born in Wyoming County, N. Y., in 1833, and came with his parents to Oakland County, Mich., in 1834. He was a farmer, sailor, mechanic, teacher, and real estate dealer. He graduated at the State University in 1864. He held several offices at Petoskey. In politics a Republican.

MURDOCH FRAZER

Representative from Saginaw County, 1848. Was born in Inverness, Scotland, Dec. 25, 1812. He was a farmer and a Democrat. He settled at Saginaw in 1835, and was Supervsior in 1844 and 1846. He died Mar. 18, 1876.

ALLEN M. FREELAND

Member of the State Board of Education, 1919—. Was born on a farm near Caledonia, Kent County, Mich., Mar. 18, 1872, of English parentage. His early education was obtained in the rural schools. Later he attended Valparaiso University, of Valparaiso, Ind., from which institution he received the degree of B. S. He then entered Hope College at Holland, Mich., where he was given the degree of B. A. He began teaching a district school at the age of seventeen and has been engaged in that profession ever since. From 1898 to 1907 he was Superintendent of the South Grand Rapids schools, and, during this period, conducted summer schools for teachers. He also served four years as member of the Kent County

Board of School Examiners. For the past twelve years he has been Commissioner of Schools of Kent County. While serving as Commissioner he has been an instructor for several summer terms in the Western State Normal School at Kalamazoo. He has also studied law and was admitted to the bar in 1916. Mr. Freeland was married to Bertha L. Dean, of Grand Rapids, in 1897, and has one child. He is a 32nd degree Mason, being a member of the DeWitt Clinton Consistory and Saladin Temple Shrine. He was appointed a member of the State Board of Education by Governor Albert E. Sleeper, Apr. 23, 1919, to fill the vacancy caused by the resignation of Thomas E. Johnson, and was elected Apr. 2, 1923.

CHANDLER FREEMAN

Representative from Clinton County, 1863-4. Was born in Hebron, Me., Jan. 18, 1814. He was a graduate of Dartmouth College, came to Michigan in 1855, and was a manufacturer at Maple Rapids. He took great interest in public schools and education. He died in August, 1865, at Central City, Colo.

CHARLES HUSE FREEMAN

Representative from the Second District of Wayne County, 1913-14. Was born at Topeka, Kan., Oct. 6, 1884, of English descent. He acquired his education in the public schools of Detroit, supplemented by a business university course. After completing his education he engaged in cement construction and the real estate business. He is a direct descendent from Edmund Freeman, who arrived from England and established Lynn, Mass., in 1630. In politics a National Progressive.

FRANKLIN S. FREEMAN

Senator from the Twenty-fourth District, 1877-8. Was born at Sutton. Mass., Feb. 14, 1829. He removed to Adrian, Mich., in 1839, and in 1843 to Ionia County. He was engaged in mercantile and agricultural pursuits until 1860, then resided in Ionia, engaged in insurance and money loaning business. He was treasurer of the People's Fire Insurance Company of Ionia and Montcalm counties. In politics a Republican.

HERBERT L. FREEMAN

Delegate in the Constitutional Convention of 1907-8, from the Thirteenth District, Genesee County. Was born in Flushing in 1859, of American descent. He received his education in the public schools at Flushing. In 1885 he was married to Miss Margaret McGinley. of Flushing. He was engaged in the farming business until 1904 when he went into real estate. He served as Supervisor and County Superintendent of the Poor.

LEONARD FREEMAN

Senator, 1911-12, from the Thirteenth District, comprising the counties of Genesee and Livingston. Was born in Crawford County, Pa., May 6, 1867, and came to Michigan in 1903. Previous to his coming to Michigan he was engaged in the mercantile business and in farming. After locating in this state he engaged in the manufacture of butter and cheese, farming, and dealing in real estate. Married. He was president of the Fenton State Savings Bank of Fenton, served as Village President of Fenton, and was a member of the Board of Control, Michigan Reformatory at Ionia, from February, 1908, up to the time of his election as State Senator; also served on the Board of Prison Industries. In politics a Republican.

RETIRE WHITTIMORE FREES

Representative from the Second District of Lenawee County, 1923—. Was born in Utica Township, Winnebago County, Wisconsin, January 2, 1864. He was the fourth son of Retire W. and Clare J. Frees. His early education was acquired in the public schools of Utica and when twenty-one he entered Lawrence University. While attending the university he entered the ministry and for twenty-five years has held pastorates in Wisconsin, Illinois and Michigan.

ALFRED FRENCH

Senator from the Third District, 1850-1. Came from the State of New York and settled in Branch County while it was a wilderness. He was a pioneer Democrat, and held almost undisputed political sway in that vicinity for many years. He was an active Legislator. He resigned as Senator, June 27, 1851.

CHARLES B. FRENCH

Representative from the First District of Monroe County, 1901-2. Was born in Geneva, O., June 13, 1852. At the early age of thirteen he was compelled to earn his living and began as train boy on what is now known as the Big Four Railroad between Cleveland and Columbus. While thus engaged he studied telegraphy which business he followed for thirty years. He then purchased the farm on which he resided near the village of Petersburg, Monroe County. He was not married. In politics a Democrat. He died at Norwalk, O., Nov. 28, 1921.

GEORGE H. FRENCH

Senator from the Thirteenth District, 1861-2 and 1863-4. Was born in Junius, N. Y., Jan. 18, 1820. He received a fair education and became a teacher. In 1841 he settled on a farm in Tekonsha, Mich., but was a merchant at Homer after 1848. He filled local offices, and in the Senate introduced the first resolution to free the slaves as a war measure. He also introduced the resolution which resulted in the "roll of honor," a lasting record of the soldiers who died for the Union. In politics he was a Republican.

JOHN M. FRENCH

Representative from Eaton and Ingham counties, 1842. Was born in New Brunswick, N. J., July 11, 1798, and removed to western New York in 1806, there learned the trade of a tanner, and was in that business in several places. He settled in Aurelius, Mich., as a farmer in 1838, and held several offices including that of Supervisor. He resided at Lansing after 1866. At the legislative reunion in 1886, he was the oldest person present. In politics he was a Democrat.

ROBERT E. FRENCH

Senator from the Eleventh District (St. Clair County), 1893-4 and 1895-6. Was born in England, Jan. 20, 1835. He came to Canada at the age of seven years, where, after a limited school education he engaged in the manufacture of boots and shoes. In 1861 he came to Fort Gratiot, Mich., where he for a time continued his trade and engaged in a general mercantile business. In politics a Republican. He held the offices of Supervisor, Township Treasurer and Mayor of the city of Fort Gratiot. He was the first Postmaster at Fort Gratiot, which position he held for fifteen years. In 1855 he was married to Henrietta Nottingham, of Canada.

WILLIAM A. FRENCH

Representative from the Second District of Monroe County, 1883-4; and Commissioner of the State Land Office, 1894-1901. Was born in Pelham, Canada, Mar. 2, 1849 and received his education in the public schools of that city. In 1867 he went to Chicago, where he was engaged as night manager of the lines of the Chicago & Northwestern Railroad, remaining in that capacity for four years when he moved to Dundee, Mich., where he was engaged as agent for the Chicago & Canada Southern Railroad. He also engaged in sawmilling, and as a railroad contractor furnished materials for the Chicago & Canada Southern Railroad west of the Detroit River. He represented the people of that district in the State Legislature of 1883-4, and at the close of his term moved to Bell, Presque Isle County where he continued in lumbering and milling. In politics a Republican. He was for four years a member of the Republican State Central Committee. Mar. 20, 1894, he was appointed Commissioner of the State Land Office to fill the vacancy caused by the removal of John G. Berry, and was elected to that office to succeeded himself for the term of 1895-7; was nominated at the Republican State Convention held in Grand Rapids in August, 1896 by acclamation to again succeed himself for the term of 1897-9; and was renominated at the Republican State Convention held in Detroit in September, 1898, for the term 1899-1901. He died at Saginaw, Mar. 1, 1903.

JOHN W. FREY

Representative from St. Joseph County, 1853-4. Was born in Canajoharie, N. Y., July 24, 1804. By occupation he was a blacksmith and farmer, in politics first a Whig then Republican. He came to Michigan in 1843, settled at Three Rivers and engaged in business as a blacksmith. About 1854 he opened a general store in Three Rivers, which he carried on several years, retiring during the late war. He died in November, 1872.

G. OLIVER FRICK

Representative from the First District of Wayne County, 1921-2. Was born Jan. 26, 1872, at Pittsburg, Pa., and is of German descent. His education was acquired in the public and high schools of Niagara and Erie counties, N. Y. After completing high school he learned the printer's trade and with his father published a weekly newspaper at Youngstown, N. Y., and continued such publication until 1902 when he entered the U. S. Government service as Mine Grant Inspector. Mr. Frick is at present secretary-treasurer of the Central Glass Casket Co. He is married and has two sons. In politics he is a Republican.

CHARLES A. FRIDLENDER

Senator, 1891-2, from the Twenty-sixth District, comprising the counties of Alcona, Alpena, Iosco, Ogemaw and Oscoda. Was born in Paris, France, Apr. 8, 1838, and came to the United States in 1854. He went into the army in October, 1861, as a private in Battery H, 1st Mich. Light Artillery, and participated in all the engagements in the Vicksburg and Atlanta campaigns, and was discharged in 1865, having obtained the grade of 2d Lieutenant. He then engaged in the mercantile business. He served as Village Treasurer, until he received the nomination of his party for the State Senate on the Democratic ticket. His Republican opponent, Benjamin C. Morse, was given the certificate of election on an alleged vote of 4,117 to 4,005 for Mr. Fridlender, who made contest and was awarded his seat in the Senate of 1891-2 on the 24th of February, 1891. He died in the State of Washington, June, 1915.

ALONZO T. FRISBEE

Senator from the Twentieth District, 1885-6. Was born Oct. 12, 1840, near Howell, Mich. He received a high school education and worked at home until twenty-eight years of age. He settled as a farmer in Isabella County in 1872 and was also a merchant. Afterwards he returned to Livingston County; was Supervisor many terms. In politics a Greenbacker.

PHILIP S. FRISBEE

Representative from Oakland County, 1859-60. Was born near Seneca Lake, N. Y. He removed from Chautauqua County to Lapeer County in 1833 and in 1840 purchased land in Springfield, Oakland County, and removed to that town. He was a Justice. He died Dec. 21, 1800.

ALMON B. FROST

Representative from Oakland County, 1871-2. Was born Sept. 17, 1826, in Covington, N. Y. He was a farmer by occupation, a Democrat in politics. He came to Michigan with his parents in 1841. They settled in Orion, Oakland County. He was Supervisor sixteen years, Township Clerk four years, School Inspector twenty-five years and held other town offices.

JOSEPH JAMES FROST

Representative from the First District of Kent County, 1917-18. Was born in Bryan, O., July 15, 1881, of German descent, and was educated in the public schools. He came to Grand Rapids in 1901, was employed in the branch office of Brunswick-Balke-Collender Co. for several years, resigning his position to enter the cigar business, and then engaged in the cigar and sporting goods business. In politics a Democrat.

CEYLON C. FULLER

Representative from Newaygo and other counties, 1869-70. Was born at Chardon, O., June 25, 1832. In 1845 he removed to Grand Rapids, Mich., where he was educated, and at Hiram College, O., a classmate and room mate of President Garfield. He studied law and was admitted in 1860; practiced at Big Rapids. He was Postmaster, Prosecuting Attorney, Judge of Probate, and Circuit Court Commissioner, and was vice-president of the Michigan Pioneer and Historical Society and contributed to local history which was published in the *Collections*. In 1882 he was elected Judge of the Twenty-seventh Judicial Circuit and served one term. His death occurred at Big Rapids Dec. 23, 1906.

CLARENCE J. FULLER

Representative from Livingston County, 1921-2 and 1923—. Was born in Livingston County Dec. 22, 1876, of American parents. He was educated in the district schools and high school at Howell. He has always been a resident of Michigan and an active farmer. He is married and has one daughter and one son. In politics he is a Republican. He served his township as Supervisor during the years 1911-12 and 1913, being chairman of Board of Supervisors in 1913.

EDWARD L. FULLER

Representative from Washtenaw County, 1840; and Senator from the Fifth District, 1841, and from the Second District, 1842. Was born at Sempronius, N. Y., May 22, 1810. He graduated at Union College in 1830, and studied law. He settled in Washtenaw County at an early day and was a distinguished orator of the Whig party. When on the stump he was followed from place to place by crowds. Every art of the speaker was at his command: Mythology, classic story, fable, anecdote, history, poetry, biography, scripture, personal observation and experience, vivid imagination, fervid enthusiasm, apt and ready wit, magnetized his hearers, and they laughed, cried, shouted, and were completely under his control. He died at San Francisco, Cal., Apr. 6, 1851.

ORAMEL B. FULLER

Representative from the Delta District, 1893-4, 1895-6 and 1897-8; Senator from the Thirtieth District, 1901-2, 1903-4, 1907-8; and Auditor General, 1909-10 to 1923—. Was born at Jersey City, N. J., Jan. 22, 1858, coming to Michigan in 1869. He received his education in the public schools of Lansing and Muskegon, to which latter city he removed in 1874. He removed to Ford River, Delta County his present home, in 1884. Mr. Fuller was married to Miss Jennie L. Van Zalingen, of Muskegon, in 1887. He is a Mason, member of the Escanaba Commandery, Ahmed Temple of the Shrine at Marquette, DeWitt Clinton Consistory, Grand Rapids, and is also a member of the Knights of Pythias and the Elks. He represented the Delta district, composed of the counties of Alger, Delta and Schoolcraft, in the House in 1893, 1895 and 1897; was speaker pro tem. of the House in 1897; represented the Thirtieth Senatorial District, composed of the counties of Chippewa, Delta, Luce, Mackinac, Menominee and Schoolcraft, in the Senate in 1901, 1903 and 1907 and was president pro tem. of the Senate in 1903. He was Supervisor of the Ford River Township for ten years, but resigned when he was elected Auditor General in 1908 and is at present prominently connected with many business enterprises of Escanaba. In politics he is a Republican. At the Republican Convention held at Muskegon, Sept. 22, 1922, he was nominated for an eighth term, and at the election held on Nov. 7, 1922, was elected.

PHILO C. FULLER

Representative from Lenawee County, and Speaker of the House, 1841. Was born in New Marlborough, Mass., Aug. 13, 1787. By profession he was a lawyer, politically a Whig. He was a member of the New York Assembly, and also Senator. He settled in Adrian in 1837, and had charge of the Erie & Kalamazoo Railroad, and bank. He was Assistant Postmaster General under Harrison, and again became a resident of New York, and was Comptroller of that State. He died at Geneva, N. Y., Aug. 16, 1855.

GEORGE A. FUNSTON

Representative from the Third District of St. Clair County, 1867-8. His post-office address was Capac. (Further data not obtainable).

ANDREW FYFE

Senator, 1905-6 and 1907-8, from the Sixteenth District, comprising the first, second, third, fourth, fifth, sixth, seventh, eighth, ninth, and twelfth wards of the city of Grand Rapids. Was born at Glasgow, Scotland, Apr. 27, 1863. He came to this country with his parents when three years of age and settled in the Province of Ontario, Canada, where he attended the common schools until the family moved to Grand Rapids, Mich., in 1879. He began life in the United States as a furniture worker and in 1884 was engaged as reporter on Grand Rapids newspapers. He was appointed clerk of the Superior Court of Grand Rapids in 1887, and while holding that office studied law, passed an excellent examination and was admitted to the bar. He resigned that office to accept the appointment as surveyor of customs for the Port of Grand Rapids, tendered him by President Cleveland in 1893. After 1897 he gave his attention to law and insurance business. Mr. Fyfe was known as a forcible campaign speaker for the Democracy until 1896, when he left that party upon the money issue and stumped the state against Bryan; then became an active Republican.

LAWRENCE C. FYFE

Representative from Berrien County, 1881-2 and 1883-4; and Delegate in the Constitutional Convention of 1907-8, from the Seventh District, Berrien County. Was born in Fort Lennox, on the Isle Aux Noix, Richelieu River, Quebec, in 1850, of Scottish descent. He received his education in Scotland, England, and at the University of Michigan. Married and lived in Michigan since 1869. He was engaged in the practice of law at St. Joseph in 1907.

GEORGE M. GAHAGAN

Representative from the Second District of Lenawee County, 1913-14. Was born in Medina Township, Lenawee County, Mich., June 13, 1878, of Irish parentage. His education was acquired in the common schools. With the exception of two years, when he was engaged in newspaper work in Chicago, Ill., he always resided in Michigan, most of this time being employed in farm work. In politics a Democrat.

JOHN L. GAGE

Representative from Genesee County, 1843. Was born in New London, N. H., Oct. 5, 1805. He removed with his parents to Ontario County, N. Y., in 1817, and lived with them until of age. He then taught school winters and worked as a carpenter summers. He came to Michigan in 1830 and settled near Tecumseh. In 1836 he settled on a farm in the town of Flint, where he lived until 1887. He held various offices, including Justice and Supervisor. He resided in Burton. Genesee County in 1887. In politics he was a Democrat.

JUSTUS GAGE

Member of the State Board of Agriculture, 1861-9. Was born in De Ruyter, N. Y., Mar. 13, 1805. He received an academical education, and became a Universalist minister. In 1837 he settled in Wayne, Cass County, was one of the first presidents of the County Agricultural Society at Detroit. For eight years he was a member of the State Board of Agriculture, and was Director of Schools at Dowagiac. He took great interest in the early development of the State Agricultural College. He died Jan. 21, 1875.

SENECA H. GAGE

Representative from Eaton County, 1859-60. Was born in Bellona, N. Y., Oct. 3, 1813. By profession he was a physician, politically first Whig, then Republican. He settled in Bellevue, Eaton County, in 1834, and in practice was more than once compelled to wait for daylight in a tree, when pursued by wild beasts. He was a member of the first nominating convention of Eaton County in 1838. He died Dec. 30, 1882.

WILLIAM GAGE

Representative from Oakland County, 1843. Was an early pioneer from the State of New York, and was the first settler in the township of Holly, Oakland County, and built the first house there. In 1838 he was a Justice of the Peace.

JOSEPH M. GAIGE

Senator, 1895-6, from the Twentieth District. composed of the counties of Huron and Sanilac. Was born in West Burlington, Otsego County, N. Y., June 13, 1848; was educated at Cooperstown (New York) Seminary, the Oneida Conference Seminary, Cazemoria, N. Y., and the University of Michigan, graduating from the law department of the latter in 1869. The following year he became member of the firm of Moss, Mills & Gaige, lumber manufacturers and real estate dealers at Croswell, Sanilac County, and continued as such until the dissolution of the firm by the death of Truman Moss in 1883. He then engaged in the real estate business and banking at Croswell. In politics a Republican. He held the office of Village President and president of the Croswell Agricultural Society.

FRANKLIN B. GALBRAITH

Senator from the Fourteenth District, 1889-90. Was born in Sanilac County, Mich., in 1839. At the age of seventeen he began the study of medicine in the medical department of the University. He was admitted to a final examination for the degree of Doctor of Medicine at the close of his second year. He then went to New York City and entered the College of Physicians and Surgeons, where he remained one year and graduated with honor from that college in 1861. He returned to Michigan, and in the same year accepted a commission as Assistant Surgeon to the 10th Mich. Vol. Infantry, with which command he served until 1863, when he was compelled to resign on account of broken down health. In the summer of 1863 he accepted the appointment of surgeon to the Board of Enrollment for the Fifth Congressional District of Michigan, and was one of the board that conducted the first and second drafts that were made in the Fifth District. After a few months he resigned his position on the Board of Enrollment and engaged in the practice of medicine with Dr. O. C. M. Stockwell, in Port Huron, where he remained in the practice of his profession until 1865, when he was appointed surgeon to what was to be the 30th Mich. Vol. Infantry. This regiment was commanded by Col. John Atkinson, and rendezvoused on the fairgrounds in Pontiac. This regiment was finally broken into fragments and the detachments were sent to replenish the depleted ranks of regiments already in the field. Dr. Galbraith was offered the appointment of Surgeon to the Fourth Michigan Cavalry, which was declined because the regiment was then with Sherman on his march through Georgia, and it looked as though the war was about over, which it virtually was, and the doctor being in Pontiac, and liking the town and surrounding country, concluded to remain here and practice his profession. In November, 1865, he rented an office and began the work which resulted in building up the largest and best practice ever done by any physician in Oakland County. In 1883-5 he was elected president of the Oakland County Agricultural Society. In politics a Republican. He was elected Mayor of the Democratic city of Pontiac.

WILLIAM J. GALBRAITH

Representative from the First District of Houghton County, 1903-4, 1905-6 and 1907-8. Was born in Montgomery County, Ill., Nov. 5, 1866, of Scotch-Irish parents. He was educated in the Illinois State Normal School from which he graduated in 1889, and then entered the literary department of the University of Michigan where he remained two years. He graduated from the law department of the University of Michigan in 1894. He was a successful educator, having been principal of schools, institute conductor and instructor in English in the Wisconsin State Normal; also Secretary of the School Board of Calumet five years. In politics a Republican.

ELBREDGE G. GALE

Representative from Genesee County, 1853-4; Delegate from Genesee County to the Constitutional Convention of 1850; and Senator from the Twenty-fourth District, 1861-2. Was born in Norwich, Mass., Feb. 2, 1811, and removed with his parents to Shoreham, Vt., in 1818. He was a teacher at sixteen, was educated at the Shoreham Academy, studied medicine and graduated at Castleton in 1834. He practiced in Niagara County, N. Y., but in 1844 settled at Atlas, Mich., continuing in practice. He was surgeon of the provost board of the 6th district until the close of the war; and Collector of Internal Revenue for two years, same district. Later he returned to Vermont. In politics he was a Republican.

MARTIN P. GALE

Representative from Mecosta County, 1881-2. Was born Nov. 20, 1847, in Barre, Vt. He received an academical education, and in 1867 removed to Chicago and engaged in mercantile business. In 1872 he removed to Big Rapids, Mich. He was elected Mayor of Big Rapids in 1877 and re-elected in 1878 and 1879. By occupation he was a lumberman; in politics a Republican.

EDWARD R. GALLOWAY

Representative from Hillsdale County, 1917-18 and 1919-20. Was born in Reading Township, June 19, 1855, of American parentage. His education was acquired in the rural schools and the Hillsdale High School. Married. He served his township as Justice of the Peace, and as Supervisor, having been twice elected chairman of the board. In politics a Republican.

JOHN GALLOWAY

Representative from Oakland County, 1845. His postoffice address was Waterford Center. (Further data not obtainable).

JOHN H. GALLOWAY

Senator from the Twenty-third District, 1861-2. Was born at Gorham, Ontario County, N. Y., Oct. 2, 1817. His grandfather was a scout and messenger for General Washington during the Revolutionary War. He came to Howell in 1844 and established a foundry. In politics he was a Republican. He filled minor offices and was a successful business man.

CALEB H. GALLUP

Representative from Huron County, 1867-8. Was born in Norwalk, O., May 10, 1834. He was the first student to receive a degree from Madison University, N. Y. He graduated from the Cincinnati Law School in 1858. In 1859 he removed to St. Johns, Mich., and in 1860 to Port Austin. He was ten years Prosecuting Attorney of Huron County, held other county and town offices, and was Deputy U. S. Marshal. He opposed municipal aid to railroads in the Legislature, and took the first steps to secure a harbor of refuge at Sand Beach. He resided at Norwalk, O., in 1887.

GEORGE GALLUP

Representative from Delta County, 1903-4. Was born at Northfield, Vt., July 31, 1858. He was educated at the Northfield High School, Wesleyan Academy at Wilbraham, Mass., Wesleyan University at Middletown, O. After attending the law department of the University of Michigan one year, he was admitted to the bar in 1881 and opened a law office at Farwell, Mich. In 1889 he moved to Delta County and opened a law office in Escanaba where he practiced his profession. He served as Mayor of Escanaba several years. Married. In politics a Republican.

AUGUSTUS H. GANSSER

Representative from the First District of Bay County, 1911-12; and Senator, 1915-16, 1917-18 and 1923—, from the Twenty-fourth District, comprising the counties of

Bay and Midland. Was born at Wurtemberg, Germany, July 5, 1872. He attended the primary schools in Germany and the public schools of Bay City where he has resided since June, 1881. He is married. From 1884 to 1886 he was employed in a mill; 1886 to 1896 collector and clerk; manager of a carpet store, and newspaper correspondent from 1896 to 1898, and insurance agent from 1898 to 1910. He has served in the M. N. G. since 1892, and participated in the battle and siege of Santiago in 1898. He has been active in many fraternities and is a member of Bay City lodges F. & A. M., R. A. M., O. E. S., Elks, Odd Fellows, K. of P., and National League of Veterans and Sons. In politics he is a Republican.

SAMUEL N. GANTT

Representative from Oakland County, 1838. Came from Central New York to Pontiac, Mich., in 1837 and established the Pontiac *Herald*, which he published as a Democratic paper until 1839. He removed to Paw Paw and started the Paw Paw *Free Press* in 1845, which he published less than a year and a half. He afterwards moved to Detroit. Nothing farther can be learned of him.

GEORGE W. GARD

Representative from Cass County, 1911-12. Was born in Cass County, Apr. 4, 1848, and was educated in the public schools. He was married in November, 1872, to Rachael Kirby. He taught school for several years, teaching nine years in one district and having at one time an enrollment of ninety-seven. A farmer by occupation. He was Supervisor, and County Treasurer. In politics a Republican. He died Nov. 9, 1913.

MILTON J. GARD

Member of the State Board of Agriculture, 1875-81. Was born in Union County, Ind., Mar. 11, 1824. He settled on a farm in Volinia, Cass County, in 1829. He became greatly interested in the education of the early settlers, and established a grammar school which he taught for four years, and it became the germ of the farmers' club of that township. He filled every township office except one, was president of the Cass County Agricultural Society for six years, and was for six years a member of the State Board of Agriculture.

EARL P. GARDINER

Delegate from Washtenaw County to the Constitutional Convention of 1850. Was born in Bosrah, Conn., in 1807. In 1827 he enlisted in Co. A, 2nd Regiment, U. S. Infantry, and was stationed at Fort Gratiot, Michigan Territory. On his discharge he married, settled in Ann Arbor, and went into business as publisher of the *Michigan Argus*. He also was Justice. By trade he was a printer; in politics a Democrat. Deceased.

AMOS GARDNER

Representative from Branch County, 1885-6. Was born in Otsego County, N. Y., Mar. 18, 1833. His occupation a farmer; in politics a Republican. He held the office of Supervisor nine terms.

RANSOM GARDNER

Senator from the Fifteenth District, 1853-4. Was born at Fort Ann, N. Y., in 1813. He came to Jonesville, Mich., in 1837, and engaged in mercantile business. His first connection with railroads was the building of the station house at Jonesville, the next a contract to grade the Michigan Southern Railroad to Chicago. This was followed by track laying on the same road. He also built the Detroit & Toledo branch of the Lake Shore road; the road from Jackson to Adrian; the Cincinnati, Wabash & Michigan, and several others. He was emphatically a leader and projector in the early days of railroad building. He was first a Whig and then a Republican. He resided at Jonesville until 1866, when he became a resident of Kalamazoo. He married Olivia A. Smith in 1839, and was the father of three sons and two daughters. He was a man of great energy and indomitable will, active, industrious, honorable and benevolent. He died at Kalamazoo, June 9, 1876.

WASHINGTON GARDNER

Secretary of State, 1894-7 and 1897-9; member of Congress, 1899-1901 to 1909-11. Was born in Morrow County, O., February, 1845. Before the war he attended the public schools in his native state; after the war he entered an academy; later was a student at Hillsdale College for three years, and graduated from the Ohio Wesleyan University in 1870. Subsequent to graduation he studied theology in Boston and law in New York. In 1861 he entered the army as a member of Co. D, 65th Ohio Vol. Infantry; served over three years as a common soldier in the ranks; was in every campaign, skirmish and battle with his regiment from the time of organization to May, 1864, when he was badly wounded in the engagement of Resaca, Ga. He was Regent of the Grand Council of the Royal Arcanum, and for several years chaplain of the supreme body; and served the Michigan Department G. A. R. as its commander. From 1889 to 1896 he was a professor in, and public lecturer for, Albion College. He was appointed Secretary of State by Governor Rich, Mar. 20, 1894, to fill the vacancy caused by the removal of John W. Jochim; was elected to that position for the term of 1895-7, and re-elected to that of 1897-9; was elected to the 56th, 57th, 58th, 59th, and 60th Congresses of the United States and re-elected Nov. 3, 1908.

CHARLES W. GARFIELD

Representative from the Second District of Kent County, 1881-2; member of the State Board of Agriculture, 1887-99. Was born in Wauwatosa, Wis., Mar. 14, 1848. He removed to Grand Rapids in 1858, attended school, and was a teacher at seventeen. He graduated at the Agricultural College in 1870; engaged in the nursery business; from 1874 to 1878 was connected with the horticultural department of the Agricultural College; for four years conducted the farm department of the Detroit *Free Press;* and was Secretary of the State Horticultural Society 1877-87. A Republican in politics.

SAMUEL M. GARFIELD

Representative from Kent County, 1871-2 and 1875-6. Was born in Pembroke, N. Y., June 23, 1816. He received a common school education, and in 1841 settled in Milwaukee County, Wis. In 1858 he settled on a farm near Grand Rapids, Mich. He was a Supervisor and held other local offices. By occupation he was a farmer: in politics a Republican.

JAMES GARGETT

Representative from Gratiot County, 1863-4. Was born in Godmanchester, Canada, July 15, 1825. He removed to Ohio in 1835; received a common school education; became a teacher and farmer; was a commission merchant in Cleveland; then in the hardware trade at Frederickstown, O.; removed to Alma, Mich., in 1858, and became a merchant and manufacturer, and dealer in real estate. He was Supervisor and held other local offices. In politics he was a Republican.

WILLIAM D. GARRISON

Representative from Shiawassee County, 1871-2. Was born Aug. 9, 1835, in Farmer, N. Y., and came with his parents to Michigan in 1837. He worked on a farm and attended winter school until twenty, then learned the trade of a carpenter, but finally went into mercantile business at Vernon, and became a leading merchant of Shiawassee County. A Republican in politics. He was director and stockholder in the National Bank of Corunna.

MATTHEW T. GARVEY

Senator from the Eleventh District, 1875-6. Was born in Clark County, O., May 13, 1821. He received a common school education, removed to Cass County, Mich., in 1846, and continued to reside there. He was five terms Supervisor; served two terms as Justice, and four years as Judge of Probate for Cass County. He was Postmaster at Dowagiac under Taylor. His occupation was farming; in politics a Republican.

JAN W. GARVELINK

Representative from Allegan County, 1873-4 and 1883-4; and Senator, 1891-2, from the Tenth District, comprising the counties of Allegan and Van Buren. Was born in the Netherlands, Dec. 6, 1833, and came to the United States at the age of fourteen years. He received a common school education before coming to this country; did not obtain a school education here, but informed himself in the English language. After becoming of age he was elected Township Clerk two years, then held the office of Supervisor about twenty years; was also honored with the offices of Justice of the Peace, School Inspector and School Director for from twenty-five to thirty-five years.

ALONZO GARWOOD

Senator from the Seventeenth District, 1857-8. Was born Oct. 15, 1824, in Logan County, O. After studying medicine he graduated at Starling Medical College at Columbus, O. He located at Cassopolis, Mich., in 1850, and engaged there in practice after that date. He was one of the organizers of the Republican party at Jackson. In 1864 he was mustered into the service as surgeon of the 28th Mich. Infantry, and served until 1866. From 1874 to 1884 he was one of the County Superintendents of the Poor.

HERSCHEL R. GASS

State Superintendent of Public Instruction, 1883-5. Was born in Ray, Mich., Mar. 7, 1844. He graduated from the University of Michigan in 1873; from 1874 to 1877 was professor of sciences and mathematics, Vincennes, (Ind.) University; principal of Vernon, Mich., and Jonesville high schools from 1877 to 1883; appointed Superintendent of Public Instruction to fill vacancy, Mar. 1, 1883. In 1884 he was elected to that office as the Republican candidate, but resigned in 1885, after serving a short time.

MYLO L. GAY

Representative from Livingston County, 1869-70; and Senator from the Twenty-second District, 1871-2. Was born in Salisbury, Conn., June 20, 1825. He lived at Ann Arbor, Mich., from 1831 to 1837, then came to Howell. He graduated at Oberlin College in 1848, studied law and was admitted in 1853. He held several town and county offices, and became a banker at Fowlerville in 1873, still residing at Howell. He died Mar. 21, 1884.

EDWARD GAYDE

Representative from the Third District of Wayne County, 1915-16 and 1917-18. Was born at Plymouth, Mich., Jan. 2, 1878, of German parents. He was educated in the Plymouth public schools. At sixteen years he entered his father's store as a clerk, which occupation he followed until Jan. 9, 1899, when he and his brother purchased the stock and formed a copartnership under the name of Gayde Brothers, dealing in groceries, crockery and hardware. He served one term as Clerk of the village of Plymouth, one term as Trustee of said village, three terms as Clerk of Plymouth Township, and ten years as a member of the Board of Cemetery Trustee of the village of Plymouth. Fraternally, he was a member of Plymouth Rock Lodge No. 47, F. & A. M., Union Chapter No. 55, R. A. M., Northville Commandery No. 39, K. T., Plymouth Chapter No. 115, O. E. S. and Moslem Temple A. A. O. N. M. S. In politics a Republican.

AUGUSTINE S. GAYLORD

Representative from Saginaw County, 1863-4. Was born in Jefferson, O., Feb. 9, 1831. He was liberally educated in the best institutions of Ohio. He removed from Ohio to Saginaw in 1851, and entered upon the study of the law. In 1852 he was appointed Deputy County Clerk, and was Clerk of the county in following years. Politically he was a Whig until 1854, then a Republican. About 1854 he became a law partner of Hon. John Moore, and as a lawyer was a success from the start. He married Emeline E. Warner, of Ripon. Wis., in 1856. He was U. S. Commissioner in 1864-5 and 1866, and as Representative was a leading member of the House and of the judiciary committee. He was appointed Assistant Attorney General of the United States by President Grant, and was solicitor of the Interior Department under Secretary Chandler until his death, June 21, 1877. He wrought many important changes in the methods of business with great advantage to the service. He died June 21, 1877 at Saginaw.

JAMES J. GEE

Representative from the Second District of Muskegon County, 1901-2. Was born in Homer, Calhoun County, Mich., Dec. 19, 1851, and received his education in the district and high school. After teaching school for one year he engaged in the mercantile business at Whitehall. He was interested in horticulture and forestry, being a successful fruit grower and farmer. Married. In politics a staunch Republican. He held the offices of Township Treasurer, Supervisor and member of the School Board.

JOHN GEDDES

Representative from Washtenaw County, 1841. Was born in Londonderry, Pa., Mar. 10, 1801, and was brought up on a farm. In 1824 he located land three miles south of Ann Arbor, in Pittsfield. In 1825, with his brother, he bought more land and settled on a farm in Ann Arbor Township. He ran a sawmill for forty years, up to 1868. In 1829 he was an anti-Mason, then a Whig and later a Republican. The Whigs elected him Representative in 1841. He was Supervisor, Assessor and Justice for more than twenty years. He died at Ann Arbor, Nov. 4, 1889.

LUDGER A. GELINAS

Representative from the First District, Saginaw County, 1909-10. Was born at Saginaw, July 31, 1867, of French descent. He acquired his education at the High School of Saginaw and North Division High School of Chicago. Mr. Gelinas was married in 1900 to Miss Julia Dieterich of Chicago. A contractor and with the exception of residence in Chicago from 1889 to 1900 he lived in Michigan. He was a member of Keystone Lodge, F. & A. M., Lawn Chapter and Lincoln Park Commandery Chicago, and Saginaw Temple of Shriners. In politics he was a Republican. He held the office of Alderman two terms, and was elected to the Legislature Nov. 3, 1908. He died in Saginaw Nov. 17, 1915.

GEORGE W. GERMAIN

State Treasurer, 1841-2; Representative from Ionia County, 1857-8; and Delegate from Ionia County to the Constitutional Convention of 1867. Was born in Marcellus, N. Y., June 4, 1818. He came to Michigan in 1843 and purchased a farm in North Plains, Ionia County. He was a Whig of the Seward-Greeley type, became a Republican and was the first of that party sent to the Legislature from Ionia County.

NATHANIEL L. GERRISH

Representative from Mecosta, Osceola and Lake counties, 1875-6. Was born in Durham, Me., Feb. 16, 1820. He came to Michigan in 1861, and settled at Croton, Newaygo County. He held the office of Supervisor, and was by occupation a lumberman.

GODFRIED GETTEL

Representative from Huron County, 1915-16, 1917-18, 1921-2 and 1923—. Was born at Sebewaing, Mich., Feb. 26, 1871, of German parents. His education was secured in the Sebewaing public schools. He was married Jan. 7, 1897, to Frankie Thompson of Kilmanagh. He has always resided in Sebewaing, where he has held the office of Supervisor nine years and member of the Board of Education eighteen years. Most of his time he has been devoted to farming and stock raising. In politics he is a Republican.

JOSEPH GIBBONS

Representative from the Second District of St. Clair County, 1889-90 and 1891-2. Was born in Ireland, June 12, 1825. During the late war he was in the government employ one year on the Mississippi River, with Commodore Rodgers. His occupation was that of farming. He was elected to the House of 1889-90, on the Democratic ticket, and re-elected to that of 1891-2.

ADONIRAM J. GIBBS

Representative from Ionia County, 1881-2. Was born in Nelson, O., Jan. 18, 1840. He removed with his father to Ionia County, Mich., in 1854, received an academical education and became a farmer in Orange. He was Justice several terms and School Superintendent. In politics a Republican.

GEORGE C. GIBBS

Representative from Calhoun County, 1839. Was born in Herkimer County, N. Y., in 1812, settled in Marshall, Mich., in 1836, and commenced the practice of law. He was Supervisor, Justice, Prosecuting Attorney, and reporter of the Supreme Court. His reports cover most of the opinions given from 1851 to 1857. In 1858 he established a general mercantile collection agency in New York City, which he closed in 1870, removing to San Diego, Calif., where he resumed the practice of law. He died there in 1886.

JAMES L. GIBBS

Representative from Grand Traverse and Manitou counties, 1877-8, and 1885. Was born in Sheboygan County, Wis., Feb. 16, 1848. He was educated at common schools with a few terms at Ripon College. He came to Michigan in 1873; was in the lumber and mercantile business. He was Supervisor, and County Clerk for six years. Politically he was a Republican. He died at Mayfield, Grand Traverse County, Jan. 20, 1900.

CHAS. F. GIBSON

Senator from the Twenty-ninth District, 1881-2; and from the Fourth District, 1893-4. Was born in Grand Blanc, Mich., July 22, 1836. He graduated from the law department of the Michigan University in 1866 and went to Bay City where he was engaged in the mercantile business until moving to Detroit, where he engaged in manufactory pursuits. In politics a Republican.

JOHN GIBSON

Representative from Wayne County, 1871-2. Was native of Devonshire, England, born in 1830. He came to the United States when nineteen years of age, reaching Detroit with a single sovereign in his pocket. He entered upon his trade, that of carpenter and builder, which was the active business of his life, he having built over four hundred and fifty houses in Detroit. For many years he engaged in building cottages upon city property of his own, which he held for sale on the instalment plan. His business enterprises yielded him an ample competence. He was for many years a member of the board for reviewing the assessments, and was two years president of the Mechanics' Society of the city. He was still living in Detroit in 1887. Politics Republican.

SAMUEL GIBSON

Representative from St. Joseph County, 1897-8. Was born in Northumberland County, Pa., Sept. 22, 1830. His early education was acquired in the common schools of Pennsylvania. At the age of nineteen he moved with his parents to Constantine Township, St. Joseph County, two and one-half miles north of the village, on what is known as Broad Street; owner of a valuable farm consisting of 433 acres. He was married in 1860 to Miss Martha J. Green. Although agriculture was his principal occupation, he engaged in banking, and was president of Central State Bank of Geneseo, Kan., vice-president of the Commercial State Bank of Constantine and director of the First State Bank of Mendon. In politics a Democrat. He was elected Representative to the House of 1897-8 on the Democratic People's Union Silver ticket.

CHARLES W. GIDDINGS

Senator, 1899-1900, from the Nineteenth District, comprising Gratiot and Clinton counties. Was born at Sherman, Fairfield County, Conn., Feb. 9, 1847. While yet a lad he removed to Ohio and received his education at the public and select school of Palmyra. He came to St. Louis with his parents in 1866. It was then a town of about 150 people. Here he followed various occupations such as a new town offered to a boy and young man until 1872 when he began the study of law. Mr. Giddings was Under Sheriff of Gratiot County from Jan. 1, 1873 to Jan. 1, 1877, and was also Deputy U. S. Marshall for the Eastern District of Michigan during the same period, accepting these positions to maintain himself and family while pursuing his studies. Mr. Giddings began the practice of law at St. Louis in January, 1877. He served as City Attorney and member of the Common Council of the city of St. Louis; was at one time connected with the First National Bank of St. Louis and one of its board of directors.

EDWIN W. GIDDINGS

Member of the Constitutional Commission of 1873. Was born at Preston, Conn., June 11, 1815. He came to Romeo in 1838, and engaged in the mercantile business until he retired in 1873. He was president of the Citizens' National Bank for several years. In 1873 Gov. Bagley appointed him one of the eighteen commissioners to revise the constitution, from which he resigned Oct. 8, 1873.

J. WIGHT GIDDINGS

Senator from the Twenty-eighth District, 1887-8 and 1889-90; and Lieutenant Governor, 1893-5. Was born in Romeo, Mich., Sept. 27, 1858. He attended the high school of Romeo, graduating in 1877; spent one year at the Oberlin University of Ohio, and three years at Amherst College, Mass.; he then entered the law department of the Chicago and Northwestern Railroad, where he remained during 1880-1, preparing for admission to the bar. In 1882 he purchased the Cadillac *News*, which he owned and published until the spring of 1887, when he again resumed the practice of law. In politics a Republican. Active upon the stump as a speaker in several campaigns, he was engaged by one of the leading bureaus of the country as a platform orator.

MARSH GIDDINGS

Representative from Kalamazoo County, 1849; and Delegate from Kalamazoo County to the Constitutional Convention of 1867. Was born in Sherman, Conn., Nov. 19, 1816; became a resident of Richland, Mich., in 1830. For some time he was a student in Western Reserve College, O.; was admitted to the bar in 1841; was delegate to the Republican National Convention of 1860, and a Presidential Elector the same year; was eight years Probate Judge of Kalamazoo County; nominated Consul General to Calcutta, but declined; and was Governor of New Mexico until his death at Santa Fe, June 3, 1875, and was buried in Kalamazoo. He was several years a member of the Republican National Committee and was an able lawyer, good debater and cultured man.

ORRIN N. GIDDINGS

Representative from Kalamazoo County, 1846. Was born in Beekman, N. Y., Feb. 21, 1814. He received a fine business education, and from fifteen until twenty-two was a clerk. He settled as a farmer in Charleston, Mich., in 1836, was a Justice and several terms a Supervisor. From 1847 to 1852 he was a merchant and produce dealer at Augusta, Mich., also Supervisor. He was Treasurer of Kalamazoo County eight years; Quartermaster General of Michigan several years; several years a Trustee of Kalamazoo. He was engaged in farming and buying and selling real estate. He was a Whig until 1854, then a Republican. He died at Climax, Kalamazoo County, Nov. 20, 1904.

TOWNSEND E. GIDLEY

Delegate from the Eighth District to the Constitutional Convention of 1835; Representative from Jackson County, 1835, 1836, 1838 and 1850; and Senator from the Fifth District, 1839-41, from the Fourth District, 1842, and from the Twelfth District, 1863-4. Was born at Poughkeepsie, N. Y., in 1805. He received a good business education, was four years a clerk, and became a merchant. He settled as a farmer on a fifteen hundred acre farm in Jackson County, and put in three hundred acres of wheat in 1833. He became at once a leading farmer and horticulturist. He resigned as Representative Feb. 22, 1836 and was succeeded in extra session by Abraham F. Bolton. He was a leading Whig, and was their candidate for Governor in 1851, but was defeated by Gov. McClelland. At the Legislative reunion in 1886 he was the oldest member present. No man had a larger acquaintance with the men and happenings of the first fifty years of Michigan as a State. He died at Grand Haven, Oct. 8, 1888.

PAUL GIES

Representative from Wayne County, 1859-60, 1865-6 and 1877-8. Was born in Germany in 1827, coming to Detroit in 1831. With a common school education he was a merchant, then a manufacturer. He was Alderman nine years, and president of the Council, was County Treasurer from 1869 to 1873, and held other local offices. He was Captain of the Company in the 27th Michigan for one year, when he resigned.

MILO E. GIFFORD

Representative from Allegan County, 1869-70. Was born in Lorain, N. Y., Aug. 19, 1832. By occupation he was a merchant, in politics a Republica... He served as Captain of the N. Y. Artillery regiment from 1862 to 1865. He died Nov. 6, 1878.

LINUS S. GILBERT

Delegate from Macomb County to the First Convention of Assent, 1836; and Representative from Macomb County, 1837. Was born in Vermont, Jan. 24, 1804. He came to Michigan in 1832, settled in Romeo, and engaged in mercantile business for some years. In 1839 he purchased wild land in Richmond, Macomb County (a portion of which is now a part of the village of Memphis), and was one of the best farms in Macomb County, where he lived until his death, Sept. 7, 1866. He held various town and village offices.

PETER GILBERT

Senator from the Twenty-fifth District, 1891-2; and from the Twenty-fourth District, 1893-4. Was born at Simcoe, Ont., Apr. 1, 1844. He came to Michigan in 1883 and purchased his farm "Inglewood," three hundred sixty acres, in Arenac County, and engaged in farming and fruit growing. He graduated from London (Ontario) Commercial College in 1868; was married the same year to Henrietta Freeman, granddaughter of Rev. D. Freeman, who preached the first Methodist sermon where Detroit now stands, in 1804. He held the office of Justice of Peace, and was elected on the Democratic ticket to the Senate for the term of 1891-2; was chairman of the committee on finance and appropriations; re-elected to the Senate for the term of 1893-4. He died December, 1920.

THOMAS D. GILBERT

Representative from Kent County, 1861-2; and member of the Board of Regents of the University of Michigan, 1864-76. Was born at Greenfield, Mass., Dec. 13, 1815, and was there educated. After five years' service as a clerk, he engaged in the lumber business at Grand Haven, Mich., in 1835, and was a pioneer in that business. He served as Sheriff of Ottawa County. He removed to Grand Rapids in 1858. He served several years on the Board of Education, was five years president of the Board of Public Works, and in 1887 president of the National City Bank, a position he had held since 1865. Mr. Gilbert was vice-president of the State Pioneer Society. He died at Grand Rapids, Nov. 18, 1894.

JOHN F. GILDAY

Representative from the First District of Monroe County, 1893-4. Was born in LaSalle, said county, May 16, 1838. He owned and occupied the farm where he was born and where he made his home. He acquired his education at the public schools and the union school at Monroe. He engaged in teaching winters and taught twenty-one terms; then gave his attention more exclusively to his farm. In politics he was a Democrat. He held the offices of School Inspector and Justice of the Peace of his township, member of the County Board of Examiners and secretary of said board two years. He died Mar. 8, 1920.

CHARLES I. GILES

Representative from Muskegon County, 1909-10 and 1911-12. Was born at Coldwater, Mich., Dec. 20, 1864. He was educated in the Coldwater public schools. Mr. Giles was engaged in cigar making from 1879 to 1883, after which he located on a farm in Muskegon Township. He was Supervisor of Muskegon Township from 1895 to 1902, and resigned Jan. 1, 1902, to accept the office of Register of Deeds of Muskegon County, which office he held for four years; was defeated for a third term at the primaries, in a field of nine candidates; was also chairman of the Board of Supervisors for two years. In politics a Republican.

FRANK H. GILL

Representative from the First District, Grand Rapids, Kent County, 1889-90. Was born in Middlebury, Summit County, O., Feb. 12, 1845. His father, John C. Gill was of Irish origin, although his ancestors came to America with William Penn. His mother was of English birth. The subject of this sketch received but a limited education, and that under most adverse circumstances. He began the real battle of life at the age of fourteen years when he began his apprenticeship, during which time he read incessantly but in no particular direction, greatly to his regret. On Apr. 21, 1861, he enlisted under James B. Steadman, and took part in the Battle of Phillippi, the first engagement of the war. He afterwards enlisted in the 25th O. V. V. Infantry. After hostilities had ceased he was made master of transportation for the coast division at Orangeburg, S. C. In 1878 he went to California and took part in the agitation for adoption of the new constitution, and at last returned to Michigan and settled in Grand Rapids. He was elected to the House of 1889-90 on the Fusion ticket.

GEORGE EDWIN GILLAM

Representative, 1897-8 and 1899-1900, from the Iosco District, comprising the counties of Alcona, Iosco, Ogemaw and Roscommon. Was born at Coldwater, Branch County, Mich., Dec. 20, 1863. His early days were spent in the counties of Branch and Hillsdale, where he acquired a common school education, supplemented by a course at Hillsdale, graduating in 1881. After completing his course he went to Montague, Mich., and engaged as lumber inspector, which occupation he followed for three years. During the winter of 1884-5 he entered the law office of Frank Braclin, at Montague, where he studied law, and at the same time assisting in the publication of the local paper at that place. In 1885 he went to Detroit, where he was engaged in local work for the Detroit dailies, which occupation he continued until Dec. 12, 1886, when he purchased the *Review*, published at Harrisville, Mich. On June 12, 1889 he was married to Miss Rena B. Tillotson, of Oneida, N. Y. In politics a Republican. He was President of the village of Harrisville and a member of the School Board.

GEORGE F. GILLAM

Representative from Branch County, 1871-2. Was born Nov. 7, 1836, at Middlesex, N. Y., and received a common school education. He removed to Hillsdale County,

Mich., in 1854. He lived in Bronson, Branch County, from 1858 to 1872, where he was Town Clerk, Supervisor, and Justice from 1877 to 1881, and Probate Judge of Ingham County from 1881 to 1885. He was practicing law in Lansing in 1887. In politics a Republican.

AMASA GILLETT

Representative from Washtenaw County, 1849. Was born in Litchfield, Conn., June 23, 1779, moved to Western New York when twelve years of age; came to Michigan and located his land in what is now called Sharon. From early manhood he was a leading member of the M. E. Church, very prominent in the temperance cause, and as an anti-slavery man. His house was known as a station on the "under-ground railroad." He held many positions of honor and trust, such as Supervisor and Justice. In politics he was a Whig. He died Dec. 22, 1854.

JOEL H. GILLETTE

Representative from the Second District of Berrien County, 1899-1900 and 1901-2. Was born in Bertrand Township, Berrien County, Mich., Mar. 22, 1851. His education was begun at a district school in his native township and completed at the Niles High School, after which he engaged in teaching, and taught several years with marked success. His services as teacher were repeatedly sought after, but he declined all offers, preferring to devote his time and energies to his occupation of farmer. Farming was his only occupation until 1888, after which time the real estate and loan business, and management and settlement of estates were prominent features of his business career. In politics an active Republican. He was twice elected School Inspector; filled the office of Superintendent of Schools under the old law; was elected Town Clerk, and Supervisor of Bertrand Township three terms; in 1892 was elected Register of Deeds of Berrien County, and again in 1894. In 1880 he served as Census Enumerator. In 1890 he was president of the Berrien County Farmers' Institute Association.

JOHN E. GILLETT

Representative from the Missaukee District, comprising the counties of Missaukee and Kalkaska, 1923—. Was born in the Township of Clearwater, Kalkaska County, October 3, 1878, his parents being among the earliest pioneers of the county. Mr. Gillett is not married and is a farmer by occupation. He is connected with the farm organization of the county; is serving his ninth term as Supervisor, being chairman of the board for the second term, and is director of the school board. Fraternally he is affiliated with the Valley Home Grange No. 1139, P. of H.; I. O. O. F.; Knights of Pythias and F. & A. M. He was elected to the Legislature November 7, 1922, without opposition.

MARTIN S. GILLETT

Representative from St. Clair County, 1849. Was born at Hartford, Vt. He had a limited education and came to Port Huron, Mich., in 1839, engaged in lumbering and mercantile business, and built several stores and a fine residence. He was first a Whig, then a Republican. He was gifted in music, and for many years was leader of the choir in the Congregational Church, of which he was a member. He was Justice of the Peace, for a long time chairman of the Board of Supervisors; and Postmaster under Lincoln. He died in 1865.

SHADRACH GILLETT

Representative from Wayne County, 1841. Was born in Lyme, Conn., Jan. 22, 1801. He settled in Detroit in 1815, and resided there through life, except seven years in the Upper Peninsula. He built the first wharf in Detroit where the "Walk-in-the-Water" first landed. His house was on the site of the Fort St. Presbyterian Church. He was first a clerk, but became a leading forwarding and commission merchant. He was interested in fisheries, owned a steamer and several vessels and mills. He retired in 1858. From 1865 until his death he was clerk in the office of the comptroller of Detroit. He died Feb. 15, 1876.

JOHN GILLULY

Representative from Livingston County, 1859-60. Was born in Boston, Mass., in 1826. He was a graduate of the law school at Ann Arbor in 1861, and went into practice at Brighton. In June, 1861, he went into the service as Captain of Co. I, 5th Mich. Infantry. He served in many battles and was made Lieutenant Colonel July 18, 1862. On Dec. 13, 1862, he was killed at the battle of Fredericksburg, while leading the regiment to a charge. He was a brave officer and his death was greatly felt by his regiment.

JOSEPH GILMAN

Representative from Van Buren County, 1855-6. Was born Apr. 24, 1816, at Woodstock, Vt. He was a farmer, politically a Republican. He removed from the State of New York to Michigan in 1837, and settled upon a farm in Paw Paw. He was prominent in Grange work and was Justice of the Peace. He was injured by a tree falling on him Oct. 20 and died from the effects Dec. 18, 1884.

ARTHUR D. GILMORE

Representative from Lenawee County, 1873-4; and Senator from the Fifth District, Lenawee County, 1889-90. Was born at Blissfield, Lenawee County, Mar. 3, 1847. He attended Adrian College from 1863 to 1866, and entered the Michigan University in 1868, graduating from the law department in the spring of 1870. He was clerk of the judiciary committee of the Senate in 1871. He was admitted to the practice of law in Michigan and also in Ohio; followed the banking business after 1873.

HENRY DILWOOD GILPIN

Governor of the Territory of Michigan, 1834. Born in Lancaster, England, Apr. 14, 1801. He graduated from the Pennsylvania University in 1819; was admitted to the bar in 1822. He was State Attorney and afterward Attorney General for the United States. He furthered Gen. Jackson's financial policy and was named Territorial Governor for Michigan but his appointment was rejected by the United

States Senate. In 1837 he was made Attorney General of the United States. He was the author of several literary and legal articles. He died at Philadelphia, Jan. 29, 1860.

JOSEPH E. GIRARDIN

Representative from Wayne County, 1879-80. Was born Apr. 6, 1838, at Berthier, Ont. He received a common school education, and moved to Detroit in 1856. He was engaged for many years in the mercantile line, but retired from active business on account of ill health. In politics a Democrat.

CLARENCE E. GITTINS

Senator from the First District of Wayne County, 1913-14. Was born in Plymouth Township, Wayne County, Sept. 21, 1884, son of George I. and Josephine A. Gittins. His early life was spent on his father's farm in Plymouth and Canton Townships, Wayne County. He was educated in the district schools, supplemented by a short term at Ypsilanti Normal College. In 1902 he began teaching district school, which he continued for four years. He was principal of the Lyon Graded School, Hamtramck, for three years. Mr. Gittins graduated from the Detroit College of Law, and was admitted to the bar in 1909. Married and a resident of Highland Park. In politics a National Progressive.

CASSIUS L. GLASGOW

Senator, 1903-4 and 1905-6, from the Fifteenth District, comprising the counties of Barry and Eaton. Was born of Scotch parentage in Allen Township, Hillsdale County, Mich., Feb. 16, 1859. He received his education in the district and union schools and Hillsdale College. He remained on his father's farm until ready to start life for himself which he did by clerking in a hardware store in Jonesville, Mich. After a few years he went West, obtaining employment in the office of a wholesale hardware house in Sioux City, Iowa. He moved to Nashville, Barry County, in 1881 and engaged in the hardware and implement business, adding a large furniture store in 1896. He is a member of the orders of F. & A. M., K. of P. and Modern Maccabees. In politics a Republican. He held the offices of President and Treasurer of his village.

HENRY C. GLASNER

Representative from Barry County, 1911-12 and 1913-14. Was born in Johnstown Township, Barry County, Mich., Sept. 23, 1872. The first fifteen years of his life were spent on a farm. He attended the public schools of Battle Creek, working in a store during his spare time. At the age of eighteen he began teaching in the rural schools of Barry County and taught four years, after which he engaged in the mercantile business at Lacey, Mich. He was Postmaster here until he removed to Nashville. He was a successful merchant and owned and operated a farm. In 1898 he married Miss Maude Wilcox, of Hastings. He served as chairman of the Democratic County Committee, Deputy Sheriff, Village Assessor two terms, member Board of County Canvassers, and a member of the Board of Education. A member of the F. & A. M., K. of P., O. E. S., K. O. T. M. M. and the Grange. In politics a Democrat.

ANDREW B. GLASPIE

Representative from the Second District of Oakland County, 1917-18 to 1923—. Was born at Oxford, Nov. 21, 1876, of Scotch-Irish parentage. His father was a veteran of the Civil War, his grandfather served in the War of 1812, and his great-grandfather in the Revolutionary War. Mr. Glaspie served one year as a member of Company G, Thirty-first Mich. Infantry, during the Spanish War. He was educated in the public school, the Oxford High School and the Michigan Normal College at Ypsilanti. In 1899 he engaged in the printing and publishing business at Oxford, and is at present engaged as one of the publishers of the Oxford *Leader*. He served eight years as Deputy Factory Inspector and eight years as Postmaster at Oxford. Mr. Glaspie is married. In politics he is a Republican.

JOHN M. GLAVIN

Representative from Berrien County, 1867-8. Was born in Ireland, Mar. 25, 1822. By occupation he was a surveyor and civil engineer; in politics a Republican. He came to America in 1850, lived in Chicago until 1854, then went to Owosso, Mich., and was engaged in the construction of the Detroit & Milwaukee railway from that place to St. Johns and Grand Rapids, until 1857, when he removed to Berrien County, and resided at New Buffalo. He was County Surveyor of Berrien County from 1877 to 1883: Postmaster of New Buffalo from 1881 to 1855; and for nine years was Supervisor of New Buffalo. He was a Republican after 1854.

FRANK P. GLAZIER

Senator from the Tenth District, 1903-4; and State Treasurer, 1905-7 and 1907-8. Was born at Jackson, Mich., Mar. 8, 1862. At the age of five he moved with his parents to Chelsea, Washtenaw County, Mich., where he received his early education in the village schools, afterwards attending the University of Michigan where he was graduated from the pharmacy department in 1880. He then took up a practical course at Eastman's Business College of Poughkeepsie, N. Y., and completed his education by a special course of study at the University of Heidelberg, Germany. From 1882 to 1890 he was engaged in general merchandising and banking at Chelsea and Stockbridge; in 1890 he organized the Glazier Stove Company and began the manufacture of the popular B. & B line of oil heaters and cook stoves. He erected as a memorial to his father the late George P. Glazier, one of the finest bank buildings in the state. He was President of the Glazier Stove Co., and stockholder and director of many concerns throughout the state and elsewhere. He served six terms as President of Chelsea village, eleven years as a member of the Board of Education, and represented his district in the State Senate for the term of 1903-4. He was the unanimous choice for State Treasurer of the Republican State Convention held at Detroit, June 30, 1904, and was elected for the term of 1905-6 and re-elected Nov. 6, 1906. He resigned Jan. 22, 1908. He died at Cavanaugh Lake, near Chelsea, Jan. 1, 1922.

DANIEL G. GLEASON

Representative from Macomb County, 1883-4 and 1885-6. Was born at Friendship, N. Y., Sept. 26, 1824. He received a common school and academical education, came to Birmingham, Mich., in 1845, studied medicine, and in 1848 commenced practice at Chesterfield. In 1887 he resided at Richmond engaged in practice, and was also interested in other business pursuits. In politics he was a Democrat.

JAMES GLEASON

Representative from Livingston County, 1853-4. Came from Orleans County, N. Y., in 1837, and settled on a farm in the town of Hartland, and became a prosperous farmer. In religion he was a Catholic; politically a Democrat.

JOHN P. GLEASON

Representative from the Second District, of St. Clair County, 1853-4. His post-office address was Memphis. (Further data not obtainable).

JAMES L. GLENN

Representative from Cass and Van Buren counties, 1846 and 1847. Was a native of Pennsylvania, and when young lived in Philadelphia. He acquired a good education and became a civil engineer, which he followed successfully until he came west in 1834. He first located at Niles, but finally settled upon a farm on Beardsley's Prairie, Cass County. He was Sheriff of Cass County from 1842 to 1844. He made the plan and survey of Lansing when it was selected as the capital, and had charge of the building of the old state house. He was also State Engineer of the Sault canal. He died Jan. 1, 1876.

AUGUSTUS S. GLESSNER

Representative from Branch County, 1859-60. Up to the time of the rebellion he had been a Democrat, but then became a Republican. A carpenter and joiner by trade, but for many years he loaned money. He was distinguished for his fairness and integrity as a citizen and as a business man.

ASA CHAPIN GLIDDEN

Member of the State Board of Agriculture, 1889-95. Was the son of Jehiel Glidden of New Hampshire and Harriet (Chapin) Glidden of Onondaga County, N. Y. He was born June 21, 1835, near Batavia Village, Genesee County, N. Y. He married Esther Gould, of Orange County, N. Y., on Mar. 12, 1868. She was born 1843 and died Mar. 17, 1890; he then married Loretta Bicknell of Cedar Springs, Mich., who was educated in the high school and taught school for some years. Mr. Glidden was educated in a common school previous to 1852, when the family moved to Paw Paw, Mich., where he attended high school; taught district school eleven winters. A Congregationalist; and a Republican from Fremont to Taft. He managed his mother's farm; served as Township School Inspector for some years; Supervisor one year; secretary of the County Agricultural Society six years; secretary of the County Insurance Company two years; president of the First Michigan Association of Agricultural Societies continuing for three years; 1884 for four years an editorial contributor to the *Michigan Farmer;* editor of the *Grand Visitor* for three years; member of the State Board of Agriculture 1889-95; correspondent of several papers; in 1895 sold out and moved to Cedar Springs, Mich., where he worked his farm.

ANTHONY GLUECKLICH

Representative from the First District of Wayne County, 1893-4. Was born in Bohemia, in the year 1844. At the age of seven years he came to America with his parents who intended locating in the United States, but were prevailed upon to remain in Canada, where they had landed. He attended public school in Canada, also the Queen's City Commercial College at Cincinnati, O. On graduating from the latter returned to Canada and taught public school the four years prior to his majority. At the age of twenty-one years he came to Detroit, Mich., and engaged in the grocery business, and where he made his home, with the exception of two or three years in Monroe and Adrian where he was engaged in the hardware business. He then engaged in the life insurance business. In politics a Republican.

JOSEPH GODFREY

Senator from the Second District, 1865-6. Was born in Cortland County, N. Y., in September, 1822. He was a painter, and came to Michigan in 1847, and went into business at Ann Arbor, where he remained until 1854. He was the first City Marshal there. Removing to Detroit in 1854 he prosecuted a successful business until the time of his death, Jan. 7, 1875. He was an Alderman, an active member of the old fire department, and a member of the Fire Commission at the time of his death. In politics he was a Democrat.

JAMES J. GODFROY

Representative from Monroe County, 1835 and 1836. Was born in Detroit, Mich., in 1804. He was educated at Beardstown, Ky., and studied law. When quite young he married Miss Victoire, daughter of Col. Francois Navarre of Monroe, and soon after removed to Monroe. He early abandoned practice from ill health. He became a member of the firm of Indian traders, P. & J. J. Godfroy. He was very popular with the Indians and with the French, and exercised a greater influence over the French population of Monroe County than any other man. He removed the last of the Indians from Detroit. In politics he was a Democrat. The French confided in him and called him "Father Jaques," although he was still a young man. He died in 1847.

PETER GODFROY

Representative from Wayne County, 1843. Was born in Detroit in 1797. His ancestor, James Godfroy, settled there in 1716, and was a fur dealer, which his descendants followed for more than a century. With his brother, Jacques, he was in this business during the first half of the present century. The family had trading posts from Detroit to the Mississippi. He was a Democrat and a Catholic. He owned the Peter and Jacques Godfroy farms, now occupied by fine residences. He died May 26, 1848.

AUGUST GOEBEL

Representative from Wayne County, 1879-80. Was born in Munstermaifeld, Rhenish Prussia, Sept. 2, 1839. He received a common school education. In 1855 he emigrated to Detroit, where he worked at book-binding seven years. In 1861 he enlisted as a private in Co. A, 2d Mich. Infantry, and was promoted gradually to the rank of Captain. After participating in many pitched battles he resigned on account of loss of hearing. Returning to Detroit he was appointed Superintendent of Public Works in 1870. He engaged extensively in the brewing business. In politics a Democrat.

SEWELL S. GOFF

Representative from Lenawee County, 1853-4. Was born in Royalston, Mass., Jan. 29, 1811. By occupation he was a farmer, in politics a Democrat until 1854, then a Republican. He came to Michigan in 1829 and settled at Blissfield, where he was Supervisor five years and Justice of the Peace twelve years. He was a Lieutenant in the Black Hawk War. He died Jan. 23, 1865.

ALFRED GOODELL

Representative from Macomb County, 1847. His postoffice address was Armada. (Further data not obtainable).

DANIEL GOODELL

Representative from Wayne County, 1843. Was born in Vermont, May 11, 1795. He settled in Ecorse at an early day, and married into a French family. He served in General Hull's army. He was Supervisor as early as 1829 and held the office of Justice, and other local offices. He was a farmer, and a Democrat in politics. He died Apr. 28, 1882.

JAMES M. GOODELL

Senator from the Eighteenth District, 1873-4. Was born Oct. 1, 1841, in Leroy, N. Y. He received a common school education. In 1855 he came to Michigan, and settled in Corunna. He was admitted to the bar in 1863. He was Prosecuting Attorney four years, and Circuit Court Commissioner two years.

SOLON GOODELL

Representative from the Third District of Wayne County, 1897-8 and 1899-1900; Senator, 1901-2 and 1903-4, from the Fourth District, comprising the twelfth fourteenth and sixteenth wards of the city of Detroit, the city of Wyandotte, and the townships of Brownstown, Canton, Dearborn, Ecorse, Huron, Monguagon, Nankin, Romulus, Springwells, Sumpter, Taylor and Van Buren. Was born in Superior, Washtenaw County, Mich., Nov. 30, 1840. He attended the district school until he was sixteen years of age, and worked on his father's farm until he was twenty-one. In 1860 he settled on a farm in the township of Canton. His occupation was that of a farmer and stock breeder. In politics a Republican. He represented his district in the Legislature four terms, two in the House and two in the Senate. He died Jan. 29, 1920.

ALONZO A. GOODMAN

Representative from Macomb County, 1857. Was born in Pittsfield, Mass., Jan. 28, 1813. By occupation he was a farmer, in politics, first a Whig, then a Republican. He came to Detroit in 1835, and settled at Harrison, near Mt. Clemens, in 1842. He removed to Missouri in 1865 and lived at Kansas City in 1887.

FRANCIS GOODMAN

Representative from Allegan County, 1881-2, and 1883-4. Was born in Hesse Darmstadt, Germany, Mar. 3, 1827. He came to Baltimore in 1830, lived in Pennsylvania and then in Ohio, where he was educated. He settled in Salem, Allegan County, Mich., in 1855. He was Supervisor nine years, Justice four years, and held other local offices. He served ten months in the 9th Mich. Infantry. In politics he was a Republican.

GEORGE GOODMAN

Member of the Board of Regents of the University of Michigan, 1841-3. Was born in Philadelphia, Pa., Sept. 29, 1793. He settled at Niles, Mich., in 1836. He kept a bookstore there, and was for many years agent of the American Express Company. During the administration of President Fillmore he was Postmaster of the place. Apr. 5, 1841, he was appointed Regent of the University for the full term of four years, but after two years's service resigned the office. He died at Niles, Apr. 10, 1862.

LOWELL GOODMAN

Representative from Wayne County, 1838. Was born in Hadley, Mass., Aug. 17, 1789. He was a farmer and in politics a Whig. He came from Willoughby, O., to Detroit in 1835, settled on a farm in Greenfield. He died at Mt. Clemens, Mich., Mar. 18, 1842.

CHAUNCEY GOODRICH

Representative from Eaton County, 1861-2. His postoffice address was Lansing. (Further data not obtainable).

CHAUNCEY B. GOODRICH

Representative from Allegan County, 1857-8. Was born in the State of New York in 1818. By profession he was a physician, in politics a Republican. He settled in Allegan County in 1843, and practiced medicine until a year or two prior to his death, which occurred in 1871. He was the first physician in Saugatuck in 1842.

ENOS GOODRICH

Senator from the Twenty-eighth District, 1853-4. Was born at Clarence, N. Y., Aug. 11, 1813. He settled in Atlas, Genesee County, 1836. He voted to remove the capital to Lansing. With his brother Reuben, he built the Goodrich flouring mills, and gave life and business to that section for many years. In politics he was a Democrat, while a Legislator. He died at Fostoria, Sept. 16, 1897.

JOHN S. GOODRICH

Justice of the Supreme Court, 1851. Was born at Clarence, N. Y., Oct. 7, 1815. He was an earnest student, especially excelling in mathematics, and had a limited academical education. He studied law in Buffalo, came to Michigan in 1836, and worked at civil engineering on the line of the Port Huron & Lake Michigan railroad. He finished his law studies at Pontiac and was admitted to the bar in 1840, and became a member of the firm of Hanscom & Goodrich, and a leading lawyer of Oakland County. In 1851 he was elected Judge of the 7th circuit, by which he would have also been a Supreme Judge, but was taken sick on boat returning from Buffalo where he had been attending to law business and died at the Michigan Exchange hotel, Detroit, Oct. 15, 1851.

JOHN V. B. GOODRICH

Representative from the Second District of Ottawa County, 1887-8 and 1889-90. Was born in the township of Pompey, Onondaga County, N. Y., Oct. 10, 1839. He was formerly a mechanic but later by profession a lawyer. During the war he served in the 4th Michigan Infantry and held the office of President of the village of Coopersville. He was elected Representative on the Republican ticket to the House of 1887-8, and re-elected for 1889-90.

LESTER ADORAN GOODRICH

Representative from Hillsdale County, 1899-1000 and 1901-2. Was born in New Haven, Oswego County, N. Y., Mar. 2, 1854. He moved to Cambria, Hillsdale County, Mich., in 1863, lived on a farm until eighteen years of age, and attended the graded school during the winter months. He entered Hillsdale College in the fall of 1875, taught school during the winter months, and graduated in the scientific course in 1879, receiving the honorary degree of master of science two years later; entered the University of Michigan in 1880 and graduated in 1882, receiving the degree of pharmaceutical chemist, and entered the drug business at Hillsdale, Mich., in 1883. Politically a life-long Republican. He was elected an Alderman in 1890 and re-elected in 1891; also elected Mayor of Hillsdale in 1892, and held the office for three consecutive terms.

LEVI N. GOODRICH

Representative from Jackson County, 1869-70 and 1873-4. Was born in Fairhaven, Vt., Sept. 9, 1820. He received a common school education. He removed to Concord, Jackson County, in 1844. He held several local offices. By occupation he was a farmer; in politics a Republican.

REUBEN GOODRICH

Senator from the Twentieth District, 1855-6; and Representative from Genesee County, 1857. Was born in Clarence, N. Y., June 28, 1819, and settled in Atlas, Mich., in 1836. He engaged in milling and mercantile business for many years. In 1845 he founded the village of Goodrich and was for twelve years its Postmaster. In 1860 he moved to Traverse City, appointed land office receiver but removed by Johnson and reappointed by Grant. One of three to formulate the county road system. He was twenty-three years on School Board. He was trustee of Traverse City, and held other positions. In politics he was a Republican. He died Jan. 8, 1899.

DANIEL GOODWIN

Delegate from Wayne County to the Second Convention of Assent, 1836; Justice of the Supreme Court, 1843-6; Delegate from Wayne County to the Constitutional Convention of 1850 and to the Constitutional Convention of 1867. Was born in Geneva, N. Y., Nov. 24, 1799. He was the seventh in descent from Ozias Goodwin, who settled at Hartford, Conn., in 1635. His mother, Lucretia Collins, was granddaughter of Timothy Collins, the first pastor of Litchfield, Conn. He graduated at Union College in 1819, and was a classmate of Wm. H. Seward and of Bishops Doane and Potter. He took one of the honors of the class, and studied law with John C. Spencer, at Canandaigua, N. Y. After practicing a short time at Geneva, N. Y., he removed to Indiana, where he was stricken with consumption, and entirely lost the use of one lung. On account of the death of his father at Detroit in 1825, he removed to that city, entered into practice, and acquired so high a standing as a lawyer that he was endorsed by the Michigan bar for United States District Judge when the State was admitted to the Union. This was declined on account of small salary, but he accepted the position of district attorney and held it several years. In 1843 he was Judge of the Supreme Court of Michigan, which he resigned in 1846. In 1851 he was Judge of the circuit comprising the Upper Peninsula, and held it until 1881, residing at Detroit and practicing law in court vacations, also officiating at times in other circuits, and in the recorder's court of Detroit. In two elections he was the only Democrat holding a State office. Twice he lacked but one or two votes of being elected United States Senator. He was a model judge and lived a spotless life. He was president of the Constitutional Convention of 1850. He died at Detroit, Aug. 25, 1887.

JUSTUS GOODWIN

Delegate from Calhoun County to the Second Convention of Assent, 1836; Representative from Calhoun County, 1839, 1842, 1843 and 1847; and member of the Board of Regents of the University of Michigan, 1848-52. Was a native of Lenox, Mass., afterwards a resident of Oneida County, N. Y. He graduated at Hamilton College in 1821, read law and entered into practice. In 1831 he emigrated to Ann Arbor, where he remained two years. In 1833 he purchased 568 acres of land in what is now Union Township, Branch County, the purchase including the present site of Union City, and was the first settler there. He was the first Postmaster at Union City, then called Goodwinsville, and somewhere about 1852 to 1854 was agent of the State Prison at Jackson. He was the first Supervisor of Burlington, Calhoun County, and served eight years; also eight years Justice. In politics he was a Democrat. After leaving his position as agent of the prison he removed to Coldwater, entered into the practice of the law and afterwards removed to Texas, where he died Sept. 6, 1858.

WILLIAM F. GOODWIN

Representative from Jackson County, 1857-8 and 1859-60; Delegate from Jackson County to the Constitutional Convention of 1867; and Senator from the Seventh District, 1881-2. Was born in Canandaigua, N. Y., Mar. 25, 1812. In 1816 he removed with his parents to Monroe County, N. Y., where he lived on a farm and received a common school education. He came to Michigan in 1842, and settled at Concord in 1845, where he resided, being engaged in milling, mercantile business and farming. He has been Postmaster, and Supervisor two terms.

HENRY A. GOODYEAR

Representative from Barry County, 1847 and 1875-6; and Senator from the Twenty-second District, 1855-6. Was born in York County, Pa., June 30, 1818, and became a citizen of Michigan in 1838. He received a common school education and was a merchant at Hastings for more than forty years. He was President and Mayor of Hastings and filled other positions of trust. In politics he was a Democrat. He died at Hastings, May 5, 1901.

SAMUEL C. GOODYEAR

Representative from the First District of Genesee County, 1897-8 and 1899-1900. Was born in Lincolnshire, England, July 18, 1843. Nine years later he came to America with his father's family, locating at Pontiac, Oakland County, Mich. Four years later he moved to the township of Gaines, Genesee County. He acquired a common school education, by working on the farms summers and teaching school winters. In 1870 he was married, and since that time he devoted his attention to farming and stock raising. In politics a Republican. He was Supervisor six years and a member of the county committee for a number of years; was a candidate for Representative in 1890, and elected to the House of 1897-8 and was re-elected to the House of 1899-1900.

HENRY GORDON

Representative from Wayne County, 1873-4. Was born in Geneseo, Ill., Mar. 15, 1837. He received a common school education. In 1856 he removed to Michigan and settled in Detroit. In 1861 he enlisted in the 1st Mich. Infantry and participated in the first Battle of Bull Run. He returned to Detroit, was mustered out of service, and soon after removed to Flat Rock, Wayne County. His occupation was that of a teacher of vocal music.

JAMES WRIGHT GORDON

Senator from the Sixth District, 1839; Lieutenant Governor, 1840-1; Acting Governor, 1841. Was born at Plainfield, Conn., in 1809. His father was a noted politician and gentleman of culture, and gave his son every educational advantage. He graduated at Harvard College, and for a time was professor at Geneva, N. Y., where his father had removed. While there he studied law and was admitted to the Supreme Court of New York. In 1835 he settled as a lawyer at Marshall, Calhoun County. In politics he was a Whig. On the election of Gov. William Woodbridge to the United States Senate, he became Acting Governor. He was also a candidate for the United States Senate, and was the Whig caucus nominee against Gov. Woodbridge. The contest of the two state offices created great excitement. Mr. Gordon accepted a consulship to South America under Gen. Taylor, hoping to restore failing health by a change of climate, but died December, 1853, from a fall from the balcony. He was a man of great natural ability and force of character, and acquired distinction as a lawyer, public speaker and politician.

JOHN R. GORDON

Representative from the First District, Marquette County, 1899-1900, 1901-2, 1905-6 and 1907-8. Was born at Silver Hill, Canada, Feb. 15, 1851, of Scotch parentage. He received but little education in the common schools of the country, attending in the winters only until the age of fourteen. At that age he commenced work in the lumber woods as chore boy, and with the exception of seven years in the hotel business at Hancock he engaged in lumbering all his life, in the several capacities from chore boy to general manager, having operated for himself for many years. In politics a Republican.

WILLIAM D. GORDON

Representative, 1893-4, 1895-6 and 1897-8, from the Midland District, composed of the counties of Gladwin, Midland and Arenac. Was born in Bayfield, Ont., June 7, 1858. He graduated from the law department of the Michigan University at the age of twenty-one years, and located at Midland, where he engaged in the practice of law. A prominent member of several secret societies. In politics a Republican. He was chairman of the Republican County Committee; held the offices of Circuit Court Commissioner, Prosecuting Attorney, Probate Judge of his county, City Attorney of Midland, was a member of the Legislature of 1893-4, during which he served as chairman of the judiciary committee; was elected to the House of 1895-6 and re-elected to that of 1897-8. Mr. Gordon was unanimously chosen speaker of the House of 1895-6 and 1897-8 on their organization.

VICTOR M. GORE

Delegate from the Seventh District to the Constitutional Convention of 1907-8; and member of the Board of Regents of the University of Michigan, 1914—. Was born Sept. 29, 1858, at Plainview, Ill., of English parentage. He was educated in the public schools and at Blackburn University, at Carlinville, Ill., and at the University of Michigan, receiving the degree of B. L. from the latter institution in 1882. He has devoted himself exclusively to the practice of law since that time. He served twenty-one years as a member of the Board of Education, and was a member of the Constitutional Convention of 1907-8. Mr. Gore is married and has four children, two daughters and two sons. He was elected a member of the Board of Regents of the University in April, 1913, for the term ending Dec. 31, 1921, and re-elected Apr. 4, 1921.

CHARLES T. GORHAM

Senator from the Thirteenth District, 1859-60. Was born in Danbury, Conn., May 29, 1812. He prepared for college but became a clerk. He settled in Marshall, Mich., in 1836, and was a merchant until 1840, was then a private banker until 1865, then president of a national bank. He was Major General of State militia; was minister to the Hague from 1870 to 1875; Assistant Secretary of the Interior,

1875-7; delegate to National Republican Conventions several times, and declined several high positions. He was a Democrat until 1848, a Whig until 1854, then a Republican. He died at Marshall, Mar. 11, 1901.

PATRICK GORMAN

Representative from the Second District of Monroe County, 1871-2. His postoffice address was Grafton. (Further data not obtainable).

FRANK E. GORMAN

State Treasurer, 1919—. Was born at Forester, Sanilac County, Mich., Mar. 28, 1874, of Scotch-Irish parents, and has always lived in Michigan. He acquired his education in the public schools of Sanilac County and various summer normals. After leaving school he taught in the public schools of Sanilac County for eight years, and during this time served one year as Postmaster at Forester. Mr. Gorman was married Sept. 29, 1898, to Clara L. Jenkins and has one daughter, Marguerite Jean. He is a Mason, an Elk, a member of Lansing Commandery, and Elf Kurafeh Temple. In politics he is a Republican. He entered the State Treasurer's office in April, 1906, as bookkeeper, and was promoted to cashier in 1909, and appointed Deputy State Treasurer Jan. 1, 1913, which position he held until May 22, 1919, when he was appointed State Treasurer by Governor Albert E. Sleeper. He is affiliated with the Capital National Bank of Lansing, being a director and cashier of that institution. He was nominated for State Treasurer at the Republican Convention at Saginaw in 1920 and was elected Nov. 2, 1920; and re-elected Nov. 7, 1922.

JAMES SEDGWICK GORMAN

Representative from Washtenaw County, 1881-2; Senator from the Fourth District, 1887-8 and 1889-90; and member of Congress, 1891-3 and 1893-5. Was born on the farm in Lyndon Township, Washtenaw County, Dec. 28, 1850. He began his education in a log schoolhouse. At the age of eighteen he lost his left arm in a threshing machine accident. He commenced a preparatory course in the study of law with Hon. A. J. Sawyer, attended the union school of Chelsea, graduating therefrom at the age of twenty-four, and from the law department of Michigan University two years later. He commenced the practice of law in Jackson and served two years as Assistant Prosecuting Attorney under James A. Parkinson. Removing to Dexter in the fall of 1879 he was elected Justice of the Peace at the next election, and in November, 1880, was chosen Representative in the lower House of the State Legislature, where he soon rose to prominence as one of the leaders of the House. Owing to the failing health of his father, at the close of the session, Mr. Gorman went back on the farm to redeem it under a foreclosure mortgage, which he did. In 1886, he was elected to the State Senate, representing Washtenaw and Monroe counties, and was re-elected in 1888. He was nominated by the Democrats for the Fifty-second Congress in 1890, against his earnest protest and was elected.

AMOS GOULD

Senator from the Twenty-sixth District, 1853-4. Was born in Aurelius, N. Y., Dec. 3, 1808. He received a fair education and for a time was a student in Hamilton

College. On the temporary suspension of that institution he engaged in teaching at Auburn, N. Y., at the same time entering the office of William H. Seward as a student. He was admitted to the bar in 1832, practiced law with ability in western New York for several years, and came to Owosso, Mich., in 1843, where he practiced his profession until 1865. In 1844 he was elected Probate Judge of Shiawassee County. He was also Prosecuting Attorney of the County, and Supervisor of Owosso from 1844 to 1850. In 1855 he was the Democratic candidate for Attorney General but was defeated. After the rebellion he was a Republican. In 1865 he organized the first national bank of Owosso, and was its president, owning a majority of the stock. He also managed a farm of twelve hundred acres. He was engaged in extensive land and lumber speculations and was a wealthy man. He died May 14. 1882.

JAMES GOULD

Representative from Jackson County, 1879-80. Was born in DePeyster, N. Y., Nov. 24, 1831. In 1836 he removed to Moscow, Mich. In 1850 he removed to Jonesville. He received a common school education. In 1854 he commenced the study of law. He removed to Litchfield and from thence to Jackson in 1861, where he entered into the real estate, insurance and loan business. In 1870 he was admitted to the bar. He was Prosecuting Attorney, School Inspector and Alderman. In politics he was a Republican. He died at Jackson.

JAMES J. GOULD

Representative from Eaton County, 1877-8. Was born in Hector, N. Y., Sept. 1, 1823. He received a common school education. In 1854 he removed to Michigan and settled in Reading, where he held the office of Township Treasurer. In 1866 he removed to Kalamo, where he engaged in farming and held the office of Justice. In politics he was a Republican.

HERBERT W. GOWDY

Representative from the First District of Berrien County, 1919-20 and 1921-2; and member of the State Board of Agriculture, 1923—. Was born Aug. 27, 1874, on a farm near Union Pier, of Scotch and English parentage. He was educated in the public schools of Berrien County. Later he attended school in Chicago for two years. He then returned to the farm where he engaged in fruit growing until 1897, when he removed to Chicago where he worked in the office of the L. Wolff Manufacturing Company, plumbing supplies. In 1902 he purchased farms at Union Pier where he has since been engaged in fruit raising. Mr. Gowdy is married and has one son. In politics he is a Republican.

CORNELIUS A. GOWER

State Superintendent of Public Instruction, 1878-81. Was born at Abbott, Me., in 1845. He entered Waterville College in 1863, but coming to Michigan before graduation, he entered the senior class of the University in 1867. Graduating from the classical course in that year, he entered the law department in 1868. His tastes, however, inclined him to the profession of teacher, and he taught four seasons in Maine and one year in Ann Arbor; he was Superintendent of Schools

at Fenton three years; was County Superintendent of Schools in Genesee County
three and half years; was Superintendent of Schools in Saginaw City four years;
and was president of the Michigan City School Superintendents' Association in
1878. He was appointed Superintendent of Public Instruction, Sept. 1, 1878, to fill
the vacancy caused by the resignation of Hon. H. S. Tarbell. He was also nominated
to fill the vacancy on the Republican state ticket for that office, caused by Mr.
Tarbell's declination. He was elected, with the rest of the Republican ticket, and
was re-elected in 1880. He was appointed Superintendent of the Reform School
by Gov. Jerome, and resigned the office he held. He was in charge of the Reform
School in 1887 and had a State and national reputation as an able and efficient
superintendent.

BENJAMIN GRACE

Representative from Genesee County, 1859-60. Was born in Lyons, N. Y., Nov. 19,
1820. By occupation he was a merchant, in politics a Democrat. He came to
Michigan in 1831, settled at Livonia, moved to Fentonville in 1851, and resided at
Deerfield, Livingston County, in 1887.

WILLIAM CHARLES GRACE

Senator, 1913-14, from the Sixth Senatorial District, comprising the counties of
Kalamazoo and St. Joseph. Was born in Jackson County, Mich., June 15, 1881,
of Irish and German descent. He removed with his parents to Lucas County, O.,
when he was five years of age, the family afterwards returning to Michigan and
locating at Clinton, Lenawee County. In 1904 he entered the law department of
the University of Michigan from which he graduated in 1907, and began the practice of law at Kalamazoo. In politics a Democrat.

JAMES GRAHAM

Representative from Berrien County, 1865-6. Was born in Stoyestown, Pa., Mar.
5, 1831. He removed with his parents to Berrien Springs, Mich., in 1846. He
received a common school education and for a time was a student at Albion College.
In private business he was a lumber dealer, merchant and farmer. He was Deputy
Sheriff of Berrien County, and was Sheriff for two years. He was also Deputy
Revenue Collector, and filled other minor offices. In politics he was a Republican.
He died June 5, 1877.

JAMES W. GRAHAM

Representative from the Fourth District of Saginaw County, 1891-2. Was born
in Ireland, on the 28th day of March, 1843; moved to Canada when he was four
years old, and Michigan in 1867, and made Fremont, Saginaw County, his home.
A farmer by occupation. He held several offices of trust in his township and county
previous to his election as Representative at the fall election of 1890.

JONATHAN B. GRAHAM

Representative from Hillsdale County, 1846; and Delegate from Hillsdale County
to the Constitutional Convention of 1850. Was born at Windsor, Conn., Feb. 26,

1811. He was bred to farming, received a common school education, and at twenty-one became a traveling agent. He employed other agents and speculated in horses and cattle. He settled at Jonesville in 1837, became a farmer and dealt in live stock. Politically he was a Democrat. He held prominent local offices.

ROBERT D. GRAHAM

Representative from the Third District of Kent County, 1895-6 and 1897-8; Senator, 1899-1900, from the Seventeenth District, comprising the tenth and eleventh wards of the city of Grand Rapids and the townships of Kent County; and member of the State Board of Agriculture, 1902-19. Was born in Union, Ont., Nov. 11, 1855. When about one year of age he moved with his parents to Minnesota, and eight years later came to Michigan, locating on a farm near Grand Rapids. His early education was acquired in the district school and the schools of the city of Grand Rapids. He studied law four winters in a law office in Grand Rapids, attending the farm summers; was admitted to the bar, but did not engage in the practice of his profession to any extent. He devoted his time principally to farming and fruit-growing. He was a member of the executive board of the State Horticultural and State Agricultural Societies; also a director of the West Side Building and Loan Association; a director of the Citizens' Telephone Company and president of the Fifth National Bank of Grand Rapids. In politics a Republican. He was a member of the Legislature of 1895-6, and served on the judiciary, university and liquor traffic committees, was elected to the House of 1897-8, and elected to the Senate of 1899-1900.

BRADLEY F. GRANGER

Member of Congress, 1861-3. Was born in the State of New York; received a public school education; removed to Ann Arbor and engaged in the practice of law. He was elected to Congress as a Republican. Deceased.

ELIHU GRANGER

Representative from St. Clair County, 1848. Was born in Phelps, N. Y., Sept. 17, 1803. In early life he worked at wool carding and cloth dressing. In 1832 he married Maria L. Perkins, in 1834 removed to Cuyahoga County, O., worked at his trade until 1836, when he settled on a farm in Columbus, Mich., which he exchanged for a farm in Berlin in 1839, where he died Dec. 8, 1886. In politics he was a Democrat. He was the first Clerk of Berlin, and was several times Supervisor.

GEORGE H. GRANGER

Representative from Tuscola County, 1879-80 and 1881-2. Was born in Wayland, N. Y. He received his education at the Dansville Seminary, and the Genesee, Wesleyan, Seminary at Livonia, N. Y. At Wayland he studied medicine, graduating in the Michigan University in 1867. He was an assistant surgeon of a New York regiment in the War of the Rebellion. He located at Unionsville, Mich., in 1865, where he resided in 1887. A Republican in politics.

LYMAN GRANGER

Senator from the First District, 1842-4. His postoffice address was Columbus, St. Clair County. (Further data not obtainable).

ALEXANDER GRANT

Representative from Macomb County, 1881-2 and 1883-4. Was born at Ypsilanti, Mich., Mar. 24, 1838. In 1849 he removed with his parents to Livonia, N. Y., where he received a common school education. In 1855 he returned to Michigan, working in a store, and teaching school at Birmingham, removing to Utica in 1858, where he resided. He held the office of Postmaster at Utica; Justice of the Peace; Trustee of the village of Utica; member of the School Board, and of the Macomb County Republican Committee. In politics a Republican.

CLAUDIUS B. GRANT

Representative from Washtenaw County, 1871-2 and 1873-4; member of the Board of Regents of the University of Michigan, 1872-80; and Justice of the Supreme Court, 1890-1909. Was born at Lebanon, York County, Me., Oct. 25, 1835. At the age of twenty he entered the University of Michigan, graduating from the classical course in 1859. The following three years he taught in the Ann Arbor High School, the last two years of which he was principal. He served in the Civil War, entering the United States service as Captain of Co. D, 20th Mich. Infantry, was made Major Nov. 21, 1863, and Lieutenant Colonel Dec. 20, 1864; resigning this position Apr. 12, 1865, he returned to Ann Arbor and entered the law department of the University; was admitted to the bar in June, 1866, and began the practice of law in Ann Arbor. He was elected Recorder of Ann Arbor in 1866, and appointed Postmaster in 1867; was a member of the House of the State Legislature in 1871-2, 1873-4; was elected Regent of the University in 1871, and in 1872 was appointed Alternate Commissioner of the State of Michigan under the law authorizing the Centennial Commission. In 1873 he moved to Houghton, where, until his election, he was engaged in the practice of law. He was elected Prosecuting Attorney in 1876; Judge of the Twenty-fifth Judicial Circuit in 1881, and re-elected in 1887; was elected Justice of the Supreme Court in the Spring of 1889, for full term, and re-elected Apr. 3, 1889.

JOHN HENRY GRANT

Member of the Board of Regents of the University of Michigan, 1909-14. Was born at Burlington, Ind., Sept. 22, 1857. He was educated in the University of Michigan where he received the degrees of Bachelor of Arts in 1882 and Bachelor of Laws in 1883. He married Henrietta Mason of Burlington, Apr. 5, 1883. He was a lawyer by profession and began to practice in Manistee in 1883; member of the firm of McAlvay and Grant, 1887-1902; and Grant and Neal, 1905-11; director of the Manistee County Savings Bank and the Northern Assurance Co. In politics a Republican. He served as Probate Judge, Manistee County; member of the Board of Education of Manistee; City attorney; and was appointed a member of the Board of Regents of the University Dec. 23, 1909, to succeed Arthur Hill, deceased.

ROBERT J. GRANT

Representative from Barry County, 1869-70 and 1871-2. Was born at Ballston, N. Y., Feb. 17, 1822. He came to Michigan with his parents in 1836, living at

Marshall one year, and settling at Bellevue in 1837. He removed to Hastings in 1849 and became a merchant. He was Treasurer of Hastings eight years. Mayor three terms, and member of the Board of Education nine years. In religion he was a Methodist; in politics a Republican.

ROBERT J. GRAVERAET

Senator from the Thirty-second District, 1857-8. His postoffice address was Marquette. (Further data not obtainable).

BENJAMIN F. GRAVES

Justice of the Supreme Court, 1857, 1868-81. Was born at Rochester, N. Y., Oct. 18, 1817, of New England parents. He worked on his father's farm when a boy, but at the age of twenty was disabled by dangerous illness from physical labor. Having commenced the study of law in 1837, he was admitted to the bar at Rochester in October, 1841. During the following winter he was journal clerk of the New York Senate. In 1843 he went to Battle Creek and practiced law there until 1857, being meanwhile made a master in chancery and three times elected Magistrate. In 1857 he was appointed Judge of the fifth circuit to fill a vacancy, and was therefore for a short time a member of the Supreme Court under the old system. When his term expired under his appointment he continued in the circuit judgeship by regular election. He held sixteen circuits a year, kept full and accurate minutes, in his own hand, of the work of his court, wrote out his charges, and held evening sessions, until, in 1866; he was threatened with an attack of paralysis. He then resigned. In 1867 he was elected Justice of the Supreme Court, and re-elected in 1875. He was originally a Democrat, then a Free Soiler in 1848, and at the repeal of the Missouri Compromise and the attempt to force slavery into the territories, he became a Republican. He refused to be a candidate for Judge in 1884, and in 1887 resided at Battle Creek, universally respected by the citizens of Michigan.

BENJAMIN F. GRAVES

Representative from the Second District of Lenawee County, 1911-12. Was born in Chautauqua County, N. Y., May 19, 1839, of American parentage. He was educated in the public and select schools of Chautauqua County. In June 1864, he married Miss Elizabeth Bailey, of Warsaw, N. Y. Mrs. Graves died in March, 1876, and in June, 1877 Mr. Graves was married to Miss Elizabeth Kirney, of Seneca, Mich., Apr. 23, 1860 he enlisted in Co. G. 19th Ohio Vol. Infantry, and served five months under first call for troops in what was then called three months' service. He re-enlisted in Co. L, 2nd Ohio Cavalry and served two and one-half years. Mr. Graves practiced law for a number of years with marked success, but retired. In 1888 he was appointed by Governor Luce upon the Board of Managers of the Soldiers' Home at Grand Rapids. In March, 1893, he resigned to become Commandant of the Soldiers' Home. In politics he was a Republican. He died at Adrian, Mich., Oct. 8, 1917.

WILLIAM GRAVES

Secretary of State, 1853-5. Was born at Southampton, N. H., July 19, 1809. He became a resident of Michigan in 1835, and for many years was agent of the great stage line from Albany to Chicago, residing at Niles. He was commissioned Major by Gov. Mason in 1836. He was twice Mayor of Niles and four times its Treasurer. He held the last office at the time of his death, Apr. 26, 1881. In politics he was a Democrat. He was a prominent Mason, often master of the lodge at Niles, and was several years deputy grand master.

EDGAR L. GRAY

Representative from Newaygo and other counties, 1871-2; and Senator from the Thirtieth District, 1873-4 and 1875-6. Was born in Troy, N. Y., Oct. 10, 1832. He received an academical education. In 1839 he emigrated to Michigan and settled on Goguac Prairie, Calhoun County. He removed to Grand Rapids in 1844, and in 1854 to Newaygo. He was admitted to the bar in 1854, and was in the practice of law in 1887. He was Prosecuting Attorney and County Treasurer. He especially distinguished himself by securing the taxation of lands, belonging to railroads holding grants of land by act of Congress, which had long been held without taxation. This just act was carried against a bitter and determined opposition. In politics a Republican.

HUMPHREY SNELL GRAY

Representative from Mason County, 1899-1900. Was born in the county of Huron, Ont., Canada, Sept. 8, 1869. He was educated in the common schools, attended high school at Clinton, Ont., for two years; took the entrance examination to Toronto University in 1885, but did not matriculate; taught school two years in Simcoe County, and came to Michigan in January, 1888. He learned measuring and inspecting lumber, and worked at this summers, and went to school winters after 1890. He attended Oberlin College, O., from 1890 to 1892, and Michigan University from 1892 to 1894, receiving the degrees of A. B. in 1893, LL. B. in 1894, and A. M. in 1896, for special work in constitutional law, constitutional history, and political economy. During these years of study Mr. Gray supported himself by tallying lumber, and sometimes scaling logs in the woods. After leaving school in 1894 he practiced law and was Prosecuting Attorney of Mason County.

JAMES S. GRAY

Representative from Oakland County, 1883-4. Was born in Troy, Oakland County, Dec. 2, 1851. He received a common school education, and engaged in farming and teaching in the primary schools of his county. In politics he was a Democrat, but was supported by the Nationals of his district.

MYLES F. GRAY

Representative from the First District of Ingham County, 1909-10. Was born at Parkhill, Ont., Apr. 25, 1869, of English descent. He received his education in the public and night schools at Parkhill. He spent his boyhood as a newsboy. At the age of sixteen he became editor of the *Review* at Richmond Hill, Ont., and when twenty-two years of age purchased the Plymouth *Mail* at Plymouth, Mich., which paper he published for eight years. He then purchased the Lansing *Record* but sold it within a year and conducted a job printing business. Mr. Gray was married to Myrtle M. Baker of Wayne, in 1892. In politics a Republican. He was elected City Clerk of Lansing in 1904 and re-elected in 1905 and 1907.

NEIL GRAY, JR.

Senator from the First District, 1843-4. Was born in Ayrshire, Scotland, Jan. 2, 1803. He worked on his father's farm until eighteen, when he entered Glasgow College, where he studied five years, two of them for the ministry. He abandoned this idea, and studied medicine three years, graduating in 1830 from Glasgow Medical College. In 1831 he came to America, and in 1837 he married Mrs. Maria Webster, and settled on two hundred acres of land in Bruce Township, near Romeo. After marriage he gave up the practice of medicine and went into the milling business, buying and operating a flouring mill near Romeo. In 1851 in company with his brother, he built a flouring mill at Clifton, Macomb County. He was one of the founders of the Frst National Bank of Romeo, of which he was president until his death. He was a Scotch Presbyterian. In politics he was a Republican. He died Dec. 14, 1868, having accumulated a large fortune, and leaving four sons, all engaged in milling.

THOMAS GRAY

Representative from Lenawee County, 1851. His postoffice address was Ridgeway. (Further data not obtainable).

THOMAS GRAY

Representative from Isabella County, 1913-14. Was born in Hastings County, Ont., Mar. 20, 1854, of Scotch and Irish descent. He was educated in the common schools of Ontario, coming to Michigan in December, 1880. He worked in the lumber woods and May 1, 1881, purchased 120 acres of wild land, clearing the same, and after seven years leased the farm with other lands in other parts of the township. Mr. Gray was in the grain business until 1894 when he was elected Sheriff, re-entering the business after the expiration of his term as Sheriff. He served several years as Supervisor and was Chairman of the board. Married. In politics a Republican.

ALBERTUS L. GREEN

Representative from Eaton County, 1861-2, 1865-6 and 1870; and Senator from the Twentieth District, 1867-8. Was born in 1824, in Herkimer County, N. Y., and was educated at Lima Seminary and Oberlin College. In 1840 he came to Olivet, Mich., with the colony that founded Olivet College, and was one of its first students. He was for many years a merchant, was also engaged in milling, manufacturing, and building of railroads. He was a trustee of Olivet College, also a Justice and Supervisor. In politics he was a Republican; in religion a Congregationalist. He was elected Representative in 1870 in place of Almon A. Thompson resigned. He died Oct. 21, 1875.

ALONZO B. GREEN

Representative from Alpena County, 1914-15, 1917-18 and 1923—. Was born at Dover, Me., June 6, 1860, of American parents. He was educated in the common schools of Alpena County. He came to Michigan with his parents in 1869, who settled on a farm in Green Township, Alpena County, in 1880. He served as Clerk of Green Township and Supervisor, eight years as chairman of the board. In politics he is a Republican. He is married and has one son and one daughter.

CHARLES M. GREEN

Representative from the First District of St. Clair County, 1897-8. Was born in Erin, Macomb County, Mich., Mar. 9, 1854. He received a district school education. In 1867 he went to Detroit and learned the trade of sign writing and moved to Port Huron in 1879, where he followed the occupation of painting until June, 1889. In politics a Republican. He was elected Alderman in 1888 and served two years; was appointed Deputy Collector and Inspector of Customs under Harrison Geer, June, 1889; resigned Mar. 1, 1892 and engaged in farming and real estate.

COGSWELL K. GREEN

Representative from Berrien County, 1835-6. His postoffice address was Niles. (Further data not obtainable).

DAVID A. GREEN

Representative from the First District of Oakland County, 1909-10, 1911-12 and 1921-2. Was born in the Bloomfield Hills district of Oakland County, Nov. 2, 1862, his parents being among the early settlers of the county. He received his education in the public schools, supplemented by a course in a normal school. He was married in 1891, and has two children. Mr. Green was appointed Postmaster of Clarkston in 1891 under the Harrison Administration, and resigned in 1896 and engaged in the produce business; also held village and township offices, and was president of the Clarkston Board of Education. In 1902 he engaged in the mercantile business in the city of Pontiac, which business he conducted for seventeen years. In politics a Republican. He is a member of all the Masonic orders to and including the Shrine; also a member of the Elks and Knights of Pythias.

EDBERT B. GREEN

Senator, 1889-90, from the Twenty-fourth District, comprising the counties of Gratiot, Midland, Isabella, Clare and Gladwin. Was born at Olivet, Eaton County, Mich., Mar. 24, 1853. He served as messenger in the State Legislature during the session of 1865, acquiring in early life a knowledge of and taste for public affairs. He graduated from Olivet College in 1875. In October of that year he was called home, while attending an eastern college, by the death of his father, A. L. Green, and soon after he engaged in business in his native place. He was President of the village of Olivet two terms. In the year 1884 he removed to Alma, Gratiot County, and as a member of the firm of Hamlin & Green engaged in the manufacturing and lumber business. He was President of the village of Alma at the time of his election to the State Senate. In politics a staunch Republican.

EDWARD H. GREEN

Representative from Mackinac, Emmet, Charlevoix, Antrim and Otsego counties, 1873-4 and 1875-6. Was born in Reamstown, Pa., Oct. 31, 1834. He was educated at the State Normal School at Lancaster, Pa. In 1866 he removed to Michigan, entered the law department of the State University, graduating in the class of 1868. He entered the 10th Penn. Regiment of Infantry in April, 1861, as private, and served three months. He immediately re-enlisted at the expiration of that time in the 107th Penn. Infantry as private, and, for gallant and meritorious service, was promoted to Major. At the Battle of Spottsylvania Court House, he was captured and held prisoner for ten months. He long held the office of Prosecuting Attorney of Charlevoix County.

GEORGE C. GREEN

Representative from the First District of Wayne County, 1893-4. Was born in England in 1844. In 1862 he came to the United States, locating at Lexington, Mich., where he began work on a farm. His only education was acquired at the district school and private study. In 1870-1 he was Under Sheriff of Sanilac County, at the close of which term he began the study of law. He studied privately and also in the office of Devine & Wilson at Lexington. He was admitted to the bar of the State Court in 1875 and to the United States Court in 1878; was for six years Circuit Court Commissioner of Huron County. He located in Detroit, where he engaged in the practice of law. In politics a Republican. He was elected to the House of 1893-4 on the general legislative ticket of the city of Detroit.

ISAAC GREEN

Representative from Sanilac County, 1875-6. Was born in England, Apr. 5, 1824. He was educated at Quaker Seminary, Prospect Hill, Ireland. He removed to Michigan in 1852. By occupation he was a merchant. He was Postmaster eighteen years and Supervisor ten years, Treasurer four years, and Township Clerk four years. In politics he was a Republican.

JAMES A. GREEN

Representative from Bay County, 1887-8. Was born at Fort Edwards, N. Y., Jan. 4, 1836. He received a fair education, was in California three years, two years in Virginia, building and repairing saw mills, and in the same business in Minnesota, where he also engaged in reading law. He served in the 3d Minn. regiment a year, was discharged from ill health, removed to Iowa, and was admitted to the bar. In 1864 he again enlisted, in the 8th Iowa, and served until the close of the war. Soon after he came to Michigan and became a member of the firm of Green & Stevens. He served as a Supervisor and member of the Board of Education. In politics a Republican.

NELSON GREEN

Delegate from Lenawee County to the Constitutional Convention of 1850; Representative from Lenawee County, 1853-4; and Senator from the Thirty-first District, 1861-2; and from the Thirtieth District, 1863-4. Was born in Wayne County, N. Y., May 29, 1803. He was married in 1826, and lived in Otto, N. Y., from 1826 to 1847, when he settled in Rollin, Lenawee County. He was a member of New York Legislature of 1828. By occupation he was a farmer and surveyor, politically first Whig, then Republican. He removed to Oceana County in 1856, was for many years County Surveyor and did a large amount of surveying in Oceana and Muskegon counties. He was Judge of Probate for Oceana County. He removed to Addison, Lenawee County, in 1879, where he resided in 1887.

NOAH K. GREEN

Representative from Lenawee County, 1850, 1861-2 and 1863-4. Was born in Windsor, Mass., Dec. 24, 1808. He received a common school education, was brought up a farmer, and taught school. He settled on a farm in Medina, Lenawee County in 1835, where he lived until his death in 1886. He aided in organizing the town in 1837; was Supervisor for ten years. In politics he was a Republican. He died at Medina, May, 1886.

ORSON GREEN

Representative from Lenawee County, 1859, 1871-2. Was born in Palmyra (now Macedon), N. Y., Mar. 5, 1812. His father was a Captain in the War of 1812. The son received a limited education. In 1833 he traveled afoot to Adrian, Mich. In 1834 he located a farm in Rollin. He was a Justice in 1837 and held that office for eighteen years. He was Supervisor for twelve years.

SANFORD M. GREEN

Senator from the Sixth District, 1843-4 and 1846-7; Justice of the Supreme Court, 1848-57. Was born in Grafton, N. Y., May 30, 1807, his ancestors settling in R. I., in 1673. He received a fair education, became a teacher, and worked alternately at farming and teaching until 1828. He studied law five years, was admitted, commenced practice first at Brownville, then at Rochester, N. Y., but in 1837 settled at Owosso, Mich., in practice. He was Prosecuting Attorney of Shiawassee County. By appointment he made a revision of the laws of the State, known as the Revised Statutes of 1846. In 1848 he was appointed a Judge of the Supreme Court and assigned to the 4th Circuit to succeed Judge Whipple, and then to the 3d, in place of Ransom. He held that position until 1857 when the present Supreme Court was organized. He continued to act as Circuit Judge until 1867, when he resigned, removed to Bay City and engaged in practice. In 1872 he became Judge of the 18th circuit which he held until the close of 1887. In 1860 he published his well known work, "Practice in the Circuit Court"; in 1866-7 his work in two volumes on practice in the courts of common law jurisdiction; and in 1879 his work on "Township and the Powers and Duties of Township Officers," of which the State ordered 10,000 copies in 1882. He died at Bay City, Aug. 13, 1901.

DANIEL C. GREENE

Representative from Macomb County, 1879-80. Was born in Berlin, N. Y., June 8, 1821. He graduated at Williams College in 1843. For a time he was a teacher in the South, but from 1846, for many years, was bookkeeper in a wholesale commission house in New York City. He removed to Romeo, Mich., in 1866, and engaged in the hardware trade. In politics he was a Democrat.

ALSON GREENFIELD

Representative from Tuscola County, 1867-8. Was born in Ohio, and became a resident of Michigan about 1855. He held the offices of Supervisor and County Treasurer. He resided at Unionville, Tuscola County, in 1887. In politics he was first a Republican, later a Greenbacker and Democrat.

JOHN GREENFIELD

Representative from Ontonagon County, 1859-60. Was born in Renfrewshire, Scotland, Mar. 10, 1810. By occupation he was an engineer, politically a Democrat. He came to Michigan in 1832, was Deputy Sheriff of Wayne County in 1836; Collector of Customs at Ontonagon in 1858; and Sheriff of Ontonagon County in 1860. He died Mar. 6, 1861.

WILLIAM L. GREENLY

Senator from the Second District, 1839-40, and from the Third District, 1842-3; Lieutenant Governor, 1846-7; and Acting Governor, 1847-8. Son of Thomas and Nancy Greenly, was born at Hamilton, N. Y., Sept. 18, 1813. He attended school at Hamilton Academy, entered Union College and graduated in 1831, at the age of nineteen. He studied law with Stoner & Gridley, at Hamilton, where he remained three years. He was admitted to the bar at Albany in 1833, and practiced law at Eaton, Madison County, until October, 1836. He came to Adrian, Mich., Oct. 20, 1836, and commenced the practice of law. The next year he was a candidate for the Legislature but was defeated. In 1845 he was nominated by the Democratic State Convention for Lieutenant Governor, Alpheus Felch heading the ticket for Governor, and was elected. He served as Lieutenant Governor until Mar. 4, 1847, when by the election of Governor Felch to the office of United States Senator, he became ex-officio Governor, and filled that position until Jan. 3, 1848. During his administration the bill was passed removing the capital from Detroit to Lansing, and the bill abolishing the court of chancery, and the office of chancellor, and transferring its duties to the Supreme Court, Gov. Greenly was Mayor of Adrian in 1858, and was Justice of the Peace twelve years. He took part in the dedication of the new capitol at Lansing in 1879. He was a scholarly, cultured and genial man. He died at Adrian, November, 1883.

CHARLES GREGORY

Representative from Hillsdale County, 1851. Was born in Danbury, Conn., Aug. 12, 1810. He came to Jonesville in 1834 with a stock of general merchandise, and continued in business several years. In politics he was a Democrat. He was Justice for eight years, and Postmaster at Jonesville during the term of Buchanan, and held various offices. He removed to Chicago in 1863. He died July 23, 1879.

CHARLES S. GREGORY

Representative from Washtenaw County, 1861-2 and 1883-4. Was born near Auburn, N. Y., Aug. 16, 1817. He came with his parents to Washtenaw County in 1834, and settled on a farm in Scio. His occupation was farming until 1840, when he became a merchant for fifteen years. He was also a banker for many years, and secured a competency. He was always a Democrat. He held nearly all town offices from Supervisor down, and for twenty-one years was a trustee of Dexter Union schools. He was president of the village for five years, and president of the Washtenaw County Agricultural and Horticultural Society for four years. He resided at Dexter in 1887.

JOHN M. GREGORY

State Superintendent of Public Instruction, 1859-65. Was born in Sand Lake, N. Y., July 6, 1822. With a common school education at seventeen he became a teacher.

In 1842 he entered Union College and graduated in 1846. He studied law two years, but finally became a Baptist minister. In 1852 he became the head of a classical school in Detroit. He became conspicuous in the cause of education, and 1854 established the *Michigan Journal of Education*, of which he was sole editor for five years. In 1858 he was elected Superintendent of Public Instruction, and was twice re-elected, holding that position from Jan. 1, 1859 to Jan. 1, 1865. He then became president of Kalamazoo College for two years, and then Regent of the Illinois Industrial University, which he held many years. He was appointed one of the three Civil Service Commissioners and held it until 1885. He was a distinguished educator, and was an earnest worker, a man of broad views, of trained thought, and a careful, successful officer in all educational positions.

JOHN VAN NEST GREGORY

Representative from the First District of Washtenaw County, 1889-90 and 1891-2. Was born in the township of Howell, Livingston County, Mich., Jan. 5, 1839. He held the offices of School Inspector, Commissioner of Highways, and Supervisor being chairman of the Board of Supervisors in 1887-8-9; was elected three times president of the Agricultural and Horticultural Society of Washtenaw County.

WILLIAM H. GREGORY

Representative from Wayne County, 1853-4 to 1857-8. Was born at Perrinton, N. Y., June 8, 1824, and came to Plymouth, Mich., in 1830. With a common school education he became a teacher, and was ordained a Baptist minister. He was for a time associated editor of the *Michigan Christian Herald*, and was also pastor of the Baptist Church at Northville. A fluent speaker, ready debater, he was a strong anti-slavery and temperance man. In politics he was a Republican. He died Nov. 2, 1858.

WILLIAM S. GREGORY

Representative from Wayne County, 1840. Was born in Fairfield County, Conn., Feb. 9, 1790, and removed to Plymouth, Mich., in 1830. He was a farmer, and is presumed to have been a Whig in politics from the political revolution of 1839-40, when he was chosen to the Legislature. He was also one of the Superintendents of the Poor for Wayne County, 1841-3. He died Feb. 6, 1863.

MICHAEL GREINER

Representative from Wayne County, 1875-6; and Senator from the First District, 1885-6. Was born in Alsace, France, Nov. 1, 1830, and removed with his parents to the United States in 1831, taking up his residence in Grosse Point, Wayne County, Mich., where, with the exception of three years in Eagle River, Lake Superior, and Saginaw, he continued to reside. He acquired his education principally at night schools. He was Postmaster at Conners Creek for fourteen years and Justice of the Peace for eight years and held other positions of public trust. By occupation he was a farmer and merchant; in politics a Democrat.

JUDSON GRENELL

Representative of the First District of Wayne County, 1887-8. Was born in Elmira, N. Y., Apr. 21, 1847. He resided in Honesdale, Pa., Patterson, N. J. and Port

Jervis, N. Y., and at the latter place entered a printing office to learn the printer's trade. Before attaining his majority he removed to New York City, thence in 1868 to New Haven, Conn., where, while working at his trade, he continued his education by attending the Yale College scientific lectures. Here in 1874 he married, and in 1877 he removed with his family to Detroit. In the spring of 1884 he left the printer's case to accept a position on the staff of the Detroit *Evening News*. He resigned a year later to accept the office of Deputy State Oil Inspector. During all these years he was a close student of what is known as "The Labor Question." He became identified with the Union, the Knights of Labor, and similar organizations and held prominent positions in all. He was also a constant writer for the labor press in this and other states, his subjects embracing the entire range of labor questions. He was nominated for Representative by the Independent Labor party, endorsed by the Republicans.

JOHN GREUSEL

Representative from Wayne County, 1871-2 and 1873-4; and Senator from the Second District, 1875-6, 1881-2 and 1883-4. Was born at Bliescastel, Bavaria, Dec. 4, 1809, and with a common school education learned the trade of a shoemaker. He held a position as forester for two years, and came to America in 1833. He lived at Brooklyn, Newburgh, Haverstraw, Glasgow, N. Y., and worked at brick making, and was foreman of large brick yards. He married an American lady, and in 1848 removed to Detroit and established a large brick yard in Springwells, in which he continued until his death in November, 1886. He held several local offices, was a delegate to the Republican National Convention in 1872, and several terms a member of the Detroit Board of Estimates.

JOSEPH GREUSEL

Representative from the First District of Wayne County, 1903-4, 1905-6, 1907-8 and 1913. Was born at Glasco, Ulster County, N. Y. Mr. Greusel's family is of Colonial and Revolutionary antecedents; settled in Michigan in the territorial days; figures in the military history of the nation, and for long periods in affairs of state at home. In politics a Republican. He represented his district in the Legislatures of 1903-4, 1905-6 and 1907-8 and was again elected to the Legislature Nov. 5, 1912. He died at his temporary home at Lansing, Feb. 13, 1913.

THEOPHILUS C. GRIER

Representative from Bay County, 1867-8. Was born at Ravenna, O., Jan. 2, 1834, and was a descendant of Rev. John Cotton of Pilgrim fame. At fifteen he was apprenticed to learn the printer's trade. He studied law in Ohio, commenced practice at Pine Run, Mich., removed to Bay City in 1859, where he secured a lucrative practice. In 1860 he was Prosecuting Attorney and Circuit Court Commissioner of Bay County; in 1865 City Attorney. In 1870, without opposition, he was elected Judge of the 18th Circuit. In politics he was a Democrat. He died June 5, 1872.

CLINTON G. GRIFFEY

Representative from Marquette County, 1879-80; and Senator, 1889-90, from the Thirty-first District, comprising the counties of Iron, Marquette, and Menominee.

Was born in Erie County, Pa., Sept. 2, 1845, and removed to Michigan in 1875. He held the office of Supervisor and was a member of the Legislature in 1879, and Postmaster at Negaunee from April, 1880, to April, 1884.

JAMES W. GRIFFIN

Representative from Cass and Van Buren counties, 1844. His address was Adamsville. (Further data not obtainable).

JOHN GRIFFIN

Judge of the Supreme Court of the Territory of Michigan, 1805-23. Was a native of Virginia, born about 1799, and probably studied law in that State. At the time Michigan Territory was created he was one of the Judges of Indiana Territory. He made a tour of Europe and when he returned he was appointed Territorial Judge for Michigan by President Jefferson, Dec. 23, 1805, in place of Samuel Huntington who had declined to serve. He was subservient to Judge Woodward and invariably voted with him on the bench. In 1823 when Judge Woodward resigned, Griffin followed his example and it is said went to Philadelphia and died there between 1842 and 1845.

LEVI T. GRIFFIN

Member of Congress, 1893-5. Was born at Clinton, Oneida County, N. Y., May 23, 1837. His parents moved to Rochester, Oakland County, Mich., in 1848. He graduated from the University of Michigan in 1857, and entered upon the study of law at Detroit. He entered the U. S. Army in August, 1862, as Second Lieutenant, Fourth Mich. Cavalry, and served as First Lieutenant, Adjutant, Captain, Brigade Inspector, Acting Assistant Adjutant-General, Cavalry Corps, Military Division of Mississippi, and Brevetted Major. At the close of the war he resumed practice of law in Detroit; appointed Fletcher professor of law in the University of Michigan in 1886; defeated candidate for Judge of the Supreme Court in 1887; elected to the Fifty-third Congress to fill the place made vacant by the death of Hon. John Logan Chipman.

ALBERT G. GRIGGS

Representative from the First District of Oakland County. 1913-14 to 1919-20. Was born in Wyoming County, N. Y., and came to Michigan in 1864. He received his education in the public schools of Rochester, Mich. His chief occupation was farming although also interested in real estate, being part owner of the Bloomfield Highlands plat; also connected with the Commonwealth Savings Bank of Pontiac. He served as Supervisor, Register of Deeds and Superintendent of Schools. In politics a Republican; was elected to the Legislature in November, 1912; served continuously after that time and was re-elected Nov. 5, 1918.

THOMAS GRIMES

Representative from Livingston County, 1879-80. Was born in Courtland County, N. Y., Nov. 10, 1825. He received a common school education and removed to

Michigan in 1846, locating in Pinckney, where he engaged in carriage making, afterwards in mercantile business, and finally in general collecting and farming. He held the office of Township Clerk and Justice. In politics he was a Republican.

JOHN GRINNELL

Representative from St. Clair County, 1863-4. Was born in Killingsworth, Conn., in August, 1809. He removed to Putnam, N. Y., in 1819, remaining there until 1837, when he came to Riley, Mich., and settled on a farm, and was Justice in 1841, and also in 1845. He removed to Brockway, Mich., in 1847, and engaged in farming and lumbering. Several times he held the office of Supervisor, was Justice twenty-two years and Postmaster eight years. He was retired from business in 1887. Politically he was a Republican.

AUGUSTUS D. GRISWOLD

Representative from Kent County, 1863-4 and 1865-6. Was born in Oneida County, N. Y., Oct. 11, 1823. By profession he was a lawyer, in politics a Republican. He came from Rome, N. Y., to Michigan in 1856. He was U. S. District Attorney for western Michigan from 1865 to 1869, except six months, when he was removed by Johnson and re-appointed by him. He was speaker pro tem. in 1865, and chairman of the judiciary committee. He was engaged in the practice of law at Ovid, Mich., in 1887.

GEORGE R. GRISWOLD

Senator from the First District, 1848-9 and 1853-4. Was born in the State of New York. By profession he was a lawyer. He settled in Detroit at an early day, and was clerk of the first Michigan House in 1835. In 1839 he was owner and publisher of the Detroit *Morning Post*, a daily paper. He was Register of Deeds, 1837-41, and Clerk of Wayne County, 1843-7. He was president *pro tem* of the senate in 1853, was Acting Lieutenant Governor, 1853. He was appointed a purser in the navy Sept. 10, 1853, and died on board the U. S. brig, Dolphin, at sea off the African coast, Apr. 5, 1857.

HARRISON W. GRISWOLD

Representative from Berrien County, 1853-4. Came to Michigan about 1835, and was a grocer at Niles. In politics he was a Democrat. He died in 1885.

STANLEY GRISWOLD

Secretary of the Territory of Michigan, 1805-8. Was a native of Torringford, Conn., and a graduate of Yale College in 1786. He was a son of Capt. Shubael and Abigail Stanley Griswold, born Nov. 14, 1763. He was a Lieutenant in his father's company in the War of the Revolution. He studied for the ministry and became the pastor at New Milford, Conn., in 1790 where he remained twelve years. Several of his sermons were printed. In 1804 he established a weekly newspaper in Walpole, N. H. and obtained considerable renown for his ability as an editor. He was appointed Secretary of Michigan Territory in 1805 by President Jefferson, and served three years. Gov. Huntington of Ohio appointed him to a seat in Congress to fill a vacancy and after this he was given the office of Territorial Judge of Illinois. While occupying this office he died in Shawneetown, Ill., in 1815.

ALEXANDER J. GROESBECK

Attorney General, 1917-19 and 1919-21; and Governor of Michigan, 1921—. Was born Nov. 7, 1873, in Warren Township, Macomb County, Mich. His father, Louis Groesbeck, was of Dutch-French ancestry, and his mother, Julia Coquillard Groesbeck, was of French ancestry. He received a common school education at Mt. Clemens, Mich., and at Wallaceburg, Ont., where he resided with his parents for two years. He worked in a saw mill from the ages of thirteen to seventeen, then studied law in Port Huron with the firm of Stevens & Merriam. Mr. Groesbeck entered the law department of the University of Michigan in 1892, graduating in July, 1893, and has since that time practiced law in Detroit. He was elected to the office of Attorney General Nov. 7, 1916, and re-elected Nov. 5, 1918; was nominated for Governor at the August primary of 1920 and was elected Nov. 2, 1920; and was re-elected Nov. 7, 1922.

CHARLES C. GROESBECK

Representative from Macomb County, 1863-4. Was born in Warren, Mich., Nov. 3, 1833. His father was a farmer. The son attended the public schools of Detroit. He was Supervisor of Warren several years; County Clerk from 1871 to 1879; and Justice for more than twenty years. He moved to Mt. Clemens in 1871, owned two farms in Warren, dealt in real estate and was a manufacturer of lumber and staves. In politics a Democrat.

FRANK A. GROGER

Senator, 1915-16, from the Nineteenth District, comprising the counties of Lenawee and Monroe. Was born in Cambridge Township, Lenawee County, Mich., July 3, 1857, of American parentage. He was educated in the district schools. Married. Occupation a farmer. In politics a Democrat.

ANTHONY GROSFIELD

Senator from the Third District of Wayne County, 1889-90. Was born in Germany, Jan. 4, 1843. He was a real estate dealer and insurance agent. He served as Alderman of the Twelfth ward of Detroit; member of the Board of Education and member of the Board of Estimates; was elected on the Democratic ticket to the Senate of 1889-90.

EBENEZER O. GROSVENOR

Senator from the Fourteenth District, 1859-60 and 1863-4; Lieutenant Governor, 1865-7; State Treasurer, 1867-71; and member of the Board of Regents of the University of Michigan, 1880-7. Was born at Stillwater, N. Y., Jan. 26, 1820. He received a common school and academical education, and from fifteen to seventeen was clerk in Chittenango, N. Y., and from 1837 to 1839 was a clerk for his brother at Albion, Mich. He was in 1839-40 a clerk in the State Commissioner's office at Monroe, and from 1840-44 a clerk at Jonesville. In 1844 he married Sally Ann Champlin, and became a merchant at Jonesville. In 1854 he established the banking house of Grosvenor & Co., of which he was president and manager. He held all important town offices; president of the military contract board in 1861, and afterwards president of the State Military Board; member and president of the Board of State Building Commissioners from 1871 to 1879; long vice-president of the Jackson & Fort Wayne Railroad Company; and was effective in completing the road; and a director in insurance companies and other corporations. He was a Whig until 1854, then a Republican. He died at Jonesville, Mich., Mar. 19, 1910.

IRA R. GROSVENOR

Representative from Monroe County, 1871-2. By profession a lawyer, and long a resident of Monroe, and engaged in practice there. He went into the service during the late war, and was made Colonel of the 7th Mich. Infantry, June 10, 1861, and served in the field until July 7, 1862, when he resigned.

JOHN GROVES

Representative from Berrien County, 1845 and 1846. Was a native of Maine. He removed to Buchanan from New Albany, Ind., in 1844, and was the first attorney in that village, commencing practice in 1848. He died in 1852.

ISAAC J. GROVIER

Representative from Macomb County, 1839. Was born in Ballston, N. Y., Feb. 15, 1797. He was a manufacturer of glass by occupation, politically a Democrat. He came to Michigan in 1835, and in company with Dr. E. Hall organized the Clinton Glass Works Company at Mt. Clemens, and erected a large glass factory, ashery, blacksmith shop, lime kiln and store, all of which they operated until failing health compelled him to stop. He died July 26, 1850.

NICHOLAS GULICK

Representative from Shiawassee County, 1853-4. Was born in Orion, N. Y., May 13, 1818. He received a common school education and taught five winters. In 1842 he settled in Byron, Shiawassee County, Mich. In 1846 he became a merchant there, held various town offices. He was eight years Postmaster at Byron. In politics he was a Democrat.

ALFRED GULLEY

Representative from Wayne County, 1857-8. Was a native of Rhode Island, born in 1793. He resided subsequently in Vermont and New York, and came to Michigan in 1835, settling at Dearborn, where he first engaged in keeping a public house, and afterwards bought a farm west of the village, where he died in 1862. He was a Democrat in politics.

ALFRED B. GULLEY

Representative from Wayne County, 1851. Was born at Potsdam, N. Y., Dec. 22, 1819. His education was academic. He was reared a farmer in his father's family, which he accompanied to Michigan in 1835. He resided at Dearborn, except from 1875 to 1878, when he was connected with the State Agricultural College at Lansing, as professor and superintendent of the farm. He had business connections at various times in Detroit. He was a Democrat up to 1856, then a Republican.

FREEMAN O. GULLIFER

Senator from the Twenty-ninth District, 1883-4. Was born in Oldtown, Me., Apr. 7, 1847. He received a common school education, served in 20th Me. Infantry from August, 1864 to the close of the war, and came to Bay City in 1867, and soon engaged in lumbering. He was Supervisor, and held other offices. Later he was chief clerk in the office of the Commissioner of Labor. In politics he was a Republican. In 1870 he removed to Alcona County living at Au Sable. Later he removed to Lansing and Detroit but in 1902 went to California where he died at Los Angeles, Dec. 4, 1920.

JAMES GUNNING

Representative from Wayne County, 1842. Was born in New York, Dec. 22, 1801. He was self-educated, worked in a glass factory as a boy, and later for three years had charge of a gang of men in the building of the Erie canal. He settled in Southfield, Mich., in 1825, removed to a farm in Livonia in 1831, and lived there until his death, Apr. 14, 1874. He was Postmaster, Justice twelve years, Deputy Sheriff, and Coroner, and was also a merchant, attorney and Methodist minister. In politics he was a Democrat.

THERON S. GURNEY

Senator, 1889-90, from the Twenty-second District, comprising the counties of Lake, Mason, Newaygo and Oceana. Was born at Chester, Geauga County, O., in 1836. He finished his academic course at Willoughby, O., University, and graduated from Ohio State and Union Law College at Cleveland, O., in 1862. He was principal of Chardon, O., Union Schools from 1863 to 1865, and came to Hart, Oceana County, in 1866, and followed the practice of law at that place. He held the offices of Supervisor, Town Clerk, Village President, County Clerk and Register of Deeds.

HENRY K. GUSTIN

Representative, 1897-8 and 1899-1900, from the Alpena District, comprising the counties of Alpena, Crawford, Montmorency, Oscoda and Otsego. Was born in Bay City, Mich., May 12, 1868. His education was acquired in the Bay City public schools, supplemented by a course in the literary department of the University of Michigan in 1885. In July, 1887, he located in Alcona County, where he engaged in the lumber business; entered the law department of the University of Michigan in 1892; was admitted to practice in 1893, and located at Alpena, where he formed the partnership of Dafoe & Gustin, with Hon. L. G. Dafoe of Alpena. In politics a Republican. He was Circuit Court Commissioner.

BERNARD HAACK

Representative from Saginaw County, 1871-2. Was born in Wesel, Rhenish Prussia, emigrated to this country in 1849, and settled in Michigan in 1850. By occupation he was a farmer; politics a Republican. He was Supervisor of Blumfield, Saginaw County, for thirty years, first term in 1856; and Justice after 1860.

WILLIAM A. HAAN

Representative from the First District of Kent County, 1919-20 and 1921-2. Was born at Grand Rapids, Mich., Mar. 3, 1891, of Dutch parentage. He was educated in the parochial school and at Calvin College, of Grand Rapids. He was connected with the Grand Rapids Gas Light Company two years; secretary-treasurer of the Grand Rapids Merchants Mutual Fire Insurance Company; and now secretary-treasurer of the Fisher-Mar.hman-Haan Company, general insurance. During the war he served as a member of the government draft board. Mr. Haan is married and has two sons. In politics a Republican. He served two terms as Supervisor.

JOHN W. HAARER

State Treasurer, 1913-15 and 1915-17. Was born at Ann Arbor, Mich., Apr. 21, 1870, and acquired his education in the public schools of that place. He was engaged in the insurance business for a number of years and later was appointed Deputy State Treasurer. He is now vice-president and cashier of the City National Bank of Lansing. From 1901 to 1903 he was president of the Council of Ann Arbor. As a member of the Michigan National Guard he has served as Battalion Adjutant, Captain, Major, Assistant Inspector General and is now retired as Major. He is a Mason, member of Ann Arbor Commandery and Moslem Shrine, also an Elk. and a member of the British Numismatic Society and Royal Societies Club of London, England. He was married Jan. 6, 1903, to Klara A. Bissinger. He was elected State Treasurer in 1912, and re-elected Nov. 3, 1914.

WALTER HACKETT

Representative from Monroe County, 1881-2. Was born in Ida, Mich., July 5, 1845. His parents removed to Raisinville, Monroe County, in April, 1850. He received a common school education, and held the office of Township Treasurer six years. His occupation was farming; in politics a Democrat.

JOSEPH B. HADDEN

Senator, 1913-14, from the Twenty-third District, comprising the counties of Muskegon and Ottawa. Was born at Otsego, Mich., July 30, 1865, of American parentage. His education was acquired in the Otsego High School. He was married Feb. 19, 1890, to Miss Frances E. Scott, of Plainwell. He was connected with the West Michigan Furniture Company, of Holland, Mich., served as Alderman, was appointed by the Common Council as a member of the committee on public buildings and also served as Superintendent of the Poor. In politics a National Progressive.

JOHN HADLEY, JR.

Representative from the Third District of Oakland County, 1861-2. His postoffice address was Holly. (Further data not obtainable).

HENRY S. HADSALL

Senator, 1897-8, from the Fourteenth District, composed of the counties of Ingham, and Shiawassee. Was born in Batavia, Genesee County, N. Y., Oct. 14, 1858; came to Michigan in 1868 and attended the district schools, supplemented by a course in the Byron public schools; taught school three years, after which he read law in the office of B. W. Huston of Vassar; was admitted to practice, before the Circuit court of Tuscola County, in 1882; later, going to Owosso, entered into partnership with Gilbert R. Lyon, where he engaged in the practice of his profession. In politics a Republican until 1896. He was elected to the Senate of 1897-8 on the Democratic People's Union Silver ticket.

FRANCIS H. HAGERMAN

Representative from Lenawee County, 1843. Settled as a farmer in Medina, Mich., about 1834. He came from the State of New York. In politics he was a Democrat. He died at Medina about 1845.

CHARLES F. HAIGHT

Representative from the First District of Ingham County, 1923—. Was born in North Newburg, Shiawassee County, March 21, 1865. His father died when Charles was four years old, and a few years later Mrs. Haight and her two sons removed to Pontiac. He attended school in North Newburg, Northville and Pontiac. Several years of his early life were spent as a railroad employee, part of the time as locomotive fireman and part as telegraph operator. Later he studied law, which profession he still follows, being at present senior member of the law firm of Haight & Hittle, of Lansing. On August 29, 1889, he was married to Miss Harriet B. Lightbody of San Jose, California. They have no children living. In 1903 Mr. Haight removed to Lansing, where he acted as assistant secretary of the Grand Lodge I. O. O. F. of Michigan. In 1911 he was elected judge of municipal court of the city of Lansing, and was re-elected in 1915. During the summer of 1918 he resigned and went to France with the A. E. F. as a Y. M. C. A. secretary, having charge of the educational work among the American soldiers in the Nantes, France, division. Mr. Haight has been a life-long Republican.

SALMON L. HAIGHT

Representative from Washtenaw County, 1849 and 1853-4. Was born in Leyden, N. Y., Feb. 22, 1805. In 1813 he removed to Steuben County, N. Y. At the age of thirteen he was left a penniless orphan. He married in 1826 and removed to Saline. Mich., in 1833, and became a farmer. He held various local offices. In politics he was a Whig. He died at Tecumseh, January, 1881.

ELIAS HAIRE

Representative from the Fourth District of Washtenaw County, 1865-6. His postoffice address was Manchester. (Further data not obtainable).

JOHN HAIRE

Representative from Ottawa County, 1861-2. His postoffice address was Grandville. (Further data not obtainable).

ROBERT A. HAIRE

Representative from Ottawa County, 1873-4. Was born July 20, 1836, at Bombay, N. Y. He came with his father to Marshall, and in 1846 to Grand Rapids. He received a common school and commercial education. He engaged in the lumber business near Grandville in 1852. He enlisted in 1862 in the 5th Mich. Cavalry, and rose to the rank of Captain and took part in many battles, serving until the close of the war, being in command of the regiment in the winter of 1864. In 1865 he settled near Spring Lake and engaged in the lumber business as head of the firm of Haire, Savidge & Cutler. He was President of Spring Lake, 1877.

HORACE HALBERT

Senator from the Seventeenth District, 1879. Was born in Yates County, N. Y., Mar. 1, 1827. He received an academical education, graduated at the State University in 1858, and became a teacher at Kalamazoo for four years. He purchased a farm in Conway in 1867, and in 1867-8 was professor of mathematics in Kalamazoo College. He was Supervisor several terms and treasurer of Livingston County. In politics he was a Republican.

DAVID B. HALE

Representative from Eaton County, 1875-6. Was born in West Windsor, Vt., Feb. 14, 1820. He settled in Eaton County in 1844, and held many local offices in Eaton Rapids, including Supervisor five terms. He was a farmer; in politics a Republican; served several years as member of the board of control of the State Reform School. He was vice-president of the Michigan Pioneer and Historical Society. He died at Eaton Rapids in 1909.

WILLIAM HALE

Senator from the First District, 1845-6; and Attorney General, 1851-5. Was born in Oneida County, N. Y., in 1809. He became a lawyer in New York and removed to Detroit in 1837, and early acquired legal and political prominence. He was Prosecuting Attorney of Wayne County two terms; was Alderman in 1859-60; was reporter of the Supreme Court in 1847; and in 1857 purchased the National Hotel in Detroit, and rebuilt it and named it the Russell house. He removed to California in 1862 and took high rank there as a sound and able lawyer. He died at San Francisco, Feb. 4, 1874.

WILL ERWIN HALE

Representative from Eaton County, 1909-10 and 1911-12. Was born at Eaton Rapids, Mich., Oct. 3, 1858. He acquired his education in the district schools, Eaton Rapids public school and the State Agricultural College, graduating from the latter with the class of 1882. With the exception of four years residence in the city of Eaton Rapids, Mr. Hale lived on the farm. He was married Apr. 8, 1866, to Elida Brainerd. Mrs. Hale died Dec. 3, 1909. In politics a Republican. He held the offices of Township Clerk, Supervisor of Hamlin Township, Supervisor of Eaton Rapids City, and chairman of the Board of Supervisors.

ADNEY ADELBERT HALL

Representative from the Second District of Ingham County, 1899-1900. Was born in the township of Waterloo, Jackson County, Mich., Feb. 27, 1852. For the first fifteen years of his life he lived with his parents upon his father's farm, working summers and going to school winters. For the next ten years he worked out by the month, paying his father his wages until he was twenty-one, after which he saved enough from his wages to take a course of study and graduate from the Grass Lake Union schools. Then by teaching school winters and practicing strict economy, he saved sufficient from his earnings to pay his way through the State Normal school at Ypsilanti, where he graduated in 1884. Since graduating he has had the Superintendency of the Cadillac, Dansville, Chelsea, and Stockbridge union schools, was for two years president of the Washtenaw County Teachers' Association, and member of the Ingham County Board of School Examiners; then in the hardware and furniture business at Stockbridge, Ingham County, Mich.

ALFRED D. HALL

Representative from Lenawee County, 1877-8 and 1879-80. Was born at Byron, N. Y., Jan. 6, 1824. With a fair education he settled at Tecumseh in 1845; held various local offices, including Supervisor four terms. For many years he was president or secretary of Farmers Mutual Insurance Company of Lenawee County, also president of the County Agricultural Society. He was a farmer and a Republican.

DE VERE HALL

Representative, 1891-2, from the Ogemaw District, comprising the counties of Crawford, Ogemaw, Oscoda and Roscommon. Was born in Bedford, Monroe County, Aug. 22, 1854. He was educated in the union school at Holly, and was principal of the union schools at Goodrich and Gaines, Genesee County; Byron, Shiawassee County; and Caseville, Huron County, at the latter place five years; was a member of the Board of School Examiners of Huron County and secretary thereof for two years, and was admitted to the Bar at Bad Axe, Huron County, in the Spring of 1883; resigned said office in the summer following and removed to West Branch, forming a partnership with the Hon. D. P. Markey, ex-Speaker of the House of Representatives, in law and real estate business. He was elected Prosecuting Attorney of Ogemaw County in 1884, and re-elected in 1886 and 1888, resigning therefrom Nov. 1, 1890, to stand as candidate for Representative. In politics a Republican. His seat was vacated by removal from the district before extra session of 1892.

EZRA S. HALL

Representative, 1917-18, 1919-20 and 1921-2, from the Missaukee District, comprising the counties of Kalkaska and Missaukee. Was born at Ailsa Craig, Ont., in 1860, of Irish descent. He attended the public schools, the Collegiate Institution at Parkhill, Ont., and the Model School in London, Ont. He came to Michigan in 1882, taught school eleven years, and in 1895 was elected School Commissioner of Missaukee County. He resigned this office in 1910 to become Postmaster at Lake City, which position he held for four years. Since 1914 he has devoted his entire time to farming. He was Assistant Postmaster in the Legislature of 1915-16. Mr. Hall is married.

FREDERICK HALL

Representative from Ionia County, 1850. Was born in Shelburn, Vt., Mar. 24, 1816. With a common school education he came West in 1835 and in 1836 was clerk in a store at Lyons. He settled in Ionia in 1841, where he died in 1883. He held many offices, including Justice, Register of Deeds, Receiver of the U. S. Land Office eight years, Mayor of Ionia, president of the National Bank, director in the Ionia & Lansing railroad, etc. He was a Democratic candidate for Congress in 1864, and a candidate for elector in 1876. In politics he was a Democrat. A large dealer in pine lands, he left a fortune. He was a man of fine personal appearance, genial manner, and was widely known and numbered many friends.

HENRY HALL

Representative from Washtenaw County, 1844; and Senator from the Sixth District, 1853-4. Was born in Sterling, Conn., May 2, 1800. With a common school education he was clerk six years, then taught school at Charleston, S. C., one year, then a merchant in Connecticut for ten years. He settled on a farm in Dexter, Mich., in 1833, on which he remained until 1867, after that time residing in the village of Dexter until his death, Oct. 28, 1873. He was Town Clerk sixteen years, many years a Justice, and several times Supervisor. In politics he was a democrat.

HENRY C. HALL

Representative from the Second District of Calhoun County, 1889-90. He was the first white child born in Battle Creek. He received his education partly at the Battle Creek schools and partly at the Vermontville Academy. At the opening of the rebellion he enlisted and served as Captain of a company in the 13th Michigan during the entire war. Married. A mason by trade, and in connection with his brother Charles he became the leading contractor in that line of business in Battle Creek and vicinity. He served as Alderman in the City Council, and also as Mayor. In politics a Republican.

JAMES H. HALL

Delegate in the Constitutional Convention of 1907-8. Was born in Orange County, N. Y., in 1846, of Dutch and English descent, his great grandfather. John Hall, having served in the war of the Revolution. His maternal grandfather, Henry Wannamaker, and his wife, Mary Dator, were of Holland parentage. Mr. Hall received his education in the common schools and graduated in 1874 from the law department of the University of Michigan with the degree of LL.B. His wife was Miss Jessie Emery. His early life was spent upon a farm. He practiced law, also was a banker; was owner and manager of a 700 acre farm called "The Clover Blossom Farm." He was interested in the *Independent Farmer*, a newspaper, which he founded, February, 1903, at Kinde. In 1874 Mr. Hall went to Port Austin, where he resided and practiced law. He died at his son's home in Highland Park, January, 1916.

HORATIO HALL

Representative from Eaton County, 1851. Was born in Byron, N. Y., Aug. 7, 1816. He settled in Bellevue, Mich., in 1844. He was a volunteer in the Patriot War of

1837. He was a farmer, and held various town offices, including Town Clerk and Supervisor.

MOSES HALL

Representative from Calhoun County, 1844. Came from Vermont to Battle Creek in 1832 and settled on a farm. He held various local offices. He was one of the founders of the Presbyterian Church at Battle Creek, of which he was an active member. He was a Justice for many years and was acting in that capacity at the time of his death, May 12, 1860.

SALMON C. HALL

Representative from Kalamazoo County, 1851. Was born in Litchfield, Conn., Nov. 9, 1809. By occupation he was a surveyor; in politics a Democrat. He came to Michigan in 1835. He was Register of Deeds and Treasurer of Barry County, afterwards Recorder of Vernon County, Mo., and corresponding clerk in contract office of Postoffice Department at Washington. He was with Major Ransom on survey work in Kansas. He served as First Lieutenant in the 1st I. H. G. under Col. Wattles of Kalamazoo. He was pensioned by the U. S. government. He resided at Pittsfield, Mass., in 1887.

TALMAN W. HALL

Representative from Calhoun County, 1855-6. Was born at Sudbury, Vt., Sept. 1, 1805. He was educated at an academy and for several years was a teacher. He settled as a farmer in Battle Creek in 1834, and became a merchant in 1842. He held local offices. both Territorial and State. and was Associate Circuit Judge of Calhoun County from 1836 to 1845. He was admitted to the bar but never practiced. He was Mayor. Postmaster and Alderman of Battle Creek; and took great interest in education. Until 1854 he was a Democrat, then a Republican. He died at Battle Creek July 2, 1890.

FRAYER HALLADAY

Representative from Osceola County, 1903-4. Was born in Leeds County, Ont., Oct. 15, 1848, of Scotch and Dutch ancestors. He was educated in the district schools of Ontario, supplemented by a commercial course at Hamilton, Ont. He came to Michigan in 1871, locating in Osceola County and opened a general store in the village of Ashton. Interested in the lumber manufacturing, wood and coal business at Grand Rapids. A widower. In politics a Republican.

CORNELIUS A. HALLENBECK

Representative from Eaton County, 1901-2 and 1903-4. Was born in Ghent, N. Y., Feb. 1, 1839. and removed to Vermontville, Mich., where he entered the academy and received his education. He engaged in farming until the Civil War, when he enlisted in Co. H. 6th Mich. Infantry and Heavy Artillery, on Aug. 6, 1861. He was severely wounded at the Battle of Baton Rouge, La., Aug. 5, 1862, and discharged from service Sept. 5, 1865. Married and a successful farmer since the close of the war. He was elected Justice of the Peace in 1882 and served in that capacity until July, 1902, and was commander of Edward Dwight Post No. 163, at Vermontville, for seven years. In politics a Republican.

WILLIAM B. HALLETT

Representative from the First District of Kalamazoo County, 1917-18. Was born at Adrian, Mich., July 1, 1860, of New England parents. At the opening of the Civil War his parents removed to Ohio, where his father enlisted in the 67th Ohio Vol., and fell at the Battle of Deep Bottoms in the seven day fight. Mr. Hallett received his education in the public schools of Ohio, taking up newspaper work at an early age. Returning to Michigan in 1881, he was married and then went West, conducting a newspaper for three years in Kansas. He returned to Kalamazoo and established a printing business, which included the publishing of the *Advocate*. In politics a Democrat.

PATRICK J. H. HALLY

Delegate in the Constitutional Convention of 1907-8, from the Third District, Wayne County. Was born in Wales, Mich., in 1867, of Irish parents. A few years after his parents moved to Detroit, where he was educated, graduating with the degree of B. A. from the Detroit College in 1888. He then took up the study of law and graduated from the University of Michigan in 1891. In 1896 he married Miss Mary G. Walsh. He occupied the position of Assessor in Detroit, and in 1900 became Assistant Corporation Counsel.

JOSEPH F. HAMBITZER

State Treasurer, 1893-4. Was born in Fond du Lac, Wis., in the year 1856. At the age of three years he removed with his parents to Grant County, Wis., where he acquired a common school education. At the age of 15 years he accepted a position as clerk in a general store where he remained three years and went to Houghton County, Mich., to clerk, but being unable to secure a position at once, he went to work in the Concord copper mine where he remained two years. While thus engaged he devoted his evenings to study and in 1878 was granted a teacher's certificate and taught school one year; he then accepted a position as Assistant Postmaster in the Hancock postoffice, which position he held for nine years. In the fall of 1884 he entered the law office of Chandler, Grant & Gray, in Houghton, where he remained for two years when he was nominated for County Treasurer, to which office he was elected; was renominated to a second term, endorsed by the opposing party and elected without opposition. He held the position of cashier of the Superior Savings Bank of Hancock. He was nominated by the Republicans at the convention of 1892 for State Treasurer, to which position he was elected; served to Mar. 20, 1894.

EDWARD L. HAMILTON

Member of Congress, 1897-9 to 1919-21. Was born in Niles Township, Berrien County, Mich., Dec. 9, 1857. He was educated in the public schools and was admitted to the bar in 1884. Married. In politics a Republican. He was elected to the 55th Congress, in November, 1896; served continuously; was elected to the 66th Congress Nov. 5, 1918.

EVA McCALL HAMILTON

Senator from the Sixteenth District, 1921-2. Was born in St. Clair County, Mich., of Scotch-Irish and English parents. She received her education in high school, normal college and special courses. She has been engaged in teaching school and as instructor in physical culture. She has been active in many committees and commissions having to do with civic affairs, and has devoted years to the study of public questions, and has had actual experience in an unofficial capacity before both branches of the Legislature. She is the first woman elected to the Michigan Senate; was elected at the general election Nov. 2, 1920.

JOHN HAMILTON

Representative from St. Joseph County, 1879-80. Was born in Wayne County, O., Sept. 1, 1812. He received a common school education; and came to Michigan in 1832 and engaged in farming. He was Commissioner of Highways a number of times. In politics he was a National.

NATHANIEL A. HAMILTON

Representative from Berrien County, 1877-8. Was born in Lansing, N. Y., Mar. 1, 1836. He was a resident of Whitewater, Wis., from 1842 to 1859, and there received an academical education, studied law, and was admitted to the bar in 1870. From 1859 to 1868 he was in practice at Placerville, Calif., then returned to Wisconsin, and in 1870 became a resident of St. Joseph, Mich., and in 1887 resided there engaged in his profession. He was Prosecuting Attorney, and in 1876 was a delegate to the Cincinnati Convention. In politics a Republican.

ANDREW G. HAMMOND

Representative from Kalamazoo County, 1839. Was born in Wyoming County, N. Y. He settled at Kalamazoo, in 1836, and was cashier of a branch of the Michigan State Bank. He removed to Greenfield, Mass., in 1840, and afterwards resided in Hartford, Conn., where he died in 1856. In politics he was a Whig.

CHAS. F. HAMMOND

Representative from the First District of Ingham County, 1893-4. Was born in Jackson, Mich., July 31, 1856. He acquired his education at the Mason High School, attended the law department of the Michigan University, and in 1879 began the practice of the law in Lansing. He held the office of Prosecuting Attorney for Ingham County, also a member of the Board of Education, and City Attorney for the city of Lansing. In politics a Republican.

CHARLES G. HAMMOND

Representative from Branch County, 1840 and 1841; and Auditor General, 1842-5. Settled in Union City, Mich., as a lawyer in 1836, his father being formerly at Smyrna, N. Y. He purchased the village site and sold it to a company. He removed to Chicago, became prominent in railroads and a leading citizen. He died prior to 1887 and left a fine record as a Christian and business man.

DAVID A. HAMMOND

Member of the State Board of Education, 1891-6. Was born in the township of Augusta, Washtenaw County, Dec. 16, 1855. From the time he was ten years of age he largely supported himself, and after he became thirteen wielded his own paddle, working on the farm by the month in summer, and attending a district school in the winter, doing chores for his board. In this way he earned the money that paid his expenses at the State Normal School, which institution he entered in 1872, but was unable to pursue his studies continuously on account of lack of funds. When his money gave out he had to leave school and go to work to earn more. His vacations at the holidays were usually spent in chopping wood by the cord, and his summer vacations in the harvest fields. As soon as he had advanced sufficiently to get a teacher's certificate, he began teaching in the country schools. In June, 1878, he graduated from the Normal School, and in September following became principal of the graded schools in Blissfield, Lenawee County. Here he remained four years, and during a part of that time served as Township Superintendent of Schools. Then the law establishing the County Board of School Examiners went into operation, he was elected a member of the first board. The following year he became secretary of the board and was also elected Superintendent of Schools at Tecumseh; continued in the Superintendency of the Tecumseh schools for six years and had been re-elected by a unanimous vote of the board for a seventh, when he was called to the Superintendency of the Charlotte city schools. He was married to Miss Cora E. Folwell, of White Pigeon, in 1880. In politics a Democrat. He was elected a member of the State Board of Education Nov. 4, 1890; resigned Aug. 1, 1896.

D. JUDSON HAMMOND

Representative from the First District of Oakland County, 1897-8 and 1899-1900. Was born on a farm in Oakland Township, Oakland County, Mich., Jan. 15, 1841. He acquired a common school education and commenced life for himself on a farm. At the commencement of the war he had charge of a large farm near Rochester; was drafted but furnished a substitute, and at the expiration of his lease he enlisted and served in the 22d and 29th Mich. Vol. Infantry. At the close of the war he went to Canada and engaged in the speculation of oil, but returned and purchased a farm in Oakland Township. He was married in 1866; sold his farm in 1871 and moved to Pontiac, where he engaged in the business of dealing in produce, in which occupation he continued nine years. Later he disposed of his interest and engaged in banking and real estate, in which he was engaged for ten years. Then he dealt in real estate and loans; a prominent member in the G. A. R. and I. O. O. F. circles; served on the Board of Water Commissioners of the city of Pontiac during its existence and acted as clerk most of the time. In politics a Republican. He held the office of Alderman of his city.

HORACE N. HAMMOND

Representative from St. Clair County, 1885-6. Was born in Bolton, N. Y., Nov. 18, 1832. He came with his parents to St. Clair County in 1833. He was a teacher for twenty years, then a bookkeeper, and in 1871 settled on a farm in East China. He was Town Clerk eighteen years, Justice several years, and held other local offices. In politics a Democrat.

JASON E. HAMMOND

Superintendent of Public Instruction, 1897-9 and 1899-1901. Was born in Ransom Township, Hillsdale County, May 17, 1862. His education, begun in the district school, was continued in both Hillsdale and Michigan agricultural colleges. Graduating from the latter in 1886, he entered the teachers' ranks, utilizing the long vacations by work in summer schools or by reading law. In 1888 he was elected member of the Hillsdale County Examining Board; in 1891 was made County Commissioner, and in 1893 was chosen as Deputy Superintendent of Public Instruction. His successful conduct of the important duties devolving upon him in this position four years later elected him to the head of this department; was re-elected Superintendent of Public Instruction on the Republican ticket for the term of 1899-1901.

WILLIAM HAMMOND

Representative from Eaton County, 1849. Was born in Deerfield, N. Y., in 1815, and removed to Genesee County, N. Y., when young. He came to Michigan in 1838, and engaged in the mercantile business until 1844; afterwards a farmer in Eaton, Eaton County. In politics he was a Whig.

CHARLES S. HAMPTON

Representative from Emmet and other counties, 1885-6. Was born in Medina, Mich., Sept. 10, 1856. He lived in Texas from 1858 to 1862, then at Hudson and Muir, Mich., settling at Harbor Springs in 1875. He was a graduate of Adrian College, for several years published the *Independent*, a Greenback paper, and was long a leading Greenbacker. He published a Democratic paper at Petoskey. He was a defeated candidate for Congress for the Tenth District. He moved to Detroit and practiced his profession of law. He died at Detroit Apr. 21, 1917.

JOHN W. HANCE

Senator from the Twenty-fourth District, 1883-4. Was born at Marengo, O., in 1848, of German and Welsh parentage. He came to Michigan in 1865, and resided in Isabella County, being engaged in farming and real estate business. Republican in politics.

BENJAMIN SAWTELLE HANCHETT

Member of the Board of Regents of the University of Michigan, 1911—. Was born at Grand Rapids, Mich., Oct. 1, 1868, and has always lived in that city. He was educated in the public schools, after which he entered the employ of the Street Railway Company of Grand Rapids as office boy. He has remained with the same concern ever since, although the name of the company is now the Grand Rapids Traction System, and of which he is now president and general manager. In 1900-1 he built the Grand Rapids, Holland and Lake Michigan Railway, which was the first interurban lines operated in western Michigan, and for a time was president of that company. Mr. Hanchett was married in 1897 and has one son and one daughter. He served as President of the village of East Grand Rapids for three successive terms, and was elected a member of the Board of Regents of the University in April, 1911. On April 13, the same year, he was appointed Regent to fill the unexpired term of Judge Loyal E. Knappen, who had resigned; was re-elected Apr. 7, 1919.

GEORGE E. HAND

Representative from Wayne County, 1846. Was born in Connecticut in 1809, graduated at Yale College in 1829, and came to Detroit, where he studied law and was admitted to practice. In 1835 he was appointed Judge of Probate of the county. As member of the Legislature he was chairman of the committee for the sale of the public works, and prepared the bills for providing for the sale of the Central and Southern railroads and the incorporation of companies for their purchase. Judge Hand held the office of United States District Attorney under President Pierce. He was a Democrat in politics. During his later years he held no office and was not an active practitioner, but handled landed property as buyer and seller. He was a man of vigorous physical build, cultivated by exercise, being known as an athlete. He was never married, and declining faculties threw the management of his large estate into the hands of his friends. He died Aug. 30, 1889.

MICHAEL HAND

Representative from Berrien County, 1853-4. Was born in Butler County, O., Jan. 18, 1806. He arrived in the town of Berrien, Berrien County, in 1831, and cleared a large farm, which became his home for life. He held several positions of trust, including those of Supervisor and Justice. He was a man of public spirit, a leader in politics, and a Democrat. He died Jan. 29, 1877.

SHERMAN T. HANDY.

Representative, 1899-1900 and 1901-2, from the Dickinson District, comprising the counties of Dickinson, Iron and Baraga. Was born at Morpeth, Ont., Apr. 3, 1867. He attended the public schools there, graduated from the Ridgetown Collegiate Institute in 1885, took a course in Stratford College, graduating in 1889, entered the law department of the University of Michigan, and was graduated from that school in 1891. In 1892 he entered upon the practice of law at Crystal Falls, Mich., with W. F. Cairns, under the firm name of Cairns & Handy, which continued until Mr. Cairns removed in 1892. Mr. Handy continued the business until June, 1895, when he formed a partnership with Fred H. Abbott, of Detroit, under the firm name of Handy & Abbott. This partnership was dissolved in October, 1897, by mutual consent. He was elected Circuit Court Commissioner on the Republican ticket in 1895; Prosecuting Attorney of Iron County in 1896; was renominated in 1898, but declined the nomination to run for Representative from the Dickinson District; was elected to the House of 1899-1900, and re-elected to the House of 1901-2.

PATRICK HANKERD

Representative from Jackson County, 1877-8, 1883-4 and 1885-6. Was born in Dexter, Mich., Mar. 22, 1845. In the year 1850 he removed with his parents to Henrietta, Jackson County. He received a common school education; taught school seven years. He held the office of Township Clerk one year, and the office of Supervisor fourteen years. He was the Democratic candidate for Congress in the Third District in 1886.

JAMES W. HANLEY

Senator from the Third District of Wayne County, 1913-14, 1915-16 and 1917-18. Was born at Detroit, Mich., Feb. 27, 1886, of Irish parentage. He was educated in the public schools of Detroit. He served as Estimator of the first ward of Detroit and was also a member of the Republican City Committee from the same ward. He engaged in the contracting business. In politics a Republican.

MARTIN HANLON

Representative from the Second District, Ingham County, 1905-6 and 1907-8. Was born at Dunkirk, N. Y., Aug. 7, 1853, of Irish parentage. He was a blacksmith by trade, having worked at his trade in Imlay City and Almont, Lapeer County, for nearly seven years. At the age of twenty-three years he began attending the high school at Almont, from which school he graduated. He continued his school work, graduating from the State Normal College at Ypsilanti, in 1882. A widower, his wife having died in January, 1895. He was Superintendent of the Williamston Public Schools for three years, 1882-5. He then bought an interest in a drug business at Williamston and later acquired the entire stock. In politics a Republican. He held the offices of School Trustee, Village Trustee, Justice of the Peace, Township Clerk. School Examiner, Commissioner of Schools.

PERRY HANNAH

Representative from Grand Traverse County, 1857-8. Was born in Erie, Pa., Sept. 22, 1824. He removed to Port Huron, Mich., in 1837, where he remained ten years, much of the time employed in rafting saw logs from Port Huron to Detroit. In 1846 he went to Chicago, landing in that city without a cent in his pocket. For four years he was employed as clerk in a lumber yard. In 1850 he formed a partnership with A. T. Lay and James Morgan in the well known firm of Hannah, Lay & Co. They commenced the lumber business with a borrowed capital of $6,000. In 1851 the firm purchased the present site of Traverse City, where they built a steam saw mill and opened a store. This business increased to immense proportions, and the firm owned lines of steamers which ran to Chicago and up the shore to Mackinac, and had the largest mercantile establishment, outside of Detroit, in the State. Mr. Hannah was for twenty-seven years a school officer, many years Supervisor, four years a member of the State Republican Committee, and was a Presidential Elector in 1864. He gave a site for nearly every church in the city, one for the Carnegie Library and the city park. He died Aug. 16, 1864.

GEORGE HANNAHS

Senator from Van Buren County, 1871-2. Was born at Cobleskill, N. Y., Mar. 17, 1823. In 1831 he removed to Utica, N. Y., and received a fair education. He came with his father to Albion, Mich., in 1837, where they were engaged in merchandise and milling. He also was in the salt manufacture at East Saginaw. He moved to South Haven in 1864, and built up a large lumber business and dealt in real estate. He served several times as President of Albion village and of South Haven; was a trustee of Pontiac and Kalamazoo asylums, and resided in California in 1887. In politics he was a Republican.

ALFRED H. HANSCOM

Representative from Oakland County, 1842 and 1845. Was a native of Rochester, N. Y., and was admitted to the Oakland County bar in 1838. He was an eloquent advocate, and an able political speaker. He was speaker of the House in 1845, and District Attorney of Oakland County for several years. He was married. He removed to Ontonagon County about 1850, and died on shipboard returning from Pontiac about 1857. He was a Democrat, and one of the greatest political orators in that party in the early days of Michigan.

CHARLES A. HANSCOM

Representative, 1889-90, from the Ontonagon District, comprising the counties of Baraga, Gogebic, Isle Royal, Keweenaw and Ontonagon. Was born at Buffalo, Erie County, N. Y., Mar. 19, 1859. By profession he was a lawyer, insurance agent and real estate dealer. In politics he was a Republican. He died at Ironwood, January, 1916.

DAVID E. HARBAUGH

Representative from Wayne County, 1840. Was born in Lisbon, O., in 1807, was educated at Washington College, Pa., was admitted to practice as an attorney in Ohio, in 1832, and became a resident of Detroit in 1834. He was elected Justice of the Peace and was president of the Detroit Young Men's Society in 1837; was City Attorney, 1844-5; member of the Board of Education, 1848; City Recorder, 1850; Prosecuting Attorney, 1861-3; Collector of Internal Revenue, 1865-9, and Police Justice, 1873-8. He was in active practice, except as interrupted by official duties, until his death, May, 1884. He was a Whig and Republican, but sympathized with the Greenbackers when they developed their greatest strength in 1878. He was a gentleman of broad views, generous and public spirited.

WILLIAM F. HARDEN

Representative from Allegan County, 1874. Was born July, 1831, in Wayne County, N. Y. He was educated in the common schools, in 1858 removed to Michigan, and lived in Martin, Allegan County, and was many years Supervisor. He was elected to fill a vacancy in the Legislature of 1874 caused by the resignation of Charles W. Watkins. In politics a Republican.

FISHER A. HARDING

Representative from Wayne County, 1841. Was a native of Massachusetts, born in 1811. He was a graduate of Harvard, and a law student under Daniel Webster. He spent two years in practice in Chicago, 1835-7, and in the latter year removed to Detroit, forming a law partnership with Fletcher Webster, who subsequently returned to Boston. He was appointed a master in chancery in 1840. Mr. Harding became connected editorially with the Detroit *Advertiser* in 1841, and so continued, with the exception of an intermission of about a year, until the time of his death, Aug. 4, 1846. He is described as a man peculiarly gentle in manner and pure and classical in thought. In politics he was a Whig.

ANSON R. HARDY

Representative from the First District of Ingham County, 1901-2. Was born in Concord, N. H., Feb. 3, 1855. He came to Michigan with his parents in 1860, and settled on a farm near the Agricultural College. By hard study at home he fitted himself to teach school winters, and by working on the farm summers was enabled to take short courses in business colleges and normal schools. He was a successful teacher fourteen years, and a member of the Board of School Examiners for six years, the last two years having the immediate superintendency of the schools. In politics a Democrat. In 1888 he was elected Register of Deeds, which office he held four years. He located in Lansing in 1893, where he engaged in the real estate business.

WILLIAM M. HARFORD

Representative from Muskegon County, 1881-2. Was born in Holmes County, O., Feb. 15, 1842. He worked at farming, attending district school. He graduated at the Ohio Wesleyan University in 1868. He was successively Superintendent of Schools at West Jefferson, Waynesville and London, O. In 1875 he was part proprietor and editor of the Fremont *Journal*. In 1878 he removed to Muskegon, Mich., and soon became editor and proprietor of the Muskegon *Chronicle*.

SEELEY HARGER

Representative from Oakland County, 1849. Was born in Ballston, N. Y., in 1801. In 1817 he removed to western New York. He came to Oakland County, Mich., in 1837, and resided in West Bloomfield.

JOHN U. HARKNESS

Representative from Lenawee County, 1883-4. Was born in Raisin, Mich., May 12, 1840. In 1848 he settled with his parents in Rollin, same county, where he resided most of the time since. He received a common school education, with two or three terms at Friends' Seminary, near Adrian, Mich. He learned the carriage-maker's trade, which business he carried on several years. After 1879 he engaged in farming. He filled various township offices, having been Supervisor three years. In politics a Republican.

CHARLES I. HARLEY

Representative from Mason County, 1901-2 and 1903-4. Was born in the State of Ohio, Aug. 6, 1864, and obtained his education in the public schools. He came to Michigan with his parents in 1882, and engaged in farming, milling and lumbering. Married. He held the offices of Township Treasurer and Supervisor. In politics a Republican.

WILLIAM HARLEY

Representative from Mason County, 1891-2. Was born in Sandusky County, O., May 22, 1843. He lived on the farm up to the breaking out of the Rebellion, when he enlisted in the 55th Ohio Vol. Infantry; served up to the time of the veteran enlistment, when he re-enlisted as a veteran, again in the 55th, and served as a Sergeant to the close of the war. After the war he again took farming as his occupation and moved to Steuben County, Ind., where he lived two years; sold out and moved to Michigan, near Marshall, lived in that locality three years, then sold out and moved back to his old homestead in Ohio, where he remained nine years, when he moved to a beautiful farm of 160 acres in the township of Riverton. In politics a Democrat.

HENRY H. HARMON

Representative from Livingston County, 1863-4. Was born in Manchester, N. Y., June 2, 1823. He came to Oakland County with his parents in 1838. He received a common school education; taught school in Howell in 1847; commenced the study of law and was admitted to the bar in 1849. He began practice at Howell. He held the offices of Town Clerk, Circuit Court Commissioner, Prosecuting Attorney and Judge of Probate; also for some years edited a paper. He was a Democrat in politics.

EGBERT P. HARPER

Representative from the Second District of Washtenaw County, 1885-6 and 1887-8. Was born Oct. 24, 1832, in Wayne County, N. Y. He came to Michigan about 1837; held the office of Supervisor fifteen years. He was elected to the Legislature of 1885-6, and re-elected to the House on the Fusion ticket.

WILLIAM HARPER

Representative from Livingston County, 1891-2. Was born in Berlin, Erie County. O., Mar. 5, 1841, and a resident of Michigan since he was four years old. He was a practicing physician and a resident of Deerfield Township, Livingston County. Mr. Harper enlisted in the Eighth Infantry during the war, but failed to muster. He held various township offices, and in 1880 was a candidate for Representative from Genesee County, but was defeated by A. S. Partridge, the Republican candidate. He was made the Democratic candidate for Representative from Livingston County in 1888, but refused to run; in 1890 accepted the nomination and was elected.

ANSON R. HARRINGTON

Senator, 1917-18, from the Seventeenth District, comprising the county of Kent. Was born in Walker Township, Kent County, Mich., Apr. 6, 1870, son of Vernon and Martha Ellis Harrington. He was educated in the district schools. He was married Dec. 27, 1899, to Ella M. Bailey, daughter of Joseph S. and Ann Mary Cross Bailey. In politics he was a Democrat. He was elected to the Senate Nov. 7, 1916; was renominated in 1918 but defeated. He died Dec. 1, 1918.

CHARLES F. HARRINGTON

Representative from St. Clair County, 1877-8. Was born at Port Huron, Mich., Sept. 20, 1842. He received a classical education at Canandaigua Academy, N. Y., and in 1861 commenced the study of law. In 1864 he commenced practice at Port Huron. He was Circuit Court Commissioner for St. Clair County one term, and Prosecuting Attorney two terms. In 1873 he abandoned practice and was instrumental in organizing the Port Huron Savings Bank, with which he was connected as cashier and director, and was also interested in railroads.

DANIEL B. HARRINGTON

Representative from St. Clair County, 1847; and Senator from the Thirty-first District, 1853-4. Was born at Sodus, Ontario County, N. Y., Apr. 23, 1807. He settled with his father on Black River, St. Clair County, in 1824, attended school, was a clerk in Detroit, and in 1833 went into business at Black River. In 1835, with Judge White, he bought eighty acres of land, now part of the site of Port Huron, purchased other lands, and engaged in lumbering and real estate. He was Postmaster, president of the First National Bank, and of the Port Huron Savings Bank. In 1874 he built the city opera house. He was of Puritan ancestry and his ancestors served in the Revolutionary War. In the State Historical Museum at Lansing there is a picture of Mother Rod, a noted Indian woman of St. Clair County, given by Mr. Harrington. He died at Port Huron, July 7, 1878.

EBENEZER B. HARRINGTON

Senator from the Fourth District, 1839. Was born in Lyons, N. Y. By occupation he was a lawyer, in politics a Democrat. He came to Michigan in 1831. He studied law in Whitesboro, N. Y., and was admitted to practice law in Michigan in 1837. He edited and published the Lake Huron *Observer* at Port Huron. From 1838 to 1844 he practiced law in Detroit, being associated with James A. Van Dyke. Governor Mason appointed him master in chancery in 1838. In 1839 he was appointed to superintend the publication of the revised statutes of Michigan. The same year he was appointed reporter of the Court of Chancery, and in 1844 he also became reporter of the Supreme Court. He died in August, 1844, the volume known as Harrington's Chancery Reports being prepared for publication in November, 1844, by Henry N. Walker, his successor in office.

EDWARD W. HARRIS

Delegate from Oakland County to the Constitutional Convention of 1867. Was born May 4, 1831, at Bradford, Vt. In 1837 he came to Michigan with his parents, who settled at Rochester, Oakland County. He attended the academy at that place for several years. In 1854 he graduated at the state and national law school at Poughkeepsie, N. Y., and located at Port Huron. In 1855 he formed a co-partnership with the Hon. O. D. Conger, in the law business, under the firm name of Conger & Harris. In 1862 he was appointed Judge of Probate of St. Clair County, in the place of Major Scarritt, resigned, and served as such for three years. In 1866 he was elected Prosecuting Attorney, and served two years, in 1868 he was elected Judge of Probate and served four years. In 1873 he was appointed Judge of the sixteenth circuit, in place of Judge Mitchell, resigned, and in 1875 was elected to the same place without opposition.

ISRAEL V. HARRIS

Senator from the Twenty-third District, 1853-4. Was born in Pine Plains, N. Y., Apr. 2, 1815. He received an academical education, and was engaged in farming until he came to Michigan in 1836. In 1837 he settled in Tallmadge, was a merchant with his brother at Grand Rapids, then engaged in lumbering and real estate. He was six times Supervisor of Tallmadge. Later he lived at Grand Haven. He died at Grand Rapids, Oct. 17, 1886.

JAMES A. HARRIS

Representative from the First District of Saginaw County, 1919-20 and 1921-2. Was born on a farm in Jefferson County, N. Y., Oct. 17, 1861, of English parents. He is the youngest of a family of seven. He was a student at the Grand Rapids High School, Ives Seminary, Antwerp, N. Y., and the law department of the University of Michigan, graduating from the latter institution in 1890. He has been engaged in the practice of law at Saginaw since that time. Mr. Harris is married and has two children. He held the office of Recorder for the city of Saginaw and also local white slave officer for two years. In politics he is a Republican.

MICHAEL HARRIS

Representative from Menominee County, 1905-6, 1907-8, 1909-10 and 1917-18. Was born in Ireland, Sept. 19, 1852. He received his education in the National School of that country. He came to the United States in the year 1866, settled in Hancock, Mich., and engaged in mining for three years. He removed to Marquette in 1869 and was employed as lumber inspector. He was married in 1872 to Margaret Barry. He moved to Spaulding, Menominee County, in 1876, purchased a farm and engaged in lumbering and general store business. He held the offices of Township Clerk and Justice of the Peace of Spaulding Township, and was elected Supervisor of Harris Township in 1903 and re-elected in 1904. In politics an active Republican.

MYRON HARRIS

Representative from Ottawa County, 1875-6. Was born at Pine Plains, N. Y., Mar. 2, 1820. At the age of nineteen he came to Michigan and located at Tallmadge, Ottawa County, where he resided. In 1844 he built a saw mill, and lumbered for about twenty years, building up a most successful business. In politics he was a Democrat. He was a Captain of militia. He died at Tallmadge Sept. 1, 1880.

SILAS G. HARRIS

Representative from Ottawa and Kent counties, 1847, 1848 and 1850. His postoffice address was Tallmadge. (Further data not obtainable).

THOMAS W. HARRIS

Representative from Wayne County, 1869-70. Was a carpenter by trade, born in New Jersey in 1817. He resided in Newark, N. J., up to 1852, when he located at Detroit. He was a Democrat in politics, nominated for the Legislature in 1869 by his party as a representative workingman, he being at the time president of the Trades Assembly, an organization composed of delegates from the various labor unions of the city. He died in 1884.

WILLIAM HARRIS

Representative from Keewenaw County, 1871-2 and 1873-4. Was born in Cornwall, England, Mar. 17, 1819. In 1847 he came to the United States and settled in Ontonagon County. He received an ordinary public school education, and was by occupation a mining superintendent. In politics he was a Republican.　　　. . .　.

WILLIAM HARRIS

Representative, 1889-90, 1895-6 and 1897-8, from the Antrim District, comprising the counties of Antrim, Charlevoix and Kalkaska. Was born at Burmot Hills, Saratoga County, N. Y., in 1832; came to Michigan in 1836, locating on a farm near Battle Creek; attended district school and one term at Kalamazoo College; taught school several winters, and worked on the farm summers; his principal occupation that of a farmer. He was married in 1860, and his wife died in 1887. In 1866 he moved to Norwood, where he engaged in real estate and money loaning. In politics a Republican. He was Supervisor of Battle Creek Township in 1864-5, and of Norwood twenty-three years; held the offices of Register of Deeds, Judge of Probate and School Examiner.

WILLIAM HARRY

Representative from Houghton County, 1891-2. Was born in Cornwall, England, Aug. 14, 1842, where he received a common school education. He was left an orphan at twelve years of age, and at nineteen he came to this country and settled in New Jersey, and engaged to work in an iron mine as time keeper. In the Spring of 1863 he removed to Lake Superior and settled in Hancock, Mich. He secured work in the copper mines and in 1864 learned the tinsmith's trade. In the spring of 1869 he started in the tin, sheet iron, copper and hardware business, and continued it up to Jan. 1, 1890, when he sold it out and retired from active mercantile life. Then he devoted his time to his banking, mining and other interests in Houghton County. In politics an ardent and active Republican. He was elected to the House of 1891-2 on the Republican ticket.

ANDREW HARSHAW

Senator, 1887-8 and 1889-90, from the Twenty-sixth District, comprising the counties of Alcona, Alpena, Iosco, Ogemaw and Oscoda. Was born near Banbridge, Ireland, Feb. 4, 1839. In the year 1849, when yet a lad, he came with his widowed mother to Michigan and settled in Oakland County. When seventeen years of age he commenced an apprenticeship at the tinsmith's trade. He worked at the bench successfully for many years in Pontiac. He afterwards engaged in business for himself in company with Hon. S. H. Norton. He served as Alderman of the city of Pontiac with credit two terms. In 1872 he went to Alpena and opened a hardware business. He served as a member of the Alpena City Board of Education in 1874, 1875, 1877 and 1879, and Supervisor of the third ward in 1876; also held the position of Alderman during the years 1872 and 1873, and again in 1881. In 1884 he was elected Mayor of Alpena, and was re-elected in 1885. In June, 1886, on the death of Mayor Richardson, he was unanimously chosen by the Common Council to fill the vacancy. In 1884 he was one of the Butler Presidential electors on the Fusion ticket. A prominent Odd Fellow. He was State Senator in 1887, and was re-elected to the Senate of 1889-90 on the Democratic ticket.

ALVIN N. HART

Representative from Lapeer County, 1885-6 and from Ingham County, 1871-2; and Senator from the Sixth District, 1844, 1845, 1848-50. Was born in Cornwall, Conn.,

Feb. 11, 1804. He graduated at Amherst College, came to Lapeer, Mich., in 1831; was Justice, and Sheriff of Lapeer County. He was chief Judge of the Lapeer County Court, 1846-50. He became a resident and merchant in Lansing in 1860, and was many years an Alderman. He was interested in real estate, milling, and the building of railroads. In politics a Democrat. He died Aug. 22, 1874.

BURTON LLOYD HART

Representative from the Second District of Lenawee County, 1898 and 1899-1900. Was born at Lagrange, Ind., Nov. 23, 1871. When the subject of this sketch was about three years of age his parents removed to Blissfield, Mich. At school age he entered the West Blissfield public schools, from which he graduated in 1887, being president of his class. After graduating he engaged in teaching until the fall of 1890, when he entered the law department of the Universtiy of Michigan. After a year he resumed teaching until the fall of 1894, when he resumed his law studies in Michigan University and graduated with the class of 1895. After graduation he taught school one year, then went to Morenci and engaged in law practice. In politics a Republican. He served as School Inspector of Blissfield Township, Township Clerk of Seneca Township, Village Clerk of Morenci, and was elected to the Legislature in April, 1898, to fill a vacancy caused by the removal of William R. Edgar from the State; was re-elected to the House of 1899-1900.

HENRY HART

Representative from Midland and other counties, 1875-6. Was born May 13, 1840, in China, Mich. He was raised on a farm, and received a common school education. He graduated from the law department of the University in 1865, and commenced practice at Midland the same year, where he resided. He was Justice of the Peace one year, Prosecuting Attorney of Midland County four years, Circuit Court Commissioner four years, Supervisor three years, a member of the Midland School Board five years, and in 1875 he was elected Judge of the Twenty-first Judicial circuit.

JONATHAN HART

Representative from Calhoun County, 1840. Was born in the State of New York, Oct. 25, 1795. He settled in Battle Creek, in 1836, and built a flour mill, continuing in that business until his death in 1858. He also engaged in the manufacture of lard oil. He was President of the village of Battle Creek and Mayor of the city. In politics he was a Whig and one of the first seven of that party in Calhoun County. In religion he was a Friend. He was a public spirited citizen and a successful business man.

NOAH H. HART

Delegate from Lapeer County to the Constitutional Convention of 1850; and Representative from Lapeer County, 1851. Was born in Litchfield, Conn., Oct. 30, 1813. By profession he was a lawyer, in politics a Democrat. He settled in Lapeer, Mich., in 1832, held various local offices, and was Justice for thirty years. He raised a company and entered the army in 1861, as First Lieutenant in the 10th Mich. Infantry, was promoted to Captain Mar. 31, 1863, and was mustered out Feb. 6, 1865. He resided with a daughter at Toledo, O., in 1887.

PATRICK HART

Representative from the Second District of Calhoun County, 1893-4. Was born in Monaghon County, Ireland, in 1852. Three years later he came to America, locating at Battle Creek, Mich. His only education was received at the public schools. He early engaged in the cooper business, and, with the exception of four years of grocery experience, his life was devoted to that occupation, being a member of the firm of Hart Bros., of Battle Creek. In politics a Republican. He was elected Alderman of his ward in 1886 and re-elected by increased majority in 1888.

RUSSELL A. HART

Representative from the First District of Wayne County, 1921-2. Was born at Marine City, Mich., Sept. 21, 1889, of American parentage. He received his education in the public school of Marine City and graduated from Detroit College of Law in 1912. He is now engaged in the practice of law in the city of Detroit. Mr. Hart is unmarried. In politics he is a Republican.

WILLIAM W. HARTSON

Representative from St. Clair County, 1869-70 and 1893-4. Was born in Eaton, Madison County, N. Y., Feb. 27, 1835. He engaged chiefly in farming though engaged in dealing in real estate. During the war he served as private in the 4th Mich. Infantry. In politics a Republican. He was Supervisor of Wales Township, member of the Legislature of 1869-70, Register of Deeds, Supervisor of the fourth ward of Port Huron, and elected to the House of 1893-4.

JOSEPH L. HARTSUFF

Representative from Livingston County, 1849. Was born in Onondaga County, N. Y., May 1, 1810. His early life was spent in farming, boating on the Erie canal, and later teaching school. He came to Michigan in 1835, and settled on a farm near Coldwater. He soon removed to Unadilla, Livingston County, where he was a farmer until his death, Nov. 14, 1867. He was a Justice of the Peace several years. In politics he was a Democrat.

WILL C. HARTWAY

Representative from Macomb County, 1919-20 and 1921-2. Was born on a farm in Ray Township, Macomb County, Mich., Dec. 9, 1877, of German parentage. He attended the district school and worked on his father's farm (which he now owns) until 1914, when he was elected Sheriff. Since that time he has resided in Mt. Clemens. He served as Supervisor two years, Township Treasurer two years, Highway Commissioner five years and Sheriff four years. In politics he is a Republican.

BARZILLA J. HARVEY

Representative from Lenawee County, 1857-8. Was born in Ontario County, N. Y., Sept. 29, 1808. He came to Michigan in 1832, and purchased lands in Adrian, which he occupied until his death, Sept. 25, 1863. In politics he was a Republican.

JAMES MARK HARVEY

Senator, 1919-20, from the Sixth District, comprising the counties of Kalamazoo and St. Joseph. Was born in Michigan, Nov. 26, 1873, of American parents. He was graduated from the Constantine High School, and, after attending the Michigan Agricultural College, he entered the University of Michigan, graduating from the law department of that institution. He was Postmaster at Constantine and served as County Clerk and President of the School Board. In addition to his law practice also interested in farming. Married. In politics a Republican.

ANDREW HARVIE

Representative from Wayne County, 1845; and Senator from the First District, 1850-1. Was born in Scotland before 1810, came to Michigan in 1837, and was principal of the Tecumseh branch of the University in 1839-40. In 1840 he became a lawyer at Detroit. He was master of chancery in 1848. Later he removed to Chicago. He was a Democrat in politics. In behalf of Michigan, he presented the copper block to be placed in the Washington monument.

WILLARD HARWOOD

Representative from Lapeer County, 1891-2 and 1893-4. Was born in Monroe County, N. Y., in 1843. The next year he came with his parents to Michigan, locating in Macomb County. While here he acquired his education at the public schools and during the war enlisted in Co. A, 22d Mich. Vol., and served three years. In 1868 he moved to Lapeer County, locating on a farm. In politics a Republican. He held the offices of Township Clerk and Township Treasurer.

CHARLES C. HASCALL

Member from Oakland County in the Legislative Council, 1832-3 and 1834-5; and Senator from the Fifth District, 1835-6. Was born in Cayuga County, N. Y., Nov. 6, 1799. He came to Michigan in 1819, settled in Pontiac, built a woolen mill, and owned the first printing press brought to Pontiac. He was one of the first Justices of the Peace and was Town Clerk of Pontiac in 1829-30. He kept in 1825 the first hotel in the village of Auburn, three and a half miles east of Pontiac. He built there another woolen mill, a hotel, dwelling and store, and embarked in the dry goods business. He removed to Flint in 1836, having been appointed U. S. receiver for the District of Michigan, which office he held 1836-40. He was a commissioned General of State militia and went to the "Toledo War". He was the Democratic candidate for Congress in 1850. He had a contract from government to construct a portion of the "Northern railroad," and had done considerable work when the project was abandoned. He traded in lumber and was partner in a general store. He established the *Flint Republican*, a Democratic paper conducted for him by the late Royal W. Jenney, which was discontinued in 1853. He was always a Democrat. He resigned as Senator at the close of the extra session of 1836, the vacancy being filled by Randolph Manning. He died Oct. 5, 1862.

VOLNEY HASCALL

Delegate from Kalamazoo County to the Constitutional Convention of 1850. Was born Feb. 2, 1820, in Leroy, N. Y. He came with his father to Kalamazoo in 1830.

was educated at the Kalamazoo branch of the University and became a finished scholar in Latin, English literature and mathematics. He read law and was admitted to the bar in 1843. He had mastered the art of printing while a minor. He practiced law three years, and in 1846 became owner and editor of the Kalamazoo *Gazette*, to which he gave his time for sixteen years. He sold out from failing health in 1862. He was in politics a Democrat. He was register of the United States Land Office at Kalamazoo in 1857-8, and held several local offices. He was an able and convincing editorial writer, and made his paper a political power. He died Feb. 21, 1879.

NELSON HASKIN

Representative from Lapeer County, 1887-8. Was born in Ontario County, Ont., Oct. 20, 1849, and became an acknowledged citizen of the United States, Apr. 10, 1874. He became a resident of Michigan about 1872, and held the office of Village Trustee in Imlay City. In politics a Republican.

HARAN HASKINS

Representative from Oakland County, 1837. Was born in Dutchess County, N. Y., in February, 1806. By occupation he was a farmer, in politics a Republican. He settled in West Bloomfield, Oakland County, in 1832. He was Town Clerk for eight years. He was a Captain in the "Toledo War," a deacon in the Baptist Church, and Superintendent of a Sunday school. He died in November, 1858.

FRANKLIN A. HASSENGER

Representative from St. Joseph County, 1917-18. Was born in the village of Constantine, Mich., Feb. 5, 1853, of French-German parents. He was educated in the common schools supplemented by a course in Raisin Valley Seminary, from which institution he graduated. At an early age his parents removed to what was then a wilderness where he had a chance to wield those agencies of physical development, the ax, mattock, maul and wedge. Apr. 28, 1873, he began teaching school and taught continuously until Dec. 22, 1916, resigning to take up legislative duties. Mr. Hassenger was married Mar. 23, 1882, to Miss Ida M. Young. In politics a Democrat.

ERNEST W. HASTINGS

Representative, 1901-2, from the Grand Traverse District, comprising the counties of Grand Traverse, Benzie and Leelanau. Was born in Lansing, Mich., Apr. 16, 1855, and attended the public schools until nine years old, when, his father having died in the army, he went with his mother to Traverse City, where he finished his education in the public school, and afterwards following the trade of machinist, he had charge of a mill for a number of years. He entered the real estate and insurance business in 1890. He served as Alderman of the second ward of Traverse City. Married. In politics a strong Republican.

EUROTAS P. HASTINGS

Auditor General, 1840-2. His nativity is not accurately known, although he was born in the State of New York, and was past middle age in 1840. He was trained as a business man and banker under the Dwights, of Geneva, N. Y., and was the first president of the Bank of Michigan, organized in 1825. He was a Whig in politics. He held the office of Recorder of Detroit for a term, was a U. S. Commissioner, and Pension Agent from 1837 to 1854. He took an active interest in public affairs, was earnest and zealous in his religious connections, which were Presbyterian, and was a man of refinement and character, but inclined to be over-confiding in his disposition. He died in 1866.

BARNABAS C. HATCH

Representative from Jackson County, 1849. Was born in August, 1809, and emigrated from Steuben County, N. Y., about 1837. He was self-educated. He was a farmer and settled in Spring Arbor. He was Supervisor several years; Justice twenty years; and County Judge. He acquired a valuable estate, and was a man of public spirit, fine intellectual endowments and was deservedly popular. He died Feb. 22, 1874.

HERSCHEL H. HATCH

Member of the Constitutional Commission of Michigan in 1873; and member of Congress, 1883-5. Was born at Morrisville, N. Y., Feb. 17, 1837. He received common school training until 1856, when he entered the law school at Hamilton College, N. Y. He graduated in 1859, and was at once admitted to the bar. He practiced law in his native county until 1863, when he removed to Bay City, where he re ided, and actively followed the practice of his profession. He was elected a member of the first Board of Aldermen of Bay City; elected Judge of Probate of Bay County in 1868; and member of the Law Commission of Michigan in 1881. In 1882 after the 347th ballot and a deadlock of three days he was nominated for Congress. He was elected Representative to the Forty-eighth Congress upon the Republican ticket. He moved to Detroit where he died Nov. 30, 1920.

JESSE MONROE HATCH

Representative from the First District of Calhoun County, 1909-10. Was born in Lee Township, Calhoun County, Mich., May 27, 1858, of Scotch and Irish descent. He received his education at the Marshall High School and the law department of the University of Michigan. Married. In moderate circumstances, a lucrative law practice, and owner of considerable real estate in Marshall and Battle Creek, Calhoun County; also owner of a half interest in the Calhoun County Abstract Company. In politics a Republican. He held the offices of Circuit Court Commissioner, and Prosecuting Attorney.

HIRAM HATHAWAY

Representative from Macomb County, 1842 and 1855-6; and Delegate from Macomb County to the Constitutional Convention of 1850. Was born in Massachusetts June 5, 1799. He settled in Richmond, Mich., in 1826. He also served as Associate Judge of Macomb County, was Supervisor of Richmond, and President of Armada village.

GILBERT HATHEWAY

Senator from the Fourth District, 1871. Was born in Plymouth County, Mass., in 1812. He came to Michigan in 1846, and inaugurated extensive business enterprises at New Baltimore, Macomb County. During his early life. in Massachusetts he was well known, and was Colonel in the State militia. His life in Macomb County was characterized by deeds of charity and benevolence. He was Senator from Macomb County in 1871, but died Oct. 21, 1871, before the close of his term. He gave $15,000 to erect a building for the school known as the Hatheway Institute at New Baltimore. He left a large property. He was succeeded by Seymour Brownell in the extra session of 1872.

OTTO HATZENBUHLER

Representative from the First District of Detroit, 1899-1900. Was born at Detroit, Wayne County, Mich., Jan. 7, 1862, and received his education at the German-American Seminary and the public schools. Engaging with S. Freedman & Co., he learned the trade of cigar making, packing and classing. During the winter nights of 1880-1 he took a course at Mayhew's Business College, and from 1881 to 1884 he worked at his trade for Burk, Rich & Co. He then took a position as book-keeper with the Heck Lumber Company. From 1886 to 1895 he worked for the firm of George Moebs & Co., the last three years as city salesman. In politics a Republican. July 1, 1895, he was elected paymaster of the Board of Public Works, and held that position until Oct. 15, 1898, when he was elected to the House of 1899-1900.

MARTIN HAVEN

Representative from Calhoun County, 1867-8. Was born in Livingston County, N. Y., July 21, 1823. He came to Albion in 1851. By occupation he was a builder, farmer and drover, in politics a Republican. He was Postmaster of Albion from June 20, 1875, to Dec. 31, 1886, when he was suspended by President Cleveland. He was a member of the Albion Common Council for two years, and was elected Supervisor of the third ward in 1887.

JAMES MATTHEW HAVILAND

Representative from the Second District of St. Clair County, 1909-10, 1911-12, and 1914-15. Was born at Hanover, Jackson County, Mich., July 9, 1859, of English, Scotch and Irish descent. He was educated in the district schools of Canada and Michigan. His father, James M. Haviland, enlisted in Co. A, 20th Mich. Infantry, in 1862. In the year 1865, Mr. Haviland emigrated with his parents to Townsend, Norfolk County, Ont., residing in Ontario for nine years. In 1875, he removed with his parents to St. Clair County, Mich. He was married Apr. 5, 1877, to Maggie Kearn, of Greenwood, St. Clair County. He remained in Michigan until 1882 when he removed to Kansas, remaining there two years, after which he returned to Michigan. In politics an active Republican. He served on the Board of Supervisors in the township of Columbus and as City Assessor; proprietor of Belle River Valley Farm, engaged in farming and stock raising; a member of Archie Campbell Camp No. 216 Michigan division Sons of Veterans.

DUANE HAWKINS

Representative from Easton County, 1881-2. Was born Feb. 17, 1840, in Vermontville, Mich. His parents moved from the State of Vermont in 1838. His education was received in common schools. His life was spent on a farm, except a period of nine months. That was spent in the army during the Civil War, he having enlisted Aug. 30, 1864, in the 2d Mich. Cavalry, and having been discharged June 2, 1865. He was elected Justice of the Peace; was president of the Eaton County Agricultural Society, and held many other minor offices within the gift of the community in which he lived.

LUCIUS D. HAWKINS

Senator from the Seventh District, 1875-6. Was born in Oswego County, N. Y., in 1824. His education was attained in common schools. He removed to Michigan in 1835, and settled in Spring Arbor, Jackson County. He was a farmer and machinist by occupation.

OLNEY HAWKINS

Senator from the Fifth District, 1839-40. His postoffice address was Ann Arbor. (Further data not obtainable).

VICTOR· HAWKINS

Delegate in the Constitutional Convention of 1907-8 from the Sixth District, Hillsdale County. Was born in Jonesville, in 1867, of English parents. He was educated in the public schools and at the University of Michigan. In 1897 he married Miss Jennie Eckler, of Jackson. He sold newspapers when a boy and before attending college was employed as a bookkeeper. He practiced law since 1889 and was very successful in his profession.

AUGUSTUS D. HAWLEY

Representative from Jackson County, 1841. His postoffice address was Jackson. (Further data not obtainable).

CHAUNCEY HAWLEY

Representative from Jackson County, 1842. Was born in Granby, Conn., Sept. 26, 1797. He settled at Napoleon, Jackson County, Mich., in 1834, and died Mar. 31. 1880. He was probably a farmer.

ELIJAH HAWLEY, JR.

Representative from Wayne County, 1844, 1846 and 1849. Was born in Arlington, Vt., Apr. 17, 1812. He studied law in that State and was admitted to the bar in Illinois, but never engaged in practice. He became a resident of Wayne County. Mich., in 1835. He held various town and county offices for twelve years.

RICHARD HAWLEY

Representative from Wayne County, 1865-6 and 1877-8. Was born at Shrewsbury, Shropshire, England, Dec. 10, 1815. He came to this country with his parents in 1818, and resided successively in Pennsylvania, Massachusetts, West Virginia and Ohio. He received a good common school education. He came to Detroit in 1840 and was engaged in the brewing business until 1875 with the exception of two years. He was for many years an active member of the Detroit Board of Trade, and several times represented it at the national and dominion boards. He was also an Alderman, and a member of the Board of Estimates. He was a Whig until 1854, after that a Democrat.

THOMAS D. HAWLEY

Representative from Wayne County, 1867-8: and Senator from the Second District, 1885-6. Was born at Erie, Pa., Feb. 27, 1843, and the same year came with his parents to Detroit. He received a classical and collegiate education at Toronto, Canada. He became a lawyer in 1879. He was a member and secretary of the Democratic State Committee, delegate to the Democratic National Convention, member and president of the Detroit Common Council, and held many other official and honorary offices.

WILLARD HAWLEY

Representative from the Second District of Ionia County, 1889-90 and 1891. Was born on a farm near Brantford, Ont., Dec. 28, 1834. He was educated in the common schools, under very adverse circumstances, working a farm during the summers and attending school winters. In April, 1854, he came to Michigan and during that summer worked by the month on a farm in Kent County. In November of the same year he went into Ionia County, and soon after purchased the farm upon which he resided. He was married Nov. 28, 1856, to Miss Caroline L. Marble, and had a family of three sons and three daughters. He was elected to the offices of Highway Commissioner, Justice of the Peace, and was serving his third term as Supervisor when elected as a Republican to the Legislature of 1889-90; was re-elected to the House of 1891-2. He died Apr. 9, 1891, at his boarding place in Lansing.

HENRY HAYDEN

Representative from Bay County, 1855. Was born in Essex, Conn., Feb. 8, 1819, and was educated at Hill's Academy in that town. He settled at Portsmouth, now a part of Bay City, in 1855, and was a salt and lumber manufacturer for fourteen years, and for several years Supervisor. He returned to Essex, Conn., in 1869, where he lived in retired life. He died Sept. 18, 1875.

HENRY A. HAYDEN

Representative from Jackson County, 1863-4. Was born in Otsego County, N. Y., Mar. 28, 1817. He received a common school education, was a clerk in Buffalo from 1829 to 1834, then served as sailor. He studied civil engineering, and in 1837 helped survey the line of the Michigan Central Railroad, and remained in service of the road until 1844, and was general superintendent of repairs and paymaster. He became a resident of Jackson in 1838. He was in the milling business after 1845. He was County Surveyor, Supervisor, Mayor, etc. For many years he was president of the Jackson, Lansing & Saginaw Railroad Company. In politics he was a Democrat.

PHILOTUS HAYDEN

Representative from Cass and Van Buren counties, 1844, and from Van Buren County, 1847 and 1850; and Senator from the Fourth District, 1851, and from the

Nineteenth District, 1859-60. Was born in Montgomery County, N. Y., in 1810. When young he went to Brandon, Vt., and engaged in mercantile business. In 1836 he located one thousand acres of land in Hamilton, Van Buren County, Mich., and owned and occupied a farm of seven hundred acres at the time of his death, Mar. 10, 1866. He was a prominent Republican. He was ten times Supervisor.

JAMES G. HAYDEN

Senator, 1905-6, from the Seventh District, comprising the counties of Berrien and Cass. Was born of Scotch and Irish parents in Calvin Township, Cass County, Mich., Nov. 10, 1854, and from early childhood was practically thrown upon his own resources through the death of his father. He attended the common schools of Cass County, finishing his education at the Bryant & Stratton's Commercial College. He worked for four years on the grade of the C. & G. T. and Air Line roads, and for six months as section hand. He was a successful farmer, business man, and was engaged in the insurance and real estate business, and a member of the Board of Superintendents of the Poor. He was a Mason and charter member of Cassopolis Lodge K. of P. He held the offices of Township Treasurer, served as County Treasurer, and was president of the Cass County Agricultural Society. He died at his home at Cassopolis, July 14, 1917.

ELEAZAR B. HAYES

Representative from Tuscola County, 1883-4 and 1885-6. Was born in Geneseo, N. Y., May 31, 1832. He came to Michigan in 1841, and settled in Tuscola County, in 1855. His occupation was farming. He was Supervisor fourteen years, and secretary of the Tuscola County Agricultural Society for seven years. In politics he was a Republican.

NATHAN B. HAYES

Representative from Ionia County, 1877-8. Was born at Bristol, N. Y., Dec. 13, 1835. In 1836 he removed with his parents and settled in North Plains, Ionia County. He was president of the First National Bank at Muir from its organization. He was extensively engaged in farming, also in lumbering and manufacturing. In politics he was a Republican. He died at North Plains, May 31, 1922.

WALTER J. HAYES

Senator from the First District, 1919-20, 1921-2 and 1923—. Was born Oct. 1, 1871, at Holly, Mich., of American parents. He was educated in the public schools and received his high school training at Farmington, Mich., and at the Cass High School of Detroit. He has been engaged in the banking business the greater part of the time since leaving school, and has served as trustee of Grosse Pointe Village. Mr. Hayes is married. In politics he is a Republican.

JOHN HAYNES

Representative from Midland, Isabella, Iosco and Alpena counties, 1871-2. His postoffice address was Midland City. (Further data not obtainable).

HARVEY HAYNES

Representative from Branch County, 1865-6 and 1871-2. Was born at New Paltz, Ulster County, N. Y., Jan. 24, 1817. He came to Michigan in 1836, and settled in Coldwater. In early life he studied law and was engaged in teaching. His taste, however, was farming, which he pursued as an occupation. He was Supervisor and Assessor for many years, and was efficient in securing the location of the State Public School at Coldwater. He died at Coldwater, Mar. 2, 1903.

ANDREW L. HAYS

Representative from Calhoun County, 1845. Was born in Sanborton, N. H., Aug. 27, 1803. He came to Michigan in 1829, and settled at Marshall in 1831, where he resided until his death, Dec. 9, 1864. He was the first physician in Calhoun County. He was made a Brigadier General by Gov. Mason and took part in the Black Hawk and Toledo Wars. In politics he was a Democrat. He married Clarissa S. Hunt in 1830, and his son, Luther, was the first white boy born in Calhoun County.

JOHN W. HAYWARD

Representative from the First District of Kent County, 1891-2. Was born in Niagara County, N. Y., in 1841. He entered a general store as a clerk at eighteen, enlisted in the McClellan Dragoons at twenty, was transferred to the 12th Ill. Cavalry, and mustered out at expiration of term of service, three years. Married. He acted as traveling salesman, lumberman, druggist and electrician, and superintendent of the Grand Rapids Electric Light and Power Co. He served as Alderman and was elected to the House of 1891-2.

JAMES E. HAYWOOD

Representative from Huron County, 1871-2 and 1873-4. Was born in Haverhill, N. H., May 23, 1834. He received a common school education and attended Haverhill Academy one term. He settled in Rubicon, Huron County, Mich., in 1857. He filled various town offices. By occupation he was a merchant, in politics a Republican. He died at Port Huron, Mar. 16, 1916.

CHESTER HAZARD

Representative from Livingston County, 1848. Was born in Arlington, Vt., June 23, 1796; came to Michigan in 1836 and located 320 acres of land in Genoa. In 1842 he was elected Treasurer of Livingston County and served two terms. He was for many years Supervisor, and was Justice for forty years. By occupation he was a farmer; in politics a Democrat.

CHARLES W. HAZE

Representative from Livingston County, 1853-4. He was born at Wilson, N. Y., Aug. 14, 1820. He removed with his parents to Farmington, Mich., in 1837. He received a common school and classical education, studied medicine and graduated from the medical department of the Western Reserve College, and located at

Pinckney, Mich., in 1845. He held several offices in village and town, and during the war was examining surgeon for Livingston County. In politics he was a Democrat and was a member of the State Committee. Besides his practice he was a farmer on a large scale.

WILLIAM H. HAZE

Representative from Oakland County, 1863-4. Was born at Port Hope, Canada, of American parentage, Apr. 13, 1816. His parents soon removed to Wilson, N. Y., and he was educated at Genesee College, Lima, N. Y. In 1838 he settled at Farmington, Mich., and became a farmer and teacher. In 1840 he married Lydia Emrich, of Wooster, O. He became a Methodist minister in 1843, but failure of voice compelled him to give up preaching, and he graduated as a physician from a medical college in Cleveland, O., in 1852, and practiced in Oakland County. He removed to Lansing in 1864, and was Alderman, Mayor and City Assessor; lay delegate to the general Methodist conference at Philadelphia; and one of the board of control of Albion College. He was a Republican until 1872, then an Independent, later a Prohibitionist. He died at Lansing, Jan. 21, 1910.

EZRA HAZEN

Senator from the Twenty-sixth District, 1861-2; Representative from St. Clair County, 1865-6 and 1871-2; and Delegate from St. Clair County to the Constitutional Convention of 1867. Was born at Byron, N. Y., June 1, 1817. He settled near Romeo, Mich., in 1834, removed to Almont in 1839, and to Memphis in 1854. He was a Justice for forty years, Supervisor of Riley twelve years, Deputy Collector of Customs from 1872 to 1885. He was a Republican after 1854. Deceased.

LUKE HAZEN

Representative from Hillsdale County, 1848. Was born in Vienna, N. Y., Dec. 2, 1812. He attended district and high schools and was a teacher. He came to Michigan in 1835, and settled on a farm in the town of Allen in 1839. He was Supervisor three terms, held other offices, was a farmer and merchant. He moved to Litchfield in 1853. He was a Whig until 1854, then a Republican. He was Town Clerk of Litchfield three years, and Treasurer eleven years; County Clerk, 1875-9. Latterly he lived in DeWitt, Mich.

GEORGE H. HAZELTON

Representative from Genesee County, 1845 and 1846. Was born in Morrisville, N. Y., Jan. 24, 1809. He came to Ann Arbor in 1836 and opened a land office. He removed to Flint in 1839, and purchased a large portion of the land on which that city is built. He was a merchant and lumberman, running two mills. He was one of seven Whigs in the Legislature, and was the Whig candidate for Congress in 1845. In 1854 he was appointed visitor to West Point. He was a Whig candidate for Lieutenant-Governor. He removed to Chicago in 1854 and engaged in banking until 1860. Then he was a manufacturer in Philadelphia until 1877, afterwards in same business in Chicago and New York, then five years at Baltimore running machinery by water motors. He died at Atlantic City, N. J., Dec. 24, 1893.

HENRY T. HEALD

Representative from the First District, Kent County, 1905-6; and a member of the Constitutional Convention of 1907-8. Was born at Montague, Mich., Mar. 25, 1876, of English parents. His father, Joseph Heald, was one of the pioneer lumbermen of Michigan. He received his education in the public schools of Grand Rapids, and graduated from the University of Michigan, receiving the degree of Bachelor of Philosophy in 1898. He afterward studied law in the office of Butterfield & Keeney, and was admitted to the bar in 1900. He became a member of the law firm of Stuart & Heald Jan. 1, 1902. In politics an active Republican.

PERLEY C. HEALD

Senator, 1869-1900, from the Twenty-fourth District, comprising the counties of Bay, Midland and Arenac. Was born at Lovell, Oxford County, Me., May 5, 1849, and was educated in the schools of his native place, and at Fryeburg, and removed to Midland County, Mich., in September, 1865. Mr. Heald was elected the first Mayor of Midland in 1887 and re-elected in 1888, for many years pursued the avocation of a surveyor and also a dealer in real estate. He also served three years under Land Commissioner French, as inspector of lands held by the State. A prominent Mason and belonged to several secret societies. In politics a Republican.

WILLIAM P. HEALEY

Representative from Marquette, 1867-8. Was born in Ireland Apr. 14, 1842, and came with his parents to America in 1846, who settled in Michigan. He received a fair education, and became a resident of Marquette County in 1863. He was Supervisor of Negaunee six years, chairman of the County Board, and President of the Village of Negaunee in 1865. He was admitted to the bar in 1870, and then in practice at Marquette. He was a Democrat until 1884, then a Republican. He died at Chicago, April, 1918.

JOHN S. HEATH

Representative from St. Clair County, 1835-7. Was born in Hillsboro, N. H., in 1807, and was a schoolmate of President Pierce. He studied medicine at Glenns Falls, N. Y., and took up his residence at Port Huron, Mich., in 1832, which was then Desmond. He filled many public positions, and was Collector of Customs and Sheriff of the county. He owned mills and manufactured lumber at a place then called Point Au Barques. Deceased.

CHARLES HEBARD

Member of the Board of Regents of the University of Michigan, 1888-96. Was born at Lebanon, Conn., Jan. 9, 1831, son of Learned and Persis Elizabeth (Strong) Hebard. His ancestors on both sides were English. He received his early education at a boarding school in Westfield, Mass. He taught in the country schools for one year, and in 1850 took the overland trip to the then remote State of Iowa. The following year found him at Scranton, Pa., in the employ of the Lackawanna Iron and Coal Company. In 1853 he removed to Tobyhanna Mills, and erected a sawmill for the manufacture of lumber, becoming in time partner in the firm of Dodge, Meigs and Dodge. He married Mary Cornelia Case, Jan. 5, 1857. In 1867 he began a lumber business at Williamsport, Pa., under the firm name of Dodge and Hebard. Three years later he removed to Detroit, Mich., and entered into business with Mr. R. K. Hawley, the firm, known as the Hebard and Hawley Lumber Company, having sawmills at Cleveland, O., which were supplied with logs towed from Lake Huron ports. It was in the handling of logs for these mills that Mr. Hebard first put into use his invention of the bag boom. In 1872 he sold his interest in this firm, and returned to Williamsport, where he was in business until 1877. Having become interested in the white pine timber of the Upper Peninsula of Michigan, he purchased a large tract of land on Keweenaw Point and erected a sawmill at Pequaming. This business was begun under the firm name of Hebard and Thurber; but in 1882 the latter sold out his interest to Mr. Hebard, and the firm from that time on was known as Charles Hebard and Son. Some years later, in connection with his sons, he purchased the immense Okefenokee Swamp in southeastern Georgia, containing approximately 350,000 acres of cypress, yellow pine, and gum timber. He was elected Regent of the University of Michigan in 1887, serving the full term of eight years. During his later years he resided the greater part of the time in Philadelphia. He was a member of the Union League Club of that city and of the Military Order of the Loyal Legion; was also a trustee of Jefferson Medical College. He died at Philadelphia June 11, 1902.

CHARLES A. HEBARD

Representative from Lapeer County, 1844 and 1847. Was born in Leyden, Mass., July 5, 1805. By occupation he was a teacher and farmer, politically a Democrat. He moved to Orleans County, N. Y., in 1834, and from there to Attica, Lapeer County, in 1839. He was several years Supervisor of Attica. He moved to Kasota, Minn., in 1855, and died there May 16, 1855.

GEORGE R. HECK

Representative from the First District of Ingham County, 1899-1900. Was born at St. Johns, Mich., Mar. 18, 1864. His early life was spent on a farm, and his education was obtained at the union schools of Maple Rapids and St. Johns, supplemented by a literary course at the Northern Indiana Normal School at Valparaiso, Ind. He also graduated from the law department of the same institution in the spring of 1891, and on May 5 of that year was admitted to the practice of law in the Circuit Court of the United States at Indianapolis, Ind. Returning to his home at Maple Rapids, he spent the next two years superintending his farm. In the spring of 1893 he removed to the city of Lansing and engaged in the practice of law. He was a candidate on the Republican ticket for Prosecuting Attorney of Ingham County in 1896, but defeated. A Republican in politics. A zealous worker in the order of Patrons of Husbandry, and also a Royal Arch Mason and an Odd Fellow.

BENJAMIN FRANKLIN HECKERT

Delegate to the Constitutional Convention of 1907-8; and Representative from Van Buren County, 1909-10 and 1911. Was born in Wayne County, O., in 1840, of American parentage. His education was acquired in the common schools, Canaan Academy, and Vermillion Institute—a Presbyterian College, all in Ohio. He enlisted Apr. 20, 1861, in the 16th O. Vol. Infantry, under the first call for troops;

re-enlisted August, 1861, for three years, or during the war, in the same regiment.; was promoted from private to First Lieutenant, successively. He was captured at the Battle of Chickasaw Bayou and was held a prisoner of war five months, being exchanged from Libby prison. At the close of the war, he returned to college and was graduated from the law department of the University of Michigan, in 1869. In the same year he located in South Haven, Van Buren County, Mich., and began the practice of law, later was elected Circuit Court Commissioner and Prosecuting Attorney, serving in these capacities eight and one-half years. He also served eight years as Probate Judge. His wife died Nov. 14, 1908. In politics he was a Republican. He was a 32nd degree Mason and belonged to the DeWitt Clinton Consistory and Saladin Temple of Shriners, Grand Rapids. Mr. Heckert died at his temporary home in Lansing Apr: 12, 1911.

ALBERT OSCAR HEINE

Senator, 1905-6, from the Twenty-fourth District, comprising the counties of Bay and Midland. Was born in Hamburg, Germany, Dec. 5, 1868, and came to Mt. Clemens, Mich., in 1870. A few years later he moved with his parents to Saginaw, and received his education in the public schools of that city. In 1884 he moved to Bay City, entering the employ of S. V. Wilkin, clothier, and remained with him several years. Mr. Heine then entered the clothing business with C. E. Janett under the firm name of Heine & Janett. This partnership continued until early in the year 1904, when Mr. Janett retired on account of ill health. Mr. Heine reorganizing the business under the name of A. O. Heine Co., Ltd. In politics a Republican.

DAVID E. HEINEMAN

Representative from the First District of Wayne County, 1899-1900. Was born in the city of Detroit, Oct. 17, 1865. A son of the late Emil S. Heineman, a prominent wholesale merchant and a citizen of Detroit since the early fifties. David E. Heineman graduated from the public schools of Detroit, and was president of the Detroit High School class of 1883. He graduated from the literary department of Michigan University in the class of 1887, with the degree of Bachelor of Philosophy, and subsequently remained a year in the law school of the University. He was a student in the law offices of E. C. Walker, Judge C. I. Walker and C. A. Kent, of Detroit; was admitted to the bar May 4, 1889, and formed a partnership with ex-Senator Joseph M. Weiss, which was maintained from 1891 to 1893, at which date he was appointed chief Assistant City Attorney of Detroit, which position he held for three years, with entire control of the court work of the office. He compiled and revised the present ordinances of the city of Detroit, a volume of over 700 pages. Upon retiring from the City Attorneyship, he opened a law office at 28 Moffat Building, and entered the active practice of law. In politics a Republican. He traveled extensively in this country and in Europe and Africa; widely acquainted among all classes of his townsmen, and a member of many social, political and fraternal societies.

AUGUST HEINEMANN

Representative from Huron County, 1889-90. Was born at Volkmarsen, Province of Messe-Germania, on the 5th day of November, 1844. His parents died and he emigrated to this country, arriving June 25, 1862. He settled in Michigan and engaged in mill work for a number of years until through diligence he established a home of his own in Huron County, where he bought a farm. He was married on Feb. 15, 1870. He was a citizen of Michigan after 1872, and held township offices a number of years and was elected to the House of 1889-90 on the Democratic ticket.

CARL HEISTERMAN

Senator from the Eighteenth District, 1885-6. Was born in Germany Nov. 5, 1820. He had been a resident of Michigan thirty-seven years. He was formerly a gardener by occupation, but later a farmer. He held the office of Register of Deeds six years, and Supervisor fifteen years. Politically he was a Democrat.

JAMES W. HELME, JR.

Senator, 1899-1900 and 1901-2, from the Fifth District, comprising the counties of Lenawee and Monroe. Was born in the city of Adrian, Mar. 3, 1860. He graduated from Adrian High School at the age of fifteen years, and at eighteen was for a time night editor of the *Daily Press*. For three years he taught school winters and read law summers, and on Mar. 2, 1881, was admitted to the bar and began the practice of law in Adrian city. In 1882 he was elected Circuit Court Commissioner for Lenawee County, being the first Democrat to hold that office for thirty years. He was re-elected to that office in 1890. In 1884 he was appointed City Attorney of the city of Adrian, and served for six years by successive reappointments. In 1892 he was appointed Assistant Prosecuting Attorney for Lenawee County, and served two years. He was candidate for Prosecutor on the Democratic ticket in 1896, but was defeated. He resided on his farm within the city of Adrian; an authority on all dairy topics and a frequent speaker at farmers' institutes and dairy conventions; also a contributor to many farm journals; a member of the Michigan Jersey Cattle Club, the Michigan State Dairyman's Association, Adrian Grange, and other agricultural societies. In politics, although generally acting with the Democrats, he was independent of all parties. Unmarried. He was elected to the Senate on the Democratic ticket.

LAWTON T. HEMANS

Representative from the Second District of Ingham County, 1901-2 and 1903-4; and Delegate in the Constitutional Convention of 1907-8, from the Fourteenth District, Ingham County. Was born at Collamer, N. Y., in 1864, where his father followed the trade of a blacksmith. He was of English and Dutch descent. In 1865 his parents moved to Michigan, settling in Eaton County. The family later removed to Ingham County. Mr. Hemans graduated from Eaton Rapids High School in the class of 1884, and later after spending some time in the law department of the University of Michigan, took up the practice of his profession at Mason. He married Miss Minnie P. Hill, and they had one son. For many years he was in almost continuous public service, either as Mayor of his city or member of the Common Council. He served as a member of the Legislature of 1901-2 and 1903-4 and in other capacities, and was the author of several works of a historical and public nature. He died Nov. 17, 1916.

GEORGE F. HEMINGWAY

Representative from Midland County, 1861-2. Was born in Monroe County, N. Y., June 21, 1817. He came to Michigan in 1837 and resided in the State ever since. He resided at Midland City in 1887. He held the offices of Town Clerk, School Inspector, Justice of the Peace, Supervisor, and Prosecuting Attorney three times. By profession he was a lawyer, in politics a Prohibitionist.

WILLIAM HEMINGWAY

Representative from Lapeer County, 1863-4. Was born in Chili, N. Y., Nov. 10, 1815; was a lawyer by profession, and a Republican in politics; settled in Lapeer County in 1835, and with the exception of a few months, was a resident of that county until his death, Dec. 28, 1885. For twenty years he was a Circuit Court Commissioner, and was president of the Lapeer Bar Association. In politics he was a Republican.

DONALD HENDERSON

Representative from the First District of Saginaw County (Saginaw city), 1895-6. Was born in Aberdeen, Scotland, in 1856, and acquired his early education in the public schools of that place. In 1870 he emigrated with his parents to Canada, where he learned the machinists' trade, and in 1876 he came to Saginaw, where he was in the employment of Wickes Brothers. He was a member of the board of directors of the People's Building and Loan Association of Saginaw. In politics a Republican. He was Alderman of his ward of the city, and was elected to the House in 1895-6 on the general legislative ticket of the city.

EBEN F. HENDERSON

Representative from Calhoun County, 1861-2; and a Delegate from Calhoun County to the Constitutional Convention of 1867. Was born in Royalton, N. Y., Jan. 5, 1828, and came with his father to Michigan in 1839. He purchased a farm near Battle Creek in 1852. He served as County Treasurer and Probate Judge, each for four years; and filled other offices. He was elected for a second four years as Probate Judge but died Sept. 29, 1873, before the first year of his term had expired. He was a Republican, an elder in the Presbyterian Church, and a man very popular with the people.

HENRY PERRY HENDERSON

Representative from Ingham County, 1879-80. Was born in Tully, N. Y., Sept. 23, 1842, and removed to Michigan in 1845, and settled in Oakland County. In the fall of 1845 he removed to LeRoy, Ingham County, and in 1854 to Mason, same county. He received an academical education. He held the office of Deputy County Clerk, County Clerk, a member of the Common Council, Prosecuting Attorney, a member of the School Board of Mason, and a director in the First National Bank, and other minor offices. He was admitted to the bar in 1867. In politics he was a Democrat. In 1887 he was a United States Territorial Judge in Utah. He died at Salt Lake City June 3, 1909; buried at Mason, Mich.

CHARLES R. HENRY

Senator from the Twenty-ninth District, 1885-6. Was born in Macon, Mich., Dec. 29, 1856. He received a public school education and taught for two years. He graduated at the law department of the University in 1875, and began practice in Au Sable. He held various village and county offices, and was Prosecuting Attorney. In politics a Republican.

JAMES HENRY

Representative from the Second District of Calhoun County, 1907-8 to 1915-16; and Senator, 1919-20, 1921-2 and 1923—, from the Ninth District, comprising the counties of Branch and Calhoun. Was born at Pittsburgh, Pa., Sept. 12, 1859, and received his education in the public schools of that city. He has resided in Battle Creek thirty-five years. In 1902 he platted and promoted the village of Urbandale, which is now a beautiful suburb of Battle Creek. Mr. Henry has two sons. In politics he is a Republican. He held the office of Police Judge four years; was a member of the Board of Supervisors twelve years, part of the time as chairman of the Board; and served three terms as City Assessor.

JOHN HENRY

Representative from the First District of Saginaw County, 1901-2. Was born in Philadelphia, Pa., Oct. 5, 1856, and received his early education in the public schools of that city. He located in Saginaw when eleven years of age and at the age of fourteen began work as fireman on a steamboat. He afterward became a marine engineer, which business he followed four years, when he became engineer of the Power Block. Married. In politics a strong Republican. He was Alderman of his ward in 1898-1900, and was elected to the Legislature of 1901-2 on the general legislative ticket of Saginaw County.

JOHN F. HENRY

Representative from the Second District of Allegan County, 1893-4 and 1895-6. Was born in Brantford, Canada, Apr. 12, 1835. He was a student at Princeton College, N. J., 1853-55. After leaving college he engaged as bookkeeper, and in that capacity in 1871 he entered the service of O. R. Johnson & Company, lumber manufacturers, Saugatuck, Mich., of which Senator Stockbridge was a partner. In 1885, with Wallace B. Griffin, he formed the lumber firm of Griffin & Henry. In politics a Republican. He served as President of the village of Saugatuck, and a member of the School Board.

WALTER A. HENZE

Representative from Dickinson County, 1921-2 and 1923—. Was born at Detroit, Mich., Oct. 18, 1886, of American and German descent. He received his education in the public schools in Detroit and Iron Mountain, Mich., and at a private school in Biltmore, N. C. After completing school he engaged as forest engineer for six years, and is at present business manager of the Upper Michigan Products Co. Mr. Henze is married. He has served as Supervisor. In politics he is a Republican.

WILLIAM E. HENZE

Representative from the First District of Wayne County, 1891-2. Was born in Nordheim, Germany, in 1860. He was educated at the Gymnasium in Germany; arrived in the United States in June, 1875, and in Detroit in the same month; graduated from the Detroit High School in 1878 and from the Ann Arbor law department in 1881. Married. He was Probate Clerk of Wayne County from 1883 to 1886, and in the practice of law since 1887. In politics a Democrat. He was elected to the House of 1891-2 on the general ticket in November, 1890.

HENRY H. HERKIMER

Representative from Monroe County, 1903-4 and 1905-6. Was born Sept. 4, 1842, in the township of Exeter, being a descendant of General Herkimer. He received his education in the public schools. In 1862 he enlisted in Co. K, 5th Mich. Cavalry, and remained in the service until the close of the war. After the war he married and settled on a farm in the township of London.

PETER HERRIG

Representative from the First District of Saginaw County (Saginaw city), 1895-6, 1897-8 and 1899-1900. Was born in Bingen-on-the-Rhine, Germany, Oct. 22, 1847. When two years of age he came with his father to America, locating at Saginaw, Mich., where he remained. His early education was acquired in the Saginaw schools; at the age of sixteen years he was employed in a lumbering mill, in which occupation he continued, becoming in 1885 general manager of the firm of Green, Ring & Co. During this time he was engaged in other industries and served in other capacities, being president of the building and loan association, member of the Saginaw Ice and Coal Company, of the Hemmeter Cigar Company, the City Milling Company and other enterprises. In politics he was a Republican. He was elected to the House of Representatives of 1895-6 on the general legislative ticket of the city of Saginaw, and re-elected to that of 1897-8 and of 1899-1900. He died October, 1915, at Saginaw.

CALEB HERRINGTON

Delegate from Wayne County to the Constitutional Convention of 1835; and a Representative from Wayne County, 1837. Was a native of the State of New York, born Jan. 24, 1788. He came to Michigan in 1833, and settled in the township of Plymouth, two miles west of the village of Northville, where he lived until his death, Mar. 30, 1849. The confidence of his townsmen was manifested by his frequent election to local offices of trust. He was a Captain of a volunteer company in the War of 1812, and was engaged in the Battle of Queenstown and other battles of the war. He was a farmer, and in politics a Democrat.

CASS E. HERRINGTON

Representative from Oakland County, 1887-8. Was born in that county, at Four Towns, Dec. 23, 1856, and there resided until he was seventeen years of age, when he attended the Michigan Agricultural College three years, teaching winters. He began the study of law in 1878, and was admitted to the bar in Oakland County the same year. He graduated at the Michigan University in 1879 and has practiced law at Pontiac since that time. He held the office of City Clerk of Pontiac two terms, and Circuit Court Commissioner from Jan. 1, 1883, to Nov. 1, 1886, at which time he resigned the office. He was elected Representative on the Democratic ticket.

CHRISTIAN HERTZLER

Representative from Monroe County, 1873-4 and 1875-6; and Senator from the Fifth District, 1885-6. Was born in Marietta, Lancaster County, Pa., May 25, 1830. He came to Michigan with his parents in 1835, and settled in Vienna, and resided in the same place, with the exception of twelve years, four years in Toledo, O., and eight years in Philadelphia, Pa. He received a common school education, and was a farmer by occupation. He held the office of Supervisor twenty-one years in succession, and was chairman of the Board seven years. He was elected Representative in the Legislature as a Democrat.

JOHN M. HERZ

Representative from the First District of Wayne County, 1891-2. Was born in Detroit, Nov. 10, 1859, and was educated in the public schools. When quite young he began learning the trade of cabinet maker with Messrs. Mills & Barker, and later went into the employ of John Phillips & Co. He then branched out in the grocery line for himself on Elmwood Ave., built up a lucrative business. Politically, a strong Democrat. He was elected to the House of 1891-2 as such.

ALEXANDER HEWITT

Representative from Hillsdale County, 1873-4 and 1875-6; and Senator from the Ninth District, 1879-80. Was born in Edinburg, N. Y., Mar. 25, 1818. He removed to Alleghany County in 1822, thence to Ontario County. He received a common school education. He came to Michigan in 1844, and settled in the township of Allen, on the farm. He was a farmer by occupation; and a Republican in politics. He was for two years president of the Hillsdale County Agricultural Society.

CYRUS HEWITT

Commissioner of the State Land Office, 1865-7. Was born in Greenfield, Saratago County, N. Y., Feb. 19, 1808. He came to Marshall, Mich., in 1836, and engaged in his profession as surveyor and civil engineer, platting several towns along the Michigan Central railroad and surveying for the United States a large portion of the lands in Calhoun, Hillsdale, Jackson and other counties. He removed to Lansing in 1858 and became a clerk in the State Land Office and was Deputy from 1861 to 1865. In 1864 he was elected State Land Commissioner. He was also mayor of Lansing. He engaged in banking business, which he conducted successfully until 1877, when he retired from business. In politics he was a Republican. He died Nov. 23, 1882.

HENRY HEWITT

Senator from the Fourth District, 1842. Was born in Byron, N. Y., Oct. 15, 1812. He was educated in common schools and at Middlebury Academy. N. Y. He came to Marshall, Mich., in 1835, and was a merchant, and politically a Democrat. He was Justice in 1837, and Associate County Judge in 1840. He died Mar. 7, 1842.

LAUREN K. HEWITT

Senator from the Twenty-second District, 1863-4. Was born in Palmyra, N. Y., June 14, 1816. By occupation he was a lawyer, in politics a Democrat. He was educated at Mt. Morris Academy, N. Y. He came to Washtenaw County in 1836. He studied law, settled at Howell in 1840 and commenced practice with his brother, Lewis H. Hewitt. He continued in practice there until 1857, when he removed to Lansing and was engaged in the banking business with J. C. Bailey for several years, afterwards with Daniel L. Case, and then with Cyrus Hewitt. He was also interested in insurance, and for many years was U. S. Circuit Court Commissioner. He died Jan. 11, 1877.

WALTER B. HEWITT

Representative from Washtenaw County, 1842. Was born at Stillwater, N. Y., Feb. 4, 1800. At the age of twenty-five he located near Walled Lake, Oakland County, in 1825, where he remained a year, and then engaged in the boot and shoe trade at Detroit for four years. In 1831 he moved to Ypsilanti, where he was engaged in business for many years when he retired to private life. In 1850 he bought a farm near Ypsilanti. In politics he was a Democrat. He died Sept. 4, 1886.

WILLIAM F. HEWITT

Senator from the Eighth District, 1874. Was born at Byron, N. Y., Feb. 4, 1835. He had common school education. He was a member of Merril Horse in Civil War, held several town offices, and was elected Senator in place of Philip H. Emerson, who had resigned, and he served in the extra session of 1874. After 1879 he left farming and became a grain dealer. He died at Marshall, Oct. 3, 1889.

RAY L. HEWLETT

Representative from the First District of Jackson County, 1923—. Was born in Jackson, May 14, 1879, of American parents. His education was acquired in rural and city schools. In 1907 he was married to Alma R. Howard and they have three daughters. In 1913 he established a real estate and insurance business, in which he is at present engaged. Mr. Hewlett is a Democrat and held the positions of deputy city treasurer and city treasurer for eight years.

HARRIS H. HICKMAN

Attorney General of the Territory of Michigan, 1809—. Was appointed Sept. 22, 1809. Little is known of him. He was appointed a Captain in the War of 1812, and was included in the surrender of Detroit, and is supposed to have been killed before the close of the war.

BYRON P. HICKS

Senator, 1919-20 and 1921-2, from the Fourteenth District, comprising the counties of Ingham and Shiawassee. Was born on a farm in the township of Tyrone. Livingston County, Mich., Nov. 27, 1873, of American parents who trace their lineage to the early settlers of New York and New England, one of his grandmothers being a Bradford and a descendant of Governor Bradford of the Mayflower. Another grandmother of Mr. Hicks was a Jayne, whose family was prominent in the early history of New York. He was reared on a farm in Livingston County, educated in the public schools and was engaged in school teaching for about five years, after which he entered the University of Michigan and graduated from the law department of that institution in 1898. He entered the practice of law at Durand in September, 1898, and continued in that profession until 1913, when he gave up the practice of law temporarily and entered the banking business as an officer of the Shiawassee County Bank of Durand. In 1919 he resigned this position and formed a partnership with Roy D. Matthews of Owosso, for the practice of law in that city, and has since that time been a member of the firm of Matthews-Hicks, at Owosso. He served as Prosecuting Attorney of Shiawassee County four years, during which time he fought successfully to the Supreme Court of the United States, the celebrated court house loan cases of Shiawassee County. He is a past master of the F. & A. M., past high priest R. A. M., past commander of Corunna Commandery No. 21. past patron of the O. E. S., and a member of Elf Khurafeh Temple, A. A. O. N. M. S. of Saginaw, Mich. In politics he is a Republican.

EUGENE HICKS

Representative from Livingston County, 1893-4 and 1895-6. Was born in Cayuga County, N. Y., in 1842; he attended the common schools, the high schools of Dexter and Ann Arbor, Mich., and the business college of Poughkeepsie, N. Y. From 1863 to 1808 he was a private in a company of scouts with James P. Bridger. commander of Fort Bridger, Utah Territory, of the Mountain Department Indian Service. He afterwards returned to Michigan and engaged in farming, in which occupation he continued until he removed to Brighton, and engaged in lumbering. In politics he was a Republican. He died Sept. 20, 1921.

JOHN FULLERTON HICKS

Representative from the county of Menominee, 1893-4. Was born in Kent County, Ont., May 27, 1838. He received his education at the Michigan University, graduating from the medical department in 1865. He practiced his profession at his home in Canada until 1878, when he came to Menominee, Mich., where he resumed his practice. He served several years as County Physician, a member and secretary of the Board of Pension Examiners, a member of the American Medical Association and of the American International Public Health Association. In politics a Republican. He held the office of Alderman of the city of Menominee.

MELANCTHON W. HICKS

Representative from Oakland County, 1851. Was born at Champlain, N. Y., July 14, 1805. By occupation he was a merchant, in politics a Democrat. He married Sarah Fox, of Champlain, N. Y., in 1831 and settled at Southfield, Oakland County, in 1844; was Supervisor in 1847-50; and Town Clerk in 1846. He moved to Wenona (now West Bay City) in 1867, where he engaged in the flour and feed business. He died Nov. 20, 1867.

ORREN V. HICKS

Representative from Cass County, 1913-14. Was born in Milton Township, Cass County, Sept. 27, 1869, of English-German descent. Reared upon the homestead farm, he was educated in the district schools and Edwardsburg High School. He was married to Miss Bertha Florence Thompson, a native of Ontwa Township, Jan. 13, 1892. In 1896 he was elected clerk of Milton Township on the Democratic ticket and served three years, following this in 1901 by seven consecutive years as Supervisor. In 1908 he was elected a Superintendent of the Poor for Cass County and filled that position until he resigned to accept a place in the Legislature. In politics a Democrat.

JAMES W. HICOCK

Senator from the Twenty-second District, 1853-4. Was born in Lansingburg, N. Y., Dec. 2, 1798, and received an academical education. He studied law, then followed the life of a boatman for many years. He settled with his family at Walton, Eaton County, Mich., in 1836, and ploughed the first furrow in that township. He farmed it until 1865, then removed to Charlotte. He was Postmaster, Supervisor and held other local offices. He was Senator in 1853, as a Democrat.

THOMAS T. HIGGINS

Representative from Cass County, 1903-4 and 1905-6. Was born in Randolf County, Ind., Feb. 10, 1844, and came to Michigan with his parents in 1858 and settled on a farm in Cass County. He was educated in the common schools, married and engaged in farming. He was elected to the Legislature of 1903-4 and was re-elected to the Legislature of 1905-6. He died in Jefferson Township, Cass County, May, 1910.

HIRAM M. HIGH

Senator, 1901-2, from the Nineteenth Senatorial District, composed of the counties of Clinton and Gratiot. Was born at Pleasant Valley, Wis., Apr. 11, 1860, and obtained his education in the Kansas Normal School, having followed the occupations of farmer and school teacher up to 1886, after which time he engaged in the practice of law. He was a self-made man.

FRANCIS JOHN HIGGINSON

Member of the Board of Regents of the University of Michigan, 1840-1. Was born in Massachusetts about the year 1804. He was graduated Bachelor of Arts from Harvard College in 1825, and Doctor of Medicine from the Harvard Medical School in 1828. In 1835 he removed to Grand Rapids, Mich., at that time a mere frontier settlement with a sparse population largely made up of Indians. After practicing in his profession in this wilderness for a few years he finally wearied of frontier life and returned to Massachusetts. Feb. 20, 1840, he was appointed Regent of the University for the full term, but resigned the office early in the following year. He died at Boston in 1872.

OLIVER HIGH

Representative from Washtenaw County, 1857-8. Was born in the State of New York in 1811. He was an early pioneer in Washtenaw County and a highly respected citizen. By occupation he was a farmer, politically a Democrat. He died in Sharon, Oct. 17, 1870.

HIRAM HIGLEY

Representative from Oakland County, 1835 and 1836. Was born in East Windsor, Conn., Mar. 5, 1804. By occupation he was a tanner, in politics a Democrat. He settled in Rochester, Mich., in 1827, removed to Leipsic, O., in 1853, and died there Jan. 8, 1860. He held several local offices in the town of Avon.

ARTHUR HILL

Member of the Board of Regents of the University of Michigan, 1901-9. Was born at St. Clair, Mich., on Mar. 15, 1847, son of James H. and Lucretia (Brown) Hill. His parents were both born in Michigan. He entered the University of Michigan in 1862 from Saginaw, and was graduated Civil Engineer in 1865. A few months following graduation were spent in railroad engineering in Minnesota, and later in the year he entered the law department of the University. He returned to Saginaw to enter upon a business career in lumbering, manufacturing, and shipping, which rapidly grew to large proportions. In addition to his many business cares he found time to maintain his interest in public questions, and kept himself well informed on historical and economical subjects. He was chosen three times Mayor of Saginaw, and served as president of the Board of Education of that city for five years. In 1899 he became a member of the State Board of Forestry Commissioners, having been one of the first two appointees. On the death of Regent Cocker, May 19, 1901, he was appointed to the vacancy and served out the term ending Jan. 1, 1906. At the April election of 1905 was elected to succeed himself for the full term of eight years. He was the founder of four Saginaw High School Fellowships, with an annual income of two hundred and fifty dollars each, designed to aid needy graduates of that school in securing a university education. He also bought and presented to the University the Saginaw Forest Farm, a tract of eighty acres near Ann Arbor, for the purpose of facilitating instruction in forestry at the University. He died in 1909.

BENJAMIN L. HILL

Representative from Saginaw County, 1861-2. Was born in Elkland, Pa., Dec. 18, 1813. He studied law at Norwalk, O., in 1839-40, and studied medicine in 1842-3. He was appointed demonstrator and assistant professor of anatomy in the Eclectic Medical of Cleveland, O., and after that became a professor in the college. He became a resident of Michigan in 1860. In 1863 he was appointed Consul to Nicaraugua, but resigned in 1865. He wrote two large volumes on surgery, and several other medical works. He died at Marysville, Calif., May 13, 1871.

E. PARKER HILL

Representative from Van Buren County, 1877-8 and 1879-80. Was born in Yates County, N. Y., May 11, 1819. In 1825 he removed to Waterville, N. Y., where he received a common school education. In 1856 he removed to Davenport, Ia., and from thence, in 1858, to Decatur, Mich., where he resided. He held the office of Supervisor for five years in succession. He was Register of Deeds for Van Buren

County, one term. At the organization of the First National Bank of Decatur, he was elected cashier. He was engaged in the hardware business in 1887. In politics he was a Republican.

FITCH HILL

Representative from Washtenaw County, 1845. His postoffice address was Ann Arbor. (Further data not obtainable).

FREDERICK H. HILL

Representative from Lapeer County, 1882. Was born in Lyndonville, N. Y., Nov. 29, 1852. He removed to Kalamazoo, Mich., in 1858, where he attended school until 1864, then moved upon a farm in Calhoun County, where he remained until 1870, when he settled at Attica, Lapeer County, and went into business as a dealer in lumber and grain. He was elected Representative to succeed Frank Kendrick, deceased. He removed to Council Bluffs, Ia., where he resided in 1887 and was a wholesale dealer in hardware. He was Treasurer of Attica three terms, and a member of the School Board for five years. Politically a Republican.

JAMES W. HILL

Representative from Washtenaw County, 1835 and 1836. Was a native of New York, born about 1794. He located a farm in Washtenaw County in 1831. As a Democrat he was a Representative. He built the first house and barn in what is now the town of Freedom, kept the first school, entertained the first minister, and the first sermon was preached in his house. He lived many years at Prescott, Wis., and died in 1864, at Clinton, Mich.

LOYAL W. HILL

Representative from Clinton County, 1887-8. Was born in Minerva, N. Y., July 9, 1843. He came to Eagle, Mich., in 1854, where he resided ever since. He had no school advantages until he was twenty-three years of age, when he entered the Portland Union School. He afterwards taught school eight winters. He was a student in the law department of the Michigan University in 1878-9 and was admitted to the bar in 1879, and to practice in the United States courts in 1885. He was elected Township Clerk in 1869, School Inspector in 1870, and Justice of the Peace in 1873. He was also Supervisor in Eagle.

NICHOLAS R. HILL

Representative from Kent County, 1871-2. Was born in Clarkson, Monroe County, N. Y. He lived in Ohio several years, but removed to Nelson, Kent County, in 1856 and platted and named the village of Cedar Springs, in 1855 and was first Postmaster. He held the office of Supervisor several terms, and was for many years a Justice of the Peace. He died Sept. 16, 1887, at Cedar Springs.

SAMUEL W. HILL

Representative from Keweenaw County, 1867-8 and 1871-2. Was born at Starksboro, Vt., Nov. 6, 1815. He was well educated and taught school several winters.

He became a surveyor, and as a topographical engineer in the army was engaged in the survey of lake harbors and internal improvements until 1845, then was associated with Dr. Houghton in the geological and lineal survey of the Upper Peninsula, and completed the work unfinished by Dr. Houghton, in 1846. Afterwards he was in the employ of government in the same work, and made the survey of Isle Royal. He was for many years manager of the interests of mining corporations. He saw the first log cabin built, and the first ton of copper and iron mined in the Upper Peninsula. He was a Republican in politics. He lived at Marshall winters and spent his summers in the Upper Peninsula. He died at Marshall. Aug. 28, 1889.

LOUIS N. HILSENDEGEN

Senator from the First District of Wayne County, 1915-16. Was born at Detroit, Mich., Mar. 29, 1856, of German parentage. He was educated at Notre Dame University, Ind. He engaged in the real estate business and served as president of the Hilmore Land Company. He was elected President of Grosse Pointe three terms. Married. In politics a Republican.

GEORGE E. HILTON

Representative from the County of Newaygo, 1893-4 and 1895-6. Was born in Leighton, Bedfordshire, England, Aug. 25, 1846. When six years of age he came with his parents to the United States, and five years later to Hillsdale, Mich. While here he acquired a common school education, and five years later located at Fremont. His occupation was that of a mechanic, and for several years he followed the business of contractor and builder; a member of the firm of Hilton Brothers, general contractors, and best known in the apiarian world by his many inventions of useful articles for bee keepers and his study and attention to bee culture. In politics a Republican.

EMANUEL HIMEBAUGH

Representative from Branch County, 1883-4. Was born in Columbia County, Pa., Feb. 27, 1822. He moved with his parents to Niagara County, N. Y., in 1833, and to Michigan in 1836, settling in Bronson, Branch County. He continued a resident of Branch County, engaged in farming, and also engaged in raising, fatting, and shipping live stock. He was a Fusionist in politics.

THEODORE H. HINCHMAN

Senator from the Second District, 1877-8. Was born in Morris County, N. J., Mar. 6, 1818. He removed to New York City in 1825. Mr. Hinchman received a common school education, and for five years was employed as clerk there. In 1836, he removed to Detroit, to engage with Chapin & Owen in the drug and grocery business, and in 1842 became a co-partner, when Detroit had six or seven thousand population and the State sixty or seventy thousand. He served one month in the Patriot War. He was president of the Merchants' and Manufacturers' Bank. He was for five years Sewer Commissioner, and for ten years Fire Commissioner. In politics he was a Democrat. In 1886 he was a member of the Semi-centennial Commission. He wrote a valuable book on banking and bankers of Michigan. He died May 12, 1895.

HENRY H. HINDS

Senator from the Twenty-seventh District, 1878-4. Was born Oct. 9, 1840, near Montrose, Pa. He received an academic education. In 1861 he enlisted as Sergeant in the 57th Penn. Infantry Volunteers, and took part in many battles. He was a prisoner for twenty months, being confined at Libby, Dansville, Va., Macon, Ga., Charleston, Va., Columbia, S. C., and Goldsboro, where he was paroled and entered the union lines, Mar. 1, 1865. He was mustered out of service July, 1865, as Captain. He engaged in the dry goods trade at Little Meadows, Pa., but came to Michigan in 1866, settled at Stanton, and continued in the mercantile business. He was also in the real estate and lumber business and fine stock raising. A Republican in politics.

JAMES W. HINE

Senator from the Twenty-second District, 1883-4. Was born in West Meredith, N. Y., in 1846. He received an academical education, served in the army, and settled at Lowell, Mich., in 1867. He was three years in the drug trade, then purchased an interest in the Lowell *Journal*, became editor, and in 1873 sole proprietor. He removed to Detroit after his senatorial term and was one of the editors of the Detroit *Tribune* in 1887.

MILTON B. HINE

Senator from the Twenty-fifth District, 1879. Was born at Meredith, N. Y., Feb. 2, 1828, where he resided until 1847, when he removed to Canon, Mich. He received a common school and academic education. He was a farmer and held the position of president and treasurer of the Farmer's Mutual Fire Insurance Company of Kent County for many years. In politics he was a Greenbacker.

DANA HARRISON HINKLEY

Representative from Emmet County, 1911-12, 1913-14 and 1915-16. Was born May 17, 1878, and received his eductaion in the Benton Harbor School and at the University of Michigan. Married. Engaged in the manufacture of broom handles. In politics a Republican.

GEORGE HINKSON, JR.

Representative from the First District of Sanilac County, 1889-90. Was born in Ontario, July 22, 1830, of New England parentage on his father's side. In the fall of 1845 he removed with his father's family to Worth Township, in Sanilac County. At that time Sanilac County formed a part of St. Clair County, and was an almost unbroken wilderness. He received such an education as the common schools among the poor people of that period afforded, which was followed by a course of study and reading pursued during intervals of labor long after leaving school. When of age he commenced in the woods to make a farm and home for himself, teaching winters and occasionally during the whole year, for twelve years. He then devoted his entire attention to farming as a business calling. He held the offices of Township Clerk and School Inspector for many years, and Supervisor nine years, seven of which were consecutive, including 1888; chairman of the Board of Supervisors twice, and represented Sanilac County before the State Board of Equalization in 1886. In politics a Republican.

EDWIN CHAUNCEY HINMAN

Member of the State Board of Education, 1905-6. Was born in Battle Creek Mar. 1, 1852. He graduated from high school in 1869 and from the University of Michigan in 1874. He was employed by the United States in engineering work in Wisconsin for some time. In 1880 he returned to Michigan and for two years was employed in Port Huron. In 1882 he returned to his native city and built up one of the most successful business ventures in the State. It is called the American Steam Pump Co. He was appointed as member of the State Board of Education by the Governor to fill out the time of J. H. Thompson, who resigned. His commission was dated Nov. 10, 1905. He resigned in January, 1906.

JAMES H. HITCHCOCK

Representative from Cass County, 1881-2. Was born in East Aurora, N. Y., Jan. 5, 1826. Educated in common schools, he settled in Cass County in 1831. He was in California, mining, 1852-5. He was Supervisor and held many other local offices. He was a Republican in politics.

JOHN P. HITCHINGS

Representative from Jackson County, 1851. Was born in Onondaga, N. Y., May 20, 1810. By occupation he was a farmer and teacher, politically a Democrat. He settled in Pulaski, Jackson County, in 1837, serving there as Supervisor several terms. He removed to Illinois before 1861, went to the war as Captain of an Illinois Company, and had a son killed in the war. He resided at Harrel, Montgomery County, Ill., in 1887.

DANIEL HIXON

Representative from Washtenaw County, 1843 and 1855-6; Delegate from Washtenaw County to the Constitutional Convention of 1850; Senator from the Seventh District, 1853-4; and Delegate from Washtenaw County to the Constitutional Convention of 1867. Was born in Cayuga County, N. Y., Oct. 17, 1803. He was a farmer, and politically a Democrat. He located at Tecumseh in 1826, and in 1828 was the first settler in what is now the township of Bridgewater, where he resided until his death. He was a Colonel in the Black Hawk War, and a Justice of the Peace. He died Feb. 3, 1870.

FREDERICK F. HOAGLIN

Representative from the First District of Calhoun County, 1887-8 and 1889-90. Was born on his father's farm, four miles from Albion, on the 29th of April, A. D. 1848, where he spent his early life, attending school in winter and working on the farm in the summer. At the age of twenty-two he accepted a position in a store at Albion. In 1875 he went into business for himself, which increased yearly, until he was the proprietor of one of the finest and best stock clothing stores in central Michigan. In 1872 he was married to Miss Mary M. Cunningham, of Albion. He held with credit the offices of Village Trustee and President, and Township Clerk, Alderman, City Treasurer and Mayor of Albion. He was elected on the Republican ticket Representative for 1887-8, and re-elected for 1889-90.

RICHARD M. HOAR

Representative from Houghton County, 1873-4. Was born in the county of Cornwall, England, in 1830. He received a common school education. In 1854 he emigrated to the United States and settled in Houghton, Mich. He was formerly President of Houghton village. In business he was a merchant; Republican in politics.

DAVID HOBART

Representative from the Second District of Oakland County, 1889-90. Was born in 1840, near Jamestown, Chautauqua County, N. Y. He was reared on a farm, and farming was his occupation in earlier life. He came to Michigan at the age of 19 years. For six years he was employed in the Old David Preston Bank, Detroit. In 1865 he moved to Holly and engaged in mercantile pursuits. In 1869 he was appointed Postmaster of Holly, a position he held continuously until March, 1887, a period of 17 years; agent and manager of the Holly Express office since 1866. He served on the Holly Board of Education, represented Holly on the Board of Supervisors for the year 1887, and in 1889 was President of the village.

NORTON P. HOBART

Representative from Calhoun County, 1849. Was born in Middlesex, N. Y., in 1816. By occupation he was a farmer, in politics a Republican. He came to Athens, Calhoun County, in 1833, was Supervisor in 1848, and also held the position of Postmaster. He resided in Athens in 1887.

HIRAM C. HODGE

Representative from Jackson County, 1872; and Senator from the Seventh District, 1879. Was born Feb. 22, 1821, at Stamford, Vt. In 1822 he removed with his parents to Adams, Mass., and in 1836 to Pulaski, Mich. He received a common school education. He was a lawyer by profession and by occupation a farmer and while located in Nevada County, Calif., was County Treasurer and Prosecuting Attorney. He was elected to the Lower House in 1872 for a special session in place of John Landon, deceased. He was a delegate from Michigan to the Baltimore Convention in 1872. In politics he was a National. He died at Concord, Mar. 19, 1897.

ISRAEL S. HODGES

Representative from Lenawee County, 1861-2. Was born in Onondaga County, N. Y., June 29, 1801. By occupation he was a farmer and lumberman, in politics a Republican. He came to Michigan in 1835, and was living at Blissfield in 1887.

BRADSHAW HODGKINSON

Representative from Wayne County, 1863-4. Was born in Stafford, England, May 20, 1815. He learned the trade of a hatter, came to this country in 1837, and was a farmer in Canton. He was Supervisor twelve years, and nine years a Superintendent of the Poor, later clerk and bookkeeper of that board. In politics he was a Democrat.

JOHN HOEFT, JR.

Representative, 1909-10, from the Presque Isle District, comprising the counties of Crawford, Montmorency, Oscoda, Otsego and Presque Isle. Was born at Detroit, Mich., Nov. 29, 1874, of German descent. He acquired his education in the public schools, high school, and business university of Detroit, Mich. He was married in 1896. Mr. Hoeft engaged in farming for a number of years and held the following offices: Township Clerk, County Treasurer, Justice of the Peace and Township School Inspector; also Deputy Register of Deeds. He located in Presque Isle County in 1893. In politics a Republican.

HERBERT H. HOFFMAN

Representative from Sanilac County, 1915-16. Was born at Granby City, Mo., July 16, 1871, and was educated in the public schools of Buffalo, N. Y., and the University of Buffalo, graduating from the latter in 1891. Fifteen years ago he removed to Sandusky, Mich. He was married July 16, 1895, to Jennie Brozil, of Bay City, Mich. In politics a Republican.

MICHAEL HOFFMAN

Member of the Board of Regents of the University of Michigan, 1837-8. Was born at Clifton Park, N. Y., in 1788. He studied law and was admitted to the bar at Herkimer, N. Y. He was a Representative in Congress from his district from 1825 to 1833. In 1836 he was appointed Register of the United States Land Office at Saginaw, Mich. In 1837 he was appointed Regent of the University, and drew the three year term; but he resigned the office in 1838 and returned to Herkimer, N. Y. He afterwards served in the New York Legislature three terms, was a member of the State Constitutional Convention of New York in 1846, and later was Naval Officer of New York. He died at Brooklyn, N. Y., Sept. 27, 1848.

EDWARD HOFMA

Senator, 1915-16, from the Twenty-third District, comprising the counties of Ottawa and Muskegon. Was born on a farm in Vriesland, Ottawa County, Mich., Apr. 12. 1859, of Dutch parentage. He received his education in the district schools and Hope College. In 1884 he graduated from the department of medicine and surgery of the University of Michigan, and engaged in the practice of his profession in Grand Haven and vicinity. He was married in 1886 to Elizabeth Pruim of Spring Lake, Mich. In politics a Republican.

CHARLES A. HOFMEISTER

Representative from the First District of Tuscola County, 1897-8 and 1899-1900. Was born at Tiffin, O., Apr. 8, 1853. When only one year old he moved with his parents to Huron County, Mich., where they took up a homestead. His early days were spent on his father's farm during the summer season and working in the lumber woods during the winters. His early education was acquired in the district school, supplemented by a course in the public schools of Sebewaing and Saginaw. He was married in 1886 to Miss Bertha A. Cartwright, of Unionville.

His principal occupation was that of a farmer and well driller, but he spent a portion of his time in prospecting for coal. In politics a Republican. He was Township Treasurer, Supervisor, and chairman of the Board of Supervisors.

JOHN HOLBROOK

Senator, 1887-8 and 1889-90, from the Twelfth District, comprising the counties of Ingham and Shiawassee. Was born Oct. 1, 1848, in North Chili, Monroe County, N. Y. By occupation he was a farmer. He was a school teacher twelve years. He held the offices of Supervisor, Township Clerk, Township Treasurer and lecturer of the Michigan State Grange and overseer of that organization. He was elected on the Republican ticket to the Senate of 1887-8 and was re-elected for 1889-90.

JAMES E. HOLCOMB

Senator, 1891-2, from the Twenty-seventh District, comprising the counties of Cheboygan, Crawford, Kalkaska, Missaukee, Montmorency, Otsego, Presque Isle and Roscommon. Was born in Johnstown, N. Y., July 17, 1831. He was in the mercantile business, then engaged in farming and lumbering. He served as Supervisor of the township of Nunda, and was a candidate for the Senate in 1888. He was elected to the Senate of 1891-2 on the Democratic ticket.

MARTIN H. HOLCOMB

Representative from Montcalm County, 1911-12 and 1913-14. Was born at Vernon, Trumbull County, O., Sept. 21, 1867, and was educated in the Pierson High School, supplemented by a course at the Central Michigan Normal School and a postgraduate course at Brown's University, Valparaiso, Ind. He was engaged in the lumber business until 1894, when he began farming. He was married Sept. 13, 1893, to Miss Lenora H. Hager. He was Supervisor of Pierson Township six years. In politics a Republican.

CHARLES HOLDEN

Representative from the First District of Kent County (Grand Rapids), 1895-6. Was born in Grand Rapids, Mich., Feb. 7, 1860. He acquired his education in the Grand Rapids city schools, was clerk in the Department of State at Lansing for eight years, and clerk of the joint committee on appropriations and finance and state affairs of the Senate of the State Legislature of 1883. Returning to Grand Rapids, he studied law for two years, and later engaged as fire insurance adjuster of several companies in western Michigan. In politics a Republican. He was elected to the Legislature on the general legislative ticket of the city of Grand Rapids.

DENNISON F. HOLDEN

Representative, 1891-2, from the Leelanau District, comprising the counties of Leelanau and Benzie. Was born in Ashford, Cattaraugus County, N. Y., Apr. 5, 1835. His parents were natives of Massachusetts. His early years were spent on a farm and he received his education at a village common school; after the age of 19 his winters were spent in teaching school until he was 40. He was married in 1860 and removed to Dodge County, Minn., where he resided until the fall of 1865, farming in the summer and teaching in the winter; returned to New York in 1865. In the spring of 1869 he purchased a farm in the Grand Traverse region, town of Almira, Benzie County. In politics an active Republican. He served as a school district officer, Supervisor, County Surveyor and School Examiner.

EBENEZER G. D. HOLDEN

Secretary of State, 1875-9. Was born at Kirkland, O., Feb., 18, 1834. His father settled in Byron, Kent County, Mich., in 1845. The son at the age of seventeen left home to care for himself. He learned the trade of a carpenter, qualified himself for college, and was a student in Knox College, Ill., for two and half years. He studied law and was admitted to the Kent County bar in 1859. In 1862 he was elected Prosecuting Attorney of Kent County and filled that position four years. For six years he was chairman of the Kent County Republican Committee, and for many years a School officer and Trustee of Grand Rapids. In 1869 he, with his partner, organized the Grand Rapids Savings Bank, the first in the city. In politics he was a Republican. He engaged in law and insurance business. He died at Coquille, Ore., Aug. 20, 1912.

HORACE HOLDRIDGE

Representative from the First District of Lenawee County, 1893-4. Was born in 1841 and a resident of the township of his birth. His early education was received at the district school, supplemented by one year's study at the Raisin Institute and one and one-half years at Adrian College. In 1862 he was married to Miss Adaline Holloway, of Fairfield, Lenawee County, and the following year purchased and moved on the farm. In politics a Democrat. He served as Supervisor of his township, and was elected to the House of 1893-4.

CHARLES E. HOLLAND

Representative from Houghton County, 1871-2. Was born at Indianapolis, Ind., June 30, 1835. In 1853 he went to Ontonagon, where he lived five years. He returned to Indianapolis in 1858, and in 1862 settled at Hancock, Mich., where he lived until the fall of 1886. As a resident of the Upper Peninsula he was a merchant, and actively engaged in developing its resources. His energy and perseverance led to the building of the railroad from Hancock to Calumet, of which he was long president and manager. He also placed Ontonagon in telegraphic communication with the business world. In politics a Republican. He was a member of the State Republican Committee some years.

JOHN HOLLAND

Representative from Gogebic County, 1911-12, 1919-20, 1921-2 and 1923—. Was born at Fall River, Mass., Jan. 14, 1861, of Irish parentage. He was educated in the common schools of Greenland, Ontonagon County, Mich. He was the eldest of six children, and at the age of twelve it became necessary for him to contribute to the support of the family. He went to work as "head tender" in the stamp mill of the Old Ridge Copper Mine. Later he started in the general blacksmithing business at Bessemer and continued in that occupation for twenty-eight years. After engaging in the grocery and real estate business for several years he was appointed superintendent of the City Water Department. Mr. Holland is not married. In 1906 he was elected Mayor of Bessemer; was twice re-elected to that office. He was elected to the Legislature of 1911-12 as a Democrat and re-elected Nov. 5, 1918, this time as a Republican, and again re-elected in 1920 and in 1922.

FRED W. HOLLISTER

Representative from the First District of Saginaw County, 1889-90. Was born in Gainesville, now Silver Springs, Wyoming County, N. Y., Aug. 19, 1847. He was the only son of Major W. and Elizabeth Hollister, and traced his lineage to the illustrious Hollisters of colonial and ante-colonial days. The family removed to Saginaw when Fred W. was eight years old. He enjoyed the privilege of the Saginaw common schools, which were supplemented with one year in Prof. Taft's school at Oxford. Then in 1864 he entered the office of John B. Dibble, the leading architect in this section of the country at that time. In 1869 he formed a partnership with Porter & Watkins, architects, of Bay City, and the firm established a branch in Saginaw, of which Mr. Hollister had charge. In 1870 he purchased the business at this end of the river, and during the same year he married Miss Libbie Madison, of Silver Springs, Wyoming County, N. Y. The Soldiers' Home at Grand Rapids, the Iowa State Soldiers' Home at Marshalltown, Ia., the court houses of Saginaw, Isabella, Ogemaw, Gladwin and Huron counties, and numerous churches, school houses, colleges, seminaries and other public buildings in various cities in Michigan are among the buildings that owe architectural beauty and utility for the purposes for which they were intended to Mr. Hollister. He was elected Alderman from his ward in 1879 on the Democratic ticket, and served in the council for two years. In 1881 he was a candidate for City Treasurer, but was defeated. In 1882 he was again a candidate and successful; was re-elected in 1883 and again in 1884, the last term being for two years. In politics a Protectionist Democrat.

HANNIBAL HOLLISTER

Representative from St. Clair County, 1846. His postoffice address was Port Huron. (Further data not obtainable).

HENRY S. HOLLISTER

Representative from Jackson County, 1847. His postoffice address was Gidley's Station. (Further data not obtainable).

ISAAC T. HOLLISTER

Senator from the Twenty-second District, 1857-8. Was born in Sharon, Conn., Nov. 29, 1801. He resided in that State until 1824, and became a physician, and was in practice forty years. He settled in Victor, Mich., in 1846. He was a Justice thirty years and held other local positions. He was a Whig, then a Democrat, a Republican after 1854. At the age of eighty-five he attended the legislative reunion in 1886. He died at Victor, Dec. 7, 1890.

JOSEPH A. HOLLON

Representative from Saginaw County, 1875. Was born in Utica, N. Y., Dec. 9. 1842. He removed with his parents to Michigan in 1843, and settled in Calhoun County. He made abstracts of the records of Jackson, Calhoun, Kalamazoo, and Van Buren counties, was afterwards cashier of the First National Bank of Paw Paw, and removed to Saginaw in 1866. He was a banker and an Alderman in East Saginaw, also controller. In 1872 he was Democratic candidate for State Treasurer. In politics he was a Democrat. He died May 2, 1875.

GEORGE R. HOLLWAY

Representative from the First District of Kent County, 1913-14. Was born in Middlesex County, England, Nov. 14, 1870, and came to Grand Rapids, Mich., with his parents when he was five years of age. He received a common school education. At an early age he began to learn the trade of furniture maker in the furniture factories of Grand Rapids, studying law at night until admitted to the bar. Later he became a member of the law firm of Carroll, Kerwin and Hollway. A widower. In politics a Democrat.

JOSEPH H. HOLMAN

Representative from Oakland County, 1885-6. Was born at Greencastle, Pa., July 28, 1843. He came to Michigan in 1866. Mr. Holman served in the late war, in the 126th Penn. Vol., and Mississippi Squadron. He was a lawyer at Rochester. Oakland County, and was elected to the Legislature on the Fusion ticket.

ALFRED HOLMES

Representative from Saginaw County, 1849. Was born in Charlton, N. Y., Mar. 22. 1805. He removed to Chautauqua County, N. Y., in 1834, and from there to Livingston County, Mich., where he remained six years, and from thence to Tuscola. then to Saginaw County. He was a mechanic, and served an apprenticeship at blacksmithing, made pails, tubs, boots, shoes, wagons, framed buildings, and worked at joiner and mill-wright business, and became a miller. In politics he was a Democrat.

ARTHUR L. HOLMES

Representative from the First District of Wayne County, 1895-6; and Senator from the First District of Wayne County, 1901-2. Was born in Detroit, Mich., June 17. 1862. He was educated in the public schools and early engaged in the business of lumbering. Married. In politics a Republican. He died at Detroit May, 1916.

CHARLES D. HOLMES

Delegate from Calhoun County to the Constitutional Convention of 1867. Was born in West Boylston, Mass., July 20, 1814, and received an academical education. In 1833 his father and himself located the farm in Albion, Mich. He was Register of Deeds of Calhoun County from 1873 to 1877. In politics he was a Republican. He died at Albion, Mar. 24, 1894.

JOHN H. HOLMES

Representative from the First District of Bay County, 1893-4. Was born in Goderich, Ont., Jan. 21, 1864. He came to Michigan when two years of age with his parents, locating at Bay City. His education was acquired at the high school of Bay City and the University of Michigan. He practiced law for a short time, and then engaged as contractor and builder. September, 1891, he was married to Miss Lucia Eastwood, of Bay City. In politics a Democrat.

JOHN W. HOLMES

Representative in the Legislature, 1901-2, 1903-4 and 1905-6; and Delegate in the Constitutional Convention of 1907-8, from the Nineteenth District, Gratiot County. Was born in Livingston County, N. Y., in 1840, of English and French descent. He was educated in the primary schools of his native town and in the public schools of Hillsdale County, Mich. Married. He came to Michigan in 1858 and located on a farm in Hillsdale County. In 1861 he enlisted in the 7th Mich. Vol. Infantry, and served with the regiment until honorably discharged on account of physical disability. He taught school in Hillsdale and Jackson counties for ten years, afterward engaging in mercantile business in Mosherville and Horton until 1884, when he moved to Alma where he engaged in mercantile business and farming. He was several years president of the Board of Education of Alma and served twice as Mayor of that city. In politics a Republican.

LYMAN A. HOLMES

Senator, 1917-18 and 1919-20, from the Eleventh District, comprising the counties of Macomb and St. Clair. Was born at Buffalo, N. Y., Nov. 7, 1858, of English and Irish parents. He was educated in the public and high high schools of Buffalo, and Cleveland, O. At the age of sixteen he accepted a position under Sir John McDonald as assistant timekeeper and paymaster during construction of the Q. M. O. & O. R. Railway from Montreal to Ottawa. Upon completion of this work he entered the foundry business, as apprentice, at Springfield, O., and was later promoted to the superintendency of the plant. Afterwards he filled similar positions in several large foundries in the eastern states. In 1906 he removed with his family at Romeo, Mich., where he organized and operated the first of his three foundries. In 1915 he was elected director and vice-president of the Romeo Savings Bank. In politics a Republican.

SILAS M. HOLMES

State Treasurer, 1855-9. Was in the fifties a leading dry goods merchant in Detroit. He was nominated in 1854 on the first Republican State ticket, was elected State Treasurer, and was re-elected in 1856. He removed from Detroit to San Francisco, and was engaged in business in that city in 1887.

HENRY H. HOLT

Representative from Muskegon County, 1867-8 to 1871-2, 1879-80 and 1887-8; Delegate from Muskegon County to the Constitutional Convention of 1867; and Lieutenant Governor, 1873-7. Was born at Camden, Oneida County, N. Y., Mar. 27, 1831. He received an academical education, studied law, and graduated from Union Law

College in Ohio; came to Michigan in 1857; was admitted to practice and settled at Muskegon, which remained his home. He was Circuit Court Commissioner four years, and Prosecuting Attorney four years. While in the Legislature he was chairman of the committee of ways and means for four years. He was a Republican, and a gentleman of good address and fine ability. He engaged in the practice of the law at Muskegon. He died at Muskegon, Aug. 23, 1898.

WILLIAM MARCY HOLTON

Representative from the Third District of Wayne County, 1891-2. Was born in Kildare, County Kildare, Ireland, Sept. 21, 1847; came to the United States in the spring of 1849, and settled at Verplanks, Westchester County, N. Y.; came to Michigan in 1855 and settled on a farm in the township of Taylor, Wayne County, with his mother and three older brothers. His father died when the subject of this sketch was but two years old. He moved to Dearborn in 1869. He was educated in the common schools of Taylor and public schools of Ypsilanti; and took a course of bookkeeping at Bryant and Stratton's Commercial College in Detroit. He was married in Dearborn in 1871. He held the offices of Justice, School Trustee, Supervisor of Dearborn, was Postmaster under Cleveland for four years.

SAMUEL R. HOOBLER

Representative from Alcona, Arenac and Iosco counties, 1887-8. Was born in Middleton, O., Oct. 24, 1844. He taught school in Ohio, and came to Bay City in 1868, and engaged in schools, and was a farmer near Worth, Arenac County. He held local positions. He was elected as a Fusionist.

JOHN G. HOOD

Representative from Monroe County, 1861-2 and 1863-4. Was born in Seneca County, N. Y., Aug. 3, 1810. He came to Michigan in 1845, and settled on a farm in Ash, Monroe County, which he had located in 1836, where he lived until his death, Apr. 5, 1880. He was Supervisor and Town Clerk several years, and held other town offices. In politics he was a Republican.

AZEL HOOKER

Representative from Monroe County, 1839. Came to Petersburgh, Mich., from Penn Yan, N. Y., in 1832, and was then about thirty years old. He was a merchant, and a Whig. He was a Justice several years. He moved to Buffalo, N. Y., in 1840, engaged in the transportation business, and nothing further is known of him.

CORTEZ P. HOOKER

Representative from Macomb County, 1850; and Senator from the Thirtieth District, 1855-6. Was born at Hampton, N. Y., in 1814, and was a descendant of Rev. Thomas Hooker, who came to New England in 1632. He came to Michigan in 1837, and located lands in Clinton, Macomb County, and after three years went to Washington, same county. After 1851 he lived at New Baltimore. He was a leading merchant for a few years, later, for many years one of the most prosperous farmers in the county.

FRANK A. HOOKER

Justice of the Supreme Court, 1893-1911. Was born at Hartford, Conn., Jan. 16, 1844. When twelve years of age he removed with his parents to Maumee, O., and later to Defiance; attended the public schools, the law department of the University of Michigan, and was graduated from the latter in 1865. He began the practice of law at Bryan, O., and after one year came to Charlotte, Mich., where, until his election to the Supreme bench, he was engaged in the practice of his profession. Mr. Hooker was married Aug. 5, 1868, to Miss Emma E. Carter, at Defiance, O. Mrs. Hooker died at Lansing, Nov. 24, 1909. In politics he was a Republican. He held the office of Superintendent of Schools of Eaton County; was Prosecuting Attorney for two terms, and in 1878 was appointed Judge of the Fifth Judicial Circuit by Governor Croswell to fill vacancy; was continued as Circuit Judge by a vote of the people at the following election and held that office until resigning to accept a position on the Supreme Bench, made vacant by the resignation of Chief Justice Morse. He was elected to that position at the general election of 1892, and re-elected Apr. 3, 1893, for the full term to succeed himself; was again re-elected Apr. 6, 1903, for a term of ten years. He was Chief Justice during the years 1893, 1902, 1903. He died July 10, 1911.

ARLIE L. HOPKINS

Representative from Manistee County, 1915-16 to 1921-2. Was born at Manistee Aug. 13, 1870, and was educated in the Bear Lake High School and the Michigan Agricultural College. His early life was spent in the woods assisting his father in the manufacture of lumber. It was then he conceived the idea of turning the cut-over land to agricultural purposes. In 1888 he began clearing, stumping and fencing and now has eight hundred acres under cultivation. During the last sixteen years he has been farmers' institute lecturer for the Michigan Agricultural College. Mr. Hopkins is married. In politics he is a Republican.

GEORGE H. HOPKINS

Representative from Wayne County, 1879-80 to 1883-4. Was born in White Lake, Mich., Nov. 7, 1842. In 1862, while a student at the State Normal School, he enlisted in the 17th Mich. Infantry and served until the close of the war. He graduated at the State Normal School in 1867, from the law department of the University in 1871, and was then in practice in Detroit. He was four years private secretary to Gov. Bagley and Gov. Croswell, and served as chairman of the State Republican Committee. He died at Detroit, Mar. 6, 1906.

HARVEY J. HOPKINS

Representative from Saginaw County, 1881-2. Was born in Oneida County, N. Y., Apr. 15, 1830, and was a resident of Oakland County, Mich., in 1835, and after a residence in other parts of the State, in 1871 in Saginaw County. With a common school education he was a teacher from 1853 to 1861, and served as a soldier from 1861 to 1865. He was several years in the hardware trade, but most of the time a farmer. He held many local offices, and was a Republican in politics.

MORDECAI L. HOPKINS

Senator from the Twenty-third District, 1855-6. His postoffice address was Millpoint, Ottawa County. (Further data not obtainable).

MOSES B. HOPKINS

Representative from Ottawa County, 1867-8. Was born in Huron County, O., June 16, 1820. He was a descendant of Stephen Hopkins of the Mayflower, and of Stephen Hopkins, of Rhode Island, one of the signers of the Declaration of Independence. By profession he was a lawyer, politically a Republican. He was admitted to the bar at Geneva, Ill., in 1840, and settled at Grand Haven in 1851. He held the several positions of Justice of the Peace, Circuit Court Commissioner, Prosecuting Attorney, and Circuit Judge. He died at Grand Haven Oct. 24, 1869. while filling the position of Circuit Judge.

R. HENRY HOPKINS

Representative from the Second District of Kalamazoo County, 1913-14. Was born at Charleston, Kalamazoo County, Mich., Jan. 25, 1859, his education being acquired in school district number one, Charleston, and in the Augusta schools. The Hopkins family were residents of the New England colonies some generations before the Revolutionary war, in which Robert Hopkins and his son, David, served in a New York regiment from Charlotte, afterwards called Washington County, and David. who was born in 1748, was in 1778 elected, while a soldier, to represent his county in New York Assembly. His seventh son, Henry, was born in 1794, and served in the War of 1812. He came with his family to Michigan in 1835. His son, Robert, was born in Mentz, N. Y., in 1830, was in his fifth year when the family came to Michigan Territory early in 1852. In 1853 he planted a nursery in California, using seed sent him by his father, and taken from the fruit of Michigan orchards. He returned to Michigan and was married to a daughter of Joel Chandler. From this ancestry R. Henry Hopkins was born. In politics a Democrat.

SAMUEL W. HOPKINS

Representative from Isabella and Clare Counties, 1877-8 and 1879-80; and Senator. 1893-4, from the Twenty-fifth District, composed of the counties of Newaygo. Mecosta, Isabella, and Osceola. Was born in Kent County, R. I., Apr. 1, 1845. When eleven years of age he moved with his parents to Coventry, Conn., where he attended public school and received private instructions. At fifteen years of age he entered the Ellington Academy and the next year attended the academy at Manchester. He taught school the two following winters and later attended the union business college of Cleveland, O., and the law department of the Michigan University. On graduating from the latter in 1872, he located temporarily at Grand Rapids, where he was admitted to the bar. After a short time he located at Mt. Pleasant, Isabella County, where he engaged in the practice of his profession. He held numerous local offices of public trust and gave considerable attention to the advancement of the public schools. In 1874 he was elected Prosecuting Attorney of Isabella County. In politics a Republican.

JOHN SCOTT HORNER

Secretary and Acting Governor of the Territory of Michigan, 1835. Was born at Warrenton, Va., Dec. 5, 1802. He was the third son of Dr. Gustavus Brown Horner, assistant surgeon, and nephew of Dr. Gustavus Brown, surgeon general of the Revolutionary army. He graduated from Washington College, Pa., in 1819 and practiced law in Virginia until 1835. On Sept. 9, 1835, President Jackson appointed him Secretary and Acting Governor of the Territory of Michigan, inclusive of Wisconsin and Iowa. In November, 1835, the people of Michigan elected a Legislature and state officers, with Stephen T. Mason as Governor, although not admitted by Congress as a State, and hence refused to recognize the authority of Governor Horner. He was subsequently Secretary of Wisconsin, and was a man of ability and integrity. Subsequently he became register of the Green Bay Land Office, and held that position thirteen years. He founded the city of Ripon, Wis., naming it from the home of his ancestors in England, and lived to old age respected and honored. He died at Ripon, Wis., Feb. 3, 1883.

ROSWELL G. HORR

Member of Congress, 1879-81 to 1883-5. Was born in Waitsfield, Vt., Nov. 26, 1830. In 1834 he removed with his parents to Lorain County, O., and worked on a farm until nineteen years of age; graduated at Antioch College in 1857; was clerk of the Court of Common Pleas for six years; practiced law two years, was six years in charge of a lead mining company in Missouri; and was a resident of East Saginaw after 1872; for some years engaged in lumbering and banking. He was defeated for Congress in 1884 and 1886. A fine speaker, logical and convincing, he had a national reputation as a humorist. In politics he was a Republican. After his retirement from Congress he became associate editor upon the staff of the New York *Tribune* until he died Dec. 9, 1896.

BENJAMIN S. HORTON

Representative from the First District of St. Clair County, 1865-6. His postoffice address was Bell River. (Further data not obtainable).

DEXTER HORTON

Representative from Genesee County, 1869-70. Was born in Groveland, Mich., in 1837. With a common school and academical education, he settled at Fenton, Mich., in 1859, and was Postmaster in 1861. He enlisted in the 5th Mich. Cavalry, and rose to the rank of Major, serving until 1865. He was again Postmaster at Fentonville, later in the agricultural implement business. He was Supervisor, and held other local positions, and was a delegate in the Republican National Convention of 1868.

GEORGE B. HORTON

Member of the State Board of Agriculture, 1887-8; State Senator, 1891; and Delegate in the Constitutional Convention of 1907-8 from the Fifth District, Lenawee County. Was born in Medina County, O., in 1845, of English and American descent. He was educated in the country district schools with some college work. In 1877 he married Amanda M. Bradish, of Lenawee County. He engaged as a farmer and cheese manufacturer, settling on a farm in Fairfield Township, Lenawee County, with his father in 1853. He was appointed a member of the State Board of Agriculture under Governor Luce, but resigned because of private business. He was elected to the State Senate in 1891, but lost seat after sixty days in order to give Democratic majority. He was master of Fruit Ridge grange from

1873 to 1893, of Lenawee County Grange from 1890 to 1908 and master of the Michigan State Grange from 1892 to 1908; also served as President of the Lenawee County Fair from 1867 to 1908.

NORMAN B. HORTON

Senator from the Nineteenth District, comprising the counties of Lenawee and Monroe, 1923—. Was born at Fruit Ridge, July 18, 1881, of American parentage. He attended district school and Adrian College and is a graduate of M. A. C. agricultural course, class of '02. He was associated in business with his father, George B. Horton, until about 1912, when he engaged in the cheese manufacturing business in Osceola County. In 1917 he sold out the business and entered the 2nd officers training camp at Fort Sheridan. He was commissioned captain and served in various camps in this country until discharged in 1919. Since that time he has been at Fruit Ridge assisting his father and handling his estate since his death. He was elected to the Senate Nov. 7, 1922, without opposition.

FRANK H. HOSFORD

Representative from Wayne County, 1887-8. Was born at Henrietta, O. He removed to Michigan with his parents in 1868, settling at Lowell, Kent County. He studied law at Lowell and Grand Rapids, and then entered journalism on the now defunct Grand Rapids *Times*, and served successfully in advancing positions on the *Leader, Eagle,* and *Democrat* of that city. In 1882 he was interested in the Kalamazoo *Daily Commercial* as editor and part owner. In 1883 he went to Detroit and entered the service of the *Free Press.* He was city editor and assistant editorial writer of that journal. Mr. Hosford received the complimentary vote of the union Senators in 1885 for secretary of the Senate.

ORAMEL HOSFORD

State Superintendent of Public Instruction, 1865-73; and member of the State Board of Agriculture, 1869-75. Was born in Thetford, Vt., May, 1820. His parents removed to Oberlin, O., in 1834, and he was educated in Oberlin College. He came to Olivet in 1844 as professor of mathematics and philosophy. He was an efficient officer, and had the full confidence of the people of Michigan. In 1875 he was for some time president of Olivet College. He was a member of the State Geological Board and of the State Board of Agriculture. He helped organize the Republican party and always acted with that party. His wife was Atta Heallen, of Oberlin, O. He was professor in Olivet College in 1888.

JOHN HOSKING

Representative from the Second District of Marquette County, 1923—. Was born in Camborne, England, Apr. 9, 1869. He was educated in the Ishpeming public school. Mr. Hosking is a widower and is retired after twenty-nine years in the cigar business. He is a Republican.

ORCUTT V. HOSNER

Representative from Leelanaw and Benzie counties, 1873-4. Was born July 26, 1849, in West Bloomfield, Mich. He was mainly educated at the State Normal

School. In 1870 he removed to Frankfort, Benzie County, and purchased an interest in the Frankfort *Weekly Express*. He held several official positions in Frankfort. Deceased.

LAUREN HOTCHKISS

Representative from Lenawee County, 1838. Settled in Adrian, Mich., as early as 1833, and came from the State of New York. He built a house in Adrian and lived there several years. He then became a resident of Medina, where he died about 1855. He was a Baptist preacher, and was also engaged in milling business.

LEWIS CASS HOUGH

Senator from the First District, 1893-4. Was born in Canton, Mich., July 9, 1846. He attended the high school at Plymouth, from which he graduated at the age of seventeen. He taught school in 1864; the next year attended business college of Detroit, and again taught in 1867-8. In 1866 was married to Marietta Baker, of Plymouth, and began farming, which occupation he continued until 1875, when he moved to Plymouth and engaged in dealing in grain and produce. In politics a Democrat. He held the office of Superintendent of Schools, Supervisor and President of the village of Plymouth.

OLMSTEAD HOUGH

Senator from the Second District, 1835-7. His postoffice address was Tecumseh. (Further data not obtainable).

CHARLES A. HOUGHTON

Representative from the First District of Bay County, 1917-18. Was born in Quebec, Canada, Jan. 29, 1870, and came to Michigan with his parents fourteen years later. He attended the public schools, and at the age of fourteen entered the printing business. After serving the required time at printing he branched out for himself, and engaged in the printing business. He was a member of the Board of Supervisors on two occasions. In politics a Democrat.

GEORGE E. HOUGHTON

Representative from the First District of Genesee County, 1891-2. Was born Oct. 8, 1840, in the township of Mantua, Portage County, O.; in 1856 he came to Michigan with his parents who settled on a farm in Gaines Township, Genesee County. He received such an education as he could attending the district schools winters and two terms in the Flint High School, after which he taught school for six winters, working on his farm in the summers. His occupation was that of a farmer in Clayton Township. He held the offices of School Inspector and Supervisor, the latter position for five years, being Supervisor of his township when chosen to the Legislature. In politics he was identified with the Democratic party until the election of 1890 when he was the Patron of Industry candidate for Representative.

CALVIN ELIAS HOUK

Delegate to the Constitutional Convention of 1907-8 from the Thirty-second District, Gogebic County. Was born in Ann Arbor, in 1860, of German descent. He received his education in the public schools of Owosso. In 1885, Mr. Houk married Miss Susan M. Kelly, of Alpena. He went to Ironwood in 1887, when the town was in its infancy and engaged in the drug business. He held various offices in Ironwood, holding the office of Alderman for two terms from 1892 to 1896; was appointed Postmaster in 1898, and served as Mayor in 1899 and 1900; also a member of the Board of Education and for several years the secretary of the Republican County Committee.

THEODORE G. HOUK

Representative from Oceana County, 1885-6 and 1887-8. Was born in Seneca County, O., Aug. 2, 1833. He removed to Kent County in 1850. He followed various occupations, farming, ship and house carpentering, brick making, and sailing. He enlisted as a private in Co. A, 3rd Mich. Vol. Infantry, in the spring of 1861; re-enlisted in the fall of 1863; was promoted to the rank of corporal; was wounded at Cold Harbor, Va., June, 1864, and honorably discharged in August, 1865. He returned to Kent County and engaged in farming. He removed to Oceana County in the spring of 1873. He was elected Supervisor seven years in succession; held the offices of Justice of the Peace and School Inspector.

ELISHA J. HOUSE

Representative from Van Buren County, 1857-8. Was born in Chesterfield, N. H., Nov. 29, 1813. He was a merchant and a Republican. He came from Leroy, N. Y., to Paw Paw in 1842, and was intimately connected with the growth of the village and surrounding country for many years. Later he made his residence in Kalamazoo and Detroit.

JULIUS HOUSEMAN

Representative from Kent County, 1871-2; and member of Congress, 1883-5. Was born in Zeckendorf, Bavaria, Germany, on Dec. 8, 1832. He received a common school education and commercial training in his native town. Mr. Houseman emigrated to the United States in 1851, and engaged in mercantile pursuits until 1876 (twenty-four years in the city of Grand Rapids); after that time he was principally occupied in the manufacture of lumber. He served eight years as Alderman, and two terms as Mayor of Grand Rapids. He was the candidate for Lieutenant Governor on the Democratic ticket in 1876. He was elected to the United States Congress in 1882 on the Union ticket. He died Feb. 8, 1891.

JOHN HOUSTON

Representative from Calhoun County, 1875-6. Was born May 16, 1824, in Clarkson, Monroe County, N. Y., removed to Michigan in 1833, and settled in Fredonia, Calhoun County. He was a farmer by occupation, and vice president of the National City Bank of Marshall, and was for four years Sheriff of Calhoun County. In politics he was a Republican. He died at Marshall Sept. 7, 1906.

CYRUS HOWARD

Representative from Wayne County, 1848. Was born in Massachusetts in 1791. He settled in Dearborn in 1836. He served as Justice and Supervisor at various times, was Associate Judge of the county, 1837-41, under the judicial system then prevailing, and second Judge under the county court system, 1846-50. He was a farmer by occupation, and a Democrat in politics. He died in Dearborn in 1856.

HARVEY H. HOWARD

Representative from Van Buren County, 1881-2 and 1883-4. Was born in Monroe County, N. Y., Sept. 6, 1825, received a common school education, moved to Bloomingdale, Mich., in 1851. He was Supervisor and Justice several terms, and held other local offices. He was a farmer by occupation, and a Republican in politics.

HENRY HOWARD

State Treasurer, 1836-9; and Auditor General, 1839-40. Was born in Hinsdale, Mass., Sept. 15, 1801. He was by profession a banker and business man, and came to Detroit in 1827 and engaged in the lumber business in company with Ralph Wadhams. He served as Alderman in Detroit, 1833-4, and as Mayor in 1837. He removed to Buffalo, N. Y., in 1840, and was for nearly thirty years treasurer of the Buffalo Savings Bank, and died in Buffalo July 15, 1878. His political lot in Michigan was cast with the Democratic party, but in later life he was a Republican.

HENRY HOWARD

Representative from St. Clair County, 1873-4 and 1875-6; and member of the Board of Regents of the University of Michigan, 1892-4. Was born Mar. 8, 1833, in the city of Detroit, Mich. He received his education in common schools. He removed with his parents to Port Huron in 1834. He served as Alderman ten years, and vice president of the First National Bank of Port Huron. By occupation he was a lumber merchant. In politics he was a Republican. He was elected a member of the Board of Regents of the University of Michigan for the term beginning Jan. 1, 1892. He died May 25, 1894.

JACOB M. HOWARD

Representative from Wayne County, 1838; member of Congress, 1841-3; Attorney General, 1855 61; and United States Senator, 1862-71. Was born in Shaftsbury, Vt., July 10, 1805. In early life Mr. Howard worked at farming, then fitted for college and graduated at Williams College in 1830. He studied law, removed to Detroit in 1832, and was admitted to the bar in 1833. In 1835 he married Catherine A. Shaw, of Ware, Mass. He strongly supported the claims of Michigan to the disputed territory on the Ohio border, and enlisted in the Michigan troops that mustered on the border line. In 1838 he was a leading member of the Michigan House. In 1840 he was nominated by the Whigs as their candidate for Congress, and was elected. He took an active part in the support of the Whig candidates in the campaigns of 1844, 1848 and 1852. In 1854 he united with Whigs and Free Soilers to effect a union, which was accomplished at Jackson, July 6, 1854, the resolutions adopted being drawn by Mr. Howard, and the party taking the name of Republican. In 1862 he was elected United States Senator to fill the vacancy caused by the death of Gov. Bingham, a position he filled most ably until 1871, having been re-elected in 1865. He was an active member of the judiciary committee and that on military affairs. He favored the constitutional amendment abolishing slavery and drafted the first and principal clause as it now appears. In the winter of 1870-1 he refused the presidency of the Southern Claims Commission. He died of apoplexy at Detroit, Apr. 2, 1871.

JOSHUA A. HOWARD

Representative from Wayne County, 1838 and 1840. Was born in Eaton, Mass., Apr. 13, 1793. He was a Lieutenant in the 9th U. S. Infantry and served in the War of 1812. He came to Detroit in 1815, and was Lieutenant of Ordnance, was promoted to Captain, and served at many posts in the states, coming back to Detroit in 1830, and superintended the building of the arsenal at Dearborn. He resigned in 1835, and returned to Dearborn. He served as Lieutenant Colonel in the Mexican War and was made a Colonel. He was Paymaster in the army in 1861-5. He was Supervisor several terms, Marshal of Michigan in 1841-4, Sheriff of Wayne County, 1855-7. He removed to Detroit, where he died July 12, 1868. In politics he was a Whig, then a Republican.

MANLY D. HOWARD

Representative from Ottawa County, 1863-4 and 1865-6. Was born in West Winfield, N. Y., Aug. 31, 1817. His father served in the War of 1812. The son received his early education at Fredonia Academy, N. Y. He came to Detroit in 1836, studied law, clerked in a commission house, and served two years as Deputy U. S. Marshal. From 1842 to 1847 he was a member of a produce and commission house. He removed to Ann Arbor and in 1854 to Holland and engaged in the lumber business. In 1867 he opened a law office in connection with land collections and insurance business. In politics he was a Democrat.

ORRIN H. HOWARD

Representative from St. Joseph County, 1865-6 and 1867-8. Was born in Bolton, Conn., July 13, 1812. By occupation he was a farmer, politically a Republican. He settled in Florence, Mich., in 1832, and was one of the first assessors of the town, and for twelve years a Justice of the Peace. He lived on his farm forty-five years. He died Nov. 19, 1875.

SUMNER HOWARD

Delegate from Genesee County to the Constitutional Convention of 1867; and Representative from Genesee County, 1883-4. Was born in Massachusetts in 1836; a farmer and lawyer; in politics a Republican; U. S. Judge in Arizona several years; later engaged in practice there. He was Prosecuting Attorney and held other positions.

WILLIAM A. HOWARD

Member of Congress, 1855-7 to 1859-61. Was born at Hinesburg, Vt., Apr. 8, 1813. His parents were poor, and his early life was a protracted struggle. Physically not strong enough for farm labor, he journeyed to Albion, N. Y., apprenticed himself to a cabinet maker, and worked diligently at the trade until nineteen. He then attended an academy at Wyoming, N. Y., for three years, then entered Middlebury College in 1831, and graduated in 1835. He taught school in Genesee County, N. Y., and came to Michigan in 1840, making his home in Detroit. He was engaged as a mathematical tutor in a branch of the State University, commenced reading law with Witherell & Buell, and was admitted to the bar in 1842. From that time until 1854 he was in active legal practice, a part of the time as the partner of Alexander W. Buel. In 1858 he received his seat in Congress for the third term, the certificate of election having been first given to Geo. B. Cooper, his competitor. As a Congressman from the first he took a leading position, and was second on the committee of ways and means for two terms. In 1861 he was appointed Postmaster of Detroit and held the position for five and a half years, until removed by Andrew Johnson. In 1869 he was appointed Minister to China, but declined the position. The same year he was appointed Land Commissioner of the Grand Rapids & Indiana railroad, which he held until 1877. He was then appointed Governor of Dakota, and ably filled the position. Among other positions filled by him was that of Chairman of the Republican State Central Committee from 1860 to 1866, and for several years member of the National Republican Committee. In politics he was a Whig until 1854, then a Republican. He died at Washington, Apr. 10, 1880. In 1841 he married Ellen Lane Burchard, who survived him. He left four adult children. In religion he was a member of the Presbyterian Church.

ELIJAH B. HOWARTH, JR.

Representative from the First District of Oakland County, 1923—. Was born in Orion Township, Oakland County, Oct. 2, 1885, of American parentage. He was educated in district school, Orion High School, Ohio Northern University and the Detroit College of Law, graduating from the last named institution in 1910. He began the practice of law in Rochester, Mich., but in 1913 removed to Royal Oak and became a member of the firm of Dondero & Howarth. In 1911 he was married to Laura M. Smith and they have four children, a son and three daughters. Mr. Howarth served as Circuit Court Commissioner for two terms and as a member of the draft board for the Second District of Oakland County during the World War. He was elected Representative on the Republican ticket Nov. 7, 1922.

ABEL N. HOWE

Representative from Jackson County, 1883-4. Was born in Newstead, N. Y., Oct. 15, 1841. He received a common school education, and settled in Jackson County, Mich., in 1854. By occupation he was a farmer. He held several local offices, and served in the House as a National.

GEO. HOWE

Representative from Lenawee County, 1835-6. His postoffice address was Clinton. (Further data not obtainable).

JOHN HOWE

Representative from Livingston County, 1857-8. Was born in Dalston, England, Apr. 9, 1814. He came to this country with his father in 1821. He lived in New

York City and Yonkers, N. Y., until 1833, when he settled in Deerfield with his father, on a farm of six hundred acres. He received a good common school education and became a prominent man. He was Supervisor many years and Town Clerk.

M. J. HOWE

Representative from Monroe County, 1919-20. Was born Sept. 15, 1878, at Azalia, Monroe County, Michigan, of English-Irish parents. He was educated in the public schools of Azalia and the Milan High School. He is a farmer and, with the exception of five years, has lived on a farm all his life. He has served two terms as Justice of the Peace. Mr. Howe is married. In politics a Republican.

ORIN HOWE

Delegate from the Fourth District to the Constitutional Convention of 1835; and Representative from Washtenaw County, 1835-7 and 1843. Was born in Danbury, Conn., in 1786. He settled in Lodi, Michigan, making the first land entry in 1824. He was speaker pro tem in 1835 and 1836. He was postmaster at Lodi from 1827 to 1848, and from 1831 for many years was a Justice. He was a Democrat in politics, a high Mason, and in religion a Universalist. He died Feb. 12, 1848.

ANDREW HOWELL

Senator from the Eleventh District, 1865-6 and from the Ninth District, 1867-8. Was born at Covert, N. Y., Dec. 18, 1827. His father, Joseph Howell, a member of the first Constitutional Convention of this State, removed to Macon, Lenawee County, in 1831. Judge Howell commenced the study of law with F. C. Beaman, at Adrian in 1850, and graduated at the law school of the Cincinnati College in 1853, taking the first honors of his class. He was admitted to the bar at Adrian in 1854, and practiced law there with Judge Beaman, and afterwards with R. R. Beecher. He was elected Circuit Court Commissioner of Lenawee County in 1858, and for two terms thereafter. He edited and published several editions of the justice's guide, and of Tiffany's criminal law, and was author of a compilation of the general laws of the State, known as Howell's annotated statutes of Michigan. He was elected Circuit Judge in 1881, entering upon the duties of his office on the first of January, 1882. He resigned in 1887 as Judge, and engaged in law practice in Detroit. He died at Detroit, Dec. 22, 1904.

CHESTER MILTON HOWELL

Representative from the First District of Saginaw County, 1923—. Was born in Muskegon, Sept. 10, 1884, of American parents. He paid his way through school, selling papers and doing odd jobs and then worked on a farm for a year, following his graduation from the Muskegon High School. He entered newspaper work, following it in Muskegon, Grand Rapids, Detroit and Saginaw, in reportorial and correspondence capacities, and also handling promotion publicity. He was for four years assistant secretary of the Saginaw Board of Commerce and is serving his third term as member of the County Board of Supervisors, elected from the city at large. Mr. Howell is married and has two daughters. He is a member of all Masonic bodies except Knights Templar; also of the Kiwanis, Elks, Metropolitan, Auto, Lincoln and Caravan clubs; and of the Congregational Church. He is a Republican.

GEORGE HOWELL

Representative from the First District of Lenawee County, 1883-4, 1885-6 and 1899-1900; and Senator from the Fifth District, 1887-8. Was born at Macon, Lenawee County, Mich., Nov. 4, 1836. His education was acquired at the district school, Tecumseh High School, and Hillsdale College. In 1860 he entered the medical department of the Michigan University and graduated in 1863. For more than twenty years thereafter he practiced medicine in his native town, and in 1886 he removed to Tecumseh. In 1864 he was united in marriage to Ann Amelia Remington, a schoolmate of his early school days. He was elected to the House of Representatives in 1882, and again in 1884, and to the State Senate in 1886. From the close of the session of 1887 he engaged continuously in the practice of his profession. In 1898 he was again nominated by the Republicans, and was elected to the House of 1899-1900.

WILLIAM T. HOWELL

Representative from Hillsdale County, 1842; and from Newaygo and other counties, 1861-2 and 1863-4; and Senator from the Third District, 1843-6. Was born in the State of New York, in 1811. He came to Jonesville, Mich., in 1836. He was by profession a lawyer, in politics, first a Democrat, after 1854 a Republican. After a few years' practice at Jonesville, he removed to Hillsdale, thence to Jackson in 1853, and from there to Newaygo. He held the position of United States Judge in the Territory of Arizona. He was also County Judge of Hillsdale County in 1847. He was president pro tem. of the Senate in 1845, and was speaker pro tem. in 1861-2 and 1863-4. He died Apr. 3, 1870.

NATHANIEL HOWLAND

Representative from Lapeer County, 1839. His postoffice address was Bristol. (Further data not obtainable).

SIMPSON HOWLAND

Representative from Kalamazoo County, 1875-6 and 1877-8. Was born May 18, 1822, at Stillwater, N. Y. His education was that of common schools. He removed to Ross, Kalamazoo County, in 1836. He held a number of township offices, including Supervisor and Justice. By occupation he was a farmer and the proprietor of a flouring mill and saw mill; in politics a Republican. He was alive in 1897.

CHARLES L. HOYT

Representative from the Second District of Ottawa County, 1893-4. Was born in Waterloo, Jackson County, Mich., June 18, 1859. He lived with his father on the farm until twenty-one years of age, attending district school until eighteen, when he began teaching. At twenty-one he went to Hanley, Ottawa County, where he continued in teaching. Nov. 18, 1880, he was married to Esther M. McEachron, and moved to Hudsonville. He spent two years here, teaching, and then moved to Pierson, to take charge of the books of F. F. Taylor, mercantile and lumbering firm. In 1885 he returned to Hudsonville, and engaged for himself in the mercantile business. In politics a Republican. He held the office of Township Clerk, School Inspector, and Postmaster at Hudsonville.

HERBERT H. HOYT

Representative from Saginaw County, 1877-8. Was born in Ashville, N. Y., Sept. 4, 1840. At an early age he removed to Panama, N. Y. He received a liberal education and graduated at the Cleveland Law College in 1862. He was admitted to practice in Ohio. He came to East Saginaw in 1862 and soon obtained a lucrative law practice. He was elected Judge of the Recorder's court in 1866, Alderman in 1869-71, and Mayor in 1874. He was delegate to the Cincinnati Convention in 1876. In politics he was a Republican, but later a Greenbacker, and a candidate of that party for Congress.

JAMES M. HOYT

Senator from the Sixth District, 1859-60. Was born at East Aurora, N. Y., Oct. 5, 1817. He received a fair education, studied medicine and graduated at Geneva, in 1839. He settled in practice at Commerce, Mich , in 1840, removed to Walled Lake in 1842. In politics he was a Democrat. He held many local offices. He was re-elected Senator in 1864, was given seat, but his seat was contested and he was defeated. Deceased.

JOHN P. HOYT

Representative from Tuscola County, 1873-4 and 1875-6. Was born in Austinburgh. O., Oct. 6, 1843. He served during the war in the 87th O. Infantry, and rose to the brevet rank of Major. He was educated at Oberlin College, and graduated at the law college at Cleveland, O., in 1867. In 1867 he engaged in practice at Caro, Mich., and was Prosecuting Attorney. He was a Federal Judge in a western territory for several years.

MARCUS HOYT

Representative from Leelanau District, 1923—. Was born in Muir, Ionia County, Feb. 6, 1871, of Welsh ancestry. He was educated in the district schools and the Saline High School. He engaged as a druggist at Mio and McKinley in Oscoda County, and for the past twenty-five years has followed the same business at Sutton's Bay. Mr. Hoyt is married and has two sons. He is a member of the F. & A. M. and M. W. of A. He is a Republican and has held various township and village offices and has been County Road Commissioner.

WILLIAM C. HOYT

Representative from Wayne County, 1871-2. Was born in Montgomery County, N. Y., Sept. 3, 1815. With an academical education he became a teacher, then studied law and was admitted in 1838. He settled at Milford, Mich., in 1842, and there practiced law until 1853, when he removed to Detroit. He was for three years a County Judge of Oakland County. He retired from business in 1874. He was a Democrat until 1854, then a Republican.

A. B. HUBBARD

Representative from the Second District of Oakland County, 1923—. Was born in that county on a farm in White Lake Township. His education was acquired in the rural school and the Pontiac High School. With the exception of seven years as field-man for the State Tax Commission, he has always been a farmer, his early life being spent on the farm where he was born. He is a Republican.

COLLINS B. HUBBARD

Representative from Wayne County, 1881-2. Was born Feb. 8, 1852, in Detroit. He was the son of Bela Hubbard, who removed from Utica, N. Y., and settled there in 1835. He received a liberal education in Michigan and Massachusetts. He lived in Springwells, and engaged in real estate transactions and building and also owned and operated a large stock farm ten miles from Detroit. He was a director of the Art Museum at Detroit, a member of the Light Guards and had an orange grove in Florida. In politics a Democrat.

EDWARD R. HUBBARD

Representative from Menominee County, 1921-2. Was born in New Brunswick, Canada, of Scotch-Irish parentage. He received his education in the Canadian public schools. He is engaged in farming and building contracting. He has always taken particular interest in rural school education, and in the past fifteen years has built more than twenty rural schools. In Marinette County, Wis., he built a rural school that has been made a model for the State of Wisconsin. Mr. Hubbard has served as Township Treasurer and on the School Board. He is married and has a family of ten children. In politics he is a Republican.

GILES HUBBARD

Senator from the Fourth District, 1865-6. Was born in Marbleton, N. Y., in 1817. He learned the cooper's trade and followed it some years. He settled at Mt. Clemens in 1837, and became a leading lawyer there. He also dealt largely in real estate. He was Prosecuting Attorney, Collector of Internal Revenue, and Presidential Elector in 1868. He was one of the founders of the Republican party. He died at Mt. Clemens, Nov. 6, 1876.

JOHN H. HUBBARD

Representative from Jackson County, 1869-70. Was born in Waterloo, N. Y., Jan. 27, 1828. He was educated at Lima Seminary, and removed to Waterloo, Mich., in 1850. For many years he was engaged in milling and farming, but later devoted his entire time to farming. He was Supervisor six years, Town Clerk three years, and held many minor offices. In politics he was a Democrat.

LEONIDAS HUBBARD

Representative from Hillsdale County, 1875-6. Was born in Portage County, O., in 1822. He acquired his education principally by his own exertions, and for several years engaged in teaching school. In 1851 he removed to South Wright, Hillsdale County. In 1856, he went to California, and engaged in mining and hunting. He returned in 1859. He held the position of Supervisor five years and Treasurer two terms. He was a farmer by occupation; in politics a Republican.

LUCIUS LEE HUBBARD

·Member of the Board of Regents of the University of Michigan, 1912—. Was born at Cincinnati, O., Aug. 7, 1849, of English descent. He was educated in the Woodward High School, of Cincinnati, Phillips' Exeter Academy, Harvard College, Boston Law School and the University of Bonn, receiving the degree of Ph. D. from the latter institution in 1886. He was instructor in minerology in the Michigan College of Mines from 1891-3, State Geologist from 1893-9, and a member of the Board of Control of the Michigan School of Mines from 1905-17. He is a member of the Geological Society of America and is the author of two books, and several papers on minerology and geology. He was married in 1875 to Frances Johnson Lambard, of Augusta, Me. He was elected a member of the Board of Regents of the University in 1911, and re-elected Apr. 7, 1919.

JAY A. HUBBELL

Member of Congress, 1875-7 to 1881-3; and Senator from Houghton, Ontonagon, Baraga, Keweenaw and Isle Royal counties, 1885-6 and 1887-8. Was born at Avon, Mich., Sept. 15, 1829; graduated at the University of Michigan in 1853; was admitted to the practice of law in 1855; removed to Ontonagon, Mich., in November, 1855; was elected District Attorney of the Upper Peninsula in 1857, and again in 1859; removed to Houghton, Mich., in February, 1860; was elected Prosecuting Attorney of Houghton County in 1861, 1863 and 1865; was engaged in the practice of law until 1870, and was identified with the development of the mineral interests of the Upper Peninsula; was appointed by the Governor of Michigan in 1876 State Commissioner to the Centennial Exhibition, and collected and prepared the State exhibits of minerals. He was elected to the 43d, 44th, 45th, 46th and 47th Congresses from the Ninth Congressional District of Michigan. He was an active Republican in politics.

SARDIS F. HUBBELL

Representative from Oakland County, 1851. Was born in Newburg, O., June 10, 1820. He attended common and select schools. He removed to Hartland, Mich., in 1835, where he assisted his father, who was a hatter, until he was nineteen. He commenced the study of medicine but abandoned it after one year. He studied law, and was admitted to the bar in 1846. He commenced practice at Milford, but removed to Howell in 1845. He served as Circuit Court Commissioner; six years as Prosecuting Attorney; was five years President of the village of Howell; and several years director and moderator of School Board. He was a Democrat in politics. He died at Milford June 16, 1887.

ISRAEL HUCKINS

Representative from Sanilac County, 1867-8. Was born in London, Ont., July 11, 1822. By occupation he was a farmer, politically a Republican. He came to Michigan in 1839, and settled at Lexington. He was Treasurer of Sanilac County from 1856 to 1860, and was Captain in the 10th Mich. Infantry from Oct. 1, 1861, to Sept. 25, 1864, when he resigned.

BRADLEY P. HUDSON

Representative from Calhoun County, 1853-4. Was born in Albany, N. Y., Apr. 28, 1826. By profession he was a lawyer, in politics a Whig. He came to Michigan in 1834; graduated at Albany Law School in 1848; located at Galena, Ill., in 1849; and at Marshall, Mich., in 1850. He died Apr. 22, 1853.

DANIEL HUDSON

Member of the Board of Regents of the University of Michigan, 1840-1. He was a retired physician of Marshall, Mich., was appointed Regent of the University, Feb. 20, 1840, to succeed Joseph W. Brown resigned. He died at Marshall shortly after the expiration of his term in 1841.

GRANT MARTIN HUDSON

Representative from the Second District, Kalamazoo County, 1905-6 and 1907-8; and member of Congress, 1923—. Was born cn a farm in Eaton Township, Lorain County, O., July 23, 1868, of English descendants. A part of his childhood was spent in that locality and a part in Clinton County, Mich. He came to Michigan when seventeen years of age and entered the high school at Pentwater, and from there he entered Kalamazoo College, graduating in 1894. In 1892 he was ordained to the Christian ministry of the Baptist denomination, first serving the church at Schoolcraft as pastor, afterwards at Dowagiac. Being compelled on account of ill health to relinquish the active duties of a pastorate, Mr. Hudson returned to Schoolcraft in 1895, and next started in the dry goods business, in a small way, at that place. Later he had a general store and attended to his farming interests. He has held the offices of Village Trustee, Village President, School Inspector and member of the School Board. In politics he is a Republican.

JONATHAN HUDSON

Representative from Wayne County, 1850. Was born in Reading, Pa., Jan. 10, 1813. His early education was academical, and his profession at first that of a Methodist minister, although his subsequent occupation was mercantile. He was a Republican in politics. He was Chaplain of the 1st Mich. Cavalry (Col. Brodhead's), 1861-4, serving during the time, however, six months' captivity in Libby Prison. He was mustered out of the service in 1864 with impaired health, and resumed business at Newton, where he died Jan. 7, 1876.

GEORGE C. HUEBNER

Representative from the First District of Detroit, Wayne County, 1889-90. Was born in Detroit, Mar. 6, 1857. He was president of the Union Credit Co. of Detroit, vice president of the same association at Grand Rapids, and secretary of Huebner Manufacturing Co., and member of the firm of Ed. Huebner & Co. He was elected to the House of 1899-90 on the Democratic ticket.

JAMES HUESTON

Senator from the Third District, 1883-4 and 1885-6. Was born near Newburg, N. Y., Feb. 22, 1833. When young he lived in Connecticut, and at the age of fifteen commenced the study of medicine. He lived in New York and Ohio, was a student in 1865 of the medical department of the University, and soon after commenced practice at Northville, where he still resided in 1887. A Democrat in politics.

HENRY HUFF

Representative from Hillsdale County, 1871-2. Was born in Jersey City, July 29, 1817. At the age of seven he removed with his parents to Ontario County, N. Y., and in 1834 settled on a farm in Fayette, Mich., where he lived until his death, Nov. 26, 1877. He was nine years Supervisor, and in 1871-2 was a Representative as a Republican.

DAVID HUGGETT

Representative from Barry County, 1893-4 and 1895-6. Was born in Sussex, England, Sept. 11, 1836. The following year he came to New York, and in 1856 to Michigan, locating with his father's family on a farm in Calhoun County. He received a district school education; was married in 1864, and three years later settled on a farm in Assyria Township, Barry County. In politics a Republican.

GEORGE HUGGETT

Representative from Eaton County, 1875 6. Was born at Pittsford, N. Y., June 27, 1842. In 1854 he removed to M:chigan, settled first in Calhoun County, where he was educated in the common schools. He enlisted in the 1st Mich. Cavalry in 1865, and served one year. In 1867 he began the study of law; in 1870 he was admitted to the bar. In 1886 he was the Mayor of Charlotte. He held the office of Circuit Court Commissioner, Justice, and Trustee of Bellevue village. In politics he was a Republican. He died at Charlotte, Nov. 15, 1915.

ARTHUR D. HUGHES

Senator, 1897-8, from the Fifteenth District, composed of the counties of Barry and Eaton. Was born of English parentage, in Oakland County, Mich., July 6, 1853. His education was acquired in the public schools, and at the Ann Arbor High School; taught school and began his business experience as a traveling salesman, in the states west of the Mississippi, which occupation he followed two years; returning he chose milling for his occupation. He was connected with the mills in Marine City, Grand Ledge and Greenville, and in 1885 he moved to Irving, Barry County, where he built a flour mill. In politics he was a Republican, but owing to the adoption of the financial plank in the Republican platform he felt justified in affiliating with the Silver Party. He held the office of Justice of the Peace.

ROSSEL B. HUGHES

Representative from Eaton County, 1871-2. Was born in Camillus, N. Y., Oct. 4, 1828. He came to Michigan in 1840. From 1850 to 1852 he was in California. He came back to Bellevue and was a merchant. In 1861 he became Second Lieutenant in the 2d Missouri Cavalry, "Merill's Horse," a regiment made up of a battalion from Michigan, one from Ohio and one from Missouri. He retired at the close of the war with the rank of Captain, and engaged in mercantile business at Bellevue. In 1875 he removed to Big Rapids, and was the station agent of the Grand Rapids & Indiana railroad in that city.

EDWIN J. HULBERT

Representative from Houghton County, 1875-6. Was born at Fort Brady, Mich., Apr. 30, 1829; educated at Michigan University, and adopted the profession of mining engineer and explorer. During the pursuit of his vocation he discovered in 1864 the celebrated Calumet & Hecla vein of copper, organized the companies and opened the mines. He died in Rome, Oct. 20, 1910.

ORVY HULETT

Representative from Macomb County, 1923—. Was born in Armada, on the farm which he now owns and which is still his home, Nov. 13, 1874, of Scotch parentage. His education was acquired in the district school and the Armada High School. He has held various township offices and for the past fifteen years has been secretary-manager of the Armada Agricultural Society. He is also secretary-treasurer of the Macomb County Farm Bureau and a director of the Armada State Bank. Mr. Hulett was elected to the Legislature on the Republican ticket, Nov. 7, 1922, without opposition.

TYLER HULL

Representative from Eaton County, 1883-4. Was born in Auburn, O., Oct. 10, 1840. He removed to Green Oak, Mich., with his parents in 1845, and to Windsor in 1850. He attended common schools and Olivet College. He taught school eleven terms, studied medicine and was a graduate of the Detroit Medical College. He held several local offices and was Assistant U. S. Marshal. In politics a Republican.

WILLIAM HULL

Governor of the Territory of Michigan, 1805-13. Was born in Derby, Conn., June 24, 1753. He graduated at Yale College in 1772; was admitted to the bar in 1775; but soon after entered the Revolutionary army as a Captain; was rapidly promoted and became inspector of the army under Baron Steuben; participated in many battles, and was thanked by Washington for his services at Morrisiana. On the organization of the Territory of Michigan, he was appointed its first Governor, Mar. 1, 1805, and held the position by re-appointments until he was superseded by the appointment of Gen. Cass in 1813. He surrendered Detroit in 1812 to the British without firing a gun, was court martialed therefor in 1814, at Albany, N. Y., and sentenced to be shot, but the sentence was remitted by President Madison. He published letters to vindicate his conduct in 1824. He died at Newton, Mass., Nov. 29, 1825.

CHARLES A. HULSE

Representative from Clinton County, 1913-14, 1915-16 and 1917-18. Was born on a farm in Greenbush Township, Clinton County, Oct. 10, 1852, of English and Scotch parentage. He was educated in the Greenbush district schools. At the age of nineteen he entered the employ of O. W. Baker, blacksmith, where he worked two years. In 1873 he enlisted in Co. A., 8th Regular Cavalry. Dec. 1, 1878, he was united in marriage to Charlotte Hatley, of St. Johns, Mich. Mr. Hulse followed the occupation of farming for two years, after which he engaged in the mercantile business. In politics a Republican. He died Feb. 19, 1918.

ELIJAH O. HUMPHREY

Senator from the Twentieth District, 1863-4. Was born in Caledonia, N. Y., Aug. 1, 1821. By occupation he was a farmer, in politics a Republican. He filled important positions, such as president and treasurer of the State Agricultural Society, and trustee of the Insane Asylum at Kalamazoo. He resided at Kalamazoo in 1887.

JAMES W. HUMPHREY

Senator, 1899-1900 and 1901-2, from the Eighth District, composed of the counties of Allegan and Van Buren. Was born in Powell, Delaware County, O., Aug. 19, 1846. He passed his childhood and youth on his father's farm, attending school and preparing for the University. He enlisted in the 26th O. Infantry, saw active service in Tennessee and Georgia, was severely wounded at Kenesaw Mountain, June 18, 1864, but recovered sufficiently to rejoin his regiment in November, to take part in the Hood campaign. At the close of the war he accompanied his regiment as part of "Sheridan's Army of Observation" in Texas. Returning home he began his studies in the Ohio Wesleyan University. He came to Michigan in 1869, and was married to Miss Beulah A. Sooy, of Dorr, Oct. 13, of that year, after which time he engaged almost exclusively in education work—six years in the village school of Dorr, ten in Wayland, one as Superintendent of Holland city schools, and one as teacher of pedagogy in Hope College. He had charge of the schools of Ottawa County one year, and was serving his sixth year as School Commissioner of Allegan County when he resigned to become a candidate for the State Senate. For eight years he conducted the summer normal classes at Hope College, and in 1894 this college conferred upon him the degree of M. A. He wrote two books for the teacher's desk—*Review Diagrams* and *Manual of Reading,*—both of which have met with favor, *Review Diagrams* passing through its fourth edition. He was much interested in Sunday school and church work. For six years he was president of the Allegan County Sunday School Association; was a member and an ordained minister of the Church of Christ (Disciples). In politics he was a Republican. Deceased.

JOHN HUMPHREY

Representative from Hillsdale County, 1845. Was born in Hopewell, N. J., May 21, 1798. He learned the trade of a blacksmith, and worked at his trade in several places. In 1828 he established a foundry at Canandaigua, N. Y., which he carried on ten years. In 1828 he married Jane Hall. In 1838 he settled as a farmer at Wheatland, Mich., where he died Oct. 15, 1870, survived by his wife, one daughter and four sons. He held many local offices, and was in politics a Democrat.

LEVI S. HUMPHREY

Representative from Monroe County, 1841-2. Was a native of Vermont, and was a settler in Michigan at a very early day. He was many years the stage coach king of the lake country, and did more to improve the breed of horses than any other man in the Northwest. He was for years engaged with Daniel S. Bacon in mercantile pursuits; was one of the commissioners to locate the Michigan Central Railroad; was register of the government Land Office at Monroe, and United States Marshal for Michigan. He was a large contractor on the Great Western and Grand Trunk railroads in Canada. He was a man of large stature, imposing personal appearance, and of gentle manners and kind heart. He died at Monroe in 1869.

WILLIAM HUMPHREY

Auditor General, 1867-75. Was born in Ontario County, N. Y., June 12, 1828. He came to Hillsdale County, Mich., with his father in 1837. He worked on a farm, received a common school education, and was a student at Spring Arbor. When old enough he engaged in teaching winters. Prior to 1861 he was for several years clerk in a store in Adrian. At the beginning of the war he enlisted in the 2nd Mich. Infantry, was appointed Captain in May, 1863, was promoted to Colonel, and in 1864 was made Brigadier-General, and was in command of a brigade at the close of the war. He was engaged in many battles and was always at the front. At the close of the war he purchased an interest in the Adrian *Watchtower*, changing it to a Republican paper. In October, 1875, he was appointed Warden of the State Prison, and held that office until 1883. In politics he was a Republican. He died Jan. 15, 1899, at his home in Adrian, Mich.

CLEVELAND HUNT

Representative from Wayne County, 1875-6. Was born in Detroit in 1835. He studied law and was admitted to the bar in 1856, and devoted himself chiefly to chancery and estate practice. He was a member of the Detroit Board of Education, and a director of the Detroit Locomotive Works and the Detroit Ice Company. In politics a Democrat.

EDMUND W. HUNT

Representative from Eaton County, 1869-70. Was born in Lodi, Mich., Oct. 14, 1828. He was brought up to farming, afterwards worked as a mechanic; settled on a farm in Benton, Mich., in 1863, enlisted as a private in the 13th Mich. and became a Lieutenant in the 1st U. S. Engineers, and served until the close of the war. He removed to Dimondale in 1866, was the first Postmaster there and a director of the Lansing branch of the Lake Shore railroad. He owned and operated flouring mills. In politics he was a Republican.

FRED A. HUNT

Representative from the First District of Wayne County, 1901-2, 1903-4 and 1905-6. Was born in Goshen, Mass., May 1, 1855. His early education was received in the high school of his native State, supplemented by a course at the Michigan State Normal and the law department of the University of Michigan.

Mr. Hunt was a student of the law office of Cutcheon & Allen of Ypsilanti, and a law partner of Ex-Congressman E. P. Allen for two years. He held a contract with the city of Detroit for lighting gasoline street lamps from 1880 to 1882. He was engaged as traveling salesman from 1884 to 1888, and collection attorney for North, Orrison Company, Kansas City, Mo., from 1888 to 1893. After 1893 he practiced law in Detroit. He held the office of Circuit Court Commissioner for Washtenaw County and was also a member of the Board of Estimates from the tenth ward of the city of Detroit for two terms. He was married in 1885. In politics a Republican.

JOHN HUNT

Justice of the Supreme Court of the Territory of Michigan, 1824-7. Was Associate Judge and his courts were held in the Lower Peninsula. Justice Hunt died in 1827 and was succeeded by Henry Chipman.

JAMES B. HUNT

Delegate to the Second Convention of Assent, 1836; and Member of Congress, 1843-5 and 1845-7. Was born in New York in 1799; received an academical education; studied law, was admitted to the bar in 1824, commenced practice in the city of New York, and was a partner of Michael Hoffman. He removed to Michigan in 1836 and located at Pontiac. He was Prosecuting Attorney of Oakland County by appointment of Gov. Barry from 1841 to 1843. He was elected Representative to Congress as a Democrat. His health failing, he returned to New York, and died at Washington, D. C., Aug. 15, 1857.

LEONARD H. HUNT

Representative from Kent County, 1887-8. Was born in Manchester, Mich., Aug. 13, 1840. He removed with his parents to Lowell, Mich., in 1855. He received a common school education and was a drug clerk until he entered the army as Second Lieutenant, 26th Mich. He was wounded and promoted to be Captain. He was druggist at Lowell in 1887. He was Supervisor and held other local offices. In politics a Republican.

GEORGE G. HUNTER

Representative from Clinton County, 1919-20 and 1921-2; and Senator from the Fifteenth District, 1923—. Was born in Ovid Township, Clinton County, Mich., Aug. 16, 1872, of English parentage. He was educated in the common schools and graduated from the Ovid High School in 1892. After studying law for two years in a law office in Ovid, he entered the law department of the University of Michigan, and in 1898 was admitted to the Michigan bar. From 1898 to 1907 he was employed in Chicago, during which time he was admitted to the practice of law in Illinois. Leaving Chicago he went to Marion, Ind., where he remained until late in 1919, when he took up his residence at St. Johns, where he is now engaged in the practice of law with the firm of Smith, Hunter & Spaulding. Mr. Hunter is married and has one son. In politics he is a Republican.

GEORGE M. HUNTINGTON

Senator from the Seventeenth District, 1875-6. Was born at Ludlowville, N. Y., Mar. 20, 1836. In 1838 his father removed to Michigan and settled in Aurelius, Ingham County. At the age of fourteen he went to Rockford, Ill., where he received an academical education. In 1855 he commenced the study of law at Mason with Hon. O. M. Barnes. Having been omitted in 1857 he formed a co-partnership with Mr. Barnes, which continued until 1866. After this he was associated with J. Barnes Root, and later with Hon. H. P. Henderson, of Mason. He continued the active practice of his profession until 1876, when he entered upon the duties of Circuit Judge. He held the office of Prosecuting Attorney for Ingham County in 1863 and 1864. He was Senator for Clinton and Ingham counties in 1874. Having been elected Circuit Judge during the session of 1875, he resigned the Senatorship. He served as Judge several years, and practiced at Mason where he lived thirty-four years, and died Apr. 2, 1889.

VICTOR F. HUNTLEY

Representative, 1909-10, from the Wexford District, comprising the counties of Lake and Wexford. Was born at Belmont, Franklin County, N. Y., June 6, 1854, of English descent. He was educated in the Grand Rapids and Big Rapids high schools and also attended Albion College for one year. Married. Mr. Huntley located in Manton, in May, 1886, coming from Jennings, Mich., where he had resided for three years. He received a medical education in Chicago and was a student in the office of W. A. Whippy, Goshen, Ind. He was Township Clerk, Village Assessor, and also served on the Board of Education; a member of the Michigan State Medical Society and the Tri-county Medical Society; also served two terms as pension examiner on the Kalkaska Board and was Postmaster nine and one-half years, after Oct. 1, 1897; a 32d degree Mason, a Shriner, and Past Master of Blue Lodge 347, Manton. In politics a Republican.

HOMER C. HURD

Representative from Jackson County, 1855-6 and 1861-2. Was born at Roxbury, Conn., Aug. 23, 1808. He came to Michigan and purchased a farm in 1832, and settled upon it in 1833, in the township of Burlington, Calhoun County, where he resided until his death, Feb. 12, 1873. He was a prominent citizen and was Town Clerk, and Supervisor from 1844 to 1853. He was first a Whig and Free Soiler, but a Republican after 1854.

JOHN S. HURD

Representative from Jackson County, 1857-8. Was born at Gorham, N. Y., June 2, 1815. He settled at Lima, Mich., in 1836, and removed to Jackson in 1841. He held the offices of Supervisor and Alderman, and was a leading business man, engaged in mercantile, live stock and real estate business. He built the Hurd House at Jackson. In politics he was a Whig until 1854, then a Republican. He died Aug. 7, 1880.

WILLIAM H. HURLBUT

Representative from Van Buren County, 1869-70 and 1871-2. Was born Aug. 25, 1819, at Richland, N. Y., at the age of sixteen years he went to work at Hamilton,

N. Y., where he stayed five years. In 1840 he located a farm in Bangor, Van Buren County. He afterwards exchanged for a large tract of land and became identified with all improvements in that part of the county. He was Register of Deeds from 1851 to 1853. He was first a Democrat, then a Republican, then a member of the National or Greenback part.

WILLIAM A. HURST

Representative from the First District of Wayne County, 1901-2. Was born in Courtright, Ont., Apr. 8, 1862. He came to Michigan when eight years of age and received his education in the common school at St. Clair, supplemented by a course at the Detroit College of Law. He was Circuit Court Commissioner in 1896 and elected again in 1898; president of the Alger Republican Club in 1896; secretary of the Republican County Committee in 1893 and president of the State League of Republican Clubs in 1899. Married. In politics a strong Republican. He was elected to the Legislature of 1901-2, on the general legislative ticket.

ERASTUS HUSSEY

Representative from Calhoun County, 1850; and Senator from the Thirteenth District, 1855-6. Was born in Scipio, N. Y., Dec. 5, 1800. Brought up a farmer he became a teacher; removed to Plymouth, Mich., in 1824, and was a farmer until 1836; removed to Battle Creek in 1838 and was a merchant until 1847; then editor of the *Michigan Liberty Press*, an anti-slavery paper; had charge of the "underground railroad" and made it a success, sometimes taking forty slaves through in a body; was a delegate to the Buffalo Convention of 1848; was County Clerk, and president of the Convention at Jackson in 1854, when the Republican party was organized and named; was Mayor of Battle Creek, and delegate to the Republican National Convention in 1880. He died Jan. 21, 1889, at Battle Creek.

BENJAMIN W. HUSTON

Delegate from Tuscola County to the Constitutional Convention of 1867; Representative from Tuscola County, 1869-70 and 1871-2; and Senator from the Twenty-second District, 1879-80. Was born in Rochester, N. Y., Mar. 5, 1831. In 1836 he came to Michigan with his father, who settled at Canton. As a young man he worked at farming and taught school, and attended the Ypsilanti Seminary several terms. He studied law and was admitted to the bar in 1854. In 1855 he commenced practice at Vassar. He was appointed Prosecuting Attorney and elected to that office, and was Circuit Court Commissioner on the Democratic ticket. In 1862 he went into the service as Captain in 23d Mich., saw active service, became Major, and served until January, 1865. In 1866 he was elected Circuit Court Commissioner. He was speaker pro tem in 1869, 1871-2, and served as chairman of the judiciary committee. He was delegate to the Republican National Convention in 1872, and was several times actively supported for a nomination to Congress. A Democrat until 1860, then a Republican.

ALLEN HUTCHINS

Delegate from the Third District to the Constitutional Convention of 1835; and Representative from Lenawee County, 1835 and 1836. Came to Adrian, Mich., from Orleans County, N. Y., as early as 1832-3. He was a lawyer, and probably the first who settled in Lenawee County. He was an active, prominent business man. In politics he was a Democrat.

J. WESTON HUTCHINS

Senator, 1913-14, from the Tenth District, comprising the counties of Hillsdale and Jackson. Was born in Pulaski Township, Jackson County, June 14, 1854. His father was a native of Pennsylvania, of German-English descent; his mother was a native of Western New York, her father having come from Massachusetts. Mr. Hutchins attended the public schools in Pulaski and Hanover townships and was for a short time a student at Hillsdale College; taught school winters and worked on the farm in the summer seasons until his marriage, Nov. 24, 1880, to Sarah E. Lambert, of Pulaski; he then engaged in farming. From 1898 to 1906 he was a Farmers' Institute Lecturer during the winter months, mostly in Michigan but with one season in Wisconsin and a part of three different years in Rhode Island as college extension worker for the Agricultural College of that State. A member of the Methodist Episcopal Church and of the Grange. In 1906 he was elected secretary of the Michigan State Grange. In politics a National Progressive.

LOOMIS HUTCHINSON

Representative from Calhoun County, 1869-70. Was born in Smyrna, N. Y., Apr. 21, 1818. He worked on his father's farm, receiving a common school education and taught school winters, working on the farm summers. In 1844 he came to Michigan and bought a farm in Emmet, Calhoun County. He was Supervisor of Emmet ten years. He was first a Whig, then a Republican.

BENJAMIN F. HYDE

Representative from Wayne County, 1851. Was born at Ferrisburg, Vt., Sept. 24, 1819. He was of the well known Hyde family who gave their name to Hyde Park in Vermont. He came to Detroit in 1846, studied law, was admitted to practice, and was for a time a law partner with Hon. Geo. Jerome. His tastes were more for politics than law. He was a Democratic Alderman in 1856. His political career terminated with his election as Judge of the Recorder's court, November, 1863. He filled the office only from Jan. 16, to May 16, 1864, when ill health compelled his retirement. He died July 8, 1865.

CHARLES W. INGALLS

Representative from Ionia County, 1853-4. Was born in Bristol, N. H., Apr. 21, 1812. He came to Michigan in 1837. Most of the time he was a resident of Ionia County; resided at Harbor Springs in 1887. He served as Supervisor and Postmaster. By occupation he was a farmer, politically a Democrat.

DANIEL F. INGALLS

Representative from Oakland County, 1840. Came to Michigan about 1835, and to Oxford, in 1837. Politically he was a Whig. He was Supervisor of Oxford in

1838-41, and Town Clerk in 1844. He removed to Ohio and died there. He built a foundry at Oxford with Benjamin Knight, and a cannon cast at their foundry was used at many celebrations in Oxford.

JOHN N. INGERSOLL

Representative from Chippewa County, 1849; and from Shiawassee County, 1869-70; and Senator from the Twenty-eighth District, 1861-2. Was born May 4, 1817, in North Castle, Westchester County, N. Y. He moved to New York City when young, and lived for a time with an uncle in Connecticut. At the age of thirteen he commenced to learn the printer's trade in New York City, and worked with Horace Greeley, with whom he was always on familiar terms. In 1837 he came to Detroit, was a compositor in the *Free Press* office, then foreman in the office of the *Advertiser*. In 1839 he became editor of the Mt. Clemens *Statesman*, then published the St. Clair *Banner* from 1842 to 1846. He then started the Lake Superior *News*. He was a clerk in the Legislature and in 1848 secretary of the Senate. He then became editor of the Detroit *Daily Bulletin*, and of the *Hesperian*, a monthly magazine, organ of the Odd Fellows; was manager of the Detroit *Daily Times;* editor and publisher of the Rochester, N. Y., *Tribune;* then from 1858 to 1862 editor and publisher of the Owosso *American;* then started the Shiawassee *Journal*, He was a Democrat until 1858, then a Republican. He was four times Mayor of Corunna; was Justice of the Peace, Postmaster, and United States Assessor. He was a leading Odd Fellow, and held the highest office in the grand lodge and the grand encampment, representing Michigan in California and Maryland. For the last years of his life he was blind. He died at Corunna, May 13, 1881.

FREDERICK FREMONT INGRAM

Delegate in the Constitutional Convention of 1907-8 from the Third District, Wayne County. He was born in Barry County, of English descent. His father's parents were pioneers, settling in Barry County in 1835, where they secured land and became farmers. Mr. Ingram received a common school education. In 1889 he was married at Hudson, Wis., to Miss Laura Mayo, a native of Kentucky. When a young man Mr. Ingram was a telegraph operator for a short time. He then learned the drug business while clerking in a drug store in Hastings. On his twenty-first birthday he became the proprietor of a drug store in Ypsilanti, and after that travelled six years over the United States as a commercial traveler; was proprietor of a manufacturing establishment in the drug line in Detroit and vice president of the National Manufacturing Perfumers' Association and active in numerous other commercial organizations. He was appointed and served as a member of the Detroit Public Lighting Commisson for six years.

SILAS IRELAND

Representative from Berrien County, 1877-8. Was born Nov. 10, 1818, in Concord, O. He received his education mostly by his own exertions, and came to Michigan in 1839. In 1842 he removed to a farm near Berrien Springs. He held the office of Supervisor in Berrien Township five years. He was Superintendent of the Poor for twelve years. By occupation he was a farmer and surveyor; in politics a Republican.

JOHN D. IRVINE

Representative from Mackinac County, 1850 and 1851. His postoffice address was Mackinac. (Further data not obtainable).

ROBERT IRWIN, JR.

Member of the Legislative Council from Brown and other counties, 1824-5 to 1830-1. (Further data not obtainable).

WILLIAM W. IRWIN

Representative from Wayne County, 1853-4. Was a native of Pennsylvania, born in 1811. He was Supervisor of Springwells, 1851-5. By occupation he was a farmer; in politics a Democrat. He died in 1855.

NELSON G. ISBELL

Senator from the Second District, 1849-50 and 1850-1; and Secretary of State, 1859-61. Was born in Charleston, N. Y., Feb. 18, 1820. He received an academical education and settled at Howell, Mich., in 1844, engaging in mercantile business. He was Justice, soon became a farmer, and was Supervisor, Town Clerk, and Senator. He was one of the first board of control of the State Reform School. From 1861 to 1869, except a short interval, he was Collector of Customs at Detroit. In politics he was a Whig, a Republican after 1854. In 1848 he was the only Whig in the Senate. He was a resident of Lansing for several years prior to his death. In 1869 Mr. Isbell purchased the Lansing House and conducted it for many years. He died July 21, 1878, at Lansing and was buried at Howell, Mich.

EDWIN B. ISHAM

Senator from the Thirty-second District, 1873-4. Was born May 9, 1819, in the town of Canaan, Conn. He received a common school education. In 1868 he emigrated to Michigan, and settled in Negaunee, Marquette County. Occupation was mining and iron manufacture.

FRIEND IVES

Representative from Allegan County, 1850. Was of English descent, born in Plymouth, Conn., Dec. 22, 1790. At twenty-one he traveled through the South selling clocks. He made his first home at New Lebanon, N. Y., and afterward at Medina, O. He bought a farm at Gun Plain, Allegan County, in 1833. His wife was Harriet Warner, born July 17, 1792, and who died Mar. 17, 1867. He filled several town offices and was elected Associate Judge of Allegan County on the Democratic ticket. He was a farmer and died Feb. 22, 1874.

SAMUEL GIBBS IVES

Representative from Livingston County, 1855-6 and 1857-8. Was born in Lansing, Tompkins County, N. Y., Dec. 21, 1812. He settled in Unadilla Township, Livingston County, Mar. 17, 1835. He served as Justice of the Peace for sixteen years.

For many years he was a member of the Methodist Episcopal Church. He was the First Republican Legislator elected from Livingston County and re-elected in 1856, also served at extra session. In 1848 he was commissioned Captain of Livingston Troop 2d Battalion National Guards by Governor Epaphroditus Ransom. In 1872 he was Presidential Elector on the Republican ticket. Governor John J. Bagley appointed him Commissioner for the building of the asylum for the insane at Pontiac, in 1874, also a member of the board of control of the same institution in 1875. During the Civil War he was enrolling officer for his district from 1861 to 1865, and active in raising men for the prosecution of the war. He removed to Chelsea in 1876 and was a member of the Common Council and President of the village. For nearly two decades he was president of the Chelsea Savings Bank. He died at Chelsea Aug. 7, 1894.

WILLIAM E. IVORY

Representative from Lapeer County, 1905-6, 1907-8, 1917-18 and 1919-20. Was born in the township of Hadley, Lapeer County, Mich., Oct. 14, 1866, of American and English parents. He secured his education in the district school and the Hadley High School. He was a member of the Board of Supervisors and served as chairman. He conducted a private banking business in Hadley for a number of years. A member of several orders including the F. & A. M., O. E. S., Bay City Consistory, A. A. S. R., Eif Khurafeh Temple, A. A. O. N. M. S. and the Grange. Married. In politics a Republican.

ANDREW JACKSON

Representative from Cheboygan, Mackinac, Chippewa and Schoolcraft counties, 1879-80. Was born Oct. 29, 1844, in Henry County, O. He received a high school education at Toledo; entered the army in 1861; was promoted gradually to the rank of First Lieutenant and Adjutant, and resigned on account of wounds in August, 1863. He re-enlisted as a private in 1864, and served through the war, receiving the rank of Brevet Major. In 1872 he removed from Louisville, Ky., to Sault Ste. Marie, Mich. He was chairman of the Board of Supervisors in 1877. Occupation was government and railroad contractor. Politics Democratic.

CHESTER E. JACKSON

Representative from Clinton County, 1897-8. Was born at Racine, Wis., Nov. 19, 1845. His early education was acquired in the public schools, and at the age of sixteen he took charge of the homestead, working on the farm summers and attending the Racine High School winters. He was appointed United States Consul to Antigua, British West Indies, in 1878, and held the position twelve years. On account of the good record he made in the consular service he was not removed during Cleveland's first administration; returned in 1890, and settled at Ovid, Mich., where he became identified with the Clinton County Fruit Company, of Ovid, of which he held the position of secretary and treasurer, at the same time managing a farm. In politics a Republican. He was elected President of Ovid in 1895.

JOSEPH JACKSON

Representative from Monroe County, 1835-6. His postoffice address was Perry's Grove. (Further data not obtainable).

JOHN W. JACKSON

Representative from the Second District of Saginaw County, 1917-18 and 1919-20. Was born at Hamilton, Ont., Jan. 15, 1858, of English parents. His education was acquired in the public schools of Arkona, Lampton County, Ont. He commenced work in a general store at the age of fourteen years. He came to Michigan in 1880, locating at Chesaning, where he engaged in the bakery business for two years. In 1887 he entered the general merchandise business and continued in the same until 1914, when he retired from active business. Treasurer of the Che- saning Milling Company and of the Chesaning Home Telephone Company. Married. In politics a Republican. He served two years as Supervisor.

SAMUEL P. JACKSON

Representative from the First District of Monroe County, 1889-90 and 1891-2. Was born in Londonderry, N. H., in 1817. His father moved to the adjoining town of Manchester in 1819. From that time to 1845 he had the advantages of farm life education aided by the common schools, the *New Hampshire Patriot* and the *New York Tribune*, each representative of the political parties of the olden times. In that year he commenced mercantile life in the city of Manchester, from which he retired in 1874. He served on the school board in that city and was twice elected to the Legislature of his native state, and to the Constitutional Convention in 1876. In 1883, after a residence of sixty years in one town, he removed to Monroe, Mich., and with his sons engaged in the manufacture of paper and con- tributed somewhat to the success of the Monroe Manufacturing Company. In politics a Democrat. He was elected to the House of 1889-90 on the Democratic ticket and re-elected to that of 1891-2.

WILLIAM B. JACKSON

Representative from the First District of Wayne County, 1891-2. Was born in Thompkins County, N. Y., Jan. 28, 1831, and came to Michigan in 1848. Married. He was formerly a school teacher; practiced law in Oakland County from 1853 to 1873, removing to Detroit in October, 1873, where he continued his law practice. He was elected to the House of 1891-2 on the Democratic ticket.

JAMES J. JAKWAY

Representative from the Second District of Berrien County, 1913-14. Was born at Benton Harbor, May 20, 1863, of Scotch and French parentage. He was edu- cated in high school and at the Michigan Agricultural College. Married. He taught school eight years and engaged in fruit-growing twenty years. He served as Supervisor and also presided as chairman of the board. In politics a Democrat.

DELBERT C. JAMES

Representative from the First District of Wayne County, 1919-20. Was born Apr. 11, 1872, in the township of Maple Grove, Saginaw County, Mich., of English parentage. He received his early education in the public schools of that township. He moved to Saginaw in 1890 where he attended the International Business Col- lege. In 1895 he removed to Detroit and engaged in the fire insurance business,

In addition to this work he studied law and was graduated from the Detroit College of Law in 1903. He began the practice of law with Arthur W. Kilpatrick, under the firm name of James & Kilpatrick, which partnership was dissolved in 1910. Engaged in the fire insurance business, being president of the Delbert C. James Company. From 1898 to 1908 he was secretary of the Orion Light and Power Company of Orion, Mich., also treasurer of the Lake Orion Resort Association of the same place. Married. In politics a Republican.

W. FRANK JAMES

Senator from the Thirty-second District, 1911-12 and 1913-14; and member of Congress, 1915-17 to 1923—. Was born at Morristown, N. J., May 23, 1873, of Cornish descent. He was educated in the Hancock High School and at Albion College. He served as Treasurer of Houghton County, Alderman and Mayor of Hancock. Mr. James is married and has four children, two boys and two girls. He has been engaged in the real estate and insurance business since 1898. He participated in the Spanish-American War, being a member of Co. F, 34th Michigan. In politics he is a Republican.

JULIUS M. JAMISON

Senator, 1895-6, from the Sixteenth District, composed of the city of Grand Rapids, except the tenth and eleventh wards. Was born on a farm in Wayne County, O., Apr. 30, 1854; was educated in the Indiana Normal School, commercial college and University of Michigan, graduating from the law department of the latter in 1880; made three trips to Europe, writng as foreign correspondent, and in 1882 settled at Grand Rapids, where he engaged in the practice of law. In politics a Republican.

OSCAR A. JANES

Senator, 1895-6, from the Sixth District, composed of the counties of Branch, Hillsdale and St. Joseph. Was born in Johnston, Rock County, Wis., July 6, 1843; attended district school winters and worked on farm summers; later attended college. After two months in college he enlisted in the 4th Mich. Vol. Infantry., and participated in the Battles of the Wilderness, Spottsylvania, North Ann, Cold Harbor and the battles around Petersburg, Va.; lost his left arm as the effect of a wound received at Jerusalem Plank Road, Va., June 22, 1864; returned to Hillsdale College, from which he graduated in 1868; entering a law office, he was admitted to the bar in 1871 and engaged in the practice of law in Hillsdale. In politics a Republican. He held several offices of public trust, including City Clerk, City Attorney, Alderman, Circuit Court Commissioner and Judge of Probate, served on the staff of Governor Alger, was deputy commander of the G. A. R. of Michigan in 1883; and was trustee and auditor of Hillsdale College.

WILLIAM LOUIS JANUARY

Representative from the First District, Wayne County (Detroit), 1897-8. Was born in Green County, O., July 9, 1853. He was educated in the public schools of his native State, and later in the University of Michigan. He took an elective course in the literary department, afterwards transferred to and graduated in the law department, class of '83. While in the law department he acted as private secretary for ex-Governor Felch, who was at that time Tappan Professor of law in the University. After graduating he was admitted to the bar, and at once located in Detroit, where he continued in the practice of his profession.

ADOLPH JASNOWSKI

Representative from the First District, Detroit, of Wayne County, 1889-90. Was born at Detroit, Jan. 4, 1856. By occupation a cigar manufacturer. In politics a Democrat.

WILLIAM JAY

Senator from the Seventh District, 1863-4 and 1865-6. Was born at Pennington, N. J., July 22, 1820. He was a clerk two years in New York City; then became one of the firm. He was a merchant at Trenton, N. J., filled several city offices, was a member of the New Jersey Legislature in 1855, and a delegate to the first Republican National Convention in 1856. He settled on a farm at Whitmore Lake, Mich., in 1859. In 1869 he removed to Emporia, Kan., and was Mayor of that city. In 1887 he was president of the Citizens' Bank of Emporia, and a prominent and successful business man.

FREDÉRICK ALBERT JEFFERS

Member of the State Board of Education, 1915—. Was born at Farmington, O., July 24, 1869. He was taken, when an infant, to Connecticut, where he was left an orphan at five years of age. He came to Jackson County, Mich., in 1875, where, in the township of Napoleon, he received his elementary education. He taught school on the border of Jackson and Washtenaw counties; attended Michigan State Normal College at Ypsilanti, from which he graduated in 1891, and from which he later received the degree of Master of Pedagogics. After graduation he went to Atlantic Mine as Superintendent of the Adams Township Schools which position he has held for thirty years, living for the past twelve years at Painesdale, where the new township high school is located. He has been a school examiner for Houghton County for twenty-five years; was an instructor in the summer schools of the Northern State Normal School for more than ten years, teaching history, civics, public school administration and other subjects. He has also done institute work, besides filling most of the offices of the Upper Peninsula Educational Association, including that of president. Mr. Jeffers is married. He has been prominent in fraternal circles and is a 33rd degree Mason. He was elected a member of the State Board of Education Apr. 5, 1915, and re-elected Apr. 4, 1921.

HENRY H. JENISON

Senator from the Fourteenth District, 1883-4. Was born in Eagle, Clinton County, Mich., Sept. 25, 1842, where he resided. Occupation was farming; in politics probably a Democrat.

WILLIAM F. JENISON

Representative from Clinton County, 1863-4. Was born in Byron, N. Y., Dec. 19, 1812. He attended common schools, and the college at Brockport, N. Y. He taught school seven years; settled as a farmer in Eagle, Mich., in 1837. He was Supervisor ten years, held many town offices, and was for four years Sheriff of Clinton County. He kept a hotel for thirty years. He was a director of the Ionia and Lansing railroad, secured $10,000 subscription, and gave two years of his time to secure the road. In politics he was a Democrat. He died at Eagle, June 14, 1897.

BALDWIN JENKINS

Delegate from the Twelfth District to the Constitutional Convention of 1835. Was born at Fort Jenkins, Pa., and moved with the family to Ohio and then to Michigan. He was the first Justice of the Peace in Cass County. He was noted for his remarkable memory and intimate knowledge of his section. He was one of the first County Judges. He died at his daughter's in Berrien Center in 1847.

BELA W. JENKS

Senator, 1905-6 and 1907-8, from the Twentieth District, comprising the counties of Huron and Sanilac. Was born in Essex County, N. Y., of Welsh parentage, July 18, 1849. A resident of Michigan since 1860, he received his education in the public schools of St. Clair; a successful business man and engaged in various business enterprises. In 1874, he became a member of the firm of J. Jenks & Co., was secretary and treasurer of J. Jenks & Co., Inc., from 1882 to 1902, secretary of the Huron Milling Co., and treasurer of the Mihlethaler Co., Ltd., from 1902. He held the office of Treasurer of Sand Beach Township and Trustee of Sand Beach Village.

BELA W. JENKS

Senator from the Twenty-fourth District, 1869-70 and 1871-2. Was born at Crown Point, N. Y., June 6, 1824. He was educated at Charlotte, Vt., and settled at St. Clair, Mich., in 1848. He became a successful merchant, and dealt in lumber and real estate. He was a Republican, and held several local offices.

CASSIUS M. JENKS

Representative from the First District of Jackson County, 1903-4. Was born at Marshall, N. Y., Sept. 15, 1850. His education was acquired in the Grass Lake public schools. A lawyer by profession and one of the leading criminal lawyers in central Michigan. A widower. A Democrat in politics.

JEREMIAH JENKS

Senator from the Twenty-third District, 1875-6. Was born in Sullivan County, N. H., Dec. 13, 1810. He received a common school education. He removed from Essex County, N. Y., to Michigan in 1854, and resided in this State. He was Inspector of Customs from 1861 to 1864, and was also Deputy Collector of Internal Revenue two years. He held various other offices of public trust. By occupation he was a lumberman; in politics a Republican.

JOHN S. JENNESS

Representative from Lapeer County, 1865-6; and Senator from the Twenty-fifth District, 1867-8. Was born at Newbury, Vt., Apr. 27, 1813. He was bred a farmer, then a clerk, and for thirty years a merchant. He opposed railroad aid in 1867, none of the thirty bills passing over the veto of Gov. Crapo. He was President of the village of Almont in 1866-7. He resided in Detroit in 1887. In politics he was a Whig and Republican.

JOHN S. JENNESS

Representative from the First District of Washtenaw County, 1867-8. His post-office address was Ypsilanti. (Further data not obtainable).

WILLIAM JENNEY

Senator from the Twentieth District, 1877-8; and Secretary of State, 1879-83. Was born at Poughkeepsie, N. Y., June 18, 1837. In 1843 he removed with his parents to Mt. Clemens, Mich. He graduated at Brown University in 1859. In 1861 he went out as Captain of a company in the 9th Mich. Infantry, served four years, and became a Major. He became a lawyer at Mt. Clemens, also engaged in farming. He was Colonel of State Militia and aid-de-camp. He was a Republican in politics.

IRA JENNINGS

Representative from Livingston County, 1839 and 1847. Was a farmer and an early settler in the town of Green Oak, in 1836. He was Supervisor of the town in 1844, and served eight terms in that capacity. Deceased.

HIRAM JENNISON

Representative from Ottawa County, 1853-4; and Delegate from Ottawa County to the Constitutional Convention of 1867. Was born in Canton, N. Y., May 11, 1813. He was a lumberman and farmer by occupation; a Democrat in politics. He came to Michigan in 1834. He was the first settler in Georgetown, Ottawa County, and for eleven years was Supervisor of the township. The village of Jenisonville, in Georgetown Township was named after him.

PETER JENSEN

Representative from Delta County, 1909-10, 1911-12, 1913-14, 1919-20 and 1921-2. Was born Nov. 14, 1863, in the Province of Schleswig, Denmark, of Danish parents. He was educated in the common schools and came to America in 1881, locating at Escanaba. In 1893 he engaged in the general fish business under the firm name of Hansen & Jensen, which firm is in active business at the present time. He has also been interested in the general oil business since 1913. Mr. Jensen is married and has four sons and two daughters. He is a member of the F. & A. M. and the M. W. of A. He served four years on the City Council and has held the office of Township Highway Commissioner. In politics he is a Republican.

DAVID HOWELL JEROME

Senator from the Twenty-seventh District, 1863-4 and 1865-6, and from the Twenty-sixth District, 1867-8; member of the Constitutional Commission of 1873; and Governor of Michigan, 1881-3. Was born at Detroit, Mich., Nov. 17, 1829, the son of Horace and Elizabeth Rose (Hart) Jerome. His father died when he was an infant, and his mother removed to central New York, but in 1834 returned to Michigan and settled in St. Clair County, where Governor Jerome was educated. In 1853 he went to California and engaged in mining. In 1854 he settled in Saginaw and engaged in mercantile pursuits. In 1862, under appointment of Governor Blair, he raised the 23d Mich. Infantry in a short time, and was commandant of camp with the rank of Colonel, until the regiment went to the field. In 1865 and 1866 he was military aid to Governor Crapo, and in 1865 was appointed on the State Military Board, of which he was a member and president until 1873. In 1862 he was elected to the State Senate, and served six years, being chairman of the committee on state affairs throughout that time. He opposed municipal railroad aid and supported the vetoes of those measures. He served several years on the board of Indian Commissioners; was active in building the railroad from Saginaw to St. Louis, and long its president; also president of the Saginaw Street Railroad Company; also trustee of the Michigan Military Academy. In 1859 he married Lucy Peck, daughter of E. W. Peck, of Pontiac. He was a Republican in politics; in religion an Episcopalian. He died at Watkins, N. Y., Apr. 23, 1896.

JAMES D. JEROME

Representative from the First District of Wayne County, 1905-6 to 1921-2. Was born in Detroit Oct. 29, 1875. Both of his parents were also born in Detroit. He received his early education in the public schools of that city, graduating from the high school in 1894. He entered the literary department of the University of Michigan, and subsequently studied in the law department receiving his degree of B. L. in 1898. He immediately took up the practice of law in Detroit. In politics he is a Republican. He was first elected to the Legislature in 1904; served continuously from that time to and including the session of 1921-2.

GEORGE JEROME

Senator from the Second District, 1855-6 and 1857-8. Was born in Tompkins County, N. Y., in 1824, coming with his parents to Michigan in 1827. His father, Horace Jerome, in connection with Thos. Palmer, built the first lumber mill in the West on Pine River in St. Clair County. Except some four years spent at the East in pursuing his education, he lived continuously in Michigan after 1827, and in Detroit after 1844, having previously to that time lived in St. Clair County. He was admitted to the bar in Detroit in 1848. During his senatorial term he was chairman of the judiciary committee. He was the general attorney of the Detroit, Grand Haven & Milwaukee railway under all changes of management from 1859 to 1887. He was Collector of Customs at Detroit, 1869 to 1875, when he was relieved at his own request. He was one of the commissioners on the plan of the city, 1857 to 1869, and held other positions of trust. Politically he graduated from the Whig into the Republican party. He died Mar. 6, 1897.

TIMOTHY JEROME

Representative from Saginaw County, 1857-8. Was born in Trumansburg, N. Y., Feb. 16, 1820. His occupation was a lumberman; politics first Whig, then Republican. He came to Detroit in 1828, was an active business man and lumberman in St. Clair County until 1853, then removed to Saginaw, where he was a manufacturer of lumber and salt, also engaged in steamboating, mining in the western territories, and in cattle ranches.

WILLIAM F. JEROME

Representative from Hillsdale County, 1915-16. Was born at Andover, England, Dec. 15, 1863. He was educated in the Bothwell and Toronto, Ont., schools and the Detroit Institute. He engaged for many years in the ministry, his first actual work being at Mio, Mich. He afterwards removed to Carsonville and later to Croswell, where he had charge of a church at Lexington.. He was rector of St. Mark's Church, at Marine City, removing from there to Detroit, where he was rector of St. George's Church and Chaplain of St. Luke's Hospital for five years. He then removed to Algonac because of ill-health and was rector of St. Andrew's Church for five years and was elected Mayor of Algonac for one term. In 1895 he was appointed a delegate to represent the I. O. O. F. in Europe. During 1913 and 1914 he was grand chaplain of the I. O. O. F. In politics a Republican.

AUGUSTUS JEWELL

Senator, 1893-4 and 1895-6, from the Seventh District, composed of the counties of Cass and Berrien. Was born on a farm in La Grange Township, Cass County, Mich., Dec. 3, 1845; acquired his early education in the Dowagiac High School and Baptist College at Kalamazoo; studied law and was admitted to the bar but never engaged in the practice of the profession. His home was in Dowagiac, but for a number of years his time was occupied to a considerable extent in attending to western investments. In politics a Republican. Deceased.

CHARLES A. JEWELL

Representative from the First District of Lenawee County, 1869-70. His post-office address was Medina. (Further data not obtainable).

EDWARD JEWELL

Representative from Kent County, 1865-6 and 1867-8. Was born in Greene County, N. Y., Dec. 13, 1818. By occupation he was a farmer, in politics a Republican. He came to Michigan in 1855, and was four terms Supervisor of Solon, Kent County. His residence in 1887 was Petaluma, Calif.

JAMES FRANKLIN JEWELL

Representative from the Second District of Houghton County, 1921-2 and 1923—. Was born at Cornwall, England, July 6, 1867, of English parentage. He came to Houghton County, Mich., when fourteen years of age, his education being acquired in the public schools in England and night schools in Houghton County. Mr. Jewell is married and has two children, a boy and a girl. In politics he is a Republican.

JOSEPH B. JEWELL

Representative from Newaygo County, 1877-8. Was born in Grattan, N. Y., in 1826. From 1836 to 1856 he lived in Allegany County, N. Y., working the last ten years as a carpenter and joiner. He settled on a farm in Newaygo County in 1856, and was also engaged in lumbering. Twice he served as president of the County Agricultural Society, several years as Supervisor of Dayton, and held other positions. In politics he was a Republican.

GEORGE W. JEWETT

Delegate from Washtenaw County to the Second Convention of Assent, 1836. Was born in Connecticut, and came to Ann Arbor, Mich., in 1830 from Ohio. In politics he was a Democrat, by profession a lawyer. He was also Justice of the Peace. He died at Ann Arbor before 1860.

WILLIAM JIBB

Senator, 1897-8, from the Fifth District, composed of the counties of Lenawee and Monroe. Was born in England, Oct. 20, 1843, and came to America with his parents in May, 1851, locating at Genesee, N. Y., for two years, where he acquired his early education in the public schools, supplemented by a high school course; then coming to Michigan, locating on a farm in Hudson Township, Lenawee County, where he again attended the public school winters and worked on the farm summers. At the outbreak of the Civil War he enlisted in Co. B, 2d Mich. Infantry, but not being of age his father objected and he was taken out, but having an earnest determination to take part in the defense of his country, he again enlisted in Co. F, 4th Mich. Infantry, and was again objcted to by his father, and again taken out. On Aug. 24, 1861, he again enlisted in Co. F, 11th Mich. Infantry, where he served over three years with General George H. Thomas; was wounded twice. Returning, he worked at farming and blacksmithing until 1876, when he was elected Collector and Marshal of the village of Morenci; was appointed Deputy Sheriff, in which position he served for eight years; was Deputy Oil Inspector but resigned to take the position of Superintendent of the Michigan Stone & Supply Company quarry, located at Maybee, Monroe County. He was twice commander of the G. A. R. post at Adrian, Mich., and senior vice commander of the state department one year; a member of the F. & A. M. and of the K. of P., and past captain of U. R. K. of P. In politics a Republican.

JOHN W. JOCHIM

Secretary of State, 1893-4. Was born in Motala, Sweden, Oct. 12, 1845. He acquired his education at the schools of Wadstena and Linkoping. The following four years he was engaged as bookkeeper for a firm in Stockholm. In 1869 he came to America, locating at Ishpeming, Mich., where he began work for a mining company; like most beginners, he first found a place upon the stock piles of iron ore. Within a year he had obtained a position as clerk for a responsible hardware firm. In 1874 he started in the hardware business for himself, in which he persisted with great success. In politics a Republican. He served as Alderman and member of the School Board of Ishpeming for a number of years. He received the unanimous nomination for Secretary of State in the Republican convention of 1892, and was elected to that office. He served to Mar. 20, 1894.

AUGUSTUS S. JOHNSON

Representative from Oakland County, 1845. His postoffice address was Springfield. (Further data not obtainable).

CHARLES C. JOHNSON

Representative from Mecosta County, 1909-10. Was born at Plainwell, Allegan County, Mich., Oct. 3, 1864, of American parentage. He was educated in the common schools. Mr. Johnson was married in 1888. He moved to Mecosta in 1886 and in 1905-6 served as Township Clerk, and in 1907-8 was Supervisor of his township. In politics a Republican.

DANIEL F. JOHNSON

Representative from Oakland County, 1840. Was born in Canton (now Cairo), N. Y., Jan. 29, 1801. In 1834 he settled on a farm in Groveland, Oakland County. He was Supervisor in 1836, and in 1851. In 1840 he was elected by the Whigs. He became a Republican in 1854.

DANIEL S. JOHNSON

Senator from the Twenty-ninth District, 1853-4. Was born in Haverstraw, N. Y., in 1821, and was a capitalist and lumberman. He came to Michigan in 1846, founded Zilwaukie, Saginaw County; was an extensive ship timber dealer in New York City, and also a leading lumberman in the Saginaw valley from 1847 to 1858. He died Aug. 6, 1860.

DAVID JOHNSON

Representative from Jackson County, 1845; and Justice of the Supreme Court, 1852-7. Was born in Sangerfield, N. Y., Oct. 20, 1809. He removed to Genesee County, N. Y., in 1824, studied law, and was admitted to the bar in 1824. He went to Painesville, O., in 1836, came to Michigan in 1837, and settled in practice at Jackson in 1838. He was in the first rank of lawyers; was Prosecuting Attorney, School Inspector in 1839; Circuit Judge of Jackson County, 1846-50; and Democratic candidate for Judge of the Supreme Court, 1857. He practiced at Jackson forty-eight years. He had a strong constitution, and active temperament, was decided in his convictions, well versed in law, and a leader at the bar. He stamped his impress upon the early history of Michigan as one of the ablest of the pioneers. He died July 28, 1886.

ELIAS F. JOHNSON

Member of the State Board of Education, 1898-1901. Was born June 24, 1860, at Van Wert, O., and brought up on a farm. His primary education was obtained at the common schools, and he subsequently attended the National Normal University, and graduated from the Ohio State University with the degree of B. S. To enable him to graduate from college, Mr. Johnson engaged as a table waiter, and worked at various odd jobs during vacations, and also taught in rural school districts for several terms. After graduating he was elected Superintendent of Schools of Van Wert for five years; was appointed Surveyor of his native County, and served until elected to the Ohio Legislature in 1885. The county was Democratic, but he was elected by a handsome majority, and served until the close of 1887. In 1888 he came to Michigan, and in 1890 was appointed to a professorship in the law department of the University of Michigan. In May, 1898, he was appointed a member of the State Board of Education by Gov. Pingree, and was nominated for the same position (short term) in 1898 by the Republican State Convention, and elected for the term 1899-1902. He resigned in 1901 and was succeeded by Patrick H. Kelley.

HIRAM JOHNSON

Representative from the First District of Shiawassee County, 1891-2. Was born in Venice in that county, on Sept. 7, 1839. His parents came to Michigan in 1834 and first settled in Livingston County, where they resided until 1837, when they bought a farm in Venice and moved on to it the same year, being the second family in town. Mr. Johnson's early years were spent on the home farm, he received the benefit of the common district school until he attained his majority, and was preparing to go away to school to finish his education when the war broke out. He was one of the first to go to his country's call, enlisted the 28th day of August, 1861, as a private of Co. "H", T. B. Stockton's First Mich. Independents, afterwards known as the 16th Mich. He served through the Peninsular campaign and was wounded three times in the Battle of Gaines' Mill, Va., June 27, 1862. In the second Bull Run fight he was also wounded. He was discharged upon the expiration of his term of service, Aug. 18, 1864. He then returned to his home in Venice, where he resided, engaged in farming and bee culture. He served as Supervisor of his town for six consecutive years; held most of the minor offices of the town; was defeated in 1888 by Dr. J. B. F. Curtis for the Legislature; and was candidate for Sheriff on the Greenback ticket in 1868.

JAMES JOHNSON

Representative from St. Joseph County, 1883-4 and 1885-6. Was born in Summerset, O., Feb. 22, 1814; removed to St. Joseph County, Mich., Apr. 18, 1832. His occupation was farmer, lumber manufacturer, and dealer in real estate; in politics a Democrat.

J. EASTMAN JOHNSON

Member of the Board of Regents of the University of Michigan, 1858-70. Was born at Alstead, N. H., Dec. 6, 1805. He was admitted to the bar of St. Joseph County, Mich., in 1837, and practiced law until his death, which occurred at Niles,

Mar. 14, 1888, at the age of 83 years. He was Probate Judge of St. Joseph County for twelve years; and was a Presidential Elector in 1884. Politically he was a Republican. He was a distinguished Mason, was long secretary of the grand lodge, and had also been grand master.

LUKE S. JOHNSON

Representative from Huron County, 1891-2. Was born in Avon, Lorain County, O., Dec. 30, 1847. He was raised on a farm until fifteen years of age, when he entered the service, from which he was discharged at the close of the war. He was in the 43rd O. Infantry. He came to Michigan in 1869 and worked in the mills at Saginaw for five years, then moved to Caseville, Huron County. He was elected to the House of 1891-2 on the Democratic ticket.

MILO N. JOHNSON

Representative from the Third District of Wayne County, 1919-20, 1921-2 and 1923—. Was born June 30, 1867, on a farm in Northville Township, Wayne County, Mich. His father died when he was ten years of age and his mother when he was sixteen. Finding himself without a home, he went to live with a neighboring family doing chores for his board and schooling. He graduated from the Northville High School. He was engaged in the mercantile business six years, after which he worked in the County Treasurer's office for the same length of time. He was Postmaster ten years. Mr. Johnson is married. In politics he is a Republican.

OREN G. JOHNSON

Senator, 1921-2 and 1923—, from the Twenty-first District, comprising the counties of Lapeer and Tuscola. Was born July 30, 1872, at Mayville, Mich., of English and Danish descent. He was educated in high school and the Detroit College of Medicine. After completing high school he taught for one year, and then entered the railway service, being promoted to engineer at the age of 25 years. Later he entered the Detroit College of Medicine, graduating in 1905, and has since practiced medicine at Fostoria. In July, 1918, he applied for a commission in the Medical Corps, U. S. Army, and served overseas one year with the Saumer Artillery Hospital and Base Hospital 103, being honorably discharged from such service July 26, 1919. Mr. Johnson is married. In politics he is a Republican.

RANSOM C. JOHNSON

Senator, 1895-6, from the Thirteenth District, composed of the counties of Genesee and Livingston. Was born in Mundy Township, Genesee County, Mich., July 12, 1849; educated at district school and Flint High School; studied law, and in 1876 engaged in the practice of that profession in the city of Flint. In politics a Republican. He served as member of the Board of Health and Alderman of his city; an active member of the I. O. O. F., serving as chairman of grand lodge two years.

SAMUEL JOHNSON

Representative from Cass County, 1877-8 and 1879-80. Was born July 7, 1839, in Springfield, N. Y. He received an academical education, and graduated at Cazenovia Seminary, N. Y. He removed to Michigan in 1864. He was elected Township Clerk six years; Supervisor of Wayne Township three years; County Superintendent of Schools in 1873. He was a teacher, but engaged in farming and the breeding of fine stock, in which he was deeply interested. In politics he was a Republican. He was a professor of practical agriculture in the State Agricultural College at Lansing, 1879-89; secretary of the State Agricultural Society, 1891; and president of the Farmers' Mutual Fire Insurance Co., of Cass County, 1900-12.

SIMEON M. JOHNSON

Representative from Ionia, Kent and Ottawa counties, 1843. His postoffice address was Grand Rapids. (Further data not obtainable).

THOMAS EDWARD JOHNSON

Member of the State Board of Education, 1917-19; and Superintendent of Public Instruction, 1919—. Was born near Thetford, Ont., Mar. 10, 1883, and removed to Michigan with his parents when he was six years of age. His father is a Methodist minister and has held numerous charges throughout the eastern part of the State. Mr. Johnson received his education in the public schools, graduating from the Flint High School in 1900. After teaching country schools for a time he entered the University of Michigan but left there in his second year, and later completed his college work at Alma College, where he received his degree of A. B. He has been Superintendent of Schools at Montrose, Dryden, Stockbridge, Onaway and Coldwater. In addition to his school work he has been active in civic, religious and fraternal affairs, and is a member of several Masonic bodies, the B. P. O. E., and K. of P. Mr. Johnson was married Aug. 7, 1907, to Mildred M. Milks, of Saginaw County. He has two children, a son, Stanley H., and a daughter, Patricia H. On Sept. 12, 1917, he was appointed by Governor Sleeper a member of the State Board of Education to succeed Thomas W. Nadal, resigned; and on Apr. 5, 1919, was appointed by Governor Sleeper to fill the vacancy in the office of Superintendent of Public Instruction caused by the death of Fred L. Keeler, which occurred Apr. 4, 1919. The Republican State Central Committee, on Apr. 4, 1919, substituted the name of Mr. Johnson for that of Mr. Keeler as a candidate for the office of Superintendent of Public Instruction for the term ending June 30, 1921. He was elected Apr. 7, 1919, and re-elected Apr. 4, 1921, and again re-elected Apr. 2, 1923.

WELCOME W. JOHNSON

Representative from Kent County, 1877-8. Was born at Williamston, Mass., Oct. 26, 1817. His parents removed to Oneida County, N. Y., in 1819. He came to Michigan in 1835. He received a common school education. He served several years as Town Treasurer in Dundee, Monroe County. In 1849 he united with the Michigan conference as preacher. He resided near Grand Rapids in 1887, where he had a farm, and preached occasionally. In politics he was a Republican. Deceased.

CARLOS J. JOLLY

Representative from the Third District of Houghton County, 1923—. Was born at Atlantic Mine, Mich., July 8, 1888, of English parents. He attended the public school of Adams Township, graduating from high school in 1906. He is also a graduate of the Michigan College of Mines, of Houghton, and of the Detroit College of Law. In 1915 he started in the practice of law at South Range and was appointed Assistant Prosecuting Attorney of Houghton County in 1917, holding that position until he returned to private practice four years later. He has been secretary of the Houghton County Republican Committee since 1920. Mr. Jolly is married and has two children. He was elected to the Legislature Nov. 7, 1922, without opposition.

COULTER W. JONES

Representative from Midland County, 1923—. Was born at Lono, Ark., May 13, 1881. His education was acquired in district schools and the Arkansas Agricultural College and University. To defray expenses while attending the university, he worked in spare time on the agricultural experiment station, caring for the greenhouses. For two years he was assistant chemist in the experiment station and for the past eighteen years has been a manufacturing chemist. In 1907 he was married to Miss M. Eola Gardner, of Ypsilanti, and they have three children. Mr. Jones is a Democrat and served on the Midland City Council.

DE GARMO JONES

Senator from the First District, 1840-1. Was born in Albany, N. Y., in 1787, and came to Detroit as a sutler in the army under Gen. Harrison in 1813, and subsequently settled there. He established a store and became a leading business man, and at a later date was prominent in the development of the Lake Superior copper mines. He was Mayor of the city in 1839, several times Alderman, and took an active interest in business, church and educational affairs, and left a valuable estate. He was on the board of the Detroit French College. He erected the first plaster mill in the State. He was a Whig in politics. He died in 1846.

EDWARD H. JONES

Representative from the First District of Cass County, 1861-2. His postoffice address was Constantine. (Further data not obtainable).

EDWARD L. JONES

Representative from Jackson County, 1850. Was born at Chesterfield, Mass., Jan. 1, 1814. He removed to the State of New York and became a clerk. In 1833 he became clerk in the Commercial Bank of Cleveland, O., and in 1838 cashier of the Merchants and Mechanics' Bank of Monroe, Mich., which failed in 1840. He removed to Jackson, became a druggist, and sold out in 1849. From 1852 to 1859 he was in the banking business at Cleveland, O., then in same business at Milwaukee, Wis., until 1863, then in the Sanitary Commission at Atlanta and Chattanooga until the close of the war; organized national banks at Atlanta and Columbus, Ga., but retired from business in 1879. He resided at Atlanta in 1887. He was first a Whig, then a Republican.

GEORGE JONES

Representative from Eaton County, 1853-4. Was born in Manchester, N. Y., Aug. 18, 1816. He came with his father's family to Novi, Mich., in 1831. He was Captain of militia in 1838. He removed to Oneida, Mich., in 1843, and settled near Grand Ledge, where he resided in 1887. He served nine years as Supervisor, four years as Town Clerk and was Justice two terms. In politics he was a Democrat, by occupation a farmer.

GEORGE C. JONES

Representative from Ontonagon County, 1865-6. Was born in Orleans County, N. Y., Oct. 1, 1829. By occupation he was a lawyer, politically a Republican. He came with his father in 1843 to Springfield, Mich., where he lived until 1853. He studied law and settled in Ontonagon in 1854. He removed to Appleton, Wis., in 1869, where he resided in 1887.

GEORGE N. JONES

Senator, 1903-4 and 1905-6, from the Eleventh District, comprising the County of St. Clair. Was born at Bellevue, Mich., in 1859, of English ancestors. He was educated in the normal school of Canada. Married. He engaged in the grocery business for years. In politics a Republican.

GEORGE W. JONES

Territorial Delegate in Congress, 1835-7. Was a delegate until Michigan became a State, with his residence in Wisconsin, which was then a portion of the Territory of Michigan. (Further data not obtainable).

GILMAN C. JONES

Senator from the Seventeenth District, 1861-2. Was born at Hopkinton, N. H., July 26, 1820, was brought up on a farm and became a teacher. He settled on a farm in Cass County in 1844, taught school, was a clerk, in 1850, became a merchant at Dowagiac, where he resided in 1887, and was a dealer in wool. He was President of the village several time, repeatedly a Supervisor. He was a Republican, but after the war affiliated with no political party.

JOHN JONES

Representative from the Second District of Marquette County, 1893-4 and 1895-6. Was born in Detroit, June 20, 1841. At the age of seven years he moved with his parents from Detroit to Eagle River, Keweenaw County, and from there to Sault Ste. Marie. He acquired a common school education and in 1871 went to Ishpeming, Marquette County, where he was in the employ of the American Express Company; also engaged in the retail of coal and wood. In politics a Republican. He held the offices of Alderman and Mayor of the city of Ishpeming.

JOHN D. JONES

Representative from St. Clair County, 1877-8. Was born in London, Ont., Jan. 17, 1825. He removed to DeKalb County, Ill., in 1838, thence to St. Clair County, Mich., in 1843, and resided in Brockway. He engaged in lumbering and farming.

He received a common school education. He was Supervisor for six terms, Justice twenty-six years, School Director twenty-three years, and held all town offices, except Treasurer and Clerk, for a number of terms. He was Postmaster at Merrillsville for many years. In politics he was a Republican.

JOHN H. JONES

Representative from Branch County, 1865-6 and 1867-8; and Senator from the Thirteenth District, 1869-70, and from the Tenth District, 1875-6. Was born at Hopewell, N. Y., Apr. 27, 1828, and was educated at the Genesee Wesleyan Seminary at Lima, N. Y. He afterwards became a teacher. In 1854 he settled on a farm at Quincy, Mich. For several years he was Supervisor. He voted to sustain Gov. Crapo's position on railroad aid bills, and was one of the five Senators who voted against the passage of the railroad law. He resided at Quincy in 1887.

LOSS E. JONES

Representative from Jackson County, 1847. His postoffice address was Brooklyn. (Further data not obtainable).

RICHARD JONES

Representative from Barry County, 1867-8. Was born in Otsego County, N. Y. He came to Michigan in 1848, and lived at Battle Creek in 1887. By occupation he was a farmer, in politics a Republican. He was Supervisor and Town Clerk.

WALTER C. JONES

Delegate to the Constitutional Convention of 1907-8 from the Seventh District, Cass County. Was born at London, Monroe County, in 1875, of English descent. He received his education in the district schools, Union City High School, and studied law in the office of Judge Chester, of Hillsdale, Mich. He was admitted to the bar in 1897, and actively engaged in the practice of his chosen profession at Marcellus, Mich. Married.

WHITNEY JONES

Representative from Eaton and Ingham counties, 1845 and 1846; Auditor General, 1855-9; and Senator from the Twenty-second District, 1859-60. Was born in Chautauqua County, N. Y., May 2, 1812. He moved from New York to Michigan in 1839. He was a country merchant, and took up his residence in Delta, Eaton County. He was Supervisor and Postmaster; Postmaster of Lansing, 1849-53; United States Assessor for the Third District, comprising the counties of Washtenaw, Jackson, Calhoun, Eaton and Ingham, 1862-6; Postmaster at Lansing, 1868-71; and Treasurer of Ingham County, 1883-7. He was a leading Whig until 1854, when he helped organize the Republican party at Jackson, and was the first nominee of that party for Auditor General. He supported Greeley in 1872, and eventually became a member of the Greenback party. In 1887 he removed to Alameda, Calif. He died at Lansing, Mich., Feb. 29, 1892.

WILLIAM H. JONES

Representative from the First District of Wayne County, 1915-16 and 1917-18. Was born at Detroit, Mich., Apr. 28, 1855. He was educated in the Detroit public schools and the high school. After working for some time for his father, who was in the shoe business, he entered into partnership with his brother in the same line of business, where he remained until 1891, when the partnership was dissolved. On account of ill-health, he removed to a small farm in Pontiac and in 1893 he returned to Detroit where he secured employment as a street car conductor. He was married in 1889 to Ida L. Gray. In politics a Republican.

WILLIAM T. JONES

Representative from Mecosta County, 1885-6 and 1887-8. Was born in Watertown, Ont., Mar. 10, 1846, and was a resident of Michigan after 1873. By occupation he was a lumberman. Mr. Jones held various offices of public trust, among which were Township and Village Treasurer, Supervisor and Superintendent of Poor, Village President, and president of the Mecosta County Agricultural Society. He was elected Representative on the Republican ticket.

THOMAS JEFFERSON JOSLIN

Member of the Board of Regents of the University of Michigan, 1864-8. Was born at Cohocton, Steuben County, N. Y., Apr. 29, 1829, son of Thomas and Mary Ann (Sleeper) Joslin. His paternal ancestors came from Wales and settled in Rhode Island in colonial times, on the mother's side he was descended from the Pennsylvania Quakers. He received his early training in the public schools. After completing a high school course he took up special theological studies under the direction of the Detroit Conference of the Methodist Episcopal Church, on the completion of which he was ordained a minister in that denomination and continued in active service until retired in September, 1903. His labors have been confined to the Detroit Conference, where he has held some of the most important pastoral charges. He held the office of presiding elder for fourteen years and was delegate to the General Conference in 1880. He was elected to the Board of Regents of the University in April, 1863, and entered upon the duties of the office Jan. 1, following. He drew the four year term, and at the end of that period did not seek re-election. He was married Dec. 24, 1849, to Susan Willover, of Holly, Mich., and they had five children.

CHAUNCEY JOSLYN

Representative from Washtenaw County, 1844; and member of the State Board of Education, 1851-5. Was born at Throopsville, N. Y., June 28, 1813. He was educated at Temple Hill, Livingston County. After leaving school he engaged in teaching for five years, when he began the study of law. In 1837 he removed to Ypsilanti. He was appointed member of the State Board of Education Apr. 2, 1851, in the place of George N. Skinner, deceased; elected Nov. 2, 1852, for a term of two years. He was Judge of Probate, Washtenaw County, in 1852. In 1853 he was appointed one of the commissioners to construct the St. Mary's falls ship canal. He was Mayor of Ypsilanti in 1858. Mr. Joslyn was elected Judge of the Twenty-second Judicial Circuit in April, 1881, on the Democratic ticket, and served until the close of 1887. He died at Ypsilanti, Oct. 31, 1889.

JAMES F. JOY

Representative from Wayne County, 1861-2; and member of the Board of Regents of the University of Michigan, 1882-6. Was born at Durham, N. Y., Dec. 20, 1810. He graduated at Dartmouth in 1835, and subsequently at the Cambridge Law School. In his junior years he was a teacher, and instructed classes at Dartmouth, after graduating. He settled at Detroit in 1836, studied law, and became a partner of Geo. F. Porter, under the firm name of Joy & Porter. As a lawyer he was eminently succesful. He early gave attention to banking, land and railroad interests, and his law practice was largely in those directions. In 1846 he was a principal agent in organizing the Michigan Central Railroad Company, and he was many years connected as attorney, counselor, director and president. He built the Chicago, Burlington & Quincy, and the Hannibal & St. Joseph railroads, and in connection purchased for those companies 800,000 acres of valuable land. The building of the Chicago & East Michigan; the Jackson, Lansing & Saginaw; Detroit, Lansing & Northern; and Detroit & Bay City railroad, was greatly indebted to him for aid. Later he directed his attention to the Wabash, opening up a new route between Detroit and St. Louis. His success was largely due to the confidence eastern and foreign capitalists had in his sagacity and financial ability. Formerly he was a Whig, later a Republican. He was a Regent of the University from Jan. 1, 1882, to Dec. 21, 1886, when he resigned. He died at Detroit, Sept. 24, 1896.

ETHEL JUDD

Representative from Hillsdale County, 1855-6 and 1857-8. Was born in Herkimer County, N. Y., Apr. 24, 1807. By occupation he was a farmer, in politics a Republican. He settled on a farm in Adams, Mich., in 1837, and built the first church and school house in the town, also the first six frame dwelling houses. He was five years Supervisor. He raised a company for the 10th Mich. Infantry in 1861, and went south with them, but returned in 1862 from ill health. He died Feb. 11, 1883.

GEORGE E. JUDD

Representative from the Second District of Kent County, 1889-90. Was born in Massachusetts, Mar. 23, 1838. In the War of the Rebellion he served in the 3d Mich. Infantry. His occupation farming. He was elected to the House of 1889-90 on the Republican ticket.

MARTIN KALLANDER

Representative from the Ontonagon District, 1887-8, comprising the counties of Baraga, Isle Royal, Keweenaw and Ontonagon. Was born in Sweden, Sept. 28, 1852. He landed in this country in 1872 and went direct to Eau Claire, Wis., and continued a resident of that State until July, 1885, when he located at Bessemer, Mich. His principal occupation was that of railroad and timber contractor. He was running the largest boarding house at Bessemer in 1887 and was a leader of his fellow countrymen in that region. Mr. Kallander was nominated for Representative by the Labor party and then endorsed by the Democrats.

JOHN KALMBACH

Representative from the First District of Washtenaw County, 1911-12. Was born in Sylvan Township, Washtenaw County, Mich., Sept. 30, 1861, of German parents. He was educated in the district schools and in 1902 graduated from the Detroit College of Law. In the same year he was admitted to practice and opened an office in the village of Chelsea, where he built up an extensive practice. He was married Nov. 25, 1887. He helped organize the Farmers' and Merchants' Bank at Chelsea, and became one of its directors. In politics a Republican.

HARRY J. KANE

Senator, 1905-6 and 1907-8, from the Twenty-fifth District, comprising the counties of Isabella, Mecosta, Newaygo and Osceola. Was born in Middlesex County, Ont., Canada, Sept. 20, 1860, of Irish ancestors. He acquired his education in the common schools of Middlesex County, Canada, and came to Michigan in 1880 and engaged in farming. Mr. Kane continued on the farm until elected Sheriff of Isabella County in 1890, which office he held four years. In 1895 he engaged in the mercantile business at Mt. Pleasant. In politics a Republican.

JACOB KANOUSE

Representative from Livingston County, 1861-2. Was born in Morris County, N. J., Aug. 23, 1817. He came to Michigan at an early day and settled in Livingston County as a farmer. He was a resident of Chohoctah Township; held many offices, among them, Justice, Judge of Probate four years, and was special commissioner to take the vote of the several Michigan regiments during the war. He was a Representative as a Republican.

LUTHER C. KANOUSE

Representative from Livingston County, 1901-2. Was born in the township of Burns, Shiawassee County, Mich., June 29, 1842. His education was obtained in the common schools, supplemented by one year at the State Normal School. He was in the Civil War, enlisting in Co. D, 6th Mich. Cavalry, and was wounded three times. He was promoted to a First Sergeantcy in September, 1863, and was made First Lieutenant in 1864. He belonged to General George A. Custer's Mich. Cavalry Brigade and was present at the surrender of General Robert E. Lee at Appomattox, Va., and was also on the grand review in Washington, D. C., in May, 1865. In June, 1865, he was sent to Wyoming to fight the Indians, being mustered out of service in the following November at Fort Leavenworth, Kan. He returned to Michigan and engaged in farming. Married. In politics a Democrat. He held the offices of Supervisor, Township Treasurer and Highway Commissioner.

EDWARD KANTER

Representative from Wayne County, 1857-8. Was born in Breslau, Germany, in 1824, and came to this State in 1842. From 1847 to 1867 was in active mercantile life, then was at the head of a banking house, of which he was president. He was for five years an Inspector of the Detroit House of Correction, four years a member of the Poor Commission, and was a member and treasurer of the State Commission to the New Orleans exposition in 1885. In politics a Democrat, four years a member of the State Committee and eight years of the National, twice on the electoral ticket, twice a candidate for State Treasurer, and delegate to the National Convention in 1876. He was president of a number of German societies.

FREDERICK KAPPLER

Representative from the Second District of Houghton County, 1909-10, 1911-12, 1913-14 and 1919-20. Was born in Negaunee, Mich., Nov. 16, 1866, of German parents. He acquired his education in the public schools of Negaunee and Lake Linden. He was in the employ of the Calumet and Hecla Mining Company for twenty-four years, leaving their service to engage in farming. Married. A member of the Grange, the K. of C., and the German Aid Society. He served two years as Alderman. In politics a Democrat.

HORATIO S. KARCHER

Senator from the Twenty-eighth District, 1923—. Was born in Clinton County, Michigan, June 7, 1868. His early education was obtained in the district school and later he attended the St. John's High School and M. A. C. He removed to Rose City in 1887 and was employed as Superintendent of the Rose City High School for ten years. For the past thirty years he has been engaged in the general store and drug business. Mr. Karcher is married and has one son and one daughter. He has held various public offices, having been School Examiner, Judge of Probate, Mayor, Postmaster, Supervisor and Clerk.

JONATHAN KEARSLEY

Member of the Board of Regents of the University of Michigan, 1838-53. Was born in Virginia in 1786, and graduated at Washington College, in 1811. In 1812 he was appointed First Lieutenant of the 2d artillery corps, and during the war held the positions of Captain, Major and Assistant Adjutant General. He was engaged in many battles, and lost a leg at Fort Erie. In 1817 he was appointed receiver of taxes in Virginia and in 1819 became a receiver of the U. S. Land Office in Detroit, which he held for thirty years. He was a member of the Michigan Historical Society in 1828. He was Mayor of Detroit, and Judge of the Recorder's Court. A Democrat in politics. He died at Detroit, Aug. 31, 1859.

ROBERT C. KEDZIE

Representative from Ingham County, 1867-8. Was born in Delhi, N. Y., Jan. 28, 1823. He graduated at Oberlin College in 1847, and from the medical department of the Michigan University in 1851. He settled at Kalamazoo, but in 1852 removed to Vermontville, where he remained until 1861, when he entered the army as surgeon of the 12th Mich. Infantry. On his return he settled at Lansing, and was professor of chemistry in the State Agricultural College after 1863. He was for many years a member of the State Board of Health, and its president. He was president of the State Medical Society in 1874, and was a member of various societies, and has a national reputation as the author of valuable papers on health, hygiene and agriculture. He was a Representative as a Republican. He died at his home Nov. 7, 1902.

FRED LOCKWOOD KEELER

Superintendent of Public Instruction, 1913-19. Was born July 4, 1872, on a farm in Sharon Township, six miles from Grass Lake, Washtenaw County. He attended a district school, and later the Grass Lake High School, from which he graduated in 1889. He entered the University of Michigan in the fall of 1889, graduating from there in 1893. In 1894 he did graduate work, also doing assistant work in the University of Michigan. He took three summer terms of work in the University of Chicago. Mr. Keeler was married in 1894 to Miss Bertha Bliss, of Ann Arbor, and had two children. In the fall of 1894 he was appointed principal of the high school at Houghton, which position he held for one year. In the summer of 1895 he was placed at the head of the department of science at the Central Michigan Normal School at Mt. Pleasant and continued in that work for thirteen years. He was appointed Deputy Superintendent of Public Instruction by Superintendent L. L. Wright in 1908 and continued to hold that office until Nov. 15, 1913, at which time Governor Ferris appointed him Superintendent of Public Instruction to fill the vacancy caused by the resignation of Luther L. Wright. Mr. Keeler devoted his life to educational work. He was a Mason and a member of the DeWitt Clinton Consistory. In politics he was a Republican. At the convention held at Grand Rapids, Feb. 12, 1915, he was unanimously nominated for Superintendent of Public Instruction and was elected Apr. 5, 1915, and re-elected Apr. 2, 1917. He died Apr. 4, 1919.

LUCIUS KEELER

Representative from the Second District of Cass County, 1865-6. His postoffice address was Union. (Further data not obtainable).

MINER S. KEELER

Senator, 1895-6, from the Fifteenth District, comprising the counties of Barry and Eaton. Was born in Middleville, Barry County, Oct. 18, 1862; educated in Middleville High School, and Grand Rapids Business College. At the age of sixteen years, he engaged in general merchandising, which was his chief occupation; interested in the Keeler Brass Manufacturing Company; a director of the Hastings City Bank and of the State Bank of Middleville, and had various other interests in the village and county. In politics a Republican. He held the offices of Village Trustee and Village President.

RICHARD KEELER

Representative from Calhoun County, 1877-8. Was born in Ridgefield, Conn., Mar. 1, 1825. He moved to New York in 1834, and thence to Michigan in 1847. He received a common school education, and was Town Clerk of Pennfield for twelve years. By occupation he was a farmer, in politics a Republican.

WALTER A. KEEN

Representative from Isabella County, 1915-16. Was born at Winn, Isabella County, Mich., June 3, 1881, of Scotch and German parentage. He was educated in the common schools and the Central Michigan Normal School. He taught school for several years and was County Clerk of Isabella County. Married. In politics a Democrat.

ANDREW J. KEENEY

Representative from Monroe County, 1863-4. Was born in the State of Pennsylvania, Feb. 26, 1819. By occupation he was a farmer and stock raiser, and was largely engaged in lake fisheries. He was a member of the Michigan Pioneer and Historical Society. Politically he was a Democrat. He was Supervisor, Justice, and held other positions. He came to Michigan with his father's family in 1828, and lived in Erie, Mich. Deceased.

EDWARD R. KEEP

Representative from the First District of Calhoun County, 1899-1900. Was born on a farm in the town of Homer, Cortland County, N. Y., May 27, 1848, and received his early education at the common schools of his native town, attending school winters and farming summers. He subsequently attended the Cortland Academy, in Homer village, about two years, and taught school nearly six years; then engaged in the saw and planing mill business with his brother-in-law for three years. He removed to Michigan in 1875, and engaged in the retail lumber and coal business in Tekonsha.

EDWIN W. KEIGHTLY

Member of Congress, 1877-9. Was born in Van Buren, Ind., Aug. 7, 1843. He received an academical education and graduated at the law department of the University in 1865. He engaged in law practice in St. Joseph County, and in 1872 was elected Prosecuting Attorney. He was appointed Judge of the 15th Circuit to fill a vacancy, and in 1875 was elected to that position for six years. In 1876 he was elected Representative to Congress from the Fourth District as a Republican, and served one term. He was engaged in the practice of his profession in 1887.

WILLIAM A. KEITH

Representative from Berrien County, 1883-4. Was born in Indiana, Feb. 26, 1843, and was educated in that State and in Illinois. He served in the 10th Ill. Cavalry from September, 1861, to January, 1866, rising from private to Captain. Then he settled as a farmer in Berrien County, Mich. Politically he was a Greenbacker.

LOUIS L. KELLEY

Representative from the Clare District, 1905-6 and 1907-8; and Senator, 1913-14, and 1915-16, from the Twenty-eighth District, comprising the counties of Alcona, Arenac, Clare, Crawford, Gladwin, Iosco, Ogemaw, Osceola, Oscoda and Roscommon. Was born near Rutland, Vt., Dec. 29, 1848, of American parents. He came to Michigan in 1861, attended the Ann Arbor High School, clerking and teaching until the fall of 1872, when he entered the medical department of the University of Michigan. He graduated in March, 1875, and located at Farwell, Mich., May 1, and actively engaged in the practice of his profession. Mr. Kelley was married in 1871. He held the offices of Village Trustee, Village President, Supervisor and several terms chairman of the Board of Supervisors. In politics a Republican.

MARK N. KELLEY

Representative from the First District of Lapeer County, 1885-6 and 1887-8. Was born at Pontiac, Oakland County, Oct. 17, 1831. Mr. Kelley removed with his parents, in 1844, to Lapeer County, where he resided. He received a common school education, and at an early age began farming, which he followed until 1868, when he engaged in mercantile business. In 1873 he built an elevator at Metamora, still continuing farming, and also engaged in the produce business. He held the office of Supervisor and Township Treasurer. In politics a Republican.

PATRICK HENRY KELLEY

Member of the State Board of Education, 1901-5; Superintendent of Public Instruction, 1905-7; Lieutenant Governor, 1907-9 and 1909-11; and member of Congress, 1913-15 and 1921-2. Was born in Cass County, Mich., Oct. 7, 1867, of Irish parentage, and removed to Watervliet, Berrien County, when eight years of age. He obtained his education in the public schools, the Valparaiso, Ind., Normal School, from which he graduated in 1887, and the Michigan State Normal School, at Ypsilanti, from which institution he received a teacher's life certificate. Mr. Kelley has held the position of principal of schools at Galien and Hartford; and served five years as Superintendent of Schools at Mt. Pleasant. In 1889 he entered the law department of the University of Michigan and received his degree in June, 1900. Since September of that year he has been engaged in the practice of law at Lansing and Detroit. In politics he is a Republican. In April, 1901, he was appointed a member of the State Board of Education to fill vacancy caused by the resignation of E. Finlay Johnson, and was elected to the same position in 1902. Two years later he was elected Superintendent of Public Instruction. In 1906 he was elected Lieutenant Governor, and served two terms. Mr. Kelley is married and has three children, one son and two daughters. He was elected Congressman-at-large in 1912, and two years later was elected to Congress from the Sixth District; was re-elected in 1916, 1918 and again in 1920.

ROBERT J. KELLEY

Representative from Alpena and other counties, 1877-8. Was born in Monroe County, Mich., Sept. 3, 1844. He received an academical education, and in September, 1862, enlisted in Co. K, 5th Mich. Cavalry, and served until the close of the war. He took a commercial college course in Detroit, graduated from the law department of the University in 1868, and commenced practice at Bay City, but after 1869 practiced at Alpena.

SAMUEL HARLAN KELLEY

Representative from Berrien County, 1905-6 and 1907-8. Was born at Marion, Grant County, Ind., Mar. 27, 1861, of Scotch-Irish parentage. When five years of age he moved with his parents to Savannah, Mo., attended the public schools of Savannah, and the Missouri State University, 1878 to 1880; taught district school in 1881, and was appointed clerk in the railway mail service for eight months in 1881. In 1882 he was appointed adjudicator of claims in the U. S. Treasury at Washington, which position he held until November, 1885, when he resigned to become chief clerk of the U. S. Land office at Wakeeney, Kan. While in Washington he studied law and was graduated from the Columbian University Law School in 1884. In November, 1886, he resigned his position in the land office and purchased the *Scott County News*, a Republican paper, and moved to Scott City, Kan., where he practiced law and conducted his newspaper. In 1889 he moved to St. Joseph, Mo., and practiced law until 1893, when he came to Benton Harbor, Mich., where he practiced law. Married. In politics a Republican. For twelve years he was a member of the county committee, and chairman of the city committee five years. He was elected to the Legislature of 1905-6 from the First District, and re-elected from the Second District, Nov. 6, 1906.

CHARLES B. KELLOGG

Representative from the County of St. Joseph, 1893-4. Was born in White Pigeon, Mich., Feb. 6, 1840. His early education was acquired at the common schools of White Pigeon, and when fourteen years of age he began work for a mercantile firm in White Pigeon. He continued in this occupation for fourteen years for firms in White Pigeon, Mich., Mishawaka and Middlebury, Ind., and Constantine, Mich. He purchased a farm on Pigeon Prairie, two miles east of Constantine, where he made his home, being engaged in farming and stock raising. Mr. Kellogg was the eldest son of Charles Kellogg, one of the founders of the White Pigeon village and a member of the firm of Kellogg Bros., merchants and merchant millers, originators of the scheme of navigation on the St. Joseph River. He was elected to the House of 1893-4 on the Democratic and People's party tickets.

EDWIN KELLOGG

Representative from St. Joseph County, 1850. Was born in Sheffield, Mass., Feb. 17, 1803. He settled at White Pigeon in 1830. He was a merchant at Schoolcraft and Sturgis, and one of the firm of Kellogg & Brothers at White Pigeon engaged in merchandise and flour milling. He removed to Kansas in 1854, where he was a farmer until his death, Jan. 6, 1876.

FRANCIS W. KELLOGG

Representative from Kent County, 1857-8; and member of Congress, 1859-61 to 1863-5. Was born in Worthington, Mass., May 30, 1810; received a limited education, and removing to Michigan, entered into the business of lumbering at Kelloggsville, Kent County. As a Republican he was elected to the Legislature of 1857. During the rebellion he raised six cavalry regiments for the service. In 1865 President Johnson appointed him Collector of Internal Revenue, for Alabama, and he was afterwards elected to Congress from that State. He died at Alliance, O., November, 1878.

JOHN R. KELLOGG

Representative from Allegan County, 1838; and member of the State Board of Education, 1855-61. Was born in New Hartford, N. Y., in 1793, was a clerk as a young man, and from 1818 to 1836, a successful merchant at Marcellus, N. Y. He settled at Allegan, Mich., in 1836, where he resided until his death in 1868. He was elected Nov. 7, 1854, a member of the State Board of Education for a term of six years. He was an intimate friend of Seward and Cass, and kept up a friendly correspondence with them through life. He was largely interested in lands and acquired a competence; often a delegate to State conventions, he had great weight in party councils. He was a Republican in politics.

OLIVER KELLOGG

Representative from Washtenaw County, 1837. Was born in Sharon, Conn., Oct. 2, 1797. He came to Detroit, July 4, 1832, and with an ox team conveyed his family to the western part of Washtenaw County. He purchased a large tract of land in Sharon. Held various positions of public trust, was Associate Judge under the county court system, Postmaster, Justice, etc. In politics a Democrat. He sold his farm and moved to Ann Arbor in 1856, where he died Feb. 24, 1859.

ROBERT RANSOM KELLOGG

Member of the Board of Regents of the University of Michigan, 1844-5. Was born at Hudson, N. Y., May 18, 1813. He received the degree of Bachelor of Arts from the University of the City of New York, in 1835. He was ordained to preach in 1838, his first charge being in Brooklyn, N. Y. In 1840 he removed to Michigan and was for some years pastor of the Presbyterian Church in Romeo. Mar. 11, 1844, he was appointed Regent of the University in place of DeWitt C. Walker resigned, and served out the term, retiring in 1845. During the years 1848-52 he was pastor of the Second Presbyterian Church in Detroit, and from 1853 to 1855 he was secretary of the American and Foreign Christian Union. From 1861 to 1866 he was pastor at Milford, Pa., and died there Sept. 25, 1866.

SHIVERICK KELLOGG

Representative from Ionia County, 1871-2 and 1873-4. Was born in Murray, N. Y., Sept. 9, 1817. He was educated at Potsdam Academy, and settled as a farmer in Easton, Ionia County, in 1849. He was a charter member of the Michigan Pioneer Society in 1874. He held several local offices. In politics a Republican.

HARRISON KELLY

Representative from St. Joseph County, 1859-60. Was born in Jefferson County, Va., Nov. 28, 1797. A farmer, in politics a Whig, Abolitionist, Republican and later a Greenback Prohibitionist. He came to Michigan in 1833, and purchased a farm in Burr Oak, in which he resided in 1887.

WILLIAM D. KELLY

Representative from the First District of Muskegon County, 1895-6, 1897-8 and 1899-1900; and Senator, 1901-2 and 1903-4, from the Twenty-third District, comprising the counties of Muskegon and Ottawa. Was born of Irish parents, Nov.

26, 1865, in Ferrysburg, Ottawa County, Mich. His education was acquired in the public schools of Grand Haven and Muskegon, having moved to the latter place in 1879. From 1881 to 1885 he was engaged as bookkeeper for a large mercantile establishment in the city of Muskegon; purchasing an interest at the latter date in the planing mill and box factory of that place, in which business he continued until 1889, when he sold out and engaged in the wholesale lumber business. He remained in this occupation a short time, purchased timber lands, and then gave his attention to real estate and insurance business. He was married to Zepha E. Wheeler, daughter of Joseph E. Wheeler.

WILLIAM J. KELLY

Representative from the First District of Monroe County, 1895-6. Was born in Dauphin County, Pa., Aug. 26, 1837. In the spring of 1847, he came with his parents to Monroe City, and in the fall of the same year, moved to the farm in La Salle Township. The public schools and home study were his means of early education; his life occupation that of a farmer and stockbreeder. In politics a Republican. He was a member of the Republican County Committee; and a director in the Farmers' Mutual Fire Insurance Company of Monroe and Wayne.

NEWELL J. KELSEY

Representative from Calhoun County, 1883-4. Was born at LeRoy, Mich., June 20, 1843, received a high school education, and was a teacher at sixteen. He served in the war from August, 1861, to September, 1865, first in the 2d Mich. Infantry, then "Merrill's Horse," 2d Mo. Cavalry, and rose to the rank of Lieutenant. In 1887 he was a farmer, in politics a Republican. He was several years a Supervisor, and chairman of the board. He died at Lansing, Mar. 8, 1902.

SULLIVAN R. KELSEY

Representative from Shiawassee County, 1847, 1859-60 and 1861-2. Was born in Fairhaven, Vt., Aug. 16, 1805. He was educated in private and common schools. He was clerk in a store, then engineer in a paper mill, and traveling salesman. At twenty-one he became a merchant in Fairhaven, and from 1831 to 1833 was in the same business at Brockport, N. Y. In 1833 he removed to Bloomfield, Mich., and opened the first store in what is now the village of Birmingham, where he continued in business for eleven years, and was Postmaster from 1837 to 1844. He became a resident of Byron, purchased the water power, and with B. W. Dennis, built and operated the Byron mills until 1856, then alone until 1858. He then engaged in the hardware trade until 1865. In 1864 he was elected Judge of Probate, and held that position from 1865 to 1881. He was eight years justice, nine years Supervisor at Byron, and was Alderman and Mayor of Corunna. He was first a Whig, then a Republican. He died Nov. 28, 1886.

C. WESLEY KEMMERLING

Representative from Monroe County, 1909-10, 1911-12 and 1915-16. Was born in Raisinville Township, Monroe County, Feb. 15, 1872, of German descent. His education was acquired in a district school and State Normal. He was married

Dec. 24, 1895, to Ethel Faye Loudenslager. With the exception of two years spent in the Ohio oil fields, Mr. Kemmerling engaged in farming. In politics a Republican. He held the office of Highway Commissioner.

REUBEN KEMPF

Senator from the Fourth District, 1885-6; and Representative from the First District of Washtenaw County, 1895-6. Was born in Pennsylvania, Mar. 5, 1835; came to Michigan in 1841 and received his education at the public schools of Ann Arbor. He began life a merchant, in which occupation he continued twenty years; then engaged in banking. In politics a Republican.

FRANK KENDRICK

Representative from Lapeer County, 1881. Was born in Waterford, Me. He removed to Michigan with his parents when about six years of age. Having received an academical education he engaged in teaching. Aug. 18, 1861, he enlisted as a member of Co. A, 5th Mich. Cavalry, and served until the war closed, being discharged June 3, 1865. During his service he participated in forty battles; was wounded three times, and returned home in poor health and with a broken constitution. He engaged in farming, but was obliged to abandon that pursuit on account of his health. He then taught for three years, when his health failed so completely that he had to abandon all pursuits, and, for a number of years, was a confirmed invalid. In 1880 he was elected Justice of the Peace. In politics he was a Republican. He died Nov. 16, 1881, and was succeeded in the Legislature by Frederick H. Hill.

FREDERICK G. KENDRICK

Representative from Macomb County, 1869-70. Was born in Germany, May 14, 1836. Came to Michigan in 1844. He was at first a farmer, then a merchant, and was in the lumber, sash and blind business for nine years. He was Sheriff of Macomb County from 1870 to 1874; member of the Mt. Clemens Board of Education for nine years, and president of the Mt. Clemens bitter water company. He was Postmaster in 1887, and in politics a Democrat.

LUCIUS KENDRICK

Representative from Lapeer County, 1869-70. Was born at Darien, N. Y., Oct. 9, 1817, and settled in Lapeer County in 1836. He held several offices of trust in Dryden, and in the county. He was for many years a local correspondent of the Detroit *Tribune*, and contributed a valuable series of articles to the Lapeer *Clarion* of reminiscences of Lapeer County. He was a Republican in politics. He died Oct. 12, 1883.

FREDERICK A. KENNEDY, SR.

Representative from Lenawee County, 1850. Was born in England, Dec. 27, 1785. He came to America in 1817, and resided in Pennsylvania and New York until 1831, when he removed to Michigan, settling in Lenawee County in what was afterwards called Ridgeway. He was cooper by trade, but after coming to Michigan followed farming principally. In politics a Democrat. In 1857 he removed to Jackson, where he resided until his death, Feb. 26, 1872.

FREDERICK A. KENNEDY, JR.

Representative from Jackson County, 1846. Was born in Brighton, England, Feb. 18, 1811. He came to Pennsylvania in 1819, but soon removed to Lodi, N. Y. In 1831 he became a farmer in Ridgeway, Mich. He settled in Hanover, Mich., in 1837, and was Supervisor four years, Justice eight years, and after 1875 Superintendent of the Poor. He was the County Agent of the State Board of Charities in 1887. In politics he was a Democrat.

MUNNIS KENNEY

Representative from Washtenaw County, 1840. Was born in Newfane, Vt., Dec. 10, 1788. He received an academical education, was three years in Williams College, and the fourth at Middlebury, graduating in 1809. Studied law, and was in practice at Townshend, Vt., and was a member of the Vermont Assembly in 1816-21. He lived at Brighton, Mass., a few years, and in 1829 settled on a farm in Webster, Mich. He was an anti-slavery Whig, the founder of the Washtenaw Mutual Insurance Company, and for many years its secretary. He died Apr. 23, 1843.

MYRON C. KENNY

Representative from Lapeer County, 1865-6; and Delegate from Lapeer County to the Constitutional Convention of 1867. Was born in Perry, N. Y., in 1823, and came to Michigan in 1842. By profession he was a physician, in politics a Republican. He received an academical education at Romeo, Mich., and taught several terms in Macomb County and at Lapeer. Studied medicine and went into practice at Lapeer in 1848, where he resided in 1887. He was three years President of the village and twice Mayor of the city of Lapeer, School Inspector seven years, and member of the Board of Education for sixteen years.

HENRY KENT

Representative from the Second District of Montcalm County, 1895-6. Was born in Tompkins County, N. Y., Jan. 28, 1837. In the spring of the same year the family came to Oakland County, Mich., where he attended the district school, and in 1853 removed to Fairplain Township, Montcalm County; his life occupation was that of a farmer. During the war he served in Co. A, 1st Regiment of Engineers and Mechanics; was with Sherman on his march from Atlanta to the Sea, through the Carolinas to Goldsborough, and thence to Washington. In politics a Republican. He held the offices of Town Clerk, Justice of the Peace, Supervisor and County Treasurer.

RICHARD KENT

Senator from the Ninth District, 1853-4. Was born in Newburyport, Mass., Oct. 30, 1786. He received a good academical education, taught school and practiced surveying several years. He was an early settler in Adrian, Mich., where he followed farming. He was also Supervisor and held other town offices. He died in 1867.

WILLIAM A. KENT

Representative from Branch County, 1838. He was a typical pioneer; full of force and energy—a leader in the Democratic party until the time of his death in 1862. He was Associate Judge under the old system, and was known as Judge Kent.

JOHN KENYON, JR.

Representative from Livingston County, 1850; and Senator from the Twenty-seventh District, 1855-6. Was born in Queensbury, N. Y., July 28, 1806, came to Tyrone, Mich., in 1840, and purchased a farm, and followed that occupation for life. For nine years he was Supervisor of the township. He died Nov. 12, 1874.

BENJAMIN B. KERCHEVAL

Delegate from Wayne County to the First Convention of Assent, 1836; and Senator from the First District, 1838-9. Was born at Winchester, Va., Apr. 9, 1793, and was the son of an officer of the Revolution. Came to Detroit at an early age. In 1821 he was appointed Pension Agent of Indiana, and removed to Fort Wayne, but returned to Detroit. He was Alderman in 1830; director of the Detroit & St. Joseph Railroad Company in 1835; trustee of the Detroit Savings Bank; a corporator of the Peninsular Bank in 1849; and for many years a forwarding and commission merchant, doing business at the foot of Woodward avenue. In politics he was a Democrat. He died Mar. 23, 1855.

JOSEPH W. KERNS

Representative from the First District of Saginaw County, 1911-12. Was born at Stratford, Ont., Jan. 2, 1852, of Scotch-Irish descent, and received his education in the public schools of Saginaw, Mich. Married. He was in the Michigan State Military Service about sixteen years. He held the offices of Sheriff, County Road Commissioner and Alderman, chairman of the Republican City Committee, and a member of the Republican County Committee at various times during the past thirty years. In politics a Republican.

ANGUS W. KERR

Representative from the First District of Houghton County, 1899-1900 and 1901-2. Was born in Ontario, May 24, 1873, and came to Michigan while yet a mere boy, settling at Lake Linden. His education was largely received in the schools of that place and he graduated from the high school of the village. He attended the law department of the University of Michigan during the school year of 1891-2 and at its close entered the office of A. T. Streeter of Calumet, Mich., and was admitted to the bar July 12, 1895. He held the office of City Attorney of Calumet and Circuit Court Commissioner of Houghton County. In the Spanish-American War he served with Co. D, 34th Regiment of Mich. Vol. from the time of its muster into the service of the United States until it was mustered out, being assigned to recruiting duty. In politics a Republican. He was elected to the Legislature of 1899-1900 by the full vote of his district, having no opponent, and was re-elected to the House of 1901-2.

JAMES KERR

Representative from the Second District of Saginaw County, 1897-8. Was born in Ayrshire, Scotland, May 16, 1850, where he acquired a common school education and in 1865 came to this country and worked nine years in the lumber woods of northern Michigan and Wisconsin; was married in the fall of 1876 and located on a farm in Taymouth Township. In politics a Democrat. He was elected Representative to the House of 1897-8 on the Democratic People's Union Silver ticket. His seat was contested and declared vacant by House, Mar. 4, 1897. At a special election held Apr. 5, 1897, Mr. Kerr was elected to fill the vacancy.

JOHN CLARK KETCHAM

Member of Congress, 1921-2 and 1923—. Was born in Toledo, O., Jan. 1, 1873, of English-American parentage. The family came to a farm in Maple Grove Township in the summer of 1873 and Mr. Ketcham has been a resident of Barry County ever since. He was educated in the rural schools and the high schools of Nashville and Hastings, graduating from the latter in 1892. He taught school in 1899, when he was elected Commissioner of Schools, serving eight years. In 1907 he was appointed Postmaster and served until 1913. In 1912 he was chosen Master of State Grange and served eight years. In 1916 he was chosen lecturer of the National Grange, which position he still holds. He was married to Cora E. Rowlater June 30, 1897, and they have three children. In politics he is a Republican.

DANFORTH KEYES

Representative from Lenawee County, 1875-6. Was born in Ashford, Conn., May 27, 1816. He received a common school education, removed to Clinton, Mich., in 1836, and resided there. He was Supervisor of Tecumseh in 1863-5, and after the division of the town in 1869 was Supervisor of Clinton in 1869-70. He engaged in the milling business, and also a grain dealer. In politics he was a Democrat. He died at Clinton, January, 1889.

KARL D. KEYES

Senator, 1907-8, from the Fifteenth District, comprising the counties of Barry and Eaton. Was born at Olivet, Eaton County, Mich., Jan. 12, 1867. He received his education at Olivet and Oberlin Colleges. He was married to Minnie E. Evans of Bellevue, Mich., July 18, 1893. He was a member of the firm of George W. Keyes & Son, bankers, and also in the retail book and stationery trade. He served as President of the village, Trustee and Treasurer. In politics an active Republican. He died May 3, 1915, at Olivet, Mich.

HENRY C. KIBBEE

Senator from the First District, 1851. Was born in Orange County, Vt., Oct. 22, 1818. He came to Michigan in 1839, and commenced milling in 1844 at Mt.

Clemens. He was contractor for the Erie and Kalamazoo canal in 1847, and in 1849 contractor for the Buffalo & Blackwell canal, N. Y. In 1851 he re-organized the bank of Macomb County, and was president, vice president and cashier until 1858, when he sold out and went into the lumber firm of Kibbee, Fox & Co. In 1861 he was a large contractor in buying horses for the army, and in 1863 was elected cashier of the First National Bank of Detroit. In 1857 he was appointed Pension Agent, and served through the term of Buchanan. He also organized the banking firm of Duncan, Kibbee & Co. He was not active in business after 1887. In politics a Democrat.

PORTER KIBBEE

Commissioner of the State Land Office, 1851-4. Was born in Orange County, Vt., in July, 1813. He came to Michigan in 1836, and for many years was a resident of Mt. Clemens. He was for two terms Judge of Probate for Macomb County. He held a partnership with his brother in flouring and lumber mills, the firm being P. & H. C. Kibbee. In 1858 he was elected president of the bank of Macomb County. By occupation he was a merchant, in politics a Democrat. In 1887 he was an invalid and resided at Detroit.

RUFUS KIBBEE

Senator from the Third District, 1846-7. Came from the State of New York, and was a physician and druggist at Canandaigua. He removed to Coldwater about 1867, where he died about 1883-4. In politics he was a Democrat.

CHARLES B. KIDDER

Representative from Lapeer County, 1901-2 and 1903-4. Was born in Almont, Mich., Mar. 4, 1848. His education was obtained in the State Normal School at Ypsilanti, after which he was a successful teacher for ten years, when he bought a farm which he managed seventeen years, finally removing to the village of Almont where for twelve years he held the office of Supervisor of his township. He was secretary of the Lapeer County Farmers' Mutual Insurance Association for twelve years. In politics a Republican.

HERMANN KIEFER

Member of the Board of Regents of the University of Michigan, 1889-1902. Was born in Sulzburg, Baden, Germany, Nov. 19, 1825, son of Conrad and Frederike (Schweykert) Kiefer. His father and paternal grandfather were both physicians and surgeons. On the maternal side his grandfather was director of the Botanical Gardens in Karlsruhe. Until his ninth year he was educated under private tutors, and from then, until he was eighteen, he attended the Gymnasia of Mannheim, Freiburg, and Karlsruhe. His later studies, including medicine, were carried on at the Universities of Freiburg, Heidelberg, Prague, and Vienna. On May 13, 1849, he passed examinations as physician and surgeon before the State Board of Examiners in Karlsruhe; and after a short term of service as surgeon of a volunteer regiment, he came to the United States in October of the same year. He was married to Franciska Kehle July 21, 1850. He settled in Detroit where he followed the practice of his profession, with the exception of two years, 1883-5, when he was United States Consul at Stettin, Germany. He was a member of the Detroit Board of Education in 1866-7, and of the Public Library Commission in 1882-3. He was a presidential elector in 1872 and delegate to the Republican National Convention of 1876. Mar. 15, 1899, he was appointed Regent of the University to succeed the late Moses W. Field, and at the expiration of the term was elected for the full term of eight years.

JOSEPH H. KILBORN

Representative from Ingham County, 1847 and 1849. Was born in Westbury, Lower Canada, May 8, 1809. He settled in 1839 in Meridian, Mich. He was Postmaster in 1840, in 1844 County Superintendent of the Poor, and Supervisor in 1846-7. He is said to have been very effective in the removal of the capital from Detroit to Lansing. He was a farmer and a Democrat. He was a Colonel of the Militia in 1848. He died at Okemos, Ingham County, Nov. 1, 1891.

SAMUEL L. KILBOURNE

Representative from Ingham County, 1875-6. Was born near Toronto, Canada, in 1839. He removed with his father to Detroit in 1839, and to Okemos, Ingham County, in 1841. He received an academicial education at the agricultural college. He graduated from the law department of the Michigan University in 1860, and commenced the practice of his profession in Lansing. In 1861 he edited the Lansing *State Journal*, in 1868-9, was clerk of the Supreme Court. He was City Attorney two terms. In politics a Democrat. He had an extensive practice, and was one of the law firm of Kilbourne & Humphrey.

JOHN KILLEAN

Representative from Kent County, 1887-8. Was born at Buffalo, N. Y., Nov. 27, 1831, and was a resident of Michigan after 1864. Formerly his occupation was varied, but at present a grocer. He was Alderman of Grand Rapids twice, president of the Common Council three times, and member of the Police and Fire Commission. He was elected Representative on the Fusion ticket.

WILLIAM MARVIN KILPATRICK

Senator from the Seventeenth District, 1881-2 and 1895-6; and Delegate in the Constitutional Convention of 1907-8, from the Fourteenth District, Shiawassee County. Was born at Middlesex, Yates County, N. Y., in 1840, of Scotch and Irish descent. He worked on his father's farm until nineteen years of age, with no advantages except an intelligent community and country school. He spent one year in the Genesee Seminary in New York and taught school the two winters following. He then took a business course at the Poughkeepsie Business College and went West in 1863, going to Illinois, where he again taught school. He came to Michigan in 1864, and spent the next two years at Ann Arbor attending the law lectures and on his father's farm in Grass Lake Township, Jackson County, to which place his father had moved from New York. He graduated from the law department of the University of Michigan in 1866, and came to Owosso where he practiced law. He was married three times. He served as Supervisor at large and Mayor of Owosso, Prosecuting Attorney, State Senator in 1880 and 1894, alternate delegate to the Republican National Convention at Minneapolis and was a member of the Republican State Central Committee. He died Sept. 18, 1919.

EBENEZER C. KIMBERLY

Representative from Shiawassee County, 1851. Was born at Mansfield, Conn., Oct. 9, 1777. He came to Corunna in 1840, as the agent of Trumbull Cary, an extensive land holder, and devoted himself to that business as a resident. He died at Corunna, Mich., July 8, 1856.

AUSTIN N. KIMMIS, JR.

Representative from the Second District of Oakland County, 1895-6 and 1897-8. Was born June 20, 1860, on the farm in Novi, attended district school, the Milford High School and the Normal School at Ypsilanti, Kalamazoo College, and took a course in law at Ann Arbor, where he graduated with the class of 1884; was admitted to the bar upon examination in Washtenaw County, but never engaged actively in practice; at the conclusion of his studies at Ann Arbor he at once engaged actively in stock breeding and general farming. Among his classmates of Kalamazoo College was Miss Blanche Peck of Cassopolis, whom he married Aug. 30, 1881. Mrs. Kimmis died June 10, 1894. In politics a Republican. He held the offices of School Inspector, Justice of the Peace, and Supervisor.

EDWARD KING

Representative from Washtenaw County, 1881-2 and 1883-4. Was born in London, England, Sept. 12, 1830, and came to this country with his father in 1833. They resided in New York City until 1837, when they settled at Ypsilanti, Mich. He was engaged in mercantile business until 1867, when he purchased the farm upon which he lived. In politics a Democrat.

FRANCIS KING

Senator, 1913-14, from the Twenty-fifth District, comprising the counties of Gratiot, Isabella and Mecosta. Was born in Chicago, Ill., Jan. 5, 1863, of English parents. He attended public and private schools in that city, later graduating from Williams College; came to Alma, Mich., in 1902. He was twice elected Mayor, twice President of the Board of Trade, a member of the City School Board, Trustee of Alma College, director and second vice president of the First State Bank and financially interested in the large manufacturing interests of Alma. For two years he served as a member of the State Forestry Commission and represented the Eleventh Congressional District in the Republican National Convention of 1908. Married. In politics a Republican.

GIDEON G. KING

Representative from Hillsdale County, 1855-6. Was born in the State of New York, about 1820, came with his father from Lima, N. Y., to Ypsilanti in 1837, and removed to Amboy, Hillsdale County, in 1841. He was Supervisor of Amboy six years. By occupation he was a farmer, in politics first Whig and then Republican. He died at the age of thirty-nine.

JOHN KING

Representative from Washtenaw County, 1843. His address was Whitmore Lake. (Further data not obtainable).

JOHN B. KING

Representative from Monroe County, 1850. Was born in the State of New York in 1798. Came to Michigan in 1832, and settled on a farm in Summerfield, Monroe County. He was Town Clerk, Supervisor, Justice nine years, and held other town offices. He removed to Raisinville where he was Supervisor, Justice, and overseer of the poor. He was a Democrat until 1856. He died Mar. 26, 1857.

JONATHAN P. KING

Representative from Mackinac County, 1835-6 to 1839, 1842 and 1848; and Senator from the Sixth District, 1849-50. His postoffice address was Mackinac. He did not take his seat in 1835-6. (Further data not obtainable).

NATHAN G. KING

Senator from the Seventh District, 1873-4. Was born in Nassau, N. Y., Feb. 25, 1819, received a common school education, and prepared for college under private instruction; was engaged in extensive mercantile operations in early life, but in 1843 commenced the study of law, and was admitted to the bar in 1846. Commenced the practice of his profession in Albany, N. Y., in company with Hon. S. H. Hammond, and afterwards had for his partner Hon. Henry Hogeboom. He emigrated to Michigan in 1856, and settled in Berrien County. In 1865 he removed to Brooklyn, Jackson County, where he resided in 1887. Politically he was a Republican.

PAUL H. KING

Secretary of the Constitutional Convention of 1907-8. Was born in Arapahoe, Neb., in 1879, of American descent. He received his early education at home under the instruction of his mother, entered school at eleven years of age and graduated from the Dowagiac High School in 1898. He was admitted to the bar on examination after private study in 1904. In 1891 his father, who was a physician, moved from Nebraska to Minnesota for his health, and located at Wadena, where he died, and his son went to work. He served as page in the Minnesota House of Representatives in 1893 and 1895. He then moved to Michigan, locating at Dowagiac, the home of his grandparents. He was appointed floor messenger in the State Senate in 1897, secretary's messenger in 1899, assistant secretary in 1901, working as grocery clerk and factory employe between sessions. He served as journal clerk of the House in 1903-5-7-, and was elected clerk of the House at the special session of 1907. He also served between sessions as a clerk in the office of the Secretary of State from 1901-5.

ALBERT CHARLES KINGMAN

Senator, 1909-10 and 1911-12, from the Ninth District, comprising the counties of Branch and Calhoun. Was born at Corning, Steuben County, N. Y., June 18, 1850, of American parentage. He received his education in the Angelica Academy, N. Y., and Kalamazoo College. When quite young, his father removed to Angelica, in Allegany County, N. Y., where they lived until 1867, when they removed to Michigan, and settled at Cassopolis. In 1868, Mr. Kingman entered Kalamazoo College as a freshman, having received his preparatory training in Angelica Academy. He graduated from Kalamazoo College in 1872, receiving the A. B. degree and the degree of A. M. in due course in 1874. He studied law at Dowagiac and at the University of Michigan, and was admitted to the bar in 1874. In 1877 he came to Battle Creek to practice law. In politics he was an ardent Republican. He died at Battle Creek July 26, 1916.

JOHN KINGOTT

Representative from the Third District of St. Clair County, 1899-1900. Was born at Wittenberg, Prussia, Mar. 17, 1857. His education comprised seven years' schooling in his native country. He came to America Apr. 13, 1874, when about seventeen years of age, and worked one year on a farm in Connecticut. He then came to Michigan, and worked on a farm in Sloan Township, St. Clair County, for an uncle. After two years of service he removed to Capac and served for nine years as farm hand, then secured a farm of 120 acres for himself. He served his township as Commissioner of Highways and as Supervisor. He was elected to the Legislature of 1899-1900 on the Republican ticket.

SOLOMON O. KINGSBURY

Representative from Kent County, 1867-8. Was born in Connecticut, May 2, 1812. His father's family soon after removing to Painesville, O., where he received a common school education. In early life he was a clerk. He became a resident of Grand Rapids at an early day and was a merchant. He was elected County Treasurer in 1848 and 1850, serving four years, then resuming mercantile business. In 1858 he opened a real estate and insurance office and continued in that business during life. In 1867 he was appointed Postmaster of Grand Rapids, and held that position two years. He died May 16, 1886.

EDWARD L. KINGSLAND

Representative from the First District of Berrien County, 1893-4 and 1895-6. Was born in New York, Feb. 22, 1839; came to Michigan in 1854; attended district school and two years at Hillsdale College; worked on farm summers and taught school winters; married in 1865 and settled on a farm in Hagar Township. His life occupation was that of a farmer. In politics a Republican. He held the offices of Supervisor and County Superintendent of Schools.

JAMES KINGSLEY

Member of the Legislative Council from Washtenaw County, 1830-1 and 1832-3; Senator from the Fourth District, 1838, and from the Fifth District, 1839, and from the Second District, 1842; Delegate from Washtenaw County to the Constitutional Convention of 1850; and member of the Board of Regents of the University of Michigan, 1852-8; Representative from Washtenaw County, 1837, 1848 and 1869-70. Was born in Canterbury, Conn., Jan. 6, 1797, attended school until nineteen, then took a Latin course, either at Brown University or with one of its professors. From 1823 to 1826 he was the tutor in the family of Ludwell Lee, in Virginia; removed to Grand Gulf, Miss., and from there to Ann Arbor, Mich., in 1826. In 1830 married Lucy Ann Clark. From 1830 to 1838 he was Judge of Probate and was the second Mayor of Ann Arbor. In politics he was a Democrat. He died Aug. 10, 1878.

SAMUEL R. KINGSLEY, JR.

Representative from the Third District of Wayne County, 1893-4 and 1895-6. Was born in Newark, O., July 10, 1843. When ten years of age he came to Michigan with his parents; received a common school education; settled on a farm in Romulus Township. He served, during the war, in Co. D, 24th Mich. Infantry; was wounded and taken prisoner at Gettysburg; released on account of wounds and remained in the army till the close of the war. In politics a Republican. He was Township Clerk and Postmaster. He died at Romulus, Dec. 2, 1917.

JAMES H. KINNANE

Senator, 1907-8, from the Seventh District, comprising the counties of Berrien and Cass. Was born in Kalamazoo County, Mich., of Irish parentage, about 1860. He received his educational training in the high school at Kalamazoo, the Kalamazoo Baptist College and the University of Michigan, graduating from the Kalamazoo High School in 1880 and from the law department of the University of Michigan in 1884. He at once entered upon the practice of law at Kalamazoo, where he remained ten years, leaving there in 1895 under a commission from President Cleveland to enter a special branch of the United States Indian Service in the Northwest. After being in the service two years, he returned to Michigan and opened a law office at Dowagiac. He was an active Democrat up to 1896 and held the office of City Attorney two terms in the city of Kalamazoo beginning with the year 1889. He left the Democratic party in 1896 and became an active Republican. He held various municipal offices in Dowagiac city. Mr. Kinnane, in his early life, served three years in the Michigan State Troops; was married in 1887, prominent in social and fraternal orders; and for several years president of the Cass County Bar Association.

DANIEL KINNE

Representative from Hillsdale County, 1847; and Delegate from Hillsdale County to the Constitutional Convention of 1850. Was born in Vermont in 1814. He emigrated from Erie County, N. Y., in 1838 and settled on a farm in Reading, Hillsdale County. He was five years Supervisor, and held other town offices. In 1845 he was Associate Judge of the County. He was active in building a plank road from Reading to Hillsdale; in the Reading Manufacturing Company, and cheese factory. He died many years prior to 1887.

EDWARD D. KINNE

Representative from Washtenaw County, 1881-2. Was born at DeWitt, N. Y., in 1842. He prepared for college at Cazenovia Seminary, N. Y., and graduated in the classical department of Michigan University in 1864. He also graduated from the Columbian Law School, in Washington, D. C., in 1867. Having located at Ann Arbor in 1867, he practiced law in that city. He has been City Recorder and City Attorney of Ann Arbor, and Mayor two terms. In 1886, as the Republican candidate, he was elected Judge of the circuit comprising the counties of Washtenaw and Monroe. He retired from the bench in 1917. He died at Ann Arbor, July 25, 1921.

GEORGE KIPP

Representative from Genesee County, 1873-4. Was born in Owasco, N. Y., Nov. 25, 1811. In 1814 he removed to Erie County, N. Y. He was educated in common schools. In 1846 he came to Michigan, and settled at Atlas, Genesee County, where he resided in 1887. He held several local offices. By occupation he was a farmer.

JAMES KIPP

Representative from Clinton and Gratiot counties, 1857-8. Was born in Cayuga County, N. Y., June 13, 1801. He removed to Atlas, Mich., in 1836, and was Supervisor seven terms, between 1839 and 1848, Justice from 1837 to 1854, and Associated Judge of the County. He removed to Duplain, Clinton County, in 1855, where he lived two years, then became a resident of St. Johns. By occupation he was a farmer, in politics a Republican. He was Superintendent of the Poor in Clinton County from 1866 up to the date of his death, Oct. 22, 1884.

EUGENE J. KIRBY

Representative from Van Buren County, 1921-2 and 1923—. Was born in St. Joseph County, Aug. 30, 1859, of English parents. He received his education in the public schools of Schoolcraft, Mich. He engaged in the real estate business in Chicago, and for the last twenty years in farming and dairying, being for eight years secretary-treasurer of the Dutch Belted Cattle Association of America. He held the elective offices of Alderman, City Recorder and Supervisor. Mr. Kirby is married. In politics he is a Republican.

JOHN W. KIRBY

Representative from the Second District of Kalamazoo County, 1889-90. Was born in New Lebanon, Columbia County, N. Y., Oct. 24, 1824. He passed his early years until he attained his majority on the home farm. He received the benefit of the common school of his native place. This, with the instruction he received in the art of farming from his father, an intelligent and successful farmer, equipped him for the duties of his vocation. He, in 1852, was married to Miss Mary Howland, and resided on the home farm until 1867, when he removed to Charleston, Kalamazoo County, Mich. In politics he was a staunch Republican. In 1886 he received, in the convention of the Second District, a large number of votes for Representative, but withdrew his name that another might receive the nomination. But in 1888 he received the unanimous vote for the same office and was elected to the Legislature of 1889-90.

WILLIAM J. KIRBY

Representative from Kalamazoo County, 1887-8. Was born in Otsego County, N. Y., Feb. 11, 1845. His former occupation was that of surveyor and civil engineer; later a farmer. He was appointed Supervisor of Pavilion in 1882, and elected in 1883 and 1884. He was Superintendent of the building of the Kalamazoo County court house in 1884. Mr. Kirby was elected Representative as a Republican.

OTTO KIRCHNER

Attorney General, 1877-81. Was born at Frankfort-on-the-Oder, Prussia, July 13, 1846. He came to Berlin, Ont., with his father in 1854, received an academical education, and began the study of law. In 1864 he was a clerk to the Auditor General, and in 1865 clerk of the House judiciary committee. He studied law in Detroit, and was admitted in 1866. He stumped the State for Grant and Wilson in 1872, in 1876 was chairman of the Republican city committee, and was a delegate to the Cincinnati Convention. In 1885 he was appointed one of the professors of law at Ann Arbor, but resigned after a short service. He had a lucrative law practice. In politics he was a Republican. He died at Detroit, July 21, 1920.

JAMES KIRK

Representative from the First District of Tuscola County, 1891-2. Was born near Belfast, County Antrim, Ireland, Sept. 1834; in June, 1851, emigrated to this country and came to Michigan in 1854; worked by the month about seven years in Oakland County, then came to Tuscola County and settled on a farm. He held the office of Highway Commissioner, was Supervisor for four successive years, and School Director for eighteen years. In politics he was a Republican. He was elected to the House of 1891-2; died before the extra session of 1892.

JOHN PATRICK KIRK

Representative from the Second District of Washtenaw County, 1903-4. Was born in the city of Ypsilanti, Mich., Sept. 20, 1867. His education was obtained in the local public schools and the Ypsilanti High School from which he graduated in June, 1886. He entered the law department of the University of Michigan in October, 1886, graduating from that institution in June, 1888. After his graduation he engaged in the practice of law at Ypsilanti. He was City Attorney of Ypsilanti and Prosecuting Attorney of Washtenaw County; identified with the Michigan National Guard, and when war was declared with Spain he was Captain of the local company, but was mustered into the service as one of the Majors of the 31st Mich. Vol. Infantry; later Lieutenant Colonel of the 1st Regiment, Michigan National Guard. A Democrat in politics.

WILLIAM KIRK

Representative from Tuscola County, 1901-2 and 1903-4. Was born near Belfast, Ireland, in 1844, where his education was obtained in the national schools. He came to Michigan from Canada in 1861 and in 1867 went to Pike's Peak and celebrated the laying of the last rail of the Union Pacific R. R. He returned to Michigan in 1871 and located on a farm. Married. He held various offices in his township; was Supervisor and also president of the Tuscola County Agricultural Society. In politics a strong Republican.

GEORGE KIRKLAND

Representative from Monroe County, 1855-6. Was born in the State of New York, Sept. 1, 1810. By occupation he was a farmer, a Democrat in politics. He came to Bedford, Mich., in 1842. He held the offices of Supervisor, Road Commissioner, Justice sixteen years, and Treasurer of the F. M. F. Insurance Company several years. He resided at Samaria, Monroe County, in 1887.

WILLIAM M. KIRKPATRICK

Representative from Marquette County, 1885-6. Was born at Allegheny City, Pa., Jan. 17, 1849, where his early years were spent. He held the office of Justice and School Inspector. In politics a Republican.

JOHN KIRKWOOD

Representative from the County of Cass, 1893. Was born and raised on the farm where he lived all his life. His early education was received at the district school. He was fifty-one years of age in 1893, a bachelor, and had always worked upon the farm. He held the offices of Township Treasurer, Highway Commissioner and Supervisor. In politics he was a Democrat until the organization of the People's party, which he gave his support; was nominated by that party to the Legislature of 1893-4, endorsed by the Democrats, and elected. He died at his home May 14, 1893.

CLARENCE E. KISTLER

Representative from Mason County, 1917-18. Was born in Gaines Township, Kent County, Mich., July 14, 1869. He was educated in the township district schools. He was married Dec. 19, 1894, to Lillie M. Eldridge. He represented his township on the Board of Supervisors. Fraternally a member of the F. & A. M., I. O. O. F., M. W. of A., A. O. O. G. and Grange. In politics a Democrat.

HENRY KLEI

Representative from Wayne County, 1881-2. Was born in Germany, July 24, 1849. His parents emigrated to America in 1852, and located in Detroit, where he resided. Mr. Klei received his education in the public schools in Detroit. He was elected Alderman in 1878 and in 1879 for the full term of two years. He was a cigar manufacturer by occupation, and a Republican in politics.

PETER KLEIN

Representative from Wayne County, 1869-70 and 1875-6. Was born Sept. 12, 1813, in Oermingen, Alsace, and came with his parents to this country in 1828, who settled in Erie County, N. Y. He studied medicine and practiced four years at Rochester, N. Y., and two years at St. Catherines, Ont. He graduated from Geneva Medical College in 1846, and soon after settled in Detroit, where he practiced his profession. He was city and county physician and United States surgeon at the Detroit barracks. In politics he was a Democrat.

CHARLES H. KLINE

Representative from the First District of Washtenaw County, 1893-4. Was born in Tautoguay, Wood County, O., Aug. 21, 1864. At the age of seven years he came to Michigan with his mother and located at Evart, Osceola County; here he attended the high school, from which he graduated under fifteen years of age. He then entered the Michigan University, graduating from the literary department and from the law department in 1886. He remained in Ann Arbor, and was for three years with the law firm of Sawyer & Knowlton, he then began business alone, still remaining at Ann Arbor. Nov. 3, 1890, he was married to Miss Belle McLaren of Ann Arbor. In politics he was a Democrat. Deceased.

FRED B. KLINE

Senator, 1907-8, 1909-10 and 1911-12, from the Nineteenth District, comprising the counties of Lenawee and Monroe. Was born in Addison, Lenawee County, Mich., Feb. 1, 1865. His education was acquired in the public schools of Addison. At the age of twenty years he engaged in the hardware business at Addison. Married. In politics a Republican. He removed to California.

ALONZO F. KNAPP

Representative from Oakland County, 1873-4. Was born in Bristol, N. Y., Mar. 12, 1833. He emigrated to Michigan in 1834, and settled in Salem, Washtenaw County. He finished his classical education at the State Normal School. He studied medicine, and graduated from the Western Medical College, Cleveland, O., in 1865. In 1868 he removed to South Lyons, where he resided in 1887 and practiced his profession.

CORNELIUS KNAPP

Representative from Lenawee County, 1871-2. Was born in Nassau, N. Y., July 12, 1824. When young his parents removed to western New York, where they lived until 1835, when they removed to Rome, Mich. He worked on his father's farm until 1846, then learned the carpenter's trade and followed it until 1859. He bought a farm in Rome in 1850, and lived upon it in 1887. He was Supervisor for sixteen years.

JACOB KNAPP

Representative from Saginaw County, 1881-2. Was born in Wurtemberg, Germany, Oct. 14, 1846. He received a common school education and came to this country in 1866, and settled in Detroit, but in 1868 removed to Saginaw City, where he engaged in the manufacture of cigars. He was Alderman in 1877 and 1879. Politically a Democrat.

SAMUEL OLIVER KNAPP

Member of the State Board of Agriculture, 1867-73. Was born Feb. 23, 1817. In company with Governor Payne he manufactured woolen goods. He married Sarah Balch at Northfield, Mass., and moved to Michigan and made considerable money in mining copper and dealing in mines in the Upper Peninsula; in the late fifties he moved to Jackson, Mich., where he improved a very fine place, one of the finest in the State, in 1874. He was self educated in addition to a limited schooling, and learned some botany, horticulture, minerology and geology. He built and managed with great delight and success a small greenhouse adjoining his dwelling. He was one of the founders of the First Methodist Church of Jackson and was most generous in helping to build the church in 1866. He was the founder of Bay View, building the first cottage there in 1875. He gave most of his fortune to the church which he founded. He was a very generous and upright man with a positive will of his own; rather slow of speech and somewhat reserved. He served as a member of the State Board of Agriculture, 1867-73, by appointment by Governor H. H. Crapo. There were no children. He died at Jackson, Jan. 6, 1883; his wife died Dec. 12, 1899.

LOYAL EDWIN KNAPPEN

Member of the Board of Regents of the University of Michigan, 1904-12. Was born at Hastings, Mich., Jan. 27, 1854, son of Edwin and Sarah M. (Nevins) Knappen. He is of New England ancestry, and both his paternal grandfathers served in the Revolutionary War. After the regular preparatory training in the Hastings schools he entered the University of Michigan and was graduated Bachelor of Arts in 1873, taking the Master's degree in course three years later. On leaving the University he entered immediately upon the study of law, which was interrupted by six months' service as assistant principal of the Hastings High School. He then resumed his law studies with the Hon. James A. Sweezey and was admitted to the bar in August, 1875. He practiced his profession at Hastings and at Grand Rapids in connection with various law firms. He was married to Amelia I. Kenyon Oct. 23, 1876. He was Prosecuting Attorney for Barry County from 1879 to 1883, and Assistant Prosecuting Attorney for Kent County from 1888 to 1891. From 1880-8 he was United States Commissioner. He served on the School Board of Hastings and Grand Rapids. In April, 1903, he was elected Regent of the University of Michigan for the full term, and took his seat the following January. He was at once put at the head of the Committee on the Department of Law. He resigned before the end of his term.

GEORGE W. KNEELAND

Representative from Livingston County, 1850. Settled in Howell, Mich., in 1836, first as a farmer, afterwards engaged in running a steam saw mill at Howell, and was in the same business in Iosco where he died. He was Judge of Probate of Livingston County in 1840 and held other public positions. Politically he was a Democrat.

BENJAMIN KNIGHT

Representative from Eaton County, 1844 and 1847. His postoffice address was Eaton Rapids. (Further data not obtainable).

BIRDSEY KNIGHT

Representative from the First District of Bay County, 1891-2 and 1893-4. Was born in Avon Township, Oakland County, Mich., July 18, 1851; three years later he moved with his parents to Bay City where he acquired a common school education, he also attended school at Rochester, Oakland County. He was a farmer and began work for his father, as soon as able to be of any service, on the farm. In 1878 he was married to Eren A. Hillaker. In politics a Democrat. He served as Supervisor of his township, also chairman of the County Board.

GODFREY E. KNIGHT

Representative from Kalamazoo County, 1875-6. Was born Sept. 15, 1838, in Schoolcraft, Mich. He graduated from the University of Michigan in 1860. He held several village offices and was Justice of the Peace in Schoolcraft. By occupation he was a merchant, in politics a Democrat.

HENRY C. KNIGHT

Member of the Board of Regents of the University of Michigan, 1864-7. Was born in East Bethlehem, Pa., Sept. 13, 1817. He graduated at Jefferson College, spent one year in Yale Law School, came to Michigan in 1837, and settled at Pontiac. He was admitted to the bar in 1839, remained in Pontiac until 1848, and was a partner of O. D. Richardson. He then taught a classical school, and devoted himself to the ministry until 1853, when he settled in Detroit and resumed law practice. He was for many years superintendent of the Fort Street Presbyterian Sunday School. In politics he was a Republican. He was an Alderman and member of the Board of Education of Detroit; Prosecuting Attorney of Wayne County, and Regent of the University, both of which positions he held at the time of his death, Mar. 26, 1867.

JAMES BROOKS KNIGHT

Representative from Dickinson County, 1903-4, 1905-6, 1907-8 and 1911-12. Was born at Mineral Point, Wis., Mar. 19, 1850, of English parents. He was educated in the public schools of the Upper Peninsula, supplemented by work in some private schools. Married. Interested in mines and mining, having been Inspector of Mines and Commissioner of Mineral Statistics. In politics a Republican. He held the offices of Township Superintendent of Schools, Justice of the Peace, Township Clerk and Alderman.

NATHAN KNIGHT

Representative from Bay County, 1877-8, and 1879-80. Was born at Otisfield, near Portland, Me., July 14, 1817. His father removed to Michigan in 1826, and settled at Avon, Oakland County. He finished his educational studies at Austinburg Institute, O. He taught school two terms, and came to Bay City in 1854. He was Supervisor of Hampton for many consecutive years. His principal business was farming. In politics he was a Democrat. He died at Hampton, Mich., Dec. 30, 1886.

RICHARD KNIGHT

Representative from Antrim and other counties, 1883-4. Was born in the county of Surrey, England, and had a common school education. He came to Woodstock, Ont., in 1850, and was a blacksmith in Canada and Wisconsin. He removed to Banks, Mich., in 1863. He was Sheriff of Antrim County, sixteen years, a Justice and Town Treasurer. Politically a Republican.

WILLARD A. KNIGHT

Representative from the Second District of Calhoun County, 1905-6. Was born at Battle Creek, Calhoun County, Mich., Nov. 10, 1876. He acquired his education in the Battle Creek High School, Bryant & Stratton's Business College of Chicago, and a graduate of the law department of the University of Michigan; a practicing attorney. While in Ann Arbor he was connected with the *U. of M. Daily*, the college publication, as business manager, and edited and published the *U. of M. Republican*, the students' Republican organ at the University. In politics a Republican.

LEONARD F. KNOWLES

Delegate in the Constitutional Convention of 1907-8 from the Twenty-seventh District, Charlevoix County. Was born in Spring Green, Wis., Feb. 18, 1876. He came to Michigan with his parents in the year 1879, and they located on a farm near St. Louis. At the age of eleven years he started out to earn his own living. He maintained himself in the St. Louis schools from which he graduated in 1897, and followed that by a business course in Yerrington College, St. Louis. At the age of twenty-one he went to Tennessee and taught Latin in the Dibrell Normal College for one school year, then entered the law department of the University of Michigan from which he received his degree in 1901. In the latter part of July in the same year he arrived in Boyne City and began the practice of law. In 1905 he created the law firm of Knowles & Converse. Dec. 2, 1903, Mr. Knowles married Miss Florence Beardsley.

ELDRIDGE G. KNOWLTON

Representative from Oakland County, 1844. Was a farmer and innkeeper in the town of Groveland; was Supervisor in 1837-41, also Justice of the Peace. He came to Michigan in 1837 and removed in 1847.

HERMAN L. KOEHLER

Representative from the First District of Wayne County, 1913-14 and 1915-16; Senator from the First District of Wayne County, 1917-18. Was born in the Principality of Waldeek, Germany, Mar. 20, 1849, and received his education in private and high schools. In 1864 he came from Germany and located at Detroit, Mich. He started his business career as a clerk in a hardware store and read proof on the old Detroit *Daily Tribune* in 1869, when the paper was directed by James E. Scripps, when, for several years, he and Dennis Ryan, later of the Ryan Knitting Works, compiled the annual *Detroit City Directory*. In 1870 he went with the late August Marxhausen, Sr., to be city editor of the *Abend-Post*. In the early nineties, he removed to Cheboygan County and became a factor in Republican politics there, being Supervisor, Postmaster and Justice of the Peace. Koehler Township, Cheboygan County, was named for him. On his return to Detroit, he became financially interested in the Broadway market and Miles Theater. Mr. Koehler was married July 23, 1879, to Emma D. Hoenighausen. He was a delegate from Michigan to the Republican National Convention at Chicago in 1916. In politics he was a Republican. He died June 16, 1920.

JOHN KOLVOORD

Representative from the Second District of Allegan County, 1891-2. Was born in Holland, Ottawa County, Mich., Sept. 2, 1852, where his father died; in 1864 he moved to Allegan County. Married, and followed the business of merchant and milling. In politics a Cleveland Democrat, believing in tariff reform.

EZRA L. KOON

Senator from the Twelfth District, 1869-70, and from the Ninth District, 1883-4. Was born at Tyrone, N. Y., Dec. 31, 1833. He came first to Michigan in 1844, but taught school and attended Franklin Academy, Plattsburgh, N. Y., in 1854-5. He studied law in Illinois and at Hillsdale, and was admitted in 1859, where he engaged in practice. He was Circuit Court Commissioner two years, and Prosecuting Attorney four years. With Hon. Charles Upson he was commissioner to examine the compilation of 1871. He was twice Mayor of Hillsdale; after 1875 a trustee of Hillsdale College; and vice president of Second National Bank of Hillsdale after 1874. Politically he was a Republican.

GERRIT W. KOOYERS

Representative from the First District of Ottawa County, 1915-16 to 1923—. Was born in the township of Fillmore, Allegan County, Mich., Apr. 17, 1876, of American parents. He attended the public schools of the city of Holland, Hope College and the law department of the University of Michigan, graduating from the latter in 1899. The following year he engaged in the general law, real estate and insurance business at Holland. Mr. Kooyers is married and has four daughters and one son. He has held the office of Justice of the Peace and served two terms as Supervisor. In politics he is a Republican.

JACOB C. KORE

Representative from the First District of Lapeer County, 1859-60. His postoffice address was Hadley. (Further data not obtainable).

GUSTAV A. KRUEGER

Senator, 1909-10, from the Second District of Wayne County, comprising the fifth, seventh and ninth wards of Detroit. Was born in Germany in 1868, acquiring his education in Smith's Business University, Peters' German and English private school, Central High of Detroit, and the public schools. At the age of twelve he emigrated with his parents to Detroit, Mich., where he learned the cigar trade.

He was secretary of the C. M. B. A. for fifteen years. In politics a Republican. He was for four years a member of the Republican County Committee; an active member of several secret societies.

FRANZ C. KUHN

Attorney General, 1910-12; Justice of the Supreme Court, 1912-19. Was born at Detroit, Mich., Feb. 8, 1872, of German parents. He was educated in the public schools of Mt. Clemens. In 1893 he graduated from the literary department of the University of Michigan and in 1894 from the law department. From 1894 to 1896 he served as Circuit Court Commissioner of Macomb County; served three terms as Prosecuting Attorney; elected Probate Judge in 1904; re-elected 1908, resigned June 6, 1910, and was appointed Attorney General by Governor Warner. He was nominated for the office of Attorney General at the Republican State Convention held at Detroit, Oct. 6, 1910, and elected Nov. 8, 1910. He was appointed to the Supreme Bench by Governor Osborn on Sept. 6, 1912, to fill the vacancy caused by the death of Charles A. Blair. At the Republican State Convention held at Detroit in Sept. 24, 1912, he was nominated for the office of Justice of the Supreme Court to fill out the unexpired term and was elected Nov. 5, 1912. He resigned in 1919.

JOSEPH KUHN

Representative from Wayne County, 1879-80. Was born in Neustadt, Hesse Cassel, Prussia, Mar. 9, 1826. In 1846 he emigrated to Detroit. The same year he removed to Perry County, O., where he received a collegiate education. In 1849 he returned to Detroit and established a select school. He served as Justice two terms, Alderman, School Inspector, and member of the Board of Estimates. Occupation was that of general foreign and domestic business, exchanges, real estate, loans, etc. In politics he was a Democrat.

MARTIN KUNDIG

Member of the Board of Regents of the University of Michigan, 1841-2. Was born Nov. 19, 1805, at Schwyz, in the Canton of Schwyz, Switzerland. He made his classical studies and part of his theological course at the colleges in Einsiedeln and Lucerne. In 1827 he went to Rome to continue his studies. There he was found by Bishop Fenwick, of Cincinnati, in 1828, and was immediately engaged by him for his American missions. On his arrival in this country he completed his studies at Bardstown, Ky., and was ordained to the priesthood Feb. 2, 1829. He was at once appointed rector of St. Peter's, Cincinnati, and the following year was placed over the missions in Wayne County, O. Late in 1833 he came to Detroit, having been assigned to St. Anne's Church, at that time the only Catholic Church in the place. He was pastor of St. Anne's for several years and during that time built St. Mary's and Holy Trinity churches. During the frightful cholera epidemic of 1834 he labored most heroically, and converted one of the churches into a temporary hospital. Mar. 18, 1841, he was appointed Regent of the University and proved a very punctual and efficient member of the Board till his removal to Milwaukee, Wis., in the summer of 1842. There is no record of his resignation, and no successor was appointed till the close of the term in 1845.

On his removal to Milwaukee in 1842 he became rector of St. Peter's, then the only Catholic Church in the city; and two years later he was made Vicar General of the diocese, an office that he retained up to the time of his death. For many years he was a kind of wandering missionary over a wide range of country in the Northwest, where he established many parishes and churches all over the land. He died at Milwaukee, Mar. 6, 1879.

FREDERICK W. A. KURTH

Representative from Wayne County, 1879-80. Was born June 6, 1844, in Berlin, Germany. In 1852 he emigrated to America and settled in New York City. In 1854 he removed to Detroit. He received a liberal education, and in 1861 enlisted in the war. In 1865 he embarked in the retail grocery business. In 1878 he was elected Superintendent of Schools at Springwells. In politics a Republican.